D0603223

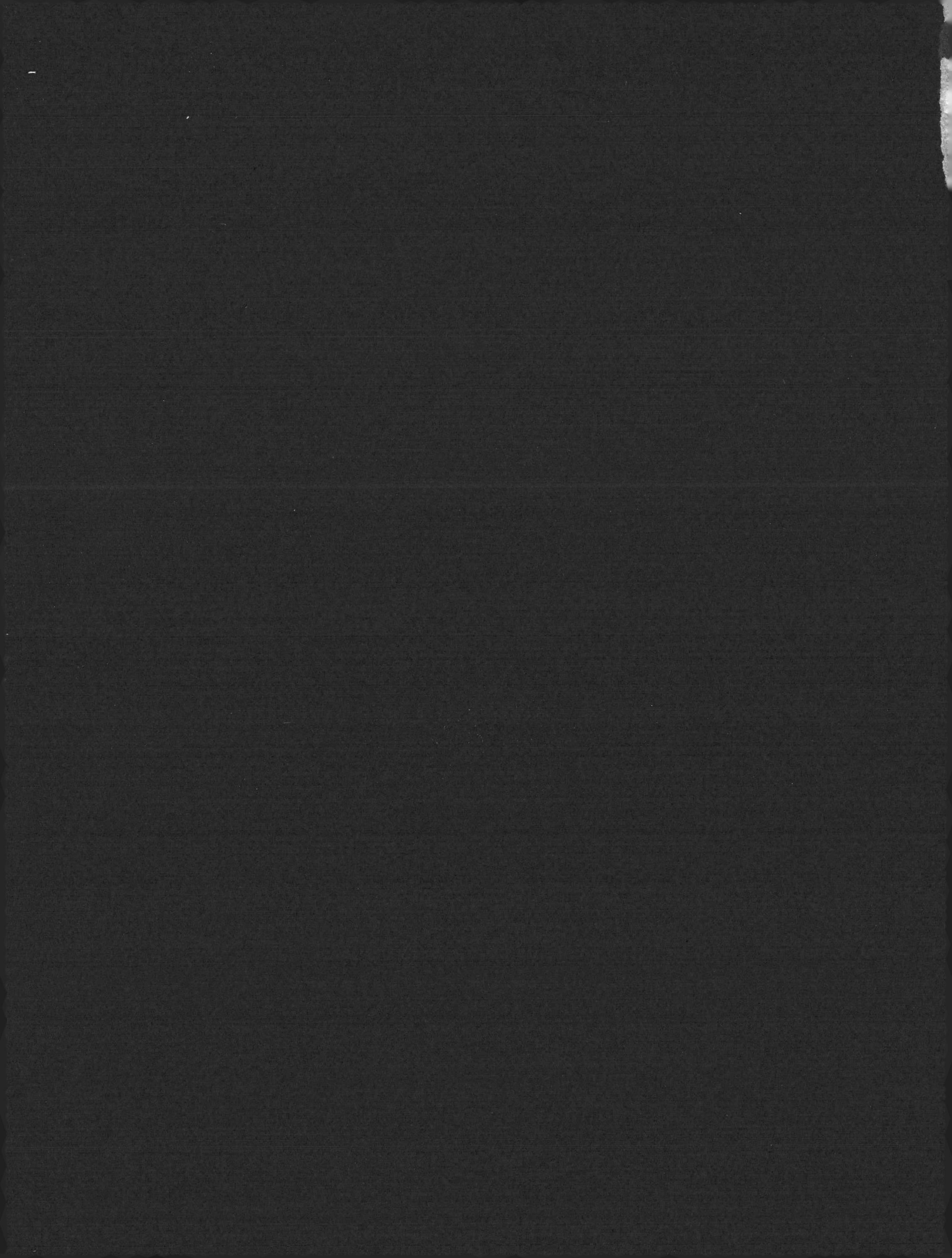

A LIFE OF

PICASSO

VOLUME II: 1907–1917

A LIFE OF
PICASSO

VOLUME II: 1907–1917

John Richardson

with the collaboration of Marilyn McCully

RANDOM HOUSE · NEW YORK

 Published in the United States by Random House, Inc., New York, and simultaneously in Canada by Random House of Canada Limited, Toronto.

Owing to limitations of space, all acknowledgments of permission to reprint copyright material and to use illustrations will be found following the index.

Library of Congress Cataloging-in-Publication information is available.

ISBN 0-394-55918-5

Random House website address: http://www.randomhouse.com/

Designed and typeset by Michael Raeburn/Cacklegoose Press
Illustrations reproduced by RAF, Florence/Summerfiield Press
Printed in Great Britain by Butler & Tanner Ltd, Frome and London

98765432

First Edition

Frontispiece: Self-portrait photograph by Picasso, Sorgues, 1912. Archives Picasso.

Opposite: Picasso. *The Letter*, 1912. Oil and postage stamp pasted on oval canvas, 16×22 cm. Whereabouts unknown. Kahnweiler photograph: Galerie Louise Leiris.

Cover image: Picasso. *Violin*, 1912. Pasted paper and charcoal on paper, 31.5×24 cm. Musée Picasso.

For Kosei Hara

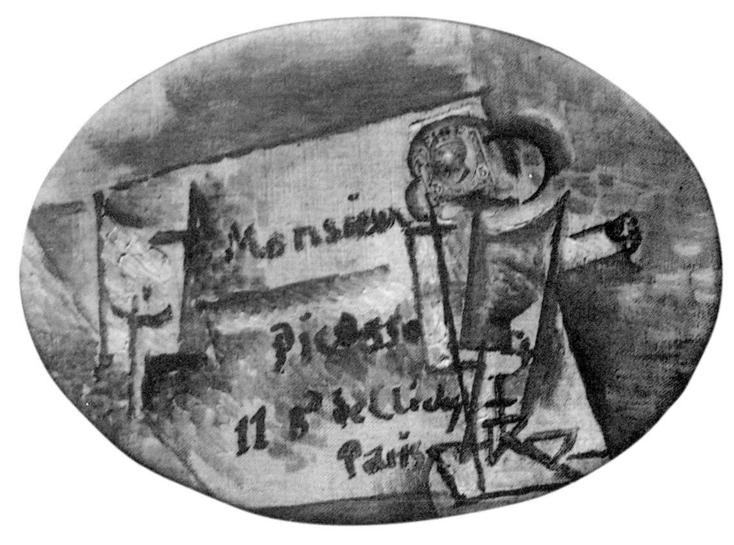

Acknowledgments

My greatest debt is to Picasso himself and his wife, Jacqueline, who encouraged me to embark on this project. After the artist's death Jacqueline gave me the run of the studios and, when necessary, provided me with a bed. I am likewise indebted to the artist's son Claude, and his wife, Sydney, for their wholehearted support. Claude's intervention has solved a number of otherwise intractable problems; his sister, Paloma, has also been wonderfully encouraging. Their mother, Françoise Gilot, has been very generous with inside information. Many thanks, too, to Maia Picasso-Widmaier, Bernard Picasso and his mother, Christine, Marina Picasso, Javier Vilató, Jaime and María Angeles Vilató and Jacqueline Picasso's daughter Catherine Hutin-Blay. My deepest thanks also go to Dora Maar for patiently answering all the questions with which I bombarded her. For their great help in providing materials and photographs from the Braque archives I am most grateful to Denise and Claude Laurens; and for providing material from the Matisse archive I thank Claude Duthuit.

The director, Gérard Régnier, and staff of the Musée Picasso have been exceedingly cooperative. Hélène Seckel has been very generous with her time and scholarship, and Anne Baldassari has made Picasso's own photographs available, for which many thanks; also to Brigitte Léal, Jeanne-Yvette Sudour, Sylvie Fresnault and Ivan de Monbrison. The director, Maria Teresa Ocaña, and staff of the Museu Picasso in Barcelona have likewise given me every possible assistance. I would also like to express my gratitude to the director, Eugenio Chicano, and Rafael Inglada of the Fundación Pablo Ruiz Picasso in Málaga and to Joaquim Ferràs i Boix and the Centre Picasso d'Horta. At the Picasso Administration Sandra Poupaud valiantly complied with all our requests.

Warmest thanks to Françoise Cachin, Director, Musées de France, and to Michel Richard, Chief of the Agence Photographique de la Réunion des Musées Nationaux, and, in particular, to Caroline de Lambertye, who has made hundreds of photographs available to us; also to Colette Giraudon, formerly of the Musée de l'Orangerie, for many kindnesses. François Chapon of the Bibliothèque Doucet and the staff of the Bibliothèque Nationale have likewise been of enormous help. In London, the librarians at the British Museum, the Victoria and Albert Museum and the London Library have been very accommodating.

This book owes a great deal to the support of my friends at the Museum of Modern Art, above all William Rubin, Director Emeritus, whose *Picasso and Portraiture* exhibit came as a godsend just before this book went to press. Agnes Gund, President, Glenn D. Lowry, Director, Kirk Varnedoe, Kynaston McShine and Carolyn Lanchner of the Department of Painting and Sculpture, and Clive Philpot, the former librarian, have also been unfailingly helpful. All of us connected with this book would like to bless Judith Cousins, MoMA's invaluable research curator, for sharing her resources with us. She has been an indefatigable source of information. At the Metropolitan Museum of Art William Luers, President, and Philippe de Montebello, Director, have given me every assistance. Special thanks to William S. Lieberman for many kindnesses, also to Sabine Rewald and Gary Tinterow. At the Beinecke Rare Book and Manuscript Library Alfred Mueller and the staff have been most helpful and I am grateful to them.

My publishers have left me mercifully free to go my own way, for which I am most grateful, especially to Harry Evans for his support of this daunting project, to my editor, Daniel Menaker, and his assistant, Adam Davies, and to Ann Godoff. Thanks also to Virginia Avery for further editing, to Kathy Rosenbloom and Amy Edelman for their heroic efforts to keep things on schedule; and to Andy Carpenter for designing the cover. My agent, Andrew Wylie, and his assistant, Bridget Love, have done wonders to resolve problems. Ann Warnford-Davis and Bob Tabian have also helped. Many thanks to my British publisher, Jonathan Cape, especially to Mark Holborn, who has been consistently encouraging. My gratitude also to Thomas Tilcher at Kindler Verlag in Germany; Carmen Criado at Alianza Editorial in Spain; and my Italian publisher, Leonardo Mondadori. Theodore Feder and Elizabeth Weisberg at ARS have been extremely cooperative and helpful over the matter of permissions. I thank Thekla Clark and Mara Puccini at Summerfield Press in Florence for achieving the highest quality photographic reproduction in the shortest possible time.

This volume has entailed five years of research. Here I have been very fortunate in the services of John Field, who put his vast archives (not least family records of his cousin Hamilton Easter Field) at my disposal and produced dossier after dossier of invaluable information in any number of areas, so copious that I have not been able to include as much as I would have liked. This is especially true of the section on Kahnweiler and his *Ostpolitik* (Field's concept), where I have been obliged to relegate much of his more detailed material to notes. Deepest thanks and apologies to him. Pepe Karmel, who has also had access to Kahnweiler's stockbooks, has likewise shared his research with me. Besides lending me the manuscript of his unpublished dissertation, Karmel has made valuable suggestions. I would also like to acknowledge the great help with research that Michael FitzGerald, Peter Read and Jeffrey Weiss have provided. In Paris, the eminent Picasso scholar Pierre Daix has frequently come to our rescue. Catherine Giraudon has worked tirelessly, copying out correspondence in archives and also canvassing the *ayant droits* for permission to do so. My friends Bernard Minoret and James Lord have been most generous with their help.

Of all the scholars who have proffered advice, none has been more sustaining than my old friend John Golding. His book on cubism, first published in 1959, has never been surpassed. I am greatly indebted to it. An even older friend, Richard Wollheim, has time and again come to my rescue and helped me put my ideas in order. Robert Rosenblum has likewise proved a fount of wisdom and wit. Lydia Gasman has also been extraordinarily generous with her guidance, without which I would never have made it through the sacred wood. Robert Silvers, editor of *The New York Review of Books*, has been as supportive as always; so has Robert Hughes. I have also been fortunate in the friendship and help of Billy Klüver and Julie Martin, the recording angels of twentieth-century art.

Collectors have been very generous in allowing us to photograph works in their collections. I cannot name them all, but would like to single out my mentor Sally Ganz for her enthusiastic support. Many thanks also to Gianni and Marella Agnelli, Natasha Gelman, Christian Peter Henle, Pauline Karpides, Leonard Lauder, Jacqueline Nordmann, Paul Padgette, Emily Rauh Pulitzer, David Rockefeller, Paul Sacher, the late Florene Schoenborn, Sanford Schwartz, Stanley J. Seeger, Philippe Solvit, Betsey Whitney and Richard S. Zeisler.

Dealers have been very generous with details of provenance, catalogs, photographs and much more. Heinz Berggruen, through whose hands so many Picassos have passed, has been a great source of help; as has Quentin Laurens and the staff of the Galerie Louise Leiris, formerly the artist's dealers. I would also like to thank William Acquavella, Doris Ammann, Ernst Beyeler, Marianne and Walter Feilchenfeldt, Arnold and Marc Glimcher, Emmanuel Hutin, Jan Krugier, Alex Maguy, Klaus Perls, Ray Perman, Lionel Prejger, Angela Rosengart, James Roundell, Robert Stoppenbach, Eugene Thaw and Hasegawa Tokushichi.

The auction houses have been very supportive, particularly the modern painting departments of Christie's and Sotheby's both in London and New York; special thanks to Charles Hindlip, the chairman, and Jussi Pyrkkänen at Christie's, and to Laurel J. Beckett and Lucy Tage at Sotheby's. Eberhard Kornfeld, Matteo Lampertico at Finarte and Lucrèce Recchi at Guy Loudmer have also provided assistance.

Besides the above, I am indebted to the hundreds of people, some of them friends, many of them strangers, who helped to make this book possible (deepest apologies if I have inadvertently omitted anyone): Marie Adams, Pierre Marcel Adéma, Ancilla Antonini, Irina Antonova, Eduardo Arroyo, the late Lily Auchincloss, Jean-Paul Avice, Alexander Babin, Rosaline Bacou, Christine Baker, François-Marie Banier, Vivian Barnett, Sabine Barnicaud, Sid and Mercedes Bass, Henri de Beaumont, Pierre Bergé, Yves and Michèle Berger, Marie-Laure Bernadac, Georges Bernier, Kathrin Binder, Bill Blass, Margarita Christiansen Patri di Bosch, Gilbert de Botton, Gilbert Boudar, Alain Bouret, Edward Burns, Anselmo Carini, Jean-Bernard Cahours d'Aspry, Pierre Caizergues, Vivian Cameron, Lucien Clergue, Françoise Cohen, Philippe Colin, Elizabeth Cowling, Paul Crowther, Nicole and José-Emmanuel Cruz, Olivier Daulte, Stelly Delecourt, the late Edouard Dermit, Caroline Eichenberger, Maxime de la Falaise, Fèlix Fanés, Hector Feliciano, Jack Flam, Francesc Fontbona, Lucian Freud, the late Edward Fry, Susan Galassi, Kate Ganz, the late Vicente García Márquez, Pierrette Gargallo, Victoria Garvin, the late Christian Geelhaar, the late Walter Goetz, Georges González Gris, Nicholas Gormanston, Thomas D. Grischkowsky, Marta Guthová, Kosei Hara, Mildred Hathaway, Linda Dalrymple Henderson, Wolfgang Henze-Ketterer, Anne Herme, Adrian Hicken, Madame Huin, Ron Johnson, the late James Joll, Lewis Kachur, Christian Kaufmann, Michel Kellermann, Martin Kemp, Robert

Kerzner, Dorothy Kosinski, Albert Kostenevich, Gilbert and Carmen Krill, Mary Louise Krumrine, Geneviève Laporte, Jane Lee, Anne Leguy, Carlos Lozano, Jean-José Marchand, Anne de Margerie, Josephine Matamoros, Mary McDougal, Camilla McGrath, Neil MacGregor, Isabella McIntyre, George Melly, Jean-Paul Monery, Isabelle Monod-Fontaine, Nelida Mori, Charlotte Mosley, Francis M. Naumann, Percy North, Mary Anne Ordona, Roberto Otero, Josep Palau i Fabre, Francesc Parcerisas, Fabienne Pariente, Peter Perrone, Mikhail Piotrovsky, Antoni Pitxot, Stuart Preston, Sam Raeburn, Marika Rivera Phillips, Angelica Rudenstine, John and Rosamond Russell, Arlette Sarrazin-Verdaguer, Monique Schneider-Manoury, Nicholas Serota, Roger Shattuck, Richard Shone, Julia Shmeleva, Valeria Soffici Giaccai, Susan Sontag, Hilary Sperling, Werner Spies, Mariuccia Sprenger, Ronald Strom, Elizabeth Stuart, David Sweetman, Geneviève Taillade, Josiane Tricotti, Gertie Utley, Shelley Wanger, RoseAnna Warren, Joy Weber, Lisa Webster, Mary Jane Wheelock, John Wilson, Rodrigo de Zayas.

I am particularly grateful to those who provided accommodation and hospitality when I was working away from home: Ahmet and Mica Ertegun, Polly Fritchey, Sarah Saint-George, Janey Longman, Oscar and Annette de la Renta, the late David Warwick, Donald Munson, Duarte Pinto Coelho, Marguerite Littman and that most generous patron of the arts, Drue Heinz.

Lastly, I could never have written this book without the Herculean support and saintly patience of my collaborator Marilyn McCully. She has helped me triumph over all manner of demons. Marilyn is a renowned Picasso scholar in her own right, and she has contributed many of her own ideas to the book. At the same time she has taken over such routine tasks as checking sources and marshaling notes, thereby leaving me free to focus my energies on the writing. I thank Marilyn with all my heart and look forward to working with her on the next two volumes.

Marilyn's husband, Michael Raeburn, has played a no less crucial role in the actual making of the book. He has assembled all the illustrations, single-handedly designed the layout, collated the index, set the type and taken care of the technical details. His selfless devotion has been a lesson to us all. No author could have been better served.

Contents

A LIFE OF

PICASSO

VOLUME II: 1907–1917

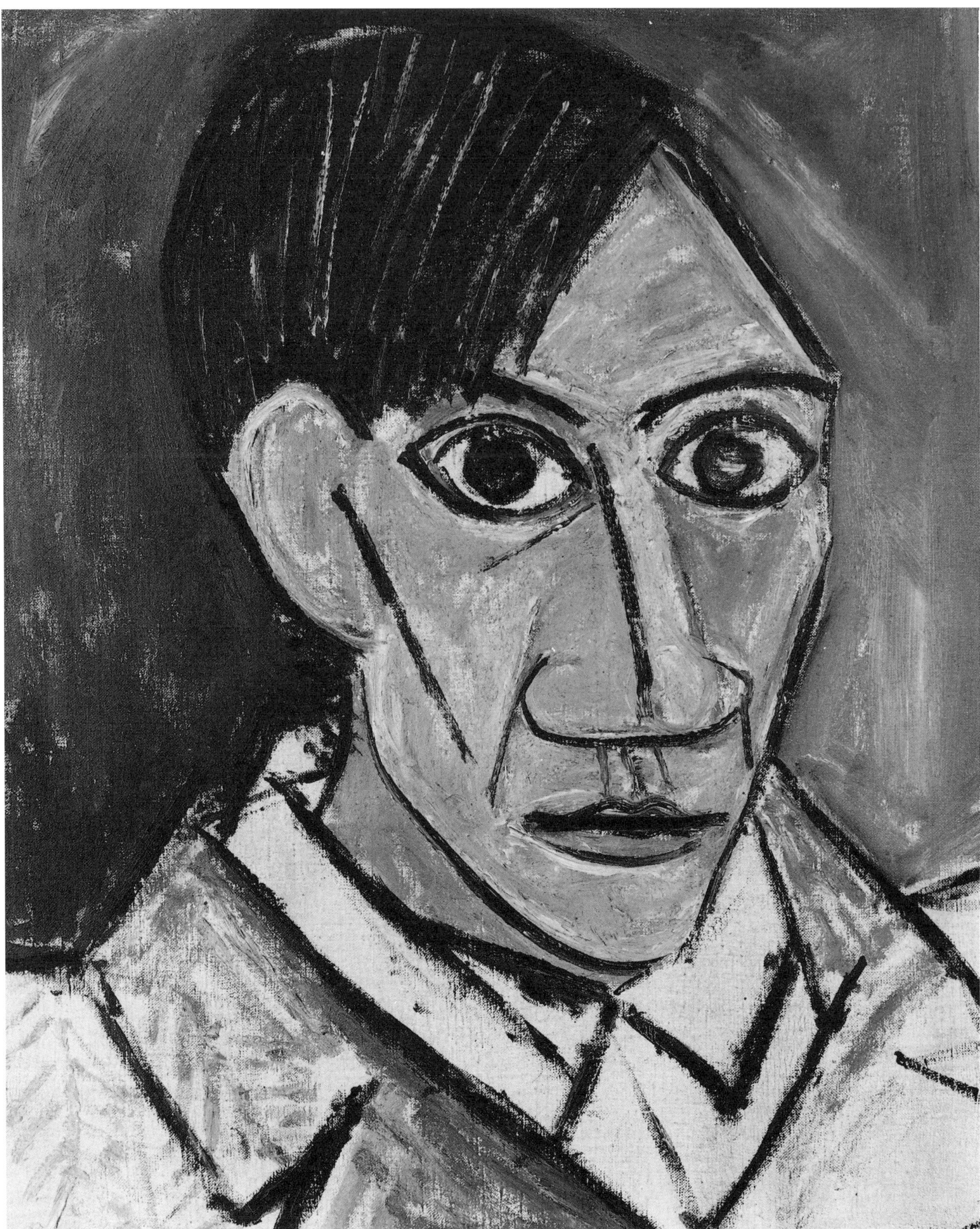

Introduction: *La Bande à Picasso*

Fernande and Picasso in Montmartre, 1906. Archives Picasso.

Opposite: Picasso. *Self-Portrait,* spring, 1907. Oil on canvas, 56×46 cm. Národní Galerie, Prague.

AT THE TIME THIS BOOK OPENS, January, 1907, Picasso was living with the languorous, auburn-haired Fernande Olivier—celebrated as "*la belle Fernande.*" Their affair had started three and a half years earlier and had reached its apogee the previous summer, when Picasso had taken her to a remote village in the Pyrenees and painted her as an incandescent goddess. In the last few months, however, things had changed. Fernande could only conclude from her lover's latest work that the honeymoon was over, and that Picasso felt far more intensely about his art—to which all the women in his life would ultimately be sacrificed—than he did about her. Now that he was starting work on the revolutionary painting that would come to be called *Les Demoiselles d'Avignon,* the artist found Fernande's presence extremely distracting, but he was too possessive and jealous to let her out. And so while he worked away demonically, she was confined to the large, chaotically cluttered studio in the Bateau Lavoir—that ramshackle tenement perched precariously on the slopes of the Butte de Montmartre where cubism is said, rightly or wrongly, to have been born. When he was not painting or, more likely, drawing, the artist relaxed in the company of a tight little group of friends who were already known as "*la bande à Picasso.*" As he told the writer Hélène Parmelin some fifty years later, "We had no other preoccupation but what we were doing and . . . saw nobody but each other. Apollinaire, Max Jacob, Salmon . . . Think of it, what an aristocracy!"[1] Picasso was right: his *bande* was as exclusive, as disdainful and as much a law unto itself as any aristocratic coterie. They had no doubts about their destiny: "You've heard of La Fontaine and Molière and Racine," Jacob announced. "Well now that's us."[2]

A storyteller of genius as well as a great poet, Guillaume Apollinaire was undoubtedly the star of this trio. To quote Gertrude Stein,

> he was extraordinarily brilliant and no matter what subject was started, if he knew anything about it or not, he quickly saw the whole meaning of the thing and elaborated it by his wit and fancy carrying it further than anybody knowing anything about it could have done, and oddly enough generally correctly.[3]

Although he had already written some of his most memorable works (*Le Chanson du mal aimé* and *L'Enchanteur pourrissant,* to name but two), he had yet to make a name for himself. To earn a living, he was toiling away in a bank, also editing and writing pornography: notably a rollicking,

Picasso. *The Duel* (caricature of Apollinaire), 1907. Graphite and colored pencils on paper, 18×13.7 cm. Private collection.

sadistic farce called *Les Onze Mille Verges*. The book includes coded references to some of their mutual friends, and its subversive sexuality has much in common with the savagery of *Les Demoiselles d'Avignon*. To further his career rather than avenge his honor, Apollinaire had recently challenged a journalist to a quite unnecessary duel.[4] He had chosen Max Jacob, with whom he had a contorted love-hate relationship, as one of his seconds. So that Max could make a good impression on the other, more aristocratic, *témoins*, Picasso lent him a top hat.[5] Alas, when he removed the hat from his head, the assembled seconds could read the name Picasso writ large inside the crown. The duel did not take place.

Max Jacob was even more tormented than Apollinaire, but by a very different set of demons: real ones insofar as he had seen them in visions. He was also a marvelous poet. This small, bald gnome—son of a Jewish tailor from Brittany—had met Picasso on his first visit to Paris in 1901 and fallen instantly in love with him; and in love (and sometimes hate) he would remain until his death in a French concentration camp in 1944. As his friend the courtesan Liane de Pougy wrote, Jacob could be mischievous, dirty, bitter, arrogant, perfidious, thoughtless, insolent and much else,[6] but he also had enormous charm and a sporadically saintly nature that enabled him to find peace as a lay brother in the monastery of Saint-Benoît.

Picasso did not return Jacob's overheated feelings, but in his cannibalistic way he lived off them. He also came to depend on Jacob's prodigious intelligence and quirkish passion for French literature, not to mention his merciless mockery and bitchy wit, his saucy song-and-dance routines and lurid accounts of louche adventures. When Picasso was in one of the black moods that bouts of intense work would provoke, Jacob could usually tease him out of it, just as he could tease—they were both extremely touchy—Apollinaire into losing his temper. André Salmon was more phlegmatic. He was not in the same league as the other two poets, but he was a more conventional *homme de lettres*—a little too polished and a bit of a lackey. Although he would soon quit his studio in the Bateau Lavoir, Salmon remained close to Picasso, who liked having his laureates at hand, the better to pit them against each other.

All three poets were young—the same age as Picasso or slightly older—poor (especially Jacob) and unknown, and obliged to do journalistic hackwork when their writings, which were steadily accumulating, went unpublished. All three liked to drink, but not to excess; Jacob and Salmon preferred drugs (Jacob favored ether and henbane; Salmon opium, a drug for which Picasso and Apollinaire, who was primarily addicted to fine food, also had a taste). All three were bachelors—unattached and sexually experimental. Jacob's private life had long been a matter of public knowledge: he plied the streets for the roughest "trade." Meanwhile the polymorphous Apollinaire, who had not entirely recovered from his rejection at the hands of an English governess, was tempting fate by taking on a handsome Belgian psychopath as a live-in secretary. The consequences for Picasso as well as himself would be disastrous. Salmon (not entirely to the surprise of Apollinaire, who is the source of the story)[7] had suddenly turned "*très tante*" (very gay) and hung out with other *tantes*. This phase was short-lived. A few months later, Salmon would marry an opiomane like himself. A fourth poet in the group, the flamboyantly

Picasso. *Portrait of Max Jacob*, early 1907. Gouache on paper, 62×47.5 cm. Museum Ludwig, Cologne.

Picasso. *André Salmon, Study for Sculpture*, 1907. Charcoal on paper, 60×40cm. Private collection.

Marie Laurencin. *Louis de Gonzague Frick*. Pen and ink on paper. Collection P.M.A.

bearded Maurice Chevrier, also turns out to have been homosexual. During the day, he worked for the Ministry of Agriculture; at night he wrote poetry under the name of Cremnitz and enjoyed the company of Picasso and his friends. Another eccentric *littérateur* whom Apollinaire introduced into the Bateau Lavoir was his childhood friend Louis de Gonzague Frick—poet, essayist and theatrical dabbler—who lived on the other side of Paris, "*sur cette rive ultra gauche*," as he called it. Frick was the parody of a fin-de-siècle aesthete. However, for all his greenery-yallery affectations—he went about monocled, top-hatted, frock-coated, a flower in his buttonhole and another in his hand—he was a fund of erudition and literary lore. Such was his devotion to Apollinaire—who had been told by his doctor to eat an apple a day before breakfast—that Frick went every morning to shop for the perfect fruit and deliver it to the poet. In return Apollinaire would read his cards.

Other habitués of the Bateau Lavoir included the clever but charmless Maurice Princet: a mathematician and actuary who supposedly provided cubism with a mathematical and theoretical rationale (Picasso and Braque furiously denied this; Princet would later put his expertise at Marcel Duchamp's disposal). After Picasso arranged for the beautiful Alice Princet —a former mistress of his—to elope with Derain, the cuckolded actuary distanced himself from the group. Rather more genial was "Baron" Jean Mollet, Apollinaire's Figaro, whom the poet had ennobled for any number of services—not least introducing him to Picasso. Nor should we leave out of account the progressive young critic Maurice Raynal, who would write eloquently about cubism and remain a lifelong friend of the artist; nor the painter André Deniker, one of three gifted sons of the librarian at the Jardin des Plantes, who would let Picasso into the zoo at night so that he could draw the animals for a bestiary that he and Apollinaire hoped to publish.[8] Mention must also be made of three actors, all soon to become stars: Charles Dullin, who had worked as a busker before becoming an instigator of French avant-garde theater; Harry Baur, the celebrated *vedette* whom Picasso called "El Cabot" (the ham)[9] and Max Jacob's "*ennemi intime*," Marcel Olin, a bellicose pacifist and anarchist, who would die in battle in 1916.[10]

Picasso's Spanish friends would always have first claim on his affections —so long as they were Catalans. He especially enjoyed visits from members of Barcelona's Els Quatre Gats group, with whom he had had his first success. Picasso's closest Spanish friend in Paris was Ramon Pichot, whose prosperous family had fed and lodged him when he was down-and-out in Barcelona. On his first trip to the French capital, Picasso had introduced Ramon to Germaine, who would be the unwitting cause of the suicide of Picasso's friend Carles Casagemas.[11] Germaine and Ramon had later married and turned their house, La Maison Rose—very near the Bateau Lavoir—into a restaurant. Picasso was also fond of three Catalan sculptors: two of whom, Gargallo and Casanovas, divided their time between Paris and Barcelona and kept him in touch with his Catalan cronies. Picasso's favorite was the third: Manolo, who had settled in France to avoid the draft. Picasso loved Manolo's dangerously anarchic sense of mischief, which was at odds with his polite Maillol-like sculpture, and would greatly regret his move in 1910 to Céret in the foothills of the Pyrenees, where his (and Picasso's) painter-patron Frank Burty Haviland had settled. Haviland, who was better off than anyone else in the group, revered Picasso. However, after urging his hero to spend the summers of 1911 and 1913 at Céret, he fell so heavily under his influence that he felt constrained to rid himself of his remaining Picassos, by way of exorcism.

Picasso's *tertulia* (the Spanish term for informal groups of kindred spirits who forgather and exchange banter on a more or less daily basis) included a likable and perceptive Italian painter/writer, Ardengo Soffici, and assorted Germans. The Germans belonged to an avant-garde group of painters and writers known as the *dômiers*: a pun on the German word for "cathedral," and the Café du Dôme, where they congregated, and, of course, the painter Daumier. In the past Picasso had reached for his revolver whenever a German threatened to bombard him with theories. Now that the *dômiers* turned out to have a greater understanding of modernism than the French, he welcomed the more enterprising and acquisitive of them—Wilhelm Uhde, Richard Goetz and their friend Alfred Flechtheim from Düsseldorf—to his studio. All three had started by collecting modern art and ended up dealing in it. A Prussian intellectual with a progressive eye, Uhde prided himself on his grasp of Picasso's cubism. It sometimes took a little time, but in the end he always got the point of the latest development and in the process acquired another painting for himself or one of the young collectors he counseled. Uhde was homosexual, as were several other *dômiers*, and it was through him that Picasso would meet the androgynous-looking, drug-addicted painter Karl-Heinz Wiegels. After arranging for Wiegels to move into the Bateau Lavoir, the artist took a liking to him and was shattered when he killed himself in 1908. Wiegels was one of a succession of good-looking young Germans whom Uhde would bring to the Bateau Lavoir (as well as to the Steins' salon) and inculcate with his passion for Picasso. After Wiegels's suicide, an infinitely more serious German artist would take a studio in the Bateau Lavoir: Otto Freundlich. Little is known about Picasso's rapport with this militant modernist, who experimented with abstraction around the same time as Mondrian. But they kept in touch; and Freundlich's death in a concentration camp during World War II would affect Picasso deeply.[12]

Gertrude Stein, c. 1908. Beinecke Rare Book and Manuscript Library, Yale University.

Although Picasso would visit his principal dealers, Ambroise Vollard and Daniel-Henry Kahnweiler, most days he was in Paris, there was no question on either side of their joining his *tertulia*. For one thing, they were not poets or painters: they were in trade. For another, Picasso had been so scurvily treated by dealers earlier in his career that he had difficulty regarding any of them, except for *marchands amateurs* like Uhde and Goetz, as friends. Besides, Vollard was too arrogant and Kahnweiler and his wife too conventional to withstand the mockery, mayhem and squalor of Bateau Lavoir life. Nor, for similar reasons, would the artist's early patrons Leo and Gertrude Stein participate in the *bande à Picasso*'s activities. Leo was becoming more and more of a curmudgeon. However, Picasso was very dependent on his cash advances and very eager to win him over to his work in progress, the *Demoiselles*. He was not successful: Leo's phenomenal eye for modern art never recovered from the shock of what he called "this horrible mess." Gertrude had less of an eye but was more of a modernist. Picasso had established a very close relationship with this formidable woman—just as he would with her lover Alice Toklas, who arrived from San Francisco in September, 1907. However, he preferred

Derain retour du service
militaire

Far left: André Derain, c. 1908. Archives G. Taillade.

Left: Georges Braque in his studio playing the accordion, c. 1911. Archives Laurens.

Henri Matisse with his wife and daughter Marguerite at Collioure, summer, 1907. Archives Matisse, D.R.

Entrance to Picasso's studio in the Bateau Lavoir. Photograph by Dora Maar.

his Montmartre turf, while the Steins preferred their *pavillon* on the other side of Paris, where Gertrude had *her* salon. The Steins' Saturday evening get-togethers were a nightmare for Picasso, whose French was still far from fluent; but he could not afford to miss them. Their walls were the best possible advertisement for his work, which Gertrude was tireless in persuading affluent friends to buy.

That Gertrude underestimated and misunderstood Picasso's *tertulia* emerges from her memoirs, which do the group scant justice and herself scant credit. True, she gushes over Apollinaire, but she characterizes him as a wit and a card—"so suave you can never tell what he is doing"[13]—never as a poet, let alone a major one. The same with Max Jacob. Gertrude's pages imply that he was a giddy little clown, not one of the most divinatory and sensitive writers of his day. As for Salmon, he would always bear Gertrude a grudge for putting him down as a nonentity. She was equally hard on Braque, who would join Matisse in denouncing Gertrude's pretensions to genius. These mutual antipathies might have been less fierce if Gertrude had learned to speak proper French. According to Braque, she was no more able to follow what he and his friends said than they were able to follow what she wrote.

There was one other personage—a man of towering importance in Picasso's life—who was conspicuously absent from his *tertulia*: Henri Matisse. The two artists took an obsessive interest in each other's work and, as their paintings often reveal, paid regular visits to each other's studios. Nevertheless, their pride, mutual mistrust (all the stronger for the mutual regard that it implied) and one-upmanship made for an extremely fraught relationship. Their rapport would become even less cordial when Matisse's two most brilliant followers, Derain and Braque, rallied to Picasso. This change of allegiance would have major repercussions at the Bateau Lavoir: the *rendez-vous des poètes* would become more of a *rendez-vous des peintres*. The *tertulia* would take on a more macho character. Flanked by the much taller Braque and Derain, Picasso looked like Napoleon with his marshals—"every inch a chief," Gertrude Stein said.

Apart from Fernande, one of the few women to play an active role in the *bande à Picasso* was Marie Laurencin, whom the artist would present to Apollinaire early in 1907, saying that he had found him a fiancée. Laurencin would later accuse the *bande* of being spiteful and decadent. Since this is what Picasso, Fernande and the rest of them thought of her, these accusations need not be taken too seriously. However, there is no denying that women had to contend with a lot of macho condescension and beastliness in this phallocentric group. Since women were traditionally excluded from *tertulias*, they played little part in Picasso's; but it would surely be unrealistic to expect anything else of a man who had been born in the late nineteenth century into the society that invented machismo. Given his childhood in a household of doting Andalusian women, Picasso could certainly behave in a manipulative and willful way. However, as anyone who knew him well can attest, the misogynistic verso had a recto that was compassionate, generous and loving. To his friends Picasso manifested an ineffable brightness of spirit and intelligence. Nobody can write about him without taking this dichotomy into account. So much for recent attacks by self-promoting "moralists," who choose to

Picasso, 1907. Archives Picasso.

judge this great artist, born into another age and another culture, by the light of today's cant. As I hope these pages will show, the artist, at least in these early years, was as much sinned against as sinning.

* * *

Before tackling the *Demoiselles*, let us take a brief look at Picasso shortly before and shortly after he embarked on it. Picasso liked to mark important anniversaries by doing a painting which would signify a change in his work as well as in his life. Around the time of his twenty-fifth birthday (October 19, 1906), he executed a group of self-portrait paintings and drawings, which, as we saw at the end of the last volume, unveil a totally new Picasso: a sunburned Dionysos in an undershirt, his hair *en brosse*, all set to challenge and subvert the tradition of European art up to and including Cézanne, whose self-portrait with a palette (p. 387) had partly inspired this image. How cool, how laconic the artist looks, before he embarks on his messianic mission.

A few months later (February or March, 1907), Picasso reveals a much harsher image of himself, wrapped up in a heavy winter overcoat of herringbone tweed, as if freezing cold. According to Salmon, Picasso had become a recluse; he had virtually forsaken painting for drawing and was busy filling sketchbooks in preparation for the *Demoiselles*. The physical and psychic strain that the portrayal of these whores caused him is reflected in this anguished image. To judge by a photograph of him which this painting bounces off rather than follows, the artist has done everything possible to give his image the smell of cordite. As Baudelaire wrote, "The charms of the horrible intoxicate only the strong."[14]

Inspiration for this portrait (now in the Prague National Gallery) did not come from any of Picasso's previous exemplars—El Greco, Cézanne or Gauguin—but from Van Gogh and a totally new source: the cinema. The artist was a past master at self-dramatization, and the look of menace on Picasso's face derives, at least in part, from the stylized close-ups in the silent movies of which the artist was such a fan: close-ups where the eyes, graphically accentuated, as here, in black, double for the silent mouth and articulate the hero's sangfroid, the villain's glee, the artist's mad resolve. This work is the quintessence of the Andalusian *mirada fuerte*, the strong gaze, that Picasso turned on people he wanted to conquer, seduce, possess and, not least, shock. Now for *Les Demoiselles d'Avignon* . . .

Below: Engraving no. 129 from *Suite 347*, May 30, 1968. Aquatint and etching, 22.5×26.5 cm.

1

"Le Peintre de la vie moderne"

Picasso. Study for *Les Demoiselles d'Avignon*, spring, 1907. Charcoal on paper, 48×65 cm. Öffentliche Kunstsammlung Basel, Kunstmuseum. Cooper Gift.

No twentieth-century painting has attracted more attention than Picasso's great brothel composition of 1907, *Les Demoiselles d'Avignon*: five confrontational whores posed theatrically on a little stage, framed by draperies, dark red on the left, blue on the right. In the foreground there is a still life of fruit, which is usually thought to have a phallic significance. Knowing Picasso, I suggest it is a sardonic joke: men do not go to brothels to eat fruit. The painting's shocking treatment of a shocking subject, its highly charged sexuality and stylistic disjunctiveness, not to speak of its role as a principal begetter of the modern movement, have brought it unprecedented iconic fame and a surfeit of stylistic analysis and interpretation. The *Demoiselles* had its apotheosis at the Musée Picasso in 1988: an exhibition including the great painting itself and the El Greco that inspired it, as well as the contents of sixteen mostly unpublished sketchbooks and studies in assorted media, comprising in all some four or five hundred items.[1] Besides reproducing every one of these works, the huge, two-volume catalog provided an exhaustive chronology and anthology of references, a masterly analysis of the carnets by Pierre Daix, a major historical study by William Rubin and a reprise of Leo Steinberg's "Philosophical Brothel" essay.[2] In some respects the profusion of preparatory drawings proved too much of a good thing: it encouraged scholars to focus on the sketches at the expense of the painting itself. The emphasis on the *croquis* for the two allegorical visitors to the brothel—a sailor and a medical student clutching a skull, as it were, Eros and Thanatos—is the more distracting, given that Picasso in his wisdom banished them from the final version. In retrospect, one can see why he kept most of this preliminary material secret; why he preferred to make misleading statements rather than elucidate the *Demoiselles.* As he later confessed, "You must not always believe what I say. Questions tempt you to tell lies, particularly when there is no answer."[3]

To justify my own approach to the *Demoiselles,* I need to bring myself into the picture. In the 1950s I shared a house in Provence with the British art historian and collector Douglas Cooper. The house contained what was then the most comprehensive private collection of cubist art in the world. Picasso was a frequent visitor. Since he was extraordinarily generous with his work, he seldom arrived empty-handed. On February 20, 1959, Cooper's forty-eighth birthday, the artist gave him an important two-sided drawing for the *Demoiselles* composition. I was away in the

Opposite: Picasso. *Les Demoiselles d'Avignon*, 1907. Oil on canvas, 243.9×233.7 cm. The Museum of Modern Art, New York: Acquired through the Lillie P. Bliss Bequest.

Constantin Guys. *Prostitute.* Wood engraving by Tony and Jacques Beltrand from Gustave Geffroy's *Constantin Guys* (1904).

Picasso. *Horseman*, inscribed "Constantin Guis," 1905. Pen and black ink on sketchbook page, 17.5×12cm. Musée Picasso.

United States at the time but would subsequently hear Picasso comment on it; not so much on the recto as on the verso of the sheet: a striking drawing of Fernande Olivier. At the time Picasso's comments seemed of little consequence. Later, when I focused on the *Demoiselles*, I realized he had unwittingly provided a key to it.

The recto of the drawing appears to have nothing to do with the verso, which portrays Fernande from the back; her torso is twisted to show her right breast; her head is twisted to show her right profile. She has laced herself into a very tight *tailleur*, shaped like an hourglass, trimmed with two buttons above a vent at the back. Her right hand holds something we cannot see: a parasol, as a related drawing confirms. Did this image have any connection with the *Demoiselles*? Picasso gave the same answer he had given Cooper. After setting aside the *Demoiselles*, he had contemplated doing a large Bois de Boulogne composition: Fernande *en promenade* with a horse and carriage in the background. Fernande had apparently bought that *tailleur* for the opening of the Indépendants. Picasso confirmed that he had soon abandoned this alternate project and returned to battle with the *Demoiselles*.

It is important to establish these details, because in his justly celebrated interpretation of the *Demoiselles* Steinberg has questioned them, indeed has accused Cooper of "patent inaccuracy."[4] This is unjust to Cooper, who faithfully recorded Picasso's words and in doing so provided an invaluable clue to the concept behind the *Demoiselles*. By revealing that he had envisaged painting a Bois de Boulogne scene at the end of the first phase of the *Demoiselles* (that is to say, sometime in July), Picasso opens up this painting to a new interpretation, one that has the added virtue of allowing for other ones, such as Steinberg's eloquent argument for sexual trauma and Rubin's for Eros and Thanatos and fear of venereal disease. Picasso's work is far too protean and paradoxical to be limited to a single reading.

Odd though it might seem, there is a thematic link between Picasso's whorehouse and his carriages in the Bois de Boulogne: Constantin Guys. Guys excelled at both these subjects—a fact celebrated by Baudelaire in his most prophetic piece of art criticism, his article on Guys entitled "Le Peintre de la vie moderne" (1863). In this essay the poet postulates two quintessentially "modern" subjects for an artist to address: the brothel and the procession of carriage folk in the Bois. The fact that Picasso intended to paint these two subjects suggests that he saw himself identifying not so much with Guys as with Baudelaire's "painter of modern life." He was not, of course, the first to do so—Manet had also assumed the role—but he fitted the bill better than any other artist of this century. We do not know whether Picasso had as yet read Baudelaire's essay, for which he later expressed the highest regard. We do, however, know that he was very familiar with Gustave Geffroy's book on Guys. This had come out three years earlier and included lengthy quotations from Baudelaire, as well as from Edmond de Goncourt's *La Fille Elisa* with its astonishingly realistic descriptions of low-class brothels. One of Geffroy's plates had already inspired Picasso's drawing of a top-hatted man on a horse, jokingly signed "*Constantin Guis* [sic]." Not only did Guys's drawings trigger Picasso's Bois de Boulogne sketches, but the whorehouse scenes reproduced in Geffroy's book—some of them even include sailors—are reflected

Picasso. Study for Bois de Boulogne composition, spring, 1907. Charcoal on paper, 65×48cm. Öffentliche Kunstsammlung Basel, Kunstmuseum. Cooper Gift.

Opposite top: Constantin Guys. *Brothel Scene*. Wood engraving by Tony and Jacques Beltrand from Gustave Geffroy's *Constantin Guys* (1904).

Opposite center: Constantin Guys. *Carriages in the Bois de Boulogne*. Wood engraving by Tony and Jacques Beltrand from Gustave Geffroy's *Constantin Guys* (1904).

Opposite bottom: Picasso. Study for Bois de Boulogne composition, May, 1907. Pen and India ink on sketchbook page, 10.5×13.6cm. Musée Picasso.

again and again in the grouping and posing of the *Demoiselles*. For instance, the salacious slouch that Guys uses for many of his whores inspired the half-lying, half-sitting pose with legs ajar that Picasso uses for the second *demoiselle* from the left. However, Guys's influence on the *Demoiselles* is less significant than the influence of Baudelaire's essay on Picasso. "Le Peintre de la vie moderne" addressed the same issues that Picasso addresses in the *Demoiselles*, notably the poet's adulation of what he called "pure art . . . the type of beauty peculiar to evil, the beauty in the horrible,"[5] or his notion of whoredom as an ideal subject for an artist.

> [The whore, Baudelaire says] is a perfect image of savagery in the midst of civilization. She has a kind of beauty which comes to her from sin. . . . Let us not forget that, apart from natural beauty and even artificial beauty, all beings have the stamp of their trade, a characteristic which may, on the physical level, express itself as ugliness, but also as a kind of professional beauty. . . . Amongst these [women], some, in whom an innocent yet monstrous sort of fatuity is only too apparent, carry in their faces and in their eyes, which look you brazenly in the face, the evident joy of being alive (in truth, one wonders why). Sometimes they effortlessly adopt poses, both provocative and dignified, that would be the joy of the most fastidious sculptor, if only the sculptor of today had the courage and the wit to seize hold of nobility everywhere, even in the mire. . . . In this foggy chaos, bathed in golden light, undreamed of by indigent chastity, gruesome nymphs and living dolls, whose childlike eyes have sinister flashes, move and contort themselves.[6]

Picasso. *The Harem*, 1905. Oil on canvas, 154.3×109.5cm. The Cleveland Museum of Art: Bequest of Leonard C. Hanna, Jr.

Baudelaire's challenge to "the sculptor of today" would be taken up by the painter of tomorrow, Picasso. Not that the artist ever admitted to doing anything of the sort. The more crucial the source, the more determined he was to divert attention from it. Daix confirms this: whenever Baudelaire's name came up in conversation, Picasso would switch the subject to Matisse, as if the poet were his rival's private property.[7] In my experience strategies of this nature were usually a sign that Picasso had something to hide.

As for the other "modern" subject that Picasso borrows from Guys, the parade of parasoled cocottes lolling in the back of carriages with grooms on the box, we have only to listen to Baudelaire's descriptions—for instance, of the coachmen: "stiff and perpendicular . . . the monotonous and uncharacterized effigy of servility . . . their whole character consists in having none"—to conclude that Picasso was familiar with the essay.[8] Slight as they are, these Bois de Boulogne sketches provide further confirmation of Picasso's identification with "the painter of modern life"—an identification that would last until his death. However, their lack of fervor equally reveals why Picasso failed to go ahead with this alternate project.

* * *

Picasso had begun to envisage a Baudelairean role for himself the previous summer, which he had spent at Gósol in the Pyrenees. There in the isolation of a mountain wilderness the artist, who sometimes chose to identify with Christ, seems to have concluded that his time had come. He was finally ready to establish that he—as opposed to Matisse, who had dominated successive Salons—would be the mahdi of modern art.

Before he left Gósol, Picasso executed a sizable but sketchy harem painting, which anticipates the *Demoiselles* in that it depicts four naked Fernandes at various stages of their toilette. It also includes a great soft, sprawled male attendant. Picasso makes a typically Andalusian joke at this *maricón*'s expense by placing one hand on his *porrón* (a phallic drinking vessel), and, no less significant, a flower in the other. He elaborates his simple joke by sketching in the attendant's lunch: a suggestive length of sausage and some round, pink things. The joke is also on Ingres, whose *Bain turc* inspired this beautiful if mocking pastiche. A related gouache, *Three Nudes*, is so profusely annotated (the inscription specifies that the women are in a brothel and one of them is smoking a cigarette) that Picasso must have intended to execute a more ambitious version. He never did. Back in Paris, he continued to do studies of naked women—notably the hefty *Two Nudes* in the Museum of Modern Art, New York—who often have their arms around each other's waists. Lesbians? Possibly: Gertrude Stein, whose portrait he had recently finished, was much in his thoughts. We would, however, do better to take another look at the self-portrait as Bacchus that Picasso did around this time.[9] If the artist saw himself as Bacchus (or Dionysos), he would have seen his female counterparts, not least the *demoiselles*, as bacchantes: those maenads "who tore Orpheus apart, at Dionysos's behest, for worshiping the rival god, Apollo."[10]

By the end of 1906, Pyrenean euphoria had evaporated. Picasso "became uneasy," André Salmon reported. "He turned his canvases to the wall and threw down his paintbrushes. For many long days and nights, he drew. . . . Never was labor less rewarded with joy, and without his former youthful enthusiasm Picasso undertook a large canvas that was intended to be the first fruit of his experiments."[11] Salmon's claim that Picasso had indeed more or less abandoned painting for drawing at the end of 1906 would not be confirmed until those hundreds of preliminary studies materialized eighty years later.

Significantly, the first idea for the *Demoiselles* is to be found in a sketchbook on the recto of a study for the *Two Nudes*, which suggests that Picasso started working towards the *Demoiselles* before 1907. In the first studies five naked whores are grouped around a male figure—a sailor, as subsequent drawings reveal—while a man clutching a book (sometimes a skull), whom Picasso would identify as a medical student, enters on the left.[12] Both these intruders will be eliminated before he executes the big painting: the sailor will simply disappear; the medical student will forfeit his place to a *demoiselle*. These interlopers were too blatantly allegorical. They recall the doctor and nursing sister who symbolize *Science and Charity* in the sickbed painting his father had obliged him to do when he was fifteen. Picasso would have hated to imply a moral, let alone tell a moralizing tale.

Meanwhile Picasso returned once again to his revered El Greco. A major work had turned up round the corner from the Bateau Lavoir in the collection of an old acquaintance from Barcelona days, Ignacio Zuloaga. An urbane painter of flashy Hispagnolist scenes, who prided himself on being a pioneer in the rediscovery of El Greco, Zuloaga had finally acquired a masterpiece by his favorite artist. (Only one of this connoisseur's nine other Grecos is still accepted as authentic.) Zuloaga had discovered

El Greco. *Apocalyptic Vision*, 1608–14. Oil on canvas, 224.8×199.4cm. The Metropolitan Museum of Art: Rogers Fund, 1956.

Picasso. Study for *Les Demoiselles d'Avignon* (on recto of study for *Two Nudes*), winter 1906–07. Black pencil on sketchbook page, 10.6×14.7cm. Musée Picasso.

Picasso. Study for *Les Demoiselles d'Avignon*, 1907. Graphite pencil and pastel on paper, 47.7×63.5cm. Öffentliche Kunstsammlung Basel, Kupferstichkabinett: Bequest of the artist to the city of Basel.

Bottom right: Picasso. Study for *Les Demoiselles d'Avignon*, May, 1907. Pen and India ink on sketchbook page, 10.5×13.6cm. Musée Picasso.

Picasso. Study for *Les Demoiselles d'Avignon*, June, 1907. Watercolor on paper, 17.4×22.5cm. Philadelphia Museum of Art: A. E. Gallatin Collection.

this altarpiece—once mistakenly known as *Sacred and Profane Love*, then, when Zuloaga owned it, as *The Opening of the Fifth Seal*, and subsequently renamed *Apocalyptic Vision*—in a doctor's house in Córdoba.[13] Zuloaga paid a thousand pesetas for the *Fifth Seal*, and soon had it hanging in his studio at 54, rue Caulaincourt.[14] And there Picasso frequently saw it over the next few years—the only old master that he was free to study in a friend's house rather than in a museum or dealer's gallery; and, as was his way with an obsessive new image, he devoured it, internalized it, much as he would the image of a new woman in his life.

Besides helping himself to El Greco's sacred fire, Picasso based the scale of the *Demoiselles* (244×234 cm) on the *Fifth Seal* (225×193 cm), and its peculiar, fortuitous proportions. Over the centuries, what had originally been a vertical altarpiece had been damaged and cut down.[15] Hence the awkward, squarish format of the El Greco: an accident which would help Picasso solve the vexing problem of giving an extended figure composition the tension and compression it required. Early studies for the *Demoiselles* reveal him trying to adapt his grouping to the format of the sketchbook page, but never quite succeeding until—with the *Fifth Seal* fresh in mind—he starts squaring the rectangle and cramming his figures together, much as El Greco has done with his writhing, resurrected nudes. Now that he had worked out the proportions to his satisfaction, Picasso could cut and stretch a canvas corresponding to them and address his apocalyptic whores in earnest.

*　　*　　*

Work on the *Demoiselles* condemned the twenty-five-year-old Picasso to a life of seclusion. Although friends sympathized with his aspirations, none of them was capable of understanding the pictorial form that these aspirations took. When he allowed Salmon, Apollinaire and Jacob to see the painting, they were baffled and took refuge in embarrassed silence, or the faintest of praise. As a result, the band of friends, whose support was so vital to Picasso, ceased temporarily to meet. One of the few visitors he welcomed to the studio was the dealer Ambroise Vollard, who came by on February 4 and bought up most of the Blue and Rose period works that he had not acquired the previous year. Since Picasso still hoped to get a contract out of Vollard—the dealer for whom he would always have the highest regard—he consented to a down payment of 1,400 francs on a total of 2,500 francs, the balance to be paid in six months.[16] Thanks also to recent purchases by Leo and Gertrude Stein, Picasso and Fernande would have enough to live on. Gertrude was working on an ambitious breakthrough project—*The Making of Americans*, that tedious *Bildungsroman*—and was disposed to be charitable.

Pierre Bonnard. *Portrait of Vollard* (detail), c. 1904–05. Oil on canvas. Kunsthaus, Zurich.

The Steins also provided Picasso with money for a second studio in the Bateau Lavoir. This was a dark room on the floor below his principal studio:[17] a sanctuary where Picasso could lock himself away from everyone, including Fernande—lock himself away with a model if need be. One of the possibilities raised by the *Demoiselles* sketchbooks is that he drew from life. He usually denied doing so—probably to imply that these exercises were no longer necessary—but evidently liked to keep his eye in. "You ask him if he uses models," the American journalist Gelett

Picasso. Study of a sailor, March, 1907. Black pencil on sketchbook page, 24.2×19.3cm. Musée Picasso.

Burgess wrote in 1908, "and he turns to you a dancing eye. 'Where would I get them?' grins Picasso, as he winks at his ultramarine ogresses."[18] Where indeed? However, a number of studies turn out to be done in the more hesitant manner Picasso uses when he has someone posing for him. And we know from the ever-carping Leo Stein that Picasso twice shared one of his models: "But [he] could make nothing of it; the few drawings he made did not, so to speak, look at the model."[19] Drawings for the sailor and details of his silk and lanyard seem to have been done from life.[20]

Although most of the *Demoiselles* studies relate generically to the image that Picasso had devised for Fernande, there are occasional intimations of another set of features. The artist, who freely admitted sleeping with most of his models, was doubtless seeing other women. Sabartès, usually the epitome of discretion, admitted that the artist was very experimental sexually.[21] Picasso may also have reverted to his old habit of frequenting brothels. Since his subjects usually reflect the circumstances of his daily life, this is more than likely. Citing Françoise Gilot's assertion that Picasso confessed to having caught and been cured of an unspecified venereal disease at some unspecified time before his first marriage, Rubin hazards a guess that this occurred in the course of this winter and that "trepidation in regard to syphilis and gonorrhea had to play some role in [the *Demoiselles'*] symbolism."[22] In fact Picasso is known to have contracted a venereal disease in Barcelona in 1902. His friend Dr. Josep Fontbona had treated him and been well rewarded with a handsome Blue period painting of a melancholy mother wandering at dusk on a beach, clutching a baby in one hand, a red flower—the traditional emblem of a prostitute who was menstruating or sick—in the other. According to Dr. Fontbona's great-nephew, Picasso was suffering from nonspecific urethritis, but the significance of his gift to the doctor might suggest a more deadly malady.[23] In view of Picasso's visits, the previous winter, to the Parisian venereologist Dr. Louis Jullien at the prison-hospital of Saint-Lazare—ostensibly to paint the syphilitic prostitutes in his care—syphilis cannot be ruled out.[24]

Since there is no evidence of further bouts of venereal disease, it is safer to attribute the coolness between Picasso and Fernande to the letdown that often afflicts sexual relationships after an initial period of bliss, or to the letdown an artist's mistress feels when she can no longer delude herself that she means as much to her lover as his work. Fernande may also have felt degraded by Picasso's use of her distinctive image for his whores. (The back-to-front whore, lower right, derives as much from Fernande on a bidet as from Cézanne's squatting *Bathers*.) This put-down must have been particularly galling to a penniless beauty born out of wedlock who had survived by marketing her body, as a model, it is true, not a prostitute, though models sometimes had to sacrifice their virtue to get or keep a job. Picasso liked to rub all this in—"jokingly," of course—by telling his friends that Fernande was one of the girls in his brothel. The joke was hardly a compliment.

Picasso. Study for squatting *demoiselle*, March, 1907. Pen and black ink on sketchbook page, 24.2×19.3cm. Musée Picasso.

"*Les Demoiselles d'Avignon*—how that name annoys me," Picasso said. "It was Salmon who invented it. As you well know it was originally called *Le Bordel d'Avignon*."[25] Salmon also seems to have been responsible for an alternate title, *Le Bordel philosophique*, which he claims was adopted by "*les familiers de Picasso*"—Apollinaire, Jacob and himself. However, there is no reference to it in any of their writings, and Picasso never used it. When he finally allowed his painting to be shown, at the exhibition L'Art Moderne en France, which was held at Paul Poiret's Salon d'Antin in July, 1916, Picasso lashed out at Salmon, who had organized the show, for foisting this facetious joke of a title onto his masterpiece: furious because the only reason for doing so was to assuage public prudishness by substituting a euphemism for the word "brothel." Convenience obliged the artist eventually to use it, albeit in a subtly different Spanish form: "*las chicas de Avignon*" (the Avignon girls). "*Chicas*" has a less facetious connotation than "*demoiselles*," which means "damsels."

When a close friend, the Argentinian photographer Roberto Otero, asked Picasso whether there was any truth in the story that the painting had been named after a brothel on the carrer d'Avinyó in Barcelona, Picasso launched into a furious denial. "Would I be so pathetic as to seek inspiration . . . in a reality as literal . . . as a specific brothel in a specific city on a specific street?" And he went on to say that it would be as misguided to tie his *chicas* down to this or that whorehouse as it would be to see his saltimbanques emanating from the Cirque Médrano, or his girls of the so-called Negro period recruited from a brothel on the rue Saint-Denis.

Picasso. *Portrait of Fernande*, 1907. Gouache on paper, 63×48cm. Private collection.

> The worst thing is that when I am asked about this and say it's not true [Picasso went on], people go on maintaining that [the *demoiselles*] are girls from a brothel on the carrer d'Avinyó. In fact, as everybody once knew, this story was invented by Max Jacob or André Salmon or some other friend in our group—it doesn't matter who [in fact it was Salmon]—and it was a reference to a grandmother of Max who was from Avignon, where his mother also lived for a time. . . . We said in jest that she owned a *maison de passe* there. . . . This was an invented story like so many others.[26]

In any case, as Picasso always maintained and Santos Torroella has recently established, a brothel was not at all the kind of establishment to be found on the carrer d'Avinyó.[27] This was (indeed still is) a respectable street of prosperous bourgeois residences, a stuffy gentlemen's club and a few shops, one of which used to provide Picasso with paper and watercolors when he lived nearby. The street also boasted a restaurant, whose proprietor, Otero believes, dreamed up this spurious Picasso connection sometime in the 1950s, to promote business. Picasso also objected to the unwarranted significance that had been attributed to the spoof identities —Max Jacob's grandmother, Marie Laurencin and Fernande—which he and his friends had invented for his "*chicas*."[28] As he said, "My characters are imaginary characters."[29]

*   *   *

Fernande was the first of Picasso's mistresses to undergo a process that a subsequent lover, Françoise Gilot, would describe as first the plinth, then the doormat.[30] In the mountain paradise of Gósol, Fernande had been treated—and painted—like a goddess. Back in the Bateau Lavoir, she was treated as a chattel and depicted as a whore. Hence no mention of the *Demoiselles* in either of her memoirs, although she was living with Picasso the entire time. Significantly, the diary on which her memoirs are based lapses into sudden silence at this point. Intense work made Picasso more misogynistic than ever. How could he wrestle the whole tradition of European art to the ground with his mistress sitting lazily by, fussing over her toilette, spraying herself with Chypre, doing precious little housework (visitors were horrified by the mess), distracting Picasso with her maddening "little ways"?[31] Then there was her new *idée fixe*: they should adopt a child. A child would bring them together again, transform them into *une vraie famille*. After all, Picasso had presented her, the previous summer, to his mother and father as his *novia*.

Whether or not Picasso was sleeping with other women, Fernande would have had reason to resent the *demoiselles* as bitterly as if they had been flesh-and-blood rivals. Had they not taken Picasso away from her? Were they not responsible for his leaving her for days and nights on end (Picasso loved to draw at night)? Daix thinks Fernande may have incurred her lover's wrath by modeling for his amorous friend Van Dongen;[32] I am not so sure. "*La belle Fernande*" was famously susceptible, very conscious of turning heads whenever she appeared in public. She is known to have had a brief romance at some point with an amusing young poet called Jean Pellerin: "*l'honneur de l'école fantaisiste*," according to André Salmon.[33] Early 1907 seems the most likely time for this escapade. Salmon remembers Pellerin visiting the Bateau Lavoir and being very struck by Max Jacob's attempts to take Picasso's mind off "the Egyptians" (code name for the *Demoiselles*) with a campy music-hall ditty:[34]

Ah! quell' joie
J'ai le téléphone;
Ah! quell' joie,
J'ai le téléphone chez-moi!

The genial Pellerin may well have consoled Fernande during the dark days of the *Demoiselles*. She was one of those women who put too much faith in the maxim that to keep a lover you have to make him jealous. All the more cause for the misogyny that fueled this *chef d'œuvre*. Where better to exorcise these feelings than in the basement studio, with or without a model? There Picasso could lock himself away and work naked, as he preferred to do when the weather was warm,[35] and paint and repaint those menacing maenads, so much taller than himself.

* * *

Apollinaire continued to frequent the Bateau Lavoir, but he was no longer able to keep up with Picasso's great forward leaps. The painter had outgrown the Arlequin Trismégiste persona, which Apollinaire had contrived for him at the time of the Rose period. A diary entry for February 27, 1907, is a measure of the poet's bafflement: "Evening, dinner with Picasso, saw his new painting; even colors, pinks of flowers, of flesh, etc., women's heads similar and simple heads of men too. Wonderful language that no literature can do justice to, for our words are preordained. Alas!"[36] Apollinaire may have seen some of the early *Demoiselles* studies but not the big painting, which had yet to materialize. He was almost certainly accompanied by Géry Pieret, a young Belgian con man, whom he sometimes passed off as his secretary. Earlier in the month, Pieret had announced that he was leaving Brussels for Paris the following day (February 4); Apollinaire should meet him at the station with a "*trousseau*" of six collars, a shirt and trousers, "*raflé*" (swiped) from his brother's closet.[37]

At the February 27 dinner, Picasso must have said something to trigger Pieret's theft of two Iberian sculptures from the Louvre—a theft that would leave its mark on the *Demoiselles* at the expense of appalling trouble four years later. Did he tell Apollinaire about the inspiration he had derived from these arcane Spanish artifacts? Did he indicate that he coveted them? Pieret would have jumped at any pretext to demonstrate his romantic belief that theft was a noble métier. He would obtain one of these sculptures for the artist. Deny it though he might, Picasso must have been privy to the project, even if he failed to take it seriously.

Honoré-Joseph Géry Pieret was born near Antwerp on October 22, 1884, one of three black-sheep sons of a distinguished barrister who had committed suicide in 1905.[38] This beguiling, bisexual psychopath is said to have met Apollinaire in 1904, when they were both working for a disreputable financial magazine called the *Guide des Rentiers*. However, Alice Halicka (the well-informed wife of the Polish artist Louis Marcoussis) suggests that the encounter took place in one of the *mauvais lieux* (pick-up places) that Apollinaire frequented in his quest for offbeat sex.[39] And the poet was probably responsible for providing his new friend with a job. When Pieret was fired for blackmailing the owner of the journal, Apollinaire took his side. He was captivated by this athletic, striking-looking adventurer, who supposedly spoke English, Spanish, German, Italian and Flemish as well as French, and who also claimed to be fluent in Greek and Latin, yet chose to be a thief. He did not steal out of a desire to be wicked or rich, Pieret told Apollinaire's friend Fernand Fleuret, but "to accomplish something rare and difficult, which required courage, psychological acumen, imagination and the strength of mind to kill if need be or jump from a third story."[40]

In 1905, Pieret had returned to Belgium to do his military service in the cavalry. Although an accomplished horseman, he deserted (probably to spend the money he had inherited from his father). Later, he rejoined his regiment, only to desert all over again. Arrested, he pleaded mental instability and was finally discharged. Apollinaire, whom he wrote to as "*mon meilleur ami*," sent him money and rescued him from a succession of scrapes; and his mother got her new husband to pay him to leave for Canada. However, the black sheep traveled no farther than Paris, where Apollinaire took him on as his *homme à tout faire*, "a job in which cooking played an important role."[41] He also ennobled Pieret as "Baron Ignace d'Ormesan," the name under which he figures as the protagonist of a number of Apollinaire's stories (notably the "L'Amphion faux messie" section of his picaresque *L'Hérésiarque*). Pieret's experiences as a hustler—also as a boxer, cardsharper, drug pusher, jockey, pimp, blackmailer and convicted felon—are likely to have been the source for the bizarre homosexual incidents (all that ferocious anal-plugging, sadomasochism and scatology) which spice page after page of Apollinaire's recently finished pornographic novel, *Les Onze Mille Verges* (his masterpiece, Picasso claimed).

Picasso was amused by Pieret, and so was Fernande—she found him "crazy, amusing, intelligent, bohemian"[42]—but not to the extent of accepting him as a boon companion for their cherished friend. Although Pieret studiously skirts any mention of sexual activity, the tone of his letters suggests that he and Apollinaire may have participated in something of the

Henri Frick. *Géry Pieret Pretending to Be a Dwarf*, 1904. Caricature in Apollinaire's appointment book. Bibliothèque Nationale, Paris.

sort. (Pieret first hints at this when he chides the poet for raising the question of his "*mœurs spéciales*," and when he evokes the poet's "ideas, tastes, appetites that I am far from not sharing.")[43] Drugs were evidently a link; and there is one reference to an evening on laudanum. That Apollinaire and Pieret had a sexual relationship would be assumed by some of the journalists covering "*l'affaire des statuettes*."[44] Whether their friendship was platonic or not, Apollinaire needed saving from this incorrigible reprobate, this latter-day Villon, this embryonic Jean Genet. A woman had to be found for him. Trust Picasso to come up with one: the quirkish Marie Laurencin.

Iberian. *Head of a Man,* 5th–3rd century B.C. Limestone, ht: 46cm. Musée des Antiquités Nationales, Saint-Germain-en-Laye.

Early in March, 1907, Pieret made his first raid on the Louvre. To believe the anonymous article he wrote for *Paris-Journal* four years later, he originally had no intention of "working"—i.e., stealing—in the museum. However, Marie Laurencin remembered his asking her on that very afternoon, "I'm going to the Louvre—anything you need?"[45] She assumed he was going shopping in the Magasin du Louvre, the department store. Her story gives the lie to Pieret's claim that theft never crossed his mind until he had entered the museum and realized the lack of security—a lack nowhere greater than in the antiquities section. This is where, on that fateful day, he just happened to find himself alone except for a solitary, sleepy guard. His article goes on to describe how he was about to move up to the floor above when he noticed a half-open door, which led to a room full of Egyptian antiquities. This in turn led to other unguarded rooms.

> Stopping now and again in a dim corner to caress an ample neck or a well-turned cheek . . . I suddenly realized how easy it would be to pick up and take away almost any object of moderate size.
>
> I was wearing a box-type overcoat, and my natural slimness made it quite possible to add a little to my dimensions without attracting attention. . . . I was then in a small room, about two by two metres, in the Gallery of Phoenician Antiquities.
>
> Being absolutely alone and hearing nothing whatsoever, I took the time to examine some fifty heads . . . and I chose one of a woman with . . . conical forms on either side. I put the statue under my arm, pulled up my overcoat collar . . . and walked out, asking my way of the guard, who was still completely motionless.
>
> I sold the sculpture to a Parisian friend of mine [Picasso]. He gave me a little money—fifty francs, I think, which I lost the same night in a billiard parlor. What of it, I said to myself. All Phoenicia is there for the asking.
>
> The very next day, I took a man's head with enormous ears—a detail that fascinated me. And three days later, a plaster fragment covered with hieroglyphs. A friend gave me twenty francs for this last: I stole it from the large room adjoining the Phoenician room.
>
> Then I emigrated.[46]

Pieret's account is not entirely believable. There was nothing unplanned about his theft. Given the weight of the sculptures, he must have gone prepared. Also, he knew exactly what he was after. Had he admitted this, his story would have fallen apart. Nobody would have believed that of all the stealable items in the Louvre he had happened on the very objects that his new friend Picasso was eager to possess. He would appear to have acted with malice aforethought. And for his part, deny it though he might, Picasso must have realized exactly what this rogue was offering him. Where else in Paris could these heads have come from except the

Iberian. *Head of a Woman,* 5th–3rd century B.C. Limestone, ht: 46cm. Musée des Antiquités Nationales, Saint-Germain-en-Laye.

Louvre? Picasso had almost total visual recall and would hardly have forgotten these small but striking pieces from his own visits to what was erroneously known as the Phoenician gallery. However, he was a past master at deluding himself and would have swallowed whatever cock-and-bull story Pieret concocted. Besides, Picasso could always rationalize that if anyone was a thief, it was the rapacious archaeologists who had made off with Spanish patrimony; if anyone was a receiver of stolen goods, it was the Louvre rather than himself. As an Andalusian and a painter, did he not have a far greater moral and artistic right to these objects than this foreign museum, which took such poor care of them that nobody noticed their disappearance?

When Pieret's raids came to light four years later, Apollinaire was arrested and briefly jailed. To exculpate himself, he claimed that he had tried to persuade Picasso to return the heads to the Louvre. The artist, he said, had refused to do so, because "he had damaged the statues in an attempt to discover certain secrets of the classic yet barbaric art to which they belonged."[47] This was nonsense—nonsense that was probably inspired by Picasso's attitude to these objects. He was convinced that people's magic and strength rubbed off on things they had wrought or cherished, worn or used. Hence the compulsion not just to handle these numinous relics but to wrest them from the jaws of officialdom. Their clunky primitivism—bulging eyes, mammoth ears, heavy jaws—provided him with an ethnic catalyst for stylistic experimentation. More to the point, these "barbarous" objects were virtually Spain's only contribution to the art of the ancient world. As such, they constituted Picasso's roots. Their atavistic power was a major, though by no means unique, source of the energy with which the artist, like Frankenstein, would galvanize his *Demoiselles* into life. Once he had extracted the magic from these stolen heads, Picasso reburied them under a lot of junk in the bottom of a cupboard.

As for Pieret, within days of the theft he returned to Brussels and embarked on yet another adventure. By March 15, he had set up as a chemist, manufacturing a pomade which supposedly restored knackered horses to health. He wrote Apollinaire asking for a testimonial. Pieret next announced that he was going to marry a woman who owned a tobacconist's shop. The only problem was that he lacked the means to buy her a suitable engagement present. Would Apollinaire do him a great favor? "Ask dear Picasso to paint me one of his best as quickly as possible and send it to me by the 25th. Tell Picasso I'll pay him 175 francs in March. I propose to spend my honeymoon in Paris. I even intend to sleep one night in the rat-infested shelter to get another taste of the horror of it."[48] When Apollinaire did not reply by return, Pieret wrote again, so desperate to have his Picasso that he enclosed a contract. As far as we know, the painting was never done. Instead Apollinaire went to Brussels to see his protégé, give him money and meet Pauline, now the owner of a racehorse trained by her fiancé. Pauline soon threw Pieret out; whereupon he tried and failed to get a job in a circus. Then, in a bid for his mother's sympathy, he slashed his arms to simulate wounds received in an attack on his life. After nursing him back to health, she made him sign on as crew on a British windjammer. Some months later, he wrote Apollinaire that he had not been able to stand the diet of ship's biscuits. After rounding Cape

Horn, he had jumped ship at San Diego, where he had found work as a cowboy. Pieret would not return to Paris for another four years, and when he did, he brought disgrace and disaster with him.

*   *   *

Around the time Picasso came into possession of the Iberian heads, he experienced yet another epiphany. He paid a visit to the seldom frequented Ethnographical Museum at the Trocadéro (now the Musée de l'Homme). It was a revelation, as he later told Malraux:

> When I went to the old Trocadéro, it was disgusting. The Flea Market. The smell. I was all alone. I wanted to get away. But I didn't leave. I stayed. I stayed. I understood that it was very important: something was happening to me, right?
>
> The masks weren't just like any other pieces of sculpture. Not at all. They were magic things. But why weren't the Egyptian pieces or the Chaldean? We hadn't realized it. Those were primitives, not magic things. The Negro pieces were *intercesseurs*, mediators; ever since then I've known the word in French. They were against everything—against unknown, threatening spirits. . . . I understood; I too am against everything. I too believe that everything is unknown, that everything is an enemy! Everything! I understood what the Negroes used their sculpture for. . . . The fetishes were . . . weapons. To help people avoid coming under the influence of spirits again, to help them become independent. Spirits, the unconscious (people still weren't talking about that very much), emotion—they're all the same thing. I understood why I was a painter. All alone in that awful museum, with masks, dolls made by the redskins, dusty manikins. *Les Demoiselles d'Avignon* must have come to me that very day, but not at all because of the forms; because it was my first exorcism painting—yes absolutely![49]

Photograph of the Fon god of war (Dahomey) in one of the galleries in the Trocadéro Museum, 1895. Musée de l'Homme, Paris.

It is no easy task to establish when this crucial visit took place. For reasons of his own, the artist was forever changing his story. His most drastic revision dates from 1939, when the foremost Picasso expert of his day, Alfred Barr, claimed that the *Demoiselles*, which he had recently arranged for the Museum of Modern Art to buy, was "the masterpiece of Picasso's Negro period."[50] The artist took great umbrage. He insisted that Christian Zervos, who was compiling his *catalogue raisonné*, issue a disclaimer:[51]

> In recent times Picasso confided to me [Zervos wrote] that the critics have never taken the trouble to study his picture closely. Had they noticed the clear similarities between the "*Demoiselles d'Avignon*" and Iberian sculpture, especially the general structure of the heads, the shape of the ears, and the delineation of the eyes, they would never have fallen into the error of suggesting that this picture derived from African statuary. The artist has formally assured me that at the time he was painting the "*Demoiselles d'Avignon*" he was unaware of the art of black Africa. It was only somewhat later that he had the revelation. One day, as he was coming out of the Musée de Sculpture Comparée, which at the time occupied the left wing of the Palais du Trocadéro, he was curious enough to push the door across the way, which led to the rooms of the old Musée d'Ethnographie. Even now, more than thirty-three years later, and despite the current events that trouble him deeply, Picasso still speaks with great emotion of the shock he received that day, upon seeing the African sculptures.[52]

This disingenuous disclaimer has caused much confusion. Originally, Pierre Daix accepted it over Picasso's statement to Malraux and went so far as to write an article called "There Is No African Art in *Les Demoiselles d'Avignon*."[53] However, he later modified his stance and now shares Rubin's view that Picasso's epiphany in the Trocadéro took place in June or July and thus predates the manifestly African repainting of the two right-hand *demoiselles*.[54] This modification does not go far enough. On the strength of Malraux's testimony and another useful crumb of evidence, Picasso must have visited the Trocadéro months earlier. He always insisted that it was very cold in there. As well as being ill lit, filthy, smelly and chaotically cluttered, he complained to Françoise Gilot, the museum was very cold—no heating.[55] "Very cold, no fire," he told Dor de la Souchère.[56] The visit is thus likely to have taken place around early March, when Derain—not only the instigator of Picasso's visit but also (according to Gilot) his companion—returned from a month away from Paris.

Further support for an earlier date is a sketchbook of major studies (Daix's Carnet 10) which are Oceanic or tribal in inspiration and must therefore have been executed *after* the Trocadéro visit, yet—for reasons that will become clear—*before* Picasso started work on the big painting.[57] Sometime in April Picasso sold this sketchbook to Leo Stein, who dismembered it. Because the paper is thin and many of the pages are heavily worked in ink, gouache and even oil paint, Stein took the precaution of having the more thickly painted ones *marouflés sur toile*, mounted on canvas.[58] Picasso was so stunned that the Steins had thought these sketches precious enough to treat in this way that he decided to have the same thing done to the *Demoiselles*.[59] Leo Stein confirms this, but with characteristic bitterness attributes this sensible precaution to the artist's vanity:

> Picasso was pleasantly childlike at times. I had some pictures relined, and [he] decided that he would have one of his pictures too treated like a classic, though in reverse order—he would have the canvas lined first and paint on it afterwards. This he did on a large scale, and painted a composition of nudes of the pink period, and then he repainted it again and again and finally left it as the horrible mess which was called, for reasons I never heard, the *Demoiselles d'Avignon*.[60]

Picasso would never have lined a canvas for the "childlike" pleasure of doing things "in reverse order": he would have had a sound practical reason for doing so. The obvious explanation is that he needed to strengthen the support. For this very large composition he had chosen a fine, almost linen-like canvas. Whether or not he had started to paint on it, the artist may well have concluded that it was too delicate to withstand the assaults of his brush. Hence the need for lining it. He would not have entrusted this job to a professional restorer. What had to be done—probably no more than restretching, without necessarily gluing, the fine canvas over a more resilient support—is likely to have been done by Picasso himself. Stein's claim to have seen the canvas in a virgin state dates from some thirty years later, when his grudge against Picasso had long since metastasized. Since the *Demoiselles* was relined sometime in the 1920s or early 1930s there is no knowing what exactly happened.

Why did Picasso lie about this visit to the Ethnographical Museum and its effect on his work? One look at the *Demoiselles* confirms that the tribalization of the heads on the right—the most striking, not to say shocking,

Picasso. *Head*, 1907. Tempera and watercolor on paper mounted on wood, 31×24cm. David Rockefeller Collection. This and the study below are pages from Stein's sketchbook.

Picasso. Study for *Nu à la draperie*, 1907. Watercolor and pencil on paper, 31×24cm. The Baltimore Museum of Art: Cone Collection.

Fang mask (Gabon). Painted wood, ht: 42cm (in Vlaminck's and, later, Derain's collection). Musée National d'Art Moderne, Centre Georges Pompidou, Paris.

feature of the painting—owes everything to what he saw at the Trocadéro; if not to specific examples of tribal or Oceanic art, then to a generalized memory of the primitive things he had seen there.[61] To understand Picasso's revisionism, we have to go back to his first public repudiation of African art, in 1920, a time when he was in thrall to classical sculpture, and to that extent in reaction against primitivism. It was not so much tribal sculpture as the vogue for it that had put him against it. These magical objects had taken the place of Tanagra figures as a decorator's cliché. The astute dealer Paul Guillaume was largely to blame for making tribal art *le dernier cri.* Prices had soared. And so when asked by Florent Fels in 1920 to contribute ten or fifteen lines on the subject to a magazine questionnaire, Picasso had snapped, "*Art nègre? Connais pas.*" ("African art? Never heard of it.")[62] Three years later, Picasso clarified his attitude: "The fact is," he told Fels, "[*art nègre*] has become too familiar to me; the African sculptures scattered all over my house are more like witnesses than exemplars. I loved popular images of circus troupes, hairdresser's heads and milliner's painted dummies. I still have a great appetite for curious and quirkish objects."[63]

We also have to make allowances for Picasso's innate caginess—caginess that became increasingly pronounced after he took on the tortuously secretive Sabartès as his secretary in 1935. He manifested an obsessive need to *cacher son jeu*—conceal his game—and he allowed Sabartès to create myths about himself, myths which he would eventually come to believe. (Sabartès's authorized memoir of the artist perpetuates many of them.) Another reason for Picasso's insistence in 1939 on the Iberianism of the *Demoiselles* has to do with the patriotic exaltation that the Spanish civil war had inspired in him. After achieving more fame and honor than ever before as the painter of *Guernica,* not to speak of his directorship (in absentia) of the Prado, Picasso became the most visible symbol of republican Spain. His political stardom was a source of fierce pride. In the climate of the time, the expatriate Picasso wanted to convince himself and the world that the *Demoiselles,* his most revolutionary painting, was as wholly Spanish in atavism, spirit and style as *Guernica.*

There is another possible reason for Picasso's attitude towards Africa. After the atrocities committed by Franco's African troops in the course of the Civil War, a Spanish Republican, especially one in Picasso's position, might have felt obliged to denounce things African. This would be in line with his decision at this time to distance himself from El Greco. El Greco's genius had been tainted by the cult that Franco, prompted by his minion Zuloaga, had inaugurated. Picasso would not take El Greco back into his pantheon until 1950.

As a source of inspiration, Iberian sculpture was very much Picasso's discovery, an exclusive treasure trove to which he had helped himself in more ways than one. No other painter had staked out a claim to it. By comparison, tribal art was already bespoke. Vlaminck had been collecting *art nègre* since 1904; Matisse had shown Picasso a piece from his collection months before he started work on the *Demoiselles;* and deny it though he might, Picasso visited the Trocadéro at Derain's urging—not, as he claimed, on a whim.[64] True, he proceeded to exploit primitive art more imaginatively than anyone else, but he was hardly the first to draw on it,

Easter card from Picasso to Leo Stein, April 27, 1907. Beinecke Rare Book and Manuscript Library, Yale University.

and first as well as foremost in the field is what this competitive artist hated not to be.

On April 27, Picasso sent the Steins an Easter postcard summoning them to see "*le tableau*" the following day.[65] Gertrude was away in the country and Leo probably not back from a trip to Rome, so they may not have seen the *Demoiselles* until mid-May. At this stage, the painting had not progressed much beyond the Iberian style of the previous fall and would hardly have shocked Leo, the only collector who might conceivably buy it. Although Picasso had begun integrating tribal elements into some of his studies, it is doubtful whether any of this had as yet rubbed off on the *Demoiselles.* At all events Picasso returned again and again to the Ethnographical Museum, sometimes alone, sometimes in the company of Max Jacob, Apollinaire or Salmon. The more Picasso identified with tribal art, the more problems he created for the *Demoiselles.* To discover how tribal masks and magic could be reconciled with Iberian stylizations, he set the painting aside. Meanwhile the lack of understanding on the part of friends—and, to judge by her silence, Fernande—exacerbated his anguish. Picasso's whores seem briefly to have lost momentum—hence his switch to the carriages in the Bois de Boulogne, the other subject that Baudelaire thought worthy of a "painter of modern life."

Picasso in his studio in the Bateau Lavoir, 1908. Archives Picasso.

2

Raymonde

Picasso. *Mother and Child*, spring, 1907. Oil on canvas, 81×60cm. Musée Picasso.

Opposite: Picasso. *Head of Raymonde*, May–June, 1907. Pen and India ink on sketchbook page, 22×17.6cm. Private Collection.

IN THE SPRING, PICASSO, WHO SELDOM STRAYED far from Montmartre, had a pretext for visiting the Bois de Boulogne. He and Fernande had adopted a young girl. An outing in the park would have been mandatory. This ill-fated adoption was Fernande's idea. She had had a miscarriage in 1901 and was apparently unable to complete a pregnancy. This and the fact that she was still legally married to Paul Percheron but too fearful of this wife-batterer to demand a divorce ruled out any prospect of marriage. At least she could adopt a child. Guilt at having persuaded an earlier mistress, Madeleine, to have an abortion may have swayed Picasso. Despite his ambivalence towards children—feelings of intense fatherly love and tenderness would alternate with childish jealousy and irritation—and despite the folly of embarking on parenthood at such a difficult moment in their relationship, to say nothing of his work, he gave in to Fernande's urging.

On April 9, Fernande and Picasso had visited a Montmartre orphanage (rue Caulaincourt). "You want an orphan," the mother superior told her, "take your choice, madame." They picked out a girl, called Raymonde, who was probably about thirteen. Apollinaire says she was nine,[1] but she looks much older in Picasso's drawings. Salmon describes her as an adolescent and in his fictionalized account as being thirteen. Raymonde was playful, intelligent and "*d'une beauté grave*."[2] The daughter of a French whore working in a Tunisian brothel, she had been rescued by a Dutch journalist named Cohen and his wife. Apollinaire accuses the Cohens of being motivated by self-interest rather than compassion: they had forced the child to learn the violin with a view to entertaining them in their old age. When she showed no musical ability, they abandoned her.[3] Salmon uses Raymonde as a Montmartroise Little Nell in *La Négresse du Sacré-Cœur* (1920), the roman à clef in which he also introduces Picasso as Sorgue, a painter. In Salmon's novel Raymonde is called Léontine and plays a central role: an over-romanticized orphan who wears a dress cut down from a grown-up's and becomes the pet of the poets and painters of the Butte. When she throws herself down a shaft in an abandoned quarry, a heroic German poet climbs down and brings her shattered body to the surface. For a more factual account of Raymonde's short, sad sojourn at the Bateau Lavoir, we have to turn to Salmon's *Souvenirs sans fin*, although he gives even the truth a fictive glint.[4]

The Bateau Lavoir tenants outdid one another in spoiling Raymonde. Max Jacob gave her a cheap little doll, Salmon bought her candy.

Fernande, who bore the scars of illegitimacy and a cruel foster mother, was overindulgent. She was forever brushing Raymonde's hair, tying it up in ribbons and seeing that she went off to school prettily dressed. Pages in several of the *Demoiselles* sketchbooks reveal that Picasso did drawings to amuse the girl: comic sketches of his dog, Frika, and her puppies, also playful groups of Catalan *castellers* (athletes from the countryside who climb on one another's shoulders to form a multitiered pyramid, with an *anxaneta*, a small boy, as the apex).[5] Picasso, who had watched *castellers* perform at folkloric festivals in his youth, showed Raymonde the tower rising tier by tier and the *anxaneta* jumping off.[6]

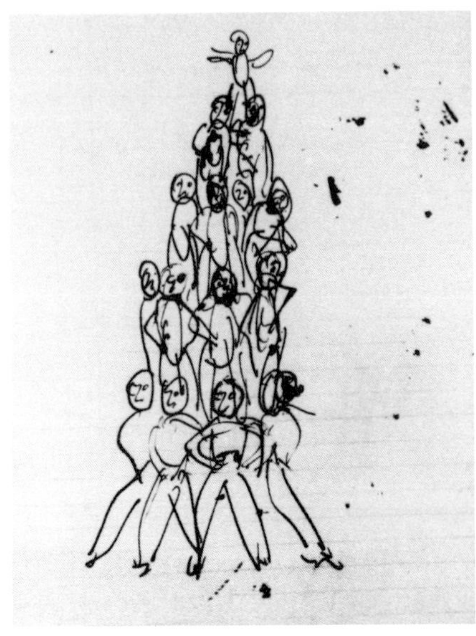

Picasso. *Human Pyramid of Castellers*, May–June, 1907. Graphite pencil on sketchbook page, 22×11.6 cm. Private Collection.

Although Raymonde lived in the studio for almost four months, Picasso made hardly any references to her in his work. The only painting is a *Mother and Child*, which reduces Fernande and Raymonde to two eerie masks, which are not only tribally primitive but also childishly primitive.[7] This new development should be seen in the light of Matisse's portrait of his daughter Marguerite, which Picasso had recently been given in exchange for one of his own paintings. Picasso had chosen this work because it revealed how Matisse had drawn on elements in his children's drawings in a bid to simplify his notation.[8] Picasso evidently followed suit. He has portrayed Raymonde in the manner of her own drawings, just as he would do in the 1950s, when he portrayed his young daughter Paloma as if she were as floppy and starey-eyed as one of her dolls. There are also some drawings of Raymonde which hint at the nature of the trouble that this exemplary child unwittingly caused. Fernande apparently made Picasso leave the studio when she wanted Raymonde to try on some new underclothes.[9] A page in one of the *Demoiselles* carnets depicting a naked Raymonde seated, legs wide apart, washing her feet, explains the reason for this precaution. There is even a painting of a girl in the same explicit pose, which looks uncannily like a grown-up Raymonde.[10] Young girls excited Picasso. They also disturbed him; they put him in mind of his dead sister, Conchita. Fernande would have had cause for alarm. The decision in late July to return Raymonde to the orphanage would have gone against her warmth of heart but not her better judgment. The girl was *de trop*—in the way.

Max Jacob's friend Henri Hertz has left an affecting account of Raymonde's last moments with her second set of foster parents.[11] They had forgathered at Apollinaire's apartment. Raymonde sat glumly in a corner while Max Jacob, who loved children, did his best to tie up a box into which he had crammed her dolls and a ball. After a few gruff words to Picasso and Apollinaire (who had Marie Laurencin with him), Max took the child by the hand—she held her suitcase in the other—and "with a profoundly sad smile," led her away. Where? Presumably back where she came from. Salmon tells a different story. ("I am not embroidering; a topic like this would not permit it.") He claims that it was Fernande who tried to return Raymonde—what is more, without success. "You wanted to take her: keep her," the mother superior reportedly told her.[12] Salmon says that the child ended up being adopted by a concierge in the Sacré-Cœur neighborhood. A postcard signed "Raymonde" (June 22, 1919) suggests that she kept in touch.[13]

On August 8, Fernande wrote to Gertrude Stein, whom she regarded as a confidante:

Picasso. *Raymonde Examining Her Foot,* spring, 1907. Graphite pencil on paper, 22×17cm. Picasso Heirs.

Picasso. *Woman Examining Her Foot,* summer, 1907. Oil on wood, 18×15cm. Musée Picasso.

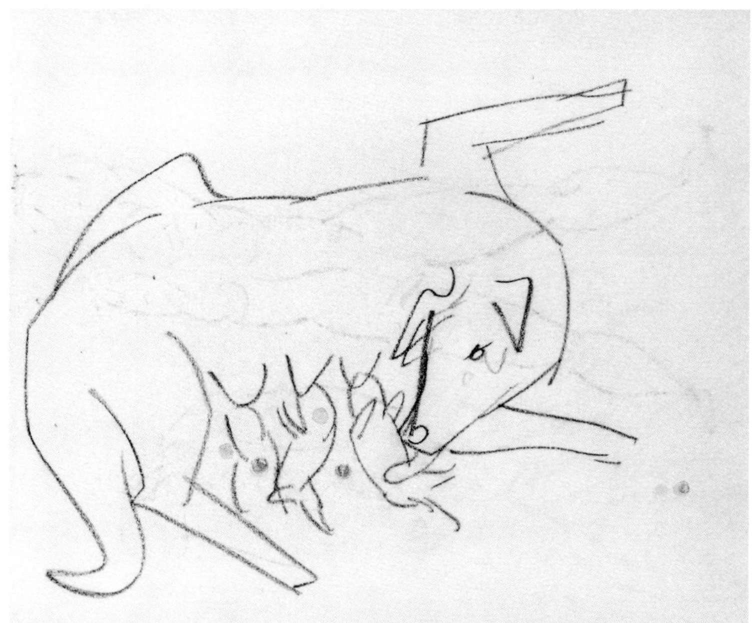

Picasso. *Frika with Her Puppies,* spring, 1907. Black pencil on sketchbook page, 19.3×24.2cm. Musée Picasso.

> I haven't yet seen Raymonde, but I intend to go next month. She has been placed in an orphanage run by sisters nearby on rue Caulaincourt and I can go and visit her the first Sunday of every month. Apparently her mother has been traced, and before the nuns are allowed to keep her there needs to be a judgment against the mother, who has to have her rights over the child annulled.[14]

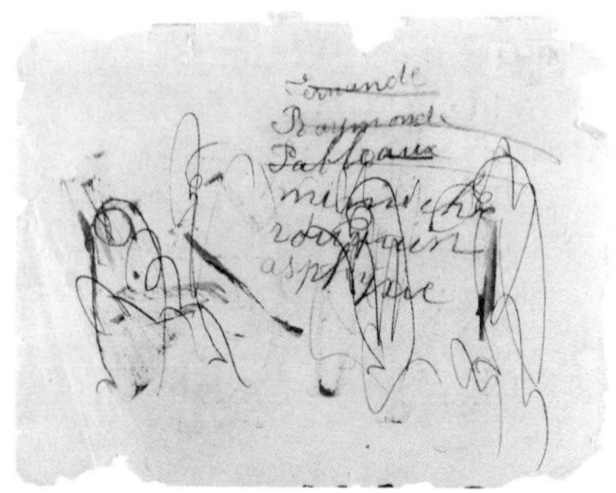

List of spelling words in sketchbook, May–June, 1907. Musée Picasso.

Salmon and another friend were in the studio when Fernande penned this letter, so she breaks off her account: "I am prevented from writing the way I would like." She was not going to divulge discreditable details with inquisitive friends looking over her shoulder any more than she would divulge them to readers of her memoirs.

Besides drawings of Raymonde, Picasso's sketchbooks include some poignant mementos: lists of words she was taught to spell; multiplication tables that have been scribbled over with the name of Picasso's mathematician friend, Princet; notes in Fernande's writing of the things that the artist had to go out and buy for her ("little girl's knickers, booties"); and lists that seem to be in the child's hand, notably one on the inside cover of Carnet 8: "*Fernande / Raymonde / Pableaux / Mimiche / rouquin / asphyxie.*" The first three names have been crossed out. Daix thinks that Picasso may have done this some years later: after he had finally sent Fernande packing.[15] The "Pableaux" pun reminds us that another Bateau Lavoir child, Van Dongen's daughter, Dolly, used to call Picasso "Tablo." But what are we to make of the last three words: tit, redhead, asphyxia? Returning Raymonde to the orphanage was probably less cruel than keeping her on in the studio.

* * *

Instead of lingering like Guys or Manet over the promenade in the Bois de Boulogne, Picasso resumed painting the *Demoiselles.* Since nobody ever bothered to photograph its successive states and the Museum of Modern Art has never X-rayed the entire composition,[16] we have very little firsthand evidence of its development beyond the ever-fading, ever-changing memories of Salmon and Kahnweiler and other friends. The final phase involved the repainting of the two right-hand heads. The synthesis that Picasso had already devised for the standing figure on the left—a frontal Egyptian eye, an Iberian ear and African facial planes—was too felicitous to repeat. Picasso was out to shock, if need be appall. Hence the jarringly discordant fright-masks he contrived for the two right-hand heads. Familiarity has inured us to the horror that these dog-faced *demoiselles* caused when they were first unveiled, almost a century ago. It was as if Picasso had unleashed a new race of gorgons on the world.

Picasso. *Les Demoiselles d'Avignon* (detail), 1907. The Museum of Modern Art, New York (see p. 10).

Some scholars see these monstrous faces as embodying Picasso's fear of syphilis.[17] They have a point; however, this polymorphous masterpiece loses much of its modernist resonance if it is narrowed down to a specific area of interpretation. Like most sexually active men of the period, Picasso was terrified of syphilis. However, his *Demoiselles* was an exorcism of more than private demons; it was also an exorcism of traditional concepts of "ideal beauty." The fright-masks constitute an assault as much on "beauty" as on women—an assault that is all the more devastating for being reinforced with Picasso's misogyny and a shot of Baudelaire's "Spleen." Years later, the artist told me that one of his snout-faced portraits of Dora Maar—a portrait not unlike the top right-hand *demoiselle*—had been inspired by the muzzle of his Afghan hound, Kazbek. "I wanted to comment on the animal nature of women," he said. And what better vehicle for this than that whorehouse staple, the dog-faced woman—the embodiment of the raunchiness that Baudelaire extolled? This, I think, is how we should see the *demoiselle* on the right, squatting post-coitally on a bidet, twisting her Medusa face around to administer the shock of horror that will leave her client wallowing in disgust—for her, her sex and himself.

These eye-catching masks made for a dilemma. Should Picasso repaint the two central Iberian girls in a similar vein or leave the painting unresolved? Once again he set it aside: this time, for good. He never signed it. After Doucet bought the *Demoiselles* in 1924, he asked Picasso to sign it. The artist refused to do so because he felt he had been duped by Doucet's hints that the painting would end up in the Louvre into letting him have it for 250,000 francs—a fraction of its real value. Picasso refused Doucet's invitations to see the *Demoiselles* in its new setting and never spoke to him again.[18] Over the years, a virtue would be made of its disjunctive state, which raises the question as to whether the *Demoiselles* is in fact finished. In early years Picasso made no bones about its being unfinished. After the Museum of Modern Art acquired the painting and it came to be seen as the greatest icon of the modern movement, he asserted ever more vehemently that it *was* finished. When he takes a vehement line over matters like this, it is best to reserve judgment—as Rubin evidently did at the time. (Steinberg persuaded him to change his mind later.) "To my surprise," he recounts, "Picasso simply did not accept the idea that the *Demoiselles* was unfinished. Whatever he said to me then—it began with something on the order of '*C'est pas du tout ça*'—left me very confused, and it was clear that he did not want to be pressed."[19] To Antonina Vallentin, Picasso was more forthcoming: he admitted to wondering whether "to redo the whole thing. Then I said to myself, 'No, people will understand what I was trying to do.'"[20] Kahnweiler, who saw the painting for the first time at the beginning of August, 1907, and many times thereafter, insisted the painting was not finished; and despite the artist's later declarations to the contrary, the dealer never vacillated on this point, as he did on many others.

Picasso's repainting of the right-hand heads is what once gave the *Demoiselles* its power to shock. But this does not, I think, entitle us to regard the highly effective disjunctiveness as anything but the consequence of a calculated risk, taken very late in the game. It was a risk that Picasso declined, after due consideration, to follow up, in the hope that people would, as he said, "understand"—presumably, understand that the *Demoiselles* had to be perceived as finished so that the artist's revolutionary endeavor could be perceived as accomplished. In fact his masterpiece is not so much unfinished as unfinishable. Hence its everlasting, open-ended fascination.

Picasso. *Woman in a Blue Hat (Dora Maar)*, October 3, 1939. Oil on canvas, 65.5×50 cm. Musée Picasso.

* * *

Earlier in the year Picasso had sent a *petit bleu* to Wilhelm Uhde, the German writer, amateur dealer and discoverer of the Douanier Rousseau, who was also one of the few people in Paris to keep pace with the artist's innovations. Would Uhde come by immediately and take a look at the *Demoiselles*? Mockery from people he respected as much as Vollard and Fénéon had demoralized the artist, and he desperately wanted reassurance from someone whose eye he could trust. Uhde failed to live up to Picasso's expectations; he was too nice to laugh, too forthright to conceal his bewilderment. "Weeks would go by [elsewhere Uhde says "several months"] before I realized what had prompted Picasso to take this new approach. Once I understood this new language, I followed [him] faithfully down this new path."[21] As soon as he adjusted to the *Demoiselles*, Uhde urged his new German friend, Daniel-Henry Kahnweiler, who had recently opened a gallery, to go and see this astonishing painting. He described it as Egyptian or Assyrian. He did not accompany him.

Picasso. *Foliage*, summer, 1907. Gouache on paper, 65×50 cm (one of the works in Kahnweiler's first purchase). Kunstmuseum Bern: Hermann und Margrit Rupf Stiftung.

Kahnweiler's first visit to the Bateau Lavoir took place much later than is usually thought. In some notes the dealer sent Gertrude Stein to clarify points in her *Autobiography of Alice B. Toklas*, he says that he opened his gallery on July 11, 1907, and that, "some weeks later, I saw Pablo at the rue Ravignan and bought three gouaches of that period (landscapes of blue, yellow and red . . . like a head [in] your collection). Some days later I bought a picture of the same style 'femme dans un hamac.'"[22] Kahnweiler would never forget the messages chalked on the studio door: "I've gone to the bistro"; "Fernande is at Azon's"; "Manolo came by."[23] Nor would he forget Picasso answering the door barefoot, wearing nothing but a shirt and hastily pulling on a pair of trousers; nor the squalor of the downstairs studio: the strips of old wallpaper that had come away from the walls, the mountain of ashes higher than the stove, the dusty stacks of canvases and "the African sculptures of majestic severity" (so much for Picasso's story that he was not yet aware of tribal art).

In his 1920 account of this memorable meeting, Kahnweiler is far from enthusiastic about the *Demoiselles*. It had struck him as an "*insuccès*" (a failure), he said: it was unfinished and did not appear to have fulfilled its purpose. Thirty years later, he was telling a very different story, except in respect of the painting's lack of finish:[24] he now claimed to have been "bowled over with admiration." Later still he further embellished the story. In the early 1960s he told Brassaï that he had "not found the painting 'Assyrian,' but monstrous, horrible. . . . At the same time I was captivated, moved, even overwhelmed by the utter novelty of the canvas. . . . Hence probably my spontaneously favorable reaction to this painting and my decision to acquire it."[25] The unfinished *Demoiselles* was not, of course, for sale; instead, Kahnweiler settled for the gouaches. The following year, however, he would acquire some forty works (though not the *Demoiselles*). And until 1914, he would mastermind Picasso's rise to fame. Except for a rift of ten years or so (during and after World War I) their association, which brought them both so much glory and fortune, would last until Picasso's death. According to the artist, friendship played little part in it—their characters were hardly compatible—and he was not especially pleased when one of his nephews married Lucie Kahnweiler's niece. On the other hand, he was very fond of the dealer's stepdaughter and eventual partner, Louise Leiris.

* * *

Kahnweiler (seated) with Hermann Rupf, 1904. Archives Kahnweiler: Galerie Louise Leiris.

Daniel-Henry Kahnweiler (known to his friends as Heini) was born in 1884 into an affluent Jewish family from Mannheim. When the boy was five, they moved to Stuttgart. His father was a banker, the German representative of a plutocratic uncle, Sir Siegmund Neumann, who had gone to London and made a vast fortune in South African gold and diamond mines. Kahnweiler had inherited his family's business acumen and cautiousness; otherwise he did not take after them. He was an intellectual, ideologically progressive—a lifelong socialist—with a passion for literature, philosophy and the visual arts. Above all he loved music, and originally aspired to be a conductor. However, his parents had other plans for their promising elder son. (Their second son, Gustav, was more of a playboy.) They wanted him to carry on the family business and make a dynastic marriage—if possible to a Rothschild. And so they apprenticed him to the Parisian brokerage house of Tardieu. Kahnweiler shared lodgings with a young Swiss whom he had met when he was a student, Hermann Rupf, the son of a prosperous haberdasher from Bern. They would become lifelong friends. When Kahnweiler opened his gallery, Rupf would be his first client and buy the dealer's first Picasso. Henceforth Rupf would come to Paris once a year and acquire a painting by Picasso, Braque, Gris or Derain. His small but exceptionally fine collection is now one of the glories of the Bern museum. Kahnweiler's other great friend was a fellow employee, Eugène Reignier, who encouraged him to haunt museums, galleries and auction houses.

Instead of courting heiresses, Kahnweiler fell in love with a humble girl from Sancerre on the Loire: Léontine Alexandrine (Lucie) Godon.[26] Picasso claimed she had worked as a maid in the pension where Kahnweiler stayed and that he married her primarily because he was nervous about his sexual orientation. (According to Françoise Gilot, Picasso was always urging Kahnweiler to admit that he liked men.) Lucie had an adored infant sister, called Louise (known as Zette), whom she and Kahnweiler would raise. After her death, Zette turned out to have been Lucie's illegitimate daughter; her father was a clockwinder from Sancerre. Liberal principles evidently gave Kahnweiler the courage to wed this "fallen woman." The prospect of such a *mésalliance* infuriated his father, but the highly principled son stood his ground and, after living with Lucie for two years, married her in 1904. In her sedate, supportive way, she proved a model wife and on that score a favorite butt of Picasso's jokes.

A year later, Julius Kahnweiler packed his son off to London to work for his rich uncle. Sir Siegmund was one of those Edwardian tycoons whose lavish hospitality—dinners of ortolans, baby lambs' tongues and *foie gras en croûte*, followed by cigars and stockmarket tips—prompted Edward VII to reward his hosts with knighthoods and invitations to shoot at Sandringham. To Edwardian society, Lady Neumann's pretensions were a standing joke. (The king's mistress, Mrs. Keppel, once scathingly asked her: "My dear Anna, may I call you Lady Neumann?") To a socialist like Kahnweiler, these pretensions were anything but a joke. He found his aunt and uncle's lifestyle vulgar and reprehensible. The huge, hotel-like mansion on Piccadilly (next door to the Rothschilds') and the materialism and worldliness that it enshrined represented everything in cultural and social life that he abhorred. The same with his job: he hated it. Whenever possible, Kahnweiler would go back to Paris and do the galleries with

Reignier. This, he realized, was where his vocation lay. When he told the Neumanns that he wanted to open a gallery in Paris, they were not pleased. They had wanted him to represent them in Johannesburg. In the end, they relented. After discussing the matter with their friend Ascher Wertheimer (Sargent's dealer), the Neumanns generously loaned their nephew £1,000 (the equivalent of 25,000 gold francs), on condition that he resume working for the family business if he did not make a go of the gallery within the year.

In February, 1907, Kahnweiler returned to Paris and took an apartment. He also rented minimal gallery space—a small room (4×4 meters) at 28, rue Vignon, near the Madeleine—from a Polish tailor. Within a month he had carpeted the floor, covered the walls with burlap and set about acquiring works by modern artists. Kahnweiler proved to have an excellent eye. When the Indépendants opened on March 21, he bought a drawing by Matisse and paintings by Signac, Derain, Vlaminck, Friesz, Camoin and, possibly, Braque. Over the next four months he built up a stock. Whenever he purchased a work, he would contact the artist and offer to be his exclusive representative. Since this enterprising German was less greedy than Clovis Sagot, better financed than Berthe Weill, and more enlightened than either, many of the brighter young painters switched to his gallery and eventually signed up with him. Although close with money and a stickler for contractual commitments—had he not trained as a banker?—Kahnweiler proved to be refreshingly honest. The one painter he desperately wanted and did not get was Matisse; he had already signed up with the prestigious Galerie Bernheim, where Seurat's brilliant friend Félix Fénéon was in charge of contemporary art.

Later, in July, Picasso came by to reconnoiter the new gallery and returned the following day with Vollard. They did not let on who they were, and for all that Kahnweiler admired Vollard to the point of adopting him as a role model, he did not recognize him; nor did he realize who Picasso was until he went to the Bateau Lavoir. For his part, the artist, who had heard good things about Kahnweiler from Derain and Braque, was as impressed by his intelligence and vision as he had expected to be. However, he still lived in hopes of a contract with Vollard; and although he would use Kahnweiler as his principal dealer and allow him to dictate cubist strategy, Picasso held off signing a contract with the future impresario of cubism until 1912.

* * *

A major by-product of the studies for the second *demoiselle* from the left is a magnificent life-size painting which Picasso worked on through the summer. Now known as *Nu à la draperie*, it was formerly called *La Danse aux voiles* (a title still used in the Hermitage, where it hangs). Daix dismisses the original title as "absurd," but I recall Picasso using it; in addition the word "*voile*" is a clue to one of the painting's sources: the Richard Strauss–Oscar Wilde opera *Salome*, which was first performed in Paris in May, 1907, around the time Picasso conceived this figure. The production was a sensation and spawned a glut of other Salomes, including a revival of Loïe Fuller's dance version later in the year. (Fuller "manoeuvres her veils . . . like a laundress misusing her paddle . . .

Loïe Fuller performing her serpentine dance in the 1890s.

Above: Picasso. *Nu à la draperie*, 1907. Oil on canvas, 152×101cm. State Hermitage Museum, St. Petersburg.

Above right: Braque. *Large Nude*, spring, 1908. Oil on canvas, 140×100cm. Alex Maguy, Paris.

Matisse. *Blue Nude*, early 1907. Oil on canvas, 92.1×140.4cm. The Baltimore Museum of Art: Cone Collection.

Picasso. *Standing Nude with Stick*, May, 1907. Black pencil on sketchbook page, 13.6×10.5cm. Musée Picasso.

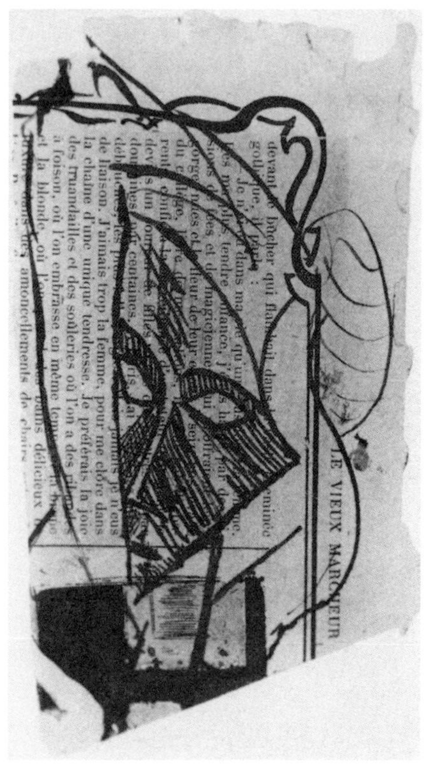

Picasso. *Head* (drawn on *Le Vieux Marcheur*), 1907. Ink on newsprint, 15.5×9cm. Private collection.

luminous without grace, with the gestures of an English boxer and the physique of Mr. Oscar Wilde," a critic had written of her original *Salome*.[27] Despite amazing lighting effects and simulated nudity, the new production was no better received.) Picasso had seen Fuller at the Exposition Universelle in 1900, when she was on the same bill as Sado Yacco (later the subject of one of his unexecuted posters) so he had firsthand experience of her inventiveness: how she manipulated unfurling veils with canes held under her skirts while dancing on a glass plaque, lit from below with shimmering lights.[28] He had also evoked the Eros–Thanatos overtones of the Salome story in one of his finest Rose period engravings.[29]

To provoke and mystify, Picasso also referred to this seemingly upright figure as "*mon nu couché*."[30] This was to demonstrate that the pose is ambivalent and the figure should be perceived as horizontal as well as vertical: as a sleeping *demoiselle* seen from above as well as a kind of Loïe Fuller. Picasso's double take does not quite work. He has put too much of the woman's weight onto her left foot for her to be envisioned, even in imagination, as flat on her back. Then again, one might take Picasso's paradox more seriously if all but one of the thirty or more studies relating to this painting were not so emphatically vertical. One in particular shows a nude standing on a dais in such an impossible contrapposto pose—her left leg would have to be twice as long to hold it—that she is obliged to support herself on a stick.

The scandal caused by Matisse's *Blue Nude* at the Indépendants had evidently spurred Picasso into going one better, and this standing/sleeping figure is the result. To confirm this we have only to up-end a reproduction of the *Blue Nude*. Braque followed suit. Under the influence of the Picasso, he embarked, a few months later, on a *Large Nude*, which is also strikingly similar to an up-ended *Blue Nude*. Braque is even less successful than Picasso at getting us to perceive his figure as both upright and recumbent. Like Picasso, he concentrates his nude's weight on one leg and then, to suggest horizontality, leaves her foot, so to speak, ungrounded. This is not enough to establish the required ambivalence. In its boldness and primitivism, the *Large Nude* constitutes a milestone in Braque's early development. It is the first move in the game of cooperation and one-upmanship that is the subtext of his and Picasso's cubism.

That Picasso worked on the *Nu à la draperie* until the end of August is confirmed by a study for it (or possibly after it) on a page of a magazine, *Le Vieux Marcheur*, dated August 23.[31] The Steins would buy the painting off the easel when they returned from Italy, in September; in 1913 they would sell it to Sergei Shchukin. Since it was not exhibited outside Russia until 1954, it never attracted the attention it deserved. A related oil sketch of more or less the same figure with legs barbarously wide apart heralds the six months or so of intense involvement with African sculpture—a period that was formerly called Negro and should now perhaps be known as Totemic. How else to describe Picasso's daunting, fetish-inspired *Dancer*, who seems to have shaken off the dust of the Trocadéro and is dancing to jungle drums?

Since the power of Picasso's primitive exemplars—what he chose to call "intercessors" or "witnesses"—resides in their being magic objects, he also aspired to do sculpture: not conventional, Rodinesque bronzes such he had formerly produced but carvings whose power would be

Above: Picasso. *Dancer*, 1907. Oil on canvas, 150×100cm. Private collection.

Top right: Picasso. *Standing Figure*, summer, 1907. Pastel, gouache and watercolor on paper, 63×48cm. Musée Picasso.

Right: Picasso. *Standing Nude*, 1907. Carved and painted wood, 31.8×8×3cm. Musée Picasso.

totemic rather than artistic. Lacking the facilities, the tools, the technical experience and the time to spare from his work in speedier media, he took to doing paintings as surrogates for sculpture. To give them a tribal air, he used herringbone hatching to simulate scarification and tattooing: witness the striated faces and bodies of the wedge-nosed, mini-mouthed figures inspired by his Trocadéro visits. Later in the year, he would obtain some chisels and hack stumps of softish wood into rudimentary totems. Far from being pastiches, these sculptures bear only the most generalized resemblance to the Oceanic and tribal artifacts which had left Picasso more in thrall to primitivism than ever. It is the artist's belief in the magic of his own handiwork that endows them with their shamanistic force. Picasso had learned from labels in the Musée d'Ethnographie that a fetish could fortify its maker's creative power and protect him against enemies, maladies and fears. He would never part with these guardian figures, any more than his uncle, the revered Canon Pablo, would have parted with the plaster saints that had served him as *intercesseurs.*

During the summer, Picasso also finished one of the most memorable paintings of the period, the highly worked *Corsage jaune (Woman in Yellow),* which he had started in early spring. This stone-faced Iberian (as opposed to tribal) figure is as wedded to her curtained setting as a figure in a bas-relief is to its support. Who is this broad-shouldered, sinewy woman? Certainly not the voluptuous Fernande. Hints of an apron and a crumpled *torchon,* not to speak of a grim, subservient stare, suggest that she might have been the *bonne à tout faire* who helped out the indolent Fernande. Picasso also did some painfully naked studies of the octogenarian Fontdevila, the smuggler who had been his model in Gósol and whose skull-like head had shown him how to resolve his Gertrude Stein portrait. He apparently envisaged a tribal carving of Fontdevila which would commemorate his deep, dark bond with this Pyrenean peasant and match an authentically primitive subject to his increasingly primitive style. In the end he switched to André Salmon, who sometimes tagged along on Picasso's visits to the Trocadéro. A large caricatural drawing (p. 5) and some related studies, in which Picasso likens Salmon's prognathous head to a tribal mask, look ahead to "a statuette in wood." This, too, was never executed. On the back of the Salmon drawing the artist has traced outlines of his hand—something he had done eighteen months before, to show how the figures in his *Saltimbanques* corresponded to the configuration of his fingers.[32] Might Picasso have envisaged his five *demoiselles* in the same form, with the thumb standing for the squatter on the right who buttresses the composition?[33]

* * *

Although Picasso "explicitly denied taking the slightest time off at [this] period,"[34] it is possible that he paid a visit to the country in the course of the summer. Salmon, his neighbor in the Bateau Lavoir, wrote that "a holiday interrupted the painful experiments" (i.e., the *Demoiselles*).[35] A harvest scene and a sudden slew of landscapes—seemingly of a specific place—might bear Salmon out.[36] So does a succession of invitations to stay in the country with Eugène Rouart (one of the sons of the celebrated collector Henri Rouart), who had just bought a major *saltimbanque*

Picasso. *Corsage jaune (Woman in Yellow),* spring, 1907. Oil on canvas, 130×96.5cm. Private collection.

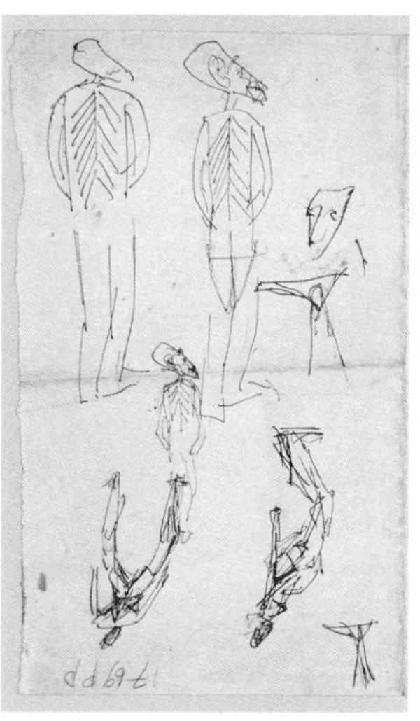

Picasso. Studies for sculpture of André Salmon (and for a female nude leaning backwards), 1907. India ink on paper, 32.5×40cm (left-hand part). Picasso Heirs.

Opposite: Bateau Lavoir studio, spring, 1908. Photograph by Picasso. Archives Picasso. The works visible include two drawings inspired by Fontdevila, a study for a standing female nude, a male head and two wooden carvings.

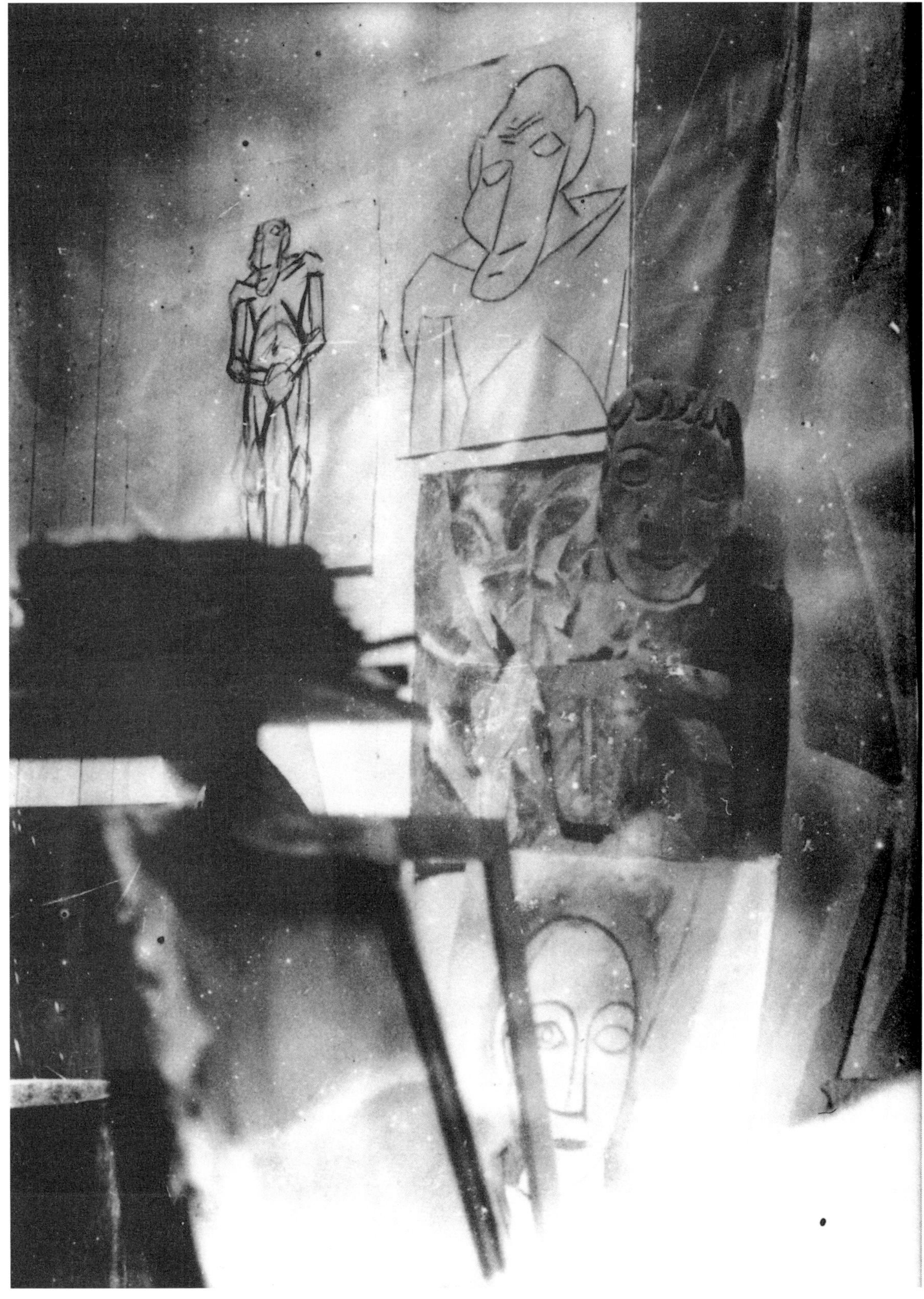

Above: Picasso. *The Harvesters*, 1907. Oil on canvas, 65×81.3cm. Thyssen-Bornemisza Foundation, Castagnola.

Right: Picasso. *Landscape*, 1907. Watercolor on paper, 17.5×22.4cm. Picasso Heirs.

painting, the 1905 *Comedians*.[37] The first of Rouart's invitations dates from April 27. Two weeks later, Victor Gastilleur, a literary friend of Picasso's and Rouart's, writes that "we are still expecting you here this summer." On July 10, Rouart writes again to say that he is going to Toulouse to see if the *Comedians* has arrived; that he looks forward to showing it to André Gide, who is staying with him; that he is thrilled to hear Picasso is working "hard and courageously" on a large painting and that he cannot wait to see it. "If you come to the south, let me know; I . . . will welcome you with great pleasure."[38] According to Eugène Rouart's son Olivier, Picasso frequently stayed at Bagnols de Grenade,[39] the family's estate in the Haute Garonne, so this might well have been where he went.[40] This trip would have taken place in the latter part of July. By August 8, Picasso was back in the studio—"working," Fernande wrote to Gertrude Stein, which implies that he had not recently been doing so.

Picasso had all manner of reasons to be secretive about his visits to the country: to cover his tracks; to imply that his work left no time for leisure; to hide a transient affair; and, most likely of all, to prevent anyone from thinking that he might actually go out and paint from nature—an activity that this foe of impressionism abhorred. Hence the denials that this or that painting or drawing had anything to do with this or that location (see also p. 114, where the artist likewise conceals the source of a specific motif). Hills and dales, Picasso would have us believe, had a mysterious way of materializing in the studio. For all his insistence that the atypically fauvish *Harvesters* had been executed in the Bateau Lavoir, it is clearly based on something he had recently witnessed. Bagnols de Grenade is the most obvious source of the distinctive countryside that unexpectedly appears in his work, but even if he did not go there at this juncture, is it not likely that he and Fernande would have taken Raymonde to the forest of Fontainebleau or some other rural area near Paris?

A glimpse of the country would also account for Picasso's sudden preoccupation with foliage—a preoccupation that manifests itself in a series of leafy abstractions culminating in the Musée Picasso's large painting of wind-tossed fronds. This rhythmically billowing alternative to bordello draperies would enable Picasso to take his whores outside and transform them into bathers. Outdoor space made for problems that he had never as yet seriously tackled. Cézanne would show him the way.

Picasso. *Landscape*, summer, 1907. Oil on canvas, 94×93cm. Musée Picasso.

*　　　*　　　*

By the end of the summer Picasso had set the *Demoiselles* aside—this time for good. It would not be exhibited until 1916 and not recognized as a great revolutionary achievement until André Breton published it in the early 1920s. In 1907 the only person to realize its importance was the artist himself. He had proved what he had set out to prove, that he was Baudelaire's *peintre de la vie moderne*, but he was too far ahead of the field to be perceived as such, hence a feeling of bitterness rather than gratification. Ironically, the most flattering recognition took the ambivalent form of invective and mockery from his principal rival, Matisse. As Gertrude Stein said, the two men had become "friends but were enemies."[41] Most Fridays Picasso visited Matisse's studio; most Saturdays they met at the Steins'; and sometime in 1907 they even exchanged paintings.[42] On

Above: Picasso. *Pitcher, Bowl and Fruit Bowl*, 1908. Oil on canvas, 81.9×65.7 cm. Philadelphia Museum of Art: A. E. Gallatin Collection.

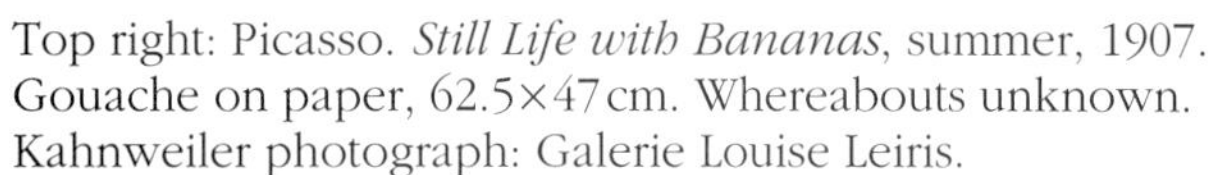

Top right: Picasso. *Still Life with Bananas*, summer, 1907. Gouache on paper, 62.5×47 cm. Whereabouts unknown. Kahnweiler photograph: Galerie Louise Leiris.

Right: Picasso. *Carafe and Three Bowls*, 1908. Oil on cardboard, 66×51 cm. State Hermitage Museum, St. Petersburg.

seeing the *Demoiselles*, however, Matisse was outraged to find his sensational *Blue Nude*, not to speak of his *Bonheur de vivre*, overtaken by Picasso's "hideous" whores. He exploded in gales of laughter; what is more he did so in front of the caustic Fénéon. In fact Matisse was anything but amused. Despite his sanctimonious statement that "a little boldness discovered in a friend's work was shared by all,"[43] he was fighting mad and let it be known that he regarded the *Demoiselles* as an attempt to ridicule the modern movement. He was going to get even with Picasso, he said, and make him beg for mercy. This threat made for some great paintings. Just as the *Bonheur de vivre* had fueled Picasso's competitiveness, the *Demoiselles* now fueled Matisse's. The modern art world would be polarized into ever more resentful Matisseites and ever more aggressive Picassoites.

Kahnweiler's report that "a short period of exhaustion followed [the *Demoiselles*]" is an understatement.[44] Besides exhaustion, Picasso suffered from a terrible spiritual isolation. There was nobody with whom he could share the exaltation and anguish of being way ahead of his time. Friends avoided the artist, Salmon claimed.[45] They thought he was crazy—crazy like Frenhofer, the painter hero of Balzac's *Chef d'œuvre inconnu*, with whom Picasso would come to identify. Just as disheartening, it was very evident that nobody would want to buy this painting, which represented more than six months' torturous work. The only possible candidate, Leo Stein, had also "brayed" with laughter, as Picasso mimicked to Antonina Vallentin, "holding his sides, doubled up."[46] Fernande, who kept in touch with her lover after they had separated, told Gertrude Stein that Picasso looked "very fed up."[47]

To take his mind off the *Demoiselles*, Picasso turned his attention to still life—a genre he had yet to tackle in any depth. The phallic features of that double-spouted drinking vessel the *porrón* had inspired some suggestive still lifes at Gósol, but the artist did not begin to see the enormous possibilities of still life until he discovered how a tight little arrangement of fruit could provide the *Demoiselles* with both emblem and fulcrum. Between the fall of 1907 and the spring of 1908, Picasso pitted himself against Cézanne in a series of deceptively simple-looking paintings of utilitarian objects—bowls, jars, saucers, jugs—which prove on closer inspection to be anything but functional. As if to make things look taller, Picasso tops some of his objects with an arbitrary excrescence, slightly different in tone or color: for instance, the small, gray, goblet-shaped thing on top of the brown container in the Hermitage still life, or the conical funnel stuck in the jar in the Philadelphia one. He teases the beholder's eye with other ambivalences: painting a concavity as if it were convex, and vice versa. Whether he is mocking Cézanne's geometrical dictum or indulging in anthropomorphic puns, Picasso dramatizes and individualizes these mundane things so forcefully—as forcefully as Van Gogh in his *Yellow Chair*—that their very tension seems to reflect the tensions of their creator's existence.

Picasso. *Still Life with Decal*, spring–summer, 1907. Watercolor and decal on sketchbook page, 22.4×17.5cm. Musée Picasso.

Picasso. Study for *Les Demoiselles d'Avignon*, March, 1907. Pastel and black pencil on sketchbook page, 24.2×19.3cm. Musée Picasso.

3

Cézanne and Picasso

"Le petit-fils de Cézanne—c'est moi."[1]
(Picasso)

Fernande Olivier, 1908–09. Photograph by Picasso. Archives Picasso.

Opposite: Cézanne in front of his *Grandes Baigneuses*, 1904. Photograph by Emile Bernard. Collection Mary Louise Krumrine.

On August 8, 1907, Fernande wrote to Gertrude Stein, who was staying in Fiesole, to complain that the summer "had been particularly hard for me, both from a physical and psychological point of view. I'm tired and often feel depressed."[2] By way of hinting that her affair with Picasso was at an end, she tells Gertrude that she is unlikely to attend the opening of the Salon d'Automne. Abandoning Raymonde had put an end to their attempt at family life. Neither party appears to have formed another attachment: Fernande had simply lost Picasso—temporarily, as it turned out—to the *Demoiselles*. The repainting of the two right-hand heads cannot have left her in any doubt as to the depths of her lover's rage. Two weeks later (August 24), Fernande wrote once again to Gertrude:

> Do you want to hear some important news? Picasso and I are ending our life together. We are parting for good next month. He's waiting for the money Vollard owes him so as to be able to give me something with which to await . . . events. What these events will be and how I will put my life together after this latest desertion I don't know. What a disappointment!
>
> But don't imagine for a minute that matters will sort themselves out again. No, Pablo "has had enough." Those are his words, although he says that he has nothing to reproach me with, he just isn't cut out for this kind of life. Forgive me if I bore you writing like this, but I need to tell someone, and you are the only person who takes a little interest in me, and I'm so downhearted. Imagine what my life is like now, although outwardly nothing has changed. I'm doing all I possibly can not to show my despair and depression, but underneath it all I feel so disgusted and the future holds out no hopes. Oh, I'm devastated, believe me, truly devastated![3]

Fernande goes on to ask Gertrude if she could help her find pupils to whom she could teach French. (She prided herself on speaking "beautiful French.") She was also looking for somewhere to live.

Next time Fernande wrote (September 2), she was in better spirits, "though still very disoriented." She had found a room on the impasse Girardon—round the corner from the Bateau Lavoir—but could not afford to move there until Vollard returned to Paris and paid Picasso the money he owed him. Meanwhile they were very hard up. In preparation for life on her own, Fernande had resumed contact with "one of my aunts" (the widow of "an uncle I loved very much when I was a child"). "We didn't get on very well before, but I'll be so bored this winter that I'll be glad to go and see her."[4] This woman sounds less like an aunt than the appalling

Madame Belvallé, the adoptive mother who had maltreated Fernande as a child and forced her into a miserable marriage.[5]

Vollard finally reappeared (September 14) and gave Picasso a check for 1,100 francs (*"pour 11 tableaux,"* according to the receipt).[6] Gertrude quotes the artist's comment: "If you love a woman you give her money. Well now it is when you want to leave a woman you have to wait until you have enough money to give her."[7] Thanks to Vollard, Picasso could now "afford to separate from her by giving her half."[8] Picasso's share of the Vollard money did not last long. Since there was no question of selling the *Demoiselles*, he decided to unload the large 1905 *Saltimbanques*—the only major early work that Vollard had not acquired, because the artist had asked such a high price for it. The dealer proposed to act as an agent and offer the painting to some of his German and Russian clients (including presumably Shchukin). Sagot, who kept his ear to the ground, heard about these overtures and informed André Level, founder of the Peau de l'Ours—the first mutual fund in modern art.[9] Realizing the significance of the *Saltimbanques*, Level went after it. Through Lucien Moline, one of the more trustworthy runners, he made Picasso an offer of 1,000 francs. At first the artist turned it down; but since he was broke, he accepted a loan of 300 francs. Vollard's clients must have failed to show any interest, for two weeks later Picasso agreed to Level's offer. The partners in the Peau de l'Ours consortium were not too happy at having a third of their annual budget tied up in a single painting, even if it was a bargain. Level soon won them over; it would prove his greatest coup.[10]

Annette Rosenshine, 1897. Photograph by Arnold Genthe. Bancroft Library, University of California, Berkeley.

Fernande lost no time installing herself in her new bed-sitting-room. She claimed to have spent "a ridiculous amount of money" buying antiques—"a very large bed and a piano and a little tea table."[11] Meanwhile Gertrude had found her a pupil. This was no less than Alice Toklas, who had just arrived from San Francisco (September 7). Gertrude had never met this bright, poised girl, who came from much the same well-to-do Jewish milieu as herself (though of Polish rather than German extraction), but she knew all about her, indeed was already in love with the idea of her. Gertrude had reached this conclusion in the course of enslaving Alice's best friend and cousin, Annette Rosenshine. Annette, who suffered from a cleft palate and harelip, was as insecure and dowdy as Alice was secure and striking. After arriving in Paris, Annette had originally been a protégée of Sarah Stein's, but Gertrude had lured her away to use as a guinea pig for literary as well as psychological analysis. Every afternoon at 4 p.m. Annette had to visit Gertrude for an analytical session, which included a perusal of the letters she regularly received from her exemplary cousin Alice. Occasionally there would be a visit to an artist's studio. Annette remembers Gertrude taking her in the early summer of 1907 to see Picasso, when he and Fernande had evidently been smoking opium or hashish.[12]

Harriet Levy and Alice B. Toklas. Fiesole, 1909. Beinecke Rare Book and Manuscript Library, Yale University.

Under Gertrude's (and occasionally Leo's) amateur analysis, Annette's psyche rapidly deteriorated, to the horror of the Rosenshine family when they arrived in Europe (summer, 1907). Despite pleas to return home to San Francisco, Annette insisted on staying close to Gertrude, whose feelings she continued to arouse with eulogies of her fascinating, sophisticated cousin. As soon as Alice appeared, Gertrude dumped Annette. So, very soon, did Alice.

Alice B. Toklas, c. 1906. Photograph by Arnold Genthe. Bancroft Library, University of California, Berkeley.

The night of their arrival in Paris, Alice and her companion, Harriet Levy, were summoned to dinner by Gertrude's brother Michael and his wife, Sarah, who lived near the Luxembourg Gardens in a former Protestant church which they had converted into a house. Gertrude sat waiting like a big predatory cat. The great woman was unusually quiet and composed: "a golden brown presence, burned by the Tuscan sun and with a golden glint in her warm brown hair." Leo came in later, but "it was Gertrude who . . . held [Alice's] attention, who . . . rang the bell in her that signified an encounter with genius."[13] Although the two women had a blazing row on the occasion of their second meeting the following day—Alice was half an hour late—it was love at first sight.

Picasso would also take a liking to Alice, indeed would end up preferring her to Gertrude. He was delighted, he said, that Alice was going to have French lessons with Fernande: "Ah, the Miss Toklas," he said, "with small feet like a spanish woman and earrings like a gypsy and a father who is king of Poland like the Poniatowskis, of course she will take lessons."[14] Half a century later, Picasso would tease his future wife, Jacqueline, by claiming that she was the image of Alice. On one occasion, he even whipped a large osprey-trimmed hat off Alice's bowed head to demonstrate the likeness. "Yes, Pablo," Jacqueline hissed angrily, "except that I don't have a mustache." Soon after they met, Picasso even attempted to flirt with Gertrude's new love. Harriet Levy described the consequences:

> "Picasso squeezed my hand under the table," Alice reported matter-of-factly. At this, Gertrude dropped her fork. "Ah," she said, looking at Alice, "and what else?" "Nothing," Alice replied. "He just squeezed my hand." Still looking hard at her friend, Gertrude tried to analyze the gesture. "It might have been a mere transient casual act," she mused. "But it may have been a more important sign. If in squeezing her hand he experienced an emotion that entered into his imagination, that would be entirely different. That might be the beginning of a permanent feeling . . ." At these words, Alice began to pale. "Might be love," Gertrude continued. Alice, Harriet thought, looked terrified. "Might even be love."[15]

By switching her affections to Gertrude, Alice exposed her cousin Annette to deep traumatic shock; in the long run, however, this betrayal saved her. Under Sarah Stein's auspices, Annette enrolled at the Académie Matisse. Then, at the end of 1908, she returned to San Francisco and became a sculptor.[16] Meanwhile Alice would settle down to forty years of happy married life.

Annette Rosenshine. *Bust of Alice B. Toklas*, 1928. Plaster. Collection Paul Padgette.

As soon as Gertrude met Alice, she set about taking her over. Fernande was a useful ally. As someone who had enjoyed an occasional lesbian escapade, she was very ready to promote the romance. On September 16, 1907, she wrote to Gertrude, asking her to drop by the following afternoon. Alice was coming "and would be quite delighted to see her."[17] She also invited Germaine Pichot, the woman responsible for Casagemas's suicide (and thus, arguably, for triggering the Blue period), and Alice Princet, who was about to leave her husband for Derain. "The conversation was not lively," Alice/Gertrude reports. "It was a pleasure to meet, it was even an honor, but that was about all. . . . Finally [Fernande] and I arranged about the French lessons, I was to pay 50 cents an hour and she was to come to see me two days hence and we were to begin."[18] Alice and Fernande would become the closest of friends.

Fernande's services as a confidante stood her in good stead. She and Picasso were soon reconciled, thanks in part to Gertrude. The first time Alice was asked to dine at Gertrude and Leo's (September 28), the couple that was no longer a couple was also invited. It was just the six of them —Alfred Maurer, the American painter, was Alice's partner—but dinner turned out to be the prelude to one of the Steins' heterogeneous Saturday soirées: "hungarians . . . all sizes and shapes . . . quantities of germans . . . a fair sprinkling of americans,"[19] the Matisses and Miss Mars and Miss Squires, whom Gertrude later "immortalized" (her word) as Miss Furr and Miss Skeene. Picasso and Fernande were unusually late for dinner. "I am very upset, said Pablo, but you know very well Gertrude I am never late but Fernande had ordered a dress for the *vernissage* [of the Salon d'Automne] tomorrow and it didn't come."[20] So the former lovers went to the Salon together after all. The section that caused the greatest sensation, the retrospective in commemoration of Cézanne's death the year before, would wreak yet another major change in Picasso's work.

* * *

Cézanne's death (on October 22, 1906) had left many of the more progressive young artists hoping that his spirit might live on in their work. Picasso saw the master's legacy in a different light, to judge by a comment Gertrude Stein made to Harold Acton, which sounds suspiciously like Picasso: "All modern painting is based on what Cézanne had failed to do, instead of on what he nearly succeeded in doing. To show what he could not achieve had become Cézanne's obsession and that of his followers."[21] To commemorate Cézanne's death Bernheim-Jeune held an exhibition in June (1907) of seventy-nine watercolors, few of which had ever left the studio. It was a revelation. Picasso was especially struck by the paradox of the watercolors' lack of finish and "intrinsic completeness."[22] As he later said of these supremely beautiful works: "As soon as he begins to make the first stroke, the picture is already there."[23] Cézanne had established an artist's right to restrict his picture surface to minimal washes of color, exploit the white ground as an active element, and use the fluidity of the medium to evoke a fluidity of space in which objects seem soluble. Veils of color homogenize everything and suggest that light as well as space is palpable. Even Robert Delaunay noted in one of his sketchbooks that "the watercolors of Cézanne announce cubism."[24]

Cézanne. *Foliage*, 1895–1900. Watercolor and pencil, 44.8×56.8 cm. The Museum of Modern Art, New York: Lillie P. Bliss Bequest.

The watercolor show heralded an even more momentous event: the commemorative Cézanne exhibition at the Salon d'Automne, which opened on October 1, and the simultaneous (October 1 and 15) publication in the *Mercure de France* of Cézanne's "Letters to Emile Bernard." These letters include the artist's famous dictum about treating nature by means of the cylinder, the sphere and the cone—a dictum that lesser cubists would exploit all too literally.[25] Picasso had surprisingly little time for Cézanne's theorizing. "I'm in complete disagreement with [his] idea about making over Poussin in accordance with nature," he later told Françoise Gilot.[26] He had nothing against "making over Poussin," he said—indeed would eventually do so himself—as long as this was not done "in accordance with nature" but with *his* (Picasso's) "dynamism." The Salon d'Automne's Cézanne section occupied two galleries and included some fifty-six works of all periods.[27] At least half the exhibits were lent by the pioneer Cézanne collector, Auguste Pellerin; in addition there were several loans from Paul Cézanne *fils* and Maurice Gangnat among others and—a fact too often overlooked—a number of Druet photographs of Cézanne's studio and paintings that were not in the show.

Letters from the German poet Rilke to his wife convey a sense of the ever-mounting excitement that this "difficult" exhibition engendered in discriminating minds. Rilke visited the Cézanne rooms so often during the three weeks the Salon was open that they became "virtually my apartment,"[28] and the artist the object of a passionate aesthetic cult on Rilke's part. At first, he confesses, he was at a loss: "The puzzlement and insecurity of one's own first confrontation with [Cézanne's] work, along with his name which was just as new. And then for a long time nothing and suddenly one has the right eyes."[29] Previously, he said, he had always found "the people walking about in front of paintings [more remarkable] than the paintings themselves." In the Cézanne rooms there was no question of this. "Here, all of reality is on [the artist's] side."[30] He found several other enlightened Germans worshiping at the same shrine: Julius Meier-Graefe, Count Harry Kessler, Julius Elias (the Ibsen translator) and Karl-Ernst Osthaus (founder of the Folkwang Museum, Essen). But by far the most perceptive of Rilke's compatriots seems to have been his painter companion, Mathilde Vollmoeller, who would later marry Matisse's pupil Hans Purrmann. She compared Cézanne *sur le motif* to a hound "just looking, without any nervousness, without any ulterior motive"; it was as if he recorded only "what he knew, nothing else."[31] And how astute of Vollmoeller to perceive that Cézanne weighed objects against their color: "Here the object, there the color; never more, never less than is needed for perfect balance. It might be a lot or a little, that depends, but it's always the exact equivalent of the object."[32] And how shrewd of Rilke to observe that, for all that he was a pioneer, Cézanne was "unconcerned with being original."[33] This could never be said of Picasso, true though it might be of Cézanne's other self-styled "son," Georges Braque.

Rainer Maria Rilke.

Rilke contrasts the select few, who silently "admire Cézanne and understand something of his devotion and hidden glory," with the supercilious connoisseurs, who stalk through the Cézanne rooms of a Sunday,

> amused, ironically irritated, annoyed, outraged. . . . There they stand, these Monsieurs [sic], in the middle of this world, affecting a note of pathetic despair, and you hear them saying: *il n'y a absolument rien, rien, rien.* And the women, how beautiful they appear to themselves. . . . With their mirror image in mind, they plant themselves for a moment, without looking, next to one of those touchingly tentative portraits of Madame Cézanne, so as to exploit the hideousness of this painting for a comparison which they believe is so favorable to themselves. . . . Standing in front of [Cézanne's] work, one comes back to the thought that every recognition . . . should make one mistrustful of one's own work. Basically, if it is good, one can't live to see it recognized: otherwise it's just half good and not heedless enough.[34]

Did Rilke's path cross Picasso's in the course of this exhibition, which affected both of them so deeply and made Picasso, too, question his own work? It is more than likely. They had already met through their mutual friend, Wilhelm Uhde, who had lent the poet Picasso's *Death of*

Harlequin. Later, his Rose period masterpiece, the *Saltimbanques,* would inspire one of the most celebrated of Rilke's *Duino Elegies.*[35]

Cézanne. *Self-Portrait,* c. 1875. Oil on canvas, 66×55cm. Private collection.

*   *   *

"[Cézanne] was my one and only master," Picasso told Brassaï. "It was the same with all of us—he was like our father. It was he who protected us."[36] At one time or another all the future cubists would acknowledge Cézanne's paternity, but none of them as insistently, possessively and on occasion as resentfully as Picasso. It was as if he had come to see the Master of Aix as a surrogate for the father for whom he had such ambivalent feelings. Indeed there were certain parallels between the father and the father figure. Both of them hailed from the beautiful, backward south; both had been born around the same time into solid provincial families; both were rigid and dogged and proud upholders of traditional values. In other respects they could not have been less alike. Whereas one was an incomparable genius, the other was an indubitable hack. However, as Picasso well knew, there is almost as much to be learned from a bad example as a good one. At the very end of his life, Picasso would once again target his father, but instead of seeing him as Cézanne, he portrayed him as Degas in a series of mocking brothel scenes inspired by the latter's monotypes of prostitutes.

Cézanne. *The Sea at L'Estaque,* 1878–79. Oil on canvas, 73×92cm. Musée d'Orsay, Paris: Picasso Gift.

Picasso had long been conversant with Cézanne's work: from the paintings in Vollard's stock that he had first seen in 1901, from examples in the possession of Matisse and the Steins, as well as from the show of ten paintings at the 1906 Salon d'Automne. If he did not fall fully under Cézanne's spell before embarking on the *Demoiselles,* it was largely because he had been busy exploiting Gauguin's synthetic primitivism. Later he would gravitate to the real thing—sculpture that was Iberian, Oceanic or tribal. By the end of 1907 Picasso had absorbed so much from primitivism that he was ready to move on to a fresh source. Henceforth paintings had to be not only magical but palpable. Cézanne was the master of palpability. He was also an essentially solitary master and to that extent someone with whom Picasso could identify at this moment of isolation. Apropos the great Cézanne *View of L'Estaque,* which he would later acquire, Picasso told Hélène Parmelin of "the unbelievable solitude" to which artists are condemned when they break new ground—solitude that can be both a blessing and a curse. "Is there anything more dangerous than sympathetic understanding," he asked Parmelin, "especially as it doesn't exist? It's almost always wrong. You think you aren't alone, and really you're more alone than you were before."[37] Fifty years later, the bitterness triggered by the blindness of his poet friends—Apollinaire, Jacob, Salmon—still rankled.

"It's not what an artist does that counts," Picasso remarked to Zervos, "but what he is. Cézanne's anxiety is what interests us. That is his lesson."[38] This anxiety is what compels an artist to set his sights ever higher so that each brushstroke constitutes a little victory snatched from the maw of defeat. The greater an artist's ability, Picasso used to say, the more fiercely he has to combat facility and virtuosity by making things as difficult as possible for himself—without, of course, letting it look difficult. Whenever Cézanne embarked on a fresh painting, he would start all

Opposite: Cézanne. *Grandes Baigneuses,* 1906. Oil on canvas, 209×252cm. Philadelphia Museum of Art: Purchased, W. P. Wilstach Collection.

Above: Cézanne. *Temptation of Saint Anthony*, c. 1875–77. Oil on canvas, 47×56 cm. Musée d'Orsay, Paris.

Left: Cézanne. *Madame Cézanne in a Red Armchair*, 1877. Oil on canvas, 72.5×56 cm. Museum of Fine Arts, Boston.

Above: Picasso. *Friendship*, 1907–08. Oil on canvas, 152×101 cm. State Hermitage Museum, St. Petersburg.

Above right: Picasso. *Standing Nude*, 1908. Oil on canvas, 150.3×100.3cm. Juliana Cheney Edwards Collection: Courtesy Museum of Fine Arts, Boston.

Right: Picasso. *Study of Bathers*, 1907. Charcoal on paper, 48×60cm. Musée Picasso.

over again from scratch. The same could sometimes be said of Picasso. Even when signing hundreds of prints, he did so with total concentration, as if each time were the first.

The Cézannes in the Salon d'Automne exhibition which left the most immediate mark on works by Picasso and his new friends, Derain and Braque, were two of the large, late *Grandes Baigneuses*.[39] In the course of the next six months, these three painters would vie with one another over Cézanne's mantle. Matisse was no longer in the race. Cézanne's death had to some extent released him from the master's thrall, whereas the commemorative exhibition had had a reverse effect on Picasso, Derain and Braque. They became more Cézannesque than ever. In each case their response would manifest itself in a very large painting of three nudes.

Drawings executed immediately after the Salon d'Automne reveal Picasso reverting once again to the parental strategy of doing an ambitious figure composition that would advertise both his prowess and his progress. He originally envisaged a Cézannesque frieze of as many as five (in one case even six) bathers—outdoor *demoiselles*, who are stone-faced rather than tribally masked. This time round, Picasso felt less obliged to shock. His aim was to consolidate the great leap forward he had made in the *Demoiselles*, and if possible come up with a painting which, for all its modernism, would be acceptable—and with any luck salable—to the Steins. "One does not substitute oneself for the past, one merely adds a new link to its chain":[40] Cézanne's observation sums up Picasso's attitude at this juncture.

Picasso. *Study of Bathers*, 1907. Pen and sepia ink on paper, 20×15cm. Musée Picasso.

Picasso transforms Cézanne's bathers into mannish women, naked except for a towel or two, who strike physique-contest poses. He sets them off against a vault of trees on the bank of a river or lake, indicated by the front of a boat in the immediate foreground. One or two of the women are stepping into the boat, whose protruding prow—like the prow-shaped slice of melon in the foreground of the *Demoiselles*—links them to the beholder. But whereas the slice of melon leads us into the collective womb of the *Demoiselles*, the boat thrusts outwards at us and suggests that these threatening creatures—more frontal, hence more confrontational, than Cézanne's bathers—are about to cross the water and invade our space. "It's as if the artist were behind rather than in front of the canvas, pushing everything outwards," Braque said of this pictorial device,[41] which he, too, would accommodate to his requirements. Indeed, by the end of the summer, Braque would bring distant hillsides, not to speak of the sea and sky, seemingly within our grasp in the first paintings to be dubbed "cubist."

In the interests of tension, unity and drama, Picasso soon abandoned the widely extended format of the original concept and over the next six months chopped up his Cézannesque frieze into component parts: monumental threesomes, homogenized couples and androgynous single figures with raised elbows. The couple on the left of the sketches inspired the great painting of two bathers—close-knit as Siamese twins—which has come to be known euphemistically as *Friendship*. This sentimental title was devised by the painting's first owner, the prudish Sergei Shchukin, probably for fear of exposing his daughters to the hint of lesbianism. Gertrude Stein's passion for Alice Toklas may have renewed Picasso's interest in the subject of two affectionate females. This supposition is

Picasso. Study for *Friendship*, 1907–08. Gouache and charcoal on paper, 62.8×48 cm (the picture Gertrude Stein wanted to acquire). Musée Picasso.

confirmed by Gertrude's desire to acquire one of the studies for *Friendship*. Picasso devotes a further series to the single bather on the right in the original composition. In yet another major bid to synthesize the sexes, he scales her up into a monumental androgyne with a mandala-shaped diaphragm that stands for both phallus and vagina. (A related drawing depicts a woman playing with what is apparently her very own penis.)[42]

Picasso's bathers are racially as well as sexually ambivalent. The rusty red and ruddy brown pigment of these women is much darker than that of the coral-colored *Demoiselles*, but that does not mean that they are Indians or Africans. Picasso differentiated his bathers from Gauguin's Tahitians and Cézanne's *Bathers* and, for that matter, Matisse's nymphs and fauns. He wanted to synthesize a new race of raceless women—natives of no identifiable place. They would be Picasso's own Frankensteins, a bit of this and a bit of that, and by virtue of being outside time and place and even gender, they would be instrumental in establishing primitivism as the look of modernism. W. H. Auden's line "Sylvan meant savage in those primal woods" is illuminating.[43] Picasso's savagery is metaphorical.

The first and in many respects the most mesmerizing of the *Three Women* paintings is the *Nudes in the Forest*. It is a considerable advance on earlier totemic paintings in that it is not a representation of a fetish, real or imagined, although tribal scarification has inspired the way the paint has been slashed on. This painting used to hang on the walls of Douglas Cooper's Château de Castille, the house near Avignon which the artist frequently visited in the 1950s and 1960s and at one point tried to buy. Of the numerous Picassos in Cooper's collection, the *Nudes in the Forest* was the one the artist would focus on and devour with his *mirada fuerte* eyes. "*C'est bien fort,*" he would say—an accolade he reserved for works he particularly valued—"painted all at one go like a Van Gogh." As usual Picasso talked about his work as if it were by someone else. He liked the rawness, he said—the possibilities that it opened up. Besides, he always liked the first in a series—and also the penultimate drawing or painting, "the one before I manage to kill off the original idea by resolving it."[44]

In her *Autobiography of Alice B. Toklas* Gertrude Stein makes a great to-do about Alice's first visit to Picasso's studio and the paintings she saw—notably, *Les Demoiselles d'Avignon* and *Three Women*.

> Against the wall was an enormous picture, a strange picture of light and dark colors . . . of a group, an enormous group [evidently the *Demoiselles*] and next to it another in a sort of red brown, of three women, square and posturing, all of it rather frightening. . . . I felt that there was something painful and beautiful there and oppressive but imprisoned.[45]

Gertrude then tells us about a "smaller picture," which she had apparently set her heart on: "Very pale almost white, two figures, they were all there but very unfinished and not finishable. Picasso said, but he [Leo] will never accept it. Yes, I know, answered Gertrude Stein. But just the same it is the only one in which it is all there. Yes, I know, he replied and they fell silent."[46] Daix has identified this "smaller picture" as one of the studies for *Friendship*.[47] The implication of this puzzling passage is that

Above: André Salmon in front of *Three Women*, 1908. Photograph by Picasso. Archives Picasso.

Right: Picasso. *Nudes in the Forest*, 1907–08. Oil on canvas, 99×99 cm. Musée Picasso.

Gertrude's brother had lost his flair for the avant-garde ("he will never accept it"), and that she was now the one with the eye.

Once again, Gertrude gets her dates wrong. In order to make the most of Alice's first visit to Picasso's studio (a big scene early on in Alice's *Autobiography*), she conflates other visits into a single memorable occasion.[48] Fortunately, the photographs that Picasso took of various friends—André Salmon, Sebastià Junyer Vidal, little Dolly Van Dongen—in front of *Three Women* help us to follow its development from tribal scarification to cubist faceting. The first version of this painting was probably completed around the end of 1907. Picasso then put it aside for some months, while he experimented with alternate solutions. "In the spring of 1908," Kahnweiler writes about this moment of change, "Picasso resumed his quest. . . . He had to begin with the most important thing, and that seemed to be the representation of form."[49] The example of Cézanne was paramount. There were endless discussions with Braque and Derain, often in front of the paintings at the Salon d'Automne. Tribal sculpture continued to play a covert psychic role in Picasso's art, but Cézanne dictated Picasso's choice of subjects and, to some extent, his syntax.

4

Rendez-vous des peintres

Picasso's *Woman* in the Bateau Lavoir studio, summer, 1908. Photograph by Picasso. Archives Picasso.

Opposite:
Left: Derain in his studio, c. 1908. Photograph by Gelett Burgess. *Architectural Record*, May, 1910.

Top right: Braque, c. 1908. Photograph by Gelett Burgess. *Architectural Record*, May, 1910.

Bottom right: Marie Laurencin, c. 1906. Collection P.M.A.

"*RENDEZ-VOUS DES POÈTES*" WERE THE WORDS Picasso had originally chalked up on the door of his Bateau Lavoir studio. Insofar as poets predominated over painters, the place lived up to this name. By the end of 1907, however, the studio had become more of a "*rendez-vous des peintres*," thanks largely to Picasso's friendship with two prodigiously gifted young painters, André Derain, whom he met in the fall of 1906, and Georges Braque, whom he met in the spring of 1907. (Later, they would be joined by the no less inventive Juan Gris.) Braque's and Derain's fathers were prosperous suburban tradespeople, but otherwise utterly unalike: Charles Braque, a housepainter, was an amateur artist with a taste for modern art; Louis Charlemagne Derain, a *pâtissier*, was a reactionary *conseiller municipal* with a deep distrust of it. The difference in parental attitudes would be reflected in their sons' careers and their relationships to each other as well as to Picasso. Derain, who was older by two years, was the first to rally to Picasso, and the first to back away from him and revert to traditionalism. Braque, on the other hand, would play a determining role in his development.

Years later, Braque would look back on cubism and see it as a mountaineering expedition:[1] he and Picasso roped together, establishing precarious footholds as they scaled uncharted heights. Nobody had gone that way before; nobody would know how to go that way again. As Braque's wife, Marcelle, said, the climb was too steep for Picasso to have made it on his own.[2] If the expedition enabled the artists to perceive things from a new eminence, it was because the spirit of the legendary old guide, the recently deceased Cézanne, had headed the mountaineers up the most accessible face. Braque's analogy leaves out of account the presence of Derain at the start of the climb. Derain turned out to lack the faith and nerve that the ascent required: as soon as the going became arduous, he hastened back to base, Camp Cézanne, where he could venerate the old guide in safety. Just as well: Picasso and Braque proved to be far better matched. Until 1914 all three remained friends. Later Picasso would drop Derain; Braque would support him to the very bitter end.

*　　　*　　　*

Braque had turned twenty-five in May, 1907. He was thus seven months younger than Picasso. As an artist, he was in some ways less advanced and in others more mature than the moody, mercurial *Wunderkind* that

Picasso would often lapse back into being. Although they ultimately suppressed their idiosyncrasies and, for a year or two, adopted a common style, the two artists were as dissimilar in temperament as they were in physique. As Uhde put it, Braque was "*clair, mesuré, bourgeois,*" whereas Picasso was "*sombre, excessif, révolutionnaire.*" "In the spiritual marriage which they entered into," Uhde continued, "one contributed a great sensibility, the other a great plastic awareness."[3] Braque's sensibility included an unexpected streak of fatalism. "I no more made up my mind to become a painter than to go on breathing," he once said. "In fact I do not think I ever took a deliberate action in my life. I enjoyed painting and I worked hard. . . . But I never had a definite aim."[4]

Braque came of a family of housepainters and color merchants.[5] Both his father and grandfather were Sunday painters in the Barbizon manner. (Though an amateur, Charles Braque was more gifted than Picasso's art-teacher father.) Early years were spent in the sleepy Seine-side village of Argenteuil, where Renoir and Monet had painted together in 1874 and reached a pitch of stylistic similarity that sometimes made it difficult for them, as it would for Braque and Picasso in 1911, to distinguish one's work from the other's. One of Braque's earliest memories was of watching his father decorate a villa belonging to Gustave Caillebotte, the impressionists' friend and patron—the man whose bequest of impressionist masterpieces would so excite Braque when he eventually visited the Musée du Luxembourg. In 1890 the Braques left their native Argenteuil and moved downstream to Le Havre, where their business duly prospered. Like Claude Monet, Braque grew to love this great seaport. School, on the other hand, bored him, even the drawing lessons, and he preferred playing games or (again like Monet) making caricatures. "There was nothing remarkable about my early drawings," Braque said, "and even if there had been, the teacher would have been quite incapable of realizing it."[6]

Braque and his father. Archives Laurens.

Though sensitive, moody and meditative, Braque was in other respects a normal child. His favorite pleasures were solitary ones: he liked to look out to sea for hours on end, "because this put me in touch with the infinite."[7] He also liked bicycling about the country lanes and swimming and sailing in the Seine estuary. But what appealed to him most were weekend sketching expeditions with his father, or evenings spent copying illustrations from the satirical newspaper *Gil Blas*—evenings occasionally enlivened by raids on the walls of the neighboring Sous-Prefecture to peel off posters by Steinlen and Toulouse-Lautrec.

When he was fifteen, Braque attended evening classes at the local Ecole des Beaux-Arts. But he was never consumed, as Picasso was, with a fanatical urge to perfect his technique. That would have involved the unthinkable: a plan of action. The tired academic teaching merely confirmed his innate distaste for official art—an attitude that would ripen into a taste for unofficial art. No more did the dull lessons at the local lycée hold his interest. When Braque failed his baccalaureat nobody was surprised, least of all his parents, who apprenticed him to a local painter-decorator. Learning the tricks of the family trade appealed to Braque: it left him time to paint, also to play the accordion and flute. (His teacher was one of the Dufy brothers.) On days off he would go to Paris and visit the Louvre and the Luxembourg.

After a year's apprenticeship, Braque moved to Paris to study under a master decorator for a diploma, which enabled him, in 1901, to claim a reduction in his military service from three years to one. The training had far-reaching consequences. Braque's skill at lettering and decorative effects such as marbling and woodgraining would help him to equate color with texture and devise a whole new range of tactile sensations with which to enrich his paintings. And his inherent feeling for pigment —he ground most of his own colors—would allow him to exploit the intrinsic qualities of oil paint as subtly and ingeniously as any other artist in history. Braque would pass on his expertise to Picasso, who had never shown much interest in *matière*. After they started exchanging ideas, there would be an immediate refinement in Picasso's paint surfaces, and also in his use of color as a structural element rather than a source of light or pictorial enhancement. And as Picasso later admitted, it was Braque who taught him how to keep his *papiers collés* from coming unstuck.

During his military service (he emerged as an N.C.O.), Braque's interest in housepainting waned. He now wanted to be an *artiste-peintre*, a painter of pictures rather than walls. His father, who would found the progressive Cercle d'Art Moderne at Le Havre,[8] was delighted at the idea and allowed him enough money to study in Paris. Braque established himself in Montmartre in 1902, and during the next two years—apart from a brief period under the doctrinaire Bonnat, at the Ecole des Beaux-Arts —taught himself at the "free" Académie Humbert, where "the professor counted for nothing and discipline was slack."[9] At Humbert's Academy Braque's best friend (and a friend for life) was Georges Lepape, soon to become famous for the stylized fashion drawings he did for Paul Poiret and *La Gazette du Bon Ton*. One day, Lepape told Braque about a newly arrived student: a strange, sallow, severely dressed *jolie laide*, who drew attention to herself by wearing her hair in a very thick plait and peering at her work through pince-nez caught behind her ears on a ribbon. Prodigiously gifted, Lepape said.[10] Her name, they discovered, was Marie Laurencin ("at home they call me Coco"), and she was the illegitimate daughter of a socialist *député*, Alfred Toulet, and a handsome woman of humble origins and dour distinction, rumored to have creole blood. Marie was ragged by the other students but made much of by Braque and Lepape.

Mother and daughter lived together with their cat, Poussiquette, and "acted toward each other exactly as a younger nun with an older one."[11] The mother was "very quiet, very pleasant, very dignified,"[12] given to humming Norman folktunes as she worked away at the embroideries her daughter designed. She had encouraged Marie to share her deep reverence for art and literature and no less deep distrust of men. Hence the girl's ambivalent nature: frigid and flirtatious, ribald and dainty, silly and serious, coy and exhibitionistic, and so attached to her skipping-rope that when she became Apollinaire's mistress she would give three extra-fast skips to mime *Au revoir! A bientôt! A demain!* Picasso would find Marie's bluestocking whimsicality intensely irritating. However, her first lover, Henri-Pierre Roché (the man who had introduced the Steins to Picasso), doted on her and was soon sharing her favors with his German accomplice, Franz Hessel ("Jim" to Roché's "Jules," in the latter's autobiographical novel, *Jules et Jim*, and his partner in a succession of *ménages à trois*),

Marie Laurencin. *Self-Portrait*, 1905. Oil on canvas, 92×73cm. Musée de Grenoble: Gift of A. Lowengard.

Braque. *Marie Laurencin and Georges Lepape Dancing at the Moulin de la Galette*, 1904. Private collection.

Georges Lepape. *Georges Braque*, c. 1905. Graphite on paper, 13×19.8cm. Private collection.

which enabled him to bond with another man through the medium of a shared mistress.

An unusually modish lithograph by Braque (dated 1904) of Laurencin dancing with Lepape at the Moulin de la Galette reveals that the two of them had already developed a sophisticated and idiosyncratic style of dress. So had Braque, as Lepape's drawing of him in a natty striped suit reveals. He was an early exponent of proletarian dandyism: either, as here, a dance-hall Lothario in his Sunday best, or in the fastidiously chosen worker's clothes which he would always favor: Norman peasants' ties of narrow black cord, nonchalantly knotted; denim washed and faded to just the right faint tint and texture; caps and hats of all kinds worn with casual panache. Since Braque boxed, bicycled, rowed, sailed, fenced, skated, swam and did gymnastics, he kept his well-built frame in excellent shape. Since, furthermore, he played the flute and accordion, sang popular songs, danced well (he had even learned the hornpipe from English sailors), women found him very attractive. Fernande Olivier's surprising description of Braque as a white Negro who affected a certain brutality of expression and coarseness of voice and gesture is borne out by Lepape's drawing, but I suspect this extroverted image had been cultivated to conceal a melancholy, introverted sensibility. In this respect Braque would always be an odd mixture: tough, intelligent, practical, thrifty, suspicious—as Fernande says, "a typical Norman"[13]—but also a visionary. His eyes were as large and charismatic as Picasso's but without the *mirada fuerte* aggressiveness; and they hinted at a mystic sense of métier rather than a dark, psychic urge.

Laurencin's letters to Roché reveal that she had become Braque's confidante. On April 12, 1906, she wrote that "I've been grouchy and disagreeable for four days. Braque thinks I'm a lesbian."[14] On April 28, she wrote Roché that "yesterday Braque and I were being lazy together—too lazy to do anything but fight. We didn't though. Very dumb, just sitting there, each one in an armchair. To distract me he put on his blue glasses."[15] Six weeks later (June 13), Laurencin wrote again from the country: "Braque sends me his best wishes. . . . I think of him often because he has the same kind of depressions I do."[16]

In a letter to Roché written at the end of August, Laurencin complains of stupid stories going around about Braque, "that he's hooked on opium —that annoys me."[17] These stories are not all that surprising, given that Braque was currently having an affair with the notorious Paulette Philippi,[18] once described by Apollinaire's friend Réné Dalize as "*le Malherbe de la prostitution*." Not that Paulette was a prostitute. This small, blond, blue-eyed woman of "Napoleonic" energy ran a private opium den for her numerous lovers. With the exception of a few female "slaves," these were mostly bright young men. The government official who kept her apparently did not object to Paulette's romances with a succession of painters and poets, notably Paul Fort, who immortalized her as "Manon" in his ballads and memoirs.[19] Apollinaire smoked at Paulette's; so, it seems, did Picasso. (At one point even the Bateau Lavoir became an embryonic *fumerie*; it was pretty seedy—"an opium den for Chinese of the lowest class."[20]) Paulette hated to smoke alone, Salmon says,[21] and in the course of her romances initiated most of the "*bohème de la Butte*" into drugs and, on occasion, *partouses*. "One sometimes stayed for eight days, ten days," "Baron" Mollet remembered. "Life ceased to exist, there were no more days or nights. . . . There was only one condition. . . . You had to arrive with a basket of oysters and two liters of "mêlé-cassis" (a mixture of marc and cassis). . . . As I was working for Apollinaire, rather than come up with an excuse, I had him join in. I did him a good turn that day!"[22] Fernande did not like Paulette, whom she used to meet with Braque. "Sarcastic and sneering," she says, "with a typical Montmartre wit which could get tedious."[23] Others lauded her intelligence (Paulette was very well read), independence and unsentimental rationale of "*galanterie*"—better than working in a factory, she told Salmon.

Braque, who was excessively secretive about his private life, would have been mortified to know that Laurencin discussed his feelings for Paulette with Roché, who was also sleeping with her. In Roché's diaries Paulette figures as "Opia," Laurencin as "Flap" and Braque as "Cab." For instance, his entry (May 18, 1906) about the Quat'z' Arts ball: "I saw Opia with Cab, herculean and amorous. . . . She beckoned one to join their table. She takes care of Cab, tyrannizes him a bit. Flap also has a crush on Cab. Everyone finds him attractive."[24] Whether Braque indulged in opium we do not know. However Roché's journal confirms that "Cab" was an habitué of Paulette's parties; habitués were perceived, with some reason, as opium smokers. How long this affair continued is unclear. Paulette played the field quite openly. Braque went on seeing her long after he met his future wife, Octavie Marcelle Lapré, in the winter of 1907–08. After Apollinaire's lecture at the Indépendants on April 22, 1909, Braque and Paulette were part of a large group ("*ménages* Salmon, Picasso, Derain")[25] who dined together at a bistrot.

H.-P. Roché practicing his golf swing on the beach. Photograph probably by Franz Hessel. Harry Ransom Humanities Research Center, University of Texas at Austin: Carlton Lake Collection.

*　　　*　　　*

According to legend, Picasso had picked up Laurencin at Sagot's gallery in January or February, 1907.[26] Fancying himself as a Celestina (the procuress of Spanish fiction), he decided there and then that this weird young woman would be the right mistress for Apollinaire. Illegitimacy would be a bond, and she might wean him away from his mother, as well as Géry Pieret. Picasso's pimping was most effective. "I have a fiancée for you," he told the poet, who complied delightedly with his friend's choice. Apollinaire had finally had the courage to leave his raffish mother. In April, 1907, he set up on his own. He could now entertain friends *chez lui*.

The romance took some months to consummate. At the time Apollinaire met her (February, 1907), Marie had three lovers: a man whom Roché refers to as "Brète"; Roché, who complied with her request to treat her more and more roughly ("just so long as you don't make those piercing, peacock cries," he said);[27] and the plump young German-Jewish poet Franz Hessel (code name "Glob"), Roché's accomplice. Marie's affair with Hessel had started as a threesome that included Roché, but Roché for once extricated himself. Marie disgusted him, he said, by shrieking with laughter as she squatted shamelessly on the bidet in front of them both "like a man." In April, 1907, Hessel took Roché to Munich and "gave" him (Roché's expression) two of his mistresses, Luise Bücking and Franziska, Gräfin von Reventlow, in exchange for Marie. Roché said he would like to share all his women with Franz. When they returned to Paris early in

May, Marie declared that she was still in love with Franz, although his sexuality emanated from his head, or from Roché's loins rather than his own. She next turned her attention to Apollinaire, but did not become his mistress until the beginning of July. "I've finally found a lover I love," she told Roché on July 11. The affair was a week old. Marie challenged Roché to guess who her lover was. He was amazed that it was "Pollop" (code name for Apollinaire), whom he liked less than ever now that he was jealous of him. "I never loved anyone before Pollop," Marie told him. "He is shy, reserved, sweet and tough. He is proud of me. . . . We are very together. He is very temperamental, something I have nothing against. I am no longer frightened of getting pregnant."[28] (Just as well: Marie would soon find herself taunted by Max Jacob for having had an abortion.) Apollinaire waxed no less enthusiastic about Marie: "She is gay, she is good, she is witty and she has so much talent! She is like a little sun. She is myself as woman!"[29]

Bird with a Snake ("L'Oiseau de Bénin"). Benin bronze (from Apollinaire's collection). Private collection.

In his autobiographical fantasy, *Le Poète assassiné,* Apollinaire, who calls himself "Croniamantal," embroiders on this story. He relates how Picasso, whom he names "the Benin Bird" after an oddly modern-looking, long-beaked bronze in his collection, finds him a wife, "Tristouse Ballerinette." (This was written after Marie had left him: hence the sharpness.) Who is she? Croniamantal asks the Benin Bird.

> She has the somber and childlike face of women destined to make men suffer. She has a graceful way of holding out her hands to keep you off, and she has none of the nobility that repels poets because it would deprive them of their suffering. I have seen your wife, I tell you, she is ugliness and beauty; she is everything we love today; she must taste like a bay-leaf [Apollinaire's symbol of fame].[30]

Laurencin was ambitious and used her new connections to promote herself, hence the *bande à Picasso*'s dislike of her, and hers of them. She later complained that Picasso, Apollinaire and Jacob inveterately quarreled and exchanged glares and insults—their insults were an art form—while the next minute they would be full of love for each other.

> They seldom got drunk—maybe once every two months or so—and then they would behave with excessive politeness. I never paid them much heed; I would read love stories, Marivaux's *Marianne,* and feel nothing but hatred for these men who were so unlike myself, especially their negro sculpture! It grated on my nerves.[31]

Laurencin evidently equated male chauvinism with tribal art.

Picasso came to regret his pimping. Laurencin was too much of a "*précieuse ridicule*" to fit into his *tertulia*; she proved a constant challenge to his misogyny. As Fernande put it, Marie was "chiefly interested in the effect she produced on other people. She would listen to herself talking, watching her calculatedly childlike gestures in the mirror as she spoke. . . . It was never possible to untangle the real personality and the real intelligence from the pretentious little person." On one occasion in Picasso's studio, she insisted on rummaging around and examining everything through her lorgnette. Finally she sat down and seemed about to join in the conversation, when all of a sudden she gave vent to a shrill, inarticulate cry. "It's the cry of the Grand Lama," she explained as she undid her massive plait, and let a cloud of frizzy hair billow about her

Marie Laurencin. *Portrait of Guillaume Apollinaire,* 1906. Graphite pencil on paper, 15.7×9.3cm. Musée National d'Art Moderne, Centre Georges Pompidou, Paris.

shoulders.[32] On another occasion—the Derains' housewarming party—she alternately sang quaint old ballads in a tiny voice and mumbled "*merde, merde, merde . . .*"

Fernande, who tried—and failed—to paint like Marie, usually shows her in a farcical light. She is not exaggerating, however, when she describes Marie and Apollinaire making love fully dressed in an armchair. Apollinaire's bed was sacrosanct—nobody was ever allowed to sit on it, or otherwise defile it. Marie confirmed this to Nicole Groult, Poiret's sister, and subsequently her lover. She liked to play with his collar stud, she said.[33] Marie apparently shared Apollinaire's sadomasochistic tastes. In affirmation of this he made her read the works of Sacher-Masoch (just as Picasso obliged his mistresses to read the Marquis de Sade). Much as he would deny it, Apollinaire fell very much in love with Marie—the artist as well as the woman—whereas she preferred the poet to the man. Their liaison was stormy but mutually beneficial. Marie, who had an excellent ear for verse, was partly responsible for Apollinaire's return to lyric poetry. He transformed her modish whimsicality into a modern sensibility. So long as Marie could count on the poet as a publicist and muse her work prospered. After they broke up, she dwindled into mannerism (shades of Georges Lepape), self-parody and ultimately kitsch.

Marie Laurencin. *Pauline Laurencin*, c. 1906. Oil on canvas, 41×33cm. Ashmolean Museum, Oxford.

Both of them had been eager to marry—a rite that neither set of parents had bothered with. However, Apollinaire's formidable mother would not hear of her illegitimate son marrying someone else's illegitimate daughter—a penniless one to boot. Later, Marie's no less formidable mother refused, on moral grounds, to let her daughter marry someone with a prison record and a pornography charge hanging over him. It is unlikely that marriage would have held them together. By 1910 they had both become chronically unfaithful to each other—Laurencin with a series of lovers provided by the voyeuristic Roché—but they did not finally break up until the winter of 1912–13. Eighteen months later (June 22, 1914), Marie married a suitor picked out for her by Roché, Baron Otto von Wätjen, a handsome German charmer, who tried in vain to paint like Kisling. Marie was delighted to be a baroness and, given her lesbian proclivities, unfazed by her husband's bisexuality. He replaced her mother, who had recently died, she said. "Pederasts make the best friends in the world and the best husbands in the world, for they don't pester their wives."[34] (Later in life she would try to fix up her lifelong companion, Suzanne Moreau, with a homosexual husband.) Apollinaire was heartbroken by Marie's marriage, heartbroken when war was declared two months later and the Wätjens were obliged, as enemy aliens, to flee France for neutral Spain. The poet would never see Marie again. At her death, she had all his letters buried with her.

For all her preciosity, Laurencin deserves more recognition than posterity usually accords her for her early work, above all the two apotheoses she painted in 1908 and 1909—monuments to the *bande à Picasso*, even if Apollinaire is the cynosure. Much as Picasso's *Saltimbanques* (1905) reflects Apollinaire's early verse, Laurencin's two paintings reflect his mystical ideology—a symbolist one compounded of neo-platonism, the Tabula Smaragdina, the Cabala, Rosicrucianism and the belief that "love, with its unifying qualities, represents the means by which divine understanding is achieved."[35] Laurencin has given each figure in the *Group of*

Right: Marie Laurencin. *Group of Artists*, 1908. Oil on canvas, 64.8×81cm. The Baltimore Museum of Art: Cone Collection.

Below: Marie Laurencin. *Réunion à la campagne*, 1909. Oil on canvas, 130×194cm. Musée National d'Art Moderne, Centre Georges Pompidou, Paris.

Artists (1908) an appropriate attribute. For Picasso, a lamb that looks more like a dog (a reference to John the Baptist, to whom Apollinaire had once compared Picasso: "a new John the Baptist who washed the arts in a baptism of light"); for Apollinaire, a gold-bound book; for Fernande, some flamboyant flowers (she and Marie disliked each other); and for Marie, a rose—the "*rosa mystica*" traditionally associated with the Virgin Mary—hence also the virginal blue of Marie's dress—with whom Apollinaire was apt to identify his lady loves.

The second painting, *Réunion à la campagne (Apollinaire and His Friends)* of 1909, is larger and more ambitious. It includes eight figures.[36] On the left, the three graces are personified by Gertrude Stein, Fernande Olivier and Marguerite Gilot, a beautiful blond poetess, friend of Paul Fort and Paulette Philippi, who died young. Salmon quotes one of Gilot's apostrophic fragments—"*La Terre! / La Terre! / Ivresse élémentaire!*"[37]—in confirmation of her famed capacity for drink. Apollinaire is suitably enthroned at the center of this Apollonian composition, with Picasso beside him. To the right is a group consisting of Marie, a woman who may be her mother, and the poet Cremnitz, who dedicated his *Eclogues* to Marie. If this woman, who saw herself as "*la sœur des poètes*," omitted the two poets closest to Apollinaire, Jacob and Salmon, and her former best friend, Braque, it was presumably because neither she nor her lover was prepared to allow these rivals into their pantheon. Henceforth this curious apotheosis would hang above Apollinaire's inviolate bed.

*　　　*　　　*

Since the partnership between Picasso and Braque engendered the most influential art movement of the century, their first encounter should be of some importance, but neither of them could remember a thing about it. They had known about each other since the summer of 1905, which Manolo—one of Picasso's closest friends—had spent with Maurice Raynal and Braque at Le Havre and Honfleur.[38] As Salmon wrote, "Braque [was] perpetually in quest of a comrade with whom to work out seductive solutions to insoluble problems."[39] Othon Friesz was the first of these "comrades." Seconded by him, Braque came into his own this summer. He considered his luminous views of Antwerp his "first creative works":[40] for all their indebtedness to the fauvism of Matisse and Derain, not to speak of Friesz, Marquet and Dufy, they could never be mistaken for the work of anyone else. His upbringing in another great northern harbor had endowed Braque with a feeling for the play of northern light and the interrelationship of boats and buildings, of the docks and cranes that line the busy estuaries. Braque's swirls of paint evoke the scudding clouds and eddying water, but his cauldrons of color are no more evocative of the damp, gray north than they are of the burned-out south.

In September Braque returned to Paris, but instead of spending the winter in his Montmartre studio trying his hand at still lifes or figure paintings, he wanted to continue painting out-of-doors. And so he followed the other fauves to the Mediterranean. L'Estaque, where he installed himself, was little more than an industrial suburb of Marseille, but it was dramatically situated on a bay surrounded by hills, and it had a good hotel, where he could live cheaply. It was also a hallowed place—it

Othon Friesz. *The Port of Antwerp*, 1906. Oil on canvas, 60×81cm. Private Collection.

Braque. *The Port of Antwerp*, 1906. Oil on canvas, 49.8×61.2cm. National Gallery of Canada, Ottawa.

had formerly provided Cézanne and, to a lesser extent, Renoir with subjects that were not overly scenic. The impact of meridional light was something Braque would never forget. Years later, he said that he still experienced the same thrill when he returned to the south. "There is something about the light that makes the sky of the Midi look higher, much higher than it does in the north."[41] The light inspired Braque to take ever greater liberties with the natural scene and, as Matisse and Derain had done in the south, to dabble briefly with neo-impressionism. However, fauvism was too heady, too Dionysiac, for him. For all the success of his experiments with color, Braque found that by the time he was back in Paris in February, 1907, he had involuntarily grown away from Matisse.

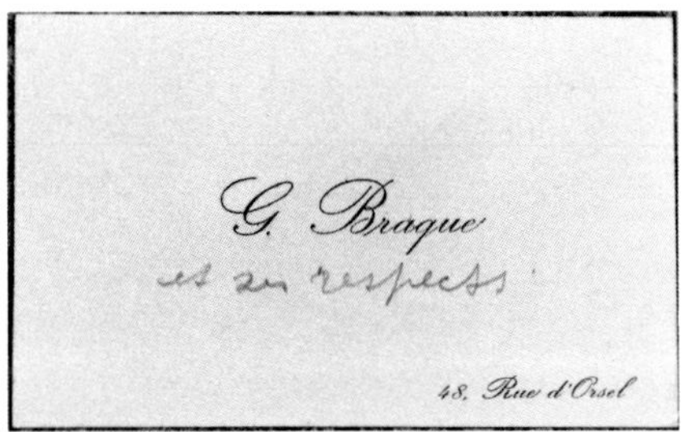

Braque's visiting card inscribed to Picasso "*et ses respects*" ("Regards"), 1907. Archives Picasso.

Braque was exceedingly shy—hence a certain timidity in his approach to Picasso. Two of his visiting cards—one inscribed "Regards," the other "Anticipated memories"—indicate the formality of their first contacts. He probably left these cards at the Bateau Lavoir in the course of the 1907 Salon des Indépendants (March 20–April 30), where he exhibited six of the fauve paintings he had done at L'Estaque. Five of these were bought by Picasso's friend Wilhelm Uhde. One of the *Demoiselles* sketchbooks done at this time contains the two entries "Write to Braque," and "Braque Friday." Their first meeting must have taken place by the beginning of May, as Braque quit Paris around then. Before leaving to visit his family in Le Havre and spend the summer at La Ciotat (near Toulon), he received a visit from Kahnweiler, who was looking for artists to show in his as yet unopened gallery. The dealer purchased a number of paintings from him. Later in the year, Braque would use Kahnweiler to submit paintings to the Salon d'Automne; only one of them was accepted. After he moved back to L'Estaque in October, his style underwent a major change. "I realized that the exaltation which had overwhelmed me during my first visit [to the Midi] and which I had transmitted onto canvas was no longer the same. I saw that there was something further. I had to cast around for another means of self-expression more in keeping with my nature."[42]

The catalyst for this change would be Cézanne. For Cézanne "painting was a matter of life or death," Braque said many years later. "That's why I have learned more from him than from anybody, and I continue to do so. . . . When I was a very young man, I wanted nothing more than to paint like Cézanne. Fortunately my wish was never granted, for, if it had been, I would never have painted like Braque."[43] The influence of Cézanne would prepare Braque for the impact of Picasso. Shortly after returning to Paris in November, 1907, he went, along with Apollinaire, to the Bateau Lavoir. The association with Picasso can be said to date from this visit.

* * *

Derain had met Picasso towards the end of summer, 1906.[44] Once again Apollinaire was responsible. The meeting took place at either the Bateau Lavoir or Azon's restaurant: Apollinaire and Derain were neighbors. The poet's mother had rented a villa—a locale for her illicit gambling parties—at Le Vésinet, next to Chatou, where Derain lived with his family. Apollinaire had met him (and through him, Vlaminck) in 1904, soon after the painter finished his military service. Besides carousing with Apollinaire and taking him to the local opium dens and brothels, Derain gave him a

Right: Braque. *Jetty at L'Estaque*, November, 1906. Oil on canvas, 38.5×46 cm. Musée National d'Art Moderne, Centre Georges Pompidou, Paris.

Below: Braque. *Viaduct at L'Estaque*, 1907. Oil on canvas, 65×81 cm. Minneapolis Institute of Arts.

crash course in modern painting (which may explain why the poet's art criticism sometimes fails to differentiate fauvism from cubism). In return Apollinaire enlightened Derain about modern poetry, above all his own, which the painter never ceased to admire. Picasso would thus have heard all about Derain from Apollinaire long before the poet produced him. When they finally met, friendship was instant.

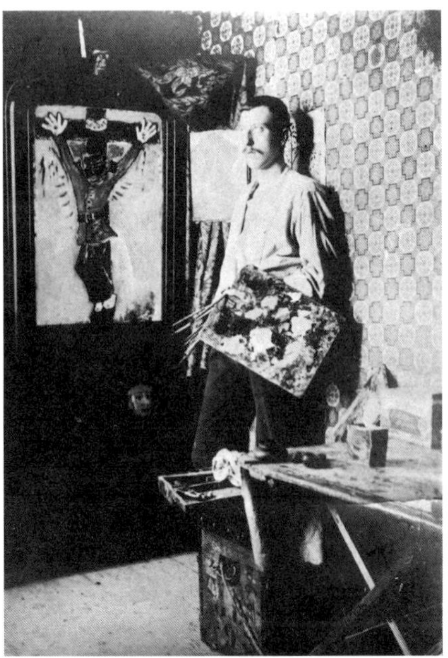

André Derain in his studio, c. 1903. Collection Michel Kellermann, Paris.

Derain was an imposing man, not just in height—he towered over Picasso—but in geniality and charm, force of intellect and character. Clive Bell—who venerated him, as all too evidently did his wife, Vanessa, and the other Bloomsbury painters—compared him with Dr. Johnson, "a dictator at once humorous and tragic but, unlike him, infinitely subtle."[45] Dictator or not, Derain was tormented by doubt—"Doubt is everywhere and in everything," he wrote Vlaminck[46]—doubly tormented in that, unlike Cézanne, who turned his doubts to triumphant advantage, Derain was ultimately the victim of them. Doubt doomed him to drink; doubt doomed him to squander his prodigious gifts in a futile effort to gentrify the modern movement by reconciling it with hallowed tradition and primitivism bordering on quaintness. Derain's fate was to be born a *petit bourgeois* and develop into a *grand bourgeois*.[47] People who talked about Picasso and Matisse *tout court* were apt to refer to *Monsieur* Derain. For all his youthful bohemianism and rebelliousness, Derain would never entirely escape being the son of a prosperous pastrycook who catered to a prosperous suburban clientele. There was an element of cuisine to his work. The father's métier might account for the son's tendency in later years to garnish his work with titillating highlights—frosting.

Derain's prosaic parents had hoped their gifted son would do better in life than they had. When he chose to exchange the parental *toque* for an artist's smock rather than the officer's *képi* on which they had set their hearts, they were dismayed. They were further dismayed when their son made friends with Maurice de Vlaminck—anarchist son of a disreputable music teacher, who lived nearby at Le Vésinet and who stipulated that he be transported to his grave in a moving van. The two young painters had met when their suburban train derailed. They had walked home together. Next morning they set off side by side to paint the Seine.

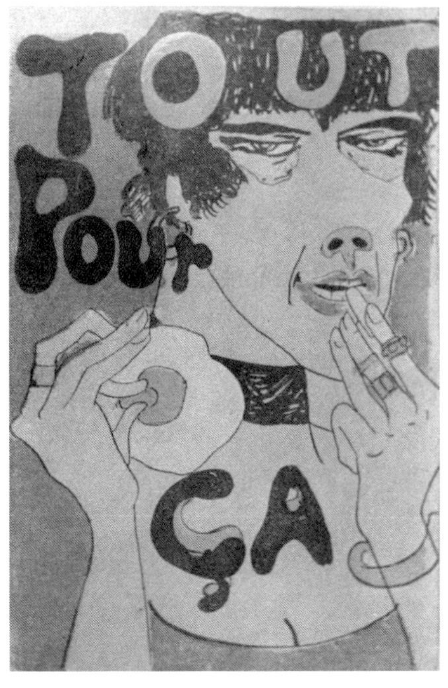

Derain. Cover of Vlaminck's novel *Tout pour Ça*, 1903.

At first it was Vlaminck—less accomplished but cruder, bolder and more of an iconoclast—who took the lead. Under his tutelage Derain adopted an anarchistic approach to life as well as art. Derain was able to live at home off his protective, if disapproving, parents. Vlaminck, on the other hand, was supporting himself (as well as a wife and family) by playing the violin in gypsy bands, bicycle racing, radical journalism and literary hackwork (lubricious novelettes, two of which Derain illustrated).[48] In the winter of 1900–01, the two artists rented a studio in a bankrupt restaurant on the Ile du Chatou—a little island close to where Renoir had painted his *Déjeuner des canotiers*, and the "School of Chatou" was born. They drew attention to themselves by wearing outrageously clownish outfits—suits checked like horse blankets, bizarre ties (Vlaminck had one made of wood), mustard-colored "American" boots, derbies worn at a rakish angle and the obligatory mustache and pipe. In the evenings they would desert the genteel purlieus of Chatou and Le Vésinet and head for the bargees' cafés that lined the Seine at Le Pecq, the brothels and hashish dens that attracted the *gens louche* who figure in Maupassant's stories about the river.[49] Drunken parties—dolled-up whores arriving in open carriages—scandalized the neighborhood; so did the artists' "drunken" (Derain's word) paintings of this nice residential area.

The Van Gogh exhibition at Bernheim-Jeune's in March, 1901, was the catalyst that jolted Derain and Vlaminck into seeing the world in a vivid new way and portraying it in raw colors slashed on with a loaded brush. Van Gogh replaced Manet as their god. Matisse, whom Derain already knew from a brief stint in Carrière's studio, also attended the Van Gogh opening. Derain introduced Vlaminck to him, and they saw each other a few times before Derain's military service in eastern France (fall, 1901–04) intervened. It would be another three years before this friendship was resumed. To keep his sanity in the army, Derain wrote constantly to Vlaminck—letters in which he takes a succession of highly theoretical positions about art.[50] Somehow he contrived to paint in his barracks, as well as on leave in the studio that he and Vlaminck continued to share.

By the time Derain returned to civilian life, he had developed a sophisticated aesthetic and a style to match. In his relief at being released from the military, he painted a series of euphorically colorful views of the Seine. So did Vlaminck; and when Matisse visited Chatou (January, 1905) to inspect their work, he was so excited he could not sleep. He invited them to exhibit at the Indépendants that spring; he also put Vollard on to them. Vollard was no less impressed and bought the contents of Derain's studio.[51] (Vollard would not buy out Vlaminck's, or for that matter Picasso's, for another year.) At the Indépendants, Derain sold three of his eight paintings, but (to believe Vlaminck, who sold only one) the principal buyer, Ernest Siegfried of Le Havre, was a malicious joker rather than a lover of modern art: he had picked out the ugliest works as an insulting present for a hated son-in-law.[52]

Derain. *Vlaminck Playing the Violin*, 1905. Oil on canvas, 110×68cm. Private collection.

Later that summer, Derain joined Matisse at Collioure in French Catalonia and worked alongside him. He was soon accepted as one of the family. Derain used to refer to the much-put-upon Madame Matisse (who executed one of his designs as a tapestry) as "Sainte Amélie, the greatest martyr of our century."[53] Matisse brought out qualities in Derain that the less accomplished Vlaminck—many of whose ideas, notably anarchism, he now repudiated—could never have evoked. For his part, Derain helped wean Matisse away from the constraints of Signac's divisionism. Indeed, if Derain's inconstancy and pride had not ruled out a long-term commitment to another living artist, he and Matisse might have enjoyed a partnership as constructive as Picasso and Braque's. In the two months he spent at Collioure Derain produced some of his most dazzling works—views of the boat-filled harbor and the Pyrenean foothills exploding in a blaze of Van Gogh–like color. Matisse had sharpened Derain's vision and refined his sense of color and design. No less important, the meridional sun had lit a conflagration in his work that would not be extinguished for another year. A manifesto-like letter (July 28, 1905) to Vlaminck summarizes the sensations that would generate the style soon to be known as fauvism: "a new conception of light . . . the negation of shadows. Light here is very strong, shadows very luminous. Every shadow is a world of clarity and luminosity which contrasts with the sunlight."[54]

Charles Camoin. *Madame Matisse Doing Needlework*, 1905. Oil on canvas, 65×81cm. Musée d'Art Moderne, Strasbourg.

During the summer at Collioure, the sculptor Maillol, who lived nearby at Banyuls, took Derain and Matisse to visit Daniel de Montfried, Gauguin's

Derain. *Dancers*, 1906. Carved wooden panels, each 64×118cm. Grosvenor Gallery, London.

friend and collector. Besides paintings, Montfried's collection included a quantity of sculpture and ceramics, manuscripts and letters. The sculptures would leave their mark on Derain's clunky carvings. Gauguin's synthesis of Peruvian, Egyptian and Oceanic elements with Western symbolism, popular imagery and folk art would inspire Derain as it had Picasso. Again like Picasso, Derain was overwhelmed by the Ingres show at the 1905 Salon d'Automne. Ingres and Gauguin as well as Matisse's *Luxe, calme et volupté* were the inspiration for *L'Age d'or*, the vast arcadian set piece in which Derain hoped to reanimate Puvis de Chavannes's moribund classicism. Derain's exemplars were much the same as Picasso's, except that he never managed to assimilate them as effectively or extract as much nourishment.

Derain came into his own at the 1905 Salon d'Automne as Matisse's principal cohort. When President Loubet refused to dignify "such daubs" with a traditional visit, their paintings were plastered all over the newspapers. Matisse and Derain's Collioure views were among the principal targets of the critic Louis Vauxcelles, whose article on the Salon coined the term "fauves" ("wild beasts"). This pleased them more than their previous nickname, "invertebrates." Vauxcelles's vilification—such as his claim that Derain's work belonged on the walls of a nursery—conferred instant fame. Vollard, most astute of dealers, decided to cash in on fauve notoriety. Prompted by the success of Monet's thirty-seven views of the Thames at Durand-Ruel's the year before, he dispatched Derain to London (Vlaminck declined the invitation) to paint the Thames between Westminster and Wapping as excitingly as he had painted the Seine between Le Vésinet and Le Pecq. Insofar as Derain's views of autumnal London blaze with meridional sunlight, they bear little resemblance to the real thing. The artist apparently wanted to brighten up the city he found so depressing. In his letters he complains about "the sad, hypocritical, bantering British spirit"; the deadness and silence he found as much in London's crowded restaurants as in its teeming workplaces; and not least "the blurred forms that emerge from the fog."[55] None of this is reflected in his paintings. The absence of fog could be explained by his newfound admiration for Turner's colorful riverscapes. Alternatively, Vollard (who had originally found Picasso's Blue period gloomy) may have stipulated cheerful color effects. Derain would also have wanted to impose a new look on the Thames, as far from Monet's aqueous impressionism as from Whistler's revered nocturnes of Battersea Bridge. Hence the hyperbolic dazzle. However, firework displays never last long. The end of Derain's fauvism was nigh: "it had been an ordeal by fire," he later wrote.[56] Back on the Mediterranean with Matisse (summer, 1906), he was once again beset by doubt. He drifted away from Matisse as imperceptibly as he had drifted away from Vlaminck and aligned himself with Picasso.

Derain. *L'Age d'or*, 1905. Oil on canvas, 176.5×189cm. Museum of Modern Art, Tehran.

* * *

When he returned from the south at the end of August, 1906, Derain moved out of his parents' house at Chatou. In October, he took a studio in Paris. Significantly, he chose Picasso's territory, Montmartre (rue Tourlaque), over Matisse's Quartier Latin, thus proclaiming that he had joined the *bande à Picasso*. An entry in one of the notebooks Derain kept some

Derain. *Bridge at Le Pecq*, 1904–05. Oil on canvas, 98.1×116.2 cm. Private collection.

Derain. *Blackfriars Bridge*, 1906–07. Oil on canvas, 80.6×99.3 cm. Glasgow Art Gallery.

time later hints at a possible reason for this change of allegiance. Derain came to see Matisse as "the dyer": "The true color of painting does not come from the prism [but from] the spirit which . . . reveals itself. . . . The color of the prism is the dyer's color. Matisse the dyer."[57] Derain was no longer able to subscribe to Matisse's "mandarin" notion that a painting's prismatic harmonies, Byzantine ornamentation and symbolist (Mallarmé-like) *poésie* should enhance, even pamper, the beholder's sensibility. As he wrote Vlaminck in the summer of 1906: "I don't see any future . . . in our tendencies; on the one hand we try to disengage ourselves from the objective world; on the other we keep it as . . . an end in itself."[58]

Derain's defection from Matisse was the more opportune for coming at a time when Picasso was mustering all his resources to win out over his rival. The two artists were ostensibly friendly, but their visits to each other's studios were dictated less by friendship than by curiosity and competitiveness. Each had to see what the other was up to. Both of them would profit hugely from the dynamics of this rivalry. They honed each other's very different strengths; they took leaves out of each other's books and rewrote them. As for Derain, he put his well-stocked mind at Picasso's disposal. His interests in literature, philosophy, mysticism, comparative religion, science, mathematics, aesthetics and musicology were the more congenial to Picasso in that they tended towards the magical and the arcane. Derain's notebooks and letters reveal that he had studied the Cabala, astrology, Pythagoras, Buddhism, the Tarot, Charles Henry's mathematical theories, numerology, Wagner's operas, Nietzsche and Plotinus (neoplatonism was one of the few constants in Derain's ideology). Much of this knowledge had already filtered down to Picasso by way of Apollinaire and Max Jacob, but they were poets. Derain had the advantage of perceiving how philosophical theories and mystic beliefs of the most diverse kind could be woven into a personal aesthetic, just as antithetical styles could be welded into a pictorial synthesis. What is more, Derain had a wide-ranging knowledge of art history—western, oriental, classical, primitive. As Vlaminck said, "he had visited all the museums in Europe"[59]—and knew the British Museum almost as well as he knew the Louvre. Here, indeed, was a mind—Apollinairean in scope, painterly in sensibility—for Picasso to gorge on.

Derain. *Harbor at Collioure*, 1905. Oil on canvas, 47×56 cm. Staatsgalerie, Stuttgart.

The 1906 Salon d'Automne's inclusion of ten major Cézannes and a commemorative show of Gauguin (who had died two years earlier) elevated these two artists to the heights of modernist veneration. Like Picasso, Derain had followed the track Gauguin had opened up through the sacred wood, but he now veered off towards Cézanne's Montagne Sainte-Victoire—something Picasso would not do for another year. A succession of large figure compositions charts Derain's progress. After the fauve *L'Age d'or*, he painted *La Danse*—a Gauguinesque jungle, complete with a Gauguinesque serpent and a frieze of maenads, in a medley of primitive styles (including the Romanesque and *images d'Epinal*)—but early in 1907 he switched to large groups of Cézannesque *Bathers*. According to Hans Purrmann (Matisse's German pupil), the first of these, *Bathers I*, was done in competition with Matisse to see who could come up with the best blue figure painting. "When Derain saw Matisse's *Blue Nude*," Purrmann says, "he conceded defeat and destroyed his canvas."[60] In fact Derain's *Bathers I* has survived. It was exhibited at the 1907 Salon des Indépendants and

Derain. *La Danse*, 1906. Oil on canvas, 175×225 cm. Fridart Foundation.

Derain. *Bathers I*, 1907. Oil on canvas, 132.1×195 cm. The Museum of Modern Art, New York: William S. Paley and Abby Aldrich Rockefeller Funds.

Derain. *Bathers III*, 1908. Oil on canvas, 180×231 cm. Národní Galerie, Prague.

caused almost as much of a stir as the *Blue Nude* for its supposed barbarousness.[61]

If he was not the first modern artist to "discover" tribal sculpture, Derain was the first to see its potential as a catalyst. However, he was too full of doubt to do much about it for another year. By urging Picasso to visit the Ethnographical Museum at the Trocadéro, he relinquished the initiative to him—much, I suspect, to his subsequent regret. When he returned to Paris six months later and saw how Picasso had transformed two of the *demoiselles* into tribal travesties, Derain claimed to be horrified; horrified that Picasso exploited the eerie savagery rather than the ethnic charm of masks and fetishes; no doubt horrified, too, at finding himself outgunned. "This can only end in suicide," Derain warned Kahnweiler: "one day Picasso will be found hanging behind the *Demoiselles*."[62] And then, once again, Derain did a turnabout. He not only came round to the *Demoiselles*; he drew on it to enliven and energize the bathers in yet another of his stiff pastiches of Cézanne. He also got together with Picasso and carved fetishes, which they hoped would make a total break with the art of the civilized world.[63] Derain's chunky figures have a numinous presence, but none of the shamanistic power of Picasso's.

Derain's place in history has not been helped by the claim in Apollinaire's poetic but otherwise unsatisfactory study of cubism that "this new aesthetic was first elaborated in the mind of André Derain."[64] This mischievous and hurtful claim was made at a time when Apollinaire had turned against Picasso. The paintings Derain did after his first visits to the Bateau Lavoir—angular views of Martigues and some Picasso-like still lifes—are among his most powerful works, but their "new aesthetic" can hardly be said to anticipate cubism. If anything, cubism did Derain in. While Picasso and Braque were laying the foundations of cubism in 1908, Derain was reduced to burning most of his recent cubistic work; his aspirations to be in the vanguard of the modern movement likewise went up in smoke.

Although Picasso soon established a working relationship with the progressive and skillful Braque, he still had occasional need of Derain. He liked him enormously; he was also very fond of the outspoken, cat-faced Alice Géry, formerly his mistress and now Derain's.[65] Picasso had not been pleased when Alice had married the actuary Maurice Princet, who was sometimes credited—to Picasso's and Braque's annoyance—with having provided cubism with a mathematical rationale. Why marry in order to divorce? Picasso had said on the occasion of their wedding (March 30, 1907). The artist liked his predictions to come true. After their marriage, Alice told Princet that she missed the Bateau Lavoir, which she had frequented since 1901. She insisted that they move back from Neuilly to Montmartre, where she could enjoy the snow-covered roofs and do paintings of the streets. Once again like Celestina, Picasso organized a lunch so that she could meet Derain. It was love at first sight. In a jealous rage Princet destroyed Alice's most prized possession—the fur coat she had bought for their marriage. Six months later, she walked out on him and moved into her lover's new studio in the Villa des Fusains, not far from the Bateau Lavoir. Alice had no problem obtaining a divorce, but she had to wait until Derain's mother died, in 1926, before they could be married. Princet had better luck as a mentor to Salon cubists like Gleizes

Derain. *Alice in a Green Dress*, 1907. Oil on canvas, 73×60 cm. The Museum of Modern Art, New York: Given anonymously.

and Metzinger, also to Marcel Duchamp (a fervent chessplayer like himself) than he had had with Picasso and Braque. Later he harnessed his mathematical skills to making a large fortune and ultimately turned to God. Princet lived to be almost a hundred.[66]

Derain. *Still Life*, 1914. Oil on canvas, 55×46.5cm. Private collection.

Derain became Picasso's yardstick. Until the outbreak of World War I, he would be the norm against which Picasso could measure the progress he was making as a cubist, the ever-increasing distance he was putting between himself and representationalism. If Picasso forged too far ahead, he could count on Derain to urge restraint—as a rule unavailingly. Derain would serve as Picasso's link with tradition: a godsend to a painter who was out to cannibalize the art of the past and remake it in his own image. Derain's shadow can be detected in the eucharistic subtext of Picasso's great 1909 *Bread and Fruit Dish on a Table* (pp. 118–20). Later the same year, Derain would persuade Picasso to try his hand at figuration: a naturalistic painting of Alice's Italian maid. In 1910, he would go to Cadaqués and paint Cézannesque townscapes alongside Picasso, who was hovering on the brink of abstraction. And, in 1914, Derain would be very much around in Avignon, when Picasso was hovering on a very different brink—Ingresque figuration—at the same time experimenting with extreme forms of cubist distortion.

During the war, in which he was commended for gallantry, Derain became even more of a traditionalist and turned bitterly against cubism. "Cubism is a truly idiotic thing that I find more and more revolting," he wrote Vlaminck from the trenches (July 18, 1917).[67] In his notebooks he condemns it as "dead magic": a mere game like "*bilboquet*" (the cup-and-ball game) or "*quilles*" (skittles). Scattering straight lines and right angles all over the place, he said, was as silly as the impressionist habit of scattering flecks of blue, yellow and red. Derain also expressed reservations about what is now called built-in obsolescence. All avant-garde movements, he claimed, were impregnated with the seeds of their own destruction—doomed, like all manifestations of fashion, to date and die. As for there being any virtue in originality, this "was an unfortunate invention of the eighteenth century," and should be suppressed.[68]

After the war, these views stood Derain in good stead with affluent collectors, who liked modern art up to a point. The *pâtissier*'s son knew just how to satisfy this public. Gertrude Stein—she and Derain never forgave each other for some ancient slight—invoked Hemingway in her dismissal of him. Both the writer and the painter, she said, looked like moderns but smelt of the museums. Archaism was Derain's cubism, Apollinaire is supposed to have said.

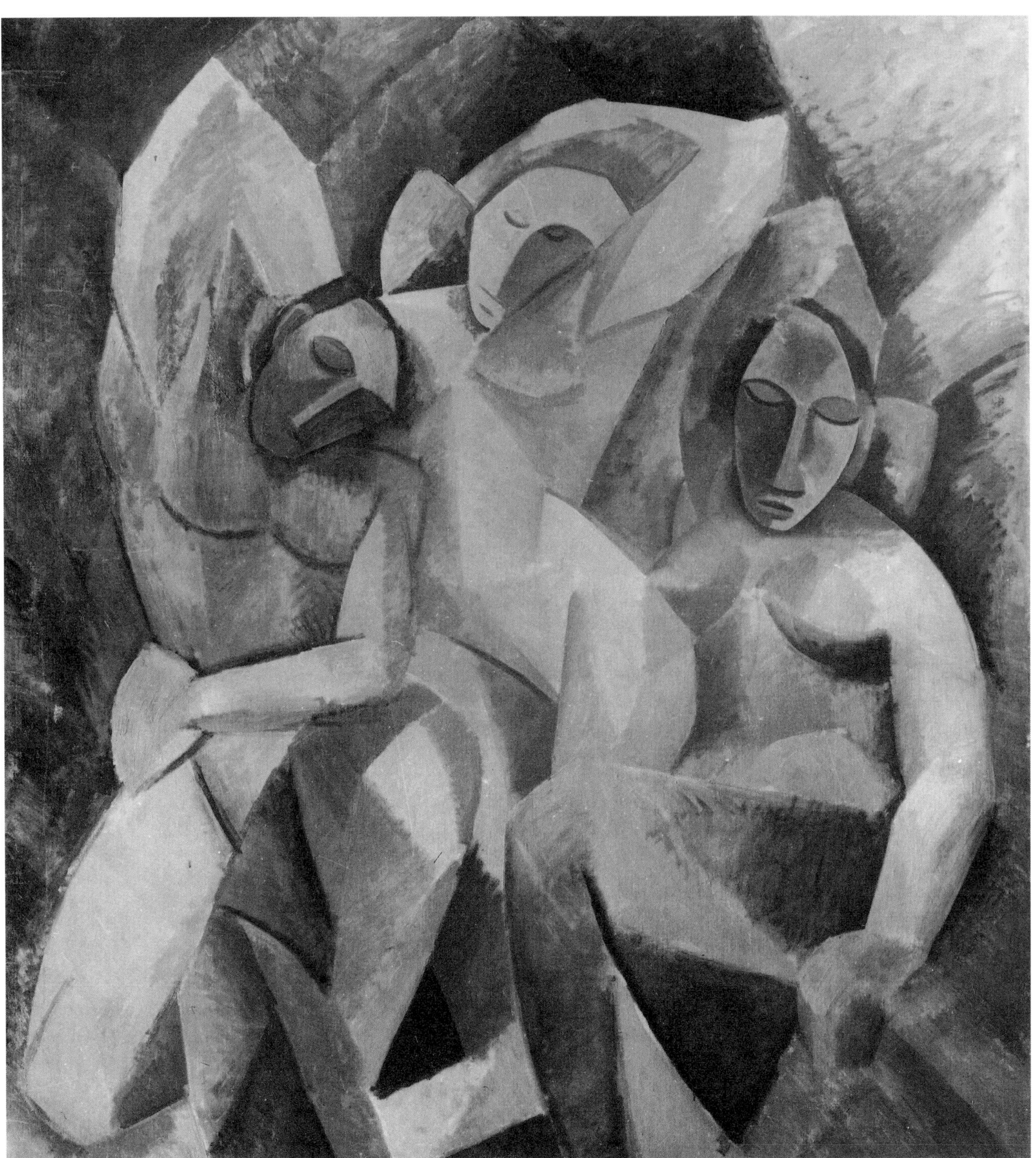

5

Three Women

Marie Laurencin. *Madame Pickaçoh.* Private collection.

Opposite: Picasso. *Three Women*, 1908. Oil on canvas, 200×178cm. State Hermitage Museum, St. Petersburg.

PLEASED AS HE WAS TO BE ON HIS OWN, Picasso had difficulty functioning without a woman around. Fernande, meanwhile, had concluded that her talents were not limited to trimming hats or playing her rented piano. She, too, would paint. And despite her "wretched taste,"[1] she turned out to have a certain naïve flair. Years later, when Picasso came upon a portfolio of her early drawings (now apparently lost), he commended her good sense in deriving inspiration from Marie Laurencin rather than him. Fernande's subjects were mostly herself: large, simplified faces with large, catlike eyes. But Fernande was too indolent to persevere with painting and soon lapsed back into *dolce far niente.* Beyond giving Alice Toklas French lessons, she did little to earn a living, even when the money Picasso had provided in August ran out. There was nothing for it but to pawn the gold hoop earrings he had given her.

> They were handmade and simple, but they really suited me and complemented my looks. I never took them off, even in bed. I was wearing my hair very long and always let it down when I went to sleep, so that despite my pale skin, the thick tresses of my chestnut hair with its golden lights and my narrow grey-green eyes slanting towards my temples made me look like a woman from the ancient Orient.[2]

Picasso must have given Fernande previous cause to visit a pawnshop, to judge by a passage in *The Autobiography of Alice B. Toklas*:

> The next time I saw Gertrude Stein she said to me suddenly, is Fernande wearing her earrings. I do not know, I said. Well notice, she said. The next time I saw Gertrude Stein I said, yes Fernande is wearing her earrings. Oh well, she said, there is nothing to be done yet, it's a nuisance because Pablo naturally having nobody in the studio cannot stay at home. In another week I was able to announce that Fernande was not wearing her earrings. Oh well it's alright then she has no more money left and it is all over. . . . And it was. A week later I was dining with Fernande and Pablo at the rue de Fleurus.[3]

The reconciliation took place two or three weeks before Christmas. Neither Picasso nor Fernande had found a substitute for the other; also there was still a mutual need and residual sexual attraction. As Alice Toklas observes, "Fernande held Picasso by her beauty. Much later, when they had separated permanently, he said of her, I never liked any of her little ways but her beauty always held me."[4] Somehow or other the two of them managed to patch up their relationship and live together for another four years, amicably if not very lovingly. Henceforth Fernande would insist on being addressed as Madame Picasso. This was not self-aggrandizement so much as the reverse: an admission that she had been demoted from fiancée to mistress. Fernande's only hope of respectability was to assume a name that she knew would never be hers.

Opium, which had served as a love potion in Picasso's seduction of Fernande, may have facilitated their *rapprochement.* This was after all a period that Fernande specifically associated with narcotics: "a time when we were eager to experience new and different sensations and were prepared to spend some strange evenings in the pursuit of them."[5] Picasso liked opium well enough—such an intelligent smell, he used to say—but had problems with hashish. So, at least, it would appear from Fernande's description of an evening in the spring of 1908, when she and Picasso joined Apollinaire, Marie Laurencin, Paul Fort, Salmon, Max Jacob and Princet for a dinner at Azon's, at which hashish "pills" were dispensed. Picasso became very hysterical on this occasion, shouting that he had discovered photography; that he wanted to kill himself, as he had nothing left to learn; that one day a wall would impede his development and prevent his understanding or penetrating "into the secrets of an art which he wanted to make new and fresh."[6] The artist's anxieties shed light on his aspirations.

Picasso. *Seated Nude,* 1908. Oil on canvas, 150×99cm. State Hermitage Museum, St. Petersburg.

Now that she was back in the Bateau Lavoir, *la belle Fernande* found herself once more enshrined in Picasso's canvases, albeit much changed. The artist no longer envisioned her as the idyllic beauty of 1906 or the dog-faced woman of 1907 but as a monumental sculptural presence, as hieratic as his portrait of Gertrude Stein—female rather than feminine, and in this respect the contrary of her alluring, womanly self. (In years to come Picasso would transform Marie-Thérèse Walter, Dora Maar, Françoise Gilot and his second wife, Jacqueline, into comparable behemoths.) Once again it seems as if a sculptor were trapped inside the painter. Heads and figures in the paintings appear to have been conceived as stone carvings. The address in one of the artist's sketchbooks of a quarry well known to Parisian sculptors confirms that Picasso contemplated tackling a material more challenging than the wood he used for his own home-made fetishes. If he endows his mistress's legs with the sturdiness of pit props, he is not doing her an injustice: *The Autobiography of Alice B. Toklas* describes Fernande as one of those women for whom the advent of short skirts would be a disaster.[7]

Cézanne. *L'Après-midi à Naples,* c.1875–77. Oil on canvas, 37×45cm. Australian National Gallery, Canberra.

A series of studies entitled *L'Offrande* (The Offering)—seemingly projects for a major composition—celebrate Fernande's return to the Bateau Lavoir. This time Picasso sets out to honor rather than dishonor her. In the end, he limited the subject to two remarkable gouaches and a smallish, uncharacteristically elongated painting on panel.[8] *L'Offrande* was inspired by Cézanne's erotic tributes to *l'éternel féminin*—compositions like *Une Moderne Olympia* or *L'Après-midi à Naples,* in which a male attendant pulls back a curtain to reveal a naked woman and, sometimes, a naked man lolling on a rumpled bed, while an admirer, evidently the artist, watches, entranced. A subject made to order for Picasso. The first idea for *L'Offrande* includes a large winged angel, but this interloper does not reappear. An inscription in Spanish on a subsequent drawing explains the subject: "She is lying on a bed and he discovers her by lifting up the

Above: Picasso. Studies for *L'Offrande*, 1908. Pencil on sketchbook pages, each 13.5×21 cm. Musée Picasso.

Above right: Picasso. *L'Offrande*, 1908. Gouache on paper, 30.8×31.1 cm. Museu Picasso, Barcelona.

Right: Picasso. *L'Offrande*, 1908. Oil on panel, 36×63 cm. Musée Picasso.

covers. Behind are the curtains of the bed and the bedroom. In his hands he holds a bouquet of flowers."

Besides the Cézannes, Picasso's own work provides a prototype for *L'Offrande*. Four years earlier, when he was pressing Fernande to move in with him, he had portrayed her asleep in two similar but contrasting situations. In one of them her then lover, the predatory Debienne, scowls menacingly down at her; in the other the artist watches gently and lovingly over her.[9] By spelling out or, rather, illustrating the options open to Fernande, Picasso hoped to coax her into leaving Debienne for him. Now, four years later, on the occasion of their reconciliation, Picasso includes a surrogate for himself in two of the *L'Offrande* gouaches: a watchful and respectful giant (all the more a giant for his resemblance to an Easter Island monolith). On the left, he is raising a curtain, as the male attendant does in the Cézanne; on the right, he is clumsily proffering flowers—a symbol of his reawakened affection. (*Gages d'amitié*—love tokens—would always play a role in Picasso's work.) To bring the supine Fernande closer, Picasso has positioned himself behind the canvas and pushed her, bed and all, out at us. Fernande thus appears to be both recumbent and upright, some distance away and yet within reach. The artist is out not so much to keep us guessing as to prevent a recumbent figure, seen feet-first, from receding perspectivally away from us, thus generating unwanted, illusory depth.

Picasso. *Still Life with Fruit and Glass*, fall, 1908. Tempera on panel, 27×21.1cm. The Museum of Modern Art, New York: Estate of John Hay Whitney.

L'Offrande is by no means the only work on panel of this period. Towards the end of 1907 Picasso had come into possession of a large wardrobe, which he had chopped up into some forty panels. With the exception of two largish nudes and *L'Offrande*, these were virtually all identical in size: 27×21 cm. And although a few depict figures and landscapes, most of them take the form of still lifes. These meticulous miniatures, in which the artist revels in his own virtuosity, seemingly for his own private delectation, provide a fascinating microcosm of the themes and subjects and stylistic concerns of early cubism. Too bad no one has ever exhibited or published these panels in sequence.

* * *

Although he was happy to have his mistress back in the Bateau Lavoir, Picasso was grateful to Alice Toklas "for taking Fernande off his hands" by continuing to take French lessons from her.[10] The lessons, Alice says, consisted of conversations about hats, perfumes and furs:

> Our only other conversation was the description and names of the dogs that were then fashionable. . . . There we were, she was very beautiful but it was a little heavy and monotonous, so I suggested we should meet out of doors, at a tea place, or take walks in Montmartre. That was better. . . . I met Max Jacob. Fernande and he were very funny together. They felt themselves to be a courtly couple of the first empire, he being le vieux marquis kissing her hand and paying compliments and she the Empress Josephine receiving them. It was a caricature but rather a wonderful one. . . . Max Jacob read my horoscope. It was a great honor because he wrote it down.[11]

Elsewhere Alice tells us that she found the end of this horoscope startling: she supposedly had "a tendency to theft."[12] She also tells us that she took "Fernande shopping, to dog and cat shows, to anything that would

Picasso. *Woman with a Fringe*, 1908. Gouache on paper, 31×24.5cm. Private collection.

give her a subject of conversation."[13] Thanks to these outings, Alice became a favorite of Picasso's. The artist may even have done a portrait of her. Although it has never been recognized as such, a gouache of a *Woman with a Fringe* in a private collection bears a striking resemblance to Alice. The woman even combs her hair over her forehead, as Alice did to hide a cyst. Picasso never, so far as I know, said that this gouache was of Alice. Maybe he suspected that Gertrude would not have approved.

*   *   *

On the occasion of his seminal visit to the Bateau Lavoir late in 1907, Braque was supposedly horrified by the work he saw. Daix has corrected this misconception by pointing out that Braque's oft-quoted comment on Picasso's recent paintings—"*ta peinture, c'est comme si tu voulais nous faire manger de l'étoupe, ou boire du petrole*" ("As for your painting, it's as if you wanted to make us eat tow or drink kerosene")—has been misunderstood.[14] Even Fernande, who was present when the remark was made, apparently did not realize that Braque was referring to fairground *cracheurs de feu* (fire-eaters), who have to swallow tow and gargle with kerosene in order to spout flames. Daix's interpretation confirms something Braque once said: Picasso had set out to shock, but (like Manet in the wake of attacks on *Olympia*), he had not been prepared for the consequences. "We were both headed in the same general direction," Braque claimed, but whereas Picasso forced the pace, he had followed his own instincts.[15] Sure enough, within a month or two, Braque, too, would qualify as a "*cracheur de feu*."[16]

After visiting Picasso's studio, Braque started work on a large composition of three nudes—the same model in three different poses, as in Seurat's *Les Poseuses*—to be entitled *La Femme* (Woman), and to be exhibited at the upcoming Salon des Indépendants. Fernande maintains that Braque managed to paint this major work unbeknownst to Picasso, even though the two of them were already in and out of each other's studios.[17] This is hard to credit, especially coming from Fernande, who took against Braque for siding against her when she broke with Picasso. Far from resenting Braque for exhibiting his three-figure *La Femme* composition, Picasso was flattered that his new friend should advertise his switch from Matisse to Picasso so openly. Besides, as Max Jacob pointed out, Picasso had a strategic reason for enlisting Braque as a "disciple." He needed him as a decoy.

If Jacob saw Picasso as a demonic Christ, he saw Braque, of whom he was inordinately jealous, as Picasso's Saint Peter. To make his point, he went so far as to cite a famous passage from the Bible: "'Thou art Peter,' said our Lord, 'and upon this rock I will build my church.'" "For the time being it would be the shoulders of Saint-Peter-Braque that would uphold the work of God, the Creator."[18] Picasso needed Braque, Jacob explained, to share the brunt of the scandal caused by his work. By holding back and allowing the stalwart young Braque the honor of exhibiting the first cubist painting, Picasso hoped to put himself out of range of attack. The authority, good sense and probity, not to speak of the broad shoulders of this "*ancien caporal et Français d'Argenteuil*" would shield the subversive young Spaniard from the threat of chauvinist assault. For all his limitless courage inside the studio, Picasso lived in fear of xenophobic ire. Indeed, this helps to explain why he would go along with Kahnweiler's decree and never exhibit at the Salons. Subsequent attacks by so-called patriots would prove Picasso right to have been apprehensive.

Picasso took pride in finding women for his friends. After fixing up Derain and Apollinaire, he now proposed to do the same for Braque. True, Braque had an on-again, off-again mistress, Paulette Philippi, but he had to share her with an aged protector as well as Paul Fort, Henri-Pierre Roché and any young painter or poet who was ready to smoke opium with her. Perhaps to save Braque from this all-too-available woman, Picasso suggested that he court a suitable girl: the attractive daughter of one of Max Jacob's cousins, who owned a Montmartre cabaret called Le Néant. For the occasion, the *bande à Picasso* rented formal evening clothes. Top hats, cloaks and canes made a great impression on Max's cousins, but the group's behavior failed to live up to their finery. The visit soon degenerated into bedlam, and they were asked to leave. Since none of them was in any condition to identify their rented apparel, they helped themselves to whatever they found in the cloakroom. After that there could be no question of further negotiations.

Marcelle Braque, 1911. Archives Laurens.

In the end Picasso came up with a much more suitable candidate for Braque: a friend of his and Fernande's, Marcelle Lapré.[19] Marcelle was not beautiful. She was short and plump and had large protuberant blue eyes: hence Max Jacob's nickname for her, "the little sea-monster."[20] However, she had abundant charm and wit and would prove to be the paragon of a wife—devoted, loyal, discreet—to a man who would ultimately forsake the outside world for the mystic realm of his studio. According to Kahnweiler, she went by the name of Madame Vorvanne, so she was either married to or living with a man of that name.[21] For his part, Braque continued to see Paulette Philippi on occasion, until he switched his affections to Marcelle in 1909. They did not set up house together until 1911 and did not marry until the 1920s.[22]

*　　　*　　　*

The 1908 Salon des Indépendants opened on March 20 and stirred up even more animosity and mockery than usual, according to an article written by Gelett Burgess, an American humorist who had come to Paris to cover the event and with the help of Alice Toklas, whom he had known back in San Francisco,[23] interview some of the artists: "I had scarcely entered the Salon . . . when I heard shrieks of laughter coming from an adjoining wing. I hurried along . . . until I came upon a party of well-dressed Parisians in a paroxysm of merriment. . . . Suddenly I had entered a universe of ugliness."[24] Much of the laughter was generated by the two large three-nude compositions that had been submitted by Braque and Derain. To the more informed visitors these paintings were portents: they revealed that Braque and Derain "had become Picassoites and were definitely not Matisseites."[25] As Gertrude Stein observed, Picasso was vicariously represented: "The first time [Picasso] had ever shown at a public show was when Derain and Braque, completely influenced by his recent work, showed theirs."[26]

Gertrude devotes several pages of *The Autobiography of Alice B. Toklas* to the opening of the 1908 Indépendants. She recounts how Alice and her companion, Harriet Levy, traversed gallery after gallery before sitting down to rest:

> Just then somebody behind us put a hand on our shoulders and burst out laughing. It was Gertrude Stein. You have seated yourselves admirably, she said. But why, we asked.
>
> Because right here in front of you is the whole story. We looked but we saw nothing except two big pictures that looked quite alike but not altogether alike. One is a Braque and one is a Derain, explained Gertrude Stein. They were strange pictures of strangely formed rather wooden blocked figures, one if I remember rightly a sort of man and women, the other three women. Well, she said still laughing. We were puzzled, we had seen so much strangeness we did not know why these two were any stranger.[27]

Derain. *La Toilette*, 1908. Oil on canvas (destroyed). Reproduction from Kahnweiler's book on the artist (1920).

The Derain was a large vertical painting, entitled *La Toilette*. It depicted three lumpen nudes with a generic resemblance to the artist's mistress, Alice Princet. The central figure is dressing her companion's hair, while the left-hand woman looks on furtively over her shoulder. In his wisdom, Derain apparently destroyed this painting.[28] The harder he tried to give his work a modernist gloss, the more stilted it became. To judge by a black-and-white photograph, *La Toilette* was strained and contrived—the prototype of much would-be progressive, would-be primitivist figure painting done in Europe over the next thirty years or so. Derain should have remained a Matisseite.

Braque's large squarish composition *La Femme* likewise included three women, or rather three views of the same woman. (The model was a deaf girl with a very white face, initials L.M., whom Picasso may also have painted.)[29] Gelett Burgess quotes Braque's explanation of this painting: "To portray every physical aspect of such a subject required three figures, much as the representation of a house requires a plan, an elevation and a section."[30] To my ear, these words sound more like Burgess, whose avocation was topographical drawing, than Braque, who would always deplore calculation in art. Like Derain, Braque is thought to have consigned *La Femme* to a similar holocaust of his early work. Fortunately, he gave Burgess a drawing (now lost) for the painting. This is illustrated in his "Wild Men of Paris" article, so we have a rough idea of its resemblance to Picasso's *Three Women*. As Picasso had anticipated, Braque bore the brunt of philistine abuse. The critic of *Le Rire* singled out *La Femme* for attack: "I particularly recommend the painting, *Hunger, Thirst, Sensuality*, in which a woman—if one may call her such—is eating her right leg, drinking her blood, and with her left hand . . . No, I could never tell you where her left hand is."[31] This was just the sort of notoriety that Picasso wanted to avoid.

Braque. *La Femme*. 1908. Ink on paper. Whereabouts unknown.

Burgess managed to interview all the more notorious Indépendants artists. The better to ingratiate himself with the natives of Montmartre, he dispensed gifts: what Fernande called "little boxes for lighting cigarettes"[32] —i.e., that new invention, the cigarette lighter. The *briquets* found favor, so did "the little American's" brash geniality. Back in Boston, Burgess had made a name for himself as a humorist, thanks to a famous quatrain, "The Purple Cow," and his invention of that useful word "blurb." (Burgess's

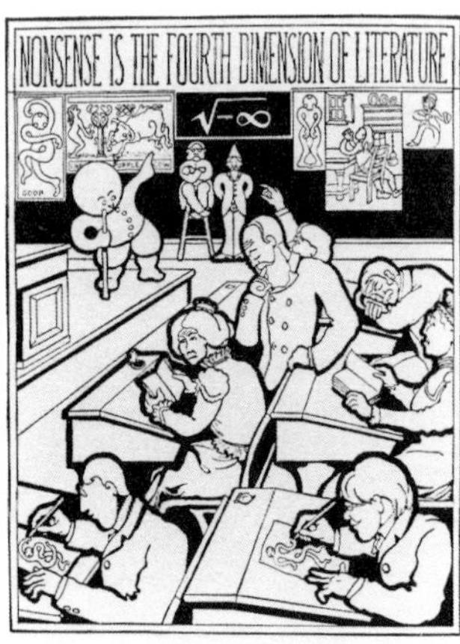

Gelett Burgess. Frontispiece of *The Burgess Nonsense Book*. New York, 1901.

books would have titles like *Are You a Bromide?* and *Ain't Angie Awful?*) He had also achieved fame of a kind by having an affair with a much older woman, Fanny, the adventurous widow of Robert Louis Stevenson. Apropos modern art, Burgess's only credential was a preoccupation with modish notions of the "fourth dimension." Accompanying him on his rounds of the studios was a kindred spirit, Inez Haynes Irwin. This pioneer feminist (the author of *Good Manners for Girls* and *Maida's Little Camp*) was equally blind to modern art, as witness her description of their visit to Picasso's studio (April 29, 1908):

> Picasso turns out to be a darling; young, olive, with bright, frank eyes, each with a devil in it, straight black hair; in an overcoat and a blue sweater that Stein brought him from San Francisco. The filthiest studio I have ever seen; a mass of bottles, rags, sketches, huge unfinished paintings, easels covered with paint, canvases turned to the wall, stove with a pile of ashes in front of it; paint brushes and bowls of water on the floor—one vast melee of dirt, disorder and disorganization. He, it turns out, painted the two monstrosities at the Steins'—the woman with the eyelashes on her nose and the other frightful, hollow-cheeked head. Two huge pictures here, one containing two heads with noses like shutters—the other with the eyes all out of gear—distinctly Aztec or Egyptian in effect; a woman made of diamond shapes; a black and white sketch of a man, absolutely conventionalized in shape; the second big picture a group of three brick-red in color, also conventionalized in shape—the maddest and most loveable of them all. Shows us a mask of the Congo and some totem-pole like hideosities that he made himself.[33]

Because he was the first writer—what is more, an American one—to photograph and publish Picasso's *Demoiselles* and *Three Women* as well as works and statements by him and other modernists, the glib, garrulous Burgess has been taken more seriously than he deserves. As he admits, his French was poor and he had no understanding of modern art, so his transcript of artists' opinions (Braque's in particular) cannot be trusted. Mark Twain might as well have described life in the Bateau Lavoir. "Is [Picasso] mad," Burgess asks, "or the rarest of *blagueurs* [bull-shitters]? Let others consider his murderous canvases in earnest—I want only to see [him] grin." As for the *Demoiselles*—"frozen stiffly upright, glaring through misshapen eyes with noses or fingers missing"—it reminds this middle-aged sophomore of nothing so much as a limerick: "There was a young girl of Lahore / The same shape behind as before." He also describes Derain's studio as "a wild place fit for dreams. But no place for mother."[34]

After a first round of interviews, Burgess departed for England. On May 23 he returned to Paris for a second round, provided, he said optimistically, "I get on with these chaps as well as I hope."[35] He was out of luck with Picasso. "The joy had died out of him," he reported (May 29) to Inez Haynes Irwin. "It is lucky I wrote the article on my first impressions, for I didn't see any sense of humor and had a hard time talking to him."[36] Poor Picasso! Burgess's waggishness must have been hard to take, but there was further reason for the artist's gloom. The drug-addicted German painter Karl-Heinz Wiegels, whom Burgess mentions meeting on his May 29 visit, was giving Picasso and other friends cause for alarm. This androgynous-looking, bizarrely dressed young man—Pascin portrays him in a bowler hat and a skirt or kilt—had been the boyfriend of Matisse's pupil Rudolf Levy.[37] After breaking with Levy, Wiegels had moved, at Picasso's suggestion, into the Bateau Lavoir. The artist was happy to have acquired this abject devotee. (Wiegels was not the first or the last homosexual to provide Picasso with the devotion on which he thrived.) However the clannish German "*dômiers*" were convinced that this affiliation would be the end of their self-destructive comrade. In fact it was not Picasso's dreaded influence but schizophrenia fueled by drugs that destroyed Wiegels. "After an eventful evening," Fernande wrote, "during which he took ether, hashish and opium in succession, he never regained his senses, and several days later, despite our efforts to care for him, he hanged himself"—apparently on June 1.[38]

The suicide was discovered the following morning by the mailman. Picasso was at work on a full-length nude on one of the doors of the chopped-up wardrobe. He rushed to Wiegels's studio and found his body hanging in the window. According to Fernande, "For some time the studio where he had died became a place of terror for us, and the poor man appeared to us everywhere, hanging as he had been the last time we saw him."[39] Once again, death left Picasso distraught,[40] all the more distraught because Wiegels's suicide reopened the scars caused by the suicide, six years earlier, of the similarly weak and sexually ambivalent drug addict Carles Casagemas: the closest friend of Picasso's Els Quatre Gats days. Wiegels had become a stand-in for Casagemas, whose death is at the root of Blue period melancholy. To make matters worse, the *dômiers* held Picasso responsible for this tragedy, which he had done his best to avert. Just as he had commemorated Casagemas's suicide in a series of memento moris (deathbed portraits and funerary scenes), Picasso proceeded to commemorate, and at the same time exorcise, Wiegels's suicide in a couple of *vanitas* still lifes with a skull, a mirror reflecting a recent painting and a palette with five brushes stuck through its hole in commemoration of the dead artist's five fingers.[41] Henceforth Picasso will nearly always proclaim his grief in painfully shrill colors.[42]

The horror of Wiegels's death was compounded by the farcical horror of his funeral at the Saint-Ouen cemetery, which has already been recounted in Volume I.[43] Afterwards, Fernande and Picasso stopped off at the Lapin Agile—"It cheered us up," Fernande says, "and we began to forget the dead man. Nobody ever went to visit his grave, but after that no one ever smoked a single pipe of opium again."[44] Nonsense. Virtually all the friends, except Picasso and herself, continued to do so. Fernande's memoirs hint at painful withdrawal symptoms: "Smoking opium without becoming poisoned by it—for that is the danger—is much easier than you would ever believe possible, although nature takes its revenge in the dreadful craving you feel for the drug when you are deprived of it, voluntarily or not, a craving that can only be overcome by the exercise of great willpower."[45]

Angst spurred Picasso on to work ever more frenetically for the next two months. The summer was stiflingly hot and the Bateau Lavoir an oven. Picasso, who suffered from the heat, often worked naked. And Fernande also went around in little more than a shift, as we can see in one of the most memorable works of the period, the painting of Fernande holding a fan and baring a breast. Ever since 1913, when it first arrived there, this down-to-earth painting, so redolent of summer heat, has been known, in

Picasso on Richard Goetz's balcony, c.1908. Musée Picasso. His companions are almost certainly Wiegels and (behind) Derain.

Picasso. *Still Life with Skull*, 1908. Oil on canvas, 115×88cm. State Hermitage Museum, St. Petersburg.

Picasso. *Woman with a Fan ("After the Ball")*, 1908. Oil on canvas, 152×101 cm. State Hermitage Museum, St. Petersburg.

Picasso. *The Dryad*, 1908. Oil on canvas, 185×108 cm. State Hermitage Museum, St. Petersburg.

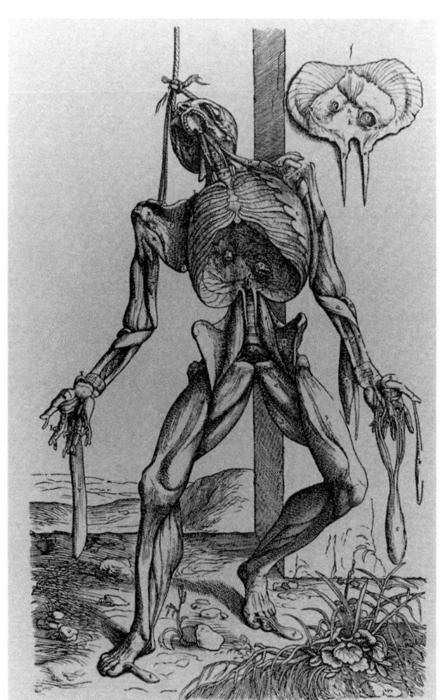

Vesalius. Seventh plate of the muscles from the second book of *De Humani Corporis Fabrica*, 1543.

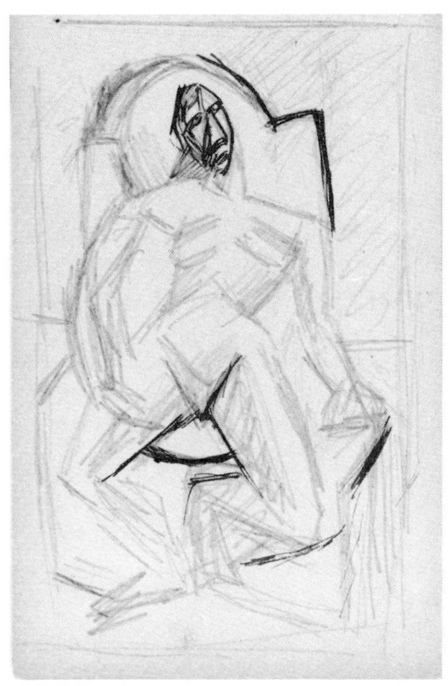

Picasso. Study for *The Dryad*, 1908. Graphite pencil, pen and black ink on sketchbook page, 19.2×13.3cm. Musée Picasso.

Russia, as *After the Ball*. This title must have been devised by Shchukin, the painting's first owner. Fernande never went to balls; even if she had, Picasso would never have condoned such a coy euphemism.

Summer permeates another great painting, *The Dryad*, which Picasso began around this time, and which would end up in Shchukin's collection. The ambivalent stance of this hefty nude slouching out of a forest at us reveals that once again Picasso wanted to paint a standing/sitting figure. In a preliminary drawing the dryad is not so much seated in a high-backed chair as sliding forwards onto the floor. Picasso was once again intent on blurring the distinction between vertical and horizontal; in the second drawing he simply removes the chair, which leaves the figure neither sitting nor standing but ambivalently in between.[46] In a closely related gouache Picasso takes her into the forest and teams her up with another woodland nymph. Finally, he reduces the composition to a single figure, whom he pushes dramatically out at us in such a way that her gaping legs form a vault, which she beckons us, laconically, to enter.

A striking precedent for this peculiar pose and other stylizations emerging in Picasso's work is a woodcut by the celebrated anatomical engraver Andreas Vesalius: the seventh plate in the second book (devoted to musculature) of his *De Humani Corporis Fabrica* of 1543. This woodcut represents a flayed cadaver strung up from a rope that has been passed through the facial cavities of the skull. Vesalius has described how he went about his task:

> I had it in mind to suspend the cadaver either with the head erect or depressed. I placed the longer end of the noose across a pulley fixed to a beam . . . and by that I drew the suspended corpse now higher now lower, taking care that it might be turned in every direction according to the requirement of the task. . . . And the cadaver was suspended in this way . . . just as it is displayed in the Seventh plate, although when that was delineated, the rope was twisted back to the occiput because of the muscles which are conspicuous in the neck.[47]

How Picasso chanced upon the work of this body-snatching anatomist, who saw his plates benefiting painters and sculptors as well as physicians and surgeons, I do not know. The most likely source would have been Apollinaire, a bibliophile with a taste for antiquarian medical books. There was also a Spanish link: Vesalius was court physician to Charles V and later Philip II. Although he was instrumental in saving the life of the king's son, Don Carlos, his scientific expertise incurred the envy of reactionary Spanish physicians and the wrath of the Inquisition. Vesalius tactfully left on a pilgrimage to the Holy Land. On his way back to take up a professorship at Palma, he mysteriously died. In his originality and vision, Vesalius would have had some of the same appeal for Picasso that another mannerist at the court of Philip II, El Greco, had. In confirmation of this hypothesis, I would point out that for the next year or so Picasso's portrayal of facial and neck muscles as well as of the musculature of arms and thighs is apt to look remarkably Vesalian.

* * *

After the Indépendants closed on May 2, Picasso concentrated on finishing the *Three Women*, which he had put aside months earlier. Daix may well be right in discerning three phases in the genesis of this painting,[48] but there is no way of knowing for sure how often the artist stopped and started work. In the final repainting, he reformulates the ideas that his stand-ins, Braque and Derain, had tried out in *their* three-women compositions. Picasso also wanted to challenge Matisse—not so much the painter of the *Bathers with a Turtle*,[49] which he greatly admired and borrowed from, as the *chef d'école*, who, at Sarah Stein's urging, had set up his own academy. This opened in January, 1908, and was attracting a growing number of students. Matisse would follow up this initiative in the fall with a retrospective at the Salon d'Automne and the publication of his "Notes of a Painter." Picasso felt challenged by all this self-promotion. When he set about repainting the *Three Women*, he worked it up into a manifesto not so much for cubism, which did not as yet exist as a concept, let alone a movement, as for himself in the role of "*peintre de la vie moderne.*" The birth pangs would be as long and agonizing as before. This time, however, Picasso would take care to involve the Steins in the execution of the project.

On May 26, Picasso wrote assuring the Steins that the large picture was going ahead,[50] also that Frika had had ten puppies (judging by studies in one of the *Demoiselles* sketchbooks, this must have been the second litter in a year). And on June 14, he again assured them that "the large picture is going ahead but what a struggle it is; besides this I am doing other things. I'm happy and reasonably quiet." He went on to report Wiegels's suicide and ended by saying that "all the painters from the Indépendants have left for the south,"[51] so he and Fernande were alone in Paris. At the end of the month he was going to see their brother, "as I have need of his help."[52] What Picasso would have wanted from Michael Stein is unclear. Surely not financial help. Leo and Gertrude apparently advanced Picasso a regular stipend against future purchases.[53] Picasso had no qualms about Gertrude's liking *Three Women*. Leo was less predictable. The *Demoiselles* had destroyed his faith in Picasso's powers; and the artist had to work very hard to win over this quirkish, doubting man, whose eye, hitherto so adventurous, no longer reacted favorably to modernism. Picasso's parity with Matisse depended on Leo and Gertrude's acquiring this sequel to the *Demoiselles* and displaying it on their prestigious, gallery-like walls—walls that carried a more permanent cachet than either of the short-lived Salons. Picasso's strategy would ultimately prevail. Leo and Gertrude's supportive patronage in acquiring *Three Women* would help to compensate for Sarah and Michael's establishment of Matisse as a *chef d'école*.

Picasso. Study for *Three Women*, 1908. Gouache on paper, 33×25cm. Musée Picasso.

In the course of rethinking his *Three Women* Picasso executed a number of highly colored, highly worked-up studies. Besides compacting the three bodies into a single ensemble, these studies show that Picasso hoped at one point to infuse his composition with movement—a reaction against the stasis of most of his more ambitious works. To set things in motion, he turned back to the gouaches of swirling foliage of the previous summer and envisioned his bathers as if they, too, were flailing. He reduces faces, torsos and limbs to identical mandala-like forms and tosses them and the women's towels tempestuously together, as if he were Jupiter in a metamorphic mode changing a trio of Daphnes into windblown shrubs. Once again Picasso may have looked to Loïe Fuller for inspiration. In their astonishing freedom of form and color and the

Sebastià Junyer Vidal seated in front of *Three Women*, 1908. Photograph by Picasso. Archives Picasso.

tenuousness of their links with figuration, these rhythmic studies sail tantalizingly close to abstraction. It would take Kandinsky another two years to reach a comparable point, and Delaunay even longer.

As always, Picasso retreated from the non-figurative brink. He abandoned the Loïe Fuller arabesques and imposed the stasis of the *Demoiselles* on *Three Women*. In so doing he turned his women to stone. The painting has ended up as conceptual sculpture—a huge reddish, Mount Rushmore–like bas-relief, which may or may not be intended as an ironical monument to womanhood. (Burgess captions this "*La Femme*," as he does *The Dryad* and the Braque.) If we compare it with the wonderfully ecstatic sketches, we can see that Picasso may, consciously or not, have pandered to his patron Leo, whose enthusiasm for modern painting was waning. Even Cézanne would ultimately be anathematized by him. By comparison with the *Demoiselles*, the *Three Women* lacks the exultation and sense of experiment that the best of the studies lead one to expect. Nevertheless it is by far the largest and, academically speaking, the most important of the paintings in which Picasso pits himself against Cézanne's *Grandes Baigneuses*. And it constitutes the foundation stone of a movement, which was still little more than a trend and months away from being known as cubism.

Right: Picasso. Study for *Three Women*, 1908. Oil on canvas, 91×91 cm. Sprengel Museum, Hannover.

6

La Rue-des-Bois

Picasso. *Landscape with Figures*, 1908. Oil on canvas, 60×71 cm. Musée Picasso.

"I HAVE BEEN ILL, VERY NERVOUS," Picasso wrote to the Steins (August 14), who had taken a villa at Fiesole for the summer, "and the doctor told me to get away and spend some time here. I worked so hard last winter in Paris. This summer in the studio with the heat and so much work to do finally made me ill. I have been here for a few days and already feel much better. Perhaps I will still be here when you get back to Paris. I am working and am very happy; my address is La Rue-des-Bois par Creil, Verneuil, Oise."[1]

Although he spent barely a month there (early August to early September), Picasso completed a dozen or so paintings—figures, still lifes, above all landscapes—as well as some works on paper, which constitute a small, self-contained chapter in the artist's development: a "green period," in that tones of viridian prevail. The Rue-des-Bois paintings evoke the tranquillity of this remote riverside farmland as distinctively as the Gósol paintings of two summers before evoke the exaltation of the high sierra. Just as he did in Gósol, Picasso uses the image of a local inhabitant—a gigantic peasant landlady—as emblematic of the place. Since he could never depict anything without to some degree identifying with it, Picasso assumes the role of genius loci in landscapes that constitute his first sustained confrontation with nature. He invests the trees with his own life force, as if he were God reinventing the universe in his image. "I want to see my branches grow," he told Malraux. "That's why I started to paint trees; yet I never paint them from nature. My trees are myself."[2] Shortly before leaving Paris, Picasso had painted a *Landscape with Figures*: on the right a man turning into the trunk of a tree; on the left a woman turning into the roots. He completes the anthropomorphic process in the Rue-des-Bois landscapes, banishing the figures and energizing the trees as if they were so many self-portraits.

Either his doctor or one of his friends had told Picasso about La Rue-des-Bois. "It was there, it could have been elsewhere" is all Picasso said, when asked about it.[3] It was an odd choice. Fernande found the place extremely pretty, but it is too flat and characterless to be anything of the sort. La Rue-des-Bois is not to be found on any but the largest-scale map. You can drive through it without realizing you have done so. There are no cafés or shops or sights to see, not even a road junction, just ten nondescript houses and barns scattered either side of a country road, parallel to a dreary stretch of the River Oise on one side, and the edge of the Forêt

Opposite: Picasso. *House at La Rue-des-Bois*, August, 1908. Oil on canvas, 73×60 cm. State Hermitage Museum, St. Petersburg.

d'Halatte on the other. Although only forty miles or so north of Paris and five miles from the porcelain-manufacturing town of Creil, La Rue-des-Bois is still as much of a backwater as it was at the beginning of the century. A high-strung artist in search of peace and quiet could not have found a better retreat, as Fernande recounts.

Madame Putman in old age. Société Archéologique et Historique des Amis du Vieux Verneuil.

> We rented a little outbuilding on a farm. It had no facilities, and we were surrounded by all sorts of animals and by villagers as ignorant as those we had met two years earlier . . . who had asked us the name of the Queen of France.[4] We had to live pretty much as if we were camping, but Pablo enjoyed the peace and tranquillity, although he didn't like the scenery. The surrounding forest was magnificent, but I realized that Picasso felt quite out of place in the French countryside. He found it too damp and monotonous. "It smells of mushrooms," he used to say. He preferred the . . . warm odors of the rosemary, thyme and cypress of his native land.
>
> Nevertheless he was able to rest at La Rue-des-Bois. He had brought his dog and his cat, which was about to have kittens, and a large and weird assortment of baggage. We ate our meals in a room that smelled like a stable and were lulled to sleep by the gentle murmur of sounds from the forest. We got up late, having slept through all the noises from the farmyard, which had been awake since four in the morning.[5]

Picasso was so fascinated by the widow Putman, his behemoth of a landlady—she was over six feet tall and weighed almost three hundred pounds—that he did a number of paintings and drawings of her. Born in Flanders in 1850, Marie-Louise Coukuyt had spent most of her life in France. After working as a cook on one of the Duc d'Aumale's properties, she had married Joseph Putman, a shepherd, and settled at La Rue-des-Bois, where they raised seven children. On Putman's death, this strapping matriarch took over the farm, tilled the soil, tended the livestock and rented out rooms. She lived on until 1939. (Her granddaughter follows in her footsteps.) Picasso, who relished gigantism, relished Madame Putman. Here in flesh and blood was one of the giantesses he had envisioned in paint. It was not only the scale of this Mother Earth figure that intrigued him. Like Fontdevila, the aged smuggler to whom he had become so attached at Gósol, she was the living embodiment of the primitivism he cherished. She was completely *inculte*, unable to read or write or speak French properly.

Madame Putman never posed for Picasso, as Fontdevila had; he simply observed her as she went about her work and devised a brutally simplistic image for her. This time the inspiration was not Iberian, tribal or Romanesque but folk art: the chunky little wood carvings of peasant types that are still to be found in tourist shops all over Europe. Picasso turns Madame Putman into a monolithic effigy seemingly hacked out of wood. Her head is treated as a columnar extension of her thick neck, her face flat as the sawn-off stump of a tree, onto which minimal features—a tiny wedge of a nose, vestigial eyes (no mouth)—have been grafted. The upward angling of the face derives from the tribal formula Picasso had contrived for Salmon's portrait, but the style derives from *art populaire* and Picasso's new enthusiasm, the naïf painting of "Douanier" Rousseau. In a preparatory drawing for his principal painting of her, Madame Putman is carrying two buckets, but in the final work Picasso omits them, for the same reason he omits the reins in his 1906 *Boy Leading a Horse*. The

Above: Picasso. Studies for *La Fermière*, August, 1908. Black chalk on paper, 48.2×62.8cm. Musée Picasso.

Right: Picasso. Study for *La Fermière*, August, 1908. Charcoal on paper, 62.5×48cm. Picasso Heirs.

Picasso. *La Fermière*, August, 1908. Oil on canvas, 81×65cm. State Hermitage Museum, St. Petersburg.

Picasso. *La Fermière (Head and Shoulders)*, August, 1908. Oil on canvas, 81×65cm. State Hermitage Museum, St. Petersburg.

Rousseau. *The Snake Charmer*, 1907. Oil on canvas, 169×189cm. Musée d'Orsay, Paris.

pose—the woman's weighed-down, wooden arms and clenched hands—speaks for itself.

Picasso had been familiar with Rousseau's work ever since his second trip to Paris in May, 1901, when he is likely to have visited the Salon des Indépendants and seen the seven paintings that Rousseau exhibited. Rousseau's champion Gustave Coquiot, who wrote the preface to Picasso's show at Vollard's, would have recommended the artist's work to him. At first Picasso seems to have taken little interest in the Douanier, who was regarded, even by his supporters, as something of a joke. He was said by some to have been a hoax perpetrated by Jarry, or by Picasso, who was rumored to have painted *The Sleeping Gypsy*.[6] Thanks to Uhde's proselytizing (his monograph on the Douanier would appear in 1911), Picasso eventually took Rousseau's work more seriously. Still it was not until he had finished exploring the possibilities of Iberian and tribal sculpture that he focused on this contemporary form of primitivism. The sheer ordinariness of the Rue-des-Bois scene lent itself to a Rousseau-like treatment. Hence the toytown look of the houses and the improbably large leaves on the trees in Picasso's Rue-des-Bois landscapes—also the disingenuous simplifications, the lack of perspective, the feigned awkwardness.

The painting that opened Picasso's eyes to Rousseau's powers seems to have been the monumental *Snake Charmer*, when it was exhibited at the 1907 Salon d'Automne. The *Snake Charmer* had been commissioned by Delaunay's mother, the Comtesse de la Rose, and executed around the same time as the *Demoiselles*. This masterpiece demonstrated once and for all that Rousseau was not an amusing Sunday painter but a genius, a caster of spells. Picasso set out to harness the Douanier's instinctive magic to his work. To exorcise the damp smells of mulch and mushrooms, he endowed the Forêt d'Halatte with the mystery and enchantment of Rousseau's exotic Arcadia. Rousseau achieves this artlessly; Picasso artfully. Picasso was also beguiled by the intensity of the Douanier's sense of reality—the intrinsic thereness of his houses and fences, his telegraph poles and flying machines. As Apollinaire wrote, "Rousseau had so strong a sense of reality that when he painted a fantastic subject he sometimes took fright and trembling all over had to open the window."[7] Rousseau also fulfilled one of Picasso's principal criteria for an artist: "You've got to make what doesn't exist, what has never been made before. That's painting."[8]

Picasso. *Landscape at La Rue-des-Bois*, August, 1908. Oil on canvas, 78×60cm. Museo d'Arte Contemporanea, Milan: Jucker Collection.

Rousseau was also useful to Picasso as an antidote to Cézanne's sway; he represented the opposite end of the pictorial spectrum. Whereas Rousseau was totally conceptual in his approach and almost as much of a devotee of high finish as Gérôme, Cézanne was totally perceptual and used lack of finish as a positive element in his work. Anything *non-finito* bothered Rousseau, who told Max Weber—where else but at the 1907 Cézanne Retrospective?—that he could finish Cézanne's paintings for him.[9] Picasso's aim was not to reconcile the examples of Cézanne and Rousseau in his work so much as to have them collide and profit from the consequences of their miscegenation. Sonia Delaunay's biographer suggests that Rousseau paid a visit to La Rue-des-Bois in the course of the summer. Unfortunately there is no confirmation of this fascinating possibility.[10]

* * *

Meanwhile Braque, who was spending the summer at L'Estaque, a small port in the vicinity of Marseille where Cézanne had once worked, was also painting landscapes—landscapes that would change the course of modern art. It was his third visit there. "I reached port safely after a rather good crossing," he wrote Kahnweiler on June 1,[11] so he must have taken a boat from Le Havre southwards around Spain and through the straits of Gibraltar to Marseille. "When I returned a third time to the south," Braque told Dora Vallier, "I found that the exaltation that had overwhelmed me on my first visit, and which I put into my [fauve] pictures, was no longer the same."[12] And to Jean Paulhan he said, "I should have had to push on down to Senegal to get the same result. You can't count on enthusiasm for more than ten months."[13]

Cézanne. *View of L'Estaque and the Château d'If*, 1883–85. Oil on canvas, 71×58cm. Private Collection, Fitzwilliam Museum, Cambridge.

Braque's passion for Cézanne—born originally of paintings he had seen at Vollard's—had been greatly reinforced by the October, 1907, show. Now that he was back in Cézanne country, he found that "there was something more secret in his painting."[14] And in the course of this summer of cubist germination, he proceeded to probe this "secret." He abandoned the last vestiges of fauve color and limited his palette to a Cézannesque gamut of viridian, ochers, grays and blacks. At the same time he did his best to liberate himself from the iron constraint of conventional perspective, not that he or Picasso would ever entirely succeed in doing so.

> You see, the whole Renaissance tradition is antipathetic to me. The hard-and-fast rules of perspective which it succeeded in imposing on art were a ghastly mistake which it has taken four centuries to redress: Cézanne and, after him, Picasso and myself can take a lot of the credit for this. Scientific perspective is nothing but eye-fooling illusionism; it is simply a trick—a bad trick—which makes it impossible for an artist to convey a full experience of space, since it forces the objects in a picture to disappear away from the beholder instead of bringing them within his reach, as painting should.[15]

In freeing himself from perspective, Braque reversed the old adage that distance lends enchantment to a view. His L'Estaque landscapes suggest that, on the contrary, proximity lends conviction to the view.

Cézanne was also the source of another painterly device to do with the elision of planes, known as *passage*—a device which Braque used to evoke space without recourse to perspective.[16] Braque took *passage* several stages further than Cézanne; within a year or two, Picasso would take it further still. *Passage*, which Alfred Barr defined as "the merging of planes with space by leaving one edge unpainted or light in tone,"[17] would play a key role in the genesis of cubism. It enabled Braque to generate what he called "*une éspace nouvelle*," a new kind of pictorial space, by having open-sided, light-refracting planes elide into one another as well as the surrounding space. This "research into space" is what cubism would be all about ("*fut la direction maîtresse du cubisme*"), he said.[18]

Braque. *Landscape at L'Estaque*, 1908. Oil on canvas, 81×65cm. Kunstmuseum, Basel.

A subtle deployment of *passage* enabled Braque to steal a march on Picasso. Compared with the views of L'Estaque that Braque did that summer, Picasso's Rue-des-Bois landscapes seem devoid of space—airless. Picasso was more interested in mass than space, and at first he practiced *passage* only insofar as it enabled him to homogenize and amplify the massiveness of his figures—notably that of *Three Women*. Unlike Braque, Picasso never had been and seldom would be much of a landscape painter, and in using Rousseau to counterbalance Cézanne, he put himself in a quandary. The hard-edged precision, the embroidered look of the details that is typical of naïf painting was incompatible with *passage*, thus incompatible with the "*éspace nouvelle*" that Braque saw as a fundamental ingredient of cubism. When Picasso returned to Paris and saw what Braque had achieved at L'Estaque, he must have realized that his own landscapes were almost as airless as scenery in a tapestry. Henceforth he, too, would use *passage* to amplify not just mass but space. Rousseau would soon fade from the picture, but Picasso would continue to exploit the Douanier's innocence of vision and even, on occasion, his hard-edgedness.

Village street, La Rue-des-Bois. Société Archéologique et Historique des Amis du Vieux Verneuil.

* * *

Given the quantity of work Picasso achieved in his three to four weeks at La Rue-des-Bois, one might think that he and Fernande lived a reclusive life. Not at all. When he was not painting, Picasso liked to be enlivened, if possible entertained. Since there was nowhere to go and no one to talk to, friends had to be enticed from Paris; and since there was only one spare room with a single bed in it, they often had to double up. Every few days or so, there would be new visitors. Sometimes problems arose, as Fernande describes. One night, an old acquaintance from Paris, the Dutch poet and novelist Fritz Vanderpyl, appeared with his highly sexed mistress, Aurélie, a peasant girl, who was proud of having started life working for the Toulouse-Lautrecs at Albi. The two of them were exhausted from having done the last seven kilometers on foot.

Fernande found Aurélie "rather too uninhibited."

> She told us in her pure southern accent she needed a good bucketful of water to wash the "dust from the road" off her feet, when she saw how astonished we were at their dark color. They were a splendidly ill-matched couple: he was Dutch, heavily built, placid, intellectual and fond of good living—a taste Amélie [sic] knew how to satisfy—and he countered his companion's energy with an implacable sense of inertia. She was vibrant and passionate and complained to him the whole time about his lack of sexual activity. She used to wake us up in the middle of the night to complain about this. She would make her way into our bedroom, half naked in her revealing blue nightgown, and sit on the end of the bed with her hands on her hips to pour out her troubles, while Vanderpyl called to her in a sleepy voice: "Amélie, you're bothering them. Come back to bed." She refused unless he promised to comply with her demands. Then she would go back to him, but next morning she would inform us in a voice full of disdain that the poor man's efforts had been unsuccessful. All this was enjoyable and amusing and helped us overcome the nervous stress, which could have become quite alarming.[19]

Derain came for a few days with Alice. She, too, caused problems. "Her face was pale and touching, with a beautiful forehead, lovely eyes and a fine complexion, but she was unable to control her aggressive nature, and this was extremely difficult to put up with."[20] After the Derains, Max Jacob arrived, which meant there were no more dull evenings. Then Apollinaire proposed himself.

Picasso. *Portrait of Apollinaire*, spring, 1908. Charcoal on two sheets of paper, 50×32cm overall. Musée Picasso and Picasso Heirs.

> As Max is already here [Fernande warned him], you will have to share his room for the eight to ten days that he is supposed to stay. Then if you want to economize—that is to say, spend no more than you do in Paris—you

> will have to take your meals with us; otherwise, there is only the local wine-merchant and he is a thief. I do the cooking, buying everything we need from the farm. There is not much variety, but the food is very good, since I get eggs as soon as they are laid and vegetables gathered from the garden. . . . I watch the cow being milked.
>
> With the room included you won't spend more than three francs a day, sometimes less. I say "room included," because we have taken only one; the woman who runs the farm rents out the other.
>
> We are surrounded by woods, in a hamlet of ten houses . . . real countryside. The Oise is ten minutes away. . . . Pablo and I are extremely happy, so much so that we are thinking of settling here definitively. We have even found a house we would like to rent . . . very pretty, an old hunting-lodge which Félix Faure visited. It's very big, very comfortable with a great field at the back, meadows out front, stables, barns, all the dog kennels one could possibly want.
>
> Anyway do come. We will be very happy. . . . You'll be able to work, never the least noise, I assure you . . . so much so that Max says the silence seems amplified.[21]

Picasso. *House at La Rue-des-Bois*, August, 1908. Oil on canvas, 92×73cm. Pushkin Museum of Fine Arts, Moscow.

Fernande asks Apollinaire to bring Picasso a bottle of Valerian, a traditional remedy for nerves; also some towels, as Madame Putman was not used to people using so many. In signing the letter, both Fernande and Max Jacob make fun of Apollinaire's habitual formula: "*la main amie de . . .*" "A friendly handshake from Madame Puthman [*sic*], the farmer," Fernande writes.[22] The idea of a bed being shared by these two old friends, who loved and sporadically hated each other and were very aware of each other's sexual proclivities, would have greatly appealed to Picasso.

In her memoirs Fernande says she thought she was going to be able to talk Picasso into renting the hunting lodge. The rent was only 400 francs a year. "But at the end of our stay, once he felt free of the obsession that had been torturing him, he wasn't prepared to settle down in this remote corner. It was too damp and green, and too far from Paris—the only place in France he considered habitable. So we returned to the city, leaving four or five of the kittens behind, as there was room for only one of them in the basket with the cat, who had had it all to herself on the journey down."[23] By early September they were back in Paris. Picasso had totally recovered from his *crise de nerfs*, although he later complained of indigestion from too much greenery.[24]

Picasso. *Still Life with Bunch of Flowers*, summer 1908. Oil on canvas, 38.2×46.5cm (formerly in Uhde's collection). Private collection.

The day after their return Picasso and Fernande called twice on the Steins; both times they were out, as we know from a postcard that he signed *Picasso peintre amateur*. A day or two later (Sunday, September 13), he sent another card—"The studio is ready. All I await is your visit"; and then a third card—"The pictures will not be ready until Thursday at midday, so we will hold the *vernissage* that afternoon. You are invited."[25] One can see why the artist was so eager to show the Steins his latest work: they bought three of the Rue-des-Bois landscapes and one of the still lifes; Kahnweiler bought most of the rest (two landscapes, two still lifes and the two paintings of Madame Putman) and later sold them to Shchukin. Most appropriate of all, Uhde, who did more than anybody to promote the Douanier Rousseau, bought the most Rousseau-like of the still lifes.

7

The Coming of Cubism

Louis Vauxcelles; caricature by André Rouveyre.

IF PICASSO HASTENED BACK FROM THE COUNTRY, it was primarily to compare notes, not to speak of paintings, with Braque, who was due in Paris by September 9—the last day for Salon d'Automne entries. To make the strongest possible showing, Braque submitted six or seven of his L'Estaque canvases to a Salon jury that included Matisse, Marquet, Rouault and Charles Guérin. To Braque's chagrin, they turned down the lot. However, each juror at this supposedly progressive Salon had the right to reinstate one of the rejected paintings; both Marquet and Guérin availed themselves of this right and voted to save two of the Braques. Although it was against the Salon's regulations, the mortified artist withdrew all his submissions.

Rightly or wrongly, Braque felt that this blow had been administered by Matisse, who was still smarting from his former follower's defection to Picasso and would have had no difficulty swaying this jury of his cohorts. To his everlasting credit, Kahnweiler came to Braque's rescue. He had originally planned a November exhibition of Pierre Girieud's unexciting Gauguinesque paintings together with Paco Durrio's unexciting Gauguinesque ceramics. He now had second thoughts. Since the Salon's refusal had not only made the remaining paintings available but also generated controversy, Kahnweiler decided to exhibit Braque rather than Girieud and Durrio.[1] To his small stock of Braque's work, he now added the fifteen views of L'Estaque. An astute stroke on his part: the show would set his gallery on a propitious new course. From now on he would see himself, with some justice, as the impresario and strategist of a new movement instead of just another *dénicheur de la jeune peinture.*

Kahnweiler's one-man show of Braque's recent work triggered the term "cubism." It was Louis Vauxcelles, the art critic responsible for dubbing Matisse and his followers "*les Fauves*," who put it into circulation. He reported that it was Matisse's idea. Matisse had drawn a little sketch for him —"two ascending and converging lines between which small cubes were set depicting a L'Estaque of Georges Braque"—to demonstrate how these paintings had been built up out of "*petites cubes.*"[2] Later, Matisse grew so weary of being asked about these "*petites cubes*" that he denied ever having mentioned them. Since the term had been applied first to Braque, and since Braque, unlike Picasso, continued to participate in public exhibitions, he alone was perceived as a cubist—not, however, for long.

Far from upsetting the usually competitive Picasso, the réclame and controversy that Braque's show stirred up worked to his advantage in

Opposite: Braque. *Houses at L'Estaque*, 1908. Oil on canvas, 73×59.5cm. Kunstmuseum, Bern: Hermann und Margrit Rupf Stiftung.

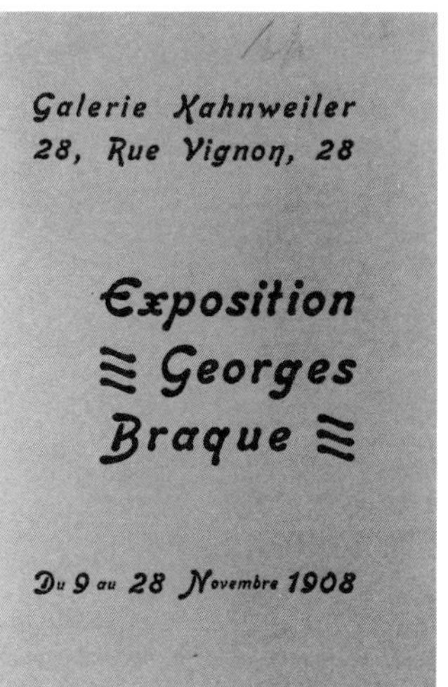

Catalogue of Braque exhibition at Kahnweiler's, November, 1908. Archives Kahnweiler: Galerie Louise Leiris.

that it enabled him to stay out of range of philistine attack. It suited him to be seen as a shadowy *chef d'école* working in secret and selling his work for rapidly rising prices. Braque's modesty ensured that Picasso need never fear eclipse. He blushed at being asked to pose for a photograph, Gelett Burgess reported. "At this period I was so shy," Braque confessed, "that I was very cautious about going to see my exhibition. I went only once at sundown when there was nobody around."[3]

Kahnweiler's Braque show—the gallery's third and last (the first had featured Van Dongen, the second Camoin)—was organized in a tremendous rush. It lasted from November 9 to 20 and included twenty-seven paintings: nineteen landscapes, six still lifes and two nudes. Since the gallery was tiny, they had to be hung extremely close, which may have determined the dealer to hold no more shows. Kahnweiler suggested that Apollinaire write the catalog preface; and Braque agreed, but was far from happy with the result. The poet was evidently baffled by the paintings—whose like had never been seen before—and took refuge in poetic gush: "In his valleys the bees of youth hum and plunder, and the happiness of innocence reposes on his civilized terraces." Worse, Apollinaire slipped in a gratuitous plug for Marie Laurencin. Meaningless phrases, Braque said. A subsequent article in which Apollinaire tried to sound as if he actually knew what he was talking about was even more embarrassing: it evoked qualities like "geometric harmonies" and "decorative intentions," which could not have been further from the artist's concepts.[4] "Apollinaire was a great poet and a man to whom I was deeply attached," Braque said, "but let's face it, he couldn't tell the difference between a Raphael and a Rubens."[5]

* * *

The word "cubism" started life as a meaningless epithet, which had as little relevance to the art it has come to denote as the caricatures of the works that appeared in humor magazines. However, it caught on with the public; even with Braque and Picasso, who loathed the word for the reason that it did not apply to what they were doing but soon found themselves obliged to use it. Over the years "cubism" has achieved universal acceptance by virtue of designating

> the most important and certainly the most complete and radical artistic revolution since the Renaissance. . . . [Nothing] has so altered the principles, so shaken the foundations of Western painting as did Cubism. Indeed, from a visual point of view it is easier to bridge the three hundred and fifty years separating Impressionism from the High Renaissance than it is to bridge the fifty years that lie between Impressionism and Cubism. . . . A portrait by Renoir will seem closer to a portrait by Raphael than it does to a Cubist portrait by Picasso.[6]

Apart from Picasso and Braque the only other artists Kahnweiler would accept into his exclusive cubist stable would be Juan Gris and, briefly, Fernand Léger. As we will see, Picasso and Braque held aloof even from them. But it would be above all the so-called Salon cubists (theoretical hacks who exhibited at the big Salons) whom the inventors of the movement held in disdain: men like Le Fauconnier, Gleizes and Metzinger, who would come along all too soon and try, and fail, to turn their discoveries into a picture-making formula based on quasi-scientific calculations. Picasso and Braque had the deepest distrust of theory: "Mathematics, trigonometry, chemistry, psychoanalysis, music and whatnot," Picasso said, "have been related to cubism to give it an easier interpretation. All this has been pure literature, not to say nonsense, which has only succeeded in blinding people with theories."[7]

Before seeing what cubism stands for, let us see what it stood against. For Picasso cubism constituted, among other things, a reaction against impressionism, whose two great luminaries, Renoir and Monet, were still hard at work and by now venerated by the public which had once ridiculed them. Picasso's attitude to impressionism was irreverent and ironical, not to say iconoclastic. The ambivalence of his feelings for Renoir would be reflected in his acquisition of some of the monstrously pneumatic nudes that the old artist did shortly before he died: "far and away his best work," Picasso would say to irritate people who prided themselves on their discrimination. He had far stronger reservations about Monet, particularly the *Nymphéas*: those huge, sumptuously painted waterlily decorations that Monet had begun in 1902 and was still touching up when he died in 1926. (Picasso would be vastly amused when American museums started buying them up in the 1950s and 1960s, as if to provide abstract expressionism with an illustrious precedent.) The *Nymphéas* reminded him, Picasso said, of a device he had once seen in a brothel: an endless band of landscape on a roll that an old woman wound past the window of a wagon lit to give copulating clients inside the illusion of movement. The thought that Nabism, fauvism, cubism, futurism, expressionism and dada came and went against this constantly unfurling yet never changing backdrop of waterlilies struck Picasso as distinctly droll.

Picasso. *Still Life with Chocolate Pot*, spring, 1909. Watercolor on paper, 61.3×47.5cm. Private collection.

However, it was not so much these elderly impressionists that Picasso and Braque were in revolt against as the whole outmoded concept of impressionism; the lack of substance inherent in the very term; the flimsy art-for-art's-sake shimmer of impressionist light effects. Cubism was also a reaction against the followers of the impressionists: against the methodology of the divisionists, the garishness of fauvism, and, in Picasso's case, against his pet aversion, Bonnard. "A potpourri of indecision" is how he described this artist's work.[8] He had caught his fear of melting in the bath like a piece of soap from Bonnard, he said.[9]

Picasso was determined to go as far as possible in the other direction and produce work that would be "*bien couillarde*"—a favorite phrase of Cézanne's that means literally "ballsy." "A painting should have balls" became a catchphrase. Picasso and Braque were famously *couillarde* and had no problem giving their work the potency, physicality and heft that the word implies. As the critic Roger Allard saw, as early as 1912, cubism was a means of registering "mass, volume and weight."[10] Henceforth, everything had to be tactile and palpable, not least space. Palpability made for reality, and it was the real rather than the realistic that Picasso was out to capture. A cup or a jug or a pair of binoculars should not be a copy of the real thing, it need not even look like the real thing; it simply had to be as real as the real thing. And so there would be no more falsehoods; no more three-dimensional simulation, no more artful trompe l'œil effects, except for the famous trompe l'œil nail with a shadow that Braque added to more than one of his 1909 still lifes in order to contrast the

Braque. *Violin and Palette*, 1909. Oil on canvas, 91.7×42.8cm. The Solomon R. Guggenheim Museum, New York.

Picasso. *Man with Tenora*. 1911. Oil on canvas, 105×69cm. Fundación Colección Thyssen-Bornemisza, Madrid.

eye-fooling mendacity of traditional notation with the cubists' realistic treatment of forms in space.

"When we invented cubism," Picasso remarked many years later, "we had no intention whatever of inventing cubism. We simply wanted to express what was in us."[11] Braque said more or less the same thing. "Cubism, or rather my cubism, was a means that I created for my own use, whose primary aim was to put painting within the range of my own gifts."[12] Both artists were loath to define what their cubism was really about. Nevertheless, at one time or another, both came out with explanations. As one might expect, Picasso's pronouncements tend to be paradoxical and contradictory: "there is no such thing as cubism," he told one interviewer and excused himself to feed his monkey.[13] Braque, however, was more forthcoming and articulate, and it is to him we have to turn for enlightenment as to the techniques that they employed at this first so-called analytic phase of cubism. This is how Braque explains his abandonment of perspective:

> Traditional perspective gave me no satisfaction. It is too mechanical to allow one to take full possession of things. It has its origins in a single viewpoint and never gets away from it. But the viewpoint is of little importance. It is as if someone spent his life drawing profiles and believed that man was one-eyed. When we arrived at this conclusion, everything changed, you have no idea how much.[14]

It followed that if the artist was ever "to take full possession of things," he must be able to represent an object from any number of viewpoints at the same time. Multiple views in one form or another recur throughout cubism; however, they are only one of Braque and Picasso's radical innovations. No less revolutionary was their reduction of the spatial element to an ever shallower recession; this enabled them to bring everything as near as possible to the surface of the canvas and as near as possible to us. Braque described this manner of dealing with space as "tactile" or "manual," because it enabled him "to make people want to touch what has been painted as well as look at it."[15] It is a complete reversal of the time-honored system of establishing a distance and making objects recede from us. To bring things within our grasp, Braque (and Picasso) took to fragmenting and faceting forms, because "this was a means of getting as close to the objects as painting allowed. Fragmentation allowed me to establish a spatial element as well as a spatial movement and until this had been achieved I was not able to introduce objects into my pictures."[16] In the same way, faceting allowed the artist (much as it does a man who cuts gemstones) to use refracted light to give his surfaces a generalized sparkle. This was a tremendous advance on the traditional device of a single source of light.

Picasso. *The Architect's Table*, 1912. Oil on canvas, 72.6×59.7 cm. The Museum of Modern Art, New York: The William S. Paley Collection.

Braque's L'Estaque landscapes set in motion a process that would totally change the way an artist represents things: a process that would enable Braque and Picasso to come up with an art that would be "simultaneously representational and anti-naturalistic."[17] and thus make modernism possible. Over the years this art would come to be divided into two phases: analytic and (after the invention of papier collé) synthetic cubism. Given their deep distrust of art historians, Picasso and Braque never took their categories very seriously. However, cubism does lend itself to this convenient, albeit arbitrary, categorization, so we are obliged to use it. Analytic cubism permitted the two artists to take things apart: dissect them "with the practiced and methodical hand of a great surgeon" (as Apollinaire said of Picasso).[18] It enabled their followers to make a further breakthrough: into the realm of abstraction—a breakthrough that they themselves would always hold back from making. Analytic cubism would make possible the achievements of de Stijl, constructivism and even minimalism. Synthetic cubism, on the other hand, permitted Picasso and Braque to put things together again, to create images and objects in a revolutionary new way, out of whatever materials they chose. It would thus make possible the achievements of the dadaists, the surrealists, even the pop artists. No question about it, cubism engendered every major modernist movement.

* * *

Before his exhibition opened, Braque allowed Picasso to borrow one of the L'Estaque landscapes (apparently the version bought by Kahnweiler's Swiss friend Hermann Rupf). Matisse reports seeing it "in the studio of Picasso, who discussed it with his friends."[19] Matisse made no secret of his dislike of what came to be called cubism—dislike that was exacerbated by a touch of envy. Picasso had changed the rules of the game so drastically, there was no way at this point that Matisse could get even. For the next three or four years, both sides would needle each other. Matisse would behave as if he were the wounded party, but in fact it was his anticubist stance—his laughter at Picasso's *Three Women*, his rejection of Braque's *L'Estaques*—that had sparked hostilities. Braque, who had the cooler head, would keep his resentment to himself. Picasso, on the other hand, enjoyed poking fun at the "*cher maître*'s" new academy and professorial pronouncements. Nevertheless, Picasso and Matisse would continue to keep watchful eyes on each other's accomplishments and pursue a policy of "Anything you can do I can do better." It would take Matisse three or four years to come round to cubism, by which time rancor would give way on both sides to respect that was no less genuine for being wary.

Matisse. *Portrait of Sergei Shchukin*, 1912. Charcoal on paper, 48.3×35cm. Private collection.

Given the animosity, Matisse would never have done Picasso the tremendous favor Fernande attributes to him in the fall of 1908: bringing Sergei Shchukin, his greatest collector, to the Bateau Lavoir studio, where he supposedly purchased two major Picassos.[20] Fernande's memory must surely be at fault. Apart from the unlikelihood of Matisse's promoting the sale of paintings he had condemned by a rival he resented to a patron he wanted to keep to himself, there is no evidence that Shchukin was in Paris at this time, or that he began buying Picassos until 1909.[21] Fernande has telescoped at least two visits into one. Matisse probably *did* bring Shchukin to see Picasso, but in 1907, or, at the very latest, spring, 1908, when the Russian was buying Matisses from Berthe Weill and Druet as well as from the artist himself.[22] Far from acquiring any Picassos, Shchukin was predictably horrified by what he saw, as Matisse doubtless hoped he would be. "What a loss for French art!" he told the Steins. Earlier, Picasso had drawn a porcine caricature of the Russian, as if to say, What a pig! If Shchukin would eventually have a change of heart and outdo the Steins as the greatest collector of Picasso's early work, it was thanks not to Matisse but to a series of tragedies in his family. Shchukin found Picasso's angst-ridden canvases in tune with his sense of grief. Among his earliest acquisitions of Picasso's work were the two painfully strident memento moris that commemorate Wiegels's suicide (pp. 87, 306).

Besides buying up most of the recent Braques, Kahnweiler acquired as many as forty Picassos in the course of 1908, including what remained after the Steins had taken first pick of the Rue-des-Bois paintings. Kahnweiler "was always on the alert," Fernande reports, "and always ready to outbid all the other dealers"[23]—the vultures who had swindled Picasso when he first moved to Paris. Now that he had the upper hand, the artist enjoyed playing dealers off against each other, just as he would soon enjoy playing the Steins off against Kramář and Shchukin. To keep abreast of what was being exhibited, what collectors were around, what was selling and what was not, Picasso took to checking out the dealers. Every evening, when the light had gone and it was no longer possible to paint, he would set off on his rounds. Being compulsive about such things, he would first call on Braque and review what he had been doing; then they would go off together on a tour of inspection, usually ending up at Sagot's, Vollard's or Kahnweiler's.

Kees Van Dongen. *Portrait of D.-H. Kahnweiler*, 1907. Oil on canvas, 65×54cm. Petit Palais, Geneva.

It was easy to trick Kahnweiler, Fernande says. "One had only to point to a picture and say: 'Not that one, my dear fellow, I've more or less promised that to so-and-so . . .' and he'd be certain to make the sacrifice (as he liked to put it) to get it."[24] But that was only the beginning. Fernande goes on to complain (just as Dora Maar, Françoise Gilot and the artist's second wife, Jacqueline, would) that "Kahnweiler used to haggle for hours on end, until . . . at the end of his tether, the painter would agree to a reduction. Kahnweiler was well aware of what he had to gain by wearing Picasso down like this." The artist would haggle back, but Kahnweiler had the advantage of patience: "At the end of it all Picasso was so exhausted that if he had been alone, with nobody to back him up, he would have given everything away for nothing, if not actually pushed the dealer violently out into the street, just to have done with him."[25] In later life Picasso would give Kahnweiler credit for his courage and persistence in establishing a market for paintings that were at first exceedingly difficult to sell. But the bargaining rankled, and he would never regard his dealer as anything but a dealer. Jacqueline said that Kahnweiler "was mistaken in choosing to see himself as Pablo's friend."[26]

Now that he was free of financial worries, Picasso could have afforded to leave the squalor of the Bateau Lavoir: no gas or electricity and only one tap and one primitive toilet for the entire building. However, pride in the simplicity, one might say the primitivism, of his life held him back. Also the availability of money was almost as much of an obstacle to his peace of mind as its absence. Picasso would always be enormously generous with his work, enormously supportive of his poorer friends; he could also be capricious and manipulative in his disbursements to those closest to him. Like a peasant, he concealed his wallet in an inside pocket of his jacket, which he kept closed with a very large safety pin.

> Every time he had to take out a banknote [Picasso] would undo the pin as unobtrusively as he could; but it was no mean task, though it certainly made us all laugh [Fernande said]. His suspiciousness was sometimes amusing and sometimes extremely irritating. I remember a day when he noticed that the pin wasn't fastened quite as usual. He looked searchingly

Clovis Sagot, spring, 1909. Photograph by Picasso. Archives Picasso. The paintings visible are *Standing Female Nude* and *Harlequin's Family.*

Picasso. *Portrait of Clovis Sagot*, 1909. Oil on canvas, 82×66 cm. Hamburger Kunsthalle.

> at everybody and remained convinced that somebody had been tinkering with his "safe."[27]

Picasso's one indulgence was to rent a studio outside the Bateau Lavoir. He found what he wanted no distance away at the bottom of a garden on the rue Cortot: a place where he could stretch and prime his canvases. It was Braque who urged Picasso to take more interest in the qualities of paint; Braque who urged him to search shops for canvas that was fine and tightly woven—hence the enhanced quality and variety of his surfaces. Did he follow Braque's example and grind his own colors? Occasionally, Picasso said, but he seldom had the time or the patience. The rue Cortot studio would also enable him to have women on the side. Fernande made jealous scenes—in part to justify her own escapades, which she claimed to have committed "out of curiosity." Henceforth there would be infidelities on both sides.

In the course of the winter, Fernande began to suffer from a kidney complaint, which might explain the relatively few appearances she makes in Picasso's work. The skinny, leggy look of the nudes in some of the drawings suggests that the artist used another, more athletic model. Picasso takes ever more outrageous liberties with the human form. The so-called *Standing Female Nude* from Philadelphia is as ambivalently posed as the Vesalian *Dryad*: apparently sitting on a nonexistent chair while straddling an impossible expanse of space. And then there are the two great bathers: a smaller, seated one (in the Hermitage Museum; p. 119) whose right flank seems to be settling a score with her left one; and a larger, standing one holding a towel. In both paintings the woman's left arm has been wrenched brutally around and popped back into a repositioned socket—a piece of surgery that, as it were, italicizes the arm, heightens our perception of its presence. Picasso must have had an articulated lay figure in the studio, on which to try out these contortions. In the more magisterial of the two *Bather* figures (the Museum of Modern Art one) Picasso pits himself against Matisse's *Bathers with a Turtle*, which he had seen earlier in the year. Like Matisse, he sets his figure off against three horizontal bands of color (sky, sea and sand, as opposed to Matisse's sky, sea and grass). This setting would imply infinite recession were it not for the shadows that both artists' figures cast on it, as if it were a painted backcloth. Picasso also has fun parodying Matisse's idiosyncratic way with feet; and he mocks Matisse's flat-bottomed women by pumping up his bather's buttocks and repositioning them on her flank.

Picasso also resumed painting portraits. Since the first of these depicts the avaricious and not very prepossessing dealer Clovis Sagot, one can only conclude that the sitter talked the artist into doing it. To avoid having Sagot around, Picasso took photographs of him—a practice he would resort to ever more frequently—and for once kept too close to them. The result is a bland map of a face which is at odds with the cubistic treatment of the rest of the composition. A portrait of Fernande in an armchair done around the same time is far more complex but also a bit pat (p. 309). However, Picasso was pleased enough to have postcards made, one of which he sent to the Steins[28]—probably a ploy to get them to buy it. But by far the finest "portrait" of this period is the so-called *Woman with a Fan* in the Pushkin Museum (p. 307). In fact it is not really a portrait. Picasso told me that although it was not done from life, it was known "in the studio"

Above: Picasso. *Standing Female Nude*, spring, 1909. Oil on canvas, 116×89cm. Philadelphia Museum of Art: Louise and Walter Arensberg Collection.

Top left: Picasso. *Bather*, early 1909. Oil on canvas, 130×97cm. The Museum of Modern Art, New York: Louise Reinhardt Smith Bequest.

Left: Matisse. *Bathers with a Turtle*, early 1908. Oil on canvas, 179.1×220.3cm. St. Louis Art Museum: Gift of Mr. and Mrs. Joseph Pulitzer, Jr.

as a portrait of Etta Cone. As he would later say of his paintings which may or not be portraits: "*Lo hice pensando en . . .*" (I had so-and-so in mind when I painted it).

* * *

Towards the end of November, Picasso's interest in the Douanier Rousseau's work was nicely rewarded. In the course of checking out the local dealers, he discovered one of Rousseau's most impressive portraits: a grim-looking woman (thought to be Yadwigha, a Polish schoolteacher with whom the artist had been in love).[29] She is staidly posed in front of an ornate curtain, holding a sapling upside down by its root, unaware of a small, dive-bomber-like bird in the background. Picasso found the painting sticking out of a stack of pictures at the shop of Père Soulié, the drunken mattress-seller who not so long before had been buying drawings from him for fifty centimes apiece (gouaches for three francs). The Rousseau cost five francs. "You can paint over it," Soulié said. Picasso would always treasure it. He admired its "penetration, clarity, decision," he told Florent Fels, and felt that it was "one of the most revealing French psychological portraits."[30]

Max Weber in his Paris studio, rue Belloni, 1906. Private collection.

Since close friends like Apollinaire and Uhde had known the Douanier Rousseau for some time, Picasso could easily have met him, even visited his studio. However he seems not to have done so. The man who claims to have brought them together was a young naturalized American of Russian origin named Max Weber, who for the last three years had been studying art in Paris—most recently with Matisse. Weber had met Picasso at one of the Steins' Saturday evenings in October, 1908. Having recently made friends with Rousseau and wheedled four little paintings and two drawings from him, the penniless American hoped to benefit from Picasso's celebrated generosity to other artists. A few days after meeting Picasso, Weber went round to his studio, accompanied by the painter Jules Flandrin and accordingly "fell in love with" a small still life on panel.[31] Although he did not have any money, he offered to buy it; and then, in the hope of getting the painting for less, or as a gift, he sent off importunate letters. For once Picasso did not give way. Weber returned to America without his painting.

In the course of showing his recent work, Picasso pulled out from behind a curtain the Douanier Rousseau portrait he had just bought. Weber was "spellbound," and invited Picasso to come and see *his* Rousseaus. During this return visit it transpired that Picasso had never been to the Douanier's studio, which happened to be close by on rue Pernety. "Sure, we can go over there," Weber said. "[Picasso] put on his coat, a flabby old coat, and we went." They found Apollinaire posing for his portrait—one of two that Rousseau did of him and Marie Laurencin, *The Muse Inspiring the Poet.* Picasso "watched every stroke of [Rousseau's] brush." Afterwards they went and had a drink in a café, but Apollinaire insisted on playing a "discordant, horrible, out-of-tune [jukebox] . . . so loud that, even if we screamed . . . we couldn't hear a word."[32]

To celebrate his new acquisition, not to mention his exploitation of Rousseau's naïf vision, and also take him up on his offer to play the violin, Picasso decided to organize a "banquet" in the Douanier's honor at the Bateau Lavoir. The date has not been recorded, but it probably took place on Saturday, November 21. Years later, when the banquet had achieved legendary status, two people whom the artist had long since ceased to regard as friends would boast that they, too, deserved credit for the evening. Sonia Terk (later Delaunay), who had just married Uhde, deluded herself into thinking that it had also been a celebration of their marriage of convenience.[33] And Leo Stein claimed that Rousseau had actually arranged to play the violin for *him*: "If I had not that drowsy afternoon asked Rousseau to play, there would have been no banquet and no post-fabricated explanations to account for it."[34] Leo's marvelous eye for modern art was beginning to play him false. He didn't even like Rousseau's painting: "I don't want that sort of thing hanging on my wall and staring me in the face all the time. I like to talk with the people of the village, but I don't want to live with them."[35]

Leo never forgave his sister for making the Rousseau banquet a set piece—a delightfully deadpan and disingenuous one, awash in local color and whimsical observation—of her celebrated memoir, *The Autobiography of Alice B. Toklas*. He accused her of turning it to her own immortal advantage. In fact, Gertrude put forward no special claims for the event beyond seeing it as "very rigolo, a favorite Montmartre word meaning a jokeful amusement."[36] Posterity would take care of that. To quote James R. Mellow, one of Gertrude's biographers, "She had taken an improvised party and propelled it into legendary status as a symbol of the freewheeling bohemian life of Paris in the decade before World War I."[37] Roger Shattuck, author of that most eloquent and entertaining study of the period, *The Banquet Years*, goes even further and sees the party as "almost a transfiguration it seems to us now, and it must have appeared so in the dizziness of that evening." Shattuck allows that it

> has been interpreted by some as a lampooning of Rousseau, as a magnificent farce organized for everyone's enjoyment at Rousseau's expense, [but it is more accurate to see the event as] a celebration of unpredictable new resources in the arts, a spontaneous display of high spirits to greet ideas being unearthed every day by . . . everyone present at the gathering, including Rousseau. . . . The banquet celebrated a whole epoch.[38]

The host and hostess disagreed most emphatically with this verdict. Some forty years later, Picasso admitted to his then mistress, Geneviève Laporte, that the banquet had been "*vraiment une blague* [really a joke]. Nobody believed in his talent. Only [Rousseau] took it seriously. He wept with joy."[39] As for Fernande, who was very much in charge of the proceedings, not least of the *paella* she had learned to cook in Spain, she describes how Picasso and his group were "overjoyed at the prospect of pulling the Douanier's leg."[40] And whatever account of the banquet one reads—Gertrude's, Raynal's, even Salmon's—there is no reason to doubt Picasso and Fernande. What could be more of a leg-pull than this spoof apotheosis *dans le style concierge*? Far from being "a transfiguration" or the celebration of the most creative decade of the century, the banquet seems to have been more like the village tease of a holy fool. The guests' supposedly bizarre behavior—Salmon and Cremnitz filling their mouths with soap and faking a fit, Salmon drunkenly eating the yellow *fantaisie* off Alice Toklas's hat, Apollinaire entreating Alice and Harriet Levy to sing "the native songs of the redskins"—seems to have blinded people to the degrading plight of the guest of honor, idiot savant of art, weeping tears

Henri Rousseau. *The Muse Inspiring the Poet*, 1909. Oil on canvas, 146×97 cm. Öffentliche Kunstsammlung, Basel, Kunstmuseum.

Henri Rousseau in his studio, 1910. Photograph by Picasso. Archives Picasso.

of tipsy joy at the mock adulation, as he sat unsteadily on a ramshackle "throne, made from a chair built up on a packing case and set against a background of flags and lanterns . . . [and] a large banner bearing the words: 'Honor to Rousseau.'"[41] Characteristically, Gertrude failed to record her brother's inebriated state. So drunk was Leo that he pinched the ribbon of the *mérite agricole* from Cremnitz's buttonhole.[42]

The proceedings started with songs and speeches composed for the occasion: a silly song by Cremnitz and an elegant if condescending toast by Apollinaire with a refrain, "*Vive! Vive Rousseau!*," in which the thirty or so guests joined.[43] Next, the Douanier took up his fiddle—a child's fiddle, according to Raynal—and without being asked, launched into his repertory of droll songs, including his favorite, "*Aïe, Aïe, Aïe, que j'ai mal aux dents.*" (Aie, Aie, Aie, what a toothache have I.) He also played some of his own compositions, notably a tepid little waltz entitled *Clémence*, which he had dedicated to his wife's memory. This led to dancing, during which Marie Laurencin, who was intoxicated, fell into a tray of jam tarts and got chastised by Apollinaire. Meanwhile candle grease dripped from a lantern and formed a pyramid like a clown's hat on the Douanier's bald head. At one point the lantern caught fire, which "made Rousseau think that it was his apotheosis," Fernande said.[44] Picasso had laid on quantities of wine; and, like most of the guests, except the American ladies—Gertrude, Alice and Harriet—Rousseau was drunk. He nodded tearfully off to sleep, snored gently, woke up, sang a bit and dozed off again. Two or three American couples in evening dress, "who had got there by accident, had to make the most excruciating efforts to keep a straight face."[45] It was only after the Steins left, taking Rousseau with them, that the guests relaxed and enjoyed themselves.

Henri Rousseau. *Self-Portrait*, c. 1900–03. Oil on canvas, 24×19cm. Musée du Louvre: Picasso Gift.

One can see why Robert Delaunay, the painter who had done more than most to further Rousseau's career, made a point of not attending the banquet. It turned out just as he had feared. For quite other reasons—one of his periodic squabbles with Picasso—Max Jacob, who had allowed his nearby studio to be used as a kitchen, told everybody that nothing would induce him to make an appearance. However, as he later confessed, curiosity got the better of him, and he went by at the end of dinner "to pick up the crumbs."[46] For his part, Picasso enjoyed the black burlesque of the evening. He was almost the only person present who genuinely admired Rousseau's work. Mockery was his paradoxical way of honoring and, in a manner of speaking, repaying his debt to Rousseau, whether or not Rousseau realized that such a debt existed. For Picasso the banquet would always be a *blague*, and so would the rosy, reverent light in which it came to be perceived. That sentimental hyperbole should have transformed this lighthearted if slightly mean-spirited charade into the apotheosis of his group's collective genius is in itself something of a *blague*.

A month later (December 19), Rousseau himself gave a farewell banquet for Max Weber, who was returning to America. The man who supposedly introduced Picasso to the Douanier had not been invited to the Bateau Lavoir party. Did the Douanier want to console him? The second banquet included many of the same guests as the first, including Picasso and Fernande, Apollinaire and Marie Laurencin, but it was more decorous and therefore less often described. In Weber's honor, Rousseau and his dim pupils, in their Sunday best, performed an American number called

Henri Rousseau. *Portrait of His Wife*, c. 1900–03. Oil on canvas, 22×17cm. Musée du Louvre: Picasso Gift.

"Tam-Tam" and other items from their repertoire. Weber, who had been a cantor in his father's synagogue, belted out bits of Handel's *Messiah*. Back in New York, Weber's encounters with Picasso, Matisse, Apollinaire and Rousseau would entitle him to the mantle of a prophet. The principal convert to his cult would be the photographer and avant-garde impresario Alfred Stieglitz. Weber taught him everything, Stieglitz averred; and it would be at Weber's prompting that in March, 1911, Stieglitz put on the first exhibition of Picasso's work at his 291 Gallery.

The Bateau Lavoir banquet wrought one small, not entirely welcome change in Picasso's life. The Douanier became an increasingly frequent visitor to the Bateau Lavoir. "We are the two greatest painters of this era," Rousseau told his new friend, "you in the Egyptian style, I in the modern style"[47]—a notion that amused Picasso, though he was not sure what it meant. In fact, the "gentle Rousseau" of legend was often anything but gentle. Fernande, who was fond of him, admitted that "his face turned purple the minute he was thwarted or bothered."[48] And another well-wisher, Gustave Coquiot, complained that "his beastliness beats anything."[49] As Shattuck says, stubbornness was at "the core of his genius."[50] Indeed it was this stubbornness and single-mindedness and not his mythic gentleness and naïveté that endeared the Douanier to Picasso. Unlike his other famous fans—Jarry, who burned all but the face of Rousseau's portrait of him, and Apollinaire, who treated him as a joke—Picasso revered the work and in his mocking way revered the man. Max Jacob reported that Apollinaire did not dare laugh at Rousseau in front of Picasso, "because he would not have allowed it."[51] Mockery was an admirer's prerogative. Apropos this mockery, Fernand Léger liked to tell the following story. He and some painter friends were sitting in one of the Montparnasse cafés amusing themselves at the Douanier's expense when the old man suddenly got up to leave. He refused to say where he was going, so Léger and his group decided to follow him and see what he was up to. To their surprise, Rousseau ended up darting into the Musée du Luxembourg. Up the stairs they followed him and caught him out gazing rapturously at a painting by their pet hate, Bouguereau. "Look at the highlights on the fingernails," Rousseau said when they taunted him. Léger confessed that he may well have had these highlights in mind when he came to paint pictures that the press described as "tubist."[52]

Henri Rousseau. *Self-Portrait*, 1890. Oil on canvas, 143×110cm. Národní Galerie, Prague.

In years to come Picasso would buy more of Rousseau's paintings: the charmingly *pompier* picture of *Representatives of Foreign Powers Arriving to Hail the Republic as a Sign of Peace* (it includes likenesses of six Presidents of the Republic and all the major crowned heads of Europe), and the beautiful pair of small heads of Rousseau and his wife, whose influence can be detected in some of the portraits of Dora Maar. During World War II, he acquired yet another painting, an *Exotic Landscape*,[53] this time from Martin Fabiani, a gangsterish dealer who collaborated with the Germans and the Vichy authorities. Picasso must have had suspicions about the painting's provenance; he was unusually insistent on obtaining proper documentation. Sure enough, the painting turned out to have been looted by the Nazis from the Wertheimer collection. Picasso immediately returned it. Fabiani went to jail for collaboration and related offenses.

* * *

Early in the spring of 1909, Picasso painted a starkly handsome *Landscape with a Bridge.* And not for the first or last time, he made a mystery of the locale. When Daix asked him, the artist said he had painted it in his Paris studio, as if that laid the question to rest.[54] He implied that he had done it from imagination, which was not quite the case. In his landscapes Picasso takes all manner of liberties with appearances, but he almost always has a specific place in mind. The *Landscape with a Bridge* is no exception. The square bell tower amid a cluster of high-raked roofs figures in several of Derain's and Vlaminck's fauve paintings of the Seine valley and, more to the point, in views that Braque painted in October, 1909. The place in question is Carrières-Saint-Denis, the next town to Chatou, where Derain and Vlaminck first became fauves. Only the bridge in the Picasso is an anomaly: there is no bridge at Carrières-Saint-Denis. Picasso has simply shifted the Chatou one a few miles downstream. The painting must indeed have been done in the studio—maybe from postcards—although the artist is likely to have reconnoitered the hillside.[55] With its plunging views down to the water, its cubistic group of buildings, its green vaults of trees (long since gone), Carrières-Saint-Denis provided Picasso with an equivalent of Braque's L'Estaque on the outskirts of Paris. If the artist was unforthcoming about his motif, it was doubtless because he did not want to be caught poaching in a fauve preserve.

Carrières-Saint-Denis is known for its quarries of a soft stone prized by sculptors, just as its views were once prized by painters. "Our hunting ground [for motifs]," Vlaminck later wrote, "was often the hillsides of Carrières-Saint-Denis which were still planted with vines, and from where you could get a view of the whole Seine valley."[56] Over the years fauve paintings of Carrières—one or two of them done from the same angle as Picasso's (without the bridge, of course)—have been wrongly identified as of nearby Chatou.

After settling in Montmartre, Derain still liked to return to his roots. Since he and Alice were not married, they could not stay under the family roof at Chatou, so they rented a house or rooms at Carrières. In 1909 they seem to have gone there in the spring and been joined by Braque, who was looking for somewhere to go and paint during the summer. In the end Braque settled farther upstream at La Roche-Guyon, a rather more picturesque village not far from his birthplace, Argenteuil-sur-Seine, which culminates in the ruin of a castle rising dramatically above a cluster of rooftops framed in trees (p. 303). A further recommendation was that La Roche-Guyon, like L'Estaque, had been painted by Cézanne. Meanwhile Derain went off to spend the summer at Montreuil, near Calais. When he returned to Carrières, in October, Braque once again joined him and, as Picasso had done, painted views of the bell-tower complex.

Picasso seems to have visited Carrières in the early spring—maybe when Braque was first there. Curiosity was probably the reason. To launch himself as a publisher, Kahnweiler had recently commissioned Derain to illustrate Apollinaire's glorious Arthurian hotchpotch, *L'Enchanteur pourrissant.* The thirty-two woodcuts that the artist executed during the summer would establish this small (27.5×20 cm), deceptively modest publication as one of the finest illustrated books of its time. Picasso, who had little experience of woodcuts, had not as yet complied with Kahnweiler's request to try his hand at book illustration and would have been

Opposite: Picasso. *Landscape with a Bridge*, spring, 1909. Oil on canvas, 81×100cm. Národní Galerie, Prague.

Above: Derain. *Carrières-Saint-Denis*, 1905 (reworked by another hand). Oil on canvas, 70.5×110.5 cm. Former collection Kimbell Art Museum, Fort Worth, Texas.

Right: Braque. *Park at Carrières-Saint-Denis*, 1909. Oil on canvas, 115×146 cm. Fundación Colección Thyssen-Bornemisza, Madrid.

Above: Picasso. Study for *Temptation of Saint Anthony*, 1909. Sepia ink on paper, 12.4×9.5cm. Author's collection.

Left: Picasso. *Temptation of Saint Anthony*, spring, 1909. Watercolor on paper, 62×48cm. Moderna Museet, Stockholm.

Picasso. *Harlequin's Family*, spring, 1909. Oil on canvas, 100.5×81cm. Von der Heydt-Museum, Wuppertal.

Picasso. *Two Nudes*, spring, 1909. Oil on canvas, 100×81cm. Private collection.

Derain. Illustration from *L'Enchanteur pourrissant*, 1909. Woodcut book illustration. Private collection.

Picasso. *Temptation of Saint Anthony*, 1909. Pencil and ink on cherrywood block, 18.5×25.7cm. Picasso Heirs.

eager to see what Derain was up to. He may also have wanted to visit the local quarries (whose names he had already noted down in a couple of 1906–07 sketchbooks)[57] and obtain stone for primitivist sculptures like the ones he and Derain had experimented with the year before. Given a cryptic sentence in a letter Derain wrote Kahnweiler later this summer (August 27)—"I would remind you of that primitive business which you should have out with Picasso"[58]—some such project might have caused a problem between the two friends.

So proud was Derain of his cherrywood engraving-blocks that he carried them around in his pocket to show friends. Sure enough, Picasso appropriated one of them, on which he sketched, though never engraved, a *Temptation of Saint Anthony* composition. After seeing the excitement that Derain derived from illustrating Apollinaire's symbolist book—besides contributing the woodcuts, he would write a commentary on it and do a related painting—Picasso decided that he, too, would turn his mind to a symbolist subject. The erotic and satanic aspects of the Saint Anthony legend had always fascinated him: in 1900, the artist had painted the walls of his rue Gabrielle studio with a *Temptation of Saint Anthony* frieze; and in 1901 he had returned to the subject when he and Pichot did a mural for their favorite bar, Le Zut.[59] Might Picasso have envisioned illustrating a text by Apollinaire about Saint Anthony? This would explain Picasso's reversion to this Apollinairean subject complete with harlequins. It is also possible that the poet descended on Carrières. He would have been curious to see what his illustrator was up to.

Cézanne was also an exemplar, to the extent that he, too, had included a self-portrait—as the saint and not, like Picasso, as the devil—in the earlier of his two versions of the *Temptation* (the one included in the 1907 retrospective). To give his *Temptation* scenes (several drawings and a large gouache) an added immediacy, Picasso has set his figures off against the bell tower and roofs of Carrières. A number of elaborately hatched gouaches of the saint (in a monk's cowl), harlequin and nude imply that Picasso envisaged a major version of the composition. In the end, however, he let the project lapse: it was too literary, too symbolist in its implications, also too confusing. The wretched saint now had two devils to contend with: one in the form of a woman, one in the form of a harlequin. (Or was Picasso referring to the Satanist belief that when two people make love, a third person, the devil, is always present?) Also, as the sketches reveal, Picasso fails to give this dramatic confrontation much pictorial tension. The figures do not pay each other any heed; their problem seems to be alienation rather than satanic enticement. And so he modified this highly charged theme beyond all recognition. The outcome is two identically sized (100×81 cm) figure paintings: *Two Nudes*, in which the church, eminently visible in the preliminary sketches, has been reduced to a ghostly white outline on an otherwise bare ground; and *Harlequin's Family*, in which three figures are homogenized into a faceted, sculptural mass like the *Three Women*, with the harlequin's droll headgear and Columbine's gable-shaped elbow standing in for the bell tower's roof.

To compensate for the limits that cubism imposed on his range of subject matter, Picasso set about giving his nudes and still-life objects an extra dimension of meaning. As was his way, he did this covertly, subliminally, often in code. Hence the hints of anthropomorphism, shamanism, sacrilege and magic. For instance, the *Woman with a Book in a Landscape* turns out to be a mocking version of the Magdalen in the wilderness —a theme very popular with seventeenth-century Spanish painters. To demonize the subject Picasso has given it a blasphemous subtext, which enables the artist to have a dig at Fernande. The book that the saintly sinner holds—a devotional one, to judge by its size—doubles as a vagina; and the finger inserted into the missal or prayerbook, as if to mark the place, makes a typically Picassian pun on masturbation. Since the mountain and three parallel trees in the top left corner denote Horta, where Picasso spent the summer, and therefore do not appear in a photograph of this painting taken in the spring,[60] they must have been added after Picasso's return from Spain, to situate the naked Fernande in a penitential wilderness rather than the Bateau Lavoir.

El Greco. *Saint Mary Magdalen in Penitence*, 1580. Oil on canvas, 156.5×121 cm. Szépművészeti Múzeum, Budapest.

As a practicing Catholic, Braque preferred to avoid these dark areas. So did Derain, who was the most spiritually and philosophically concerned of Picasso's painter friends. Derain also shared Picasso's interest in blurring the boundaries between the sacred and the profane and in harnessing the tension of sacred art to secular subjects. (Religion has a way of increasing tensions, W. H. Auden observed.)[61] The altarlike air of certain Derain still lifes—the disposition of household utensils according to ritual rather than domestic usage—is consciously eucharistic. In Picasso's work the eucharistic echoes are self-referential rather than reverent, as in the hieratic and highly charged still life *Bread and Fruit Dish on a Table.* This had started life as a Bateau Lavoir version of a Supper at Emmaus subject entitled *Carnaval au bistro*: an allegorical group of figures round a table, one of them haloed. Allegory, Picasso seems to have concluded (much as he did with the *Demoiselles*), would limit his painting to a very specific, one-on-one, reading. Why not transform the composition into a still life? This would open it up to a sacrilegious interpretation and enable the artist to perform a miracle.

If we leave out the two attendants, the original sketch for the *Carnaval au bistro* composition includes more or less the same cast as the *Temptation of Saint Anthony*: haloed saint, harlequin, temptress, plus a mystery man (who may also stand for the devil). In the margin Picasso did a rough sketch to see how the composition would work as a still life. It worked fine. And so he roughed out the *Carnaval au bistro* composition onto a large canvas and then set out, with the help of drawings, to transform his stylized figures into a group of anthropomorphic, not to say phallic, loaves of bread and a fruit dish piled with breastlike pears, disposed ritualistically on an altarlike table (the semicircular drop leaf clearly evokes an altar cloth). The artist has used art miraculously to turn flesh into bread. Besides mocking the concept of transubstantiation, Picasso gets to play Christ. This at least is how I interpret this painting.

William Rubin sees things differently.[62] As he does with the *Demoiselles*, he concentrates on the preliminary studies rather than the final painting and concludes that the still life started off as a sort of pantheon: harlequin as Picasso, the woman next to him as Fernande, the figure with the halo as the Douanier Rousseau and the man who sports a Kronstadt hat as Cézanne with a dash of Braque. I am not convinced by Rubin's canonization of Rousseau. However, I have no problem seeing the *Carnaval au bistro* sketches as a Temptation of Saint Anthony subject in a

Picasso. Study for *Carnaval au bistro*, 1909. Blue ink and pencil on paper, 24.1×27.4cm. Musée Picasso.

Above: Bateau Lavoir studio, 1909. Photograph by Picasso. *Woman with a Book in a Landscape* is on the easel; *Female Nude with Guitar* (unfinished) and the Hermitage *Seated Bather* are also partly visible. Archives Picasso.

Right: Picasso. *Bread and Fruit Dish on a Table*, 1909. Oil on canvas, 164×132.5cm. Öffentliche Kunstsammlungen, Basel, Kunstmuseum.

rendez-vous des peintres setting—a reading that would fit with a eucharistic interpretation of the final painting.

Another still life done at more or less the same time in a similar viridian tonality and sardonically reverential spirit is Picasso's handsome homage to Cézanne in the form of the artist's famous Kronstadt hat (a flat-topped derby with a curly brim). A figure wearing just such a hat appears in one of the *Carnaval au bistro* sketches. Picasso pulls off much the same trick in this painting: the substitution of an evocative object for a figure. The Kronstadt is displayed as reverentially as if it were a sacred relic on an altar; or, given its emblematic shape, a votive lingam with offerings of fruit set out in front of it.

A year later, Picasso once again incorporates a Kronstadt hat into a painting, this time of a man smoking a pipe. "It was painted in the studio without a model," the artist said. "Afterwards, with Braque we said that it was a portrait of him. He wore a hat a bit like that."[63] He also smoked the same kind of clay pipe. Braque, who fancied himself as a dandy, indignantly denied that he was the model for this painting. One of Picasso's studio jokes, he said. The only reference to him was the antiquated hat that he wore out of respect for Cézanne.[64] Despite Braque's insistence on this point, no other candidate comes to mind. And, as Baldassari has pointed out, the painting bears enough of a resemblance to a photograph that the artist took of Braque around this time for it to be accepted as a reference to him—not quite the same thing as a portrait.[65] The Kronstadt will reappear in one of Picasso's more enigmatic and private allegories: *The Reading of the Letter*, which has the added significance of dating from around the artist's fortieth birthday (October, 1921) and of having remained hidden in his lifetime. This "*mezzo del camin*" painting shows two young men seated close together reading a letter. On the floor beside them is the emblematic hat, which had come to stand for Braque and Cézanne, and a book, which conceivably stands for Apollinaire.[66] I believe the Kronstadt is an encoded reference—a rueful farewell—to the comradeship of the old *bande à Picasso* and their reverence for Cézanne. Picasso evidently had second thoughts about making his farewell public.

The artist's attempts to add an extra dimension of meaning to his work may have been a response to all the speculative talk about the fourth dimension that he complained of having to put up with at the Bateau Lavoir as well as at the Steins' Saturday-evening soirées. Discussions were apt to be instigated by Maurice Princet, the mathematician who had recently lost his wife to Derain. But it was Apollinaire—briefly one of Princet's more ardent converts—who became the principal spokesman for the fourth dimension. Indeed he became so obsessed with it that he subsequently (late 1910) translated Max Weber's article in *Camera Work*, "The Fourth Dimension from a Plastic Point of View," and also appropriated a number of Weber's ideas for a lecture he gave in 1911 at Bernheim-Jeune's.[67]

Picasso and Braque were prepared to take Princet's financial advice, but they were not going to stand for his theorizing, or for Apollinaire's rendition of it. The two of them would always be adamant that neither the fourth dimension nor any other mathematical theory had played any role in the development of cubism—*their* cubism, that is. They would pour scorn on the Salon cubists, who were forever invoking the fourth

Picasso. *Portrait of Braque*, 1909–10. Oil on canvas, 61×50 cm. Heinz Berggruen (on loan to the National Gallery, London).

Picasso. *The Reading of the Letter*, 1921. Oil on canvas, 184×105 cm. Musée Picasso.

dimension: "Beyond the three dimensions of Euclid we have added another, the fourth dimension, which is to say the figuration of space, the measure of the infinite" is how Gleizes would put it.[68] However, for all that Picasso and Braque resisted any attempt to geometrize cubism, they were not necessarily opposed to a concept of the fourth dimension (as long as the dread term itself was not mentioned) which would be spiritual rather than scientific, metaphysical rather than Euclidean. Indeed, having suppressed, insofar as they could, the third dimension in their work—out of respect for the two-dimensional nature of the picture plane—they may have felt obliged to compensate in some other-dimensional way. That persuasive popularizer of the fourth dimension Gaston de Pawlowski, a friend of Apollinaire's, proposed *his* definition of the fourth dimension: "When one reaches the country of the fourth dimension . . . one is freed forever from the notions of space and time. . . . One finds oneself blended with the entire universe."[69] This sounds not unlike what Braque came to define as "*poésie*." "What do I mean by *poésie*? For me it is a matter of harmony, of rapports, of rhythm and—most important for my own work—of 'metamorphosis.'"[70]

Below: Picasso. *Still Life with Hat*, 1909. Oil on canvas, 60×73cm. Peter Henle, Mühlheim an der Ruhr.

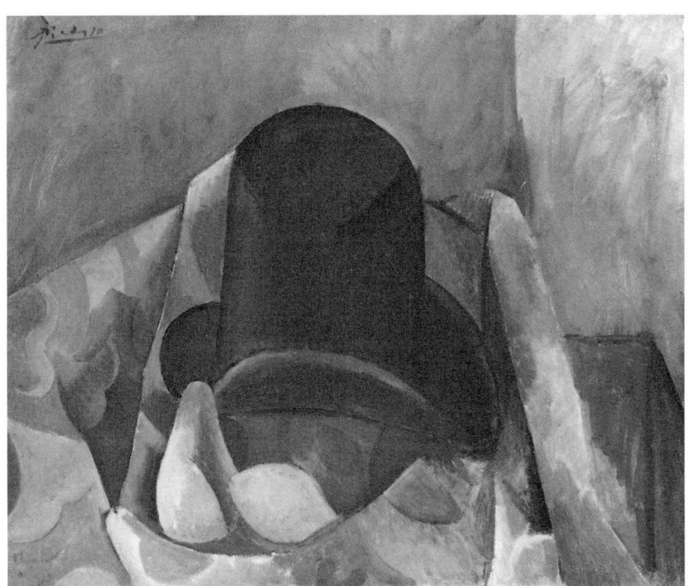

8

The Second Visit to Horta

Postcard of Calle del Marqués del Duero sent by Fernande and Picasso from Barcelona, May, 1909, to Alice Toklas. Beinecke Rare Book and Manuscript Library, Yale University.

Opposite: Picasso. *Reservoir at Horta de Ebro*, summer, 1909. Oil on canvas, 60×50 cm. David Rockefeller Collection.

IF PICASSO DECIDED TO SPEND THE SUMMER OF 1909 in Catalonia, it was partly at his family's behest. After a ten-year engagement, his sister, Lola, was finally marrying the half-Catalan, half-Andalusian neurologist Dr. Juan Vilató Gómez. The marriage was to take place in August in Málaga. A family reunion in the birthplace he disliked was not to Picasso's taste. Still, the parents deceived themselves that, once in Spain, he could be persuaded to attend. On his side, the artist wanted only to shut himself away in some remote fastness, anywhere but Andalusia, to work intensively, as he had done three summers before. After his fainthearted flight from typhus, it would have been embarrassing to return to Gósol. Fontdevila, the old smuggler, with whom he had formed such a primal relationship, was still alive—he would not die until the following year—but it would have been painful and probably pointless to rake over those old embers. An obvious alternative was Pallarès's village, Horta de Ebro, up in the *alta terra* on the border of Aragon: the other hallowed place of his youth. Horta was where Picasso claimed to have learned everything he knew, when he had first gone there in 1898.

When Picasso and Fernande arrived at the station in Barcelona on May 11, fifteen old friends—"a veritable deputation"[1]—were on hand to greet their hero. Fernande felt as mortified as she had the first time she was exposed to a Catalan welcome: she wanted to go straight back to Paris. And over the next two weeks she wrote incessantly to Gertrude Stein, who was in Rome with Leo, and to Alice Toklas, who had stayed behind in Paris with Harriet Levy, complaining about "this dreadful city": the weather (hot and wet), the attentions of the crowd ("I can't take a step outside without causing a stir"),[2] the ugliness of Barcelona (especially at night; "it's only tolerable when the sun is out"); the lack of elegance, which made it "hellishly provincial," and so on.[3] And yet she lived in hopes of the two women joining them. To the end of this plaintive letter Picasso sardonically added: *"Bonjour mes chers amis,* Spain awaits you."[4]

Had a good friend like Germaine Pichot been around, Fernande might have felt different. But apart from Casanovas, the *noucentista* sculptor, there was nobody she could count on. The lack of female allies put her at a disadvantage in Picasso's all-male world. To make matters worse, the kidney pains that she had suffered from back in Paris suddenly flared up and she started hemorrhaging. There could be no question of embarking on the arduous journey to Horta (the last twenty-five miles had to be

Picasso. *Portrait of Pallarès*, May, 1909. Oil on canvas, 67.9×49.5cm. Detroit Institute of Arts: Gift of Mr. and Mrs. Henry Ford II.

Opposite: Four drawings by Picasso of *View of Barcelona Courtyard*, May, 1909. Pen and black ink on sketchbook pages, each 17×13cm. Musée Picasso (top left and right, bottom left); Private collection (bottom right).

View of Tortosa on a postcard sent by Picasso from Horta, July 5, 1909, to Déodat de Séverac. Private collection.

negotiated on muleback) until she was better. A doctor friend (presumably Reventós) told her to stay in bed—much to Picasso's irritation. He had no patience with women's troubles, least of all now that Pallarès's brother-in-law, Onofre Godès, had found rooms for them in his cherished village. Instead of recharging his energies in the country, the artist was confined for another two or three weeks to a room in a hotel round the corner from the parental apartment. Meanwhile, his family was being impossible. They no longer perceived Fernande as a suitable fiancée but as an unsuitable mistress and refused to receive her. This, added to paternal disapproval of his work, made Picasso averse to seeing much of his parents.

Picasso had an obligation to fulfill in Barcelona: a formal portrait of Manuel Pallarès, the old friend who had introduced him to Horta. Evidently, Pallarès failed to engage Picasso's interest. The image he contrived for him is a Cézannesque compromise: a conventional likeness of a dim-looking man enlivened with halfhearted cubistic faceting. With little else to go on, Picasso has made the most of his sitter's facial hair: two cigar-shaped flanges of mustache that give this art-school teacher a dash of panache. Besides working on this portrait, which he painted in Pallarès's studio on carrer de Pelayo, Picasso spent time with Vidal Ventosa's Guayaba group, who now met in the Lyon d'Or on the Rambles, a celebrated literary and artistic café.[5] Although he now found his Catalan cronies irredeemably provincial, Picasso enjoyed being reunited with them, especially Angel de Soto, with whom he used to go whoring in the Barri Xino. Fernande's indisposition may well have encouraged him to resume this practice. The new owners of *Arte Joven* solicited Picasso's help in resuscitating the magazine, which he and Soler had edited eight years earlier in Madrid. O'Brian claims that this kept him "exceptionally busy."[6] In fact, all Picasso did was grant them the right to use his old letterhead.[7]

Picasso's most significant achievement in Barcelona was a sequence of small pen-and-ink drawings: views from his hotel window of a courtyard with palm trees and an arcaded building in the background. Studied in succession—from relatively figurative to relatively abstract (not necessarily the order in which they were done)—these drawings turn out to be as much of an advance in cubist notation as anything done over the next year.[8] Picasso confirmed this to Daix: "Everything stemmed . . . from them. I understood how far I would be able to go."[9] The more evolved of the series reveal Picasso taking Cézannesque *passage* a stage further and beginning to "shatter the enclosed form"—a development that Kahnweiler ascribes to 1910.[10] What is more, he managed this at a period of intense creative frustration, while he was cooped up with his sick mistress in a stifling hotel bedroom.

*   *   *

By June 5 or 6, Fernande felt strong enough to leave for the mountains. Not to overtire her, they stopped to rest at an inn in Tortosa, before going on the following day. Picasso was overjoyed at being back in the highlands where he had come of age as a painter. "The countryside is splendid," he wrote the Steins.[11] He said it reminded him of the "Overland," the railroad across the prairie that he knew from "westerns" (two years later,

the Wild West would inspire a cubist head of Buffalo Bill; p. 319). Horta rekindled the boyish spirit of adventure that had enlivened his previous visit. Picasso had brought Jarry's revolver with him and brandished it like a cowboy. To show what a good shot he was, he borrowed a gun, went off to the mountains, as he had done in 1898, and came back with a hare. At first they rented rooms from Tobies Membrado;[12] Picasso was obliged to work in a shed. After a few days they moved to Horta's one and only inn, the Posada Antonio Altès. The baker (Joaquim Antonio Vives) loaned Picasso a room he could use as a studio.

Plaça de la Missa, Horta de Ebro, 1909. Centre Picasso d'Horta. The town hall, where the jail was located, is seen behind the cross, with the Posada Antonio Altès just to the right.

The villagers were amazed by the visitors' smart clothes, specifically Picasso's velvet trousers and Fernande's hats. Never having seen a veil before, they assumed it to be a facial mosquito net. They were no less astounded by their first sight of a thousand-peseta note and Picasso's camera; they were also shocked to discover that Fernande was not married to Picasso. By dint of charm and looks, she would win most of the villagers over—not, however, the puritanical Pallarèses. They may once have treated Picasso like a son; they were not going to treat his mistress as anything but a Jezebel. If Manuel Pallarès had been in Horta to counter his family's prejudices, Fernande might have had an easier time, but he was back in Barcelona, assisting Picasso's father at La Llotja, the art school where they both taught. Fortunately, don Pepito Terrats, the mayor—"a regular tyrant who ruins anyone who comes up against him"[13]—fell under Fernande's spell and was less censorious: she and Picasso used to spend evenings playing dominoes and drinking "disgusting coffee" with his daughter.[14] The chief of the *guardia civil* was likewise friendly and provided them with an escort. As Fernande wrote proudly to Alice Toklas, "Can you imagine us travelling around with a posse of five handsome gendarmes in black uniforms with red, white and yellow insignia? . . . One of them looks exactly like Apollinaire."[15] Fernande's many conquests ("I'm more of a success here than in Paris," she boasted)[16] scandalized the old women of the village. One night, militant prudes threw stones at the windows of her adulterous bedroom. Picasso scared them off with shots from Jarry's revolver.

Fernande's long, descriptive letters to Alice Toklas about life in Horta were written with publication in mind. "Go ahead and translate them," she told Alice in July, "and get them published in America. I'll try and write better."[17] For all her sloppy orthography, Fernande is an amused and amusing observer—at pains to see things through Picasso's eyes. She has much fun with the awful wives: the baker's wife, who has a murky past; "*la segnora* [sic] *medecine*," who talks French but is such a bore that Fernande avoids her, hence very distant greetings on the evening promenade; the schoolmaster's tiresome spouse who does not give her the time of day; the nice schoolmistress who does; the German "Arturo Ullrich," who had left Leipzig to avoid military service and ended up as the village chemist. Most of all she loves the children—one a seven-year-old deaf-mute—who bring her flowers and perform "little services."

Fernande's most touching vignette concerns the local "*tonto*" (the village idiot): a man in his early twenties who, according to chauvinistic legend, had been fed poisonous herbs by nasty French people after straying across the border—hence his lunatic state. At first this large, vigorous man had terrified Fernande by barging into her room and making bizarre

Fernande and a girl of Horta de Ebro, summer, 1909. Photograph by Picasso. Archives Picasso.

noises, but when she realized that he was trying to speak French to her, she took pity on him. Since she could not understand his "French," he assumed that she, too, was a "*tonta*." He became so devoted that when she and Picasso left for the day on a picnic, he went even madder. Fernande was horrified to discover that the *tonto* was shut up at night in the local jail (located next door to the inn) because his yells and songs kept the village awake; horrified, too, that nobody gave him any water for fear of his tantrums and habit of smashing glasses. To her dismay, nothing was done about him.[18]

Since no entertainment was to be found at Horta, Picasso arranged for the pianola in the local bar to be mended, so that they could have something to dance to. He promised Alice that he would play "heroic pieces" for her and Gertrude when they arrived. Fernande wrote that on Pablo's feast day (Saint Peter and Saint Paul) she proposed to dance for him to the pianola. "It's the only present I can give him here, and it will be all the more munificent . . . as I have never yet celebrated his saint's day."[19] She goes on to describe the celebrations on that most pagan of festivals, Saint John's, or Midsummer, Day, when bonfires were lit all over the village, as they were in so many other parts of Europe, to rekindle the waning sun. Children jumped over the blazing straw and processed through the streets with torches. On the plaza peasants danced the *jota*: "an Aragonese dance which would have been rather monotonous if everyone had not been pretty drunk."[20] A young man wanted to teach Fernande the *jota*; when she refused, he told Picasso that he would rather dance with her than find two duros—several weeks' pay. Picasso was helping the local schoolmaster translate *Les Pensées de Napoléon I* from the French, Fernande adds; and please could Alice send her embroidery silks for a corsage she was making; also translations of books by Dickens (*Barnaby Rudge, Martin Chuzzlewit, Edwin Drood*) and Thackeray's *Vanity Fair*? She needed books to read in bed, when suffering from a kidney attack.

Fernande's letters to Gertrude tell a very different story, one that was certainly not written for publication. When she addresses the woman she regarded as her mentor, her humor gives way to self-pity. Fernande's tale of woe would evoke more sympathy if she were less sorry for herself. Horta is lovely, she says, the people look after her well, but "life is sad." Her kidney disease had been greatly aggravated by the journey to Spain. If she had stayed in Paris she would have had better care. In godforsaken Horta all she could do was eat minimally and rest. Sitting down was so painful that she mostly lay on her bed, bored to tears, unable even to sew.

> Now and then I have attacks of unbearable pain in my kidneys and my side; it's as if I am going to die of cold. This has happened only twice, but it has left me very weak and exhausted. A lot of blood in my urine, sometimes nothing but blood. Pablo is terribly irritated by this. . . . I hope to see you here, so you will be able to judge for yourself. . . . We will go and meet you in Barcelona; if I am still sick Pablo will go alone.
>
> Pablo is grumpy [Fernande's long letter continues] and I get nothing in the way of moral or physical consolation from him. When my pain strikes, he goes very pale—that's all—and gets as sick as I am. What's to be done? . . . You are the only person I can tell how depressed I am, ready to lose all hope. The last thing in the world I want is for Pablo to know just how

Picasso. *Portrait of Fernande*, summer, 1909. Oil on canvas, 60.5×52cm. Sprengel Museum, Hannover.

> morally shattered I am. You see, I have never really been ill, and for the two months I have been in Spain, I have not had a single day's respite.
>
> Already in Paris, I felt awful but I was strong enough to fight back. Here I'm too lonely. If this lasts another month, I assure you it'll be the end, I'll die. Pablo is no help; he doesn't want to know anything. He's too self-centered to understand that it is I who now need him; that he is responsible for my condition, that it's largely he who reduced me to this state last winter. He has completely demoralized me; all this is nerves, I know, but I don't have any nerves left, I can't go on. What's to be done? If I'm sad he gets furious. And then I've something else to tell you; it's far from certain, but I may be pregnant. . . . Only eight days have gone by since my first inkling. But what will I do, pregnant and sick as I am?
>
> Forgive me for telling you all this. . . . I didn't mean to but got carried away. Although I believe he loves me, I feel so wretched, so lonely. Pablo would let me die without noticing my condition. Only when I am suffering does he stop for a moment to bother about me. . . . You are going to say that I carry on too much about myself, but you are the only person in whom I can confide. It's a bit tragic, perhaps ridiculous, but it calms me down.[21]

Poor Fernande. To gauge the extent of her fall from favor, we need only compare the radiant image that Picasso had contrived for this beautiful girl at Gósol in 1906 with the anguished image he contrived for her at Horta. Despite the smart Parisian bonnet and scalloped bodice in what is probably the first of the Horta portraits, she already looks weary and resentful. Sickness in women was apt to evoke Picasso's irritation; he would go on to visualize her as what he later called "a suffering machine."[22] This was not the first or the last time that "women's troubles" would generate the exasperation, tenderness and guilt that fired Picasso's most powerful and disturbing portraits. Dora Maar and his second wife, Jacqueline, would be subjected to far more anguish than Fernande, but they would never have made an issue of it. As for Fernande's pregnancy, this turned out to be mere fancy, a desperate plea for sympathy.

* * *

Picasso. *The Oil Mill*, summer, 1909. Oil on canvas, 38×46cm. Private collection.

For his part, Picasso was overjoyed at being back in Horta. As soon as he discovered how to harness Fernande's suffering to his vision, his work would go exceedingly well. He also wanted to try his hand at landscape; specifically to go one better than the views of L'Estaque that Braque had painted the year before. On June 24 he had already written the Steins that he had "begun two landscapes and two figures always the same thing."[23] The landscapes take off from the Carrières-Saint-Denis view he had done two or three months earlier. Just as he had repositioned the bridge in that painting, Picasso transplants the palm trees from the courtyard of his Barcelona hotel to Horta,[24] where they would never have grown, and moves one of the chimneys for burning olive waste from the fields into the village.[25] This grafting of disparate scenic elements onto one another is even more striking in the view of the oil mill—a painting that was conceived at Horta but (according to Kahnweiler's records) finished in Paris. This time Picasso anomalously introduces a river complete with sailboat into this mountain landscape. The nearest thing to a river at Horta was the mountain torrent, which would have claimed his life on his previous visit had Pallarès not been there to rescue him. It is typical of Picasso's

Above: Picasso. *Houses on the Hill, Horta de Ebro*, summer, 1909. Oil on canvas, 65×81 cm. The Museum of Modern Art, New York: Nelson A. Rockefeller Bequest.

Right: Picasso. *Factory at Horta de Ebro*, summer, 1909. Oil on canvas, 53×60 cm. State Hermitage Museum, St. Petersburg.

Above: View of Horta de Ebro, summer, 1909. Photograph by Picasso. Archives Picasso.

Right: Man with guitar at Horta de Ebro, summer, 1909. Photograph by Picasso. Archives Picasso.

Above: Roofs at Horta de Ebro, summer, 1909. Photograph by Picasso. Archives Picasso.

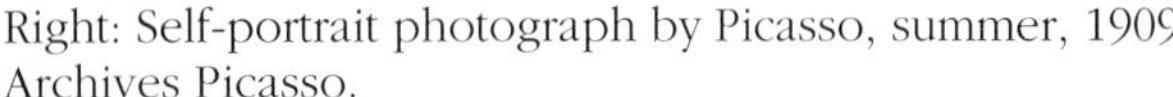

Right: Self-portrait photograph by Picasso, summer, 1909. Archives Picasso.

Picasso. *The Athlete*, summer, 1909. Oil on canvas, 93×72cm. Museu de Arte de São Paulo Assis Chateaubriand.

metamorphic humor to transform this torrent into a navigable river, like the Mattarama or the Ebro, which the traveler passes on his way up to Horta.

The local people described by Fernande turn up in Picasso's Horta photographs. "Although he hardly knows how to use a camera," Fernande wrote Alice, "Pablo could earn a lot of money taking photographs of the villagers."[26] The twenty-four sepia prints which have survived among the artist's papers disprove Fernande's assertion. The artist knew instinctively how to use a camera as an adjunct to his work. Since the photographs are not annotated, there is no knowing who the subjects are, except for the uniformed escort of *guardia civil*, in which Fernande took so much pride.[27] The well-built young man with a very trim haircut who is holding a guitar in one photograph corresponds to the bare-chested man with folded arms who figures in the Horta paintings.[28] Picasso also took photographs of himself wearing revealingly tight trousers and evidently in the midst of a narcissistic reverie.

Besides photographing the local inhabitants, Picasso focused his camera no less effectively on the local scene. Far from taking holiday snapshots, the artist used the camera to help him calculate the adjustments—tonal contrasts, formal accents, perspectival inversions—that had to be made in order to adapt the natural scene to his cubist vision.[29] Picasso had another, more mundane reason for taking photographs. He needed them to send to Gertrude Stein. He wanted to whet her appetite for the arid beauty of Horta, in the hope that she and Alice would visit him. Above all, he wanted to involve Gertrude and the increasingly difficult Leo in the process as well as the progress of cubism so that they would continue to collect.

Picasso's strategy worked. Gertrude and Leo would acquire two of the Horta landscapes—the so-called *Reservoir* view and the *Houses on the Hill*. Forever after, Gertrude would behave as if ownership of these key works entitled her to act as the high priestess of cubism. In her account of these early years, she contrives to forget about Braque, whose work she and her brother had never had the perspicacity to collect. She maintains that Picasso's Horta landscapes were not only "really the beginning of cubism" but also the proof "that cubism is a purely spanish conception and only spaniards can be cubists and that the only real cubism is that of Picasso and Juan Gris. Picasso created it and Juan Gris permeated it with his clarity and his exaltation. To understand this one has only to read the life and death of Juan Gris by Gertrude Stein."[30] By leaving Braque's partnership in cubism out of account, this preposterous claim disqualifies Gertrude as both witness and judge.

When the French translation of *The Autobiography of Alice B. Toklas* came out, in 1934, Braque was appalled by the author's malice and inaccuracy. Did his 1908 landscapes not have more right than Picasso's 1909 ones to be seen as "the real beginning of cubism"? Matisse, Salmon and Tristan Tzara also felt slighted by Gertrude, and they joined in a riposte. This took the form of a special supplement, entitled "Testimony against Gertrude Stein," to the February, 1935, issue of *Transition*, Eugene and Maria Jolas's avant-garde magazine. Jolas took issue with what he termed "the hollow tinsel bohemianism and egocentric deformations" of Stein's memoirs. Braque was dignified but forceful: "Miss Stein understood nothing of what went on around her. . . . It is obvious that she never knew French very well and that was always a barrier. But she has entirely misunderstood Cubism which she sees simply in terms of personalities."[31]

Besides making false claims for the priority of her Horta landscapes over Braque's L'Estaques, Gertrude liked to brandish the photographs that Picasso had sent her and declare, no less misleadingly, that the paintings were a "photographic copy of nature":

> When [the Horta views] were first put up on the wall naturally everybody objected. . . . When people said that the few cubes in the landscapes looked like nothing but cubes, Gertrude Stein would laugh and say, if you had objected to these landscapes as being too realistic there would be some point in your objection. And she would show them the photographs and really the pictures as she rightly said might be declared to be too photographic a copy of nature.[32]

This was to misunderstand Picasso's approach to cubism as well as to photography. The camera showed him how to convey a more heightened experience of nature by adjusting the look of it to his cubist vision rather than merely imitating it. As Picasso said, "[Art] is a lie that helps us understand the truth."[33]

Picasso. *Mountain of Santa Barbara*, summer, 1909. Oil on canvas, 54×65cm. The Denver Art Museum: The Charles Francis Hendrie Memorial Collection.

* * *

On his previous trip to Horta, Picasso had painted the Santa Barbara mountain, which rears up behind the village. He had also climbed to the top and done a drawing of the hermitage of Sant Antoni del Tossal, which crowns it—a view which Pallarès had also painted and recently given him in exchange for the portrait he had done. Picasso would hang the Pallarès in his living room at Mougins until his death. Given Santa Barbara's resemblance to the Montagne Sainte-Victoire, Picasso set about painting it in the faceted, slightly unfocused manner of Cézanne's later landscapes. Although he had no difficulty appropriating Cézanne's grasp of form, he had a problem getting his landscapes to refract light the way Cézanne's do—Spanish painters traditionally use color to heighten emotion rather than engender light. The twin gray peaks of Picasso's *Santa Barbara* fade into the faceted sky, just as the hills of L'Estaque do in Braque's breakthrough views of 1908, but with little of Braque's wonderful luminosity. But then we should remember that the natural scene, especially in its nobler, more picturesque manifestations, bored Picasso. He preferred man's handiwork to nature's and soon switched from the Cézanne-like mountain to the Cézanne-like village. His Horta ends up looking much like the Master of Aix's Gardanne.

Picasso. *Head of Woman with Mountain*, summer, 1909. Oil on canvas, 65×54.5cm. Städelsches Kunstinstitut, Frankfurt am Main.

Picasso did not entirely abandon nature; rather he harnessed it to portraiture and proceeded to depict his suffering mistress in terms of the crags of Santa Barbara by covering her in a cascade of draperies that mimic the crevasses of the mountains.[34] (This tendency to see a mountain in terms of a woman—a matter of anthropomorphism rather than cubism—was not limited to Horta. Fifty years later, when Picasso purchased the Château de Vauvenargues, including a sizable stretch of the Montagne Sainte-Victoire, he felt with some justice that Cézanne's favorite motif belonged to him; and he proceeded to "Picassify" the mountain by painting it as a recumbent Jacqueline with her right hand forming the abrupt westernmost face.) The romantic paintings in which the martyred Fernande is envisioned as the mountain of the martyred Barbara (the patron saint, as he surely knew, of *pompiers*) are a contrast to Picasso's analytical views of the village, except in one respect: the houses are virtually all as windowless and doorless as a tomb. There is not a trace of human life. By seeing Horta as a maze of blind walls, Picasso has turned this bustling agricultural village into a necropolis.

As the series of Santa Barbara–Fernandes progresses, Picasso switches backwards and forwards between long shots and close-ups. He bifurcates and crenellates Fernande's forehead like the spurs of the peak. And just as he merges the faceted head with the faceted mountain, he merges the faceted mountain with the faceted sky. As a result, sky, mountain, drapery, woman, cohere into a single organism—something that Picasso had tentatively tried three summers before at Gósol in the *Blind Flower Seller*. Then as now El Greco played a decisive role: in quasi-sacred references, in melancholy mannerist poses as well as the unifying faceting. Picasso mercilessly equates his mistress not just with Saint Barbara but with outcasts like El Greco's lachrymose Magdalens expiating their sins in the wilderness, as they cast tormented eyes up to heaven for absolution. On his return to Paris, Picasso would transform the *Woman with a Book in a Landscape* (p. 119) into a parody of one of these Magdalens. Fernande, who had in turn been deified, eroticized and bestialized—and in the process whittled down, blown up, taken apart and reconstituted—is not just faceted but flayed. Vesalius has re-entered the picture. With his help Picasso penetrates beneath the skin, not because of any special interest in anatomical technicalities but because he wants to reconcile not just back and front but inside and outside.

Besides portraying a suffering Fernande, these *écorché* paintings have been said to portray a suffering Spain. Here we should tread carefully. To judge by Picasso's, not to speak of Fernande's, letters, the artist manifested shamefully little concern about the troubles that were tearing Catalonia apart this summer—troubles that came to be known as *Setmana Tràgica* (Tragic Week). A wishful-thinking writer has recently claimed that "Picasso's concern with the workers' uprising [is] emphatically verbalized in his letters to Stein."[35] Would that he had "verbalized" something of the sort. What is surprising about the letters I have been able to see is that they show no solicitude for the cause or the victims, let alone for endangered family or friends or the city he loved. Picasso's main worry was the fate of the negatives that he had sent to be processed in Barcelona. These were indeed important. Picasso had propped up some of the Fernande paintings side by side in his studio and photographed them in such a way that he could superimpose one exposure onto another with a view to obtaining a stereoscopic effect.[36] The fate of these photographs, which he counted on to help him with his cubist procedures, was the only trouble of any real concern to him. Edifying though it might be to imagine the artist's heart bleeding for the victims of Madrid's anti-Catalan repression, there are no grounds for doing so. Twenty years would go by before Picasso became politicized enough to envisage public tragedy in terms of private trauma.

In one of the more anguished of the Horta Fernandes, Picasso Hispagnolizes Fernande by making the zigzag edges of her mantilla rhyme

Picasso. *Nude under a Pine Tree*, January 20, 1959. Oil on canvas, 182.9×244 cm. Art Institute of Chicago: Grant J. Pick Collection.

Picasso. *Female Nude*, summer, 1909. Oil on canvas, 92.5×63 cm. Whereabouts unknown.

Double-image photograph by Picasso of paintings in his Horta studio, summer, 1909. Archives Picasso (private collection). The paintings clearly visible are *Nude in an Armchair* (private collection) and *Woman with Pears* (p. 314).

Paintings in the studio at Horta de Ebro, summer, 1909. Photograph by Picasso. Archives Picasso (private collection). The three paintings are *Head and Shoulders of a Woman (Fernande)* (Art Institute of Chicago), *Female Nude* (private collection, Chicago) and *Head of a Woman* (National Museum, Belgrade).

with the zigzag formation of the mountain; and he has painted her radiant almond eyes as deep-set and lusterless—diamonds in shape only. He has constructed her face out of the same building-block elements—for instance, the wedge that stands for a nose as well as a roof—that we find in the village views. In his *Still Life with Bottle of Anis del Mono* Picasso blurs the difference between still life and figure painting by what Daix calls "*chosification*"—metamorphosis into a thing.[37] He visualizes Fernande as a conglomeration of objects. He transforms her head into the folds of a napkin; her faceted torso into a *botijo* (a jug shaped like a rooster); and the landscape background into a green curtain. For good measure he includes the most familiar faceted object to be found in Spain, a bottle of Anis del Mono; this makes a pictorial pun on the rest of this faceted composition.[38]

Picasso. *Fernande in a Mantilla*, summer, 1909. Oil on canvas, 39×30cm. Private collection. Photograph published in *Camera Work*, December, 1910.

In the end, none of Picasso's friends arrived at Horta, except Manuel Pallarès, who materialized a day or two before the artist left. The companion with whom Picasso had shared a cave in the Ports del Maestrat, where they had daubed the rocks with paint and lived like naked savages, had become a terrible bore.[39] However, this did not bother the artist. On the contrary, he would spend hours at a time sharing childhood memories and rituals with his old friend. "I'll never forget how you saved my life," Picasso would announce every time he and Pallarès, who both lived to be over ninety, got together.[40] Whereupon those who were present would know they were in for an interminable conversation in Catalan, which Picasso prided himself on speaking very badly—"like a *guardia civil*," he told Otero.[41] Fond as he was of Pallarès, Picasso would lodge him and his depressing son in a hotel rather than have them to stay in his villa. He did not want the old man dying on him—very bad luck. Death could be catching.

The high point of the summer was to have been a trip to Madrid and Toledo so that Picasso could refresh his memory of El Greco. "For a long time I've wanted to see Greco again," he wrote the Steins sometime in July.[42] He even convinced the local doctor to persuade Fernande to accompany him. But in the end they never went: Barcelona and most of Catalonia had suddenly burst into revolutionary flame. The trouble had started earlier in the year in Morocco, when mobs of unemployed laborers had attacked the Spanish employees of the supposedly Jesuit-owned mining companies in the mountains of the Rif. After troops sent to quell the uprising were decimated in an ambush (July 9), the Spanish government called up ninety thousand reservists—primarily from Barcelona. This enabled the vindictive authorities to avenge themselves on young Catalans, most of whom lacked the means to buy themselves out of the military, for being separatists, pacifists, socialists or anarchists (often all four). On July 11, the Ministry of War started shipping reservists out to Morocco, whereupon local leaders called a general strike. The revolt in Barcelona that ensued was a matter of spontaneous combustion. "No one started it! No one led it!" a leading anarchist, Anselmo Lorenzo, wrote in a letter on July 21. "Neither liberals nor Catalan separatists, nor republicans nor socialists nor anarchists. . . . A week of intoxication, of holy rage, seeing

Picasso. *Still Life with Bottle of Anis del Mono*, summer, 1909. Oil on canvas, 81.6×65.4cm. The Museum of Modern Art, New York: Mrs. Simon Guggenheim Fund.

Soldiers guarding the burned out convent of Escolapios in Barcelona during *Setmana Tràgica*, July, 1909. Institut Municipal d'Història, Barcelona.

that the fury of the masses was justified by a hundred centuries of misery, oppression and endurance."[43]

The mob's principal target was that archaic body the Church. Working-class women launched attacks on the convents—there were 348 of them in Barcelona—because of the repressive power the nuns exercised over their lives. Their worst suspicions were confirmed when they broke into the Santa Magdalena convent, just back of Els Quatre Gats, and found torture chambers—"martyrdom rooms"—in the basement. In the crypt of the Hieronymite Convent their finds were even more horrifying: the mummified bodies of twenty-five to thirty nuns with their hands and feet tied and scourges at their side. To unmask the secretive clergy, the mob dragged the corpses round the city and left one of the mummies propped up outside a church, where the father of Picasso's great friend Vidal Ventosa was sacristan. They stuck a cigarette in the mummy's mouth, as if she were a prostitute. A young man covered in coal dust grabbed another of the mummies and danced it down the Rambles, ending up in front of the house of the most hated man in the city, the hugely rich Marquis of Comillas.[44] In all, some seventy ecclesiastical buildings were burned and sacked, including the convent that had commissioned the fourteen-year-old Picasso to paint two early altarpieces, which we know only from sketches.[45] Many more churches were badly damaged. The reprisals were even more savage than they had been after the previous "troubles," in 1904. Some two thousand men were arrested and most of them put on trial; another two thousand fled to France. One hundred and seventy-five people were killed in street fights. Despite worldwide protests, five men, including the retarded coalman who had danced with the mummified nun, and the saintly anarchist Francisco Ferrer, who had played no part in the revolt, were court-martialed and shot on October 13. More violence ensued.

Picasso was not going to allow these brutal events to distract him from his work. "I haven't written to you before this," Picasso wrote the Steins towards the end of July, "because it appears that we in Spain have been in the throes of revolution. . . . Today the newspapers are beginning to arrive and they say that it is finished."[46] And in another letter a few days later he says, "We have had a big revolution in Spain. Now it's over. I feared that our stay in Spain was going to be curtailed."[47] Elsewhere Fernande says that "the events . . . had isolated us from the world for about ten days."[48] She goes on to speculate that her previous letters may have been held up by the authorities. So much for Picasso's revolutionary zeal.

The fact that the mob had blown up many of the railway bridges kept friends like Gertrude and Alice and the Pichots, who had promised to make an appearance, from visiting Horta. Likewise, Manolo and Frank Burty Haviland, who were spending the summer at Bourg-Madame on the French side of the frontier, had wanted to come and stay, but Fernande told Gertrude that "they didn't dare for fear of boring Pablo."[49] It was not, however, fear of Pablo that kept Manolo away but fear of alerting the authorities. He had fled Spain in 1901 to escape the draft. Now that young Catalans were being rounded up and sent to Morocco, it would have been madness to risk returning.

The *Setmana Tràgica* provided Picasso with an excellent excuse for not attending his sister's marriage in Málaga. He was fond enough of Lola but dreaded the prospect of seeing his provincial relatives. "Pablo's sister was married a few days ago," Fernande wrote the Steins around the beginning of August. It was celebrated in Málaga, so "Pablo had little trouble avoiding the duty of taking part in the ceremony."[50] Instead of going all the way to Andalusia, he arranged to visit Barcelona for two weeks at the end of August. Things would have calmed down by then; the witch-hunt that newspapers compared to the Inquisition would have run its course; and Picasso's parents would be back from Andalusia. No sooner had Fernande arrived at the Grand Hôtel de l'Orient in Barcelona than she fell ill again. "I am decidedly very sick," she wrote Gertrude Stein on September 7. "A friend here, who is a doctor, has advised Pablo to take me back to Paris as soon as possible. I am too exhausted to write any more."[51] But on she goes with details of nephritic crises and hemorrhages. Two days later, she wrote to Alice Toklas that they would leave Barcelona on Friday—by express and first class so that she would be more comfortable—and arrive in Paris at nine in the morning on Saturday, the 11th. That very afternoon, she promised, she would visit Gertrude. And then there would be specialists to see and the new apartment on the boulevard de Clichy to be readied and a proper maid to be found. Life would be very different.

Below: Man and dog at Horta de Ebro, summer, 1909. Photograph by Picasso. Archives Picasso (private collection).

9

Farewell to Bohemia

Picasso. *Seated Woman in Green*, winter, 1909–10. Oil on canvas, 100×81 cm. Stedelijk Van Abbe Museum, Eindhoven.

Opposite: Picasso. *Head of Fernande*, 1909. Bronze, ht: 40.5 cm. Photograph by Stieglitz published in *Camera Work*, December, 1910.

THE FIRST MAJOR PAINTING PICASSO EXECUTED in his new Montmartre studio —*Seated Woman in Green*—was a half-length nude of Fernande. Its sober color—dark green, gray and ocher—and the faceting of the face and upper body hark back to Horta, except that the sitter no longer looks anguished. The other great work that absorbed him was a very similar sculpture of Fernande's head; it, too, harks back to Horta. During his summers in mountain areas Picasso was always finding bits of wood and rock that lent themselves to sculptural transformation. In Gósol he had sent for chisels. In Horta he did not bother: he made drawings of Fernande that would serve as blueprints for what would be his most important cubist sculpture. As soon as he was back in Montmartre, he went to his sculptor friend Manolo's studio—not to Paco Durrio's, where he had done the ceramic of Fontdevila in 1906;[1] Durrio could not abide cubism—and modeled this head, which is as jagged as the heights of Santa Barbara, in clay. After casting it in plaster, Picasso sliced away at the facets with a blade to make them diamond sharp. The head bears out a claim he made some years later that there were enough specifications in cubist paintings for an exact three-dimensional equivalent to be made.[2]

Although Picasso had moved on from primitivism, Fernande's sculpted hair—a mass of protuberances like a cluster of tropical fruit—bears traces of tribal art, Fang masks in particular. (Picasso was always devising strange formulae for women's hair: chignons like bunches of bananas, breasts or buttocks.) This coiffure might also have a prehistorical derivation: the monstrous, steatopygic fertility symbol the *Venus of Lespugue*, which would also leave its pneumatic mark on Picasso's sculptures of Marie-Thérèse twenty years later.[3] Nor can we leave Vesalius out of account. The Flemish anatomist's *écorché* figures continued to inspire Picasso to flay Fernande: to strip off the epidermis and reveal the underlying musculature of the face; also to make plinths of the platysma, the muscles that extend from the shoulders and collarbone up to the head. Significantly, Fernande went under the knife shortly after this sculpture was finished. Picasso liked to think of himself as a prophet.

The dynamism Picasso gives to this faceted head would catch the eye of the futurist Boccioni when he visited Paris in the spring of 1912. He probably saw it at Vollard's and was so impressed that he temporarily abandoned painting for sculpture.[4] His first attempt to "surpass" Picasso's cubism was an ornately faceted, centrifugally twisted head of his mother,

Umberto Boccioni. *Head + House + Light*, 1912. Sculpture (destroyed).

entitled *Antigrazioso*. Cubism with knobs on, but nothing like as ornate and busy as the other heads (*Fusion of a Head and a Window* and *Head + House + Light*, both destroyed), in which he demonstrated his portentous theories of "physical transcendentalism." Boccioni's later sculpture works better. But for all their futurist *dinamismo*—cubism jazzed up with cinematic simultaneism, art nouveau biomorphism and tailfins reminiscent of 1950s automobiles—these pieces suffer from the same sense of static movement that we find in a Muybridge photograph of a runner. Boccioni's cubist-derived paintings are likewise done in by an incoherent windiness that passes for speed. Kahnweiler objected to his painters exhibiting alongside the futurists because they made too much noise.

Picasso respected the durability and versatility of bronze—how else could he cast or market his sculpture?—but it was too rich and grandiose for his taste. Later, he would often paint over it. He much preferred his original plasters—with their matte, neutral-colored planes like those in a cubist painting—to the expensive-looking bronzes that arrived from the foundry.[5] Two small sculptures done at the same time as the head of Fernande—an apple and a head—which Picasso kept for himself, were never cast.[6] The apple is a two-dimensional version of the fruit in many 1909–10 still lifes, their faceted roundness a contrast to the faceted squareness of the ubiquitous little casket. Once again, Picasso has taken a knife to the plaster apple and faceted it as if it were a prism. For all its smallness, it has an imposing presence: a monument to an apple, also apparently a portrait of one. (Picasso gave the apple he claimed to have worked from to the Czech collector Vincenc Kramář, who preserved the shriveled memento until he died.) The small, somewhat clumsy woman's head may have been a sketch for a larger work,[7] but I believe it also served as an experimental model, which Picasso could turn this way and that—as he must have done with the plaster apple—to see how faceted forms in his paintings would take the light and interact with other elements.

"It was pointless to go on with this kind of sculpture," Picasso said of his breakthrough head of Fernande.[8] One can see why. At Horta the artist had found a way of conveying a seemingly tangible experience of a subject in paint on canvas. Now that he had achieved this goal two-dimensionally, why go to the trouble of doing it three-dimensionally, especially since he lacked the requisite facilities and was obliged to work in friends' studios? However, this does not mean that Picasso ceased to conceive things sculpturally. Many a drawing done between 1909 and 1912 could as well be executed in clay or metal or wood as paint. At some point he tried to blur the distinction between painting and sculpture even further by incorporating a three-dimensional element—a plaster candelabra—into a painted still life. The experiment was apparently a failure,[9] and the resultant hybrid was either lost or destroyed. Three years would go by before Picasso returned to the problem of reconciling the flatness of the picture surface with sculptural relief. Papier collé would show him the way.

* * *

After a summer trip, Picasso liked to summon friends whose eyes he trusted to inspect and discuss the latest paintings. As soon as he arrived back from Horta, he sent out invitations to what he jokingly called a "*vernissage*"—jokingly because the traditional ritual of varnishing, which

Above: Picasso. *Head of Fernande*, 1909. Plaster, ht: 42cm. From the Envoy and Latner Family Collections.

Above left: Picasso. Study for *Head of Fernande*, 1909. Ink and watercolor on paper, 33.3×25.5cm. Art Institute of Chicago: The Alfred Stieglitz Collection.

Left: Picasso. *Apple*, 1909–10. Plaster, ht: 11.5cm. Musée Picasso.

initiated exhibitions in France, was anathema to Picasso and Braque. On no account were their paintings to be given a shine. Picasso felt so strongly about this that he threatened to confiscate two paintings that the Steins had varnished without his permission. He left their house "pale with pent-up rage" and refused to resume his visits until they promised never to repeat the offense.[10]

A *vernissage* would also enable friends to see Picasso's new apartment on the boulevard de Clichy. To placate Fernande, the lease had been put in her name. The Steins and other potential buyers were originally invited for the afternoon of Wednesday, September 15, but were put off until the following day, as the place was not ready. The real purpose of the *vernissage* was of course to sell as many paintings as possible to cover the costs of the move and Fernande's illness. The views of Horta were instant favorites: the Steins bought two of them, also one of the best Fernandes. Frank Haviland acquired the brick factory with palm trees, which was subsequently sold to Shchukin.[11] Vollard took most of the remaining paintings.

Studios at 11, boulevard de Clichy.

Kahnweiler, who had bought so much the year before, tried to strike a hard bargain and ended up with little of note. His stockbook entries for this period list a few gouaches and drawings, many of them dating from earlier periods. Later, Picasso would hold the dealer's lack of support against him—unfairly. Kahnweiler cannot have been happy about the Steins' advances to Picasso, which entitled them to a "*droit de première vue*" (first pick). He had to let the artists who had signed contracts with him have first call on his modest resources, especially at the end of summer, when they returned to Paris laden down with new work and in need of money. Why should he give special treatment to someone who refused to sign up with him? For his part, Picasso had counted on Kahnweiler to help him with Fernande's medical expenses, and felt let down. In future, when he was irritated with the dealer, he would use supposed derelictions like this as pretexts for reneging on agreements.

Thanks probably to Vollard, Picasso was able to provide Fernande with the best possible treatment. In January she had an operation.[12] It put an end to her kidney problems, but not her difficulties with Picasso. She continued to provoke more irritation than compassion. The move from the Bateau Lavoir was a mixed blessing. Although he would move five times over the next ten years, Picasso loathed uprooting himself. In later years he chose to remember his five years of bohemian squalor at the Bateau Lavoir as the most exhilarating period of his life. It was where he had made his first and probably greatest breakthrough, where he had fallen in love for the first time, where he had made his mark as the rebel leader of modern art. The move to the boulevard de Clichy meant an end to the free-and-easy camaraderie of his youth, a rite of passage most dedicated painters have to undergo. Fame now loomed—a prospect that threatened Picasso's peace of mind. And there was another tiresome development: his mistress, whom he had no intention of marrying, was not just signing herself "Fernande Picasso," she had assumed the role of a conventional young wife with a conventional household to run. Gertrude Stein describes a row between Picasso and Fernande at one of her Saturday soirées around this time. To provoke her lover, Fernande declared that there was more to be said for *apaches* than artists.

> Picasso said, yes apaches of course have their universities, artists do not. Fernande got angry and shook him and said, you think you are witty, but you are only stupid. He ruefully showed that she had shaken off a button and she very angry said, and you, your only claim to distinction is that you are a precocious child.[13]

Fernande and Picasso, 1910.

* * *

"These people must have hit the jackpot," one of the packers said to Maurice Raynal, who was helping Picasso and Fernande with their move.[14] And indeed there was a vast contrast between the Bateau Lavoir and the amenities of their new quarters: the top floor of a building, owned and lived in by Théophile Delcassé (the former foreign minister who had masterminded the Entente Cordiale). Picasso was torn between bourgeois pride—the new apartment was after all a measure of his success—and bohemian shame. In banishing want, success had opened the door to respectability. Picasso and Fernande blamed their *embourgeoisement* on each other. Both had a point. After the cruelty and rejection she had suffered at the hands of her foster mother, *la belle Fernande* yearned for security—marriage if possible. After the shabby gentility of his boyhood and the deprivations of his early days in Paris, Picasso wanted a lifestyle which would permit him to work in peace without material worries—"like a pauper," he used to say, "but with lots of money." For the rest of his life he would generate the same disorder, discomfort and dust (never dirt: Picasso was obsessively clean) that had appalled genteel visitors to the Bateau Lavoir. At the same time he would always count on the woman in his life for the simple domestic rituals and support that his hardworking mother had provided. Try as he might, Picasso could no more shake off the stigma of his bourgeois origins than the stigma of his Catholic faith. This ambivalence was not really a problem. His sense of irony enabled him to exploit these stigmas and give them a subversive twist. Hence a touch of mockery to the décor of the new apartment.

Picasso consigned the Bateau Lavoir furniture, such as it was, to the maid's room and replaced it with oddities from local junk shops. He was sufficiently amused by Fernande's famously trivial taste to cater to it. In the dining room, for instance, he hung a set of chromolithographs, which even Fernande condemned as more suited to a concierge's *loge*. One day, he returned to the apartment followed by "a man doubled up beneath the weight of a superb and immense Louis Philippe sofa and matching fauteuil upholstered in violet velvet with gold buttons," which figures in a number of cubist compositions.[15] *Passementerie* (tassels and fringe)—the kind one associates with draperies in period photographs—had a special appeal for Picasso; so did bits of hideous machine-made tapestry, not so much antique as old, which hung on the studio walls and inspired the beautiful patterned draperies in many a work of 1909–10. He would likewise use all manner of bric-à-brac—corny ornaments, fairground prizes, silly souvenirs—for compositions of utmost gravity. "If inexpensive things were costly," Picasso once said, "I'd soon find myself penniless, because they're the only ones I care for."[16]

Still-life photograph by Picasso, 1911. Archives Picasso.

Not all the furniture was a joke. Picasso was proud of the things his father sent him from Barcelona: an Italian cabinet inlaid with ivory, mother-of-pearl and shells, and part of a set of Hepplewhite chairs that

ECLIPSE
ECLIPSE

his grandfather had bought at the sale of an English wine merchant's effects in Málaga. These chairs would remain with the artist until he died. He also owned paintings by fellow artists and an ever-growing group of African and Oceanic sculpture. Besides providing Picasso and his friends with an endless source of inspiration, primitive art was the only "collectible," apart from one another's work, that interested them; it also engendered fierce competitiveness. Fernande describes how the new apartment filled up with masks and ceremonial figures, many of them hung about with "beads, necklaces, bracelets and amulets decorated with bits of glass, which would be pilfered by the artists' girlfriends for their adornment."[17]

As the apartment was on the top floor, it had a good view of the Sacré-Cœur, which would inspire a shimmering, silvery painting the following spring. The main advantage was a large, airy studio with a north light that

> no one could enter without permission, where nothing could be touched and where, as usual, the chaos . . . had to be treated with respect. . . . The maid soon came to understand Picasso's character and learned how not to anger or irritate him. The studio was never cleaned unless Picasso gave orders. . . . No sweeping was done, because he could not stand dust being disturbed. Dust in the air and sticking to his wet canvases made him wild with rage. . . . He used to shut himself into his new studio at two o'clock, earlier if he could, and work there until dusk. In the winter someone would go in to check the stove.[18]

Only his large, fat dog, the gentle Frika (purchased from Raynal), the three Siamese cats he had brought from the Bateau Lavoir and his recently acquired monkey, Monina, had the right to wander in and out of the studio as they pleased. Monina developed a passion for Picasso. She insisted on eating with him, stealing fruit and even cigarettes from his fingers, and teasing Max Jacob, who was terrified of animals. "We had to be careful not to leave anything fragile around," Fernande says. "Out of sheer devilry, [Monina] would toss all her . . . stolen treasures on the ground."[19] Surprisingly, Monina makes no appearance in the artist's work.

Every two or three months Picasso would tidy up his canvases and possessions and stash them away in huge closets. This made it possible to clean the studio—provided nothing was rearranged. A maid in cap and apron served meals in the small, cheerful dining room that looked out over the trees on the avenue Frochot.[20] Writing twenty-five years later, Fernande recalled the sun lighting up the old cherrywood sideboard, the walnut cabinets piled with their finds—bronze, pewter, porcelain—and the little walnut church organ, from which a faint smell of incense would waft whenever anyone pumped the bellows.[21] Although he was always complaining about guests, Picasso liked to keep open house, and the oval dining-room table was usually obliged to seat far more than its basic complement of four or five.

The Taverne de l'Ermitage, which was immediately opposite Picasso's apartment building, took the place of the Lapin Agile, which had been invaded by tourists. This lively, flashy bar catered to pimps, people in sports and show business, as well as clowns, acrobats, equestriennes and tightrope walkers, who rekindled his delight in the circus. They all became great friends. Fernande told Gertrude Stein how one of the performers, a San Franciscan who had a repertory of Negro songs and dances, had

Opposite: Photographs taken by Picasso in his studio at 11, boulevard de Clichy, 1910–11.
Top left: self-portrait;
top right: Frank Burty Haviland;
bottom left: Max Jacob (next to one of Picasso's Hepplewhite chairs);
bottom right: Guillaume Apollinaire.
Archives Picasso.

Picasso. *Woman in an Armchair*, winter, 1909–10. Oil on canvas, 81.3×63.5cm. Whereabouts unknown.

entertained them.[22] Another member of the troupe—an acrobat, who may or may not have been called Léonie—agreed to pose for Picasso. Her gamine looks and lean little body inspired a group of figure paintings that bear little or no resemblance to Fernande.

Gertrude Stein observed the transformation in Picasso's circumstances with amusement. Now that Fernande had a *comme il faut* apartment and a *comme il faut* maid who served up soufflés, she should have been happier than ever before, but she was not. Nor was Picasso. It was not just that their feelings for each other had burned out; it had to do with Picasso's ambivalence about social conventions. He grumbled at having to go out but usually went; he grumbled at having to entertain people but never stopped inviting them. He even gave in to Fernande and agreed to have an At Home day, like the Steins. "He chose Sunday," she said, "and in this way managed to dispose of the obligations of friendship in a single afternoon. Picasso always appeared to be delighted to see his friends . . . though he'd often have willingly seen them all in hell."[23] According to Gertrude, "there were a great many people there and even afternoon tea."[24] These Sundays soon petered out. For their first Christmas in the apartment Gertrude sent round a tree, which Picasso decorated. The candles burned dangerously low and had to be hurriedly extinguished. Gertrude received a letter of thanks, which included Christmas wishes from Cremnitz and the Pichots and was signed "Fernande Picasso."[25]

Picasso. *Mademoiselle Léonie*, 1910. Oil on canvas, 65×50 cm. Private collection. The name may have been that of the model or a reference to one of the principal characters in Max Jacob's *Saint-Matorel.*

Depending on how his work was going, the artist veered between antisocial sulking and gregariousness. He much preferred to eat at home, but he also liked to attend dinners given by prosperous friends—the Van Dongens, Paul Poiret, Richard Goetz, Frank Haviland—in order to complain about them. Likewise, he had come to dread the increasingly crowded Saturday-night soirées at the Steins', but he seldom missed them. He could on occasion be euphoric, but he usually appeared morose and dejected, bored by people trying to draw him out and get him to explain matters he had no intention of explaining in his far from fluent French. And then the Steins were always landing him with American visitors: Max Weber, who had done his best to scrounge a painting; Steichen and Stieglitz, who proposed exhibitions; and a succession of affluent lesbians, whom Gertrude would bring to the studio and oblige to buy a drawing or two—sometimes off the floor. Of the many new friends Picasso made through the Steins, Fernande singles out "the very talented Polish sculptor called Elie Nadelman, whose works now joined the Steins' already abundant collection."[26]

Now that most of the *bande à Picasso* had begun to make names for themselves, there was an increasing envy and resentment, which Picasso was not above fanning. Fernande wrote that despite his biting wit,

> which could momentarily wipe out the lines that work and worry had etched on his face; despite the youthfulness that animated [the group], I could already sense a premature aging, an imperceptible flagging in their friendships, occasional unwonted harshness (quickly repressed), boredom at seeing the same old faces every day, at thrashing out the same ideas, at criticizing the same talents and envying the same successes. Beneath the surface and still unperceived, a gradual process of disintegration was causing . . . a split between these artists who had once been so united—a split that they now tried in vain to conceal.[27]

Max Jacob. *Heads of Fernande and Maid in Cap and Apron.* Pen on paper. Picasso Heirs.

After 1909 Picasso would never again have to worry about money. This simplified his life; on another level it complicated it. Fernande found herself with nothing much to do except primp and sew and gossip and wait for her lover to emerge from the studio—seldom in a friendly mood. Whenever she asked Picasso what was wrong—was he bored or ill?—he would turn huge, astonished eyes on her and say, "No, not at all, I'm thinking about my work." "He rarely spoke during meals; sometimes he would not utter a word from beginning to end. He seemed to be bored, when he was in fact absorbed."[28] Fernande could no longer get Picasso to relax. Only Apollinaire or Max Jacob could distract him from his painting. Max would goad Marcel Olin—soon to become a celebrated actor—into a rage. After throwing the contents of their glasses in each other's faces, the two men would have a hysterical reconciliation. Picasso enjoyed that.

Ever fearful for his health, Picasso decided around the time of the move that he was ill and needed to diet. Whether his illness was psychosomatic or hypochondriacal, as Fernande suggests, or whether he was already suffering from stomach ulcers we do not know. At all events, for the next few years he would not "drink anything but mineral water or milk, or eat anything but vegetables, fish, rice pudding and grapes."[29] Perhaps it was this diet, Fernande adds, that made him sad and bad tempered—except with poets and pets. But, then, they probably occupied a surer place in Picasso's affections than she did.

* * *

Picasso's move from the Bateau Lavoir had left Max Jacob feeling bereft, abandoned by the person he loved most in the world. Without the studio next door to wander in and out of as he pleased, without the stimulus of tiffs and teases, without Fernande's doting, disapproving eye on him, Jacob cast around for a substitute for the artist. Only God would do. Hence the poet's greatest epiphany: a vision of Christ, which would culminate in his conversion to Christianity and transform his entire life, much as a similar vision had transformed that other Jewish transgressor Paul of Tarsus.

In his contradictory accounts of this epiphany, Jacob usually turns out to be fabricating or covering up lapses of memory. Four in the afternoon on September 22, 1909, is the time he originally gave for his vision, but elsewhere he cited other dates: September 28 and October 7. Henri Dion, who consulted the records of the firm that installed a new window in the poet's room a day or two before his vision, claims that it could not have occurred before December 2 or 3. One of the poet's biographers, Andreu, concludes that the end of September is the most likely date.[30] After taking Jacob's illness and poetic license into consideration, I would settle for early October—partly because it was the time of Yom Kippur, the Jewish Day of Atonement, which the poet had been brought up to observe.

There are no inconsistencies in Jacob's description of the vision itself. After working at the Bibliothèque Nationale for most of the day, he had returned to his fetid room—"It stank of kerosene, ether, stale tobacco, mustiness and the overflowing trashcans immediately below his window"—to take a nap.[31] He had bent down to put on his slippers and then glanced up: Christ had materialized on the red wall-hangings above his bed, a figure of ineffable elegance, garbed in a robe of yellow silk with pale blue facings. In the background was a landscape with a canal that he had drawn some months earlier. Jacob fell to his knees with a cry, tears welling up in his eyes, but filled with a mysterious sense of well-being: "I was stripped of my clothes by lightning. . . . I had been no more than an animal. I was born again a new man."[32] "After the disappearance of the Sacred Image, I heard a mass of voices, of words that were very clear, sharp, judicious and kept me awake the whole night. Before my eyes unrolled an uninterrupted flow of forms, colors and scenes, which I did not understand at the time but would later be revealed as prophetic."[33] It was as if Picasso, having walked out on him, had walked back into his life as Christ. As Jacob told Cocteau some years later, he would thenceforth feel for Picasso the same love that Mary Magdalen felt for Jesus. "You are what I love most in the world," Jacob apostrophized the artist in his *dédicace* to *La Défense de Tartuffe*, "after God and the saints who regard you as one of them."[34]

The day after his vision, Jacob confided in a priest, who listened with a skeptical smirk and promised to take the matter up with his superior. Jacob was mortified to hear no more. When he complained, the priest confessed that he had dismissed the whole thing as a journalistic hoax. Nor did Jacob's friends put much credence in his vision: another of his practical jokes, they said. Mean-minded neighbors attributed it to homosexual indulgence or to the effects of henbane ("the herb that makes you see demons"), or, worse, to Satanism, now that the smell of incense had been added to that of ether. Picasso made the inevitable black jokes but chose to believe him. As the poet later confirmed: "When God allowed me to come to him, you were the first to know about it; and you've been the only one not to laugh at my repentance."[35] Picasso's belief in magic was too strong for him to question Jacob's. After all, it was Jacob who had initiated him into mysticism; Jacob who had done his best to deify and also demonize him; Jacob who would dedicate *Saint-Matorel* "To Picasso, so that I know that he knows; so that he knows that I know."[36] Virtually the same provocative words reappear in the text of this autobiographical novel. And to whom does Matorel, that is to say the author, address them but Satan? Jacob loved to wallow in guilt, loved to titillate himself with the thought of Picasso, his eventual godfather, as a satanic Christ.

Max Jacob. *Crucifixion*, 1913–14. Pastel on paper, 23×15cm. Fonds Joseph Altounian.

Another incident that Jacob associates with his vision is the arrival—the following day—of Kahnweiler to buy the rights to *Saint-Matorel*, his first published book and a milestone in his career. Since *Saint-Matorel* appears to have been rewritten or revised after the vision, this must have happened later. Jacob's ever-changing accounts of the event have given rise to further confusion. He informed another biographer, Guiette, that "M. Kahnweiler bought the rights to the manuscript for 150 francs. In addition he insisted I give him a large four-leaf screen painted by Picasso"[37] —painted, according to Carco, with a reddish nude and other motifs on a straw-colored ground, thus probably of 1906.[38] Salmon claims that Kahnweiler made off not only with the screen but all the poet's manuscripts, including the "*malle de bonne-à-tout faire*" (servant-girl's valise) in which he kept them.[39] He was very grateful to Kahnweiler, Jacob told some of his friends; he felt ripped-off, he told others. The fate of the screen, which Picasso had given him to hide his uncurtained room from the street, is also a mystery. There is no record of it in Kahnweiler's stockbooks, or in the collection of Picasso's friend Madame Errazuriz, where it supposedly ended up.[40] Picasso had told Jacob off so often for selling the presents he had given him that the poet may perhaps have tried to shift the blame for its sale onto Kahnweiler's shoulders. Or did the dealer keep it for himself?

* * *

Until 1914 Picasso made a point of visiting every Salon d'Automne (also every Salon des Indépendants) to see what other painters were up to as well as take in the retrospectives of the more progressive old and modern masters (El Greco, Ingres, Puvis de Chavannes, Manet, Cézanne, Gauguin) that were a regular feature. Although usually small in scale, these retrospectives exerted such an influence on the course of modernism that the development of early-twentieth-century art cannot be followed without reference to them. The sensation of the 1909 Salon d'Automne was a show of twenty-five figure paintings by Corot. Hitherto this artist had usually been thought of as a landscape painter. "Corot discovered the morning," Picasso once said of his early Italian scenes,[41] preferring to forget that Corot later discovered the dusk in the twilit scenes of diaphanous nymphs flitting across misty water meadows that earned him vast *fin-de-siècle* popularity. The paintings of meditative women holding mandolins, which Corot did for his own pleasure and seldom exhibited, were still relatively little known. According to Braque, these were a revelation to Picasso, Derain and himself for their gravity and austerity, also for their studio settings. "They are paintings about painting," he said.[42] Braque liked the way Corot's models held musical instruments but seldom played them, thereby establishing a silence: a silence, I remember his saying, as perceptible as Corot's space. Then again, as pretexts for painting seated women, mandolins and guitars have more mystery than the usual props —needlework or reading matter (the love letter, the upturned book)— and are less sentimental and anecdotal than accessorized children or pets. Like an old-time photographer, Picasso still filled the awkward void in the background of his seated Fernandes with looped-back draperies and a vase of flowers or a potted plant. Only when he painted men did he include studio clutter: stacks of canvases, books, vestiges of an African mask. Thanks to Corot, Picasso and Braque saw how the presence of a stringed instrument could endow a figure painting with the stasis of a *nature morte.* Corot provided the cubists with their quintessential human subject.

Camille Corot. *Gypsy Girl with Mandolin (Christine Nilsson),* 1874. Oil on canvas, 80×57 cm. Museu de Arte de São Paulo Assis Chateaubriand.

The allegorical possibilities of musical instruments had intrigued Picasso ever since *Arte Joven,* the magazine that he and Soler had edited in Madrid, published Nicolás María López's essay "La Psicología de la guitarra."[43] López likens a guitar to a woman: the passive instrument on which a man plays. Like a woman, a guitar makes a show of rebellion and then "submits like a slave." The anthropomorphic rhymes and pictorial double entendres in his innumerable guitar compositions confirm that Picasso subscribed to these sentiments. Paradoxically, he also uses an ithyphallic guitar as an aggressively masculine symbol—sometimes indeed for himself—but not as often as he uses a curvaceous mandolin, with its suggestive sound hole, to stand for his mistress.[44]

Braque. *Woman with Mandolin*, 1910. Oil on oval canvas, 91.5×72.5cm. Bayerische Staatsgemäldesammlungen, Munich.

Braque, too, liked to paint guitars, not only for their allegorical or anthropomorphic possibilities but because, unlike Picasso, he loved music. Besides being an accomplished accordionist with an extensive repertory of folk and popular tunes, he had a passion for the classics (especially Bach) as well as modern music (especially Satie). For Braque painting and music partook of each other. A vase in a still life delineated a void just as a phrase in music delineated silence. He was also fascinated by the tactile qualities of instruments that a player plucked or bowed. As he said many years later, "I was drawn to musical instruments because they have the advantage of being animated by touch."[45] For Braque a principal purpose of cubism—*his* cubism, that is—was to bring figures and objects within reach; to make us feel that it would be pleasurable to touch them. Braque's *Musician* paintings stimulate the viewer's perceptions of touch and hearing. They may look much like Picasso's *Musicians*, but they are as different in their resonance as woodwind is from brass.

The first intimation of Picasso's interest in Corot is an otherwise puzzlingly conventional painting of Derain's Italian model (also his maid) in peasant costume. Picasso did this in Derain's studio. (Derain may well have done a painting of her on the same occasion.) Daix believes that this painting reflects Picasso's "desire to compete with Derain."[46] True, but was he not also competing with Corot? Besides this *Peasant Girl*, there are several other instances of figuration around this time—drawings from the model and naturalistic passages in otherwise cubist still lifes—which hint at a desire on Picasso's part to touch base with, as well as test cubism against, traditional methods of representation. He does this more than once—usually when Derain is around. Having checked that he had not lost any traditional skills in the course of his cubist climb, Picasso could return reassured to cubism: this time to a major painting, whose subject derives from the Corots he had seen at the Salon d'Automne. Known as the *Girl with the Mandolin* as well as *Fanny Tellier*, it would mark a change in the course of cubism.

Picasso told Roland Penrose (a former owner of this painting) that Fanny Tellier was a professional model known to many of his painter friends. She made overtures to him and persisted in coming to pose. "He found her presence, to which he was unaccustomed, somewhat embarrassing, but did not let it interfere with prolonged concentration on his work."[47] This does not ring true. Picasso was ruthless about his work, ruthless with importunate women, ruthless with models, whom he was far from "unaccustomed" to employing. Around the time he was painting Fanny Tellier, he also had Léonie, the circus girl, as well as Vollard and Uhde, sit for him. Why, then, should Fanny have interfered with his concentration? Maybe Picasso did not want to admit even to himself that cubism necessitated models. A traditional artist needed to see how near he could get to appearances; a cubist one needed to see how far. Why else did Picasso's closest brush with abstraction coincide with three portraits (Uhde, Vollard and Kahnweiler), which required almost as many sittings as his Gertrude Stein?

Picasso. *Woman with Mandolin*, spring, 1910. Oil on oval canvas, 80×64cm. Private collection.

Picasso's claim that Fanny Tellier gave him "more sittings than she was in the habit of giving for a single painting"[48] is also hard to believe. Professional Montmartre models usually liked regular jobs and paid little or no heed to what transpired on canvas. Was she, on the other hand, not a professional model but a whore (as her possibly invented Maupassant-like name might suggest),[49] or a woman who had been having an affair with the artist that either went wrong or was discovered and stopped by Fernande? This is the likeliest explanation. Fanny supposedly announced that she was indisposed and would not be coming the following day. "I realized that she meant not to come back at all," Picasso told Penrose, "and subsequently I decided that I must leave the picture unfinished. But who knows, it may be just as well I left it as it is."[50] Unfinished? Every square inch of the canvas is so subtly resolved that it is difficult to see how he could have carried it a brushstroke further. Some years later the artist signed and dated it, so *Fanny Tellier* is presumably "finished" after all. Her flat ax of a face points so far ahead that Karmel thinks the painting was done after his summer in Cadaqués.[51] Most scholars disagree. I find the point too close to call.

Picasso. *Fanny Tellier (Girl with the Mandolin)*, 1910. Oil on canvas, 100×73cm. The Museum of Modern Art, New York: Nelson A. Rockefeller Bequest.

A. T. V. — 1781 - CADAQUÉS, Platja del Pianch

A. T. V. — 3269 - CADAQUÉS, Cova del Gall-Marich

10

Cadaqués 1910

Maria Gay, c. 1910. Private collection.

Postcards sent by Fernande to Gertrude Stein and Alice Toklas with views of Cadaqués, July–August, 1910. The cross on the right-hand side of the lower picture marks their lodgings at 162, carrer de Poal. Beinecke Rare Book and Manuscript Library, Yale University.

CUBISM HAD DEVELOPED AT SUCH A PACE over the previous year that by the time summer came round, Picasso was once again ready to return to his Spanish roots for sustenance. Painful memories of his previous trip ruled out Horta—above all for Fernande. Instead, what Lorca called "the murmur of Latin waves"[1] lured him back to the Mediterranean. He first thought of spending the summer at the fauves' old haunt, Collioure, in French Catalonia, but according to Fernande, there were too many painters there—Marquet, Manguin and Puy. (She fails to mention the real threat: Matisse was at Collioure.)[2] Since Spain continued to exert an atavistic tug, he settled for Cadaqués, on the coast, northeast of Barcelona. Ramon Pichot and his wife, Germaine, had tried to entice Picasso and Fernande there the year before, on their return from Horta, but they had had to hurry back to Paris and move into their new apartment. This year, Picasso accepted Ramon's invitation to join them. The long, low family villa he had built some ten years earlier at Punt del Sortell, across the bay from the stark white fishing village, had the considerable advantage of a printing press. Pichot kept his boat, the *Nabucodonosor*, there. A further inducement: Ramon's celebrated opera-singer sister, Maria Gay (known as Nini), wife of the no less celebrated Catalan conductor Joan Gay, had recently completed a concert tour in France. As was her way, she told anyone desirous of accompanying her to Cadaqués that they could travel gratis on her troupe's communal ticket (what was called a "circus discount"). Her company already included several dogs and a parrot, and eighteen to twenty people, what with a dresser, accompanist, family and friends. Picasso and Fernande, as well as their maid and dog, Frika, were promised a free trip. They left on Friday, July 1.

Before departing, Picasso sent Apollinaire a note: "I am not leaving for the beautiful country of my birth until Friday. Come if you can to shake my friendly hand."[3] He was eager to discuss a project, which would be the subject of correspondence later in the summer: a translation of Cervantes's *El Licenciado Vidriera* (*The Scholar Made of Glass*) to be done by Apollinaire and illustrated by Picasso. Picasso called *El Licenciado Vidriera* "one of the most original [tales] in Spanish literature."[4] Its ironically humorous style is as ornate as its plot, aspects of which are reflected in work the artist did in the course of the summer. The story concerns a shy but brilliant young scholar of peasant background, called Tomás, who does not respond to the advances of an amorous grandee. To seduce Tomás,

Sos Pitxot, c. 1910. Private collection.

she gives him a love potion. Far from curing his shyness, this leaves him convinced that he is made of glass, though otherwise in possession of his faculties. Tomás forbids anyone to touch him and travels around on a donkey, packed in straw like a precious bottle. Eventually a priest cures him, but the crowd continues to torment him. In the end the scholar abandons his academic gown for a sword and goes off to fight in Flanders. Nothing came of Picasso's plan to illustrate this curious story (either in 1910 or in 1917, when Apollinaire suggested reviving the project). However, the notion of a body made of glass may explain the transparency and alienation of the Cadaqués figures. It also helps to explain the transparency of the figures in the *Saint-Matorel* engravings.

* * *

Even now that the Costa Brava has become one of the most overbuilt stretches of the Mediterranean coast, Cadaqués has preserved its idiosyncratic character, thanks partly to the Pichots, who still wield local power. Ramon's mother was born there; and as she was rich and generous, with a great interest in the arts, she and her sons turned the village into an artists' colony. Members of Els Quatre Gats started going to Cadaqués around the turn of the century. During World War I, refugees from Paris, including Picabia, Gleizes and Marie Laurencin, discovered it; Dalí lured Lorca there in the 1920s; and Marcel Duchamp went every summer from 1958 to 1968. Cadaqués had the advantage of being so difficult of access—cut off by an abrupt ridge two thousand feet high—that the villagers' dialect is closer to Mallorcan Catalan than to the mainland variety. This made for a sense of alienation and isolation: it was like being on an island. Until a proper road was built soon after 1910, access was altogether easier by sea. Fishing boats in the harbor included three-masted vessels that sailed as far afield as Cuba, and many local people felt closer to Havana than to Madrid. Weird geological formations are another local phenomenon. The rocks have names: the Camel, the Eagle, the Dead Woman, the Monk, the Lion's Head and the Anvil. Dalí used them as "paranoiac metamorphic" settings for some of his best tours de force, such as *The Persistence of Memory*. He and Buñuel chose them as a locale for their film *L'Age d'or*. Dalí later described the neighboring promontory, Cape Creus—often the objective of Pichot's boat trips—as "the epic spot where the Pyrenees come down into the sea, in a grandiose, geological delirium."[5] To heighten the bleakness, phylloxera had devastated the vines towards the end of the nineteenth century and left the landscape an expanse of faceted, gray-black rocks. Olive groves have now replaced the vines.

Putrefying archbishops on the rocks at Cadaqués. Scene from *L'Age d'or*, 1930, written by Salvador Dalí and filmed by Luis Buñuel. Cinémathèque Française.

Opposite top: The Pichot family, 1908. Ramon Pichot is lying in the foreground; in the group behind him are (left to right) Ricard Pichot, Germaine Pichot, Lluís Pichot, Maria Gay, Eduard Marquina, Mercedes Pichot and Antoni Pichot; in the group to the right, the Pichot parents are seated with Maria Gay's daughters and Pepito Pichot sitting in front; on the far right Lluís's wife, Angela, holds another child. Private collection.

Opposite bottom: Ramon Pichot. *Sardana at Cadaqués*. Oil on canvas, 125×191 cm. Private collection.

Maria Gay was eager to get back to Cadaqués, to the pavilion that her brother Ramon had built for her at the back of his house. She could not wait to lock herself away and rest and practice in peace, so they did not dally in Barcelona more than a night. The ninety miles to Cadaqués took the whole day to cover. Figueres was four hours by train from Barcelona. They then switched to a covered wagon to cross terrain that was so precipitous that the trek took seven hours and required two changes of horses. By the time they arrived, it was dark. For Fernande there was none of the uplift she had felt at Gósol or Horta. She found the place horribly disappointing.

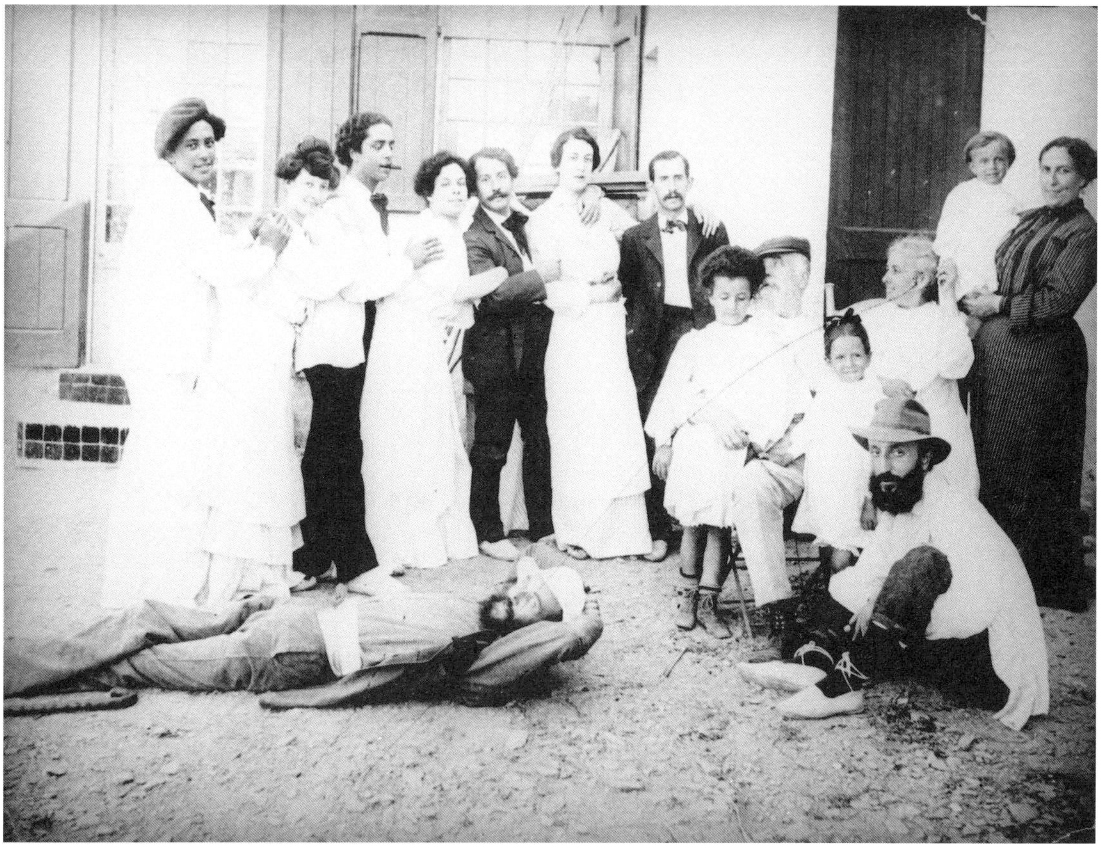

As usual, the Pichots' house was full. Besides the Gays, the family usually included Ricard, a cellist (the subject of an early portrait by Dalí), Pepito, a lawyer with a taste for the arts, another sister, Mercedes, with her husband, Eduard Marquina (an old friend of Picasso's and by that time a major force in Spanish letters), not to speak of various hangers-on. Everyone forgathered in the dining room, which had been decorated by Manolo with a handsome fireplace (now lost). To have privacy and a place to work, Picasso had rented a sparsely furnished house in the village—162, carrer de Poal (now no. 11) on the north side of the bay.[6] Fernande loathed it. As she grumbled to Gertrude Stein:

> We are paying a hundred francs a month for a house that has only two beds, two tables, and some chairs. Although I'm not bored, I find it all pretty awful. . . . Frika is happy and the maid's getting used to things. She does all the chores and although she doesn't speak any Catalan, she finds ways of making herself understood in French. . . . I don't know if we'll stay long.[7]

The house may have been spartan but it looked out to sea. Not far away was the village square, where the villagers danced the *sardana* to the tunes of Josep Maria (Pep) Ventura, a popular *sardana* composer who had recently died. Just off the square was the Hotel Miramar (later Hotel Cap de Creus; later still, a Dalí museum), where the Derains would take a room. This was run by an eccentric maid, Lídia Noguer, who had developed a passion for one of her former lodgers, Eugeni d'Ors—the celebrated Catalan art pundit, who launched *Noucentisme* and, after writing a book about Picasso, took against him. One of Noguer's many delusions was that d'Ors sent her hidden messages through his books. She would take Dalí in after his father threw him out; later she found him or sold him the shack at Port Lligat, which he turned into a surrealist folly. "She was godmother to my madness," Dalí wrote.[8] And Lorca, who fell in love with Dalí and went to stay with his family at Cadaqués in 1925, remembered this "woman's torrential conversation, shot through with extraordinary insights and oracular pronouncements."[9]

Salvador Dalí with Pepito Pichot at the first air show in Figueres, 1912. Fundación Gala-Salvador Dalí.

Dalí's father, an irascible but friendly lawyer from Figueres, had a eucalyptus-shaded villa on the beach not far from the Pichots': "On days of *calma blanca*, when not a ripple stirred the surface of the bay, the villa would be reflected as in a mirror" (Lorca).[10] The year Picasso arrived in Cadaqués, Salvador Dalí had just turned six. With his perfumed hair and sailor suit he was already disconcertingly precocious and exhibitionistic. He claimed to have met Picasso at this time—through Pepito Pichot, who was a particular friend of Dalí's father—but Picasso did not recall meeting him. It was Pepito who arranged for little Salvador to recuperate from a throat infection (this year or next) at the Pichots' estate, Molí de la Torre, near Figueres. The pointillistic paintings by Ramon that covered the walls of this house confirmed the child in his artistic vocation. Pepito gave him paint and canvas and set him to work.

On the occasion of Picasso's eighty-fifth birthday, fifty years later, Dalí evoked this summer in a long congratulatory telegram in Catalan, which began with a local saying: "*Pel mes de juliol, ni dona ni col ni cargol*" ("In the month of July, neither women nor cabbage nor snails"): a reference, Picasso told Palau,[11] to the fact that Maria Gay used to shut her husband out of her studio at Cadaqués, whereupon friends would tease him with this saying. Dalí also claimed to have sent Picasso a postcard every July saying, "In July, neither women nor oysters," but there is no trace of them in the Musée Picasso archives.[12] Dalí may also have been referring to a story he would have heard from the Pichots, that Picasso liked to shut himself away from his *dona*.

At Cadaqués, Picasso's life was almost as "hermetic" as the paintings he did there. Days that were not devoted to work were usually spent on Pichot's boat, fishing or diving for sea urchins, but only when it was calm: the artist was not the best of sailors. On one of these excursions his dog, Frika, was so incensed at being left on shore that she swam after the boat. So that Frika could catch up, Pichot anchored off the island of Es Cucurucú.[13]

Braque. *Harbor Scene*, 1909. Oil on canvas, 92.1×73.3cm. Museum of Fine Arts, Houston: The John A. and Audrey Jones Beck Collection.

Picasso initially concentrated on drawing and painting the local fishing boats—a subject that Braque, who was far more obsessive about boats than Picasso, had incorporated into cubist iconography two years earlier. Picasso seems to have had Braque's 1909 *Harbor Scene* in mind. Like him, he preferred to portray boats that were beached—"stranded in little heaps around the harbor," as Fernande described to Gertrude Stein[14]—rather than afloat on unpaintable waves (the cubists would always fight shy of the sea). At first there is some color to these paintings—touches of ultramarine sea and sky—but that soon gives way to the classic cubist gamut of grays and ochers. Picasso also abandoned boats for the female body, but he continued to draw on his experience of navicular structure—the dovetailing and the joinery. The flat forms of the Cadaqués nudes and guitar players seem mitered like so many planks.

The carpentered look of the Cadaqués paintings is also a consequence of Picasso's adoption of an orthogonal grid. This grid, which had originated with Braque, had manifested itself in Picasso's work a few months earlier. Use of the grid can be traced back to the time-honored technique of squaring-up a preliminary sketch for enlargement on canvas, which Picasso and Braque had learned at art school. Enlargement did not, of course, play any part in the cubists' use of a grid; however, as Braque said, something of the sort could equally help an artist adjust the tension, rhythm and structure of a composition.[15] Indeed, had not many an artist—Degas, for instance—allowed squared-up areas to show through the paint in order to give an artistic "weave" to a composition, to give an illusory rigor to an inert ensemble? Braque, who was much more forthcoming about cubism than Picasso, said that the grid helped him to map and animate space, reinforce the architecture.

Picasso. *Harbor at Cadaqués*, summer, 1910. Oil on canvas, 37.8×45.5cm. Národní Galerie, Prague.

The grid is much in evidence in the still lifes, which Picasso seemingly built up brick by brick: draperies corrugated to resemble a row of organ pipes form a more vertical grid in the background. In due course Picasso will go further and reduce these pipes to a rudimentary champagne-glass figuration (what Karmel calls the "stem-plus-arc motif").[16] Later he will minimalize them even further—into simple T-shapes, which "function as fragments of a discontinuous grid, rhythmically reiterating the vertical and horizontal axes of the picture."[17] This grid would be appropriated by Mondrian, when he came to Paris in 1911, as well as by Van Doesburg and Malevich, and would soon become a modernist trademark. But it is Picasso and Braque's paintings of this spring and summer that should be seen as the first modernist images: except for being executed in paint on canvas, they bear no resemblance whatsoever to any previous form of pictorial representation, and indeed might be said to have liberated artists from their dependence on retinal impressions.

Besides the grid, there is another innovation that comes into its own at Cadaqués: the large planes, opaque or transparent, out of which Picasso constructs his phantom figures. Cervantes's story about the scholar made of glass was one source for this development, but another factor should be considered. Just as Picasso had drawn on Vesalius's engravings to give an *écorché* look to Fernande's body, he now experimented with something even more invasive: X-ray photographs.[18] Röntgen's discovery of X-rays in November 1897 had taken instant hold of the public's imagination. Picasso's interest in the possibilities of radiography could have been stimulated by the futurists' "Technical Manifesto of Futurist Painting," which was published shortly before his departure for Cadaqués. It included the following challenge: "Why should we forget in our creations the doubled power of our sight, capable of giving results analogous to those of the X-rays?"[19] The artist would also have discussed the powers of the new ray with Apollinaire, who prided himself on his familiarity with the area where science and magic could be said to meet. No less likely, he would have seen Fernande's X-rays when she was in hospital in January. Given his curiosity about photography as well as any seemingly magical scientific discovery, Picasso would have been fascinated by this new ray, capable of entering the body and revealing the interpenetration of forms; capable of rendering opaque planes as transparent; capable of blurring the difference between two and three dimensions and producing an image that looks abstract but is not. The dappled passages that indicate the play of light and shadow in some of the Cadaqués studies resemble the dappled areas in X-rays and are equally indecipherable to an untrained eye. Even the identifiable items—the knobs, keys and nails—that keep Picasso's compositions from being totally illegible stick out like the foreign bodies (swallowed safety pins, forgotten forceps, fatal bullets) that X-rays detect. Some years later (1917), Picasso made a note in a sketchbook that testifies to his continuing interest in Röntgen's invention: "Has anyone put a prism in front of X-rays?"[20] he asks, as if he had not already done something of the sort.

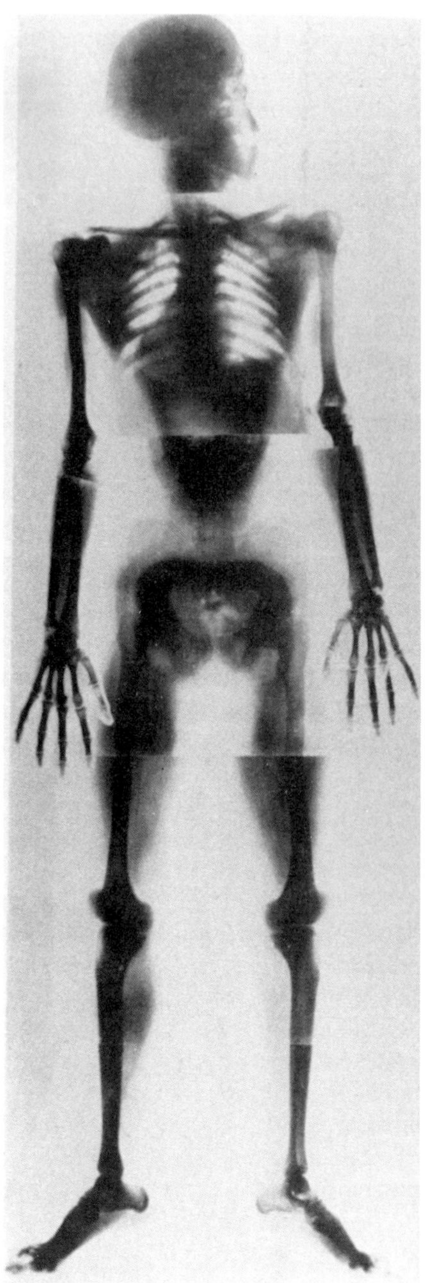

Composite X-ray by Röntgen of the human skeleton, c. 1900.

* * *

In or out of favor, the woman in Picasso's life almost always haunts his work. The Cadaqués paintings are an exception. Fernande—so closely identified with previous summer locales—is conspicuous by her absence from them. The mandolin players and nudes that preoccupied Picasso this summer are too depersonalized to evoke a specific individual. For once in his life, women are of little consequence to Picasso's art. To paint an expressive portrait of a woman, he needed to be either in the throes of a new love, sexually obsessed or consumed with rage, hatred or guilt. At Cadaqués he felt none of these things. Fernande was proving to be a livelier companion than she had been the year before—better in health and humor, as we know from her letters to Gertrude and Alice. Even though she disliked the place, she felt at ease, surrounded by people she could count on: the flirtatious French-speaking Pichots and their women, especially Germaine, who was from much the same Parisian demimonde as herself. With Germaine to confide in, Fernande did not resent being left to her own devices. She had finally accepted that her lover's work meant more to him than she ever would.

At Cadaqués Picasso vanished into his studio, oblivious to everything except the unending task of regenerating cubism, lest it lose all contact with reality or drift off into art for art's sake, or stagnate into a picture-making formula, as it would do in lesser hands. His work went very slowly, compared with the previous summer at Horta, when Fernande's anguish had inspired an avalanche of paintings. This summer, the anguish was his and not hers, and it was entirely to do with his work. Faith in his role as "*le peintre de la vie moderne*" was propelling him to the brink of abstraction—a Rubicon he would never cross. The Cadaqués images are so difficult to decipher that even the artist sometimes forgot what a particular image represented. One of the most often exhibited paintings of this summer is still cataloged as a *Rower*, although it shows a figure seated at a desk reading a book.[21] Picasso's use of the same sign to stand for different things makes it hard to distinguish figures from objects, musical instruments from boats. Indeed some of the Cadaqués drawings, apparently of domestic items, are so precisely delineated yet so indecipherable that the artist seems to be testing his own perceptions as well as ours. Zervos wisely omits titles from most of these catalog entries. A contributor to the *Burlington Magazine* would have us believe that the great *Female Nude* in the National Gallery (Washington, D.C.) is holding a baby.[22] I cannot agree. What I see as an emphatically raised shoulder the writer sees as an infant's head. Even if there had been a baby around, the artist is unlikely to have been the least interested. A baby would have been incompatible with his minimalist concepts. Palau likewise comes to grief with his interpretative titles. He either hedges his bets—*Apple and Glass (Marine View)*, *Boat–Mandoline*, *Marine–Landscape*—or hazards fanciful guesses.[23]

Ramon Pichot's printing press proved extremely useful. In April, Kahnweiler had asked Picasso to illustrate Max Jacob's autobiographical fantasy, *Saint-Matorel*, after Derain had declined to do so. ("The book is so paradoxical and disconcerting," Derain explained to Kahnweiler, "that it would make any illustrator look like a caricaturist.")[24] On July 28, Picasso wrote Kahnweiler that he and Jacob had come to an agreement—they had been having a tiff—and he was about to start work.[25] Unlike Derain's illustrations for *L'Enchanteur pourrissant*, which grow out of Apollinaire's text, Picasso's engravings for *Saint-Matorel* cast more light on his cubist preoccupations than on Jacob's prose. Picasso appears to have taken only the most cursory interest in the narrative and to have limited himself to passages that were relevant to his own concerns. The illustrations constitute a microcosm of this summer's œuvre and with a few changes—the sex of Mademoiselle Léonie, for instance—they could have done for the Cervantes story about the scholar made of glass. Jacob, who was secretly doing tentative colored sketches in the hope of converting to cubism as well as Catholicism, was flattered at the honor Picasso had done him. He would be unhappy with the result. In fact, the disjunction between word and image works to the book's advantage.[26]

For the engraving *Mademoiselle Léonie*, Picasso takes the figures he had been painting at Cadaqués a stage further and opens the forms into each other—a process he continues in a second, more elaborate, version,

Picasso. *Female Nude*, summer, 1910. Oil on canvas, 187.3×61 cm. National Gallery of Art, Washington, D.C.: Ailsa Mellon Bruce Fund.

Mademoiselle Léonie in a Chaise Longue. In order to "read" this drypoint, we need to realize that Léonie is not reclining but seated (turning slightly away from us) on the side of the chaise longue, the back of which can be seen top right and its front extension and legs bottom left. The illustration of the Lazarist monastery of Saint Theresa in Barcelona (where Matorel dies—"a sort of Hamlet . . . in a state of divine grace")[27] presents fewer problems. Picasso looks back at the premonitory drawings he had made of the arcaded courtyard in his Barcelona hotel the previous year. But this time he uses the technique of *passage* to dissolve the architecture in space—all except the curious navel-like rosette at the center of this composition. This is not a disembodied Léonie, as Palau has suggested,[28] but shorthand for the monastery fountain.

The two still lifes Picasso engraved for *Saint-Matorel* (only one was used) are a distillation of two still lifes he had painted soon after arriving at Cadaqués. The more decipherable painting—hence, probably, the first—is the vertical *Dressing Table.* At the top is one of those adjustable mirrors suspended between two columns; in the foreground an array of toilet paraphernalia: a glass with a toothbrush in it alongside Fernande's bottles and jars. Recession is not perspectivally defined but neatly suggested by the contrast of a small key in the drawer at the back with the larger key in the drawer in front. The device of focusing our attention on a familiar object that we instinctively want to grasp—a key, handle or knife—originated with Braque. By inviting us to touch it, the key lures us into what Braque called "tactile space." Picasso has given this device an anthropomorphic twist. The positioning of the key and keyhole, as it were, genitally, between the legs of the table and the angling of the mirror to reflect a face suggests that the *Dressing Table* doubles as a conceptual figure. The other major Cadaqués still life is less legible. Against an organ-pipe-like grid, Picasso sets out a conglomeration of objects, which are tantalizingly close to being identifiable—maybe a glass, fruit dish, lamp with a shade, possibly a mandolin. One of two legible details—a realistic but ghostly knob on the extreme right-hand surface of the table—conjures up a drawer not otherwise delineated. The other legible detail, the slice of lemon with radiating spokes at the very center of the composition, holds everything together as tightly as if it were a screw.

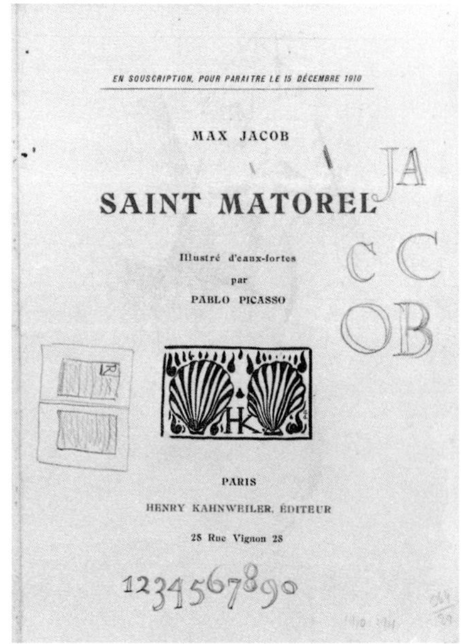
EN SOUSCRIPTION, POUR PARAITRE LE 15 DÉCEMBRE 1910

MAX JACOB

SAINT MATOREL

Illustré d'eaux-fortes

par

PABLO PICASSO

PARIS

HENRY KAHNWEILER, ÉDITEUR

25 Rue Vignon 25

Kahnweiler's brochure announcing the publication of Max Jacob's *Saint-Matorel* illustrated with etchings by Picasso, 1910. Musée Picasso.

The architectonic rigor and clarity of these monochromatic compositions has been said to reflect the minimal white houses of Cadaqués, also the gray-black rocks and *calma blanca* of the bay. However, it also reflects another kind of *calma blanca.* Hitherto Picasso's art had provided an outlet for his ravenous libido, his tenderness and misogyny, his humor, grief and anger. Just as he had sacrificed color to the demands of cubism, Picasso now found himself obliged to dispense with the emotive color that had given his Horta Fernandes of the previous summer their intensity. The *calma blanca* of hermetic cubism, as this phase is sometimes called, curtailed the artist's instinctive, visceral response to life.

* * *

Intellectual isolation was a major operational hazard of cubism. None of his writer friends, not even Apollinaire or Gertrude Stein, both of whom saw themselves as honorary cubists, could keep up with Picasso. Only

Opposite: The four etchings by Picasso published in *Saint-Matorel,* 1910. Musée Picasso:

Top left: *Mademoiselle Léonie.* 20×14.1cm.

Top right: *Dressing Table.* 20×14.2cm.

Bottom left: *Mademoiselle Léonie in a Chaise Longue.* 20×14.2cm.

Bottom right: *The Monastery.* 20×14.1cm.

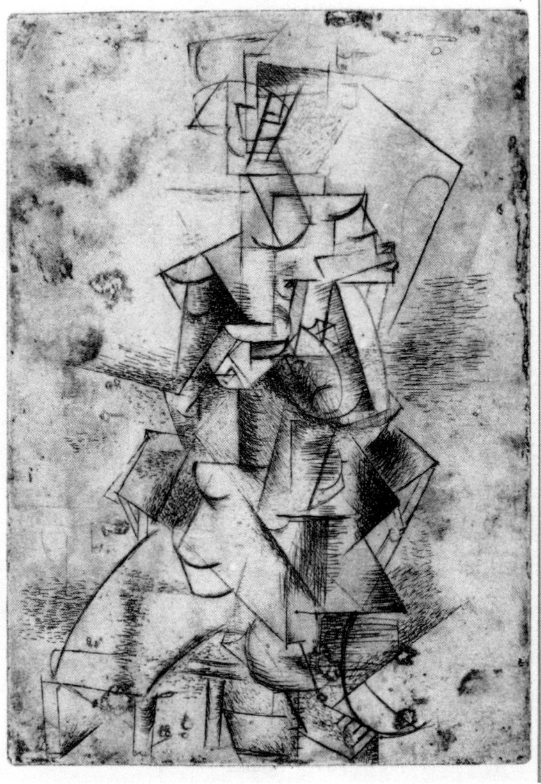

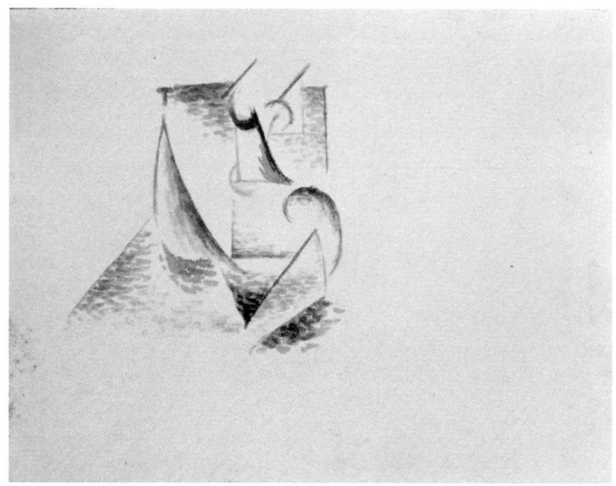

Above: Picasso. *Blotter*, summer, 1910. India ink wash on paper, 24×31.5cm. Picasso Heirs.

Top: Picasso. *Glass and Lemon*, summer, 1910. Oil on canvas, 74×101.3cm. Cincinnati Art Museum: Bequest of Mary E. Johnston.

Left: Picasso. *Dressing Table*, summer, 1910. Oil on canvas, 61×46cm. Private collection.

Braque or Derain could alleviate the problems that beset him at Cadaqués. Braque was unwilling or unable to leave Paris. Derain, however, was free to join him, not that he was in a position to provide much in the way of artistic solace. By now he was more than ever in thrall to Cézanne, and the old masters were beginning to coax him back towards classicism. Derain's desire to reform traditional art found no response in Picasso: traditional art was something to mock, bounce off or, better still, cannibalize or pillage. Nevertheless he was delighted that his friend was prepared to leave Cagnes on the Riviera and come to Cadaqués.[29] He enjoyed arguing with him and liked Alice the more for throwing Fernande off balance.

The village of Cadaqués.

Derain and Alice arrived towards the end of July. They had taken a boat to Port Vendres in the hope of finding another boat to Cadaqués. In the end they took the train from Barcelona to Figueres, where they changed to the covered wagon. Inside the wagon it was very dark. When Alice struck a match to light a cigarette, she was startled by a bearded fellow passenger jeering at her. It turned out to be Picasso in disguise. Always punctilious with old friends, he had come to meet them. The Derains spent two weeks or so at the Hotel Miramar, where they were looked after by Lídia Noguer. The visit was a success. Besides Derain and the Pichot brothers and brothers-in-law, there were visitors from Barcelona with whom he could exchange ideas—something that had been out of the question at Horta. And then there were the local fishermen, whose stories, ancient as their Phrygian caps, gave Picasso much pleasure. Did he, one wonders, encounter the fisherman, called Enriquet, who told Dalí, some years later, that he preferred his paintings of the sea to the real thing, "because there you can count the waves"?[30]

Derain did not have time to do much work at Cadaqués. André Salmon claimed he did several paintings of the place, but only a couple can be traced: both are views of the village huddled at the foot of the fortified church. Like Picasso's 1909 views of Horta, they owe a lot to Cézanne's view of Gardanne.[31] Areas of primed canvas have even been left unpainted to generate light. For once Derain's presence did not tempt Picasso to take a backward look at figuration. The two of them went their separate ways. The informal *musicales* that the Pichots organized were more to the taste of Derain than Picasso, who liked to dance and had a sense of rhythm but could carry only the simplest tune ("Tipperary" being one).[32] Derain, on the other hand, loved music: "harpsichord, spinet, flute, organ, African instruments and the gramophone . . . records of Arab and Chinese music—anything strange and unknown."[33] He even made primitive musical instruments. In the evenings, if they were lucky, Maria Gay would sing or her husband or brother play for them; Derain might also oblige and Picasso do a flamenco routine. The Corot-inspired figures playing guitars and mandolins in Picasso's paintings imply the presence of a guitarist. Every weekend, a *cobla* (a Catalan band that includes pipes called *tibles* and the nasal-sounding *tenores*, often to be found in Picasso's paintings misidentified as clarinets) would strike up the *sardana* on the village square. Picasso loved this dance. Fifty years later, Brassaï asked him about its "harsh, bitter music . . . handbags and jackets placed in a pile on the ground, and around each pile a circle of dancers weaving back and forth . . . and the expressions on their faces—serious, tense almost desperate.

Derain. *Cadaqués*, summer, 1910. Oil on canvas, 60.5×73cm. Private collection.

No sound of laughter, not even a smile."[34] Whistling a tune, Picasso demonstrated the complexity of the steps:

> It's a very serious thing, the *sardana*! [he said] And difficult! Each step must be counted. In every group, there is one person who does this for all the others. This dance is a communion of souls. . . . It abolishes all distinction of class. Rich and poor, young and old, dance it together: the postman with the bank manager, and the servants hand-in-hand with their masters.[35]

* * *

The artist's presence heightened tensions. Fernande saw to it that his neglect of her was not lost on the Pichots. She set about winning them over, particularly Ramon, and was so successful that he took her side when Picasso walked out on her in the spring of 1912. Like many another woman, Fernande was also smitten with Ramon's brother Ricard, who serenaded her (as well as his peacocks) on his cello. Derain fitted into this group well enough, but Fernande was ill at ease with Alice, who was bawdy, beautiful and quarrelsome—and in Picasso's confidence: hence a certain jealousy, which would give way in time to mutual affection. The artist enjoyed playing the pasha with these former mistresses. There was a further complication: Maria Gay was about to leave her conductor husband for an Italian tenor.

Braque. *Rio Tinto Factory at L'Estaque*, summer, 1910. Oil on canvas, 73×60cm. Musée d'Art Moderne, Villeneuve d'Ascq.

Picasso made the Derains' departure (August 6) the pretext for a trip to Barcelona. Besides wanting to show his friends the sights, he had to see his family. He may also have needed to refresh his memory of the Saint Theresa monastery, the subject of the last *Saint-Matorel* illustration. Ramon and Germaine accompanied them. The ladies went looking for junk jewelry and old medals, but it was very hot and rained a lot and they were soon exhausted. Picasso took Derain to see the sculptors Gargallo and Casanovas; and, as usual, he obliged his friends to take the funicular to Mount Tibidabo. One evening, they went to a performance of flamenco and *cante jondo*, which they greatly enjoyed; and on Sunday they attended a bullfight—very disappointing. Fernande remembers visits to a tavern on the waterfront that served very salty *tapas* to encourage drinking.[36] The Derains became so rowdy that they were all thrown out. On returning to Paris, a day or two later, Derain went to see Braque to give him the Cadaqués news. Braque immediately wrote to Picasso to say how much Derain had enjoyed his visit, and that he, too, hoped to come to Cadaqués for a few days at the end of the month.[37] In the end he never made it—probably because Picasso returned to Paris earlier than he had intended. Instead Braque went back to L'Estaque and painted two almost identical views of the Rio Tinto factory, which respond to Picasso's 1909 Hortas as elegantly as the latter respond to Braque's 1908 L'Estaques.

That Angel de Soto accompanied them back from Barcelona to Cadaqués is confirmed by a remarkable photograph that Picasso took of him there.[38] Another friend who turned up was Frank Burty Haviland. He had been spending the summer in his house at Céret, just over the frontier in French Catalonia. He needed to discuss a major commission that he had obtained for Picasso: a set of eleven large, decorative panels for a library in Brooklyn, New York, belonging to Haviland's American cousin, Hamilton Easter Field. On July 12, Field had mailed Picasso a letter, from New

York, confirming the commission and giving precise measurements and elevations of the room, but it did not reach Cadaqués until August 2. In his letter of acceptance (dated September 7), written back in Paris, Picasso told Field that he had not as yet embarked on the project. Years later, he assured Daix that he had in fact started one of the narrower panels in Cadaqués: Washington's tall *Female Nude*.[39] Another painting (subsequently overpainted or destroyed) corresponding to Field's specified dimensions can also be glimpsed in a photograph of the Cadaqués studio. There would not have been time for much more. After returning from seeing the Derains off in Barcelona (August 12), Picasso decided to curtail their stay. He was probably impatient to return to Paris and work on these huge panels in a more spacious and congenial studio.

Notwithstanding the sympathetic company, neither Picasso nor Fernande had had a good time. Fernande confessed her feelings to Gertrude Stein:

> At the risk of offending the Pichots I must admit the place is hideous. There is nothing but the sea, some wretched little mountains, houses that look as if made of cardboard, local people without any character who may be fisherfolk but have as much allure as workmen. . . . The women are like women anywhere else, except plainer, above all drab. . . . The only beaches are small and cramped . . . nothing to eat except fish, as I had been warned, fruit hard to find and mediocre, and life almost as expensive as Paris.[40]

Photograph by Picasso of paintings in his studio at Cadaqués, summer, 1910 (Picasso's original print was reversed). Archives Picasso (private collection). The largest painting is one of those begun for Field's library, while the others are *"Rower"* (top left), *Guitar Player* (bottom left) and *Harbor at Cadaqués* (bottom right).

Back in Paris by August 26, Picasso felt disappointed with the progress he had made at Cadaqués—more than ever disappointed when Kahnweiler chose to regard most of the paintings he had brought back as unfinished. The dealer would buy only one of them: the least challenging of the lot, the Braque-like *Boats*, heightened with blue. Once again, Vollard would come to the rescue; he did not understand them, but he purchased most of the remainder. Later, Kahnweiler would have a change of heart. When he came to write his history of cubism in 1916, he elevated the pictures he had failed to buy to the height of historical importance: "Dissatisfied after weeks of agonizing struggle, Picasso returned to Paris . . . with his works unfinished. But a great step forward had been accomplished. '*Il a fait éclater la forme homogène.*'" ("He had shattered the enclosed form.")[41]

In fact Picasso had "shattered the enclosed form" in his 1909 Barcelona hotel drawings; Braque had done likewise in some of his 1909 landscapes. The Cadaqués paintings are indeed milestones, in that they constitute the crux of what would eventually become one of the most momentous issues of modernism: figurative versus non-figurative. If in the end Picasso stopped short of abstraction, it was not failure of nerve but his conviction that art—his art—should be as real as the real thing. For Picasso, reality (as opposed to realism) is what his painting would always be about. Cubism was a means of enhancing, not dissipating, that reality. He did not want a painting to be an abstraction any more than he wanted it to be a facsimile. He wanted it to constitute a fact, a very specific fact. People who urged Picasso to look more favorably on abstract art because it was the pictorial equivalent of music would be told, "That's why I don't like music."

11

Cubist Commissions and Portraits

Hamilton Easter Field, c. 1915.
Photograph by Alman & Co.
Private collection.

BACK IN PARIS, PICASSO GOT DOWN TO WORK on the Field library. Had the decorations materialized, they would have constituted the most ambitious project of the artist's career—nothing less than an apotheosis of analytical cubism—in which case Field's Brooklyn house would have rivaled Shchukin's Moscow palace as a monument of modernism.[1] Besides going on with the panels he had begun in Cadaqués, Picasso now embarked on an overdoor, the exaggeratedly horizontal *Woman on a Divan*: one of the few paintings that satisfied him enough to leave in its original state. Why, then, did the Field project, which got off to such a promising start (by 1912 at least half the paintings would be more or less finished) ultimately fizzle out? Cubism was simply the wrong vehicle for a large-scale decorative scheme; and Field's specifications (eight panels of varying widths, all some six feet tall, and three overdoors) turned out to be ill suited to Picasso's vision. More to the point, Field showed little or no commitment to the project. So far as we know, he never returned to Paris to inspect the work in progress; he never had the curiosity to request photographs; and thus he was never able to visualize the masterpieces that his commission inspired. Just as well; they are unlikely to have pleased him.

Hamilton Easter Field turns out to have been one of those kindly, prissy aesthetes who like modern art in theory rather than practice and have high-minded, half-baked notions of how an artist should function. In an article he wrote a few years later Field boasts of telling Picasso that

> he made a mistake in merely painting easel pictures, for abstract art needed an entire room or better a house in which all furniture should be subordinated to the decorations which would cover the flat walls. He should get orders to decorate buildings. I could not offer him a house to decorate, but I had a library with no pieces of furniture except the bookshelves and a few low chairs.[2]

Picasso would have been extremely scornful of his patron's theories.

Field was born into a Quaker family, which had done well enough in the dry-goods business to buy the old Roebling house in Brooklyn. He had studied mining and architecture before choosing art. After reading du Maurier's *Trilby*, he had gone to Paris in 1892 to enroll at the Académie Colarossi and sit at the feet of Gérôme and, later, Fantin Latour. Although brought up in America, Field had the entrée to the Parisian art world through his mother's uncle, David Haviland, who had moved to France and becomc a leading manufacturer of Limoges porcelain (Haviland &

Opposite: Self-portrait photograph by Picasso, showing one of the paintings for Hamilton Easter Field (now lost or overpainted) in his studio, 1913. Archives Picasso.

Carved mantelpiece decorated by Robert Laurent in the home of Hamilton Easter Field, Columbia Heights, Brooklyn, c. 1913. Private collection.

Compagnie), and David's son, Charles. Charles had married the daughter of Philippe Burty, a celebrated critic and friend of Delacroix and Renoir, who had painted a memorable portrait of him. One of Charles's sons was Frank Burty Haviland, Picasso's friend, who was kept short of money for choosing to be a painter. Another son, Paul, was a photographer and critic, who became a partner of Stieglitz and married into the Lalique family. The Fields and Havilands were very close.

Field had sufficient means to live up to his elitist conviction that collecting was intrinsic to an artist's education. "I wandered along the Seine," he later wrote, "picking up a Guardi, a book of hours, a painting by Fragonard, or a sixteenth-century tapestry, and in time I had a collection."[3] He acquired drawings by Claude, Tiepolo and Puvis de Chavannes, among others, and a great many prints by Daumier, Whistler, Redon and Cassatt, but his principal passion was Japanese art. Later Field took an interest in the fauves and cubists but never acquired anything by them beyond a single Picasso drawing. As for his painting, it was genteelly Whistlerian, faintly influenced by his friends Walter Gay and Gaston La Touche. His private life was less genteel. One summer (circa 1900), he had taken a house on an estate in Brittany. The caretakers, a couple called Laurent, were not displeased when their eleven-year-old son caught the eye and captured the heart of the nice, well-off tenant. Field's solution was to adopt the family as well as the child, whom he proceeded to educate. In due course he had young Robert trained as a painter and sculptor—in part by his cousin Frank, who introduced the youth to Picasso as early as 1906–07.

Although Field lived mostly in Rome until 1910, he frequently visited Paris. On one of these visits he was taken by Laurent (so Laurent always claimed)[4] to visit Picasso, shortly before he moved out of the Bateau Lavoir. Haviland would almost certainly have accompanied them. Field had a limited understanding of Picasso's work, which he later described as "the expression of emotion through the deformation of natural forms,"[5] but he had made up his mind that the family home in Brooklyn, to which he and Laurent now proposed to return, should have a daring new feature: a Picasso library, which, he assured the artist, would be well lit at night by electricity. The idea for the library, which seems to have been a matter of modernist principle rather than modernist taste, probably originated with Haviland, who acted as middleman. Haviland had no difficulty keeping Picasso focused on the project. Field was more of a problem. Once he was back in Brooklyn, he switched his patronage to American art. With Laurent he founded two art schools—one on his family's Brooklyn property, the other in the art colony of Ogunquit, Maine, where he had a summer house that was looked after by Robert's parents. Had Field left confirmation of the library commission until his return to the United States, he would surely have chosen an American artist. At his death in 1922, his collection included quantities of American art, but only the one Picasso drawing and a set of *pochoir* reproductions of designs for *Tricorne* .

Field's commission could not have come at a more opportune time for Picasso. It challenged him to work once again on a large scale. It also pitted him against Matisse, who had just completed two great decorative panels—*Dance II* and *Music*—for the staircase of Shchukin's Moscow palace. (Originally there was to be a third, a "scene of repose," which

Right: Matisse's *Music* and *Dance II*, 1910, in the State Hermitage Museum, St. Petersburg.

Below: Picasso. *Woman on a Divan*, fall, 1910. Oil on canvas, 49×130 cm. Private collection on loan to Kunsthaus, Zurich.

Bottom: Picasso. *Pipes, Cup, Coffee Pot and Carafe*, summer, 1911. Oil on canvas, 50×128 cm. Private collection, New York.

Matisse later, in 1913–16, transformed into one of his consummate achievements, *Bathers by a River.*) Picasso knew these works from his visits to Matisse's studio; he also saw them at the 1910 Salon d'Automne, where they caused such a scandal (Apollinaire wrote virtually the only favorable notice) that Shchukin, who had come to Paris for a first glimpse of his decorations, repudiated them.[6] News of the public outcry and his patron's rejection greeted Matisse when he was summoned back from Germany to his father's deathbed. To his credit, Shchukin changed his mind on his way back to Moscow and agreed to accept these masterpieces, provided the genitalia were less explicit. Picasso, who envied Matisse his notoriety, would doubtless have seen his own *Demoiselles* as a source of *Dance II*'s ferocity and abandon and would have regarded Field's commission as a God-sent means of getting even with his principal rival.

André Warnod. *Le Vernissage du Salon d'automne.* Cartoon in *Comœdia,* September 30, 1910.

When it came to tackling large decorations, Picasso had few of Matisse's advantages. Cubism had involved too great a reduction in scale for Picasso to work comfortably on canvases that were taller than himself. During the high phase of cubism, his formats were seldom more than a meter high or wide, usually less: standard 20 or 30 F canvases, commensurate with the conventional half or three-quarter lengths that he favored.[7] Many full-length figures, it is true, are to be found in his cubist drawings, but they seldom survive the transition from paper to canvas. And try as Picasso might to ensure that more of them did, success continued to elude him. If only one of the four or five standing nudes for Field's library has survived intact, it is probably because of the artist's discomfort with his patron's Procrustean specifications. Picasso, who was sensitive about his lack of height, did not favor tall formats. To enhance gigantism, he liked a head to look as if it were bursting through the top of a canvas.

The sheer momentum of cubism also made for problems. Built into this long-term project was the impossibility of achieving stylistic consistency, given Picasso's ever-changing way of portraying things. By the summer of 1911, the relative abstraction of the earlier panels would be a thing of the past; by 1912, Picasso was speeding down yet another path, and his original 1910 concept must have seemed ever more of an anachronism. Ironically, as soon as he ceased working on the library (early 1913), cubism began to take a more decorative form. Short of radical repainting, there would have been little hope of resolving the stylistic disparity. By contrast, Matisse's panels are all of a piece—hence the intensity of their impact.

By comparison with Picasso, Matisse had the upper hand in decoration and color. Whereas Matisse had looked long and hard at Byzantine mosaics and Islamic ornamentation, Picasso had little or no idea of what decoration entailed. Hitherto the very word had been anathema to him. True, he and Braque would soon be making pictorial use of such techniques as marbling and graining, but they would do this to mock the sanctity of *belle peinture* and to enliven the picture surface with texture rather than decoration. In the absence of any decorative experience, Picasso was obliged to do the very thing that Field had counseled him against: conceive the project as a sequence of easel paintings. To judge by those that survive, the panels would never have worked as decorations: they are too dense and intricate. As easel paintings, they work perfectly.

As regards that other essential element, color, Picasso was still in something of a cubist quandary. He yearned to banish monochrome and have color play a more active role but was stymied by the difficulty of reconciling color with cubist concepts of form. According to Kahnweiler, whenever Picasso introduced color into an analytical cubist painting, he would sooner or later be obliged to paint it out.[8] The only exception was a small nude that included a luminous red drapery, but this, too, has disappeared. The dilemma would not be resolved until the spring of 1912, when Picasso and Braque took to using local color for the labels, packages and brochures they introduced into their still lifes. But that was too late to save the Brooklyn project from the one and only tendency that Field had specifically condemned in his letter: "color contrasts that are too delicate."

And then there was the matter of money—something that Field's contractual letter fails to mention. Were terms to be decided later? Or had they been settled by Haviland in his role as go-between? Since the project would take up much of Picasso's time over the next two years—a period when his prices were steadily rising—whatever terms had been arranged are likely to have required adjusting. This would have made for difficulties. For all his philanthropic impulses, Field was exceedingly stingy—a friend, the art critic Henry McBride, described him as "laughably parsimonious"[9] —and he seems to have lived up to his reputation by parsimoniously failing to make a down payment on the project. Had he done so, Picasso would have owed him a painting or two. This does not seem to have been the case. The artist would therefore have had every right to feel that he had been put to enormous trouble for little or no reward.

Except for news from Haviland (also Stieglitz, who saw the panels in Picasso's studio late in 1911),[10] Field had little or no idea, back in Brooklyn, of Picasso's progress. Now that he was setting up as a very active patron of American artists, Field began to lose interest in the library. Things might have turned out differently if he had negotiated the commission through Kahnweiler, but Picasso's 1912 contract with the dealer specifically excludes "*grandes décorations*" from their agreement.[11] Since he had more to lose than gain, Kahnweiler is likely to have discouraged Picasso from devoting so much time to an unprofitable venture. Significantly, after signing up with the dealer, the artist lost interest in working for Field.

Of all the factors that militated against the completion of the library decorations, the most decisive was Field's old mother. In his obituary, Henry McBride states that Field had no intention of installing the Picassos in his house so long as his mother was alive. This Quakeress of the old school followed "her son's activities with sympathetic interest . . . and appeared not to be too much revolted by the paintings of Maurice Sterne, Jules Pascin, Guillaumin etc. that began to appear in her house [but] it would have been too much to accustom herself to [Picasso's] extraordinary work."[12] Mrs. Field evidently found it easier to turn a blind eye to the young men who came to frolic in her son's infamous sauna than to the sinful incursion of cubism into his library. Since Field worshiped his mother, he was in no hurry to take delivery of the panels—he would indeed have dreaded their arrival. The lack of urgency that was built into the project compounded all the other problems and ensured its eventual abandonment. If the old lady had died before the war instead of in 1917, Field might have had his library. Years later, Picasso sold three of the

Picasso. *Man with Mandolin*, 1911. Oil on canvas, 158×71 cm. Musée Picasso.

completed panels (probably through Pierre Loeb) to the Italian industrialist Frua de' Angeli;[13] he repainted three others at a later date; kept back two more that were unfinished (now in the Musée Picasso); and jettisoned the biggest composition.

* * *

A very different but in the end more successful undertaking was a series of dealer's portraits—Uhde, Vollard and Kahnweiler—which Picasso had begun before he left for Cadaqués and resumed painting on his return.[14] If Picasso devoted what are arguably his finest portraits of men to dealers rather than the poets—Apollinaire, Salmon and Jacob—who were his closest friends, it was because he needed dealers as much as, if not more than, poets. Those early days in Paris, when he had to wheedle a pittance from the improvident Weill or the loathsome Libaude, had left Picasso forever fearful of poverty, forever wary of dealers. Nevertheless he was canny enough to realize that his daily bread, his burgeoning lifestyle, not to speak of fame, depended on friendly rapports with the people who bought, sold and exhibited his work. Here we should bear in mind that in the course of sitting for their portraits, Uhde held a Picasso show (May, 1910) at his Notre-Dame-des-Champs gallery, Vollard was preparing an exhibition of works from 1900 to 1910 (December 20, 1910–February, 1911) at his gallery, and Kahnweiler was supplying his compatriots with paintings for shows in Munich and other German art centers. The artist's contacts with these dealers had evidently been strengthened by the successive sittings that cubist portraiture necessitated.

Cézanne. *Portrait of Vollard*, 1899. Oil on canvas, 100×81 cm. Petit Palais Musée, Paris.

This sequence of dealers' portraits actually starts in 1909, with the one of Clovis Sagot (p. 108), whom Picasso despised as "almost a usurer" but also respected for his adventurous eye. It was almost certainly Sagot who proposed a portrait, but as a favor rather than a commission. The result is a hybrid: the progeny of Cézanne's *Cardplayers* with a nod towards Van Gogh's *Père Tanguy* (the impressionists' Père Sagot). As in the undistinguished portrait that Picasso did of his friend Pallarès a month or two later, the face is the least cubist element in the painting, far less faceted and distorted than the Fernandes done at the same time. Nevertheless the old rogue took great pride in Picasso's bland image of him. It became his "Enseigne de Gersaint" (the trade sign Watteau painted for his dealer). Sagot lent it to every modernist exhibition he could—Cologne, Munich, London, Amsterdam—until he died, in 1913, whereupon his widow sold it, as well as quantities of Picasso's drawings (quite a few to Dr. Albert Barnes), for next to nothing.

The portraits of Uhde, Vollard and Kahnweiler are far more complex. Their distortions reflect the artist's very different attitude to each of these very different men. Let us begin with the Uhde. Although started after the Vollard, it was finished earlier.[15] Uhde now had his own gallery, but he still came across as an amateur rather than a professional dealer, above all to Picasso, who saw him as a writer addicted to modern art rather than as someone in trade. This difference—one that Picasso had been brought up to respect—might well explain why he felt free to mock Uhde but not his more businesslike confrères. This and the fact that Uhde had a homosexual crush on him gave the artist an advantage that he did not hesitate to seize.

Above: Picasso. *Portrait of D.-H. Kahnweiler*, 1910. Oil on canvas, 100.6×72.8 cm. The Art Institute of Chicago: Gift of Mrs. Gilbert W. Chapman in Memory of Charles B. Goodspeed.

Above left: Picasso. *Portrait of Wilhelm Uhde*, 1910. Oil on canvas, 81×60 cm. Private collection.

Left: Picasso. *Portrait of Vollard*, 1910. Oil on canvas, 92×65 cm. Pushkin Museum of Fine Art, Moscow.

Camille Corot (?). *La petite Jeannette*, c. 1848. Oil on paper mounted on canvas, 30×27 cm (given to Picasso by Uhde). Musée du Louvre: Picasso Gift.

There is a mean edge to Picasso's portrayal of Uhde—to the Prussian prissiness embodied in the tiny desiccated cupid's bow of a mouth; the starched points of the winged collar that rhyme with the two triangles of his lofty forehead; and not least its brittle, rectilinear structure of what look like jagged shards of smoky glass. The characterization is the more mordant for being carried out with deftness, delicacy and wit. This painting did not altogether please the sitter. In one of the very few references to it in his writings, Uhde compares it unfavorably with the Vollard portrait, which he extols as Rembrandtian.[16] As for the sitter's quid pro quo, this took the form of Corot's ugliest little figure painting (if Corot it is). The ugliness endeared it to Picasso: he claimed to treasure it.

The artist's attitude to his next sitter, Vollard, was more respectful. Vollard had taken him up and dropped him and once again taken him up, but had never rewarded him with a contract. Picasso was all the more eager to keep in with Vollard because he had not only become the most important post-impressionist dealer in Paris, he had sat to every illustrious artist of his time.

> The most beautiful woman who ever lived [Picasso told Françoise Gilot] never had her portrait painted, drawn or engraved any oftener than Vollard —by Cézanne, Renoir, Rouault, Bonnard, Forain, almost everybody, in fact. I think they all did him through a sense of competition, each one wanting to do him better than the others. He had the vanity of a woman, that man. Renoir did him as a toreador, stealing *my* stuff, really. But my Cubist portrait of him is the best one of them all.[17]

Since Picasso's previous portrait of Vollard—it dated from the time of his first (1901) Paris exhibition—had been a failure, he was the more on his mettle.[18] Besides, he still hoped to convert to cubism the dealer who had done so much for Cézanne. If Vollard would only come round to art that was arguably Cézanne-inspired, he might once again buy out Picasso's studio or sign him up, instead of making irregular, albeit extensive, purchases.

Picasso's portrait neither mocks nor flatters Vollard; it honors him. The nose is blunt as a steam engine, underneath a forehead tiered like a papal tiara, and faceted to boot: an image that is daunting yet equivocal. "Do you want to know what Vollard really looked like?" Picasso asked a group of friends, many years later. And he held up a slice of tongue (we were having lunch in the studio) to demonstrate how the dealer's disproportionately large forehead resembled the fatty part of the tongue, while the rest of his features corresponded to the scrunched-up cartilage underneath. "Now that's Vollard for you."[19] According to Fernande, Picasso worked on the portrait for months.[20] Sittings were no hardship for this vain man who liked to take long naps after Lucullan luncheons in his basement. And, sure enough, the portrait looks as if the sitter were asleep. Although Cézanne presides over this great painting—as do the Spaniards El Greco and Ribera (as in the Prado's *Democritus*)—it failed to please the dealer. A year or two later, Vollard let the Russian collector Ivan Morozov have the portrait for 3,000 francs—possibly to sweeten a deal.

Vollard remained ambivalent about cubism. He made sporadic splurges —notably in the fall of 1909 and 1910, when Kahnweiler hung back—but he felt that the time for showing cubist paintings had not yet arrived; or, rather, he was not going to put his cubist paintings up for sale until

Kahnweiler had established a lucrative market for them. Hence his decision to limit his 1910 exhibition to works of the Blue and Rose periods—a decision that someone (probably Picasso) persuaded him to change: three days after the opening, Apollinaire announced in *L'Intransigeant* that several "characteristic"—i.e., cubist—works had been added to the show.[21] However, since Apollinaire complained that no catalog had been printed, no invitations mailed and no frames provided ("although works of great artistic merit can do without the boost of frames, such arrant simplicity seems excessive"),[22] one can only assume that Vollard, who was a notorious pack rat, may have wanted to propitiate Picasso, but at minimum cost.

Vollard continued to make occasional purchases but refrained from any wholehearted commitment to Picasso's work. It would be twenty years or more before they collaborated—when the dealer's interest in publishing deluxe editions coincided with the artist's preoccupation with engraving. The outcome would be Picasso's set of eighty-nine engravings known as the *Vollard Suite* (1930–37). According to Dora Maar, Vollard became so fascinated by Picasso's virtuosity as an engraver that he liked to hang around Lacourière's studio to watch him at work.[23] Picasso would always revere this dealer and never tease or torture him, as he did Kahnweiler. And Vollard's funeral would be one of the very few which Picasso suppressed his dread of death enough to attend.

Picasso. *Portrait of Vollard*, March 4, 1937, from the *Vollard Suite*. Aquatint, 34.8×24.7 cm. Private collection.

Kahnweiler's was the last of Picasso's major cubist portraits of men. Since the start of the series five or six months earlier, the artist had passed in and out of a phase of near abstraction—a development that Kahnweiler signally failed to support, as we saw in the previous chapter. The fact that the dealer had once again let him down by buying few if any examples of his recent work—possibly because he was out to manipulate him into signing a contract—might explain the lack of intensity in the characterization. The Kahnweiler portrait, which required twenty to thirty sittings, as well as a photographic session, was not always so fragmented. Picasso later told Françoise Gilot that it originally looked "as though it were about to go up in smoke. But when I paint smoke, I want you to be able to drive a nail into it. So I added the attributes—a suggestion of eyes, the wave in the hair, an ear lobe, the clasped hands—and now you can."[24] Picasso went on to equate cubism with giving a long and difficult explanation to a child: "You add certain details that he understands immediately in order to . . . buoy him up for the difficult parts." You teach people something new, he said, "by mixing what they know with what they don't know. Then . . . they think, 'Ah, I know that.' And then it's just one more step to, 'Ah, I know the whole thing.'"[25] He also told Zervos: "There is no abstract art. You must always start with something. Afterwards you can remove all trace of reality. There's no danger then . . . because the idea of the object will have left an indelible mark."[26]

Picasso. *The Student*, 1910–11. Oil on canvas, 46×33 cm (destroyed). Kahnweiler photograph: Galerie Louise Leiris.

This time there were no Cézannes or Renoirs of Kahnweiler to challenge Picasso; there was only Van Dongen's showy fauve portrait in the sitter's dining room, which makes this least theatrical of men look as if he has been overly made up for the stage. Picasso's Kahnweiler is a total contrast: low-keyed, cerebral, cool. There is no mockery, as there is in the Uhde—except possibly for the emphasis on the twin arcs of the watch chain, that badge of ironclad respectability. (Identical twin arcs

Mukuyi mask (Punu, Gabon) from Picasso's collection. Baobab wood and kaolin powder, ht: 28cm. Musée Picasso.

indicate a hairdo or a headband in a painting (destroyed in the 1940s) known as *The Student*, which seems to be a study for, or after, the Kahnweiler portrait.) Nor is there any awe, as there is in the Vollard, indeed no evidence of personal feeling. The detachment of this portrait is a measure of the distance Picasso liked to put between himself and his dealer. Whereas the *bande à Picasso* addressed one another in the intimate second-person singular, artist and dealer always used the second-person plural and treated each other formally. Outside the gallery they seldom socialized. If Picasso went most days to the gallery, it was (he told Dora Maar) "out of habit, like a Spaniard who goes to the barber every day."[27]

The mysterious object in the top left-hand corner of the Kahnweiler portrait has been said to represent a New Caledonian tiki (a roof pole).[28] In fact it is a Mukuyi mask from the Gabon,[29] and it can be seen hanging on the studio wall in some of Picasso's photographs of his friends. The inclusion of a tribal mask is more traditional than one might think. Just as a Roman bust in the background of a Pompeo Batoni portrait of an English milord establishes the sitter as a man of cultivated taste who collects classical sculpture, this Mukuyi mask establishes Kahnweiler as a man of the avant-garde who, like most connoisseurs of cubism, collected (and occasionally dealt in) primitive art. The device also enables the artist to play off a human head against a sculpted one; modernist concepts against those of another age and culture. Picasso reduces Kahnweiler to what amounts to a fetish: a hank of hair, a watch chain, a knotted tie, assorted body parts, some barely identifiable swatches of stuff stuck on to a cubist grid. The rest of this minimally accoutered figure melts into tactile space, like a snowman, who leaves nothing behind but his "attributes": his pipe, hat, muffler, and the lumps of coal that were once his eyes.

* * *

It is at this point, fall, 1910, that we should take account of a young Spaniard who was determined to be the third man of the cubist nucleus. This was the gifted young cartoonist Juan Gris, who had arrived in Paris in 1906 to escape the draft in Spain and make a new life in a new country under a new name. Four years later, this modest Madrileño, who lived in the Bateau Lavoir with a mistress and baby, surprised his neighbors by abandoning his career as a humoristic draftsman (for *L'Assiette au beurre*, *Charivari* and other journals in Paris and Barcelona) to become a cubist painter. His catalyst was his neighbor: Picasso had taken his compatriot under his wing and initiated him into the mysteries of cubism. Forever after, Gris would revere Picasso and sign himself "*ton elève et ami.*" His letters to Picasso are decidedly filial in tone, notably one in which he asks his "*cher maître*," when he was in Madrid in 1917, to visit his mother, who was looking after his son, Georges. Gris later learned that Picasso had tried to do so but found nobody at home.[30]

Gris was born (1887) José Victoriano Carmelo Carlos González Pérez —the thirteenth of fourteen children—to a once prosperous Madrileño merchant. He had studied under the academic painter José Moreno Carbonero, as Picasso had done a few years earlier. (Whereas Picasso had complained of this teacher's rectilinear formulae for drawing, Gris had evidently benefited from them.) By the age of eighteen Gris was

Picasso. *Portrait of Kahnweiler* (detail). The Art Institute of Chicago (see p. 173).

publishing drawings in *Blanco y Negro*, the magazine on which the twelve-year-old Picasso had modeled his family broadsheet. A year later (1906), he illustrated a book of verse entitled *Alma America* by a Peruvian poet, José Santos Chocano. Conversion to Jugendstil at the hands of Willy Geiger, a young German illustrator resident in Madrid, endowed him with the ability to reduce intricate subjects, such as a still life in front of a window opening onto a landscape, into terse but eloquent vignettes. For pointing out how Gris reverted to Jugendstil devices in his later cubist work—shades of Josef Hoffmann and Henry van de Velde—I was scolded by no less than Kahnweiler. He was scandalized by the suggestion that there might be a connection between the "low" art of Gris's early years and the "high" art of his maturity, let alone between modish Jugendstil and sacrosanct cubism. Kahnweiler was adamant that the early illustrations were nothing but a "*gagne pain*" (bread ticket),[31] adamant that the one and only admissible begetter of cubism was Cézanne. Kahnweiler was as intransigent on this point as a nobleman claiming descent from Charlemagne.

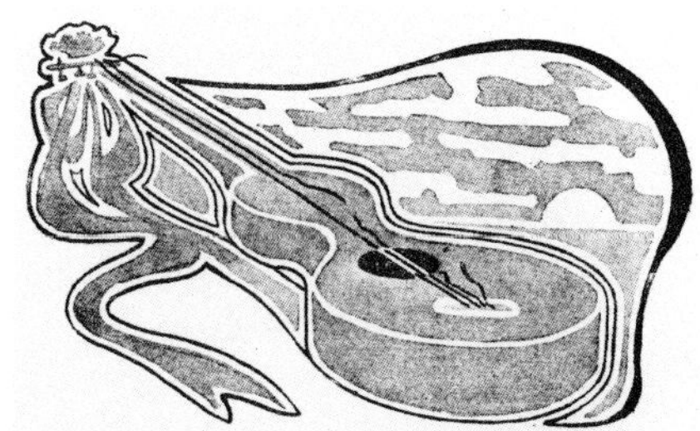

Juan Gris. *El Alma del Payador* (from *Alma America)*, 1906. Author's collection.

The Bateau Lavoir studio that Picasso arranged for Gris to rent was the one that Van Dongen had handed on to Jacques Vaillant—a painter whom Salmon repeatedly characterizes as "frenetic"—less than a year before. And there Gris lived for most of the next ten years, at first even more poorly than the other tenants. Soon there would be a dim mistress, Lucie Belin, and in 1909 a son, Georges, who was packed off to Madrid to be brought up by Gris's family. Later (1914) there would be a beautiful wife, Josette Herpin (or Grisette, as her husband sometimes called her), who helped out by working as a saleswoman in a *maison de couture*.

Few of the *bande à Picasso* warmed to Gris. "One never had fun in Juan Gris's studio," Salmon claimed.[32] Despite his dashing looks, Gris was shy, short on charm and wit, and shabby genteel rather than shabby bohemian. His letters reveal this superb painter to have been a *brave bourgeois* at heart, a little too prone to self-pity and self-righteousness (his conversion to freemasonry comes as no surprise). A saving grace was his sense of rhythm. Rhythm redeems his work from slide-rule rigidity; it also accounts for at least one social accomplishment: ballroom dancing. The chips fell from this solemn Spaniard's shoulders when he addressed himself to the rhythmic intricacies of the tango—intricacies that, back in the studio, he would transpose into cubist counterpoint.

If Gris was not destined to be as much of a pioneer as Picasso or Braque (whose "French" painterliness he held in envious esteem), at least he could work up to being the third man of cubism. By studying every move his two role models made—easy enough to do in the Bateau Lavoir—Gris soon became privy to all the innermost workings of cubism. By the summer of 1910, he felt confident enough to try his hand at watercolor still lifes, practically all of which he destroyed. A few drawings, however, have survived, and they demonstrate how rapidly and effectively Gris transformed himself, under Picasso's aegis, from a caricaturist into a budding cubist. Within a year he had developed into a painter of far more originality and intensity than any of the second generation of cubists except Léger. To establish himself in the eyes of his peers, Gris made strategic gifts of his early works to Duchamp, Picabia, Raynal and Marcoussis, who had also worked for *L'Assiette au beurre*. Most of the rest he sold

Juan Gris. *Self-Portrait*, 1910–11. Pencil on paper, 48×31.2 cm. Private collection, Zurich.

to Père Sagot. And then in January, 1912, he embarked on the portrait of his *maître*.

> Having won Picasso's friendship [Severini wrote], [Gris] could reveal his talent as an artist capable of true painting. But the portrait that introduced him into the arena was not destined to promote [their] friendship. In black and white geometric outlines Picasso looked decidedly gray and radiated a cold expression. Gris had titled the painting *Hommage à Picasso* as a way to confirm his commitment to cubism, but Picasso, far from being flattered, was extremely irritated, and Gris was rather mortified.[33]

Juan Gris. *Hommage à Picasso*, 1912. 93×74.1 cm. Art Institute of Chicago: Gift of Leigh B. Block.

Picasso must also have been mortified that Gris's portrait is more indebted to Metzinger's simpering *Le Goûter* (p. 209), which was the sensation of the 1911 Salon d'Automne,[34] than to his own cubist portraits of 1910.

Kahnweiler usually treated anyone trying to muscle in on cubism as a gate-crasher; however, he made an exception of Gris and welcomed him into the fold. That he was Picasso's protégé made little if any difference. The dealer had been enormously impressed by Gris's contributions to an exhibition at the Galerie de la Boëtie in October, 1912.[35] These included the first cubist collages ever exhibited: *Le Lavabo*, with its piece of mirror, and *La Montre*, glued to which is a bit of paper printed with *Le pont Mirabeau*, Apollinaire's melancholy poem about time ("*Vienne la nuit sonne l'heure / Les jours s'en vont je demeure*"). Gris had evidently jumped ahead of Braque and Picasso. On the strength of these highly original works, which gave rise to much comment in the press, Kahnweiler signed a contract with Gris in February, 1913 (two months after signing one with Picasso), for his entire output, in exchange for a modest monthly sum. The buttoned-up artist and buttoned-up dealer would be friends for life. None of Kahnweiler's other artists would be as close to him as Gris. Picasso would resent this closeness.

Max Jacob was likewise supportive of Gris, so was Raynal, but Apollinaire anointed him with the faintest of praise. So did Salmon, although he had supplied the captions for Gris's series of tobacco cartoons. He wrote that he had "never expected much of this handsome young man. Some of us labored under the impression that he would never rise any higher than the artistic level of the hard-working artist of *L'Assiette au beurre*."[36] Braque was also understandably ambivalent about the new arrival. He cannot be blamed for preferring to be part of a duo rather than a trio, especially when the third interloper was so beholden to Picasso. Indeed, resentment at the young caricaturist's irruption into the cubist midst never ceased to rankle, to judge by an exchange of words at a luncheon many years later. In response to an attempt by Picasso to needle him by extravagantly praising Gris, Braque turned to Cocteau and said that "the reason why so many caricaturists ended up as cubists is that they required the narrowness and '*rigueur*' of an Aristotelian discipline if they were to live down their discreditable past."[37]

Juan Gris. *Le Lavabo*, 1912. Oil and fragments of looking-glass stuck on canvas, 130×89 cm. Private collection.

Braque's distaste for Gris's former métier suggests that he himself may have once indulged in *dessins humoristiques*. Certainly his fashion-plate drawing of Lepape dancing with Marie Laurencin (see p. 62) is too accomplished to be a solitary lapse. Shame at having dabbled in this "low" genre might explain Braque's wholesale destruction of his early work; it would also explain his subtle put-down of the unnamed Gris all those years later—a put-down that was the more damning for implying that the "*rigueur*" on which Gris prided himself was a badge of bogus artistic respectability contrived out of cartoonists' formulae. To Braque's fastidious, poetic mind, this sort of slickness was as inartistic and abhorrent as the mathematical picture-making of the Section d'Or.

The difference in Picasso's and Braque's attitude to Gris can be summed up if we compare the former's verdicts—"Gris kept the accounts of cubism,"[38] and, on another occasion, "he learned his grammar all right"[39]—with the latter's favorite story about him. In the course of visiting the Bateau Lavoir to inspect his recent work (circa 1914), Braque told Gris that one corner of a still life "did not make sense." Gris ruefully agreed. After consulting his working drawings he confessed to "having made a mistake in my calculations." "Watch out," Braque replied, "else you are going to find yourself trying to fit two fruit dishes into a single apple."[40] Braque's joke must have rankled. Gris apparently came to feel that the drawings he had done with a ruler, compass, protractor and divider were somehow shameful—cheating! For he requested his widow and dealer to destroy all the evidence—several hundred working drawings—after his death. To judge by the very few surviving examples, this holocaust deprived us of invaluable insights into the working methods of the only major cubist to succeed in harnessing mathematical calculation to artistic expression.

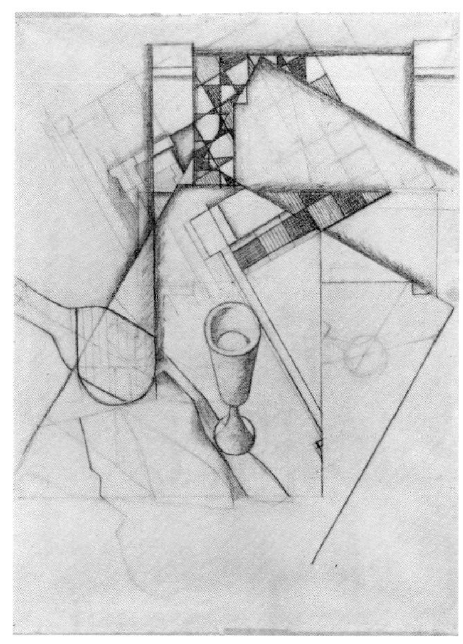

Juan Gris. *Still Life with Glass and Checkerboard*, 1913. Black chalk and pencil on paper, 63×47.7 cm. Graphische Sammlung, Staatsgalerie Stuttgart.

* * *

At this time Picasso befriended another cartoonist on the way to becoming a cubist: Lodwicz Casimir Ladislas Markus, later known as Louis Marcoussis. He was born in 1870 to a prosperous Warsaw carpet dealer and did most of his studying in Poland. By the time Markus settled in Paris, he was thirty-three, older and more proficient than his fellow students at the Académie Julian. Finding this "free" academy a little too free, he left to study at the Louvre and Luxembourg. Around 1905, a decline in his family fortunes obliged Markus to earn his living, so he started doing *dessins humoristiques* for *La Vie Parisienne* and *L'Assiette au beurre*. Since he had a sardonic, satirical eye and a knack for likenesses, his services were much in demand. At the same time he yearned to make his name as a painter and struggled desperately to keep abreast of the latest developments. However, the slickness that served him so well as a cartoonist put paid to Markus's loftier aspirations. After zigzagging from impressionism to divisionism, Nabism to fauvism, he realized that he was little more than an accomplished *pasticheur*. In despair (circa 1907) he abandoned painting and—egged on by his pretty new mistress, Marcelle Humbert—devoted himself to cartoons.

Marcelle was an ambitious *petite bourgeoise*—ambitious for the man in her life as well as herself. By her standards, a successful cartoonist rated higher than a struggling artist, however gifted. For the next three years, Markus did her bidding—with ever declining self-esteem. On the proceeds of the cartoons that he churned out they were able to move into a large apartment on the rue Delambre, complete with that epitome of genteel comfort, a suite of Dufayel furniture. Marcelle turned out to be an exemplary housekeeper, who kept scrupulously to a budget and organized nice little dinners for visiting Poles and the more respectable Montmartre

Louis Marcoussis. Collection P.M.A.

bohemians. Her pert prettiness and his sharp wit and charm made them a popular couple, above all with writers like MacOrlan, Warnod and Carco. The *bande à Picasso* held aloof until the circus brought them all together. One evening at the Cirque Médrano Markus and Marcelle fell into conversation with Braque and Apollinaire. This meeting led to a subsequent one with Picasso, which would transform all their lives.

Thanks to Apollinaire, Markus subsequently Frenchified his name to Marcoussis and converted to cubism. Max Jacob took a shine to the new couple, and Gertrude Stein was so eager to check them out that she had them to dinner. By the winter of 1910–11, they had joined the gang that hung out at L'Ermitage. Picasso liked the Pole's Jewish wit, his astuteness and, not least, his mistress. Marcoussis admired Picasso and envied him his mistress. For her part, Fernande had no problem identifying with Marcelle; they were both intent on becoming ladies, married ones, they hoped. And then, as Stein/Toklas reminds us, there was a further link between the two women: "Fernande's great heroine was Evelyn Thaw [the woman for whom her husband had recently murdered Stanford White], small and negative. [Marcelle] was a little french Evelyn Thaw, small and perfect."[41] The two women confided in each other: Fernande told Marcelle how cold and difficult Picasso was being, maybe that she contemplated taking a lover. Marcelle would have told Fernande that she and Markus were thinking of bowing to family pressure and marrying. She would not have let on that she also contemplated taking a lover—Fernande's.

* * *

Juan Gris. *Place Ravignan*, 1911. Charcoal on paper, 43.5×30.5cm. Private collection.

Meanwhile, Max Jacob was giving cause for concern. Realizing that he had not seen Max for a while, Picasso worried that he might be in trouble and sought him out in his room next door to the Bateau Lavoir. Max was indeed in terrible shape. He had overindulged in ether and henbane and passed out in the gutter. Someone had carried him home, but he was still, Fernande reports, *"à moitié empoisonné."*[42] Picasso put his old friend to bed and told the concierge to keep an eye on him. There was no point in calling a doctor: he would merely insist that the patient renounce drugs, which Jacob was not prepared to do. He prided himself on being a *poète maudit* like Verlaine, also a "pythia," a seer. Drugs sharpened his poetic sensibility, also his divinatory insights, which earned him money and enhanced his power over his friends—at least so he claimed. After conferring with Fernande, who loved Max when she did not hate him (against her better judgment, she used to slip him money for drugs), Picasso insisted that he move into the boulevard de Clichy apartment. They made up a bed for him in the studio and let him stay until he recovered.

According to Fernande, Jacob's *dégringolade* was all the fault of sinister new friends, notably a talented but unsavory journalist called Delphi Fabrice, who shared his taste for drugs and rough sex.[43] Fernande also mentions some menacing thugs, who lurked in the darkest corner of Jacob's ill-lit room, smoking away, massive white hands on their knees, patiently (Fernande says "shamelessly") waiting for guests to leave the poet's Monday-evening get-togethers ("At Homes," which bore as little resemblance to Picasso's Sundays as the latter did to the Steins' Saturdays). It was all louche and morbid and totally "*inattendu*," Fernande says—an

View from the roof of the Bateau Lavoir towards the rue d'Orchampt. Photograph by Picasso. Archives Picasso.

atmosphere to the taste of amateurs of the bizarre, not least Picasso, "who laughed indulgently at his friend's most outrageous excesses and thus encouraged him."[44]

"Despite Jacob's lack of science," Fernande said, "one left his divinatory séances more impressed than one liked to admit."[45] The poet also earned money making fetishes for his friends. According to Fernande, these consisted of

> scraps of parchment black with all kinds of strange hieroglyphs and bits of copper, iron or silver, which he would use one of my hatpins to engrave with people's astrological signs. . . . I will always treasure a piece of copper adorned with my birth sign, Gemini, of no importance as a fetish but as a present from Max—something that could only bring luck.[46]

Whether or not Picasso used Max's presence in the boulevard de Clichy apartment as a pretext, he decided he wanted even more room to work. And so he returned to the Bateau Lavoir—to a studio at the back, on the floor below his old one. "He could work better there"[47] —away from visitors, usually friends of Gertrude Stein's, who wanted to appear *à la page*. He could also get away from Fernande. As well as providing extra space in which to paint the sizable Field panels, the studio enabled him to have affairs on the side and to paint pictures which paid oblique tribute to other women—pictures which Fernande would have had no difficulty decoding, had she been allowed to see them. The return to the Bateau Lavoir is a measure of how much Picasso missed—would always miss—the bohemian camaraderie of his early days in Montmartre; a measure, too, of the widening gulf between Fernande and himself. Instead of leaving together to spend the summer of 1911 in Spain, as they had done the two previous years, they made separate plans. "Pablo is leaving for the Midi (Céret) in a few days," Fernande wrote Gertrude Stein, who was summering in Fiesole. "I am staying in Paris. I may go to Holland"—with Guus Van Dongen.[48] In the end Fernande did not visit Holland. From early July until mid-August, when she finally went to Céret herself, she stayed on alone in Paris. Bored, bereft and still a beauty, she started looking around for a lover, and to her eternal regret she found one.

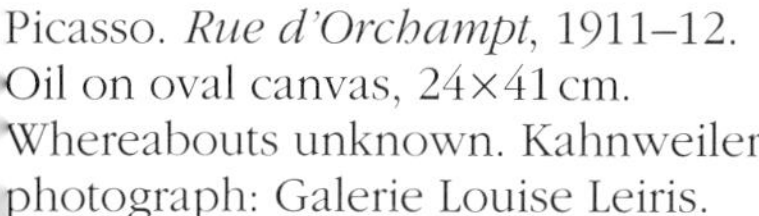

Picasso. *Rue d'Orchampt*, 1911–12. Oil on oval canvas, 24×41 cm. Whereabouts unknown. Kahnweiler photograph: Galerie Louise Leiris.

12

Summer at Céret 1911

Manolo. *Portrait of Frank Burty Haviland*, c.1908. Graphite pencil on paper, 20.8×18.3cm. Private collection.

Opposite: Picasso. *The Fan (L'Indépendant)*, summer, 1911. Oil on canvas, 61×50cm. Private collection.

FOR THE PREVIOUS TWO SUMMERS PICASSO had promised his friends Frank Burty Haviland and Manolo, the sculptor, that he would visit them in French Catalonia. Both times he had let them down. The summer of 1911 was different. There was no particular point in going back to Spain: he would not have wanted to explain why he was on his own, and in any case his parents were off for the summer in Menorca, staying with their son-in-law, Dr. Vilató. Instead Picasso decided to try Céret, in the foothills of the Pyrenees, where the Havilands and the Manolos had settled the previous year. It was cheap, they said, picturesque yet unspoiled, within easy reach of sea and mountains. The inhabitants spoke Catalan, danced the *sardana* and held bullfights, so it was almost as good as going to Spanish Catalonia. Picasso could paint in peace, above all the Field decorations, details of which could be settled with Haviland. No less important, Braque, who had promised to spend the latter part of the summer with him, liked the idea of the place.

Picasso reached Céret around July 10–12, happy for once to be alone. He put up at the Hôtel du Canigou (named after the mountain that rears up behind the town, and that Picasso—unlike Braque, Gris, Herbin, Soutine, Chagall et al.—was never tempted to paint). Haviland loaned him a room in his large house to use as a studio. The heat wave that broke out shortly after Picasso arrived explains the abundance of fans in the still lifes. Fans circulated the air in the studio; they also articulate the space in the paintings. Despite the heat, Picasso loved Céret and his work soon settled into a productive new pattern. For a companion, he had acquired a new monkey, this time a male: "He has two noble balls" he wrote Apollinaire;[1] and spends all day admiring himself in the top of a tin can.[2]

To Picasso's relief, a letter arrived on July 16, confirming that Braque would soon be joining him. Braque followed up the letter with a parcel of hats—part of a lot of a hundred gray and beige derbies that he had bought for twenty sous apiece at a Le Havre auction and distributed to his friends, including Max Jacob. "Brand new but out-of-date antique *cloches* (according to Salmon) pulled out of some dusty old cupboard, exported to Africa and shipped back to Le Havre, when the blacks showed no interest."[3] Picasso was predictably tickled (he was not the only great man to be fascinated by hats). On July 25, he wrote thanking Braque: "What a surprise, you can't have any idea how much I laughed, above all in the nude. . . . We put them on with Manolo last night to go to the café but with false mustaches and side-whiskers applied with cork."[4] Hence the glued-on, italicized look of the mustaches with which Picasso embellishes the faces of his *Musicians* and *Poets*. Braque replied that he would be arriving at Céret in a couple of weeks, that he hoped to stay on the outskirts rather than in the center of town and that he looked forward to Picasso's meeting him at the station wearing one of the hats.

While waiting for Braque to arrive, Picasso resumed working on the Brooklyn decorations, which he had now been able to discuss with Field's cousin Frank. Always very sensitive to his surroundings, Picasso proposed themes of local, that is to say Catalan, interest, and wasted no time writing to Braque and Kahnweiler about them. Although the fanciful subjects that he lists are not identified as such, they can have related only to the Field project. The most ambitious was a large painting of "a stream in the middle of the town with girls swimming and houses with round windows and areas of transparent blackness full of light and houses that are round and houses that are very square (but what language)."[5] Picasso also mentions three other subjects: "The Pearl of the Roussillon," "Poet and Peasant," and a "Christ," which would presumably have been a Crucifixion.

Beyond the description in Picasso's letter to Braque, all we know of the large painting is a partial glimpse of an unfinished canvas tacked to the wall in the background of a photograph that the artist took of himself in his Paris studio a few months later. As well as being out of focus, the painting is so obscured by other canvases that the subject is difficult to decipher, but it seems to correspond to the description in his letter. So far as I can see, it depicts what would become one of the artist's favorite motifs: a still life in front of a window framing a view—in this case the view from Haviland's house over the river Tech. (Picasso's Bateau Lavoir neighbor Auguste Herbin would paint two versions of this scene when he rented this house two years later.) The cubist clutter in the foreground represents a guitar on a fringed cloth and various other objects set on a table (identifiable by the trompe l'œil drawer knob). To unify interior and exterior space Picasso uses a looped-back curtain; this frames both the pyramidal still life, indoors, and the townscape—a conglomeration of round and square houses such as Picasso describes in his letter—outdoors. We also glimpse part of the Pont du Diable, which figures in a related view (the *Landscape at Céret* in the Guggenheim Museum). No bathers are discernible.

Auguste Herbin. *Landscape at Céret*, 1913. Oil on canvas, 94×91.5cm. Musée d'Art Moderne, Céret.

If my interpretation of this "decoration" is correct, it might have been intended to function as a surrogate window in Field's library—to brighten up a room which plans reveal to have had little natural light. Haviland, who knew the Brooklyn house of old, would have remembered how a former owner, John Roebling, designer of the Brooklyn Bridge, had watched that great feat of engineering take shape as he lay dying in an upstairs room. Might he have suggested that a view of the Pont du Diable would constitute a symbolical link between the cousins' houses? Had this painting materialized, it would have been far and away the largest and most symphonic of Picasso's cubist paintings—a change from the chamber-music scale that he had come to favor. The fate of this large composition is a mystery. Old habits die hard, and Picasso seldom if ever destroyed his botched canvases. Out of principle as much as economy, he usually

Above: Self-portrait photograph by Picasso with the largest of his canvases for the Field project (lost or destroyed), 1911. Archives Picasso.

Left: Picasso. *Landscape at Céret*, summer, 1911. Pen and sepia ink on paper, 19.4×30.7 cm. Musée Picasso.

recycled them. X-rays may well reveal this composition lurking under one of the later paintings.

Whether this would have been the largest of the Field panels we do not know. The scheme called for three sizable horizontals: 185×230 cm, 185×270 cm, 185×300 cm. One of these was presumably reserved for "Poet and Peasant," a painting about which we know nothing except that it gave Picasso trouble. "I'm going to begin the *Poet and Peasant* all over again," he wrote Braque, "I've abandoned the other one."[6] The title probably refers to Franz von Suppé's celebrated concert overture of that name, the one that is played by military bands the world over.[7] But what might the painting have represented? A bandstand? A reference to the play for which Suppé wrote the overture? An allusion to the overture's title in the form of two contrasting figures seated at a café table? The last is the most likely. The *Soldier and Girl* (spring, 1912) is not big enough for the Field panels, but it might be a study for one of them. The cubist hieroglyphs identifying the subject—a rudimentary epaulette for the soldier, skimpy tresses for the girl (signs that are not to be found in the painting, only in the preparatory sketch)—could easily have been altered to designate a poet and peasant.

Picasso. *Cobla*, 1912–14. Pen and sepia ink on paper, 10.5×13.5cm. Musée Picasso.

The only Céret drawings that would lend themselves to a group composition depict a *cobla*, the band that accompanies *sardana* dancers from a high wooden platform erected for the occasion. The musicians perched on their skeletal bandstand tootling away at wind instruments in front of skeletal music stands would have provided a suitable motif for large-scale cubist representation—all those armatures. The horizontal format would have conformed to the proportions of Field's wider panels, and the subject would have fitted in with the rest of the ensemble, especially if—to take this hypothesis a stage further—Picasso envisaged a *Sardana* as a pendant to a *Cobla*. He could then have allegorized Music and Dance, like Matisse, whose *Danse II* partakes of a *sardana*.

The Doutres *cobla* playing at the Festa de Sant Sadurní at Vernet, November, 1908.

At Céret Matisse must have been much on Picasso's mind. He was spending the summer a few kilometers away at Collioure. Ironically, both artists were working on large decorative paintings. While Picasso was struggling with the Field panels, Matisse was in the throes of an orientalist set piece, *Interior with Aubergines*, which proclaims his mastery of the genre. The two mutually mistrustful artists made no effort to see each other this summer. It was only after Picasso's departure that Braque visited Collioure and "bumped into Matisse."[8] Meanwhile Apollinaire was circulating a *canard* about this situation. Seeing the letters *KUB* emblazoned on a wall outside his house at Collioure, Matisse supposedly suspected the cubists of playing a practical joke on him, until he realized it was an advertisement for a bouillon cube.

As for the "Christ" that Picasso had told Kahnweiler he was painting, what could be more structurally appropriate to this phase of cubism than a figure on a cross? Given his messianic identification and youthful training as a religious painter, Picasso was certainly aware that the cruciform structure in a number of his cubist paintings could be subliminally emotive and evoke, albeit faintly, the most highly charged image in Western art. For all that an emphatic axial structure would have been well suited to a cubist composition—above all an exaggeratedly vertical one—a figure on a cross might well have proved too Catholic for a Quaker like Field.

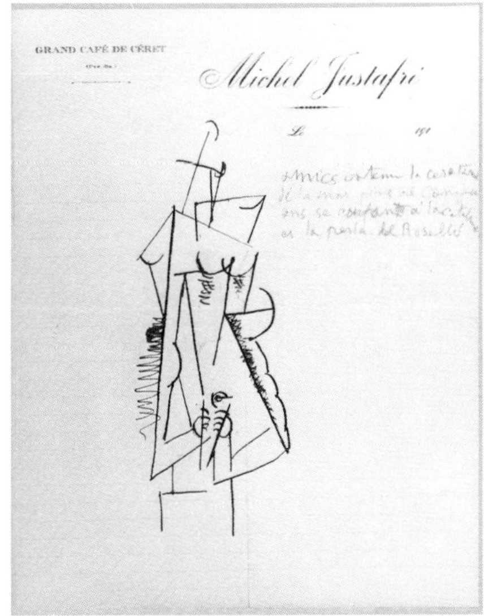

Picasso. *Woman of Céret* with lines from the "Pearl of Roussillon," summer, 1911. Pen and sepia ink on stationery of the Grand Café de Céret (Michel Justafré), 26.8×21.4cm. Musée Picasso.

No drawings of the period relate to a Christ or a Crucifixion, nor is there any record of such a painting. However, it may yet turn up under another composition.

Nor do any of the Céret images correspond to "The Pearl of the Roussillon." All we know is that the subject derives from a song in celebration of the region and its beautiful girls attributed to a local poet, Joan Amade. A few days before Picasso's arrival, Amade had organized an elaborate folkloric concert in Céret's bullring. The conductor was Déodat de Séverac, who had written music for some of Amade's songs. On a sheet of café stationery Picasso noted down the relevant lines from Amade's ditty: "Friends, come sing the praises from the sea all the way to the Canigou of the girl from Céret. Let's sing to la Catalana, who is the pearl of the Roussillon." The only major painting that corresponds to this is the magnificent *Accordionist* in the Guggenheim Museum, which Picasso told Braque he had begun soon after arriving in Céret ("very liquid to start with and [then] Signac-style methodical treatment—[scumbles] only at the end").[9] Such works as the *Accordionist*; the identically sized *Poet*, a mustachioed man—perhaps Amade?—with a pipe in his mouth (several more in a rack on the wall) and what looks like a scroll of manuscript in his hand; and the *Man with Tenora* (p. 104), which Uhde would buy and Picasso would later rediscover on Cooper's walls—such works as these are the culmination of analytic cubism.

The arcane beauty of these paintings—their subtlety, gravity and mystery—is self-evident. But their meaning is not. A work like *The Accordionist*, which is the product of phenomenal artistic intelligence as well as phenomenal artistic skill, makes far heavier demands on the acuity of our perceptions and wits than the Salon cubists' formulaic works. It also challenges our sense of structure, touch, humor, poetry (all those rhymes and double entendres) and, not least, our feelings about sex. If Picasso always insisted that his *Accordionist* is a woman, it was for good reason. As he often said, the subject of a painting is of the utmost importance. Here, the genital positioning of the "Pearl of Roussillon's" instrument is the clue. Her "squeeze box," as the accordion is vulgarly known,[10] with its little buttons and keys, not to mention the manual inflation and deflation that controls the emission of sound, turns out to be what the painting is about. Flam has suggested a coded allusion to Matisse: Picasso has borrowed the *Accordionist*'s triangular structure from his rival's magnificent *The Manila Shawl*, a portrait of Madame Matisse dressed in a flowered shawl as a flamenco dancer, which had been exhibited at the Indépendants a few months earlier. The "squeeze box" could well be a response to Matisse's no less pubicly placed splodge of a flower.

* * *

Déodat de Séverac sitting on the Pont du Diable, Céret, c. 1911.

Picasso's friendship with the charming composer Déodat de Séverac went back to Bateau Lavoir days.[11] Now almost forgotten and far less frequently played than his friend, the popular *folkloriste* Canteloube, Séverac was once regarded as the equal of Debussy and Ravel—"*le trio de la jeune musique*," Henri Sauguet said. Around the turn of the century, Séverac had been introduced to the "Apaches"—a Montmartrois group of composers, writers and painters: disciples of Ravel—by the Catalan pianist Ricardo Viñes. Through Viñes, Séverac met Haviland and Manolo, and through

Above left: Picasso. *Soldier and Girl*, 1911. Oil on canvas, 116×81cm. Private collection, Paris.

Above right: Picasso. *The Poet*, summer, 1911. Oil on canvas, 130×89cm. The Solomon R. Guggenheim Foundation: The Peggy Guggenheim Collection, Venice.

Right: Déodat de Séverac (standing left) with the Cortie-Mattes *cobla*, 1911. Archives Festival de Déodat de Séverac.

them he met Picasso. Déodat, who did watercolors and designed costumes for his own operas, claimed that each musical instrument evoked a different color: for instance the *cobla* player's *tenora* was "red, red—sunlight."

Another local luminary was Louis Codet: a mustachioed bard who might also conceivably have inspired Picasso's *The Poet.* This great-great-nephew of Voltaire and friend of Apollinaire was passionately proud of the Roussillon and had been instrumental in persuading Manolo and Haviland to settle there. So that Manolo, who was a draft dodger, could catch a glimpse of Spain, these two friends had originally gone to the frontier town of Bourg-Madame, where Picasso had promised to visit them on his way back from Horta in 1909, but was deterred by the prospect of several hours in a horse-drawn vehicle. Séverac went in his place and put the finishing touches to his first opera, *Cœur de Moulin*, which was about to open at the Opéra Comique. Manolo and Haviland had stayed on at Bourg-Madame until December, and then set off to visit Maillol at Banyuls. Icy Pyrenean winds forced them to break their journey at Amélie-les-Bains, which they could not abide—too many invalids and spittoons. To decide between Banyuls or Céret as their next stop, they flipped a coin. Céret won. They arrived on foot and put up at the Hôtel Canigou. Three days later, Séverac joined them, and Céret was launched as a *ville d'art.* Picasso and Braque would be the next arrivals, followed, in 1912, by Kisling and, in 1913, by Juan Gris, Max Jacob and Herbin. In the 1920s, Masson, Soutine, Chagall and Dalí would work there. Much later (1953), local patriots would do their best to entice Picasso to return to the area, even giving him a choice of ancient monuments where he could paint in peace. The artist declined the honor.

Picasso. *Mustachioed Man with Tenora*, summer, 1911. Pen, India ink and black chalk on paper, 30.8×19.5cm. Musée Picasso.

Toulousain by birth, Séverac felt very much at home in Céret. He settled in with Henriette Tardieu, the woman he would eventually marry, and wrote an oratorio, *Héliogabale*, which required 400 musicians, 160 singers and 40 dancers when it was first performed, in 1910, at an open-air festival at Béziers. The following year he became a local hero when he celebrated the anniversary of the Céretois music society with the first performance of his and Amade's folkloric *Cant de Vallespir.* Inspired by the *sardana*, Séverac scored more and more of his music for the dry, nasal tones of the *cobla's flabiols* (little flutes), *tibles* (rustic oboes) and *tenores*—instruments that we sometimes find in Picasso's Céret paintings.[12] If these arcane instruments intrigued Picasso, it was by virtue of their regional association rather than their musicality. They symbolized the fragile Catalan culture, which he would always hold in pious regard.

Why did the unmusical Picasso paint so many musical instruments and instrumentalists? Could it be that he wanted his amazing eye to compensate for his insensitive ear? Picasso was very conscious of this shortcoming. He never went to concerts, he told Séverac, for fear of failing to perceive the intrinsic quality of what was being played (a fear that Fernande attributes to Picasso's superiority complex: "He said he could only be touched by things to which he felt superior").[13] The prevalence of musicians in his Céretois work may also have been a response to his closeness to Séverac. For, as Picasso once said, the character, profession and language of close companions had a way of rubbing off on him. Life at Céret revolved around this charming and successful composer rather than the callow Haviland or the wacky Manolo. A cubist drawing of a

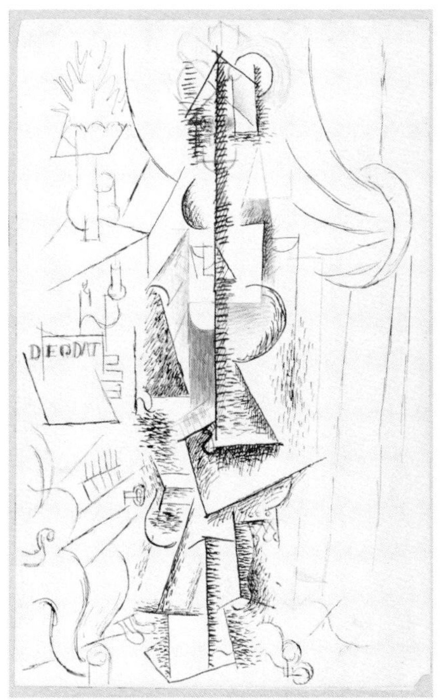

Picasso. *Pianist with Music by Déodat de Séverac*, spring, 1912. Pen, India ink and pencil on paper, 34.2×22.2cm. Musée Picasso.

Picasso. *Head* (study for portrait of Frank Burty Haviland), summer, 1912. Ink on paper. Picasso Heirs.

pianist began as a portrait of Séverac, in pencil, but ended up as a nude woman, in ink. Haviland appears in drawing after drawing. He is easily recognizable, given his distinctive sign: two scrolls of hair flanking a center parting. As Karmel has pointed out, Picasso had recently taken a photograph of Haviland, presumably with a view to doing a portrait that was never in the end executed.[14] There are, however, a number of caricatural drawings in which the man's idiosyncratic coiffure is rendered as a pair of roof tiles, setting up a double entendre: roof = hair. Some of these drawings exhibit another typically Picassian contrivance: the ivory-knobbed stick that Haviland clutches in the photograph is conjured into an erect penis.[15] Might Picasso have envisaged using Haviland as the subject of one of the Field panels?

Haviland never made a success of his own life, but he enjoyed helping his friends make a success of theirs, so long as this was not too costly. Besides enabling Manolo and his comical stick of a wife, the former barmaid Jeanne de la Rochette (known as Totote), to settle down at Céret in unwonted security, he revered Picasso to the point of self-immolation. To re-establish his identity as an artist, Haviland ultimately had no choice but to purge his style of its overwhelming Picassian taint and sell off the paintings by his nemesis. Given his insecurity, Haviland must have had a hard time trying to paint in the Maison Alcouffe, with Picasso revolutionizing art in the next room. The arrangement did not last long: Picasso soon moved to a studio of his own. Forty years later, the artist would take a group of friends, myself included, to visit Céret and its museum, of which Haviland was then curator. Tagging along was the widowed Totote: gravel-voiced and skinny (so skinny, Picasso said, "that she had to hold a broomstick to give herself volume") and, as he also observed, playing the Celestina to the extent of offering him the choice between her adopted daughter and a local *comtesse*. By contrast, the other relic of the cubist past, the ghostlike Haviland, seemed as tumbledown as the Alcouffe house, where he had once lived. However, the view of the Pont du Diable, the elegant arcaded bridge spanning the gorge of the river Tech, had hardly changed. This bridge had been built by the devil one ink-black night to the sound of mysterious Catalan music and a pervasive smell of sulfur. Picasso told us that. He jeered at legends; he also heeded them.[16]

Manolo. *Totote with Cat*, c. 1910–14. Graphite on paper, 35.3×25.3 cm. Museu Manolo Hugué, Caldes de Montbui.

From his first day at Céret, Picasso himself worked like a devil. Braque's imminent arrival would have been a goad. In Paris the two painters had kept in the closest possible touch. As Picasso told Françoise Gilot, "Almost every evening, either I went to Braque's studio or Braque came to mine. Each of us *had* to see what the other had done during the day. We criticized each other's work. A canvas wasn't finished unless both of us felt it was."[17] In the course of the spring, Braque had edged ahead. He had begun using oval canvases to emphasize the play of verticals and horizontals and solve the problem of a canvas's empty corners; he had also started to embellish paintings with stenciled letters ("forms which were outside space and therefore immune to deformation").[18] These innovations had culminated in a painting of a seated man holding a guitar, known (to distinguish it from other paintings of the same subject) as *Le Portugais*. Besides being one of the most mysterious and beautifully handled works of the period, *Le Portugais* put Picasso on his mettle, and the magnificent

Braque. *Le Portugais*, 1911–12. Oil on canvas, 117×81 cm. Kunstmuseum, Basel: Gift of Raoul La Roche, 1952.

Picasso. *The Accordionist*, summer, 1911. Oil on canvas, 130×89.5 cm. Solomon R. Guggenheim Museum, New York.

Braque. *Man with Mandolin*, 1911–12. Oil on canvas, 116.2×80.9 cm. The Museum of Modern Art, New York: Acquired through the Lillie P. Bliss Bequest.

Braque in his studio with *Le Portugais* in progress, 1912. The oval canvases in progress above the easel are *Table with Pipe* (p. 227) and *Violin*; on the right is *Man with Mandolin*. Archives Laurens.

figure paintings he did this summer, notably *The Poet* and *The Accordionist*, must be seen as responses to it.

Le Portugais was always thought to have been painted in Paris in spring, 1911, and been a response to the series of imposing mandolin players that Picasso had been painting that winter. The catalog of the 1989 Pioneering Cubism exhibition at MoMA decreed otherwise. On the evidence of a letter from Braque to Kahnweiler (undated, but probably written in late September or early October) concerning a painting of "an Italian emigrant standing on the bridge of a boat with a harbor in the background," Braque's cubist masterpiece has been mistakenly identified as this other subject and reassigned to October.[19] The point at issue is not so much the identity of *Le Portugais* as whether Picasso or, as I think, Braque had raised the stakes and edged ahead at this, the most competitive phase of their relationship. It is therefore important to establish the facts. Kahnweiler's records confirm that the Braque was done first. Karmel, who has studied the dealer's stockbooks, reports that *Le Portugais* is listed with the group of paintings that the gallery acquired in the spring and not with the later batch that Braque handed over in January, 1912.[20] No painting of an Italian emigrant appears in the inventory; it was presumably overpainted or destroyed. Nor can the subject be identified with another painting Kahnweiler acquired in the spring: MoMA's *Man with Mandolin*, a variation on *Le Portugais*, which also features a bollard in the background. Both these Braques should, I think, be seen as "Souvenir du Havre" subjects, such as Picasso would paint the following year. Shortly before he embarked on *Le Portugais*, Braque had made a series of visits to his family at Le Havre, where, as we know, he liked to spend his evenings singing, dancing and playing the accordion in waterfront dives.

Granted, *Le Portugais* is exceedingly difficult to read: it abounds in what Braque later described as "accidents which happen to suit my purpose . . . rhymes which echo other forms and . . . rhythmical motifs which help to integrate a composition and give it movement."[21] Nevertheless, it is still possible to discern that it depicts a man seated in the window of a waterfront bar playing a guitar,[22] and not a man standing on the bridge of a boat. As we can see, the window is embellished with letters and numerals, which have been simulated with the help of stencils. A configuration (upper right) reveals that Braque is as adept at punning as Picasso: it can be read as one of those heavily tasseled curtain tiebacks to be found in several cubist Picassos or as a bollard with a rope around it. Hence the indoor/outdoor ambivalence. As for the small cloud of white paint (top center), it can be read as a puff of smoke from a funnel or—more likely—something that has a purely pictorial function.

Picasso appropriates Braque's stenciled letters and pyramidal structures but, for all his abbreviations and distortions, he never goes as far as Braque in his elimination of facial characteristics. Mapping the features of *Le Portugais* is a task that nobody (not even the artist himself) has been able to perform. Paintings that he did later in the year are even more baffling. Where you might expect him to be at his most explicit, Braque is at his most allusive. When asked about the anomalous area—usually lighter in tone—to be found at the heart of these 1911–12 compositions, he talked of the need for what he called a *foyer d'intensité*: an epicenter where forms melt or evaporate. Picasso tries a similar effect at the center of his *Poet,* but as a rule his figures are anything but vaporous. His poets, smokers, musicians, are as physical as his constructions of the following year. Furthermore, they project a quirkish element of character—something that Braque ignores. But, then, Braque never showed any interest in portraiture. Even the few paintings that relate to Marcelle are too generalized to be considered likenesses.

On August 8, Picasso wrote to Fernande that he expected her to arrive with Braque sometime in the next few days.[23] Absence evidently made him more solicitous: he said he loved her; she was not to worry about money and should bring a parasol. Their finances, it seemed, depended on Kahnweiler, who had been on holiday in Corsica. Now that he was back in Paris, funds were available, and she and Braque could leave. In the end they traveled separately. Fernande took a train directly from Paris and arrived around the 15th. Braque spent several days en route, stopping off at Orléans, Guéret and Limoges—he was presumably bicycling—and arrived a day or two later. At some point during the summer Braque's mistress, Marcelle Lapré, visited Céret, as the artist later (October 13) wrote asking her to return there.[24]

Manolo. *Portrait of Fernande Olivier,* 1911. Pencil on paper, 33.5×29cm. Museu Manolo Hugué, Caldes de Montbui.

Braque's presence meant more to Picasso than Fernande's. "Braque is very happy to be here," he wrote Kahnweiler. "I've already shown him the whole area and he already has a lot of ideas in mind."[25] Picasso makes no reference to Fernande in his letters, and she is conspicuously absent from his work. *Faute de mieux,* she posed for Manolo. For a change her lover did not object; he depended on the Manolos to keep her company. Picasso, who had left Haviland's for the second floor of the Maison Delcros, a large house with a large garden, put one of the rooms at Braque's disposal. There the two artists shut themselves away and worked intensively. In the evenings they would relax in Michel Justafré's Grand Café, where Séverac had established his *tertulia.* Picasso is said to have passed the evenings drawing on marble tabletops or the paper that covered them, discussing metaphysics and aesthetics and listening to Séverac play the piano until dawn. This cannot have happened very often. In view of all the work he did at Céret, not to speak of his aversion to theoretical discussions and music, this most nocturnal and dedicated of artists is more likely to have returned to his studio after dinner for further intensive hours of drawing. (In those pre-electric days, painting stopped when the light went.)

Grand Café at Céret, c. 1910. Private collection.

Although they were together for no more than three weeks, the two artists challenged each other to such good effect that—to revert to Braque's mountaineering image—they finally made it to the summit. Over the next three years Picasso and Braque, sometimes singly, sometimes together, would conquer other peaks, but nothing would excel the feat they brought off at Céret, when the two of them pooled their prodigious resources—their very different skills and powers of invention and imagination, not to speak of Spanish *duende* and French *poésie*—to achieve parity. As Golding says, it was "a moment of poise and equilibrium."[26] The planting of the flag on the mountaintop owes as much to the visceral drive of the one as it does to the spiritual resolve of the other.

Picasso may sometimes have painted like Braque and Braque like Picasso, but both of them were adamant that they never worked on one another's paintings. Comparison of their views of more or less the same expanse of Céret rooftops dissolving into space is revealing: Braque takes

Above: Picasso. *Landscape at Céret*, summer, 1911. Oil on canvas, 65×50cm. Solomon R. Guggenheim Museum, New York.

Right: Braque. *Rooftops, Céret*, summer, 1911. Oil on canvas, 88.2×64.8cm. Private collection.

Right: Maison Delcros, c.1910. Musée d'Art Moderne, Céret.

the greater liberties and comes up with an image that has the incisiveness and sharp focus we associate with Picasso; while Picasso paints the rooftops with the soft focus and sensuousness we usually associate with Braque. Rubin, who believes this chameleonism to have been conscious, sees two of their most celebrated Céret figure paintings as exercises in each other's idiom.[27] This is truer of Picasso, who was always ready to rifle another artist's mind and, if need be, try on his boots, than of Braque, who claimed never to have committed a voluntary act. If from 1910 onwards Picasso's *facture*—the way he applied paint to canvas—plays a more active role and becomes more eloquent, subtle and versatile than ever before, it was largely thanks to Braque. Picasso made less of a dent on Braque. It was more a matter of osmosis. Picasso helped wean him away from his indulgence in *belle peinture* for its own sake and give his work a sharper, more graphic edge. It is no coincidence that Braque's best drawings were done when he was closest to Picasso. While they were together at Céret, both artists embarked on large drypoints of still lifes, commissioned by Kahnweiler. In subject and composition they are strikingly alike; in spirit utterly different. The Picasso is easy to read: a bottle of vieux Marc, a glass and three playing cards (an ace of hearts, an ace of clubs and a diamond card). It is also very direct in its impact. By contrast, the Braque is more allusive and far from easy to read. The inscription, "Fox," is a reference to Fox's Bar, near the Gare Saint-Lazare, where Apollinaire liked to hang out. The single ace of hearts might imply that, unlike Picasso, Braque had only one woman in his life. The other objects—seemingly a bottle, some glasses and a saucer denoting the price of a drink—are little more than patches of shadow on a ghostly armature of lines.[28] Braque does not raise his voice; Picasso makes a declaration.

Braque. *Fox*. 1911. Drypoint, 54.8×38cm. Private collection.

The oft-quoted joke that Picasso made many years later about Braque being his wife or ex-wife is usually treated too seriously. It is taken to imply that Braque's work is feminine by comparison with Picasso's—a notion to which Kahnweiler gave credence in the original text (though not in the final version) of his *Weg zum Kubismus*.[29] The problem with taking Picasso's quips literally is that he often reverses them. (He once told me that he could never remember whether he had said "*Je ne cherche pas, je trouve*" or "*Je ne trouve pas, je cherche*"—"not [he added] that it makes much difference.") In this case, Dora Maar is in a position to supply a corrective. When Braque was hospitalized in the late 1930s, Picasso rushed off to see him. "The nurse wouldn't let me into his room," he fumed on his return, "she said Madame Braque was with him. She didn't realize that *I* am Madame Braque."[30] Evidently Braque saw cubism as a mountaineering expedition, whereas Picasso saw it as a marriage.

In later years it was Braque who hardened his heart against Picasso rather than the other way round. Picasso's gibes at Braque's expense were fueled as much as anything by the latter's strategic withdrawal from him—a matter of self-preservation. According to Dora Maar, Braque always meant more to Picasso than any other man except the Catalan cronies of his youth. By the same token he was one of the few people capable of wounding him. Rejection was Braque's weapon, and with Marcelle's tacit encouragement ("With Picasso you can never afford to give an inch," she once told me), he occasionally used it. For instance when Picasso offered him accommodation at La Californie, the vast villa above Cannes that he

Picasso. *Still Life with Bottle of Marc*, 1911. Drypoint, 50×30.6cm. Private collection.

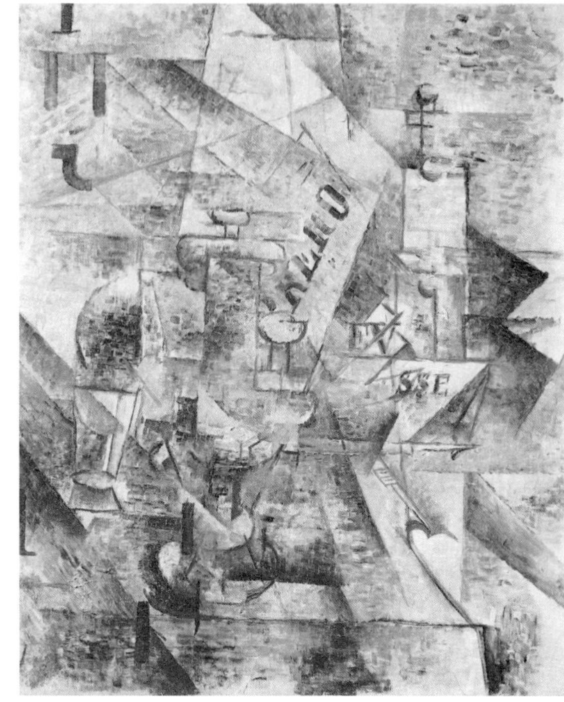

Above: Braque. *Pedestal Table*, fall, 1911. Oil on canvas, 116.5×81.5cm. Musée National d'Art Moderne, Centre Georges Pompidou, Paris.

Top right: Braque. *Still Life with Banderillas*, summer, 1911. Oil on canvas, 65×54cm. The Jacques and Natasha Gelman Collection.

Right: Picasso. *La Pointe de la Cité*, 1911. Oil on oval canvas, 90×71cm. Norton Simon Inc. Foundation, Los Angeles.

bought in 1954, in the hope that they could work together again, just as they had at Céret, Braque failed to show the slightest interest. On his annual visit to the Côte d'Azur, Braque made a point of staying with his dealer, Aimé Maeght. Picasso, who loathed Maeght, was very hurt.

*　　　*　　　*

On August 23, news broke that the Mona Lisa had been stolen two days earlier from the Louvre. Not thinking for a moment that he would be involved, Picasso treated the matter as a joke. He was more concerned with obtaining the August 24 issue of the Italian journal *La Voce*, in which his old friend the painter, poet and writer Ardengo Soffici had published the first article to establish Picasso and Braque as the two begetters of cubism and to denounce the Salon cubists for "deforming, geometrizing and cubifying . . . in the hope of concealing their . . . fatal banality and academicism behind triangles and other shapes."[31] Although written when cubism had run only half its course, Soffici's text is far more perceptive and accurate than early accounts by Salmon, Apollinaire and Raynal. Unlike them, Soffici had the advantage of being not only a painter but an insider accepted by the *bande à Picasso* and an outsider with no ax to grind: hence the insights and detachment. "Though less revealing historically than Kahnweiler's subsequent essays," Rubin has written, "[Soffici's] characterization of Analytic Cubism as a mysterious mental creation deeply tempered by lyricism and poetry rings truer in some ways to the Cubism of 1910–11 than does the later, more formal and philosophical reading of Kahnweiler."[32]

On August 29, Picasso was horrified to discover that he might be implicated in the Mona Lisa business. *Paris-Journal*, the newspaper which employed Salmon as its art critic, came out with an anonymous article by someone whom Picasso would have instantly identified as his and Apollinaire's nemesis, Géry Pieret. Pieret, who had recently returned from America, had not been able to resist boasting that he, too, had stolen from the Louvre. Picasso panicked. He entrusted his monkey to the care of local friends and raced back to Paris with Fernande. Braque stayed behind at Céret until January 19, 1912, delighted that he now had three vast studios in which to work. During the four months they would be separated, he and Picasso produced some of their greatest cubist paintings —the outcome of their cross-fertilization back in August.

Street singers with the song "L'as tu vu la Joconde?," 1911.

Pont du Diable, Céret, c. 1910. Musée d'Art Moderne, Céret.

13

L'Affaire des Statuettes

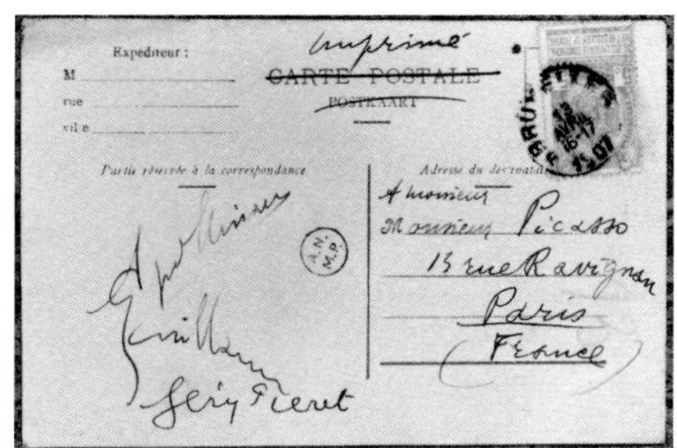

Postcard to Picasso signed by Apollinaire and Géry Pieret, April 13, 1907. Archives Picasso.

Opposite: Apollinaire in handcuffs (left) and with his lawyer (right), September, 1911. Collection P.M.A.

PICASSO WAS AT THE HEIGHT OF HIS POWERS and a month short of thirty when he found himself embroiled in what has come to be known as *l'affaire des statuettes.* Since he and the other prime suspect, Apollinaire, were foreigners with police dossiers and terrified of deportation, they were easily rattled. Summoned before a magistrate, they confessed to whatever they were accused of, unwittingly incriminated each other and later gave divergent accounts of their involvement. It is not always possible to establish exactly what happened in the course of this *affaire.* Stories leaked by Géry Pieret to the newspapers sowed further confusion. *L'affaire des statuettes* provided this narcissistic psychopath with the notoriety he craved, Apollinaire with notoriety that would darken the rest of his life and propel him into the army and contribute to his early death. Picasso would survive—scared but otherwise unscathed.

After four years in the Wild West—"*le pays des bucks et des Squaws,*" he called it[1]—Pieret had made a spectacular reappearance in Paris sometime in April. "Any dashing young man would have secretly wanted to resemble him," one of Apollinaire's poet friends, Fernand Fleuret, claimed.[2] With his boxer's muscles, great crest of fair hair and ruddy tan, Pieret looked like a Sioux warrior with an eagle's feather stuck in his headband. He dashed about in a large cowboy hat, cigar-colored American suit "made of wool as fine as the silk of his shirts,"[3] cut to show off his physique. He boasted to Apollinaire, whom he contacted on his arrival, that he was "disgustingly" flush, with large gold coins, mint banknotes and a stash of copper.[4] He also had written a novel called *Eleanor Montey,* which was about to be published. The novel never materialized and the money soon evaporated at the racetrack or poolroom. Fleuret says that Pieret aspired to be a sandwich man for Bostock's circus. Wearing nothing but a pair of leather chaps, a cowboy hat and a couple of poster boards, he proposed to gallop around Paris on a stallion bedecked with ostrich feathers, cracking his buffalo-hide whip. (Picasso may have drawn on this fantasy when he dressed one of the "Managers" in *Parade* as a sandwich man mounted on a plumed "horse"; at the dress rehearsal the "horse" and rider came to grief and were excluded from the scenario.)

On May 8, 1911, Pieret was reduced to asking Apollinaire to find him a job; otherwise, he said, he would kill himself.[5] The poet tried to fix him up with his friend Eugène Montfort. When that failed, he installed him in his apartment as a secretary. Meanwhile (May 7), Pieret had resumed his raids

Iberian. *Head of a Woman*. Stone (formerly in Apollinaire's possession). Musée des Antiquités Nationales de Saint-Germain-en-Laye.

on "his" Phoenician room at the Louvre, as he described to *Paris-Journal*:

> Although there had been more than forty [heads] when I left, I now found only twenty or twenty-five. The thought that the others had probably been removed by imitators of mine made me indignant. I took the head of a woman and stuffed it into my trousers. The suit I was wearing was of heavy material and very ample, but the statue was too bulky for me, and even though I was wearing a raincoat it was obvious despite my sex that I was pregnant with something.
>
> It took me at least twenty minutes to leave the museum. The statue [it weighed "*13 livres 150 grammes*"] kept shifting . . . from left to right, and I was afraid it would drop out and smash to bits on the floor. This did not happen, but it put quite a strain on my suit, and I decided to postpone my series of burglaries for a few weeks until I could provide myself with a pair of leather chaps and some special suspenders. Unfortunately being easily diverted, I turned to other things that necessitated a delay of several months in my antiquarian projects.
>
> And now one of my colleagues has spoiled all my plans by causing this uproar in the paintings department. I exceedingly regret this, for there is a strange, almost voluptuous charm about stealing works of art, and I shall probably have to wait several years before resuming my activities.[6]

As soon as he moved in with Apollinaire, Pieret installed the Iberian head he had stolen from the Louvre in a place of honor on the mantelpiece. The poet subsequently denied all knowledge of it. However, Pieret did this in the presence of "some ten writers and artists," who burst out laughing when told that it came from the Louvre.[7] The diadem-like hairdo reminded them of Lucie Delarue-Mardrus, the symbolist poet.

Apollinaire enjoyed Pieret's talk of their both dressing up like Fantômas or Raffles in masks of steel or black satin—*"deux jeunes gentlemen qui ne veulent pas être reconnus"*—and going off on "artistic" burgling expeditions, but was horrified when Pieret proposed putting these fantasies into practice. The poet confided his plight to the homosexual Gide: he told him that he had saved an old friend, who had recently returned from America, from the gutter, but found his presence so maddening that he was frequently driven from his own apartment.[8] Pieret had apparently reestablished his hold over Apollinaire; but whether it was the drugs with which Sonia Delaunay says he supplied the poet, or some sort of sexual predilection, or his repertoire of adventures, we do not know. Instead of sending his guest packing, the poet took off for ten days' vacation at Bois de Cise, a small seaside place on the Channel. A few days after his return, he wrote Picasso, who was in Céret, that the "Baron is working hard but I wish he would find another situation. . . . the Baron sends you his best wishes."[9]

To believe Apollinaire—in this case far from easy—he finally threw Pieret out on August 21, the very day the Mona Lisa disappeared.[10] As compensation, he gave his protégé, who was as adept at moral blackmail as he was at the other kind, some engravings to keep him going and, if possible, shut him up. Apollinaire had every reason to fear that, intentionally or not, Pieret might lead the authorities to his door. And sure enough, when newspapers started advertising huge awards for information—*Paris-Journal* offered 50,000 francs for the Mona Lisa's return, no questions asked—the narcissistic thief decided to take whatever advantage he could of this opportunity. He went to the editor, possibly through Salmon, who

Louis Marcoussis. *Portrait of Guillaume Apollinaire*, 1912. Etching, aquatint and drypoint, 49.2×27.8cm. Galerie Berggruen, Paris.

was the paper's art critic and currently on bad terms with Apollinaire, and sold him his story (much of which is quoted in Chapter 1). Pieret adjusted the facts to suggest that his principal motive had been to expose the Louvre's egregious lack of security. He also sold the newspaper his most recent theft, the head off Apollinaire's mantelpiece. *Paris-Journal* kept its promise to respect Pieret's anonymity; he was identified only as "The Thief" and described as "aged between twenty and twenty-five, very well-mannered with a certain *chic américain*, whose face and look and behavior bespeak a kind heart and a certain lack of scruple."[11]

Realizing that this article posed a threat to all of them, Apollinaire advised Picasso and Fernande to return to Paris as soon as possible. On September 3 or 4, he went to the Gare d'Orsay to meet them. Fernande's account of the ensuing farce has the ring of truth:

> I can see them both now, a pair of contrite children, terrified and thinking of fleeing abroad. Thanks to me they did not give way to their panic; they decided to stay in Paris and get rid of the compromising sculptures as quickly as possible. But how? They finally decided to put the statues in a suitcase and throw it into the Seine at night. After a hastily swallowed dinner and a long evening's wait, they set out on foot around midnight with the suitcase; at two in the morning they were back, worn out and still carrying the suitcase with the statues inside. They had wandered the streets never finding the right moment, never daring to get rid of the suitcase. They thought they were being followed and conjured up in imagination a thousand possibilities. . . . Although I shared their fears, I had been watching them rather closely that night. I am sure that perhaps involuntarily they had been play-acting a little: to such a point that, while waiting for "the moment of the crime," although neither of them knew how, they had pretended to play cards—doubtless in imitation of certain bandits they had read about. In the end Apollinaire spent the night at Picasso's and went the next morning to *Paris-Journal*, where he turned in the undesirable statues under a pledge of secrecy.[12]

By this time it was September 5. Although Fernande says he went alone, Apollinaire claims that Picasso went with him to *Paris-Journal*. Unlikely—he would not have had the nerve. *Paris-Journal* (September 6) reports a single "mysterious visitor . . . an amateur artist, fairly well-to-do [whose] greatest pleasure is collecting works of art."[13] Evidently Apollinaire. The next day, the unshutupable Pieret burst into print once again with "A PLEA FROM OUR THIEF TO HIS COLLEAGUE":

> I can only urge the person at present holding Vinci's masterpiece to place himself entirely in your [*Paris-Journal*'s] hands. He has a colleague's word . . . that your good faith is above suspicion.
>
> Adieu, I am about to leave France to finish my novel.[14]

In fact, Apollinaire had stuffed 160 francs into "The Thief's" pocket and put him on a train to Marseille so that he could set sail for foreign parts.

On September 7, the farce turned nasty. To the relief of the police, who had no other lead in the Mona Lisa affair, someone denounced Apollinaire to them. At last they could look as if they had a suspect. The Sûreté's most celebrated detective, the extravagantly mustachioed Inspector Robert, arrived at Apollinaire's apartment with a search warrant and went through his papers so thoroughly that the poet later told Salmon, "Without Robert's help, my correspondence would never have been filed."[15] Letters from Pieret proved that Apollinaire had knowingly sheltered a criminal and had

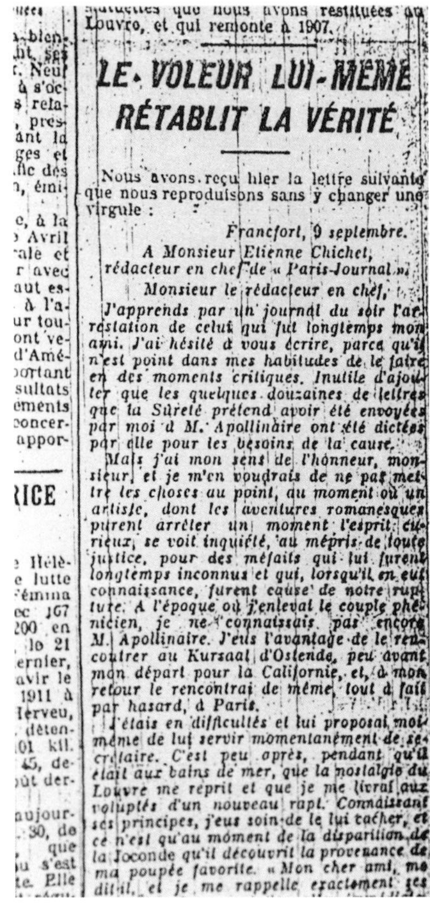

Louvre, et qui remonte à 1907.

LE VOLEUR LUI-MÊME RÉTABLIT LA VÉRITÉ

Nous avons reçu hier la lettre suivante que nous reproduisons sans y changer une virgule :

Francfort, 9 septembre.

A Monsieur Etienne Chichet, rédacteur en chef de « Paris-Journal ».

Monsieur le rédacteur en chef,

J'apprends par un journal du soir l'arrestation de celui qui fut longtemps mon ami. J'ai hésité à vous écrire, parce qu'il n'est point dans mes habitudes de le faire en des moments critiques. Inutile d'ajouter que les quelques douzaines de lettres que la Sûreté prétend avoir été envoyées par moi à M. Apollinaire ont été dictées par elle pour les besoins de la cause.

Mais j'ai mon sens de l'honneur, monsieur, et je m'en voudrais de ne pas mettre les choses au point, du moment où un artiste, dont les aventures romanesques purent arrêter un moment l'esprit curieux, se voit inquiété, au mépris de toute justice, pour des méfaits qui lui furent longtemps inconnus et qui, lorsqu'il en eut connaissance, furent cause de notre rupture. A l'époque où j'enlevai le couple phénicien, je ne connaissais pas encore M. Apollinaire. J'eus l'avantage de le rencontrer au Kursaal d'Ostende, peu avant mon départ pour la Californie, et, à mon retour le rencontrai de même, tout à fait par hasard, à Paris.

J'étais en difficultés et lui proposai moi-même de lui servir momentanément de secrétaire. C'est peu après, pendant qu'il était aux bains de mer, que la nostalgie du Louvre me reprit et que je me livrai aux voluptés d'un nouveau rapt. Connaissant ses principes, j'eus soin de le lui cacher, et ce n'est qu'au moment de la disparition de la Joconde qu'il découvrit la provenance de ma poupée favorite. « Mon cher ami, me dit-il, et je me rappelle exactement ses

Géry Pieret's letter to the editor of *Paris-Journal*, dated "Frankfurt, September 9," exonerating Apollinaire of the theft of the Iberian statuettes.

also been a receiver of stolen goods. He was taken off for questioning. At the Santé his hysterical protestations of innocence gave way to hysterical protestations of guilt—Picasso's as well as his own. Apollinaire was duly charged and locked up in a cell. The police waited a day and then announced that they were "on the trail of a gang of international thieves who had come to France for the purpose of despoiling our museums."[16]

Apollinaire did not help his case by constantly changing his story. At one point he told the police that Pieret *had* stolen the Mona Lisa; at another, he gave him an alibi. "The Thief" did not help by writing yet another letter to *Paris-Journal*—purportedly from Frankfurt, in fact from Marseille—signed "Baron Ignace d'Ormesan." In an effort to exonerate the poet, the thief muddied his reputation even further. Ironically, Pieret was never brought to justice. (In May, 1912, he was tried in absentia and given a ten-year jail sentence, which he never served.) Nosing around the Marseille docks, he found two liners about to leave: one for New York, the other for Alexandria. He tossed a coin: Alexandria. He soon charmed the captain into taking him on as a personal steward and English teacher. Another chapter in Pieret's picaresque career was about to start.

Picasso had every reason to fear that he, too, would be indicted. And sure enough, at seven o'clock on the morning of the 8th, the dreaded summons finally came. The police had arrived to take him before an examining magistrate. Fernande says he was trembling so much that she had to help him dress. He never forgot the demeaning ride to the Prefecture under escort in a bus (suspects were not allowed to take a cab). There was a long, demoralizing wait before Picasso was brought before the examining magistrate. And there he was confronted with Apollinaire in handcuffs: "pale, dishevelled, unshaven, his collar torn, his shirt open at the neck. . . . After two days of arrest, subject to long grillings like a criminal, he had confessed whatever he had been told to confess. The truth was the least part of his admissions. He only wanted to be left in peace."[17] To save his mistress and family, above all his formidable mother, from being badgered by the police, he had had no choice but to implicate Picasso.

What, exactly, ensued? In her posthumously published memoirs Fernande comes up with a sentimental rigmarole, which Picasso may once upon a time have invented for her benefit. She describes how the two contrite little boys burst into tears in front of the "fatherly magistrate, who was hard put to keep a stern countenance in the face of their childish sorrow."[18] Penrose gives another version of the same story.[19] Albert Gleizes, the cubist painter who managed to have Apollinaire's provisional release commuted to a dismissal, and André Billy are no less insistent that Picasso betrayed their hero by denying that he knew him. Almost fifty years after these events, Gilbert Prouteau, who had arranged for Picasso to see a documentary movie he had made about Apollinaire, came up with what *Paris-Presse* claimed to be the artist's confession. It went as follows:

> . . . I can see [Apollinaire] there now, with his handcuffs and his look of a big placid boy. He smiled at me as I came in, but I made no sign.
>
> When the judge asked me: "Do you know this gentleman?" I was suddenly terribly frightened, and without knowing what I was saying, I answered: "I have never seen this man."

> I saw Guillaume's expression change. The blood ebbed from his face. I am still ashamed.[20]

This "confession" sounds most unlike Picasso; however, something of the sort must have happened. Before condemning the artist for denying his old friend, we should remember that Apollinaire had behaved no less cravenly. Picasso had every reason to resent him for his incriminating avowals, which could easily have got him expelled from France. We should also bear in mind that Picasso saw himself as an artist of messianic power, an artist whose only obligation was and always would be to his work. This was sacrosanct, hence also his well-being. Too bad if friends and family had sometimes to be sacrificed; too bad for them and too bad for Picasso: he did not relish the guilt that these sacrifices entailed.

Far more puzzling than Picasso's denial of Apollinaire is his ability to escape the charges of receiving stolen goods. Surprisingly, he did not employ a lawyer, although he could easily have afforded to do so. Did he, one wonders, appeal to Olivier Sainsère, the *conseiller d'état* who had proved a powerful protector in the past and was still in a position to pull strategic strings? Help from an official quarter could explain why, after the interrogation, Picasso had no further trouble with the police. Apollinaire, on the other hand, was returned to jail and subjected to further questioning, not to speak of vilification at the hands of anti-Semites, who chose to assume that all Polish emigrés were Jews. Léon Daudet went so far as to deny having voted for him the year before, when his book *L'Hérésiarque* (partly based on Pieret's stories) had been nominated for the Prix Goncourt.

Marie Laurencin. *Self-Portrait*, 1912. Ink wash on paper, 14.2×10.2cm. Musée National d'Art Moderne, Centre Georges Pompidou, Paris.

Apollinaire was not released until September 12—and then only provisionally. His release involved still more public humiliation. He was locked in a stinking cell in the *Souricière*—the "mousetrap," as the Palais de Justice's holding cells were dubbed—handcuffed to a guard and paraded in front of a horde of press photographers, curiosity seekers and well-wishers, before being put in a sort of cage and driven back to the Santé, this time in a police car, to await the order of release, an order which by law had to be delivered on foot.

L'affaire des statuettes cast a shadow over the remainder of Apollinaire's short life. For all his brilliance and bravado, he was surprisingly vulnerable: paranoid about his illegitimate birth, his virago of a mother, his convoluted sexuality and not least his precarious expatriate status in the country that invented chauvinism. If a great many distinguished writers had not come to his defense, he might have been deported. As Picasso told Daix, one of Apollinaire's principal reasons for enlisting in 1914 was a desire to erase this blot from his record.[21]

The scandal also dealt a fatal blow to Apollinaire's faltering relationship with Marie Laurencin. She had long since ceased to have much love for him, as an earlier entry (spring, 1910) in Roché's diary records:

> Visit to "Flap." . . . She wants to distance herself from "Pollop" and the influence of his bohemian circle: Cremnitz, Picassos, Salmon. She finds them loud and effeminate, above all people you can't count on.
>
> She still dines every evening with "Pollop"—but they haven't slept together for some time—[she] finds him alright but confused—no longer his former dogmatic self.
>
> Her new lover: Eugène Montfort.[22]

Apollinaire, André Billy and Marie Laurencin at Villequier, 1913. Bibliothèque Historique de la Ville de Paris: Fonds Apollinaire.

Apollinaire in Eugène Montfort's apartment during his career as "Louise Lalanne," 1909. Collection P.M.A.

Montfort was a good friend of Apollinaire's, who had persuaded him to write a woman's column, under the name Louise Lalanne, for his magazine *Les Marges.* To make his impersonation more convincing, Apollinaire persuaded Marie to contribute two appropriately "feminine" poems to his column. After a year, "Louise" decided to shed "her wig, her bodice and her skirt" as well as her *personalité de poétesse,* and declare herself as Apollinaire.[23] The unmasking took place in the January, 1910, issue of *Les Marges,* around the time Marie embarked on the affair with Montfort.

Marie's censorious mother could not abide the thought of her brilliant daughter throwing herself away on a jailbird who was also a pornographer. She insisted that Marie leave him, but it took her almost a year to make a final break. One summer's day in 1912, Marie failed to turn up as promised to help Guillaume cook an elaborate luncheon for some friends. Serge Férat, who was one of the guests, went round to check and found Marie at home sewing. "Just tell him shit," was her message. When Férat passed this on, Apollinaire turned deathly pale. "Tell her the same from me" was all the riposte he could manage.[24] According to Serge,

> poor Guillaume suffered such terrible palpitations . . . that he abruptly decided to move out of his apartment: he has spent the last four days entirely with us and a certain Marc Brésil, a young writer who is very kind, very enthusiastic and . . . remarkably unintelligent. . . . When we go off, Apollinaire will stay on here. He proposes to look for another apartment and begin a new life. According to him . . . he has been very worn down by Marie's conduct, which is that of a concierge or seamstress.[25]

According to Serge, Brésil (the handsome son of a well-known journalist and brother of the musical comedy actress Marguerite Brésil) was too silly to fill the vacuum caused by Laurencin's departure.

The poems that Apollinaire composed in his cell and the short articles, "Mes prisons," for *Paris-Journal,* reveal how badly wounded he had been. In his agony he seems to have identified with Oscar Wilde, whose *Ballad of Reading Gaol* he would certainly have known. Like Wilde, he turned to religion and poetry writing for comfort. Hitherto his devotions had often taken the paradoxical form of blasphemy; now he cried out to God for forgiveness: "Lord, accept my homage / I believe in you, I do, I do." (He later suppressed these trite stanzas.) And in some lines he did not in the end include in *Zone*—the great poem whose subtext evokes Golgotha—Apollinaire sees himself at the time of his ordeal as Christ dying on the cross between the two thieves: the bad thief is Marie Laurencin, "who stole my life, an infamous theft," and "the good thief who will be unhappy and die in prison" is of course Pieret.[26]

Friends who had rallied round and agitated for his release now felt free to tease Apollinaire about his ordeal. Paul Léautaud used to ask him pointedly, "*Comment va la santé?*"[27] And Salmon recounts a visit to admire Apollinaire's new monkey—a macaque that may have belonged to his mother. "You see, he doesn't really have to stay in his cage," Apollinaire observed as the monkey jumped playfully from one piece of furniture to another. To which Salmon unkindly replied, "Well at least he can be provisionally released."[28] Whereupon Picasso, who was present, angrily grabbed the animal by its blue behind and thrust it back into its cage. Little by little the poet regained his sense of humor. It can only have been he who wrote (under a pseudonym, "Le Satyre masqué") in *Le Passant* that the Mona Lisa had resurfaced in cubist form.[29]

As for Pieret, he continued to keep in touch with Apollinaire, continued to feed him adventure stories, which may or may not have been true. On the boat to Alexandria, he attached himself to a fat old woman whose grubby fingers glittered with rings. She had been wet nurse to a leading Egyptian newspaper owner and stayed on as his cook. According to Fleuret, whose informant was Apollinaire, on arrival in Cairo the cook arranged for her handsome protégé to edit one of her employer's journals.[30] Once again Pieret's compulsive criminality did him in. Under the auspices of his newspaper, he organized a Christmas gala for the British and American colonies. Guests were encouraged to come *en grande tenue* —in full evening dress. As the gala drew to a close, the lights went out. "A short circuit! The lights will be on again in no time," Pieret assured the guests, as he picked their pockets and purses and helped himself to their jewelry. He supposedly pulled the same trick on another occasion and was caught. On September 6, 1912, he was had up before a Belgian consular tribunal and given a psychiatric evaluation, which found his mental state congenitally flawed. He was supposed to remain in Cairo under the auspices of the Belgian consul. However by December he had escaped via Greece to Turkey. The next we hear of Apollinaire's nemesis is in 1917: a train in which Fleuret was traveling was obliged to stop and let a Belgian troop train overtake it. Fleuret leaned out to watch; so did a young Belgian soldier, who began frantically waving his *képi*: Pieret! In the last year of the war, he resumed writing to Apollinaire, but they never met again.

Portrait of Apollinaire falsely attributed to Géry Pieret.

This is not quite the last we hear of the thief. The day of Apollinaire's death, Montfort received a letter from Pieret saying that he had redeemed himself from a life of crime by fighting on the Western Front, but was worried about Apollinaire. "A few days ago," he wrote, "I was sitting by an open window when a raven suddenly flew into the room. I felt I was getting a message from Guillaume Apollinaire. I'm very worried about him and beg you to tell me whether he's still alive."[31] And then, nearly twenty years later, Fleuret's friend Alice Halicka was in New York, working on sets and costumes for a Broadway musical. The costumier's (a firm called Eaves) employed a young English couple—penniless painters—who told Halicka that they had heard all about her and Marcoussis from a certain Monsieur Dupont or Duval. Halicka had no idea who this could be, until the painters added that Dupont or Duval was an anarchist who had been Apollinaire's secretary at the time of "*l'affaire des statuettes.*"[32]

LES PEINTRES CUBISTES

14

The Other Cubists: Jackdaws in Peacocks' Feathers

Max Jacob. *Apollinaire and His Muse*, c. 1910. Gouache on paper, 21.5×15.5cm. Musée des Beaux-Arts, Orléans.

Opposite: Jean Metzinger (?). Binding of a copy of Apollinaire's *Les Peintres cubistes*, 1913. Bibliothèque Historique de la Ville de Paris: Fonds Apollinaire.

FOR ALL HIS GENIALITY, APOLLINAIRE DID NOT readily forgive Picasso for his "betrayal." And he allowed two of the principal "Salon cubists" (cubists who exhibited at the Indépendants and the Salon d'Automne), Albert Gleizes and Robert Delaunay, to fan his resentment. Now that Apollinaire was emerging as the leading impresario of modernism, this ambitious pair was determined that he should become their spokesman. Gleizes had already made himself very useful to the poet. In September, 1911, at Marie Laurencin's suggestion, he had used his friendship with *"le substitut Granié"*—an enlightened magistrate who wrote sympathetic articles about modern art under the name Aloysius Duravel—to have Apollinaire's provisional release from prison made permanent.[1] Gleizes was not above invoking Apollinaire's support in return for this service.

To appreciate the extent of Apollinaire's change of allegiance we need only compare his statements about the Salon cubists before and after his imprisonment. In 1910 he dismissed their exhibits at the Salon d'Automne as "a listless and servile imitation of certain works, which were not included in the Salon, by an artist possessed of a strong personality and secrets that he has revealed to no one. The name of this great artist is Pablo Picasso. The cubism at the Salon d'Automne, however, was a jackdaw in peacock's feathers."[2] Six months later, Apollinaire was extolling "the jackdaws" as opposed to Picasso and Braque. Their cubism was "a noble and restrained art ready to undertake the vast subjects for which Impressionism has left painters totally unprepared. . . . Cubism is the most noble undertaking in French art today."[3]

Besides revenge, self-promotion played a part in Apollinaire's change of heart. Whether the concept of the Bateau Lavoir as "the poets' rendezvous" had been his or Jacob's or Picasso's,[4] it had emboldened Apollinaire to set himself up as the principal link between modern writers and modern painters. Since Picasso and Braque knew the poet too well to let him speak for them, or take credit for their achievements, they left him no option but to cling to the coattails of the leading Salon cubists, Gleizes, Metzinger, Delaunay and Le Fauconnier. By appearing to mastermind a cultural revolution, Apollinaire was able to enhance his reputation as poet, novelist and critic and drum up subscribers to the magazine, *Les Soirées de Paris*, which he and André Billy were about to launch. He was also able to live down his reputation as a felon and pornographer and placate his fearsome mother. His strategy was not so much divide and rule as

Picasso. *Au Vernissage du Salon*, 1911. Pen and India ink and watercolor on sheet of paper and brown envelope, 30×14.5 cm. Private collection. Picasso identified the top-hatted figure as the artist "Lombar" (Alfred Lombard).

placate and rule—placate Picasso and Braque and somehow or other reconcile them with the ambitious young painters who were out to hijack cubism. Kahnweiler was appalled by Apollinaire's switch of allegiance.

The emergence of the Salon cubists as a coherent group dated from the previous (1911) spring's Indépendants, where Le Fauconnier, Delaunay, Gleizes, Metzinger, Léger and (at Apollinaire's request) Marie Laurencin had their work hung together for the first time. The *vernissage*—on a fine spring day in May—was a sensation. The cubist Room 41 was one of the smaller galleries but it was far and away the most crowded, with people laughing, crying, protesting, arguing, exulting. By five o'clock *L'Intransigeant* appeared with Apollinaire's warily supportive article. This time he tactfully left the extent of Picasso's role to be settled by future historians, while arguing that the evidence of influences "dating back to the most noble periods of French and Italian art"[5] did not detract from the qualities of his new friends' work, whereas it clearly did. Traditionalism was one of the main charges that the futurists would level against the Salon cubists: "They worship the traditionalism of Poussin, Ingres and Corot and petrify their art with an obstinate attachment to the past, which to our eyes remains totally incomprehensible."[6]

The following morning, Salmon came out with an enthusiastic if not very enlightening review, while Vauxcelles was more than usually scathing. Picasso, who had attended the *vernissage*, was impressed by Léger's *Nudes in the Forest*, which Vauxcelles had described as "tubist": "this boy must have something," Picasso told Kahnweiler, who accompanied him. "They don't even give him the same name as us."[7] The two of them were decidedly unimpressed by the centerpiece of Room 41, Le Fauconnier's monumental (over ten foot by six foot) *Abondance*—his Russian giantess of a wife (a painter called Maroussia) carrying a basket of huge fruit accompanied by an oafish putto—which no amount of faceting could redeem from academicism. On the strength of *Abondance*, this now forgotten painter was perceived as the leader of the new school—and not just in France, either. Le Fauconnier had exhibited an earlier version of his allegory in Munich at the second Neue Künstlervereinigung, of which he was a member (Picasso and Braque exhibited as guests), and it had made such an impression that he was invited to join the Blaue Reiter the following year. After a succession of one-man shows in Munich, Berlin, Prague, Budapest, Zurich, Le Fauconnier would soon be better known in Mitteleuropa than Picasso. With his red, fan-shaped beard, imposing height and myopic air of earnestness, which drugs did much to heighten, Le Fauconnier personified the charismatic *chef d'école*. As such he was hailed in Russia (at the Golden Fleece and Knave of Diamonds group shows), also in Holland, where, after abandoning cubism, he spent World War I, wallowing in mysticism and back-to-nature expressionism. When he returned to Paris after the war, the artist whom Gleizes had once celebrated as "the master of a new generation" found that he was unremembered.

* * *

All his life Albert Gleizes would suffer from a chip-on-the-shoulder delusion that he and Jean Metzinger, as opposed to Picasso and Braque, had invented cubism. The two of them would back up each other's claims

Above: Jean Metzinger. *Le Goûter*, 1911. Oil on canvas, 75.9×70.2cm. Philadelphia Museum of Art: The Louise and Walter Arensberg Collection.

Left: Henri Le Fauconnier. *Abondance*, 1910. Oil on canvas, 146.5×98cm. Moderna Museet, Stockholm.

Marie Laurencin. *The Young Women*, 1910. Oil on canvas, 115×146cm. Moderna Museet, Stockholm: Gift of Rolf de Maré.

Fernand Léger. *Nudes in the Forest*, 1909–11. Oil on canvas, 120×170cm. Rijksmuseum Kröller-Müller, Otterlo.

Albert Gleizes. *Harvest Threshing*, 1912. Oil on canvas, 269×353cm. Whereabouts unknown.

to have done so with dubious assertions and, in Metzinger's case, revised dating of early works. Metzinger went so far as to maintain that "in 1906 Gleizes foretold cubism."[8] A critic called Chassevent referred to Metzinger and Delaunay's divisionist slabs of color as cubes two years before Matisse and Vauxcelles had even used the same word to describe Braque's L'Estaque landscapes. Chassevent was referring to unoriginal paintings that derive from Signac; Matisse to highly original paintings that laid the foundations of cubism. Nonetheless Gleizes maintained that the term "cubism" had never been used before the 1911 Indépendants and had never been applied to the work of Picasso or Braque. And on these questionable etymological grounds he maintained—like a wine grower out to promote the "*appellation contrôlée*" of his vineyard—that the "*appellation*" of cubism was "reserved for the painters of Room 41." "Overnight we had become famous. Almost unknown the day before, our names were now hawked by a hundred mouths, not only in Paris but the provinces and abroad."[9]

Robert Delaunay. *Portrait of Jean Metzinger* (or *Man with a Tulip*), May, 1906. Oil on canvas, 73×49 cm. Private collection.

Flushed with notoriety, the painters of Room 41 were determined to dominate the upcoming Salon d'Automne. When it opened in September, they repeated their *succès de scandale.* Salmon reported that "the cubists, once isolated skirmishers, engaged in their first pitched battle."[10] And indeed the Salon d'Automne's tiny Room VIII became even more notorious than the Indépendants' Room 41. As usual Picasso and Braque—who dismissed the Salon cubists as "*les horribles serre-files*" (the awful stragglers) —held aloof and left the battlefield to Le Fauconnier, Gleizes, Metzinger and Léger. (La Fresnaye, Segonzac, Lhote and Marcel Duchamp also exhibited.) Only Delaunay abstained: this juried exhibition had once rejected his work. Metzinger, the former mathematician, was the hero of the hour ("the Emperor of cubism," he was called) on the strength of his *Le Goûter* —a glib painting of a naked woman about to stir a bifurcated cup of tea. Eighty years later, it is difficult to see *Le Goûter* as anything but a traditional Salon subject genteelly geometrized. At the time, however, it was hailed as a breakthrough, and its diagrammatic organization, in which the fourth dimension supposedly plays a part, opened the eyes of Juan Gris to the possibilities of mathematics. Thanks in part to having Picasso as a mentor, Gris managed to transcend Metzinger's pedantry and calculation. His innovative paintings and collages of 1913 make the cubism of *Le Goûter* look like a prismatic trick. No wonder Metzinger's painting was so popular with the public that it came to be known as the Gioconda of cubism.

Apart from Soffici, the only critic to write perceptively about the cubist conflict was a young German, Max Raphael, a friend of Uhde's, who made regular visits to Picasso's studio to monitor his progress. In an open letter (May, 1912) attacking the expressionist Max Pechstein for the silly things he had written about cubism, Raphael concentrates his fire on Metzinger and Delaunay (identified as former followers of Signac):

> . . . [Salon] Cubism is an attempt on the part of creatively impotent but ambitious persons, who have learned to "hawk and spit" from Picasso, to mobilize the press and exhibitions with a view to drumming up publicity and doing business. Americanism in art. They say to themselves: "I've been painting as a neo-Impressionist up to now. It hasn't worked because people are familiar with Signac. Now Picasso has the direct cube. Perhaps this will work better. Picasso doesn't exhibit his work, and if he were to get known, then I, Monsieur Me-tzin-ger, will curse him out of existence."[11]

Robert Delaunay. *Self-Portrait,* 1909. Oil on canvas, 73×60 cm. Musée National d'Art Moderne, Centre Georges Pompidou, Paris.

Picasso evidently confided in this German critic the thoughts he could not share with Apollinaire or that other genial turncoat, André Salmon. At the time of the 1911 Indépendants, Salmon had reminded his readers—as usual the facts and opinions are as tangled as the prose—that cubism had been "invented five years ago by a Spanish painter after long aesthetic digressions, along with philosophers, poets and mathematicians. At first it seemed inoffensive mental juggling. But Picasso laid the first stone, the first cube of the temple, which was not the most laudable thing he has done."[12]

In a subsequent article Salmon made for further confusion: "While it is true that cubism was born of Picasso's speculations, he himself was never a cubist. The first evidence of cubism, still very hesitant . . . came from Georges Braque. . . . Much more intellectual, Jean Metzinger brought together the diffuse elements of cubism, outlined a discipline, or at least a theory; so that while cubism really does come from Picasso, Metzinger is justified in calling himself its leader."[13] Whether or not this nonsense was the cause, Picasso saw less of Salmon. This former crony never succeeded in worming his way back into the artist's confidence, as Apollinaire always managed to do. Kahnweiler may have been autocratic and Gertrude Stein egomaniacal, but at least they were fanatically supportive of Picasso. They understood what he had achieved and where he was going better than the Parisian poets who were supposedly his champions.

* * *

Apollinaire's deviousness was even remarked upon in the press, what is more in his own newspaper, *L'Intransigeant*. One of his more perceptive colleagues, Henri Guilbeaux, took him to task for his behavior at the *vernissage* of the 1911 Salon d'Automne:

> Mr. Apollinaire extols cubism. . . . To many people, and myself in particular, Mr. Apollinaire has also expressed very harsh opinions concerning it. I met him before the opening of Room VIII. He was accompanied by the genial and poker-faced Pablo Picasso, whose talent as painter, as a real painter, is undeniable. Both were sneering at the canvases in which cubes, cones and tubes were grouped and expressing rather unfavorable opinions. . . . There are those who admire Mr. Apollinaire's talent for mystification, but I am not one of them. I acknowledge Guillaume Apollinaire's education and hard work, but I question his right to contribute to the falsification of values.[14]

Jean Metzinger. Study for *Portrait of Apollinaire*, c. 1911–12. Pencil on pink paper, 42×30 cm. Musée National d'Art Moderne, Centre Georges Pompidou, Paris.

Guilbeaux did not know, at least did not relate, what transpired later that afternoon. In front of the Gleizeses and Metzingers Picasso said regretfully that he had hoped to enjoy himself but had simply found the work boring. Whereupon Apollinaire persuaded him to join the targets of his sneers—Le Fauconnier, Gleizes, Léger and possibly Metzinger and Delaunay—for a drink at a bar on the rue d'Antin. At Picasso's suggestion or Apollinaire's behest, they subsequently went on to Kahnweiler's gallery to look at his and Braque's recent work[15]—presumably the figures and still lifes done at Céret that summer. We do not know about Le Fauconnier's attitude to Picasso; we do know that Léger greatly admired his work. As for Metzinger, he had been acquainted with Picasso for some time through Max Jacob, and despite his ideological bias had written enthusiastically about his work. ("Picasso unveils to us the very face of painting. Rejecting every ornamental, anecdotal or symbolic intention, he achieves a painterly purity hitherto unknown. . . . No paintings of the past . . . belong to painting as clearly as this. Picasso does not deny the object; he illuminates it with his intelligence and feeling. He combines visual and tactile perceptions.")[16]

Gleizes, on the other hand, maintained that he had never met Picasso, never seen his work, never been to Kahnweiler's. Otherwise how could he have kept up the pretense that he had invented cubism? Gleizes was lying or very forgetful: he *had* been to his gallery, Kahnweiler said,[17] and must therefore have seen the cubist Picassos and Braques that were always on view there. He could also have seen the paintings that were shown at Uhde's and Vollard's in 1910–11. So much for the story that Gleizes had never been exposed to Picasso's or Braque's cubism. As for the myth put about by the Salon cubists to the effect that Kahnweiler resented them because he did not have them under contract, the dealer was adamant that Léger was the only one who interested him, because he did not intellectualize art like the rest of them. It was bad enough, Kahnweiler said, having Le Fauconnier pontificate about cubism without having Gleizes and Metzinger pat each other on the back for "inventing" it. That was an intolerable insult to the great artists he represented.

Jean Metzinger. *Portrait of Albert Gleizes*, c. 1911–12. Oil on canvas, 65×54cm. Museum of Art, Rhode Island School of Design: Museum Purchase.

Kahnweiler was unhappy on another score: Apollinaire was endangering the *cordon sanitaire* which he had erected around Picasso and Braque to isolate them from the Salon cubists. Now that the latter were bringing the movement into disrepute, allowing it to become the butt of newspaper and music hall jokes, a *cordon sanitaire* was more than ever necessary. Had not the *Excelsior* magazine for October 2, 1911, announced that "Metzinger and Picasso, the leaders of the new school of painting, were now known as '*les maîtres-cubes*'"?[18] The word "cubism" was becoming synonymous with anything suspect or depraved. Worse, it would soon become *passé*.[19]

It is a measure of Kahnweiler's ingenuity that he managed to turn this situation against the Salon cubists. The culprits would have to pay a price for what he called their "imposture."[20] If they were intent on being perceived as the originators of the movement, so be it. They could serve as protection against the brickbats, which were beginning to fly and might otherwise injure Kahnweiler's artists. The astute dealer urged Picasso and Braque to keep an even lower profile, lest anyone identify them with the Gleizes-Metzinger group; he also urged them to spend as much time as possible out of Paris, in the Roussillon or Provence, the better to concentrate on the real thing.

Far from reconciling the pioneers and the "impostors," Apollinaire's summit meeting with Picasso polarized them even further, much to Kahnweiler's satisfaction. Their differences were a matter of background and temperament as well as ideology. Except for Léger, who was the son of a Norman cattle-dealer, the Salon cubists were as bourgeois and unbohemian as their sobriquet suggests. Metzinger had every reason to resent the *haute bourgeoisie* of Nantes, from which he stemmed—the grandfather who had conquered Madagascar, the hypocritical, homosexual parents—but his work mirrored its conventions and stiffness. Le Fauconnier was the prodigiously clever son of a doctor from the Pas-de-Calais,

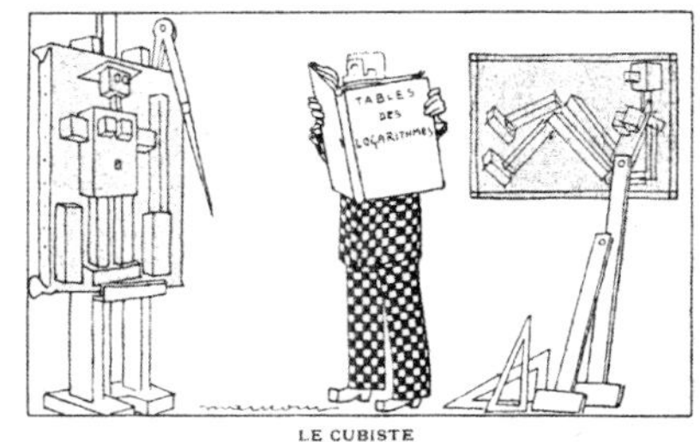

Louis Marcoussis. *Le Cubiste*. Cartoon in *La Vie Parisienne*, March 2, 1912.

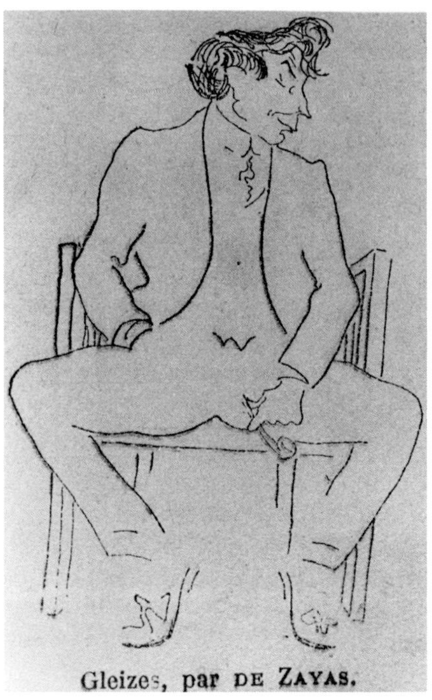

Marius de Zayas. Caricature of Albert Gleizes, c. 1912.

who had studied law and political science before becoming a painter. Gleizes was the no less gifted son of a successful designer and nephew of a fashionable academic painter. After dabbling in pacifist and socialist causes, he had joined Henri-Martin Barzun's socialist phalanstery, the Abbaye de Créteil, a utopian community of idealists who wanted to escape the materialism and corruption of the big city. Given Gleizes's envious, self-righteous nature and pompous manner (he usually wore a frock coat), it was inevitable that he should regard the visceral Picasso as the devil and dislike him and his recent work on sight. Another key figure of the Abbaye de Créteil was a brilliant young writer and exhibition organizer called Alexandre Mercereau. Insofar as he was an eloquent spokesman for the Salon cubists and a persistent promoter of their work in Eastern Europe (Moscow and Prague especially), he incurred Kahnweiler's wrath. However, Mercereau had a far sharper instinct for the avant-garde than Apollinaire and, by 1914, was exhibiting works by Mondrian and Brancusi.

A few weeks after the meeting at Kahnweiler's, Gleizes came out with what amounted to a denunciation of Picasso (and by implication Braque) in the form of a eulogy of Metzinger, entitled "L'Art et ses représentants." After condescendingly acknowledging the "efforts" of Picasso, Braque and Derain—efforts which, for all their timeliness, were "open to discussion"—Gleizes invokes Cézanne, in whose sacred name he proceeds to indict impressionism. After a tortuous argument he ends up tarring his rivals' analytical cubism with, of all things, the same anti-impressionist brush. What had shocked Gleizes about the paintings he had seen at Kahnweiler's was their "lack of legibility" and "impressionism of form"—a sin against Cézanne. "Impressionism of form" implied that a work lacked true structure and stability—what Gleizes called "volumetric relationships"—and that it was trivial in subject, concerned with ephemeral things instead of elevated themes. By contrast, Metzinger (and by implication Gleizes) was free of the impressionist taint, because—unlike Picasso and Braque, who had "betrayed" Cézanne—he had upheld the lessons of the master in works of consummate seriousness, truth and equilibrium, works that are "rigid and determined in method . . . entirely constructive, fully synthetic and pitiless toward premature or hasty realizations."[21] Works like *Le Goûter*?

Gleizes goes on to inveigh against painters who disregard "the vast subjects dear to the great epochs of the past,"[22] thereby exposing the hollowness of his and Metzinger's attempts to recast history painting in a modern mode, the hopelessness of their ambition to be the reincarnation of David, Ingres and Courbet. He fails to realize that cubism—Picasso's no less than Metzinger's—seldom, if ever, lends itself to ideological themes, panoramic subjects, symphonic effects, metaphysical pronouncements. Gleizes's cubist *chef d'œuvre*, *Harvest Threshing* (1912), exemplifies the incongruity. As a brochure for a Soviet-style Utopia, this "epic panorama of mountains, valleys, clouds and smoke, towns, workers and wheat, a simultaneous celebration of the harvest, nature and man in idealistic harmony"[23] works well enough; as cubism it creaks. Picasso came up with a good epitaph for the Salon cubists: "Once they had found themselves, they had nothing more to say."[24]

"The moment people started to define cubism," Braque told Dora Vallier many years later, "to establish limits and principles, I got the hell out."[25]

Albert Gleizes. *Portrait of Eugène Figuière* (publisher of *Du Cubisme*), 1913. 143×102 cm. Musée des Beaux-Arts, Lyon.

He shared Picasso's horror of theories and rationales. When asked by Metzinger whether feet should be depicted as round or square, Picasso replied, "There are no feet in nature."[26] A principal breeding ground of the theories that the Salon cubists revered and Braque and Picasso loathed—non-Euclidian geometry, Bergson's concept of intellectual time, notions of the fourth dimension and so on—had been the short-lived (1906–08) Abbaye de Créteil community. Besides Gleizes and Mercereau, this phalanstery numbered the writer Jules Romains among its adherents, and Metzinger, Le Fauconnier and Apollinaire among its sympathizers. And the ultimate expression of their theories is *Du Cubisme*, the book that Gleizes and Metzinger published in 1912. *Du Cubisme* is an ideological, not to say dogmatic, analysis, which purports to legitimize the authors' cubism as nothing less than a transcendental manifestation of "painting itself."[27] Although the book pays lip service to some of his achievements, Picasso dismissed *Du Cubisme* as nonsense. Likewise Braque: "Look at the daubs it engendered," he said.[28]

The chasm that opened up between Kahnweiler's artists on the one hand and the Salon cubists on the other was becoming too wide for even Apollinaire to straddle. While reassuring his old friends of his undying support—in the summer of 1912 he told Picasso that he and Braque were "the only artists he praised without restriction"[29]—he continued to eulogize their enemies. When Soffici questioned his criteria, Apollinaire tried to justify his strategy of speaking out of both sides of his mouth:

> For a new artistic concept to prevail, don't you think it's necessary to let the mediocre take its place alongside the sublime? That way you can measure the full extent of the new beauty. For this reason and out of deference to great artists like Picasso, I support Braque and the other cubists in my articles, for to align oneself with the general condemnation of [these cubists] would be to cast aspersions on a talent that only deserves to be encouraged. . . . We would surely agree on this point, in the first place with regard to Le Fauconnier.[30]

Speciousness or naïveté? A bit of both, probably. Apollinaire was determined to rally every faction of the avant-garde to his side. Hence his apparent deceitfulness; hence, too, the confusion and cronyism that flaws his account of cubism, *Les Peintres cubistes: méditations esthétiques*, which came out in 1913: a book which the author claimed (doubtless to explain the omission of Delaunay, Le Fauconnier and many more) was the first installment of a more comprehensive study. For all the poetic insights, witty acrobatics and incorrigible fantasy, one can see why Picasso, who loved Apollinaire as a man and a writer, never took his views on painting seriously; why Braque deplored every statement he ever made about art; and why Kahnweiler, who admired his poetry, threatened at one point to bar him from his gallery.

* * *

Feelings of gratitude tinged with revenge were likewise at the root of Apollinaire's bonding with Picasso's other envious antagonist, Robert Delaunay, and the affluent wife, Sonia Terk, he had lured away from Uhde. In the fall of 1912, shortly after Sonia had given birth to a son, the Delaunays invited the poet to stay with them in their vast studio at 3, rue des Grands Augustins (a few doors away from the studio Picasso would move to in 1937), while he recovered from his breakup with Marie Laurencin and looked around for a new apartment. Delaunay, whose dislike and disapproval of Picasso would be lifelong,[31] set about winning Apollinaire over to his side. This was not the first time he had tried to subvert a member of the *bande à Picasso*. Before marrying Sonia, he had urged her to turn Uhde against Picasso: Uhde had stood firm. Delaunay had also failed with Gertrude Stein, who was no admirer of his work. ("It is either big and empty or small and empty," she said.)[32]

> We have not seen much of the Delaunays lately [Gertrude wrote Mabel Dodge Luhan]. There is a feud on. He wanted to wean Apollinaire and me from liking Picasso and there was a great deal of amusing intrigue. Guillaume Apollinaire was wonderful. He was moving just then and it was convenient to stay with the Delaunays and he did and he paid just enough to cover his board. He did an article on Cubism and he spoke beautifully of Delaunay as having . . . "something or other of the *couleur pur*."
>
> Now Delaunay does conceive himself as a great solitaire and as a matter of fact he is an incessant talker and will tell all about himself and his value at any hour of the day or night to anybody, and so he was delighted and so were his friends. Apollinaire does that sort of thing wonderfully. He is so suave you can never tell what he is doing.[33]

Suave indeed. In 1910, Apollinaire had described Delaunay's paintings as "having the unfortunate air of commemorating an earthquake."[34] After accepting the painter's hospitality, he switched to rhapsody: "*La Ville de Paris* is more than an artistic manifestation; [it] marks the advent of a conception of art that seemed to have been lost with the great Italian painters."[35] In January, 1913, Apollinaire went off to Berlin with Delaunay for his one-man show at the Sturm gallery, an event which would have such an electrifying effect on Klee, Marc and Macke that they would make a pilgrimage to Delaunay's Paris studio. To coincide with this show, Apollinaire gave a lecture on modern art with special reference to Delaunay. This infuriated Kahnweiler, who suspected the Sturm's charismatic proprietor, Herwarth Walden, of plotting with Delaunay and Apollinaire to upstage Picasso's first large-scale retrospective, which was due to open the following month at Thannhauser's gallery, in Munich.

Sonia Delaunay in costume she designed for Bal Bullier, c. 1913. Getty Research Institute: Resource Collections.

Delaunay's rapid rise to fame did not cure his obsessive envy of Picasso. Rather the reverse: envy propelled him on his triumphant way, envy and his forceful mother—a lively little adventuress (in some respects not unlike Apollinaire's mother) who called herself Comtesse Berthe de la Rose, nobody quite knew why. After divorcing the wellborn Georges Delaunay, she had supposedly been kept by a politician, who had died insane. Berthe de la Rose was "artistic": known for trimming her own *outré* hats and doing watercolors of flowers, some of them pointillistic. She was prepared to go to any lengths, Gertrude Stein claimed, to make her son famous. Apollinaire remembered a lavish dinner she gave for her Robert. They ate off a Sèvres service in the shadow of Rousseau's large brooding *Snake Charmer*, which the hostess, an indefatigable traveler, claimed had been inspired by her tales of India: "Sometimes [it] feels like a venomous paradise," she had told the Douanier; it abounds in "men who play flutes and make rattlesnakes dance."[36]

Delaunay "was always asking how old Picasso had been when he had painted a certain picture," Gertrude Stein wrote. "When he was told, he

Robert Delaunay. *Window*, 1912. Gouache on canvas mounted on cardboard, 45×37 cm. Musée des Beaux-Arts, Grenoble.

always said, 'Oh, I am not as old as that yet, I will do as much when I am that age.'"[37] And he assured his wife, "I am ahead of Picasso and Braque. I am not just analyzing geometric forms. I'm trying to come to grips with the rhythm of modern life, trying to break down lines and architecture."[38] "Deconstruction" was the word he coined for this process.[39] Delaunay also maintained that he was ahead of Picasso and Braque in doing cubistic *Eiffel Towers*. For him the subject symbolized not only modern technology but phallocentric power—to judge by the inscription on the Eiffel Tower painting he gave Sonia when he was courting her: "Franco-Russian in-depth movement." Whether or not he knew that in 1906 Picasso had contemplated introducing the Eiffel Tower into his Pyrenean eclogue *The Blind Flower Seller*,[40] Delaunay assured Sonia that the tower was worthier of a modern artist's attention than Picasso's mundane guitars and fruit dishes.

That Apollinaire's muselike attentions were now Delaunay's prerogative caused Picasso intense irritation, the more so because Delaunay, unlike Gleizes and Metzinger, was an originator to be reckoned with. Apart from Léger, he was the only one of the Salon cubists to have understood how Picasso and Braque had revolutionized traditional notions of form and space, the only one to have achieved a comparable degree of optical synthesis. What is more, Delaunay had reached this point by making a virtue of color rather than scorning it. "They paint with cobwebs, these fellows,"[41] Delaunay had remarked to Léger when Kahnweiler showed them a succession of monochrome paintings by Picasso and Braque.

In reaction against cubist "cobwebs," Delaunay heightened his palette even more, and during the summer of 1912, painted a series of dazzling *Windows*, which he described as "*simultanéiste*"—a term the futurists had coined for their fusion of form and space, time and movement. However, Delaunay's simultaneism had little to do with futurism. It was primarily concerned with color, and it stemmed from the theories of Michel-Eugène Chevreul,[42] which Seurat and the divisionists had adopted. Delaunay's Chevreulian simultaneism involved juxtaposing colors in such a way that they do not merge when seen from a distance, as in a neo-impressionist painting; instead they retain their separate identities and engender not just light but pictorial form and space and, it was even claimed, musical harmonies. Delaunay's *Windows* were a major breakthrough: "Before me color was only coloring," he boasted.[43] *Windows* enabled him to break with the "deconstructive" cubism of his *Eiffel Tower* paintings, forge ahead into "pure color" and abstraction, and emerge as the leader of a new movement, which Apollinaire promptly took over and named orphism, in honor of his newly published *Bestiaire*, subtitled *Cortège d'Orphée*.

Orphism was a literary as well as artistic movement. Besides Léger, Picabia, Marcel Duchamp and, according to Apollinaire, Picasso (who adamantly denied any involvement), it included poets like the Swiss Blaise Cendrars (born Friedrich Sauser), the rich socialist Henri-Martin Barzun and the avant-garde Italian critic Ricciotto Canudo (editor of *Montjoie*, the orphists' magazine). Since his self-serving efforts to unify the opposing factions of cubism had come to naught, and Marinetti had blocked his attempts to move in on futurism, Apollinaire needed a movement in order to consolidate his platform and promote him as a cultural *conglomérateur*. As he had once hailed Picasso as a cross between Hermes and Harlequin,[44]

Robert Delaunay. *Eiffel Tower* (with inscription to Apollinaire), 1910–11. Oil on canvas, 130×97 cm. Museum Folkwang, Essen.

Marc Chagall. *Homage to Apollinaire*, 1912. Oil with gold and silver powder on canvas, 200×189.5 cm. Stedelijk Van Abbe Museum, Eindhoven.

Wood engraving by Pierre Roy after Giorgio de Chirico's *Portrait of Apollinaire* (1914), from the brochure for Apollinaire's *Et moi aussi je suis peintre*.

he now hailed Delaunay (and by extension himself) as an incarnation of Orpheus. Orphism, Apollinaire announced, was synonymous with simultaneism. This confused people who kept track of art labels; it suggested that Apollinaire was a mystifier, and orphism a rip-off of futurism, just as futurism was a rip-off of cubism. The more plagiarists accused each other of plagiarism, the more Picasso and Braque held aloof from the fray.

In 1905 it had been Apollinaire who had alerted Picasso to the painterly possibilities of symbolism. The positions of poet and painter were now reversed. This time round, it was Delaunay who alerted Apollinaire to the poetic possibilities of simultaneism, who showed him how a poet's ear could work in tandem with a painter's eye. An orphist painter or poet could metamorphose images into words, words into images—with musical overtones if need be. The first manifestation of this is the color-saturated poem "Windows," an homage to Delaunay, which Apollinaire wrote in the artist's studio for the catalog of the Sturm show. It starts, "From red to green the yellow fades" and ends, "The window opens like an orange / The beautiful fruit of light." So pleased was Apollinaire with this audiovisual conceit that he advertised his forthcoming collection of poems under a decidedly orphist title, *Et moi aussi je suis peintre*.[45]

Delaunay in front of his orphic painting *Le Premier Disque*, exhibited at the Berlin autumn Salon, 1914. Collection P.M.A.

Although Apollinaire announced in Canudo's *Montjoie* (March 9, 1913) that "the reign of Orpheus" was just beginning, orphism was already over, the victim of a row between Apollinaire and Delaunay concerning the ticklish matter of *appellations*. To keep in with the futurists, Apollinaire had allowed that simultaneism was their invention—not Delaunay's. Delaunay was furious. The control of orphism passed to Cendrars, who collaborated with Sonia Delaunay on an ambitious simultaneist poem, "Prose du Transibérien," a foldout some two meters long. Henceforth Apollinaire's rallying cry would be "*l'esprit nouveau*," a vague, omnium gatherum phrase for the multifaceted newfangledness which he was still determined to personify.[46] Meanwhile he had resumed seeing Picasso on a regular basis. Early in 1913, the artist agreed to engrave a portrait of him as a frontispiece to his forthcoming collection of poems, *Alcools*, but was distressed to discover through Max Jacob—a past master at making as well as unmaking mischief—that Apollinaire had instructed the printer to pull a proof of it in blue. On February 27, 1913, Picasso wrote the poet a terse note forbidding the use of any color but black.[47] He was not going to stand for any "*et moi aussi je suis peintre*" nonsense. Apollinaire may have unwittingly started Picasso thinking along similar lines. A quarter of a century later, the artist would get his own back and exasperate his literary friends—especially Gertrude Stein and Paul Eluard—by daring to announce, "*et moi je suis poète*."

MA JOLIE

15

Ma Jolie 1911–12

Umberto Boccioni. *Man at a Table at the Taverne de l'Ermitage,* c. 1912. Pen and sepia ink on lined paper, 20.5×13.5cm. Private collection.

Opposite: Picasso. *Woman with Guitar ("Ma Jolie"),* fall, 1911. Oil on canvas, 100×65cm. The Museum of Modern Art, New York: Acquired through the Lillie P. Bliss Bequest.

JUST AS *L'AFFAIRE DES STATUETTES* WOULD HASTEN the end of Apollinaire's faltering relationship with Marie Laurencin, it dealt the *coup de grâce* to Picasso and Fernande's affair. Picasso never forgave her for seeing him reduced to abject panic, his pride in shreds, Fernande said.[1] He was apparently so paranoid that when they went out at night he would change cabs several times to throw off nonexistent "tails"; so truculent that he knocked out a local pimp for barging into him; so disagreeable that Fernande took to going out on her own. More often than not she ended up across the road at L'Ermitage, an unwise choice for a lone woman whose lover was as irritable as he was jealous. Fernande does not seem to have cared. She was in search of adventure and possibly revenge, and since she was, if anything, more seductive than when she had first met Picasso, she soon found it.

Around the middle of October, 1911, the futurists came on a reconnoitering visit to Paris. With Severini as their guide, Boccioni and Carrà spent two weeks paving the way for the futurist jamboree that Bernheim-Jeune was organizing for the following February. They were particularly eager to see what the cubists were up to. Besides checking out the competition in Room VIII at the Salon d'Automne, they insisted that Severini take them to see Picasso, Braque, Léger and Le Fauconnier, also Apollinaire, who would write about their visit.[2] Fernande describes them as "impassioned prophets dreaming of a futurism that would oust cubism."[3] She was in a position to know: she had met them at L'Ermitage, where they forgathered every evening. Among their hangers-on was a very good-looking twenty-two-year-old Bolognese painter called Ubaldo Oppi—"highly courteous and intelligent"—who was always badgering Severini to introduce him to Picasso.

> One evening, after we had got to know each other better [Severini wrote], I made the mistake of bringing [Oppi] into the inner circle of L'Ermitage, and I was bitterly to regret this. *La belle Fernande*, who was always very flirtatious, went on the attack, partly as a joke, partly to practice her powers on a boy from the provinces, and my young friend couldn't resist at all. They embarked on a passionate affair.[4]

Severini subsequently blamed himself for the outcome, but "Picasso never reproached me for it," he wrote in his memoirs. "In the end Fernande was the hostile one. I never understood why."[5] Since this affair enabled Picasso to unload Fernande, he need not have been puzzled.

Ubaldo Oppi. *Self-Portrait*, 1911. Oil on cardboard, 60×40cm. Arco Farnese, Rome.

Eva Gouel. Archives Picasso.

Because he was friendly with Severini and Soffici, Oppi was generally assumed to be a futurist. In fact he was nothing of the sort. A pupil of Klimt, he was more of a Viennese secessionist;[6] back in Italy he became an Ingresque classicist of some distinction and ended up a reclusive painter of religious subjects in a traditional manner. Always something of a reactionary, Oppi later wrote of his years in Paris that the earlier Italian schools in the Louvre "compensated me for my spiritual bewilderment and indifference to all the isms."[7]

To carry on an affair under the ever-watchful eye of Picasso was exceedingly risky. Fernande needed an intermediary—and who better than her new confidante, Marcelle Humbert, soon to be better known as Eva Gouel, the demurely pretty mistress of Lodwicz Markus, soon to change his name to Marcoussis. Picasso had taken a liking to Markus and Eva. Since the two couples saw a lot of each other, clandestine meetings were easy to arrange. If anything went wrong, Eva was supposed to cover up for her friend, but she had other ideas. Under the pretext of being a go-between, Eva was out to compromise Fernande and grab Picasso for herself. He tacitly collaborated.

Except for Picasso, nobody in Montmartre seems to have been especially fond of Eva. This seemingly sweet-natured woman could be two-faced and calculating. Like Fernande, she went under more than one name and kept her past dark. Locally, she was better known as Marcelle Humbert, but she was not the ex-wife of a man called Humbert, as she claimed.[8] As for Picasso's assertion that it was he who changed her name to Eva—"He wanted to demonstrate that for him she was his first woman. . . . He set his heart on proclaiming [her name], establishing it in the annals of posterity"—this is yet another of the myths perpetrated by the artist and perpetuated by his amanuensis.[9] "Eve" is what her parents, Adrien Gouel and Marie-Louise Ghérouze, of Vincennes, christened her. True, Picasso Hispagnolized her name to Eva, but if he stopped calling her Marcelle, it was largely to distinguish her from Braque's Marcelle. However, the mythmaking had a point. If Picasso's mistress was Eve, the first woman, it followed that he was Adam, the first man.

Given Eva's slyness, it is difficult to determine when Picasso's affair with her began. Fernande's escapade did not necessarily trigger Picasso's. The artist's famous declaration "I love [Eva] very much and I will write this in my paintings"[10] was not made until the following June (12), but his work reveals that he had been inscribing his paintings with declarations of love for at least six months. The first of the amorously inscribed paintings—the Museum of Modern Art's *Ma Jolie*—is usually assigned to the fall of 1911, but the telltale words might well have been added later. Most of the major paintings of this period have been reworked two or three different times to keep pace with the ever-changing syntax of cubism. So as not to alert Fernande, these amorous inscriptions, which sometimes take the form of banal song titles, like "Ma Jolie," are not always easy to spot: for instance, the vertical nude where the words "J'aime Eva" appear high up on the model's thigh, like a tattoo, next to Picasso's cubist sign for pubic hair.

Fifteen years later, when he fell for Marie-Thérèse Walter, Picasso would employ a similar subterfuge. Since he was married at the time and Marie-Thérèse was under the age of consent, he would simultaneously reveal and conceal his love for his new mistress by referring to her in code—disguised initials, double entendres or allegorical imagery (bowls of peaches for her, jugs with big spouts for him)—so that everyone, above all his wife and Marie-Thérèse's mother, would be left in the dark. This process started with Eva. Although Picasso would not elope with Eva for another three or four months, these coded declarations did not rouse Fernande's suspicions. Her sardonic lover knew what she was up to and, with Eva's help, continued to pay out the rope with which she would hang herself.

Picasso was very secretive about Eva. Those assiduous monitors of his personal life, Gertrude Stein and Alice Toklas, were not aware that he had found a new love until they went to call on him at his Bateau Lavoir studio in February, 1912. As he was out, Gertrude jokingly left her visiting card. When they returned later in the week, they discovered that Picasso had painted the card into a recent still life, *The Architect's Table* (p. 105). He had also discreetly added the words "*Ma Jolie*": a phrase from a popular song, "*O Manon ma jolie, mon cœur te dit bonjour*," which the band at the Cirque Médrano was constantly playing.[11] "Fernande is certainly not *Ma Jolie*," Gertrude said as they left. "I wonder who it is."[12] She was all the more curious since Picasso's inclusion of her visiting card was having the desired effect on her vanity. She had to have this tribute to herself. On being asked the price, the canny artist wrote to her (March 19) that he had just seen Kahnweiler and could not let her have it for less than 1,200 francs. This was more than Gertrude could afford. After a second letter from Picasso saying that Kramář (an important collector of cubism) had seen her *Ma Jolie* still life and "had loved it,"[13] she bought it. So much for the significance of the visiting card.

Picasso's strategy to get Gertrude Stein collecting again—after a two-year hiatus—worked so well that Picasso kept after her. Knowing that she and Alice were leaving early in May to spend the summer in Spain, he sent her a cubistic drawing by Max Jacob and told her that he had "some things that she had not seen which I like."[14] Once again, she rose to the bait. Two days later, on May 3, Picasso confirmed an appointment with her for the following Monday. Gertrude bought two smallish but extremely fine still lifes: *The Little Glass* and *Still Life with Newspaper*. Punctilious as always with the Steins, Picasso wrote to thank her for the money: "Since you will receive this letter in Spain, say hello to the homeland that I love so much. I think you have made an excellent choice of my paintings and I am very happy that they please you."[15] Over the next two and a half years, Gertrude would buy seven more cubist paintings. They are all fine examples, some of them exceedingly fine, but the Picassos—ten in all—and the Juan Grises that she bought on her own do not compare in importance with the masterpieces by Picasso (not to speak of Cézanne and Matisse) that she and Leo had acquired during the heyday of their collecting. Nevertheless Gertrude's continuing use of her paintings as a self-promotional attraction would be a key factor in the spread of Picasso's fame.

* * *

Picasso plighted his troth in color as well as words. Hitherto his attempts to introduce color into virtually monochrome compositions had always

Picasso. *Nude Woman ("J'aime Eva")*, 1912. Oil, sand and charcoal on canvas, 98.5×63.5cm. Columbus Museum of Art, Ohio: Gift of Ferdinand Howald.

Picasso. *Nude Woman ("J'aime Eva")* (detail).

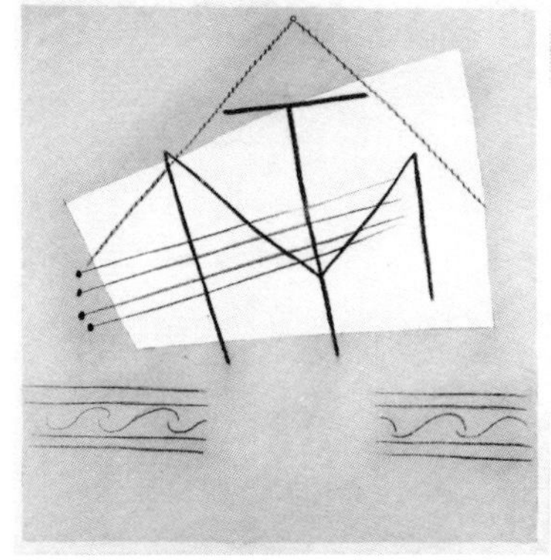

Picasso. *Guitar* (with initials MT), April 27, 1927. Oil and charcoal on canvas, 81×81cm. Musée Picasso.

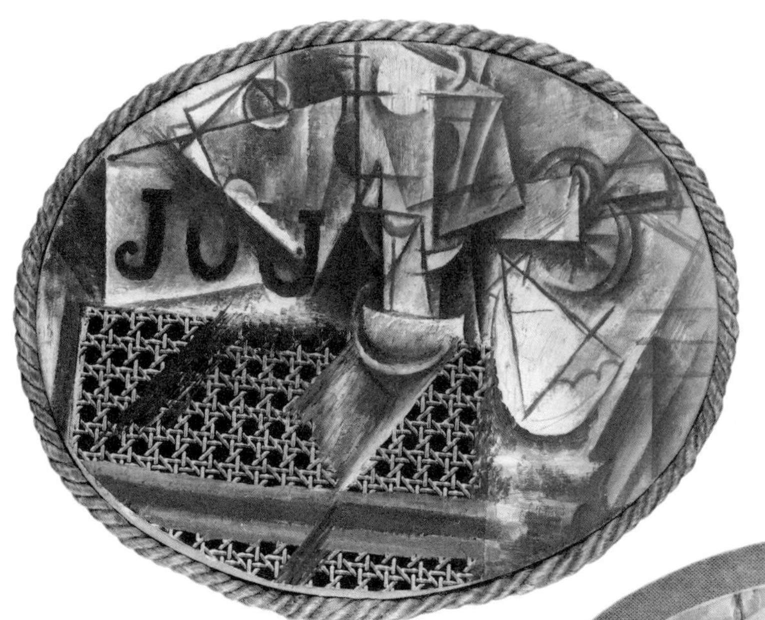

Picasso. *Still Life with Chair Caning*, 1912. Oil and oilcloth stuck on oval canvas framed with rope, 27×35cm. Musée Picasso.

Braque. *Pedestal Table ("Stal")*, 1912. Oil on oval canvas, 73×60cm. Museum Folkwang, Essen.

ended in defeat. Early in 1912, he solved the problem by using local color instead of *le ton juste*, and Ripolin (shiny house paint) instead of an artist's oil pigment. Ripolin allowed Picasso to exploit the brightness and, if need be, the shine of playing cards, flags, clothes, posters, labels, packaging, household utensils, which are the stuff of pop culture. It was so much the antithesis of impressionist *belle peinture*—all that stippling and dappling and fiddling with complementary colors—that Picasso's adoption of it might have been a response to the accusations of "formal impressionism" that Gleizes and Metzinger had leveled against his recent work. Years later, Gertrude Stein describes Picasso "talking a long time about the ripolin paints. They are, said he gravely, *la santé des couleurs*, that is why they are the basis of good health for paints. In those days (1912 onwards) he painted pictures and everything with ripolin paints, as he still does, and as so many of his followers young and old do."[16]

Advertisement for Ripolin paint.

The use of Ripolin was an assault on the integrity of a painter's traditional medium. Even the usually supportive Uhde was shocked. Informed by Kahnweiler that Uhde disliked "the recent paintings where the flags were painted in ripolin," Picasso said, "Perhaps we will succeed in disgusting the whole world and we have a lot more tricks up our sleeve."[17] Picasso's use of Ripolin coincides with his use of another alien industrial element: the oilcloth printed to resemble canework that he incorporated into his *Still Life with Chair Caning* (newspaper, glass, lemon slice, scallop shell), which is renowned for being the first cubist collage. The canework would suggest that Picasso has set the still life on a chair, but the rope frame, which the artist had added, has convinced certain scholars that it is set on a table. "A kitchen chair with a cane seat" is how Picasso described the still life's support to Françoise Gilot,[18] but ambivalence may well have been intended.

Besides opening cubism up to a new range of pictorial possibilities, this collage enabled Picasso to get back at Braque for his advances in evoking space. His recent work abounds in silvery, zephyr-like passages in which objects, even faces, evaporate or melt or turn into something that may or may not be figurative: a shimmer of woodgraining, a cloud of powdery whiteness stenciled with letters that, like as not, refer to other areas of the composition. These innovations seem to have put Picasso on his mettle. Thanks to collage, he could once again take the lead. Six months later, Braque would retaliate when, behind Picasso's momentarily turned back, he came up with the first papier collé. Whereupon Picasso would exploit this discovery in ways that Braque had never envisioned. And so on. In this friendly but deadly game of one-upmanship it is impossible to say which of the two players had the upper hand. At the height of cubism it was, surprisingly, the mercurial and temperamental Picasso who would repeatedly urge the cooler, more phlegmatic Braque to come and work with him. Later, Picasso would race ahead on his own. Emotionally, however, he would always need Braque rather more than Braque needed him. Only Picasso's tall, reserved dandy of a father, don José, had taught him as much as this tall, reserved dandy of a Norman.

Braque in Picasso's studio, 1909. Photograph by Picasso. Archives Picasso.

The month or so before May 18, 1912, would prove vital for the artist's private life as well as for the development of cubism, which once again reflects it. Coincidence or not, Picasso's abandonment of analytical cubism for synthetic cubism coincides with his abandonment of Fernande, the personification of the earlier style, for Eva, the personification of the later style. The last act of this drama starts on or around April 25, when Braque persuaded Picasso to join him on a trip to Normandy, and distance himself from the Fernande/Eva situation. The two artists stopped in Rouen to see Vlaminck, but he was not to be found, so they went on to Le Havre to visit Braque's family. A few days later, they returned by way of Honfleur to Paris. According to Daix, the ostensible purpose of this visit was for Braque to present Marcelle Lapré to his family.[19] However, she did not accompany her lover on this trip or his other visits to Le Havre in 1912. Braque's bourgeois parents doubtless knew that she was their son's mistress, also that there was no immediate prospect of marriage. Maybe they would not have welcomed her.

Brochure, "*Notre Avenir est dans l'Air*," February 1, 1912. Private collection.

The person Braque would most have wanted his family to meet would have been his partner in that other marriage—cubism. The visit to Le Havre was a success in that it made Picasso nostalgic for Barcelona. He told Jean Cassou, apropos the scallop shells in his Le Havre still lifes, "All of a sudden I could smell the port of Barcelona."[20] Braque sent happy bulletins to Marcelle: "This morning," he wrote on April 27, "I woke Picasso by playing the phonograph to him. It was delightful."[21] After he returned to Paris—"That famous return from Le Havre," mentioned by Apollinaire in *Les Peintres cubistes*[22]—Picasso celebrated his visit in a memorable oval still life, which he inscribed, on a trompe l'œil ribbon, *Souvenir du Havre*, as well as some related drawings. Severini claims that the *Souvenir* concept stemmed from him:

> I showed [Picasso] my painting, *Souvenirs de Voyage*, which he liked very much. . . . I had assembled all the things that had . . . captivated me during a trip to Italy . . . without worrying about the unity of time and place. . . . A short while later . . . [Picasso] showed me his painting, *Souvenir du Havre*, completely different from mine.[23]

In order to evoke maritime life, Picasso makes mocking but affectionate use of kitschy seaside imagery—clay pipes, anchors, lifebelts, tricolor flags, rigging, scallop shells—just as his friend Satie would make mocking use of popular melodies to evoke a circus or *bal musette*. These paintings and the first collage (the one with the scallop shells and the rope frame) initiate the next great phase in Picasso's work: synthetic cubism.

Braque was not altogether pleased when Picasso showed him the paintings he had done on his return from Le Havre. Besides borrowing the stenciled letters and woodgraining which Braque had exploited so imaginatively in his recent work, Picasso had gone ahead and solved the problem of bright color by introducing Ripolin. Severini, who was present when Braque saw these works for the first time, quotes the latter's rueful comment, "*d'un ton moitié figue, moitié raisin*" (half-sweet, half-sour): "*On change son fusil d'épaule*" (literally, "So we've changed the shoulder we shoot from").[24] To this Picasso said nothing but went on filling his pipe and smiling as if to say, "What a good joke." Severini had failed to realize that Braque was referring to a recent review of the Indépendants which commended the Salon cubists for "courageously changing the shoulder they shot from and liquidating their last cube." In other words Braque was hinting that Picasso's latest effect might be a betrayal of cubism.[25]

Juan Gris. *Les Aéroplanes*; cover of *L'Assiette au beurre*, November 14, 1908.

Three versions of a still life entitled "*Notre Avenir est dans l'Air*" form part of the same group. All three are ovals (one of them also framed, like

Above: Picasso. *The Scallop Shell ("Notre Avenir est dans l'Air")*, spring, 1912. Oil on oval canvas, 38×55.5 cm. Private collection.

Right: Picasso. *Souvenir du Havre*, spring, 1912. Oil on oval canvas, 92×65 cm. Private collection, Basel.

Left: Braque. *Table with Pipe*, 1912. Oil on oval canvas, 60×73 cm. Galerie Rosengart, Lucerne.

Futurists in Paris: Russolo, Carrà, Marinetti, Boccioni, Severini, 1912.

the first collage, in rope), and their principal feature is the red, white and blue cover of a small propaganda brochure that the French government had published (February 1, 1912) to popularize military aviation. The inclusion of the catchphrase title of the brochure is an oblique tribute to Braque. Picasso had identified Braque with Wilbur Wright (the pioneer aviator who had made many of his test flights in France) and had nicknamed him "Wilbourg" on the strength of his paper sculptures of 1911, now lost—the ones which are said to have resembled model airplanes. The challenging title of the brochure may also have constituted a riposte to the futurists, who had recently burst on the Parisian scene with a multimedia manifestation at Bernheim-Jeune's. In the cubist-baiting preface to their catalog, the futurists had vaunted the "dynamism" of such machine-age subjects as the speeding locomotives in Boccioni's *States of Mind* triptych over the cubists' static treatment of objects. It would have been typical of Picasso's sardonic humor to trounce the futurists "at their own game of modernity" by invoking "*l'Avenir dans l'Air.*"[26] Then again, as these stylistically ambivalent compositions suggest, Picasso's future was indeed in the air. He was about to abandon the monochrome of analytical cubism, which is reserved for the shells in these paintings, for the coloration and decoration exemplified by the tricolor brochure.[27] Braque would be his co-pilot. Eva, too, would be along. "AVE EST DANS L'A" is all Picasso divulges of the title. We have only to reverse the first three letters to get his gist.

* * *

Picasso and Eva, c. 1912.

To understand Picasso's switch from Fernande to Eva, it helps to remember that the artist had turned thirty in October. After the shock of *l'affaire des statuettes,* he wanted to settle down out of the limelight with a suitably attractive, suitably malleable girl and even get married. He would never have made Fernande his wife: she could not have children. Besides, she was feckless and indolent and too fearful to seek a divorce from Percheron, her abusive husband. Eva, on the other hand, was longing to prove what a perfect little wife, what a gifted *maîtresse de maison,* she would make. To this extent she appealed to Picasso's residual bourgeois streak. She was also very pretty, in a pert, Parisian way—a total contrast to the languorous, Jewish Fernande. For all her delicacy, Eva could be quite managerial. She soon established a powerful sexual hold over the artist. Hence all the genital references to her in Picasso's work—so blatantly genital that they are often overlooked. At the same time, Eva was very low-key, the perfect mate for someone eager to withdraw from the hurly-burly of bohemia and concentrate on work without having to worry about domestic details; the perfect mate, too, for someone who was increasingly solicitous of his health and obliged to follow a rigorous diet. (Alice Toklas says he liked her to cook him spinach soufflé and loin of veal.)[28] Braque had settled down happily with a woman called Marcelle. Was it not time Picasso did the same?

During the winter and on into the spring, Eva continued to manipulate this amorous tangle to her advantage, switching easily from acting as Fernande's go-between to being Markus's model mistress and Picasso's secret lover. On May 18, when all his pieces were in place, Picasso pounced; he told Fernande that he had discovered all about her affair with Oppi and was through with her. He was leaving her for Eva and giving her nothing; he hoped never to see her again. He could not throw her out of the apartment: it was in her name. Kahnweiler would sublet it from her. To survive, Fernande would be obliged to sell the few minor examples of his work that Picasso had given her.

None of Picasso's friends knew what had happened. At first Severini was thought to have been involved.

> Knowing that there was a certain friendly affection between Eva and me [he wrote in his memoirs], Marcoussis and several others in Montmartre thought that I had carried her off, and this in fact is what Fernande and her boyfriend wanted, to justify in a sense what they had done. That this was not the case became clear when it emerged that Fernande was in the young Italian's studio, and that Eva had left . . . with Picasso. As a result of this intimate drama . . . I inherited a magnificent Siamese cat, which had belonged to Picasso and which had been left alone and abandoned. It didn't live for long in my studio, as I had to get rid of it quickly, giving it either to Dufy or Braque.[29]

Louis Marcoussis. *Still Life with Chessboard*, 1912. Oil on canvas, 217.5×147.5cm. Musée National d'Art Moderne, Centre Georges Pompidou, Paris.

Besides Kahnweiler, the only person Picasso informed of his plans was Braque: "Fernande has run away with a futurist. I'm going to get out of Paris for a bit. I beg you to look after Frika [the dog] for a few days."[30] The most credible account of what had transpired comes to us from Matisse via Michael Stein:

> I think I have the true story of the Pablo business [Michael Stein wrote his sister, Gertrude, in Fiesole on June 19, 1912]. . . . Yesterday morning I was out at Robinson's riding with Leo for two hours. It was very hot and the odors in the forest were wonderful. I came home took a bath had lunch and then Matisse came in and wanted me to go to Robinson's with him. He looked so crestfallen when I told him I had already ridden that I went with him for another ride. On the way he told me he had a new model, who lived with a *littérateur*, who was one of the Montmartre crowd and that she told him all about the affair. It seems that F. had been going with the Futurist for sometime, and a note she gave her woman friend, who is always with her to deliver to the Futurist, the friend gave it to P. because she wanted P. herself. So P. confronted F. and they split. P. went to K. got money, cleared all his things out of Ravignan [Bateau Lavoir], discharged the maid, locked up the other place and decamped to Céret with the friend, where he is still working. The Futurist has no cash, so F. poses for Cinamas [movies?] and says she is going on the stage and is living with the Pichots or however you spell it.[31]

Michael, Leo and Allan Stein riding, 1912. Beinecke Rare Book and Manuscript Library, Yale University.

Leo Stein had likewise sent Gertrude a report based on stories he had heard from two sources: the Polish sculptor Nadelman, who had been briefed by his compatriot Markus, and the American synchronist Patrick Henry Bruce, who had been briefed by his friend and teacher Delaunay. Markus had told Nadelman that he had fancied Picasso's "wife" and felt that his feelings were reciprocated. The next time the two Poles met, Markus said that Pablo had gotten ahead of him and gone off to Brittany with *his* wife.[32] Delaunay's news was more accurate: "Pablo [had gone] to the Pyrenees with that little woman Fernande was constantly with."[33]

Picasso's version of the story—as given to his mistress, Geneviève Laporte, some forty years later, sheds more light in its departures from the

Louis Marcoussis. Detail of cartoon, *Schéhérazade au Bal des Quat'z' Arts*, in *La Vie Parisienne*, June 15, 1912. The three men with Eva "en route for the Palace of the Thousand and One Nights" are described as "a gentleman who has lost his illusions," "the happy bachelor" and the "newlywed."

truth than in its adherence to it.[34] He had had enough of Fernande, he told Geneviève, but did not know how to break with her. Fortunately for him, a painter in the Bateau Lavoir had fallen in love with her and written her a compromising note. Fernande had eyes only for him, Picasso boasted, so she had thrown it down the toilet. However, the toilet was one of those "Turkish" ones (a tiled hole in the floor: no pedestal) and the letter had stuck to the side of the drain. Picasso said he had found it, made a terrible, sham scene and chucked her out. According to the macho Andalusian code, he evidently felt that he would rather be perceived as a monster than as a cuckold. The toilet story explains how Picasso had probably hoodwinked Fernande into believing, at least temporarily, that she had been done in by her own carelessness—had she told Eva where she threw Oppi's letters?—rather than by the treachery of her best friend.

As for Markus, whether or not he was telling the truth, he claimed to be well rid of Eva. A month after Eva eloped, he published a cartoon in *La Vie Parisienne* (June 15) making fun of the breakup. The cartoon is a spoof of *Schéhérazade*, the ballet in which Nijinsky and Ida Rubinstein were the sensation of Paris that spring. Markus has reversed the situation. Instead of avenging himself on his faithless Zobeida when he finds her in the arms of the Golden Slave, Sultan Markus dances for joy, broken shackles dangling from his ankles. Meanwhile Eva in a turbanlike hat takes off on the arm of Picasso, who wears an overcoat patterned à la Bakst with large cubes. The ball-and-chain is now around *his* ankle. An almost identical image of her little face will resurface eighteen months later in some of the drawings for Picasso's greatest evocation of Eva, *Woman in an Armchair.*

When Picasso was asked by Daix to confirm that the face in his drawings for *Woman in an Armchair* was Eva's, he shrugged his shoulders and prevaricated, "It just happened like that. . . . Of course Eva was there at the time."[35] It was as if the artist wanted to keep this doomed woman hidden from the world, enshrined in the myth of playing Eve to his Adam; memorialized by the sort of graffiti—*"Ma Jolie," "J'aime Eva," "Jolie Eva"* —that one might find on the walls of a barracks or a prison cell. One of the more touching of these inscriptions has not survived. The only painting that we know Picasso gave Eva, *Guitar*, was originally decorated with a gingerbread heart, on which the artist had written, *"J'aime Eva"*; nothing is left of this love token except the blank area where the heart had once adhered. Picasso would certainly have married Eva if she had not contracted cancer in 1913. By December, 1915, she would be dead.

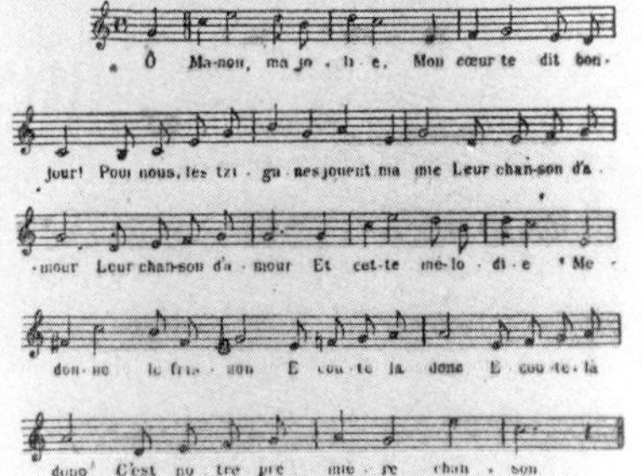

Une des chansons de Fragson à l'Alhambra

Un air délicieusement prenant dont les orchestres de tziganes ont fait la vogue et que tout Paris fredonne, d'exquises paroles pouvant être chantées par tout le monde, un ar-

tiste merveilleux qui la détaille avec un art unique : voilà ce qui explique le succès qu'obtient *Fragson* tous les soirs à l'Alhambra dans la romance *Dernière chanson.* La musique est

Refrain of Harry Fragson's "Dernière Chanson": *"O Manon, ma jolie, Mon cœur te dit bonjour! . . ."*

Deny it though he might, Picasso depicts Eva in more drawings and paintings than is generally realized. True, she does not permeate Picasso's imagery as overtly as most of his other mistresses, but, then, her reign coincided with the least representational phase of his work. As the 1911 drawings of Haviland reveal, portraiture was hardly compatible with the later development of cubism. Even figures are scarce. Between 1912 and 1914 objects outnumber human beings in Picasso's work by about ten to one.

The exigencies of cubism do not, however, explain Picasso's unwillingness to turn Eva into an icon, as he had done with Fernande in those extraordinarily expressive images, which run the gamut from ecstatic love to sadistic manipulation. One might have thought that Picasso would at

Above: Picasso. *Violin ("Jolie Eva")*, 1912. Oil on canvas, 60×81 cm. Staatsgalerie, Stuttgart.

Picasso. *Guitar ("J'aime Eva")*, 1912. Oil and collage on canvas, 41×33 cm (photographed with the gingerbread heart still in place). Kahnweiler photograph: Galerie Louise Leiris.

least have used her as a model for one of his Ingresque drawings. Since some of the neo-classical master's simpering Angelicas, Andromedas and Stratonices resemble her, this conjunction of subject and style would have seemed made to order. A desire to steer clear of the predictable and the pretty may well explain why Picasso's first Ingresque exercises portray Max Jacob, Vollard and Léonce Rosenberg rather than the odalisque-like Eva. Or did the fact that she was "small and all *pe-pe*, like a Chinese girl" (as Severini said)[36] render her prettiness unpaintable?

* * *

Fernande had difficulty surviving. The affair with Oppi lasted a few weeks at the most. Her new lover did not have the means to provide Fernande with the little luxuries to which she had become accustomed, so she broke with him. Whereupon she had another unsatisfactory romance. Férat says that Fernande treated Oppi as she treated Picasso. "She took all his money and did not even reply to the letters he wrote in ink drawn from his own veins." Now that Fernande was on her own, "it appears that she is going to give herself up to "*la 'basse' prostitution.*"[37] Férat had not seen Picasso since the latter's return to Paris; however he was sufficiently close to Apollinaire and other survivors of the *bande à Picasso* to be a reliable source of information. Still, Fernande is most unlikely to have worked as a prostitute. Had she done so, she would not have been broke by Christmas, reduced to throwing herself on the mercy of Gertrude Stein for help with the rent. She also appealed to Apollinaire for a reference—could she say that she had worked for him?—so that she could get a job as a secretary.[38] It was probably through Marcel Olin that she got a walk-on part in a play or a film. Eventually Paul Poiret came to the rescue and employed her as a *vendeuse*. When Poiret closed down, Fernande worked for an antiquaire; and when the antiquaire shut up shop, she gave poetry recitations at the Lapin Agile. At various times Fernande looked after children, worked as a cashier in a butcher's shop, ran a cabaret and read people's horoscopes—a skill she had learned from Max Jacob. In 1918, she became the mistress of Roger Karl, a gifted and very handsome actor, who could have been the greatest tragedian of his generation, Louis Jouvet said, if he had worked harder and drunk less.[39] In 1933, Fernande published a memoir, *Picasso et ses amis*, which the artist did his best to suppress but which he later admitted caught the atmosphere—the *Stimmung*—of his early years in Paris. Besides having a modest gift as a painter, Fernande turned out to be a natural writer.

Fernande at the Lapin Agile, c. 1915. Private collection.

After splitting with Roger Karl, in 1938, Fernande survived by teaching girls how to draw and speak good French. By 1957, she was in her mid-seventies and penniless. Genteel blackmail was her only option: she wrote to Picasso, threatening to publish yet another volume of memoirs.[40] Marcelle Braque acted as broker and had no problem persuading Picasso to give Fernande a million old francs on the understanding that her *Souvenirs intimes* would not be published—in his lifetime at least. Picasso need not have worried: three-quarters of Fernande's posthumous book concerns her life before she met him. After they broke up, in 1912, he never saw her again, except when she appeared on television in 1956 to be interviewed about early days in Montmartre. A disgusting performance, he said.

Fernande Olivier and Roger Karl, c. 1933–35. Private collection.

She was too old and fat and toothless to make a spectacle of herself; she who had personified beauty in his early work had made a fool of him. This woman, who had been born Amélie Lang, who was briefly Madame Paul Percheron, who called herself Fernande Belvallé, not to speak of Madame Picasso, and who achieved immortality through Picasso as Fernande Olivier, died on January 29, 1966, at the age of eighty-five, fifty years after the scheming woman who had supplanted her.

Below: Picasso. *Portrait of Fernande*, 1906. Charcoal on paper, 61.2×45.8cm. Art Institute of Chicago: Gift of Herman Waldeck.

FILS
MA
JOLIE

16

Sorgues 1912

Picasso. *Still Life with Bunch of Keys and Visiting Card*, spring, 1912. Etching, 21.8×27.8cm. Musée Picasso.

Picasso ran away with Eva on May 19, 1912. He was in such a rush that he left most of his possessions—including his cherished camera—in the boulevard de Clichy apartment, and most of his current work and painting equipment in the Bateau Lavoir studio. As soon as he arrived in Céret, he sent Kahnweiler instructions as to what he wanted done:

> Concerning the dogs, I've asked Braque to send Frika to me. As for the other animals—the monkey, the cats—Madame Pichot will take them. . . . Make a package of the canvas rolled up at rue Ravignan and the panels and send them here to me (c/o Manolo). Have the canvases . . . which are only drawn in charcoal . . . fixed by Juan Gris. As for the other paintings I have to give you . . . I want to think about it. . . . Manolo is working hard, as Déodat de Séverac says. He has a splendid house with a metal gate like the one at the Ministry of the Interior. . . . He also has an operating table and a whole lot of surgical instruments. . . . For the time being do not give my address to anyone.[1]

Over the next three weeks Picasso would write Kahnweiler every few days asking him to forward his painting materials:

> the paintbrushes that are at rue Ravignan, dirty as well as clean ones, and the stretchers that are there. . . . The palette too. . . . It's dirty. Wrap it in paper together with the stretchers, the [stencils for] letters and numbers and the [metal] combs for doing *faux bois*.[2]

He goes on to ask for all his paints—from the apartment as well as the studio:

> the tubes of white, ivory black, burnt siena, emerald green, Verona green, ultramarine, ocher, umber, vermilion, cadmium dark or rather cadmium yellow. I also have blue, Peruvian ocher. . . . I prefer to have all my paints here. . . . I need them at my side.
>
> The last etching is in the studio. . . . I'm still thinking of having a name engraved on a visiting card. But you should send me one of the two proofs so that I can draw the exact place where you should have the letters engraved by a professional engraver—of visiting cards.
>
> Send me only three or four tubes of each of the colors, however all the white . . . and a bottle of siccative and a packet of charcoal. . . . I am still at the hotel, but I've rented the house that Braque and I had last year.[3]

Now that Picasso had a house, he needed more domestic articles: "Sheets, bolsters, blankets, my linen, and my yellow kimono with flowers. I'm not sure what you'll have to do to arrange all this, but I've more faith in you

Opposite: Picasso. Fresco from Villa des Clochettes: *Guitar, Bottle of Pernod and Wineglass*, summer, 1912. Oil on whitewashed wall transferred to canvas, 104×89cm. Whereabouts unknown. Kahnweiler photograph: Galerie Louise Leiris.

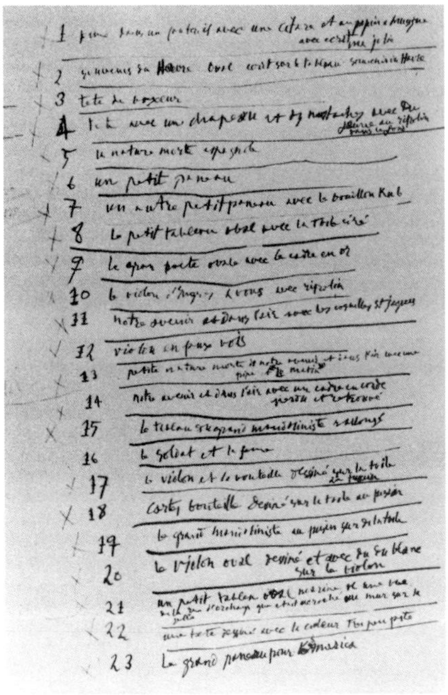

Annotated list of works left in the Bateau Lavoir studio contained in Picasso's letter to Kahnweiler, June 5, 1912. Archives Kahnweiler: Galerie Louise Leiris.

than in myself."[4] Picasso had good reason to worry about the feasibility of his requests: he may have asked Fernande to leave the boulevard de Clichy apartment, but it was still in her name, and she was not at all pleased at Kahnweiler, who had come to loathe her, barging in and removing things. When she threatened to have the dealer up for "violation of domicile," he persuaded her to sublet the apartment to him. That way he could no longer be charged with trespass.

Picasso's only other confidant was Braque. He wrote to him almost as frequently as to Kahnweiler, mostly about shipping Frika to Céret. (When she arrived, he wrote that she was "the talk of the town.")[5] He also insisted on the need to keep his whereabouts a secret. He missed Braque, Picasso said: "What's happened to our walks and our [exchanges] of feelings? I can't write about our discussions on art."[6] Braque had gone to Le Havre for his nephew's first communion. He told Picasso about the evenings he spent in bars down by the harbor (the Scandinavie and the Saint Joseph), where he liked to join the sailors in dances like the English hornpipe.

He was still waiting for his painting materials, Picasso wrote Kahnweiler on June 1—above all his palette; meanwhile he was obliged to improvise, making green "out of cobalt blue, mummy brown and cadmium yellow."[7] On June 5 he sent a letter specifying which paintings in his Paris studios were "not yet presentable" and which ones were finished and the prices for them.[8] He also listed the clothes he wanted sent. Louise, the maid, had evidently been stealing things; however, Picasso remembered exactly how everything had been left: which shirt on which chair. As for the Bateau Lavoir studio, he asked Kahnweiler to "have the concierge hang up the for-rent sign."[9] By June 7, he felt sufficiently settled into his new studio at Céret to embark on a major painting: "a man I saw playing bagpipes on Sunday."[10] Nothing came of this beyond some drawings. During this month at Céret he concentrated on still lifes. He also talked of doing a large engraving; and he wondered whether an American girl—the daughter of an art critic called Bill—who wanted to visit him, might in fact be the daughter of Buffalo Bill.

No sooner had Picasso established himself at Céret than he was appalled to hear that Fernande, having broken with Oppi, was on his track. He and Eva might have to move on. A Barcelona newspaper (*La Publicidad*, May 29) had announced that he was there (a jealous former lover of Fernande's, Joaquim Sunyer, had leaked the news), and "that jackass, Pichot," had written someone (probably Manolo) to confirm Picasso's presence: "a useless effort since no one will write back to him."[11] Picasso's worst fears were soon confirmed:

> Braque wrote yesterday [he informed Kahnweiler on June 12] to tell me he had met Pichot at Wepler's [a Montmartre café]. Pichot told him that he, his wife and Fernande proposed spending the summer at Céret. . . . I am very annoyed by all this, first because I don't want my great love for Marcelle to be disturbed by the trouble they might cause, nor do I want her bothered in any way; and finally I must have peace in order to work. I've needed it for a long time.[12]

And Picasso goes on to describe how he intends to write his love for Marcelle (soon to be known as Eva) on his paintings.

> I've done quite a few drawings and already begun eight paintings. I believe my painting has gained in robustness and clarity. . . . With all these

Above: Picasso. *Violin and Grapes*, spring–summer, 1912. Oil on canvas, 50.6×61 cm. The Museum of Modern Art, New York: Mrs. David M. Levy Bequest.

Right: Picasso. *Still Life (Fêtes de Céret)*, spring, 1912. Oil on canvas, 27×41 cm. Private collection.

> complications, I may need . . . (one never knows what might happen) a reserve of 1,000 or 2,000 francs. I should not want to be prevented from leaving for a matter of a few sous. . . . If you see Fernande, tell her that she can expect nothing from me, and I should be quite happy never to see her again. . . . And tell me if Gleizes and Metzinger's book on painting has appeared.[13]

Kahnweiler duly sent him a thousand francs.

Picasso tried to convince Kahnweiler that Fernande's imminent arrival did not bother him. "I'm not at all disturbed by Braque's letter," he wrote on June 17, "On the contrary I'm very touched that he warned me."[14] Sheer bravado! Forty-eight hours later, he was preparing for flight.

> I've learned from reliable sources that Fernande will come here with the Pichots and it goes without saying that I need some peace. So I'm going to leave. I have a lot of different places in mind. I hate to depart; it's been good to be in a large house where I've had space, and I've liked the country-side. And my painting is going well.[15]

Picasso. *Spanish Still Life*, spring, 1912. Oil and Ripolin on oval canvas, 46×33cm. Musée d'Art Moderne, Villeneuve d'Ascq: Geneviève and Jean Masurel Gift.

The following day, he confirmed that he would leave for Perpignan on the 21st, "but don't tell ANYONE, ANYONE AT ALL where I shall be."[16] Before departing, Picasso arranged for Haviland and Manolo to ship three still lifes he had just completed to Kahnweiler. Since they were not signed, the dealer had his assistant, Boischaud, simulate his signature on the back of the canvas (Boischaud would do the same for Braque) so that it would not detract from the image on the front or enable people to differentiate one artist's work from the other's. Both artists wanted to establish a communal anonymity. "We were inclined to efface our personalities in order to find originality" is how Braque put it.[17] It was an impossible dream, and they would soon revert to affixing their names to their work—usually in the form of impersonal trompe l'œil plaques, such as proud collectors put on picture frames. In due course Picasso and Braque would lay aside their principles and sign cubist paintings on the front to satisfy the demands of collectors or the trade and settle problems of attribution and authenticity.

Several of the recent paintings exhibit signs—brushstrokes that go in contradictory directions, axial ambivalences—of having been worked on upside down, the right way up, and sideways. This skews a viewer's perceptions and heightens the ambivalence. We are momentarily tricked into visualizing a violin or guitar as upright instead of supine, or vice versa; obliged to accept as right something that at first glance looks wrong. Having combined the verso with the recto of a figure, the manipulative painter gives things yet another perceptual spin. "Got you!" he seems to be saying, as we veer uncertainly between contradictory readings—a crick in the mind as well as the neck. Picasso would sometimes compound the problem by telling one friend that a still life was horizontal, another that it was vertical, and another, more truthfully, that dichotomy was the point of the picture.

This idiosyncratic way of reworking his paintings is a consequence of Picasso's transient existence. In the course of 1912, he had to acclimatize himself to four different studios. This was hard on someone who was very sensitive to his surroundings and who would always be a hostage to habits and compulsions, superstitions and rituals (like the litany of friends' names he claimed to recite every day of his life). As he told Braque, he was fed up with having to rework partly finished canvases in one new location after another. Hence the palimpsest-like nature of many works of the period.[18] Painting after painting reveals two or three phases of activity, each one different in style and coloration as well as in the telltale slant of brushstrokes and hatching. Compared with the work of other summers, when the season's œuvre was all of a piece, this summer's output was anything but homogeneous.

* * *

After fleeing Céret, Picasso and Eva spent a night at Perpignan and then took a train to Avignon, a city he had wanted to visit ever since André Salmon had nicknamed his great brothel picture after it. "You see, it was no accident after the incidents at Céret that I went to Avignon," Picasso observed to Kahnweiler apropos the *Demoiselles*.[19] Picasso looked around for a place to rent, and within a day or two had found a dreary house with a garden, the Villa des Clochettes, in the ugly little town of Sorgues, eleven kilometers north of the city. If Picasso settled on one of the most characterless urban areas in Provence, it was because he liked the idea of going into hiding, locking his mistress and himself away from nosy friends. In Avignon he would have stood out as a celebrity; word would have got back to Paris, and the Montmartre gossips would have discovered his whereabouts. In suburban Sorgues he and Eva could vanish. Besides, the downright ordinariness of the place appealed to him. Sorgues had none of the quaint, folkloric charm usually associated with Provence.

Villa des Clochettes, Sorgues.

Discomfort never bothered Picasso, and much as he loved his *jolie* Eva, he was not going to indulge her sense of decorum. To furnish his suburban villa, he had the local upholsterer provide basic beds, tables and chairs. That was that. As soon as the furniture was ready, they settled in. The house turned out to be in bad repair. When there were rain storms, the roof leaked, and Picasso and Eva were obliged to sleep under an umbrella, but they were ecstatically happy. Apart from Frika, Picasso's constant companion, the other animals were left behind in Paris, where Picasso's vet, who worked for the Cirque Médrano, looked after them. One night, Picasso took Eva to see the sixty-eight-year-old Sarah Bernhardt in *La Dame aux Camélias*—a spectacle he would remember with malicious glee; forty years later, after seeing Garbo in a movie version, he could still mimic Bernhardt's grotesque artificiality. A Montmartre acquaintance, whose name he had forgotten, introduced him to a group of congenial friends; and then in a restaurant he ran into Pierre Girieud (a friend also of Eva's, whose portrait he had painted the year before), Dufrenoy (likewise a painter), Déodat de Séverac and "everyone else we know."[20] Out of love of mystery as much as fear of pursuit, Picasso informed them all that he was on his way to Carcassonne. The only person allowed to know his whereabouts was Kahnweiler, whom he once again urged, "DO NOT GIVE MY ADDRESS TO ANYONE."[21]

Pierre Girieud. *Portrait of Eva*, 1911. Whereabouts unknown.

Even Braque was kept in ignorance for a few days. On June 27, Picasso finally wrote to him complaining about the difficulty of working on the run, at the same time boasting that he had started on some new canvases. He was counting on Braque to join him at Sorgues instead of Céret, as they had originally planned—counting, too, on letters from him. As if

Right: Picasso. *Arlésienne*, summer, 1912. Gouache and ink on paper mounted on canvas, 66×23cm. The Menil Collection, Houston.

Far right: Picasso. *Arlésienne*, summer, 1912. Oil on canvas, 73×54cm. Courtesy Thomas Ammann Fine Art, Zurich.

Below right: Picasso. *Dancers on July 14*, July, 1912. Pen and India ink and pencil on paper, 34.2×21.7cm. Musée Picasso.

Below: Picasso. *Landscape with Posters*, summer, 1912. Oil on canvas, 46×61cm. The National Museum of Art, Osaka.

he were the Sundance Kid, he signed himself, "your pard, Picasso"[22]—in ironical acknowledgment of their male bonding, their pioneering outlaw spirit.

Two days later, Picasso wrote Kahnweiler that he had begun work on three canvases, two of which we can identify. They are very different from the ones he had been doing at Céret, also very different from each other. The more conventional of the two is of an *Arlésienne* in the traditional *coif* that Provençal women still wore and that Picasso knew well from Gauguin's portrait of the Arlésienne brothel-keeper, which had inspired some of his Saint-Lazare paintings.[23] He seems to have reconsidered his decision to limit his "portrayals" of the unpaintably pretty Eva to song titles and trite declarations of love, and to have used this bland *Arlésienne* (probably inspired by a postcard) as a tryout for a portrait of her. Sure enough, it paved the way for some complex drawings and a large gouache, which Daix has identified as studies for a full-length portrait of Eva in local costume.[24] These in turn paved the way for a female nude, *J'aime Eva*, painted the following fall. Later in life, Picasso would revert again and again to this subject. In 1937 he did several paintings of a demented-looking Lee Miller wearing a Provençal coif wedged in her cracked head as if it were a meat cleaver; also a surrealist "portrait" of Paul Eluard in Arlésienne *travesti*, suckling a kitten. And, again, in 1958, a time when he was regularly attending bullfights in Arles, Picasso did at least eight portraits of Jacqueline in Arlésienne dress, one of them so *travaillé* that it bears twenty-two separate dates.[25]

Picasso. *Lee Miller as an Arlésienne*, September 20, 1937. Oil on canvas, 81×65cm. Musée Réattu, Arles.

A further identifiable Sorgues painting represents the sort of industrial, roadside scene that Picasso drove by every time he took the Sorgues–Avignon tramway (locally known as "The Buffalo" after the open, American-style carriages that were used in the summer):[26] a railroad viaduct, factory chimneys emerging from Roman-tiled sheds, and the inevitable billboards. These advertise a product named Léon; the bouillon concentrate Kub, which enabled Picasso to make a cubist pun (a cube in perspective superimposed on the letters *KUB*); and that popular Provençal aperitif Pernod, in the form of a gigantic bottle-shaped billboard—another cubist joke: it fools the casual beholder into misreading a landscape as a still life. Picasso failed to follow up this "pop" experiment. He and Braque preferred to paint things that were proportionate to the size of their canvases. Subjects that were vast in scale or scope were best left to the Salon cubists. Bright color was finally beginning to manifest itself in some of Picasso's cubist compositions, but usually in the form of Ripolin, as in the billboards of the *Landscape with Posters* or the *Notre Avenir est dans l'Air* brochure. Eye-fooling light effects had gone the way of eye-fooling perspective. To judge by a sketch of two dancers celebrating the *quatorze juillet*, Picasso envisaged yet another pretext for using local color (all that bunting). But nothing came of these attempts to take synthetic cubism outdoors. Instead the bunting was applied to still lifes.

Arlésiennes; on postcard sent by Eva from Tarascon to Alice Toklas, June 18, 1914. Beinecke Rare Book and Manuscript Library, Yale University.

*　　*　　*

In early days Picasso had frequently decorated the premises he had borrowed or rented by painting the walls with allegories, often of a comical nature. Inspired possibly by the panels he had been doing for Hamilton

Self-portrait photograph by Picasso in front of *The Aficionado*, 1912. Archives Picasso.

Easter Field, he now proceeded to embellish one of the whitewashed walls of the Villa des Clochettes with a still life which is built around a "Ma Jolie" song sheet; an allegorical portrait of the lady of the house. Picasso cherished his tribute to Eva sufficiently to have it removed from the wall when he left the house three months later. Braque was entrusted with this delicate task and had it shipped to Paris.[27] Subsequently Picasso sold it to Madame Errazuriz, his next great patron. After it had survived for fifty years, its extreme fragility was its downfall. In 1961 Douglas Cooper bought it to fill a gap in his cubist collection. Picasso happened to be present when the painting was unpacked. So did I. To everyone's horror, the crate turned out to have been damaged: the "fresco" was in fragments. "*Il ne reste plus rien de moi,*" Picasso said. His dismay would be all the greater, a year or two later, when he learned that the fragments had been reassembled and the reconstituted composition put back on the market.

The availability of bullfights had been one of the advantages of Céret; it may also have influenced Picasso's choice of the Avignon area for a hideaway. Avignon itself lacked a bullring, but the Roman arenas of Nîmes and Arles—then as now France's tauromachic centers—were little more than half an hour away. And during the summer season, between Easter and the wine harvest, there is a succession of corridas in which reputable Spanish toreros fight authentic Spanish bulls. On July 7, Picasso attended his first bullfight at Nîmes. (Fifty years later he would still be going there.) As he told Kahnweiler, "It's so rare to find an art that is so intelligent about itself. Only Mazantinito did anything of note, but despite everything, the afternoon was enjoyable and the weather beautiful. I love Nîmes."[28] And the following day he told Braque (in a letter signed "*ton Picasso, artiste peintre espagnol*") what fun it had been—not just the spectacle in the arena but the contacts with the bullfighters and their entourages before and after the corrida. Contacts like these would recharge his *alma española*.

Picasso went on to say that he had "transformed the painting of a man I had already begun (the Céret bagpiper) into an *Aficionado*. I think he would look good holding a *banderilla*, and I am trying to give him a good southern face."[29] The *Aficionado* necessitated a number of highly worked preliminary drawings; and "the good southern face" required a large mustache, a sensual mouth and, as one can see from cracks in the paint, the application of a suitably swarthy tan to a face that was formerly pink; also the addition of a high-crowned, wide-brimmed Cordoban hat. Rather than associate this man, who will crop up again and again over the next two years, with a specific character, we should see "the good southern face" as a generic Mediterranean type: one that allegorizes the Midi in Picasso's work much as cardplayers do in Cézanne's work. The metamorphosis of the Céret *Bagpiper* into the *Aficionado* is yet another example of Picasso's manipulative delight in switching the role of a figure by displaying his barely distinguishable signs—shorthand for a fringe or mustache, epaulette or fichu, pipe or *tenora*, fan or *banderilla*—in all manner of equivocal ways. If these signs compound the mystery and ambivalence, so much the better.

As usual Braque took his time arriving, possibly because Marcelle was not all that eager to join up with Picasso now that Fernande had departed.

Above: Picasso. *The Aficionado*, summer, 1912. Oil on canvas, 135×82cm. Öffentliche Kunstsammlungen Basel, Kunstmusem.

Top left: Picasso. Study for *The Aficionado*, summer, 1912. Ink on paper, 30.3×19.2cm. Whereabouts unknown.

Left: Picasso. Study for *The Aficionado*, summer, 1912. Ink and pencil on paper, 30.5×19.5cm. Picasso Heirs.

Picasso. *Souvenir of Marseille*, summer, 1912. India ink on paper, 13.5×9cm. Musée Picasso.

Grebo Mask (Ivory Coast) from Picasso's collection. Wood, white paint, plant fibers, ht: 64cm. Musée Picasso: Gift of Marina Ruiz Picasso.

"I'm already waiting for you," Picasso wrote his "pard" on July 7—would he please bring the camera Picasso had left in the boulevard Clichy apartment, also one of their favorite American-style "Singapore" suits (made of blue cotton, from *La Belle Jardinière*).[30] However, it would be almost a month before Braque and Marcelle materialized. After a few days of long walks in the *garrigue* discussing the progress they had made, the two artists decided to take Eva and Marcelle to Marseille for a couple of days. Braque, who knew Marseille well from his sojourns at nearby L'Estaque, wanted to introduce Picasso to the delights of the city, which was Barcelona's principal rival, not so much as a cultural center but as the liveliest and most licentious port in the Mediterranean. It was also the gateway to Africa.

The four of them spent their time scouring Marseille junk shops for tribal art. Since there was a constant *va-et-vien* of colonial officials, the city was the main port of entry for these artifacts. To believe Braque, they bought up *tous les nègres*. On the strength of Picasso's scrappy sketch of them at a café table with their purchases, the late Edward Fry claimed to identify one of the parcels as the finer of the two Grebo masks in Picasso's collection.[31] One of these would inspire the cylindrical eye-sockets in some of the Sorgues drawings and, a little later, the cylindrical sound hole in the cardboard and sheet-metal guitars in the Museum of Modern Art (see p. 256). A long shot, but Fry may well be right. Picasso owned to having bought "a fine mask," also "a woman with huge breasts and a young boy" on this trip. What Braque acquired we do not know. Many years later Picasso told Malraux that Braque did not really understand *art nègre*, "because he was not superstitious."[32] This reveals more about Picasso than Braque. Braque understood tribal art well enough, but less shamanistically than Picasso. "African masks opened up a new horizon to me," he told Dora Vallier. "They enabled me to make contact with instinctive things, with direct manifestations which ran counter to the false traditionalism that I abhorred."[33] Fine tribal sculptures in his collection bear witness to his discrimination.

Braque had an ulterior motive for visiting Marseille: he and Marcelle wanted to rent a house for the summer at L'Estaque or elsewhere in the Marseille neighborhood. Picasso saw to it that they did not have time for much of a search. Back in Sorgues, he prevailed upon "Wilbourg" to change his mind and settle down near him. Within a day or two Braque had found a modest house on the outskirts of Sorgues, the Villa Bel-Air, which he described to Kahnweiler as "a Japanese farm with good, old-fashioned, whitewashed walls like in France."[34] Braque knew nothing of Japanese farms; however, he may have heard that Van Gogh believed Provence to be the nearest thing to Nippon, when he settled there twenty-five years earlier. Japanese or not, the Villa Bel-Air continued to be the artist's summer home until the 1920s. Like Picasso, Braque put his stamp on the house by painting cubist still lifes directly on the whitewashed walls of the sitting room. Unfortunately these were never photographed in situ. In the last year of her life, Marcelle paid a visit to the house in the course of a pilgrimage to the various places where she and Braque had lived. According to the Claude Laurenses, who accompanied her, the frescoes had become very dilapidated.[35] Later, one of them came up for sale in a Paris auction—totally refurbished.

Marcelle Braque with Turc, c. 1912. Archives Laurens.

By the summer of 1912, Picasso and Braque began ever so slightly to diverge. Braque's Norman wariness had been sharpened by Marcelle, who was not always happy about her lover's hermetic relationship with Picasso. Nevertheless, the two men continued to "do a lot of cooking together," Braque reported to Kahnweiler (August 24):

> The other night we had *ajo blanco*, a Spanish dish. . . . We very much regretted your not being here to share this dessert-like soup (pounded almonds, garlic, bread, grapes). . . . The *ajo blanco* is a powerful insecticide.[36]

Reminiscing about Sorgues years later, Marcelle Braque—a most perceptive observer—evoked the spirit of tense camaraderie that permeated their lives. Her affection for Picasso would always be ambivalent and did not preclude a certain impatience with his childish superstitions and fears of authority, danger or adverse conditions. To illustrate her point she would describe how, when the mistral blew at Sorgues, they would go for walks in single file: the robust Braque leading the way (with the dog, Turc, that Picasso had given him), followed by Marcelle and Eva, with Picasso and his dog, Frika, huddling in their wake. As an old friend of Fernande's, Marcelle did not warm to Eva, to whom she was obliged to show rather more friendliness than she felt during their long hours alone together, martyrs to cubism—a cause that Marcelle instinctively understood but Eva sometimes found baffling. The summer of 1912 was extremely hot. This did not bother the Malagueño Picasso but was hard on the Norman Braque, who liked to work outdoors if possible. His attic studio was like an oven. The staircase up to the attic was the only airy place in the house. And there Marcelle would sit for hours, waiting for her lover to finish work for the day. She felt very alone, she said, when the two painters shut themselves away to wrestle with the problems of cubism, something which, as Braque told Dora Vallier ("with a break in his voice"),[37] nobody but they would ever be able to understand.

Although Picasso and Braque worked together as intensely as ever, the dynamics were no longer quite the same. Picasso aimed to make the objects in his still lifes increasingly discrete, whereas Braque dissolved his forms in space to a degree bordering on abstraction, as if he wanted the grin without the cat. Rubin has summed up their differences astutely: "Faced with a mark, a blot, a patch of paint, a texture or a piece of material, Picasso instinctively wants to make a figure or object out of it. Where Braque may be content to let the peg of a violin dissolve from a sign into a mark, and hence into 'painting,' Picasso will transform it into a sign for a face or figure."[38] Braque's methods sometimes made for problems, as Picasso once described to Françoise Gilot. On a visit to Braque's studio, he was examining "a large oval still life with a package of tobacco, a pipe and all the usual paraphernalia of cubism," when he suddenly drew back and said he had seen a squirrel in the painting. "'That's not possible,' Braque said." After looking carefully, however,

Braque. *Clarinet: "Valse,"* 1912. Oil on oval canvas, 91.3×64.5 cm. The Solomon R. Guggenheim Foundation, New York: Peggy Guggenheim Collection, Venice.

> he too saw the squirrel, because that kind of paranoiac vision is extremely communicable. Day after day Braque fought that squirrel. He changed the structure, the light, the composition, but the squirrel . . . somehow always managed to return. Finally, after eight or ten days, Braque was able to turn the trick and the canvas again became a package of tobacco . . . and above all a Cubist painting. So you see how closely we worked together. At that

> time our work was a kind of laboratory research from which every pretension or individual vanity was excluded.[39]

For fear of evoking sensations that would interfere with his conception of space, Braque was still wary of using any but neutral colors. Instead he drew upon his training as a craftsman and tried out textural equivalents for color. As well as passages of woodgraining and marbleizing, he now added sand to his paint. ("Work is proceeding well," he wrote Kahnweiler on September 27, "and sand painting gives me some satisfaction. I am therefore thinking of extending my stay here by another month.")[40] Next, he experimented with cinders, sawdust, metal filings, even coffee grounds and grit—and came up with paint surfaces of a subtlety and originality that have yet to be surpassed. The liberties that Braque took with the hitherto sacrosanct medium of oil paint appalled traditionalists almost as much as the liberties that he had taken with appearances. True, Braque's exploitation of texture would sometimes border on *belle peinture*, but he deserves more credit than he usually receives for establishing an artist's right to make pictures out of whatever materials he likes; credit, too, for sharing his skills and insights with Picasso and instilling him with his own passion for *matière* and his view of it as a concomitant of color.

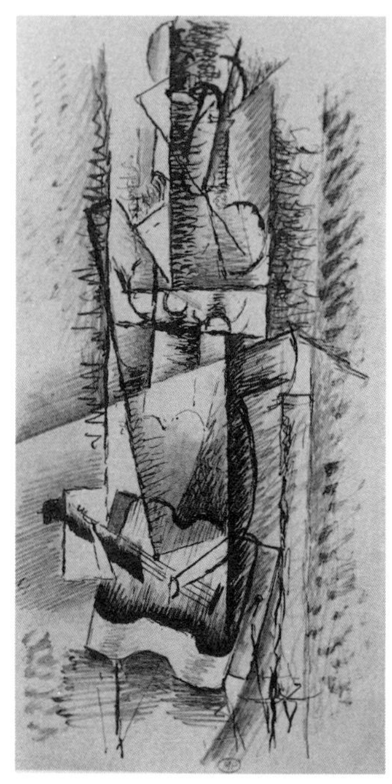

Picasso. *Woman with Guitar*, 1912. Pen, India ink and pencil on paper, 21.2×13.2cm. Musée Picasso.

The obligatory application of varnish was another tradition that Braque did away with. He and Picasso came to regard the stuff as anathema and were adamant that it should never be applied to their work. They complained that it falsified tonal values, especially of blacks, and gave paintings a nasty meretricious gleam. (For the same reason they would condemn glossy color reproductions, particularly the ones in Skira's books on modern art.) If Braque wanted a specific passage to shine, he would mix varnish with his paint. In this way he could establish a contrast between objects of identical color and tonal value: between, for instance, a shiny white jug and a matte white tablecloth. An allover layer of varnish destroyed these subtle distinctions.

The stylistic differences between Picasso's and Braque's cubism are easier to discern in drawings than paintings. By comparison with Picasso, Braque is too often dismissed as an inadequate draftsman. True, he is much more limited, but, then, Braque regarded drawing as a means to an end—the end being painting—whereas Picasso exulted in his graphic powers and, often as not, used drawing as an end in itself. Before he was wounded in World War I, Braque (unlike Picasso) never used sketchbooks but noted down ideas for paintings on bits of paper, most of which he threw away or lost. It was only during his convalescence that he started keeping sketchbooks, using them, he said, as "cookbooks" to draw on when he was "hungry" for ideas to paint.

Braque's cubist drawings are rare. They have none of Picasso's graphic bite, let alone his inexhaustible inventiveness, but then, they are much more private, done for his own purposes or pleasure—not to be exhibited or sold. Braque uses heavy black chalk (rarely pen and ink or pencil) —broadly and ruminatively—to rehearse the effects of paint on canvas. Picasso, on the other hand, prided himself on the explicit nature of his cubist drawings. At the risk of oversimplifying, one might describe Picasso's drawing as primarily sculptural, Braque's as primarily painterly; Picasso as a manipulator of form, Braque as a manipulator of space.

Picasso. *Guitarist*, summer, 1912. Ink on paper, 31×20cm. Musée Picasso.

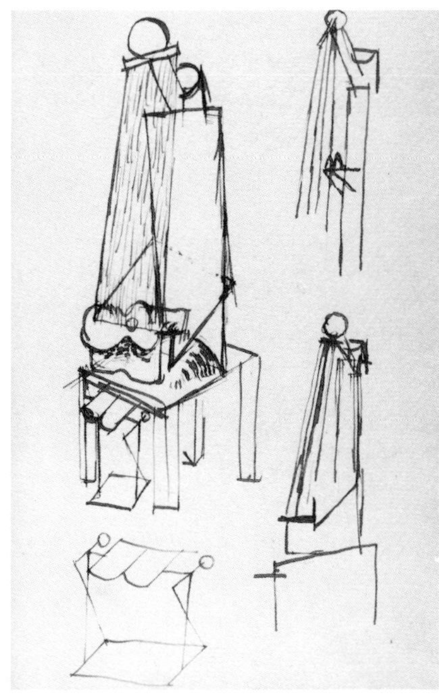

Picasso. *Guitarist* (study for construction), 1912. Pen and ink on paper, 21.2×13.2cm. Musée Picasso.

Braque. *Oboe, Sheet Music and Bottle of Rum*, spring, 1912. Charcoal on paper, 48×63cm. Öffentliche Kunstsammlungen Basel, Kunstmuseum, Kupferstichkabinett: Gift of Raoul La Roche.

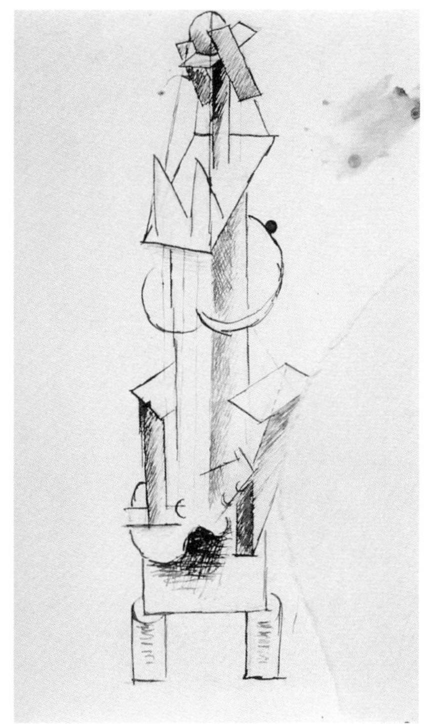

Picasso. *Woman with Guitar*, summer, 1912. Ink on paper, 31×20cm. Picasso Heirs.

Braque. *Still Life with Bunch of Grapes*, 1912. Oil and sand on canvas, 60×73cm. Private collection: Courtesy Galerie Louise Leiris.

In his sketchbooks Picasso would always generate more ideas than he could work out on canvas. This was very much the case in 1912, when the increasing complexity of cubism obliged him to paint with unaccustomed slowness. Only pen and pencil could keep pace with the outpourings of his imagination. Anyone who takes the trouble to track down the sequences of drawings in Zervos's chaotic catalog or more recently published sketchbook pages will be amazed at the profusion, the sustained inventiveness. What draftsman since Leonardo (incidentally, one of the very few Italian masters for whom Picasso had a good word) has brought off such a feat? These drawings also reveal Picasso to be a sculptor, albeit a conceptual one, of infinite imagination and ingenuity. For although many of them engender paintings or trigger changes in paintings (*The Aficionado*, for instance), some of the more intricately structured drawings—especially those of a guitar player who appears to be turning into a guitar—have evidently been conceived as conceptual sculptures rather than paintings. The great constructions of the following winter, which changed the face of twentieth-century sculpture, are the outcome.

* * *

Since Picasso had every intention of returning to Céret for the winter—provided the Delcros house was still available and Fernande no longer a threat—he had taken the villa at Sorgues for three months. He did not renew the lease. This pillar-to-post life was not to his liking. What he really needed was a permanent Parisian base, but first of all he had to make a break with the past. Returning to live in the boulevard de Clichy apartment was as unthinkable as returning to the woman or the style of painting associated with it. And so he wrote to Kahnweiler that he was coming to Paris to settle everything, above all to get rid of the apartment. "Don't you think it's high time I put my affairs into a little order?" he asked.[41]

On September 1 Picasso arrived in Paris, accompanied by Eva. They spent the next two weeks packing up the boulevard de Clichy and checking out the work stored in the Bateau Lavoir studio. Picasso looked around for somewhere to settle but decided not to make a commitment until he had got rid of the old apartment. Kahnweiler was nominally the subtenant, but the lease was still in Fernande's name. And now that she was abandoned and broke, she had to be paid off. Picasso and Fernande are unlikely to have got together to negotiate. Daix suggests that the rowdy Louise Lenoir (better known as Odette)—Picasso's mistress on his first trip to Paris and a close friend of Germaine Pichot's—may have acted as a broker.[42] The problem of the lease was soon resolved, and Picasso returned to Sorgues to vacate the Villa des Clochettes. "Picasso told me all about his trip to Paris and his encounters," Braque reported to Kahnweiler. "Everything seems to have gone well and I am happy for him."[43] One of these encounters had been with Shchukin, whom Picasso had bumped into at Kahnweiler's. Shchukin had just bought the great 1907–08 *Friendship*, "but he doesn't understand the more recent things," Picasso told Gertrude Stein.[44]

Self-portrait photograph by Picasso in his boulevard Raspail studio, 1913. Archives Picasso.

Despite an appalling cold, which he blamed on a particularly fierce mistral, Picasso stayed in Sorgues for less than a week. As soon as he heard from the concierge that the boulevard de Clichy apartment had been emptied, he would return to Paris, he told Kahnweiler, and "make another search and surely find something. I can't last much longer."[45] Kahnweiler forestalled him. He wrote back that he had rented a studio apartment for him at 242, boulevard Raspail. This was in the heart of Montparnasse, the other side of the city from the tight little village of Montmartre, where he had lived ever since he had first settled in Paris. Montmartre was associated with Fernande and the scruffy bohemianism of the Bateau Lavoir—everything Picasso now wanted to escape. Thanks largely to Frédé, of the Lapin Agile, the place was degenerating into a tourist trap. Montparnasse was now the only *quartier* for a self-respecting modern artist. On September 23, he cabled Kahnweiler that he would arrive the following morning. Though Eva was pleased to have a proper home at last, neither she nor Picasso really liked the new studio. It was on the ground floor, therefore a bit dark and gloomy: you could reach out of the back window and touch the tombs in the Montparnasse cemetery.

Braque. *Fruit Dish and Glass*, 1912. Charcoal and woodgrain paper pasted on paper, 62×45cm. Private collection. The first papier collé.

It was a relief to be rid of the Villa des Clochettes and back at the center of things; a relief, too, I suspect, to be away from Braque. While Braque was on his own at Sorgues earlier in the month, he had gone one better than his "pard." In an Avignon wallpaper store he had found a roll of paper that simulated woodgraining (shades of Picasso's first collage with its oilcloth that simulated canework). Out of three strategically placed strips of this wallpaper Braque had contrived the first papier collé: a fruit dish containing a bunch of grapes beside a glass. True, the oilcloth collage had paved the way for this development, but Picasso had failed to see the full implications of his handiwork. Now Braque had done so. As he admitted, "After having made the [first] papier collé I felt a great shock, and it was an even greater shock for Picasso when I showed it to him."[46] Picasso immediately realized that papier collé opened up a vast new range of pictorial possibilities. An object could now be presented by some foreign element that was an equivalent, as opposed to an image, of itself. A piece of newspaper, for instance, could stand for a newspaper; it could also signify anything else the artist wanted it to signify. Drawing could then function simultaneously and independently to indicate volume and integrate the real element (the piece of newspaper or wallpaper) into the composition. Furthermore, by enabling color to function independently of form, papier collé made it easier for Picasso and Braque to introduce positive color into a cubist composition. And since scissors make for a sharper edge than a paintbrush, they could now achieve much sharper contrasts of color, tone and texture.

The invention of papier collé gave him "a kind of certainty," Braque explained.[47] It enabled him to "ground" things. It also strengthened his position vis-à-vis Picasso. I got an echo of their rivalry four decades later, when I watched Picasso, on a visit to Cooper's cubist collection, give Braque's famous first papier collé a glare of mock resentment. "*Le salaud*," he said with a huge shrug. "He waited until I'd turned my back. On my way home [Cooper's château was not far from Avignon], I'll stop at that wallpaper shop and see what they have left." And he let loose a high-pitched Andalusian laugh. Wallpaper of the right degree of ordinariness had apparently been hard to find. Friends did what they could to help, as the young British painter Duncan Grant described in a letter to Clive Bell:

> [Gertrude Stein] took me to see Picasso, which I very much enjoyed. I promised to take him a roll of old wallpapers which I have found in a cupboard of my hotel and which excited him very much as he makes use of them frequently and finds [them] very difficult to get. He sometimes tears small pieces off the wall, he said. I think I shall find it difficult to know what to say, if I go alone one wants a Roger [Fry]'s tongue or a Gertrude's bust to fall back onto.[48]

Picasso. *Violin Hanging on a Wall*, 1913. Oil and sand on canvas, 65×46cm. Kunstmuseum Bern: Hermann und Margrit Rupf Stiftung.

Now that Picasso was once again installed in an apartment of his own with all his sacred rubbish and treasures around him (the dining room housed his growing collection, including a cubist Braque), he could set about adapting the concept of papier collé to his work. "I've been using your latest papery and dusty methods," Picasso wrote Braque on October 9. "I'm in the process of imagining a guitar and I'm using a bit of earth on our dreadful canvas."[49] The addition of earth or grit, sand or plaster, would explain the huge crusted scab of impasto on the *Violin Hanging on a Wall*, one of the finest paintings of the period, which Kahnweiler would soon sell to his Swiss friend Hermann Rupf. As for Picasso's first papiers collés, the earliest date to be found on one of the pieces of newspaper he used is November 10, 1912.[50] This would imply that he had been experimenting with the new medium for at least a month. The work in question, *Guitar, Sheet Music and Glass*, is so perfect—succinct and straightforward in appearance, complex and ambivalent in effect—that there must have been a great deal of preliminary study.

This papier collé is celebrated for the headline featured in it—"LA BATAILLE S'EST ENGAGÉ[E]" ("Battle has been joined")—which continues to stir up controversy. The horizontal placing of the strip of newspaper in the bottom left-hand corner suggests that it stands for itself (i.e., a newspaper), as well as for the tabletop on which the still life is set. But how should this announcement of a new Balkan offensive be interpreted? Leighten, for instance, claims that the headline reflects what she believes to be the overtly anarchist themes of antimilitarism and antinationalism in Picasso's art.[51] She does Picasso's dormant social conscience too much credit and makes insufficient allowance for his sense of irony and love of riddles and mystification.

No, the only issue of passionate interest to Picasso was cubism. In the preceding weeks it had triggered several skirmishes. The cubist room at the Salon d'Automne had prompted a reactionary *conseiller municipal*, Pierre Lampué, to make a public protest to the Ministry of Fine Arts. How could the State, Lampué thundered, allow a band of renegades who were no better than *apaches* to desecrate a public monument like the Grand Palais? A few weeks later, a Socialist *député*, Jules-Louis Breton, raised the same matter in the Chambre des Députés and was trounced by Marcel Sembat, a passionate collector and defender of modern art.[52] Yet more controversy was stirred up by the Section d'Or show (October 10–31), which had been organized by the Duchamp brothers (Marcel, Jacques and Raymond) at the Galerie La Boëtie and included virtually everyone in the Parisian modern art movement.[53] Picasso and Braque held aloof. The harmonious precepts of the "golden rule" were of no appeal to iconoclasts. Then again, the publication of Gleizes and Metzinger's *Du Cubisme* and André Salmon's unreliable "Histoire anecdotique du cubisme" (a section of his *Jeune peinture française*, and the first published account of the

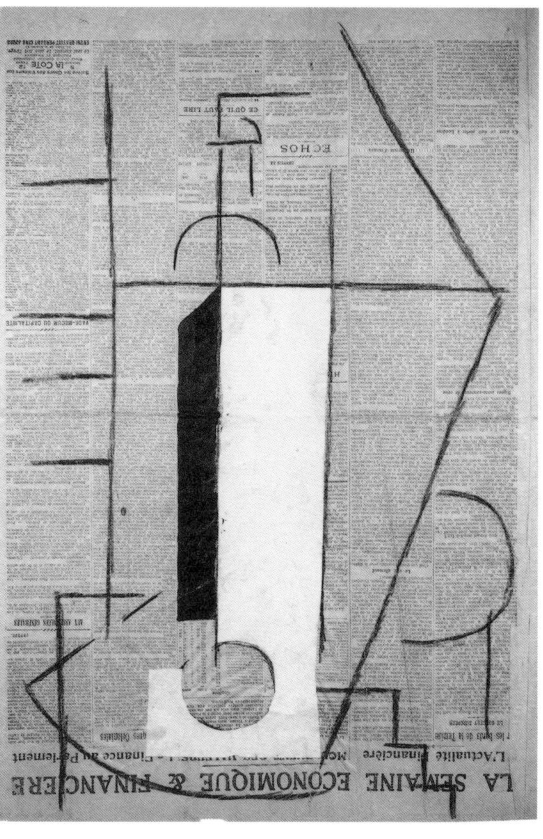

Above: Picasso. *Guitar, Sheet Music and Glass ("La Bataille s'est engagé[e]")*, late 1912. Pasted papers, gouache and charcoal on paper, 48×36.5cm. Bequest of Marion Koogler McNay, McNay Art Museum, San Antonio, Texas.

Top left: Picasso. *Bottle on a Table*, late 1912. Pasted papers, ink and charcoal on newsprint, 62.5×44cm. Musée Picasso.

Left: Picasso. *Guitar and Sheet Music*, late 1912. Pasted papers, pastel and charcoal on paper, 58×63cm. Private collection.

Joseph Hémard. *Portrait of M. Armand Fallières (in the collection of M. Lampué).* Back cover of *Le Rire*, October 26, 1912. Jane Voorhees Zimmerli Art Museum, Rutgers, The State University of New Jersey. Fallières was President of the French Republic, 1906–13.

movement) had set the cubists and their backers bickering with the establishment as well as one another. Picasso was not above fostering this animosity. For instance, when he wrote to Braque on October 31 to thank him for removing his *Ma Jolie* "fresco" from the villa at Sorgues, he could not resist revealing that Salmon's book was "revoltingly unjust" to him,[54] thus rubbing Braque's nose in Salmon's portrayal of him as a clone who followed "Picasso respectfully step by step." Salmon had likewise offended Apollinaire, who responded by publishing an article sarcastically praising the book on the grounds that "the ideas expressed here are my own."[55] Apollinaire also wrote his old friend a sharp letter, berating him for never mentioning him.[56]

With whom, therefore, was battle joined? With warmongers and nationalists? With philistines and reactionaries like Breton or Lampué, or, nearer home, with the Section d'Or and Salon cubists? Or was Picasso issuing an ironical challenge to the only living artists he regarded as his peers: Matisse and Braque? On the grounds that Picasso's recent forays into decoration had reengaged him in a dialogue, or battle, with Matisse, Jack Flam believes the adversary must have been Matisse.[57] On the grounds that the discovery of papier collé had sparked Picasso's competitive spirit, Braque strikes me as a likelier candidate, especially since the newspaper in Picasso's papier collé predates Braque's return to Paris by a very few days. Picasso enjoyed using coded references as a means of communicating with his fellow artists. And what more effective way of getting even with his "pard" than using his "papery" process, mischievously and eloquently, against him, at the same time making an ironical in-joke? Picasso may also have intended the headline in his papier collé to have wider implications: an ironical comment on the belligerence afflicting modern painters—futurists, orphists and simultaneists as well as cubists.

*　　*　　*

Around the time he executed his papiers collés—that is to say October, 1912—Picasso made a cardboard construction of a guitar. Its origins can be traced back to the hundreds of drawings of figures playing guitars, or of still lifes featuring them, which he had done earlier in the year. A few months later, early spring, Picasso envisaged a large assemblage: a canvas of a life-size figure to which he had attached a real guitar, a pair of arms made of newspaper and a real bottle on a real table. This fascinating if flimsy affair eventually fell apart. Fortunately, photographs of it survive. Next, Picasso constructed a still life—*Guitar and Bottle on a Table.* Photographs reveal that he discarded the bottle part, but saved the cardboard guitar.

These constructions hark back to the paper sculptures that Braque had made in the summer of 1911. "I am taking advantage of my stay in the country," Braque had written Kahnweiler from Sorgues, "to do things that cannot be done in Paris, such as paper sculpture, something that has given me much satisfaction."[58] None of these paper sculptures has survived, except in a single photograph. When I asked him about them, Braque told me that "they were made out of cut and folded bits of paper and cardboard: some were colored."[59] However, he attached so little importance to them that he had allowed them all to be destroyed. They had merely helped him solve pictorial problems, he said, and if they had paved the

Above: Photograph of Picasso's assemblage, *Guitarist*, in his boulevard Raspail studio, 1913. Archives Picasso (private collection). The large paper background to the assemblage can also be seen in the studio photograph on p. 248.

Top left: Paper sculpture by Braque (photographed in his studio at the Hôtel Roma), after February, 1914. Archives Laurens.

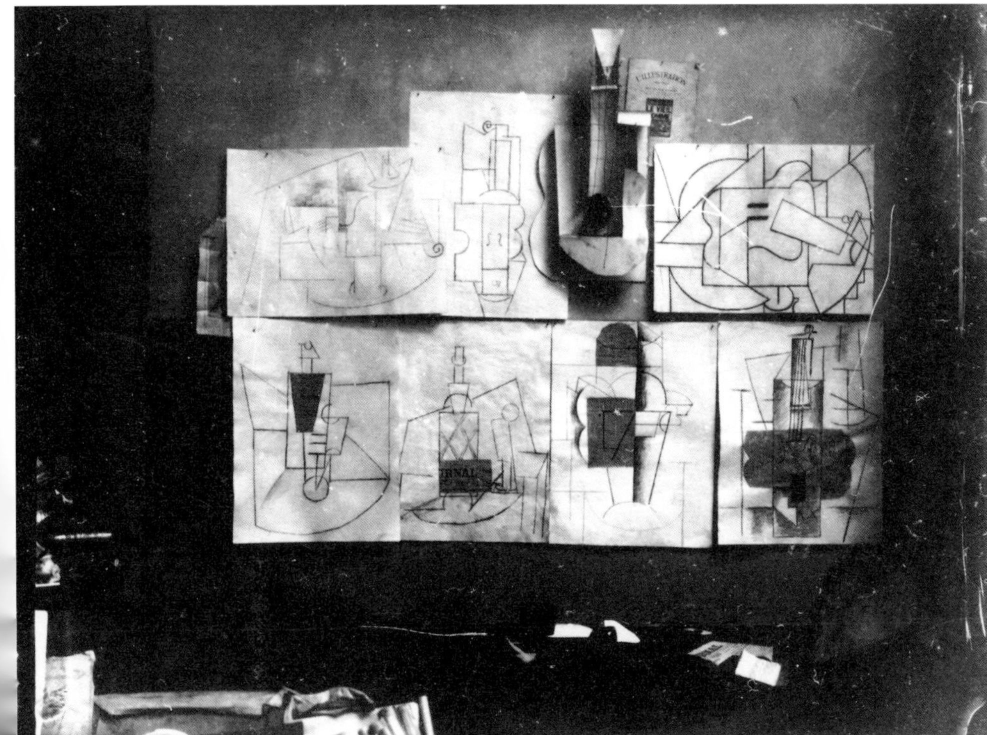

Left: Photograph of Picasso's paper constructions in his boulevard Raspail studio, 1913. Archives Picasso (private collection).

way for papier collé, "*tant mieux: il n'y avait rien de voulu dans mes idées.*"[60] I believe him. Moreover, Braque's sense of sculptural form was limited—virtually all his works in three dimensions were cutouts—and he would certainly have needed to see how his forms would function in space. Thus, although the original idea and technique for paper sculpture was Braque's, the realization of its formal possibilities was Picasso's.

Picasso is also likely to have derived technical assistance from a very different source: a Montmartre neighbor, the celebrated guitar maker Julián Gómez Ramírez, whose premises on the rue Rodier were so small that he worked on his guitars in the street.[61] The artist may likewise have studied the diagrams of different finishes and designs that were often displayed on guitar-shop walls. Another source for Picasso's cutout-paper technique, according to Cowling, was dressmakers' paper patterns: patterns that "are by definition abstract, two-dimensional blueprints for concrete, three-dimensional objects."[62] The artist would have known all about these from his childhood in a house full of females, and from the time he had his first studio—a room in the Cardonas' "hygienic" corset factory—and used to sketch the seamstresses at work.[63] Later on, he would have seen Fernande and Eva, both of whom liked to sew, cutting out patterns. Eva prided herself on her chic, on her household skills (especially with regard to domestic economy); she also did embroidery, for which Picasso drew patterns, so we can assume that she made at least some of her own clothes. Who but Eva would have shown him how to get the protruding sound hole he had contrived out of a cardboard tube to fit as snugly into his construction as a sleeve into a jacket?

Guitar maker's drawing, early 19th century. Watercolor and ink on paper, 38×26 cm. Author's collection.

Picasso likewise borrowed Eva's dressmakers' pins to try out various options for his bits of cut paper. On at least thirteen occasions he leaves the pins in; as a result we have papiers épinglés as well as papiers collés. Here Picasso makes a virtue of his own ineptitude. Getting his papers to stick properly proved a problem, and he was reduced to asking Braque for assistance. All the more likely, then, that he would have needed Eva to help him construct the far more complicated guitar. The primitivism of the method enhanced the look.

When Apollinaire later published four of Picasso's constructions made of wood, cardboard, paper and string in the November, 1913, issue of *Les Soirées de Paris,* there was an outcry. Besides the revolutionary concept, the shoddiness of the execution horrified the magazine's readers. "What is it? Should it have a base? Is it meant to hang on the wall? What is it supposed to be, painting or sculpture?" Such were the questions that Salmon says the bewildered public asked.

> Dressed in the blue of a Parisian artisan, Picasso replied in his beautiful Andalusian accent:
>
> "It's nothing, it's the guitar!"
>
> And that's it. The watertight barriers have been breached. Now we are delivered from Painting and Sculpture, themselves already liberated from the imbecile tyranny of genres. It's neither one thing nor another. It's nothing. It's the guitar! . . .
>
> Art will at last be fused with life, now that we have at last ceased to try to make life fuse with art.[64]

A year and a half later (spring, 1914), Picasso would do another version in sheet metal and wire, and in this more durable form it would change

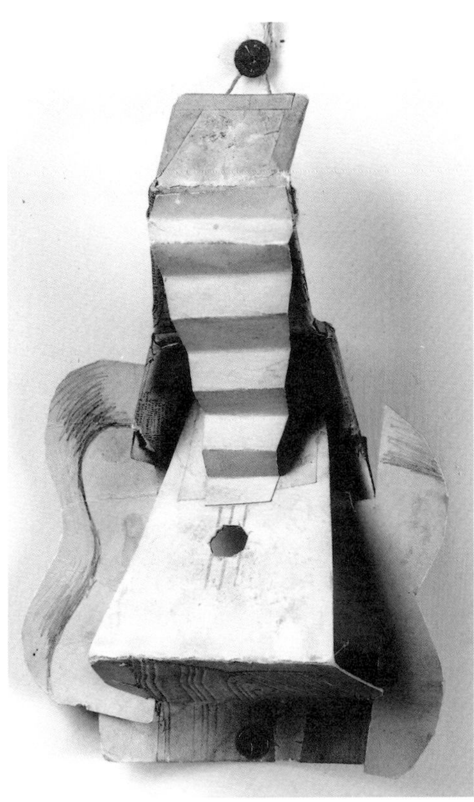

Left: Picasso. *Guitar*, fall, 1912. Paper construction, 24×14cm. Musée Picasso.

Below: Picasso. *Musical Score and Guitar*, fall, 1912. Papers pasted and pinned to cardboard, 42.5×48cm. Musée National d'Art Moderne, Centre Georges Pompidou, Paris.

the course of modern sculpture. "You'll see," the artist told Salmon, "I'm going to hold on to the *Guitar*, but I shall sell its plan. Everyone will be able to make it for himself."[65]

Word of mouth as well as photographs in *Les Soirées de Paris* spread the fame of Picasso's iconoclastic new work. Progressive young artists from all over Europe clamored to take a look. Picasso was only too happy to let them do so. The most important convert to these constructions was the Russian sculptor Vladimir Tatlin, who arrived (with Lipchitz as interpreter) sometime between April 2 and 15, 1914, and returned to Russia to spread the gospel of Picasso. Even those timid English modernists the "Bloomsberries" were impressed by Picasso's cardboard guitars. Duncan Grant visited the artist with Gertrude Stein in February; and Duncan's beloved Vanessa Bell (Clive Bell's wife, Virginia Woolf's sister) followed suit, accompanied by Roger Fry as well as Gertrude.

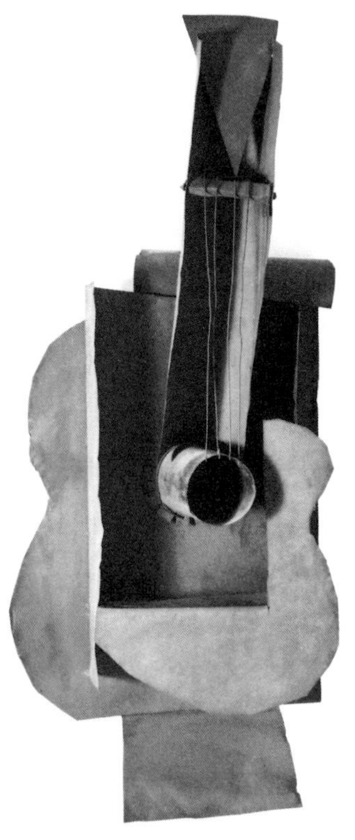

Picasso. *Guitar*, 1912–13. Construction of sheet metal and wire, ht: 77.5cm. The Museum of Modern Art, New York: Gift of the artist.

> The whole studio seemed to be bristling with Picassos [Vanessa reported back to Duncan]. All the bits of wood and frames had become like his pictures. Some of the newest ones are very lovely I thought. One gets hardly any idea of them from the photographs, which often don't show what is picture and what isn't. They are amazing arrangements of coloured papers and bits of wood which somehow do give me great satisfaction. He wants to carry them out in iron. Roger [Fry] recommended aluminium, which rather took his fancy. Of course the present things are not at all permanent. . . . I came to the conclusion that he is probably one of the greatest geniuses that has ever lived.[66]

Vanessa and Roger Fry rushed round to Kahnweiler's to buy what else but a 1909 Vlaminck landscape. "Perhaps you'll think it dull of us," she added guiltily.[67] Vanessa's evidence is useful in that it provides an approximate date for the metal version of the cardboard guitar: sometime between late March and mid-June.

* * *

Unidentified man with plaster cast of *La Dame d'Elche*, c. 1908–09. Photograph by Picasso. Archives Picasso.

One of the more imaginative and subversive of Picasso's sculptural projects exists only in the form of sketchbook drawings. The artist evidently contemplated pitting himself against *La Dame d'Elche*, the most celebrated of Iberian sculptures. The discovery of this bust at Elche in Catalonia had caused a sensation in 1897. It was supposed to date from the fifth to the fourth century B.C.; yet, far from being archaic, it was hieratically classical and perfectly preserved. Many archaeologists expressed doubts about its authenticity—doubts that recent tests have tended to confirm. However, the Louvre's expert, Pierre Paris, who had acquired the group of primitive Iberian sculptures (two of which had ended up in Picasso's hands), went ahead and purchased the piece. Its meretricious, too-good-to-be-true look and Salammbô headdress made it a major attraction. Convinced that this "national treasure" belonged to Spain, General Franco pressured the Vichy government to hand it over to the Prado in 1941. Thirty years later, the Prado ceded it to Madrid's Archaeological Museum.

Picasso photographed one of his friends leaning against a plaster cast of the *Dame d'Elche* around 1908–09.[68] Whether he admired or reviled it (the one does not necessarily preclude the other), the artist was sufficiently interested in this celebrated artifact to draw on it in some of his early cubist drawings. And then, during the spring of 1913, as his father was dying, he had the idea of doing a spoof of the *Dame d'Elche*. To mimic the *Dame*'s ornate earmuffs, he proposed to stick two B-shaped flanges (guitar-inspired signs for ears as well as other body parts) on either side of a boxlikc hcad, as if they were horse blinkers. Unfortunately he never got round to executing this construction.

Below: *Head* (project for construction), 1913. Graphite pencil on sketchbook page, 13×8.5cm. Musée Picasso.

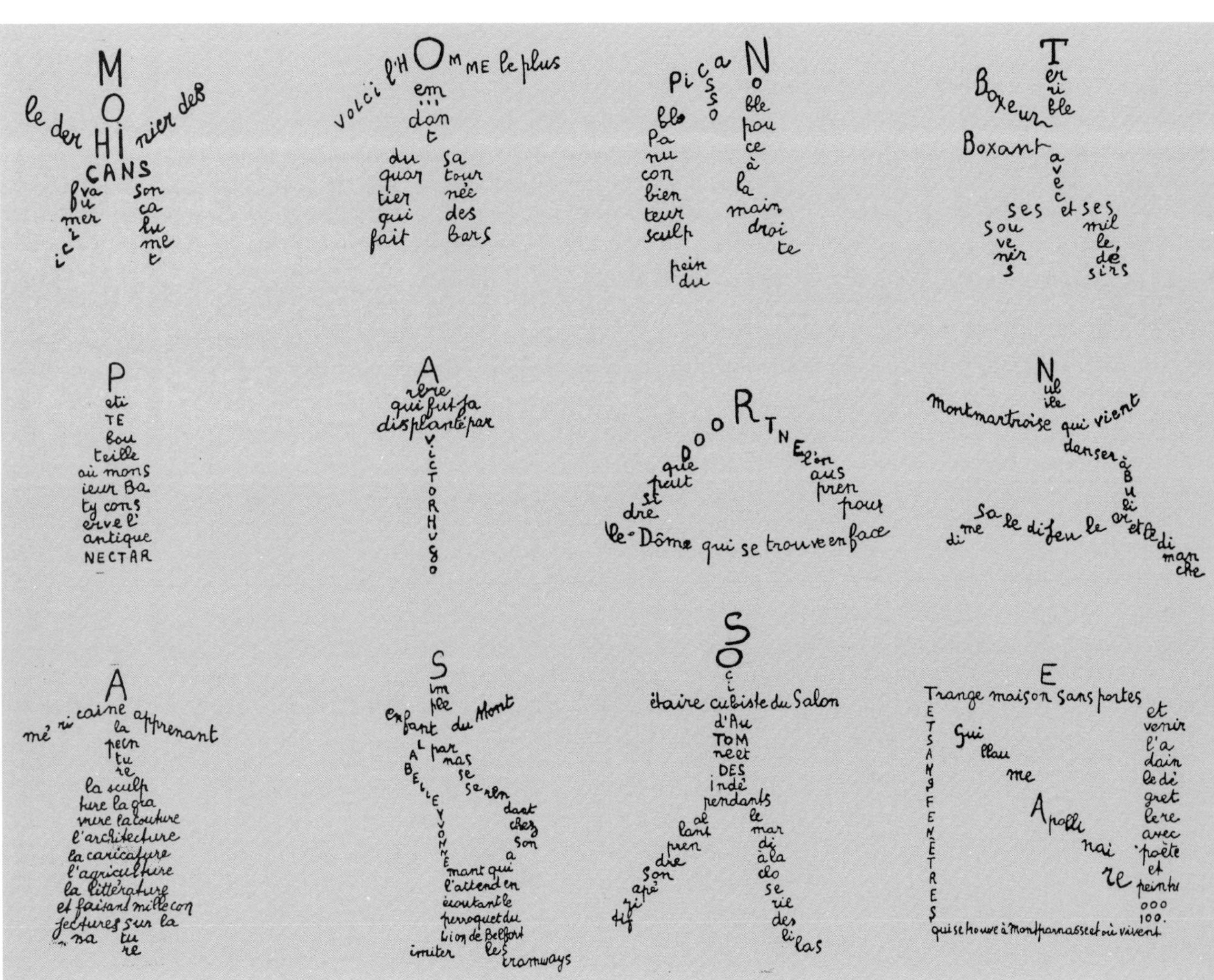

M O HI CANS
le der nier des
f va u mer ici
son ca lu me t
voici l'HOMME le plus
em ... dan t
du quar tier qui fait
sa tour née des bars
Pi ca sso N o
ble pou ce à la main droi te
blo Pa nu con bien teur sculp
pein du
Terrible
Boxeur
Boxant avec
ses sou ve nir s
et ses mil le dé sirs
P eti TE bou teille où mons ieur Ba ty cons erve l' antique NECTAR
A rère qui fut ja displanté par
VICTOR HUGO
DOORTNE
que peut st dre
l'on aus pren pour
le Dôme qui se trouve en face
N ul ile
Montmartroise qui vient
danser à Bu lier
di me Sa le di feu le ar et le di man che
A mé ri caine apprenant
la pein tu re la sculp ture la gra vure la couture l'architecture la caricature l'agriculture la littérature et faisant mille con jectures sur la na tu re
S im ple
enfant du Mont
par nas se se ren dant chez son a mant qui l'attend en écoutant le perroquet du Lion de Belfort imiter les tramways
A L BELLE YVONNE
S O ci
étaire cubiste du Salon
d'Au TOM ne et DES indé pendants
al lant pren dre son apé ri tif
le mar di à la clo se rie des li las
E
Trange maison sans portes
ET SANS FENÊTRES
Gui llau me Apolli nai re
et venir l'a dair le di gret lere avec poète et peintre 000 100.
qui se trouve à Montparnasse et où vivent

17

Life in Montparnasse

Gino Severini. *Nord-Sud*, 1912. Oil on canvas, 49×64cm. Pinacoteca di Brera, Milan: Jesi Collection.

Opposite: Apollinaire. *Montparnasse*, 1914. Calligram.

SHORTLY BEFORE PICASSO MOVED TO MONTPARNASSE the Paris Métro had opened a new Number 12 line, soon to be known as the Nord–Sud, connecting Montparnasse and Montmartre. Although brought, subterraneously, within minutes of each other, the two neighborhoods remained utterly different in atmosphere and *mœurs*. Montmartre continued to be a self-contained village dominated by two groups, which battened on tourists: artists—budding Utrillos rather than Picassos—who daubed away on street corners; and *apaches*, who touted and pimped and generated local color by throwing girls across cabaret floors. In old age Picasso liked to remember his early days there as a time of innocent camaraderie. But by 1912 he had had more than enough of Montmartre and left, never to return. Later, whenever the place was mentioned, he would sniff disdainfully and murmur, "Napoli."[1] Apollinaire explained that Montmartre had been replaced by Montparnasse, because mountain for mountain, it was more difficult to climb and

> full of fake artists, eccentric industrialists, and devil-may-care opium smokers. In Montparnasse, on the other hand, you can now find the real artists, dressed in American-style clothes. You may find a few of them high on cocaine, but that doesn't matter; the principles of most Parnassois (so called to distinguish them from the Parnassians) are opposed to the consumption of artificial paradises in any shape or form.[2]

Far from being picturesque, Montparnasse was a relatively modern quarter dating from the second half of the nineteenth century. The symbolists had put it on the bohemian map in the 1890s, when they adopted the Closerie des Lilas as their locale. After 1900, the cafés at the intersection of the boulevard du Montparnasse and the boulevard Raspail—the Dôme, the Coupole and the Rotonde—took over as the rallying place for a polyglot invasion, which had started with Germans and Austrians (the *dômiers*) but soon comprised Russians, Scandinavians and Americans. Klüver and Martin tell us why.

> The French state, with its respect for artists and understanding of the attraction they exert, allowed Montparnasse to develop into a "free zone" with less police surveillance and greater acceptance of unconventional behavior and life-styles than would have been allowed in other areas of Paris. The police kept Montparnasse free of the unsavory elements that invaded Montmartre: brothels and organized prostitution were not allowed, and criminal elements were kept away.[3]

The stretch of the boulevard Raspail where Picasso installed himself dated back no further than 1902. Number 242 is part of a studio complex called the Cité Nicolas Poussin.[4] Picasso never regarded the place as anything more than a temporary solution and moved out a year later, when his lease was up. Although it now houses a nursery school, the studio is a bit small, but that did not prevent the artist from making some of his greatest contributions to cubism while he was there. The technique of papier collé may have been conceived in Braque's Villa Bel-Air attic; it came of age in Picasso's boulevard Raspail studio.

Studios of the Cité Nicolas Poussin at 242, boulevard Raspail, 1912.

This is the first time that Dora Maar's maxim—whenever a new woman comes into Picasso's life, everything changes—can be said, in most respects, to apply. The style changed, and so did the way of life, which Eva did her best to gentrify; likewise their circle of friends. The move to Montparnasse finally dispersed the original *bande à Picasso.* Even Braque, who continued to live in the impasse Guelma (just off the place Pigalle), was no longer as available as he had been. Nor did Picasso see as much of his "pupil," Juan Gris, who was emerging as the most promising recruit to cubism: Gris could not afford to leave his "hovel" (Kahnweiler's word) in the Bateau Lavoir. Of Picasso's other painter friends, Derain and Matisse were the only ones who had settled on the Left Bank. Of the writers, Max Jacob was once again the closest to Picasso, although he would not move to the Left Bank until the 1930s. Salmon had drifted away. The silliness and verbosity of his art criticism irritated Picasso and infuriated Braque.

As for Apollinaire, he remained very close to the Delaunays. His coolness towards Picasso is reflected in the paucity and laconism of his notes after *l'affaire des statuettes.* Picasso's far more numerous letters reveal how anxious he was to resume this most sustaining of friendships. "*Je pense à toi*"; "*je t'aime, mon cher Guillaume*"; "*tu sais comme je t'aime*"; "*tu ne m'écris pas*"—such are the endearments and reproaches with which the painter pursued the poet, whose interest in him, temporarily at least, was confined to extorting photographs of recent works for his upcoming book on modern painting, or his magazine, *Les Soirées de Paris.* In the course of 1913, Picasso wrote at least eleven times to Apollinaire. (One letter included a cubist drawing.) There is no record of any answers.

* * *

Central to Picasso's new *tertulia* was a mysterious and exotic Russian couple, Baroness Hélène d'Oettingen and her "brother," Serge Jastrebzoff. (In fact Hélène had been the mistress of Serge's father.)[5] Both had a fetish for pseudonyms. Serge painted—competently enough—under the name Alexander Rudniev and later as Serge Férat. Picasso found his real name unpronounceable and always referred to him as "G. Apostrophe." Hélène painted, badly, under the name François Angiboult. Her writing, which she signed "Roch Grey" or "Léonard Pieux," was little better. When they collaborated, they called themselves Jean Cérusse: a pun on "*ces Russes*" or "*c'est Russe.*" Serge was the second son of Count Jastrebzoff, said to have been governor of the province of Moscow; Hélène claimed to be the illegitimate daughter of a royal personage, supposedly a Hapsburg—"My mother used to plunge her naked arms into massive ruby

Hélène d'Oettingen and Serge Férat. Collection P.M.A.

filled coffers," she told Max Jacob.[6] She also claimed to be the niece of Adelaide, Countess Brassov, morganatic wife of Grand Duke Michael. Countess Brassov is said to have escaped from Russia with sixty valises packed with jewels. These stories with their heady Apollinairean ring are at best partly true—like the aristocratic mayhem in Hélène's awful autobiographical novels.

"Ces Russes" were secretive about their age. Serge was probably born in 1878, Hélène around 1875. As a matter of socialist principle, he never used his title and claimed to lack funds and prefer a simple life. She, on the other hand, was worldly and snobbish and made the most of being a baroness, the consequence of a brief marriage to an elderly Estonian who had inherited an ancient Swedish title. Since Serge and Hélène were accepted as brother and sister and assumed to have had an affair, there was an incestuous aura to their relationship, which made them seem even more exotic. Whatever the truth, Hélène dominated Serge and behaved with fierce possessiveness whenever he took a mistress. For his part, he did not resent her lovers; he bonded with them, particularly Ardengo Soffici, who became his closest friend after the Italian's long affair with Hélène ended in 1908.

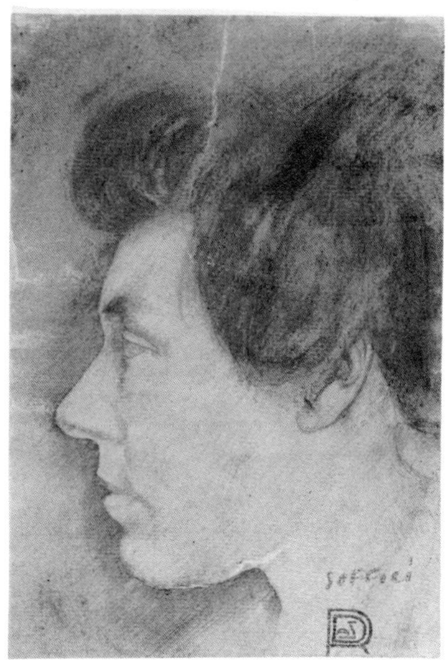

Ardengo Soffici. *Portrait of Yadwigha (Hélène d'Oettingen)*, 1903. Soffici Archive.

Serge and Hélène were prepared to be generous patrons of the avant-garde so long as the avant-garde made a show of taking their work seriously. Hitherto their principal act of patronage had been to purchase the estate of the Douanier Rousseau, whose genius they were among the first to recognize. Although they never became major collectors of Picasso's work, he welcomed their discriminating support and their no less discriminating disdain for the Salon cubists. The two ménages—the Picassos and "ces Russes"—became very close in the years immediately before and after the outbreak of World War I. Like many of his friends, Picasso had a brief affair with Hélène, when he and Fernande were drifting apart. She insisted on calling him her "gypsy" and became angry if people questioned this nickname. Fernande describes her as "the most original, the most fantastic (at least to her way of thinking) woman around," sweeping into L'Ermitage, "covered in ermine and gold, but such a good sort and so amusing that when she wanted to come off it, she enchanted us. Besides she was pretty, elegant and distinguished."[7] And, Fernande might have added, very available. The Baltic baron had liked her to strip and perform for his friends. She had remained something of an exhibitionist; after a few drinks, she would flash her blue velvet garters to arouse attention.

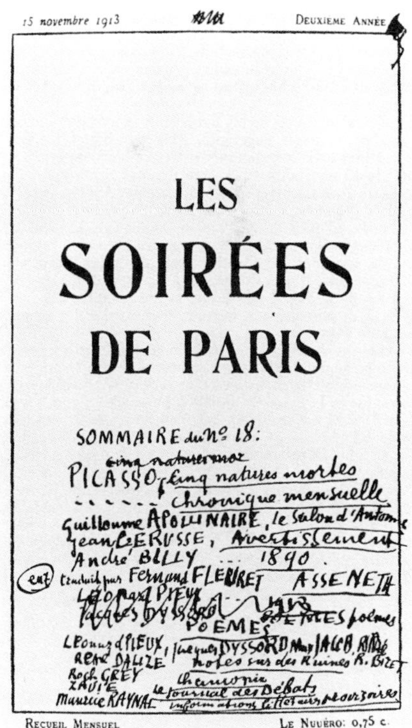

15 novembre 1913 — DEUXIEME ANNÉE

LES SOIRÉES DE PARIS

SOMMAIRE du No 18:
PICASSO, cinq natures mortes
...... chronique mensuelle
Guillaume APOLLINAIRE, le Salon d'Automne
Jean CÉRUSSE, Avertissement
André BILLY ... 1890.
traduit par Fernand FLEURET ASSENETH
Léonard PIEUX
Jacques DYSSORD
POÈMES
René DALIZE, notes sur des Ruines
Roch GREY
Maurice RAYNAL, le Journal des Débats

RECUEIL MENSUEL — LE NUMÉRO: 0,75 c.

Plan for the first number of the new series of *Les Soirées de Paris*, November 1913, handwritten by Apollinaire. Collection P.M.A.

Sometime in 1911, Hélène had sequestered Apollinaire in her *hôtel particulier* on boulevard Berthier. This "prison" was so agreeable, the poet told Fernande,[8] that he wished he had been sentenced to spend the rest of his life there, reading and writing poems to her, currying favor by suggesting that she contribute to *Les Soirées de Paris*. A year later, after his breakup with Marie Laurencin, Apollinaire moved in with Hélène and stayed on in her house while she was away for the summer. On her return he went off in his new friends', the Picabias', sumptuous motorcar for a trip to the Jura and, when he came back, moved in with the Delaunays. Whereupon he avoided Serge and Hélène: he said they reminded him of his breakup with Laurencin.[9] The truth was that Serge and Hélène distrusted Delaunay: he was manipulating Apollinaire into recognizing him rather than Picasso as the leader of the avant-garde. Hélène's first

Rousseau. *The Wedding*, 1904–05. Oil on canvas, 163×114cm. Musée de l'Orangerie, Paris.

Serge Férat. *The Book*, 1913. Oil on cardboard with pasted book pages. 39.5×28cm. Private collection, Paris.

contribution to *Les Soirées de Paris* ("Rafale," in the July, 1912, number) was her last for over a year. After quarreling with Delaunay later in the year, Apollinaire had a rapprochement with the Russians. He needed them to refinance the ailing magazine, and for two hundred francs sold them the title and subscribers' list. With Serge and Hélène as backers and coeditors, *Les Soirées de Paris*, which had not appeared for the five previous months, could now afford illustrations.[10] The first issue of the new series (Number 18, November, 1913) featured reproductions of four of Picasso's recent constructions. Most of the third issue (Number 20) was devoted to a celebration of the Douanier Rousseau. These illustrated features gave the magazine a new lease on life. Despite unreadably turgid contributions by "Roch Grey" in virtually every issue, *Les Soirées de Paris* caught on with the public and provided Apollinaire with a platform from which to dominate the Parisian avant-garde. "*Notre organe officiel Montparnassien*," Max Jacob called it.[11]

For the nine months before the outbreak of war, the *Soirées de Paris* offices occupied Serge's old studio on the ground floor of 278, boulevard Raspail. Serge and Hélène had left their *hôtel particulier* on boulevard Berthier and rented an apartment on the seventh floor of 229, boulevard Raspail, an apartment that soon became famous for its *table ouverte à la Russe*—open house. Max Jacob, who entertained the company with comic dance routines just as he had at the Bateau Lavoir, describes a morning visit to the baroness in the paneled conservatory next to her studio.[12] In yellow moiré pajamas and very high heels, she alternated between domestic and editorial duties, supervising her maid's sewing (more pajamas) and cook's activities in her *cuisine ripolinée*, while disdainfully dismissing So-and-So's book. In the evenings the baroness would switch to wearing Poiret. With red hair piled high, she would preside over gatherings which had a way of getting out of hand. For the futurists and the Chirico brothers, whom she had met when she was Soffici's mistress, she laid on lashings of ravioli and chianti and noise—Bruitist music drowning out "O sole mio." If a guest's clothes looked ragged, she would give him one of her "brother's" suits and new yellow shoes, and woe betide Serge if he objected: she would ask where on earth he had been brought up.

More public entertainments took place in the magazine's offices. Picasso was present at the most riotous of these (May, 1914): an evening of futurist music, which ended with Chirico's brother, Savinio, playing the piano with such sweat-drenched ferocity that he ended up smashing the instrument and covering himself in blood. Apollinaire was thrilled: "He broke the piano! That's what I call a musician."[13] Never one to stomach competition, especially when it was dangerously close, Gertrude Stein damned Serge and Hélène with the faintest of praise: "They were not unamusing," she wrote. "Picasso learned the Russian alphabet from them and began putting it into some of his pictures"—one of which Gertrude acquired.[14] (Kahnweiler had a different explanation for these Cyrillic letters: Picasso had copied them off posters that had been used to wrap some paintings he had loaned to a Moscow exhibition.)[15]

For a year or so Seroshka and Lialezna, as they called each other, were the acme of Montparnasse chic. They exemplified the barbarous extravagance and exoticism that Diaghilev had unleashed on Paris; also the taste for cubism that Shchukin had introduced to Moscow. Hélène's salon was

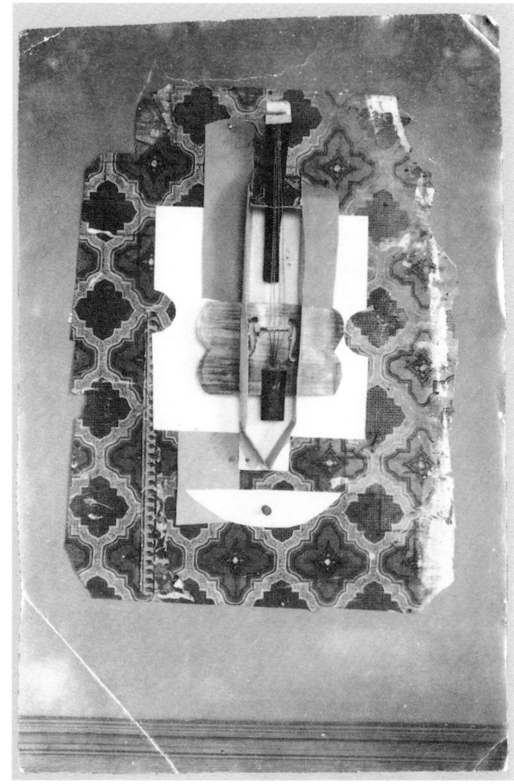

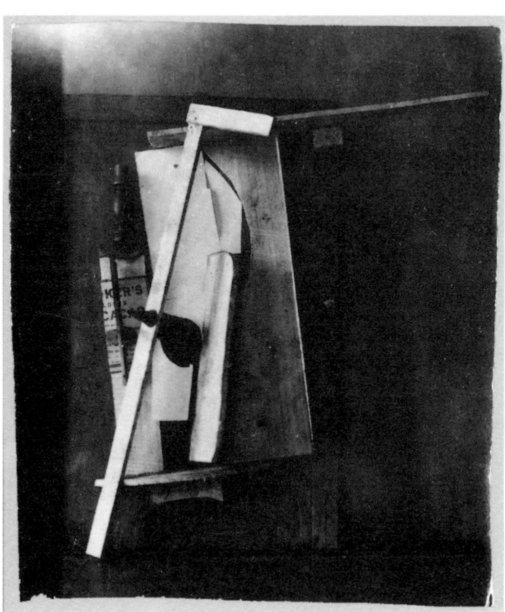

Two of the constructions illustrated in *Les Soirées de Paris*, no. 18, November 15, 1913. Archives Picasso.

Top: *Head*. String, pencil and oil on cardboard, on wallpaper (dismantled; part preserved in Musée Picasso).

Bottom: *Bottle and Guitar*. Wood, pasted paper and plasticine ball (destroyed).

Picasso. *Woman with Guitar*, 1913–14. Oil, sand and charcoal on canvas, 115.5×47.5cm. The Museum of Modern Art, New York: Gift of David Rockefeller.

not as serious-minded as Gertrude Stein's only a few blocks away, and their cubist paintings tended to be by them rather than Picasso. However their parties were a lot more lavish and a lot more fun. So long as they were in Paris, Picasso and Eva never missed them. "Ces Russes" provided him with his first taste of *mondanités*.

Like most of the competent but unoriginal painters who jumped on the cubist bandwagon, Serge was a pasticheur—better, however, than most. Much of his cubist work was executed on glass, which might explain Picasso's experiment in glass-painting around this time.[16] Picasso was intrigued by its aleatory potential. He left much of the glass surface free of paint so that the still life changes its character and meaning according to the ground against which it is set. Serge was more interested in the decorative aspects of glass-painting. Indeed his gift for decoration would prove useful when the Russian revolution put an end to his and Hélène's substantial incomes. He was able among other things to work for the theater. After he and Hélène came to the end of their considerable stock of Douanier Rousseaus, they are said to have painted several more. To believe Picasso, Serge also faked *his* work.

* * *

Montparnasse boasted its own Bateau Lavoir in the form of La Ruche, the "Hive," which housed almost two hundred "bees," as the tenants were known. La Ruche had been founded in 1902 by a philanthropic sculptor (of funerary monuments for *cimetières de luxe*) called Alfred Boucher, who aimed to ease the lot of impecunious painters, writers and actors. The main rotonda had been the wine pavilion at the 1900 Exposition Universelle. Boucher embellished this with caryatids from the British India pavilion and a wrought-iron gate from the Pavilion of Woman. There were also various auxiliary buildings—sheds in the wilderness of the garden. Virtually anyone involved in the arts was eligible for one of the cramped, segment-shaped studios; no one was ever evicted for nonpayment of rent, or for that matter anything else. As a result the place soon became dilapidated and squalid—infested with lice. (A painful abscess in Soutine's ear turned out to be a nest of bedbugs.)

La Ruche, c. 1913.

Except for Fernand Léger and Blaise Cendrars, most of the more gifted "bees" hailed from eastern Europe—Chagall, Soutine, Lipchitz, Archipenko, Zadkine, to name but a few—or, like Modigliani, Soffici and Canudo, from Italy. There were also, as Soffici remembered, "Frenchmen, Scandinavians, Russians, Englishmen, Americans, German sculptors and musicians, Italian modelers, engravers, fakers of Gothic sculpture, assorted adventurers from the Balkans, South America and the Middle East"[17]—not to speak of their women. Visitors would have to dodge nude models being pursued down corridors by lustful or jealous painters; or contend with John Noble, the American remittance man, staggering back drunk from the Dôme or the Rotonde. Chagall's memoirs evoke the atmosphere: "While an offended model sobbed in the Russian ateliers, the Italian ones rang with songs and the sound of guitars, the Jewish ones with discussions, I was alone in my studio in front of my oil lamp."[18]

The more presentable artists frequented the Baroness d'Oettingen's salon, and it is there rather than in La Ruche that Picasso met them. He felt most at ease with the Italians: they had the same Mediterranean roots as himself. He had a higher regard for Modigliani, whom he had known since 1906, than is usually thought, but found his determination to be a *peintre maudit* tedious. Of the Russians, he liked Lipchitz and his work well enough but did not warm to the others. And for their part, they were extremely mistrustful of "the mysterious and diabolical Picasso,"[19] whose work towered tantalizingly over them. Picasso got to know Chagall but was cool towards him, probably because he had aligned himself with Delaunay and Metzinger. His later work was too whimsical and folkloric to appeal to Picasso, who would express considerable irritation (circa 1960) when Chagall proposed an exchange of paintings.

Marevna. *Parade, rue de la Gaïeté, Paris: Modigliani, Soutine, Rivera, Marevna, Voloshin, Ehrenburg, Picasso, Max Jacob*. c. 1916. Drawing. Mme Marika Rivera, London.

The resentment that his painting evoked in the breasts of minor artists kept Picasso away from La Ruche. However, the friendlier "bees" would buzz around him whenever he entered one of the Montparnasse cafés: an instant cynosure, as he looked challengingly about him, opening his blazing black eyes so wide that the white showed around the pupils. The more plagiaristic painters would resort to charges of plagiarism; they would claim they had to hide their work from Picasso for fear that he would steal their *petites sensations*. They had little enough to steal. Occasionally, it is true, Picasso would lift something from a lesser painter, but he would always recycle it to greater effect. Picasso's experimental use of Férat's glass-painting is a case in point; likewise his adoption of Diego Rivera's formula for painting foliage (see p. 412).

In Montmartre, life had revolved around the circus; in Montparnasse, it revolved around the boxing ring. Pugilists took over from acrobats and clowns as Picasso's and Braque's favorite performers and, at a level of boyish fantasy, role models. A few doors from Picasso's studio on the boulevard Raspail was the Cercle Américain, where amateurs as well as professionals would train and spar in front of an audience in which *femmes du monde* and homosexuals, painters and poets, tended to outnumber the bullyboys and other more traditional fans. Picasso had a long standing passion for the sport, as Fernande's memoirs confirm: "He enjoyed going to fights and used to follow them keenly. . . . Physical strength staggered him and . . . the beauty of a fight affected him like a work of art."[20] In April, 1911, Fernande wrote to Gertrude Stein (who had once taken boxing lessons), asking whether she had gone to see the match between her black compatriots Sam MacVea—"the colored Globe Trotter"—and Sam Langford. "Pablo went."[21] He knew both the boxers: "I didn't see you at our friend Sam Langford's," he wrote Roché on April 7, probably in reference to the fight.[22] This connection inspired three 1911 drawings of a boxing match[23] and a 1912 painting entitled *The Negro Boxer* (the only reference to boxing is a patch of short, frizzy hair and the word "*onces* [sic]": a reference to the weight of the boxing gloves). While he was at Sorgues in July, 1912, Picasso wrote Kahnweiler that he had seen the film of a boxing match (probably the one in which the American Frank Claus had defeated the French champion, Carpentier, a few weeks earlier).[24] If Picasso failed to do justice to a subject which meant so much to him and whose tensions and rhythms might seem to lend themselves to cubist notation, it is because he would prefer stasis to movement. The gimmicky simulation of speed could be left to the futurists.

Picasso. *Boxers*, 1911. Pen and India ink and black chalk on sketchbook page, 16.9×24.3cm. Musée Picasso.

Picasso's acquaintance MacVea was one of the first black boxers to settle in Paris and a key figure in the pre-1914 craze for the sport. The boxing

Picasso. *The Negro Boxer*, spring, 1912. Oil on canvas, 46×27 cm. Národní Galerie, Prague.

Max Jacob. *Boxers*, 1914. Pen and ink and gouache on paper, 34×26.5 cm. Fonds Joseph Altounian.

Right: Sam MacVea, c. 1912.

Far right: Sam Langford, c. 1912.

school that MacVea opened in Paris inspired other prizefighters to join him. Soon there would be "black boxer villages"—communes where they lived together. Besides MacVea, there was Willie Lewis, who was credited by Carpentier with having been the man who "had inculcated the meaning of the pugilistic art into [French] athletes."[25] Karmel suggests that the inscription "BOX ... WI ... S" in the *Violin and Anchor* still life (p. 309) which Picasso painted after his visit to Le Havre with Braque in 1912, might refer to a poster for one of Willie Lewis's fights.[26] Since Braque was even more passionate about boxing than Picasso, and the *Violin and Anchor* painting was in the nature of a tribute to him, Karmel is probably right. As Salmon wrote in 1911, Braque "willingly practices wrestling, skating, trapeze acrobatics, and each morning, before painting, he loosens up at the punching bag."[27] In his diary (April 25, 1909), Roché records sparring with Braque and Derain in Montmartre: "afterwards billiards, dinner with Braque (at the Franc Buveur and Austens)."[28] Better known as Fox's, Austen's was the English bar near the Gare Saint-Lazare where Picasso and Apollinaire first met, in October, 1904.[29] It became one of the *bande à Picasso*'s favorite haunts, and would inspire Braque's finest cubist drypoint (1912), the still life known as *Fox* (see p. 195). Roché describes Braque as having "an impenetrable English defense. His gloves fluttered around his face like large butterflies, his elbows slid from his stomach to his sides. I quickly threw my best punches at him—all blocked. In the end I was at his mercy."[30] For Braque as well as Picasso, the art of boxing was evidently a paradigm of the fierce fights that cubism engendered.

Braque boxing, c. 1904–05. Archives Laurens.

So popular was the sport with the new generation of writers—Apollinaire, Cendrars, Colette, Cocteau, Roché and Gertrude Stein—that *Les Soirées de Paris* ran boxing articles by one of its founders, René Dalize. Dalize describes Colette taking a perverse delight in the twenty-round match between Joe Jeannette, the "Black Adonis," who looked "like a cubist dog from east Africa," and Sam Langford, who resembled "a skull in which a candle occasionally flickered."[31] Cocteau would be more rhapsodic. He described "Panama" Al Brown, a well-known fighter of a slightly later date, as "that poem in black ink, that hymn to spiritual strength."[32] The "poem" returned the poet's compliment: he loved Cocteau, he said, because the latter enjoyed getting into the tub after him and wallowing in his bathwater.[33]

However, of all the young writers in Paris, Arthur Cravan—Mrs. Oscar Wilde's iconoclastic nephew, who shocked Montparnasse with his proto-dada magazine, *Maintenant*—was by far the most dedicated boxing enthusiast. In 1914, this former amateur middleweight champion of the U.S.A. gave a series of lectures in Montparnasse on boxing (as well as dancing and poetry). Besides editing *Maintenant*, he devoted his energies to promoting the famous black boxer Jack Johnson. Cravan was at pains to identify with Johnson's notorious prowess in the whorehouse as well as the ring. "The latest passion is to pass for a negro," Cravan announced in *L'Echo des sports*.[34] He must surely have had Braque, as well as himself, in mind. Not only did Braque look like "a white Negro," he loved to pass for a professional boxer. So did Cravan. In 1917, he finally realized his dream of a professional fight with Johnson. It took place in Barcelona. Cravan lost. Not long afterwards he went to Mexico and vanished, and the dadaists canonized him.

Poster for boxing match in Barcelona between Jack Johnson and Arthur Cravan, April, 1916. Private collection.

Besides boxing with Roché, Braque liked to wrestle with the eccentric German painter/dealer/collector Richard Goetz, a friend of Picasso's from early Bateau Lavoir days and one of the original *dômiers*. Goetz had recently moved to an apartment at 58, rue Notre-Dame-des-Champs (not far from boulevard Raspail), where he continued to give lavish bohemian parties. So as to have more space, he had knocked several rooms into one. On top of the debris he would pose naked models: victims of the Messina earthquake, he would say of the resultant photographs. On the surviving walls Goetz displayed his remarkable collection, including three superb Seurats; the most important was *Le Chahut* (p. 291), which Goetz had bought from the German art historian Meier-Graefe in 1912. This painting was an icon for cubists of all persuasions. Apollinaire reproduced it in his *Peintres cubistes.* So did Picasso's German admirer Max Raphael in his *Von Monet zu Picasso*, which came out the same year. And it exerted something of an influence on Picasso's work of 1913–14. Disdain for Seurat's neo-impressionism turned suddenly into acceptance. What Picasso proceeded to appropriate—not just from *Le Chahut* but also from Seurat's drawings (which he admired to the extent of acquiring three of them)—was the great divisionist's trick of dissolving form and light into each other without any loss of substance; also his way of embedding his figures in the picture surface so that the ground appears to puff out around them, like a pillow around a sleeping head. For Picasso (and to some extent Braque) the lesson of *Le Chahut* had less to do with optical fusion than with giving cubist space a unifying skin.

* * *

"Souvenir du Havre"; postcard sent by Braque to Kahnweiler, November 27, 1912. Archives Kahnweiler: Galerie Louise Leiris.

Thanks to Kahnweiler, Picasso's work was selling well, above all in Germany. Since Vollard was not interested in giving artists contracts, Picasso finally decided to sign up with Kahnweiler. It was probably by design that he waited until Braque had negotiated *his* arrangement with the dealer. That would have put Picasso in a more advantageous position. Braque signed his contract on November 30, the day after he returned from a visit to Le Havre—as usual without Marcelle—possibly to consult his father about this forthcoming move. While there he had sent Kahnweiler a corny postcard—a view of the harbor on an easel entwined with roses—entitled "Souvenir du Havre." Braque's contract ran for only a year: he doubtless felt he could renegotiate the terms in a year's time. It specified that Braque would sell and Kahnweiler buy his entire production at mutually agreed prices: 40 francs for drawings; 50–75 francs for "drawings with wood-paper, marble or any other accessories"; 60–400 francs for canvases according to their size. A week later, Kahnweiler signed a new contract with Derain along similar, marginally more generous lines.

Picasso did not find the contractual letter that Kahnweiler sent him on December 17 satisfactory. And so the day he received it, he redrafted it in his own hand. The contract ran for three years and was five times as generous as Braque's or Derain's for the good reason that his current work had been fetching higher prices than anyone else's. Picasso's letter read as follows:

> I undertake to sell to nobody but yourself. The only works exempt from this condition are the paintings and drawings from the past which belong

Derain. *Portrait of D.-H. Kahnweiler*, 1913. Pen and India ink on paper, 32.5×15cm. Musée National d'Art Moderne, Centre Georges Pompidou, Paris.

to me. I have the right to accept commissions for portraits and large decorations destined for a specific place. The reproduction rights of the works you acquire belong to you. I undertake to sell you at fixed prices my entire production of paintings, sculptures, drawings and prints, reserving a maximum of five paintings a year for myself. I reserve the right to withhold the number of drawings I deem necessary for my work. You will allow me to decide whether a painting is finished. It is also understood that for these three years I will not have the right to sell any of the paintings and drawings I have reserved for myself. For your part you agree for the three years to buy at fixed prices everything I produce in the way of paintings and gouaches as well as at least twenty drawings a year. The prices we have agreed for the duration of our agreement are as follows:

drawings.. 100 francs
gouaches.. 200 francs
paintings up to and including No. 6................. 250 francs
of Nos. 8, 10, 12, 15, 20 .... 500 francs
of Nos. 30, 40, 50 .... 1500 francs
of No. 60 and above .... 3000 francs
prices of sculptures and prints to be discussed.[35]

A few weeks later (February 20), Kahnweiler put Juan Gris under contract. Picasso was furious with him for signing up the apprentice as well as the sorcerer. "Two Spaniards in such a small gallery was a bit much. Picasso would be merciless. For the rest of his life Gris would pay the price of this rivalry."[36] Later in the year Kahnweiler would sign up two more painters: Vlaminck on July 2 and Léger on October 20—thus completing his stable. Matisse was the only major artist whose absence he regretted. If, however, Matisse had been available, it is unlikely that Picasso would have agreed to share the same dealer. Nobody was going to abrogate his role as Kahnweiler's star. The fact that he was paid so much more than his friends was tangible proof of his supremacy.[37] One point goes unmentioned in the contract: Kahnweiler's markup of one hundred percent. As agreed with his artists, he simply doubled his cost price. Dealers and a few favored collectors were allowed a discount of twenty percent. Picasso liked the straightforwardness of this arrangement and would revert to it when Kahnweiler once again became his dealer after World War II.

Henceforth Picasso would become ever more prosperous. Although he had little or no financial sense, he guarded his savings as fiercely as a peasant. Sometime before 1914, André Level (mastermind of the Peau de l'Ours collection) introduced Picasso to one of his cousins, Max Pellequer, a banker, who would take good care of his finances for the rest of his life. The artist needed more money than ever before. Eva aspired to a more costly lifestyle than Fernande ever did. Besides, if we are to believe that inveterate gossip Gertrude Stein, they were going to get married.

18

Céret and Barcelona 1913

Picasso. *The Spaniard*, spring, 1913. Charcoal on paper, 62.5×47 cm. Private collection.

Opposite: José Ruiz Blasco and his daughter Lola, c. 1913. Private collection.

"We see a great deal of [Picasso and Eva]," Gertrude Stein informed Mabel Dodge Luhan, a few days before Christmas, 1912. "They live in this quarter and are very chummy. The new Mme. is a very pleasant hostess and quite a cheerful person. The late lamented is gone forever. I don't know anything about her. Pablo is very happy. They are at Barcelona for Christmas, she is to be introduced to his parents as a legitime, which I think she is although nothing is said."[1] Gertrude was lying about Fernande —she had recently received a begging letter from her—but correct about Picasso. Now that he was thirty-one and making good money, thanks to Kahnweiler, he was finally ready for matrimony. But first he had to present his fiancée to his family: to the ailing and chronically censorious don José, who was soon to die; to the bustling mother, who longed to see her adored son married but knew him too well to have much faith in the consequences; and to the easygoing sister, Lola, now happily wedded to the neurosurgeon Juan Vilató.

As soon as he had signed the contract with Kahnweiler, Picasso and Eva set off for Barcelona. En route they stopped for a few days at Céret to celebrate Christmas Eve with the Manolos and Havilands before leaving to spend Epiphany (the Spanish equivalent of Christmas) with his family. Picasso also wanted to earmark the Maison Delcros for the summer and discuss the Field project with Haviland. (Having arranged to exclude the panels from the terms of the Kahnweiler contract, he would have wanted his compensation to be in line with his dealer's rates. The fact that Picasso had done little further work on the panels suggests that Field was not prepared to meet the costs.) Successive postcards—from Eva to Alice and Picasso to Gertrude ("You will be the glory of America")[2]—enable us to follow Eva and Picasso over Christmas to Barcelona, where they seem to have remained for at least two weeks, possibly as long as a month.

This visit has gone unchronicled: there are no records of where Picasso and Eva stayed, whom they saw and how the family reacted to Eva. Nor do we know how Picasso got on with the father he had not seen for two and a half years. By now don José was very feeble and virtually blind, so there would have been less of the usual attacks on the iniquity of modernism. Picasso did no work on this trip, except for some notes in a sketchbook with squared-up pages, which dates from the early part of this year. Pepe Karmel relates some of its pages to a large drawing of a head, known as *The Spaniard*; and it is possible that a couple of drawings of triangular birds might have been inspired by don José's pigeons.[3] Yet another drawing of this period is annotated in Spanish, which would imply that it was done in Spain.

Sometime between January 7 and 21 Picasso and Eva returned to Paris and remained there for the next two months.[4] Although no announcement was made, they apparently envisioned a wedding—don José's health permitting—in the spring or summer, when they planned to be within easy reach of Barcelona at Céret. Stimulated by his father's Oedipal shadow, Picasso returned to work with a frenzy. Spain or its proximity brought out his dark, paradoxical spirit, and drawings poured from him in two contradictory modes: the inanimate portrayed as human, the human portrayed as inanimate. These modes have an eerie resonance that anticipates surrealism. The experience, six months earlier, of doing constructions seems to have left the artist stranded between two different dimensions: hence drawings of what look like projects for sculpture: faces in the form of large square orifices, buttressed like mineshaft entrances; and figures seemingly knocked together out of planks, or whittled down to a network of wires. Arc-tipped lines provide faces or torsos with axes ending in the curve of a hairline or browline, shoulder or clavicle. Some of these ideas culminate in paintings—mostly small ones—but the paintings lack the spontaneous vitality and inventiveness of the drawings.[5] When studied serially these emerge as one of the greatest glories of this phase of cubism. Picasso's eye was endlessly probing, his mind endlessly racing. This left him little impulse to paint.

Picasso. *Guitar Player*, 1913. Pencil on sketchbook page, 13×8.5cm. Musée Picasso.

His apparent reluctance to portray Eva in anything but song titles and encoded signs inevitably created problems for an artist whose ever-changing feelings for the woman in his life would provide an inexhaustible source of inspiration. Since the demands of portraiture had proved difficult to reconcile with the hermetic nature of cubism, Picasso had fallen back on words as a means of expressing his love for his new mistress. But words were too perfunctory, too iconographically limited to do justice to feelings that were anything but limited. And so he was obliged to cast around for other solutions. To express the physicality of his love, Picasso took to envisioning Eva metaphorically as a violin or guitar. Eva certainly throbs with more life as a musical instrument than she does as a song title or a slogan. One is inevitably reminded of Nicolás María López's essay, "La Psicología de la guitarra" (see Chapter 9). And lest there should be any doubt as to the true identity of these instruments, Picasso sometimes labels them. In one instance he has inscribed Eva's name on the side of the violin in letters so minute as to be virtually invisible. This inscription had been overlooked for eighty years, until a sharp-eyed curator at the Hermitage, Alexander Babin, spotted it.[6] Once again there is something perverse about the way Picasso keeps his mistress a secret, locked away into a painting, at the same time as he exposes her to the world transformed into a thing. That Picasso also portrayed himself in code is confirmed by a painting and a related gouache of an anthropomorphic guitar hanging under a *bec Auer*, the most popular make of gaslight—one that was frequently to be found in art schools. "*Je suis le bec Auer*," Picasso once announced. And given its ithyphallic shape and incandescent function one can see why the artist would have chosen to identify with it.

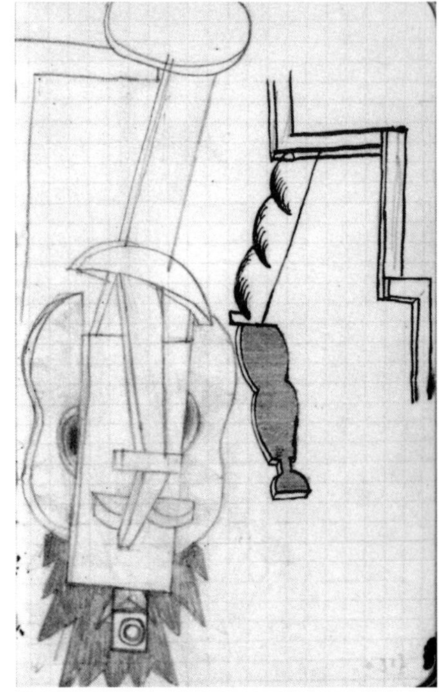

Picasso. *Head and Arm*, 1913. Pen and ink on sketchbook page, 13×8.5cm. Musée Picasso.

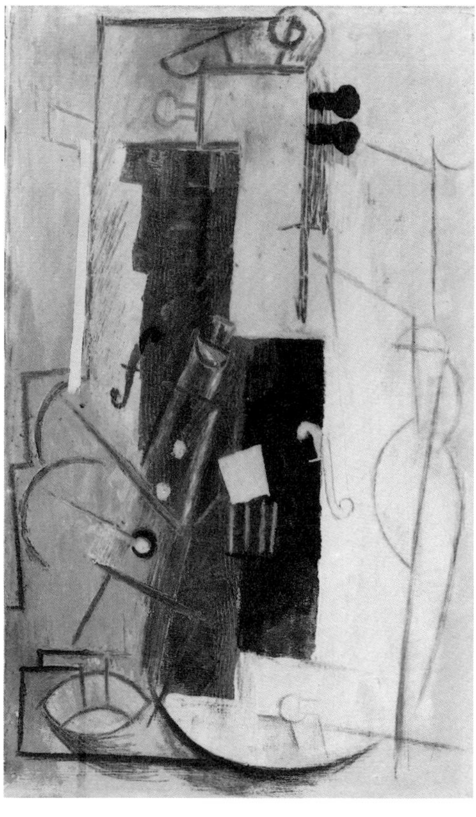

Far left:
Picasso. *Head*, 1913. Charcoal on paper, 66×51 cm. Picasso Heirs.

Left:
Picasso. *Violin and Tenora*, early 1913. Oil on canvas, 55×33 cm. State Hermitage Museum, St. Petersburg.

Far left:
Picasso. *Guitar, Gas Jet and Bottle*, early 1913. Oil, sand and charcoal on canvas, 68.5×53.5 cm. Scottish National Gallery of Modern Art, Edinburgh.

Left:
Picasso. *Violin and Tenora* (detail of passage upper left with the inscription EVA; magnified×2.4).

Picasso. *Head*, 1913. Oil on canvas, 22×18cm. Whereabouts unknown. Kahnweiler photograph: Galerie Louise Leiris.

Before Picasso left Paris, Kahnweiler visited the studio and made a major (27,250-franc) purchase at the prices set forth in the December contract. The dealer took twenty-three recent paintings of varying sizes, three earlier ones, twenty-two gouaches (including papiers collés), forty-six recent and four earlier drawings.[7] In addition Kahnweiler paid the artist 1,000 francs for repainting the background of the large 1903 group portrait of the Barcelona tailor and his family, *The Soler Family*,[8] which he had bought from the sitter. Picasso had been so bored by Soler's far from welcome commission that he never finished the landscape setting. In the end his ungifted friend Sebastià Junyer Vidal had supplied a corny woodland scene. This now had to be replaced. Picasso is said to have envisaged a cubist setting, before deciding on a blueish backdrop. Kahnweiler did not have to come up with the money until July 1, so there is likely to have been a previous transaction.[9] Otherwise Picasso might not have had sufficient funds for the summer. The dealer duly had the paintings and gouaches photographed (not the drawings: "it would have cost more than I sold them for," he said),[10] and prints sent to the artist. In acknowledging them, Picasso reported that two of the photographs were missing; he needed them, he said, because he enjoyed being surprised at the way his work looked in black and white.[11] He would scrutinize photographs of his recent work as closely as if they were successive states of an engraving.

On March 10, Picasso and Eva left Paris for Céret, where they had rented the Maison Delcros. Two days later he dutifully sent postcards to Kahnweiler and Gertrude Stein, one a group of three Catalan peasants, the ugliest of which is inscribed, "portrait of Matisse"; and on the 17th, he mailed her another, in honor of Saint Gertrude's Day. Delighted to be away from the increasingly factional art world of Paris and back among trusted old friends, Picasso immediately set to work. He concentrated on papiers collés, broadening and elaborating the possibilities of the technique. Bad news from Barcelona—his father's health was failing—obliged him to stop work and hasten to his bedside. "I've been here for a few days," he wrote Kahnweiler on March 29, "and think I'll return to Céret on Monday [March 31]."[12] Back in the Maison Delcros, he turned the front page of Barcelona's Republican newspaper, *El Diluvio* (The Deluge), which he had taken to read on the train, into a papier collé of a guitar. The page is filled with advertisements for doctors and patent medicines, and so has a certain relevance to his errand of mercy. The composition also features a black band such as bereaved family members wear on their sleeves. The prospect of his father's death was causing Picasso intense anxiety.

Three Catalan Peasants (one labeled "Portrait de Matisse" in Picasso's hand); postcard sent to Gertrude Stein, March 12, 1913. Beinecke Rare Book and Manuscript Library, Yale University.

> I'm behaving very badly towards all my friends [he told Kahnweiler on April 11]. I'm not writing to anyone, but I'm working . . . on projects and . . . not forgetting anyone or you. Max [Jacob] will be coming to Céret. Would you be kind enough to give him the money for the trip . . . also some pocket money for his expenses? Put it on my account. . . . I'm still waiting impatiently for the photos of the latest things that Deletang is supposed to have taken. . . . The news you've given me about the discussions of painting is sad indeed. As for me, I've received Apollinaire's book on Cubism. I'm quite disappointed with all this chatter.[13]

*   *   *

Picasso. *Guitar*, spring, 1913. Pasted papers, charcoal, chalk and India ink on paper mounted on ragboard, 63.5×48 cm. The Museum of Modern Art, New York: Nelson A. Rockefeller Bequest.

Max Jacob. *Céret*, 1913 (dated 1912). Pen and colored pencil on paper, 27.5×21 cm. Fonds Joseph Altounian.

Max arrived around the middle of April, exhausted from moving house—back to a room round the corner from the Bateau Lavoir, so riddled with bedbugs that it had to be replastered. "I want to change my way of life," he wrote a friend. "I'm going to Céret to spend some months with Picasso; on returning, I'll get married."[14] There had been a *dîner de fiançailles*—or so Jacob told Apollinaire[15]—and he would boast to another friend, many years later, that he had lived with an Indochinese woman for several months in 1913. Whether or not he was telling the truth, nothing came of this venture into heterosexuality. A week or two later, he wrote Kahnweiler that he had broken off his engagement.[16] If anybody could rouse Picasso from the gloom engendered by his father's illness, it was Jacob. He could also keep Eva company and under surveillance while the jealous artist shut himself away in his studio. Max had been very close to Fernande, but he did not allow this consideration to prejudice him against Eva, with whom he was soon on the friendliest terms. Max's delight at once again living with his beloved Pablo emerges in a letter to Kahnweiler:

> My day begins at six o'clock. A prose poem gets me going. At eight, Mr. Picasso in a dark blue or simple twill robe has just brought me a phospho-cocoa and a heavy and tender croissant. . . . The windows of my huge white room would like to see the Canigou (alas, rain). . . . Each day I learn to admire the greatness of spirit of Mr. Picasso, the true originality of his tastes, the delicacy of his senses . . . and his truly Christian modesty. Eva is admirably devoted to her humble household chores. She loves to write and laughs easily. She is even-tempered and directs her attention toward satisfying a guest who is dirty and phlegmatic by nature when he's not ridiculously mad or idiotic.[17]

Max was indeed a barbarous guest. According to Liane de Pougy, with whom he frequently stayed, he upset things on the tablecloth, burned holes in the sheets, left bootmarks on the bedspreads and made such a noise going to mass every morning at six that he aroused the entire household.[18]

The wet weather did not bother Max. He had no desire to go for walks in the hills, fragrant though they were with thyme, lavender and rosemary. Nor did he appreciate the frogs, toads and nightingales; they kept him awake at night. "We live in cells that are separate and vast," he told Apollinaire. "No excursions."[19] When he was not writing poetry, Max read his breviary and devotional books and made some money on the side casting horoscopes and reading cards for the local people, who found him much more "nicely spoken" than the painters who had taken over the town. And now that he was under the same roof as Picasso, Max decided to have another go at cubism, which he had neglected since his first attempts to follow the master's footsteps in 1909–10. In the letter to Kahnweiler quoted above, he says that Picasso would give his "*essais cubistes*" an indulgent glance and then retire discreetly from the room. At the end of the same letter he confesses that they "are not to the taste of my *maître* [and that] my other attempts do not satisfy me."[20] In fact the cubistic drawings (ink and black chalk, heightened with gouache or watercolor) with which Max filled two sketchbooks at Céret have more to recommend them than the banal street scenes for which he is better known. True, these cubist studies are tentative and amateurish, not to say

Max Jacob. *Still Life, Céret*, 1913. Red wash, 27.5×21 cm. Fonds Joseph Altounian.

pretty; at the same time they are evidently the work of a lyric poet—one, moreover, working in Picasso's shadow—and to that extent more sensitive than some of the deadly academic exercises of the Salon cubists. Max took pride in them: he even tried to convince Jules Romains that Picasso had pinched the idea for a cubist composition from one of his watercolors;[21] and to bolster the illusion of his own originality he subsequently dated his Céret work 1912 instead of 1913. Over the next ten years Max would occasionally dabble in cubism—for instance, the twenty-eight gouaches and watercolors with which he embellished a manuscript of his *Cornet à dés* in 1923—but in the end he lost heart and reverted to doing easily salable sketches of urban life. As Max explained to a young fan who worked as a mail sorter, there were thirteen good reasons why he was not a cubist—some more to the point than others: "Because I would like to have been the first and that was not possible"; "Because Picasso had chosen not me but Braque as a pupil"; "Because at heart I am a writer not a painter"; "Because cubism was more pleasing to my brain than my hand and I am a sensual man"; "Because cubism often seemed very ugly to me and, alas, I like what's pretty"; "Because I am an old Virgilian poet"; and finally because "all this is Picasso's fault."[22]

Meanwhile what had become of Braque? According to *Gil Blas*, "Near Avignon, the gentle giant . . . is painting cubes after cubes and teaching boxing to the children of the region."[23] Did Picasso miss him? Not that much, to judge by a letter to his old friend. "Don't be upset if I don't write you more often; I've been very worried about my father's illness. He's not doing very well. In spite of all that I'm working." Picasso missed their conversations about painting: "It's really too bad that the telephone at your place doesn't reach Céret"[24]—such good talks they could have had. But for a change he did not press Braque to join him. No longer would they both feel impelled to follow and respond to every move the other made. From June 15 onwards Braque was at Sorgues with Marcelle. He had rented an additional little house there and installed a proper studio, and in the course of the summer saw less of Picasso than of his former fellow fauves Vlaminck and Derain, who bicycled down from Paris on their way to the sea. Braque subsequently visited them at Martigues and took a number of photographs.[25]

* * *

At the beginning of May, don José took a sudden turn for the worse. On May 3, Picasso rushed back to Barcelona to the deathbed of the father he loved and hated: the father whose inept teaching had unleashed his passion for drawing and whose failure had generated so much of his power. For all his guilt and anguish, Picasso treasured the black humor of his father's demise. As he lay dying, the *déclassé* descendant of that chivalrous medieval knight don Juan de León fired off one of those disdainful squibs for which he had once been celebrated in the cafés of Málaga. When a nosy concierge pushed too close to his deathbed, he gathered enough strength to ask the family, "What have things come to? Are there no more frontiers?" These were the last words of don José Ruiz Blasco.[26] Picasso concealed his grief so successfully that he was criticized for being unfeeling; he was, as Eva reported, stricken. How could he not be? Having announced at the age of sixteen that "in art one has to kill one's father"—a feat that he performed most effectively—he would in future vindicate don José's lack of skill and restore him, pictorially, to life. "All the men in my work are my father," Picasso would say.[27] He also claimed that the countless pigeons and doves in his own work were a form of "repayment" to his pigeon-fancying parent. Especially ironical are the very late prints in which the impotent, ninety-year-old Picasso depicts don José in the guise of Degas at a brothel, observing and drawing the whores but never, never touching them.

Some years after Picasso's death, I asked his widow how he had remembered his parents. His attitude towards his adoring mother, she said, was what you would expect from a man born into the Andalusian bourgeoisie towards the end of the nineteenth century. He was undeniably fond of her but a touch ashamed of her dumpy, housewifely appearance. He apparently took her love and nurturing very much for granted—an attitude that doña María had the good sense not to question—and "to that extent it seems to have been a surprisingly uncomplicated relationship, but who knows?"[28] Picasso's feelings for his father were far more ambivalent. On the one hand, he was almost snobbishly proud of don José's *racé* demeanor, style and height (especially height), everything his mother conspicuously lacked. On the other hand, he was ashamed of his father's fogeyishness, ashamed that for all his distinction he was "*bourgeois, bourgeois, bourgeois*" (Jacqueline's words). A touch of this inherited taint, she thought, might explain Picasso's love for the *petite bourgeoise* Eva as well as his marriage to the stiflingly respectable Olga, from whom the surrealists would eventually rescue him. Having struggled to rid themselves of the very same stigma, Breton, Aragon, Eluard and the rest were well placed to show Picasso how, with a little help from the Marquis de Sade, bourgeois values could be turned upside down and given a subversive spin.

Don José Ruiz Blasco teaching at La Llotja, c. 1910. Private collection.

Don José's death indirectly put paid to Picasso's plan to marry Eva. A martyr to superstition rather than social mores, he would not have wanted to show a lack of respect for his father's memory or his mother's and sister's susceptibilities by going through a marriage ceremony when the family was still in deep mourning. He and Eva would just have to postpone things. During the period of *deuil* they suffered a further blow, which would rule out matrimony for good. Eva fell ill. She broke the news to Gertrude Stein on May 14: "Sorry not to have written to you, but we have had a lot of unhappiness and then . . . I'm suffering from an *angine* with a lot of fever, and as always in these cases it has meant that I have had to stay quiet."[29]

"*Angine*" is an imprecise term, which means tonsilitis, bronchitis or an infected throat. In the light of Eva's subsequent medical history, this diagnosis was either error or a fiction devised to cover up an unpalatable truth. Since she was to undergo an operation the following spring, Eva might have been suffering from an early manifestation of the disease that would kill her: not tuberculosis, as we are usually told, but cancer. A suspicion that Eva's disease might be life-threatening would have scared Picasso out of marriage. For once, however, the artist, who was usually so unsympathetic to his mistress's maladies (as with Fernande at Horta), did not regard her illness as a dereliction. He must have been very deeply

Picasso. *Wineglass on a Bar*, 1913. Oil, pasted and pinned papers, 21×21cm. Musée Picasso.

Picasso. *Stuffed Bird on a Branch*, summer, 1913. Oil on canvas, 33×15cm. Private collection.

in love, for as soon as he realized how ill Eva was, he behaved with a degree of compassion that he had not manifested since the fatal illness of his little sister, Conchita, some twenty years before.

Only slightly less traumatic than Eva's affliction was the mortal illness of Picasso's dog, Frika. Half German shepherd, half Breton spaniel, Frika had been his inseparable companion since his early days in Paris. Apart from a brief separation when Picasso first ran off with Eva, Frika had always been by his side. Picasso's feelings for animals were intuitive, not the least bit sentimental; he treated his pets laconically, as one animal to another. Anyone who saw Picasso with his dogs was struck by this quick rapport. No baby talk, no curt commands. Animals—other people's as well as his own—knew instinctively what Picasso wanted them to do. He was very proud of this power. When he enticed a bird out of a cage onto his shoulder, or conjured some strange, fierce hound to eat out of his hand, or coaxed an owl into fellowship with him, it was as if Picasso fancied himself as Orpheus, the poet-god, who knew how to put the animal kingdom under his spell.

Fifty years later, mention of Frika still kindled a flash of regret in Picasso's eyes. "Frika is done for," Eva's May 14 letter to Gertrude continues. "We have been to Perpignan to consult the best vet we could find, and she won't last out the year, she has been infected by another dog, which means that we will continue to nurse her, but the day there is nothing left to do she will have to be put down. I am very upset by this. Also Pablo. The news is not very gay and I hope that Pablo will resume working, for that's the only thing that will make him forget his woes."[30] Picasso asked a local *garde chasse* (game warden) to put a bullet through Frika's head. He never forgot the man's name, "El Ruquetó,"[31] nor how much he had wept.

There are no overt references in Picasso's work to his father's death or Eva's illness or Frika's end. However, there is a bleakness to his imagery, a lack of the usual high-spirited ingenuity: for example, the series of papiers collés of triangular heads and no less triangular guitars, which are so minimal it is difficult to tell one from the other. Many of these include dark mourning-band strips (such as Picasso might have been wearing) and small apertures, which alternatively stand for eyes or sound holes in a guitar but look remarkably like bullet holes. Picasso does not yet use pigeons to honor his father; though we should perhaps note that the next time he paints a bird, it is not just dead but artfully stuffed and mounted. Work was an outlet for his grief. His only large canvas of the period—the man in a tall Cordoban hat holding a guitar—which once belonged to Gertrude Stein, could well be a memorial to his father. Unfortunately the energies that Picasso put into the numerous studies are markedly absent from the painting. The way the all-black face, crisscrossed with ghostly lines, extends into a tall black hat seems to betoken death. And the oddly discordant café still life in half-mourning mauve on the right could refer to don José's heyday in the cafés of Málaga.

* * *

The resurgence of musicians and musical instruments once again reminds us that Déodat de Séverac and his musical entourage dominated Céret's cultural life. Hence possibly Picasso's switch this summer from guitarists

Picasso. *Man with Guitar*, 1913. Oil and encaustic on canvas, 130×89cm. The Museum of Modern Art, New York: André Meyer Bequest.

Picasso. *Head of a Girl in a Hat Decorated with Grapes*, late 1913. Oil on canvas, 55×46cm. Private collection, Japan.

Picasso. *Head*, 1913. Pasted papers and charcoal on cardboard, 43.5×33cm. Scottish National Gallery of Modern Art, Edinburgh.

to violinists. Out of humor or perversity, he has his violinists hold the instrument across their knees as if strumming a guitar. The bows, which these musicians clutch with fingers coiled tight as a spring, are barbed like *banderillas.* There are also drawings of men and women sawing away on cellos and double basses. Once again, musicians' heads and bodies are depicted in the guise of their own instruments—with pegs as eyes. A pity Picasso did not work up these ingenious ideas into paintings. If harlequins figure in some of the Céret paintings, it is because a traveling circus had arrived at the end of May, as Max informed Kahnweiler: "You can easily understand the charms we discover in this lively, little crowd of rowdy, peasant spectators, these equestriennes who are so respectful because they are honest-to-God working mothers, these mustachioed clowns, who seem to have had their faces painted for a farce in a cubist studio."[32]

The rain, which poured down incessantly and ruled out Picasso's walks in the woods, cleared enough for a bullfight to take place on June 10. This made the artist hungry for more, and so, the following day, he took Eva and Max off by bus to Figueres, just across the Spanish frontier, for another corrida. Eva, who had a weakness for corny, patriotic sentiments, sent Alice Toklas a card saying, "Long live Spain, America and France."[33] Her card to Gertrude suggested she "don a mantilla" and join them at Céret for the bullfight on June 29, Saint Paul's Day: "Pablo will kill a bull in your honor."[34] In some Pyrenean village, they stopped to dance the *sardana* on a square aflutter with bunting in the Catalan colors. Max was enchanted with the *cobla.* Nine years later (1922), he would publish a prose poem about this evening, "Honneur de la sardane et de la tenora," which he dedicated to Picasso. How thrilled he had been to hear the *tenora* for the first time. "Before every [*sardana*], the orchestra performed a long introduction in a grandiloquent manner. The declamation of the *tenora* was supported by the other instruments kept tightly together."[35] In the course of the *bal populaire* Max claimed that he had made out with a blond Spanish girl and a fifteen-year-old brunette—poetic license?—and then "the silence and the sadness of a mountain night once again descended on us."[36]

Picasso. *Harlequin*, summer, 1913. Oil on canvas, 88.5×46cm. Gemeentemuseum, The Hague.

Lured by the bullfights, Picasso, Eva and Max Jacob returned once again to Spain—to Figueres and Girona, around the middle of June. No sooner were they back in Céret than Picasso and Eva decided to leave almost immediately for Paris (June 20). They took Max with them and stopped en route at Toulouse, possibly to see Arthur Huc (publisher of *La Dépêche de Toulouse* and a progressive collector who had bought Picasso's *Moulin de la Galette* in 1900); also to visit the Musée des Augustins and take a new look at Ingres's *Tu Marcellus eris,* another version of which had inspired Picasso's 1905 *Woman with a Fan.*[37] Picasso's comment on this painting, as reported by Max ("made in front of us with authority behind which I hide"), is very baffling: "Ingres, not a very conscientious artist."[38] Either Max had misheard, misunderstood or missed the point of an ironical joke. Since this journey was in the nature of an Ingresque pilgrimage—the travelers stopped the following day at Montauban to see the Ingres Museum—and since intimations of his influence would soon surface in Picasso's work, the denigration of the master who would inspire the next major stylistic change should not be taken literally. If Picasso's *facture* becomes more sleek, his flesh painting more satiny, his passages of virtuoso detail sharper in focus, it will be largely thanks to "Ingres, *artiste peu consciencieux*."

Why the sudden departure for Paris? Picasso had supposedly contracted *une petite fièvre typhoïde*.[39] However, he had a mortal terror of disease and would not have stopped off to visit museums if there had been anything wrong with him. Nor would he have sent Gertrude a postcard, announcing, "*A demain*." No, I suspect the reason for this trip was Eva's health rather than Picasso's; and the need to see Gertrude and Alice had to do with finding a good specialist. Picasso certainly felt well enough on June 24 to write Apollinaire and suggest a meeting. He would indeed fall ill, but not for another two weeks. On July 10, Eva wrote Gertrude, who had left with Alice to spend the rest of the summer in Spain and was currently in Barcelona, that

> Pablo is not any better. The doctor has diagnosed a mild attack of typhoid. [He] is sending for a night nurse because he is worried that I will be the next to fall ill—which would not do at all. All the same Pablo is quite weak, and an icepack has to be put on his stomach every three hours, for the pain is in his stomach not his head, which is all to the good. . . . According to the doctor, Pablo will not recover for another twelve days.
>
> Pablo says you mustn't take such a liking to Barcelona, because the place is rife with fever [*fièvres de la mer*], at one moment the doctor was convinced that this is what he had caught. . . . The blankets are perfect and of great service to me."[40]

On July 14, Eva sent another bulletin to Gertrude, c/o Thomas Cook, Barcelona.[41] The doctor had just paid a visit. Picasso's fever had gone down, but the doctor's failure to come up with a diagnosis was disturbing. He had none of the symptoms of typhoid and was now thought to have caught Malta fever in Barcelona. On July 18 Eva reported that he was "much better and beginning to get up";[42] and, on the 22nd, that "Pablo is almost well—he gets up every afternoon. Matisse had been by frequently to find out how he was, and today he brought Pablo some flowers, and spent most of the afternoon with us. He's most agreeable."[43] He also brought some oranges. Oranges were to Matisse what apples were to Cézanne, and he was in the habit of making gifts of them to friends. Picasso, "who seems to have divined the secret meaning of this gesture,"[44] would not eat them but put them in a bowl on the mantelpiece, which he would point out to visitors: "Look at Matisse's oranges." Years later, Picasso would buy his magnificent 1912 painting *Still Life with Oranges* in commemoration of these gifts.[45]

Eva wrote Gertrude that they would probably return to Céret around the middle of August, then go to Barcelona, "unless Pablo changes his mind."[46] Meanwhile Max Jacob, who had returned to Paris with them, was writing "very pretty poems," and Apollinaire was being more and more of a brute ("*mufle*"). "As for me, I have bought three very pretty corsages at the Bon Marché."[47]

Whether Picasso's illness was Malta fever or a psychosomatic reaction to his father's death, Eva's sickness and Frika's end, it confirmed him in his hypochondria, his weakness for fads and diets. Henceforth he would drink more modestly than ever; as for drugs, ever since his sporadic indulgence in opium at the Bateau Lavoir, he had been averse to them.

Jean Auguste Dominique Ingres. Study for *Le Bain turc*, c. 1860–2. Oil on paper, 25×26cm. Musée Ingres, Montauban.

Matisse. *Still Life with Oranges*, 1912. Oil on canvas, 94×83cm. Musée du Louvre: Picasso Gift.

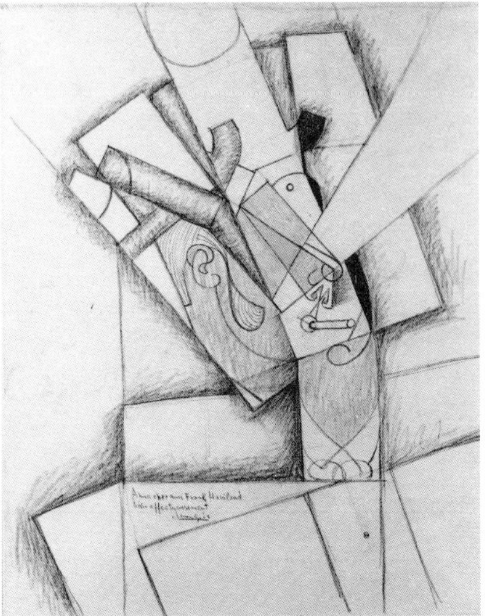

Gris. *The Smoker*, 1912. Charcoal and red chalk on paper, 72×59cm. The Jacques and Natasha Gelman Collection.

Apart from work, tobacco was Picasso's only addiction, at least until his late eighties, when his doctor persuaded him to substitute liquorice.

Picasso was now celebrated enough for his state of health to be reported in the newspapers. An item in *Le Figaro* (August 9) was taken up by the *Indépendant*, French Catalonia's principal journal:

> The little town of Céret is jubilant. The Cubist master has arrived to take a well-deserved rest. The "Cubist" to whom *Le Figaro* is referring is the likable artist Pablo Picasso. Presently gathered round him at Céret are the painters Herbin, Braque [in fact at Sorgues], Kissling [*sic*], Ascher, Pichot, Jean [sic] Gris, and the sculptor Davidson.[48]

The artist, who had returned to Céret at the beginning of August, was far from jubilant about this invasion. He had nothing against Kisling, a twenty-two-year-old Pole who had only recently begun to attract attention at the Salons (the next year his duel—sabers as well as pistols—with a fellow Pole called Gottlieb would make him a hero in Montparnasse). He had nothing against the American sculptors Jo Davidson and Michael Brenner, whom he knew through Gertrude Stein. (Brenner was in the process of abandoning sculpture for dealing and had come to Céret to sign up artists.) Nor did he have anything against Auguste Herbin—most rigid of geometrical cubists—who was an old though never very close friend from the Bateau Lavoir. However, the other old Bateau Lavoir friend, Juan Gris, posed a different problem. By signing up with Kahnweiler, Gris had unwittingly incurred Picasso's wrath. In his blind zeal to be accepted as cubism's third man, he was confident that he and his attractive new mistress, Josette Herpin, would be welcomed into Picasso's summer *tertulia* and—who knows?—take the place of the absent Braque. For his part, Picasso saw Gris as a sorcerer's apprentice—doubly dangerous for his mastery of the sorcerer's secrets—and a tactless fool for invading Picasso's preserve and setting himself up in the local café as a cubist dialectician, "arguing every inch of the ground."[49] Picasso's dudgeon worsened as he sat—in silence except for the occasional barbed remark—listening to his former pupil pontificate.

These café discussions were made all the more fraught by Manolo, whose antipathy for Gris was one that only a hot-blooded, mocking Catalan steeped in the classical tradition could feel for a cerebral and humorless modernist from Madrid, who was a much more imaginative and inventive artist. Manolo did his best to encourage Picasso's distrust of this compatriot who had developed with such amazing speed that he had caught up with his mentor. A comparison of the canted, vertical rectangles in Gris's top-hatted *Smoker* with the structure and color of Picasso's top-hatted heads suggests that Gris had stepped into Braque's shoes. During the two weeks they were together in Céret, they are unlikely to have seen each other's work: Picasso would not have been that forthcoming and Gris would have had very little to show. To his credit, Picasso would be full of praise for Gris's Céret paintings when Kahnweiler showed them to him in October. Later, the two painters would be reconciled, but Picasso would always resent his only real pupil: he had turned out too well. He came to regret not owning any examples of Gris's work and did his best to persuade Douglas Cooper to relinquish the great grisaille portrait of Josette Gris (1916, now in the Prado), which would leave a mark on his work in the mid-1920s.

Another old friend, Ramon Pichot, newly arrived in Céret, posed a very different threat to Picasso's equanimity. Few people had shown Picasso as much kindness as Ramon and his generous family of artists, musicians and writers. Ramon had been a surrogate father to him back in Barcelona, and they had been further linked when Ramon married Germaine: Picasso's onetime mistress and the cause of Casagemas's suicide.[50] Eva's treacherous treatment of Fernande had put an intolerable strain on these frayed old ties. The year before, the Pichots had put Picasso to flight by threatening to arrive in Céret with Fernande. This year, Ramon appeared in person—presumably alone, and presumably to press the prosperous Picasso to provide for Fernande, who was worse off than ever. Pichot pressed too hard. Criticism of his personal conduct by even his closest friends would always trigger intense rage in Picasso, especially when it reflected on his sacrosanct private life, his relationships with women. All we know is that Picasso "came to blows with someone in his group of friends"[51]—presumably Pichot. He and Eva left immediately, a fact that *Gil Blas* reported. "At Céret they're all fighting for a place at the guest table (*table d'hôte*). Understandably disgusted, Picasso fled this charming little spot he had discovered."[52] So ended his third and last stay in Céret.

Picasso and Eva were back in Paris by the middle of August.[53] "We had some disputes," Picasso wrote uncommunicatively to Kahnweiler, who was vacationing in Rome (August 19) "and preferred to come back to Paris to find some peace. We've found a studio with an apartment, very large and full of sunlight . . . 5*bis*, rue Schœlcher. I've also bought a Rousseau. And that's all that's new."[54]

Below: Picasso. *Landscape: Céret*, spring, 1913. Pasted papers, pastel and charcoal on paper, 47.7×63cm. Musée Picasso.

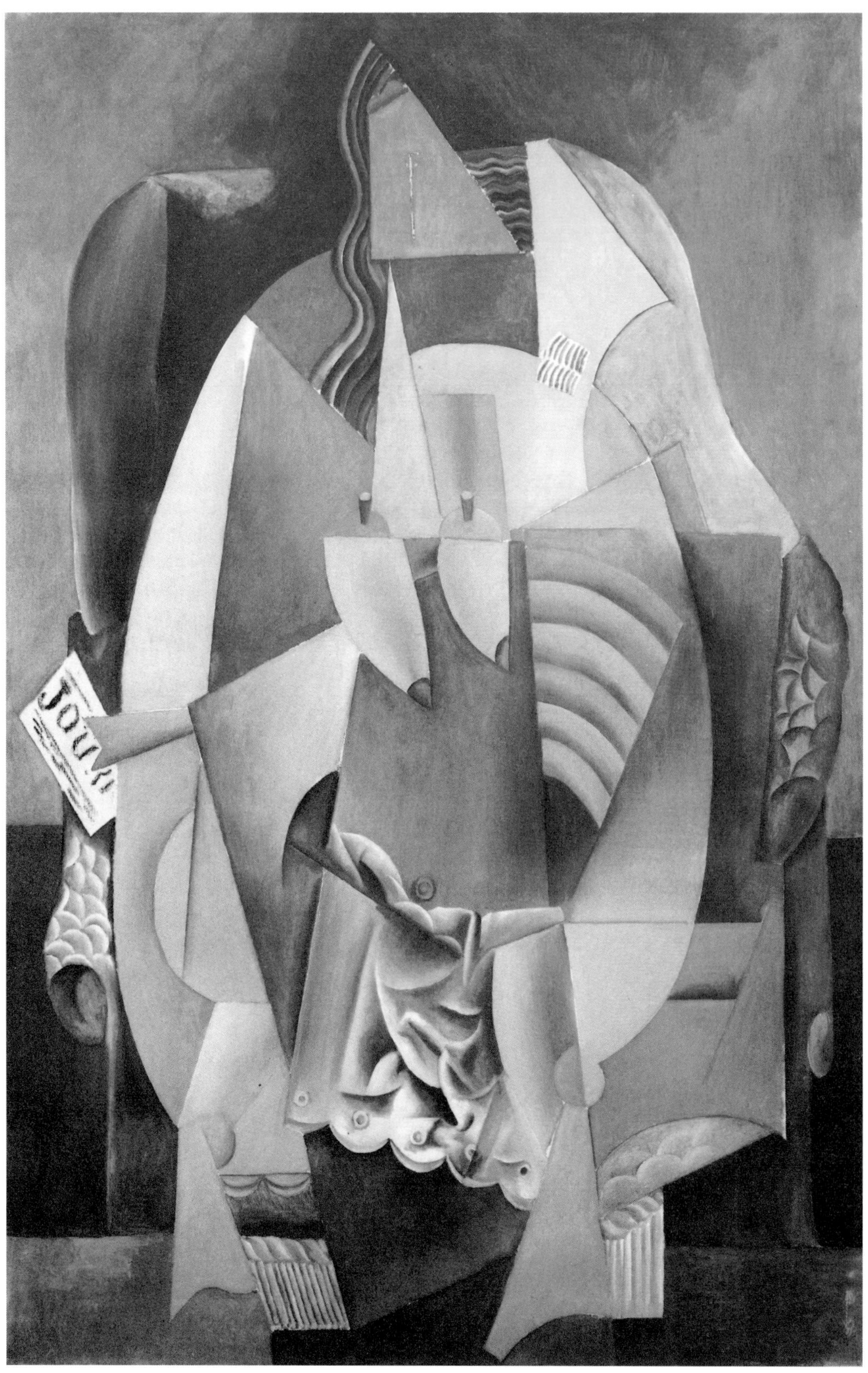

19

Woman in an Armchair

Exterior of Picasso's studio at 5*bis*, rue Schoelcher.

Opposite: Picasso. *Woman in an Armchair*, fall, 1913. Oil on canvas, 148×99cm. Collection Sally Ganz, New York.

THE STUDIO-CUM-APARTMENT AT THE HEART OF Montparnasse where Picasso would live for the next three years was much more imposing than any of his previous quarters. The building was new and catered to the monied bohemians, many of them foreigners, who were taking over Montparnasse. The stairway was carpeted and the landings lit by bronze figures of nude nymphs dangling lightbulbs. Plaster casts of the Elgin marbles lined the stairs. These had always fascinated Picasso. He had copied them as a child and drawn on them for his 1906 *Watering Place*; however, most visitors found them inexcusably fustian. Even Jean Cocteau, who would soon make classicism fashionable, recalled his youthful contempt. He would race up the stairs out of breath, averting his gaze, only to find himself, seconds later, menaced by Picasso's army of African sculptures, "which I scarcely liked any better."[1]

The fanciful staircase would have impressed Eva and amused Picasso—the more so for shocking solemn modernists. He had taken the apartment for its studio, which was "big as a church,"[2] and soon to have four or five hundred canvases stacked against the walls. Of these *Les Demoiselles d'Avignon* had pride of place, as a photograph that Picasso took of himself at the center of the clutter reveals. The floor was covered with discarded brushes, palettes and paint tubes as well as newspapers, brochures, cinema tickets, tobacco packets and other debris. Now that all this was potentially the stuff of art, Picasso had an excellent excuse for throwing nothing away. Despite the accumulation of rubbish, his studio was rapidly becoming a treasure house of incalculable riches. He was forever putting things under lock and key.

Besides being much larger than the boulevard Raspail, the new studio was much brighter, since the opposite side of the street had never been built up. This was a mixed blessing in that it made for an uninterrupted view of the Jewish section of the Cimetière Montparnasse. A strange choice for someone who was notoriously superstitious, one might have thought, but the outlook does not seem to have daunted Picasso. The same cemetery had adjoined his previous studio. It was only when Eva fell mortally ill that the view seemed painfully congruous.

Picasso settled into the rue Schœlcher at the beginning of October, 1913. Now that he had much more space at his disposal, he resumed doing constructions. At the request of Apollinaire and Serge Férat, he had Délétang photograph the latest batch as well as the ones he had done the

Picasso. *Head of a Woman*, fall, 1913. Oil on panel, 16×12cm. Musée National d'Art Moderne, Centre Georges Pompidou, Paris.

Picasso. *Head of a Woman*, 1913. Wax crayon on paper, 23×20cm. Picasso Heirs.

Above: Picasso. Study for *Woman in an Armchair*, fall, 1913. Gouache and black chalk on paper, 32.7×27cm. Musée Picasso.

Left: Matisse. *White and Pink Head*, 1914. Oil on canvas, 75×47cm. Musée National d'Art Moderne, Centre Georges Pompidou, Paris.

previous year. The appearance of four of these in the first of the new series of *Les Soirées de Paris* is said to have scared all but one of the magazines's forty subscribers into canceling their subscriptions. This is yet another of the legends perpetuated by Penrose.[3] Apollinaire's biographer, Adéma, cites at least five subscribers—Jean Sève, Raoul Dufy, Sonia Delaunay, Stuart Merrill and Vollard—who did not cancel.[4] There must have been a number of others. More to the point is the enormous influence that the publication of these revolutionary constructions in a relatively obscure periodical would exert on twentieth-century sculpture over the next few years.

Since Matisse's visits to Picasso's sickbed in July, they had resumed a friendship which meddlesome adherents on both sides had done their best to extinguish. (Salmon was the principal *agent provocateur*, Jacob the principal peacemaker.) Around 1912, the animosity had gotten out of hand. Late in life, Matisse told Brother Rayssiguier that he could never forget going to join a café table where Picasso was sitting with his cronies, and, to his mortification, being cut dead.[5] Picasso must have been showing off to his *tertulia*. From now on, the two artists regularly checked out each other's work, comparing and challenging each other's concepts. Picasso later observed that nobody could fully understand his or Matisse's pre-1914 work without realizing what they took from each other and how many ideas they shared.[6] Matisse had moved in 1909 to Issy-les-Moulineaux—a suburb that was ten minutes from Montparnasse by train (fifty-four a day, he boasted)[7]—and taken to riding. He even found horses for Picasso and Eva. "We ride with Matisse in the forest of Clamart," Picasso wrote (August 29) Gertrude Stein, who was in Granada.[8] Matisse could not resist regaling the same gossip. Did he think that this news might mitigate Gertrude's resentment of him? "Picasso is a horseman. We go out riding together, which amazes everybody"[9]—or, as Daix points out, might have amazed everybody if he had not kept it a secret from everyone except Marcel Sembat, the socialist *député*.[10] When news of the reconciliation seeped out, it did indeed surprise people, but the avant-garde did not take long to adjust to the new balance of power. By 1914, Picasso and Matisse would be perceived, in Paris at least, as twin rather than rival leaders of modern art. Instead of bad-mouthing each other, they were at pains to be civil. When the Japanese painter Riichiro Kawashima asked Picasso whether he liked Matisse, Picasso "widened his bright eyes and said, 'Well, [he] paints beautiful and elegant pictures. He is understanding.' He would not say any more." Four years later, when Kawashima asked Matisse about Picasso, the answer was "He is capricious and unpredictable. But he understands things."[11]

Picasso cannot have enjoyed being challenged to do something that Matisse, who was proud of his horsemanship, did much better. However, it was a small price to pay for a new, mutually beneficial alliance. Their disputes were now friendly. Matisse summed up their differences somewhat simplistically: "Picasso shatters forms; I am their servant."[12] When cubism was at its hermetic height, Matisse had held out against it; now that he was reconciled to Picasso, he was reconciled to cubism. Although he never actually "shatters forms," some of Matisse's 1914 paintings—the *White and Pink Head* of his daughter, Marguerite, *View of Notre Dame (on a Blue Ground)* and *Still Life (after de Heem)*—are in cubism's debt. So,

Picasso. Erotic drawing, 1903. Sepia and wax crayon on card, 13.3×9cm. Private collection.

Picasso. Study for *Woman in an Armchair*, fall, 1913. Watercolor and pencil on paper, 31.2×25.2cm. Whereabouts unknown.

Matisse. *Portrait of Madame Matisse*, 1913. Oil on canvas, 145×97 cm. State Hermitage Museum, St. Petersburg.

Cézanne. *Madame Cézanne in a Yellow Armchair*, 1893–95. Oil on canvas, 80.8×67.5 cm. Art Institute of Chicago: Wilson L. Mead Fund.

too, is *Bathers by a River*, the large panel (originally destined to be a pendant to *Music* and *Dance*) that Matisse reworked in the course of this summer, only to put it aside for another three years. Much as they owe to Picasso, these paintings owe even more—the emphatic black grid, for instance—to Juan Gris's rigid scaffolding.

Like Picasso, Matisse was concerned with reconciling the image of the woman in his life with his stylistic advances. The previous winter he had begun work on a largish portrait of his wife—the last and probably greatest of the canvases he devoted to her—but after seeing the portrait *Madame Cézanne in a Yellow Armchair* at the 1913 Salon de Mai, he decided to start afresh. During the summer and fall of 1913, he painted, painted out and repainted the portrait over and over again until he had arrived at an image that is Cézannesque in its iconic authority. Amélie Matisse wept at the disappearance of what was apparently an attractive and lifelike portrayal of her. However, besides updating Cézanne, Matisse wanted to commemorate his middle-aged wife as a lady—gracious, dignified, worthy. And so he pared her face down to a stylized gray mask (hence, possibly, Picasso's frequent use of gray as an active color) crowned with an elegant wreath of a toque. He also gave her head and torso a slight inclination suggestive of a lofty personage responding to a salutation—an attitude that presupposes a certain reverence on the beholder's part: not so much towards her as towards her husband's hieratic effigy.

After observing Matisse's portrait of his wife turn inexorably into a masterpiece, Picasso set about doing a three-quarter-length painting, similar in size and subject—*Woman in an Armchair*—but otherwise different as can be. Whereas Matisse's attitude to his martyr of a wife is essentially respectful, Picasso's attitude to the mistress he adored is anything but. To exalt Eva's sexuality he portrays her, proudly and tenderly but also monstrously, in terms of her own genitals—shades of an erotic drawing he had done in 1903.[13] He uses the voluptuously buttoned arms of the violet fauteuil as a tactile equivalent for the labia, into which he inserts the soft, pink architecture of Eva's body, much as he does in the earlier drawing. And he depicts her face as a vertical slit, which, as we know from a related study, is another pictorial pun: face = vagina. Even the colors are appropriate: bruised pinks, mauvish browns and ruddy ochers. In yet another twist, Picasso modestly covers Eva's lap with a chemise, but immodestly drapes it to attract attention to the cleft it conceals—*trou ici*, to quote a newspaper cutting in his recent *Au Bon Marché* collage. And, as we have seen, when it came to Eva's beautiful pointed breasts, so redolent of tribal sculpture, he nails them to her body with an alternate set of nipples.

Did Eva weep at the sight of herself envisaged as a sexual organ? She would have had cause, not least because the more figurative drawings for this "portrait" reveal that Picasso had no problem reconciling her frail beauty with the demands of cubism. By now Eva probably realized, as most of her successors would, that she would sooner or later be consumed in the furnace of her lover's psyche. Picasso would have told her of the vow he had made at the age of thirteen, when his younger sister, Conchita, was dying of diphtheria (a vow to God that he would never paint or draw again if Conchita's life was spared—a vow he must surely have broken).[14] Once again it would seem that Picasso was weighing the woman he loved against his art.

Whether or not Eva enjoyed life with Picasso (years later Kahnweiler would accuse him of treating her badly),[15] he was evidently very happy with her. His numerous tributes to her sexuality imply that she satisfied him in that respect, and so long as she did not exasperate him by falling ill, he remained faithful and loving in his spoiled way. The vast, cathedral-like studio soon filled up with new work, which gave his self-esteem a considerable boost—something that his rivalry with Matisse would necessitate. Meanwhile, papier collé was having an enormously exhilarating effect on his work. It liberated him from the austerity and constraints of analytical cubism and, by providing him with so many additional options, it enabled him to be even more protean and productive. Papier collé also provided an outlet for the artist's sardonic sense of paradox and wit. Picasso had often leavened his imagery with puns and double entendres (which Poggi likens to "wild cards"[16]). However, now that he—not to mention Braque—had established an artist's right to do what he liked with whatever material he liked, he was able to exploit humor more overtly and to far greater effect than ever before; he could also sometimes assume the mantle of a poet. Seemingly simple arrangements of cut paper turn out to be booby-trapped with ironical asides, in-jokes and poetic contrivances that are as mocking and subversive as anything in Jarry.[17]

Picasso. *Still Life "Au Bon Marché,"* 1913. Oil and pasted papers on cardboard, 23.5×31 cm. Museum Ludwig, Cologne.

A case in point is the *Au Bon Marché* collage, contrived from the lid of a department store box. I had hoped that this box might have contained "the three pretty corsage ornaments" mentioned in Eva's July 22 letter to Gertrude Stein, but Karmel has confirmed that this collage figures in a group of works that Kahnweiler acquired in the spring.[18] I suspect that there had been a previous box, which contained the broderie anglaise chemise of *Woman in an Armchair.* Picasso hoarded boxes like this, especially ones that had contained objects associated with the woman in his life. In this collage he uses the lid as a support for the still life, the label to imply the box, and the box to imply Eva. The wineglass on the right floats as freely in space as an astronaut; the perfume *flacon* on the left is rather more grounded. Two bits of newspaper in the gap on the front of the box spell out a coded message: "*Lun B*," which sets up a rhyme with the words "*Lingerie Broderie*" above, and "*trou ici*" ("hole here"), which is all too evidently a reference to Eva. The significance of this deceptively simple-looking composition and its seemingly crude joke has been hotly and inconclusively disputed.[19] My own view is that this collage opens up its secret if we see it in the light of *Woman in an Armchair,* which Picasso could well have begun thinking about in the course of the summer and which, as we have seen, portrays Eva genitally with the folds of her chemise arranged to make the same "*trou ici*" point in paint. In the collage, Picasso hides his mistress away in a box, or turns her into one, while also signaling that we have access to her.[20] In *Woman in an Armchair* he makes the "*trou*" the theme of the painting.

These highly charged subjects called for a highly charged style: hence the ever-increasing elaboration of Picasso's surfaces. Papiers collés are embellished with pages torn from books, decorative borders, sheet music, visiting cards, as well as colorfully patterned wallpaper and wrapping

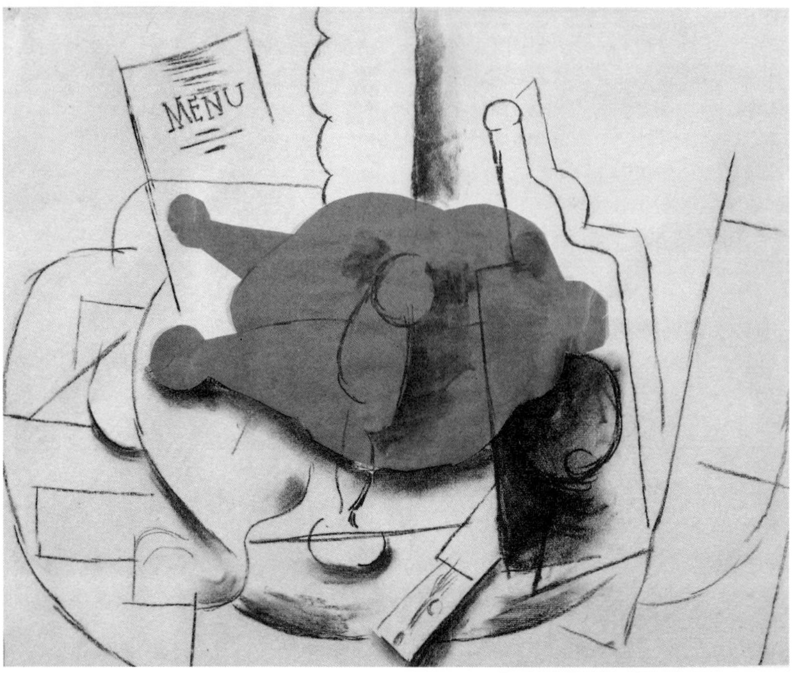

Picasso. *Chicken, Wineglass, Knife and Bottle*, spring, 1913. Pasted paper and charcoal on paper, 47×59 cm. Private collection.

Picasso. *Knife, Fork, Menu, Bottle and Ham*, spring, 1914. Oil and sawdust on cardboard, 29.5×38 cm. State Hermitage Museum, St. Petersburg.

Picasso. *Vanitas (Guitar, Skull and Newspaper)*, 1914. Oil and ashes on canvas, 43.5×61 cm. Musée d'Art Moderne, Villeneuve d'Ascq.

paper. As for paintings, Picasso mixes his pigment with the additives—plaster, grit, sand, coffee grounds—which Braque had shown him how to use. Characteristically, he goes a step farther and encrusts one of his still lifes with beads and fake pearls.[21] It is not a success. Thanks to Seurat, he turned instead to pointillism, which he had formerly dismissed as "passé." But familiarity with Goetz's *Le Chahut* had shown him how he, too, could set his forms in a spatial element as shallow, resilient and soft as a feather bed. After spending evening after evening in the course of winter, 1913, listening to his new friend Severini extol the qualities of the artist he regarded as his master, Picasso had further designs on Seurat. It was not his divisionist theories and optical calculations that attracted him; it was the master's dots he wanted to exploit, but in his own new way. And exploit them he did, in much the same spirit as a *modiste* applying sequins to a dress. Picasso's juxtapositions of colored dots do not generate light or, for that matter, shadow, as Seurat's pointillism does. They embellish specific objects and areas and make them tactile; they also set up a vibration that animates surfaces, just as passages of *faux bois* and *faux marbre* do.

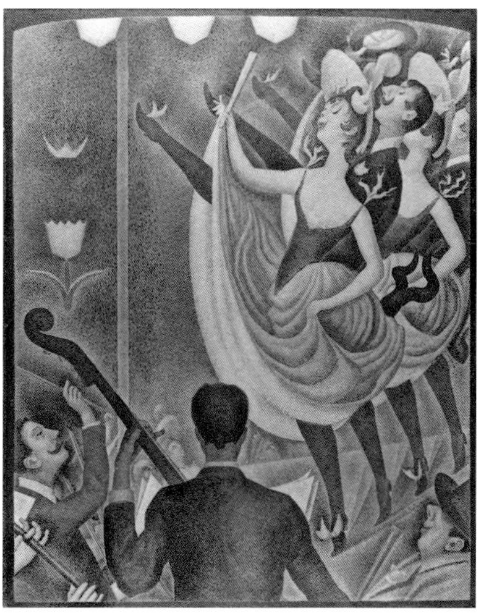

Georges Seurat. *Le Chahut*, 1889–90. Oil on canvas, 171.5×140.5 cm. Rijksmuseum Kröller-Müller, Otterlo.

The sparkle of Picasso's pointillism enhances the sparkle of his pictorial wit. He uses it to great effect in his parodic heads of a quartier Latin student in a *faluche* (the bouffant beret that students once wore). In the papier collé version that Gertrude Stein acquired, Picasso simulates the *faluche* in crumpled brown paper; in a subsequent version he goes a stage further and simulates the papier collé elements in paint, the subject's face and sleeve in monochrome pointillism. (Note how the student's newspaper, *Le Journal*, has been shortened to "URNAL," to make a pun on "urinal.") The artist follows a similar procedure in his comical treatment of a roast chicken with slices of black truffles under its skin, thereby establishing that it is a *poularde demi-deuil* ("chicken in half-mourning"). Picasso uses the brown paper from which he fashioned the *faluche* for the skin of this well-roasted bird, and then does a second version in which he simulates the papier collé in paint on canvas that he has also cut up. No less illusionistic is the still life of a ham—carved to reveal the pink lean and the white fat, its bread-crumbed outside eye-foolingly and mouth-wateringly rendered in toast-colored sawdust. These paintings suggest that the artist was influenced by shop signs.

Picasso. *Student with Newspaper*, 1913. Oil and sand on canvas, 73×59.5 cm. Private collection.

Picasso also adds ashes to his pigment, notably in the *Vanitas (Guitar, Skull and Newspaper)* he painted early in 1914, that is to say, about the time of Eva's first cancer operation. A dark aura of ash-encrusted paint—darkness made tangible—surrounds the skull. The guitar that stands for Eva is composed of two areas of woodgraining: wavy at the back in imitation of hair; vaginal in front, to indicate "*trou ici*"—a point that a superimposed keyhole drives home. Picasso's eyes seem to look out from the sockets in the skull. Might this *Vanitas* have been painted on or around Ash Wednesday or in the course of Lent? The dates would fit, so would the subject, so would the ashes, which hint at Picasso's ability to get the liturgy to work for him—if need be, sacrilegiously.

Picasso also applies pointillism to his sculpture. In the spring of 1914, he made a wax of an absinthe glass, topped with the requisite sugar cube on a slotted spoon—a real spoon and, supposedly, the first example of what would come to be called a readymade. The artist had six bronzes cast. One is thickly coated with what looks like demerara sugar but is in fact sand. The rest are painted, inside and outside, in combinations of flat color and confetti-like dots. Each cast has a very different, faintly anthropomorphic character, which has prompted the theory that these sculptures are surrogate heads—*poètes maudits* or other victims of the green goddess, absinthe.[22] True, the spoon looks a bit like a hat worn at a rakish angle; and the protruding Boccioni-like flanges, which extend the planes of the glass into the space around it, can be seen as noses, brows, or lips. However, Picasso insisted that his glasses were just that: glasses.[23] Nor were they conceived as objets d'art. They may be made of bronze and impossible to drink from, but they are sui generis, every bit as real as the real thing. If there is an allegorical side to them, it is that glasses will come to stand for Eva, much as sound boxes of a guitar had done.

Picasso. *Absinthe Glass*, spring, 1914. Painted bronze with metal sugar strainer, ht: 21.6cm. The Museum of Modern Art, New York: Gift of Mrs. Bertram Smith.

"I'm out to fool the mind rather than the eye," Picasso told Françoise Gilot, "and that goes for sculpture too."[24] This is particularly true of the new series of constructions he embarked upon once he was installed in the new studio. Earlier in the year, Picasso had experimented with figures: a tiny paper sculpture, *Guitarist with Sheet Music*, which Gertrude Stein had rescued and put in a glass case; and the elaborate assemblage of a musician playing a real guitar (p. 253), which he had dismantled. This time round, he kept to still lifes—the usual cubist repertoire of objects with the addition of assorted polygonal dice and food (round wooden slices of sausage on square wooden slices of bread). However, as usual there are anatomical references. Picasso has cobbled his assemblages together out of the junk that littered his floor—bits of cut tin, odds and ends of wood, sheet metal, "bobble" fringe, chair legs and so forth—which he painted and sometimes pointillized with a roughness and readiness in keeping with the carpentry.

One or two of these constructions are free-standing, but most are reliefs, like their prototype, the cardboard guitar done the year before, except that they are less emphatically frontal. In his paradoxical way Picasso flattens his reliefs as if to turn them into paintings; at the same time he uses every device, short of perspective, to endow the things in his paintings with the heft of sculpture. These constructions, none of which was ever sold or replicated in more durable material, cannot compare with Picasso's more important paintings in stature or technical ingenuity—indeed, clumsiness is intrinsic to their nature. Nevertheless, they revolutionized a sculptor's concept of his materials. As Golding says, "they stand directly behind the whole Constructivist ethos."[25] And their influence continues to manifest itself almost a century later.

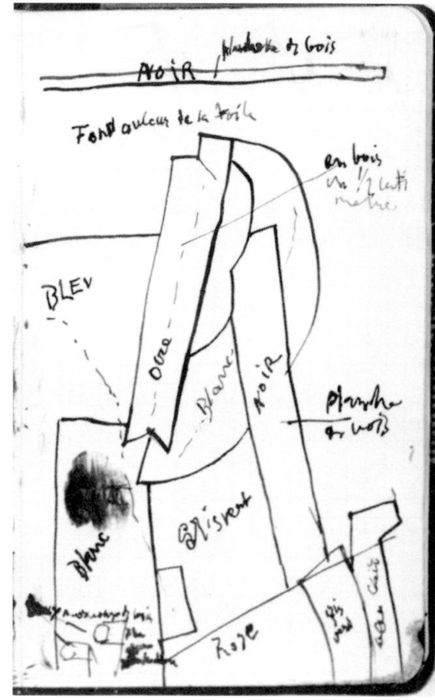

Picasso. *Head*, 1913. Pen and ink on sketchbook page, 13×8.5cm. Musée Picasso.

* * *

Around the time Picasso and Eva moved to the rue Schœlcher, Gertrude Stein and Alice Toklas returned from their summer vacation in Spain, all primed for a breakup with Leo. By the beginning of 1913, Alice had driven such a wedge between the brother and sister that reproachful notes were their principal form of communication. Leo no longer bothered with the famous Saturday soirées. As he reported to his sister in London, a few days after her thirty-ninth birthday (February 3, 1913): "A lot of Hungarians, Turks, Armenians & other jews came here Saturday to celebrate your birthday, but I told them it was the wrong day & that besides there

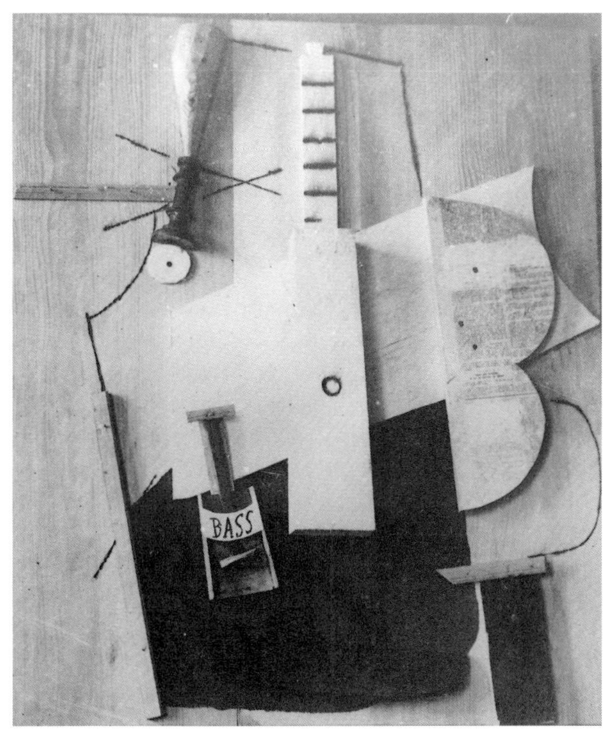

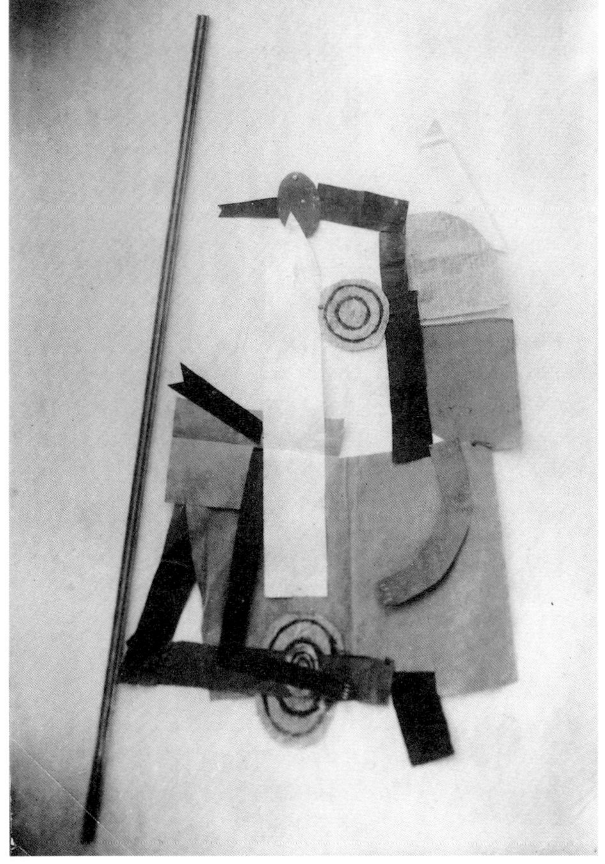

Above: Picasso. *Violin and Bottle on a Table*, 1915. Wood, string, nails, with paint and charcoal, ht: 45 cm. Musée Picasso.

Top left: Picasso. *Guitar and Bottle of Bass*, 1913. Construction, painted wood (original state), ht: 89.5 cm. Kahnweiler photograph: Galerie Louis Leiris.

Left: Picasso. *Guitar Player*, 1913. Construction (destroyed). Photograph by Picasso. Archives Picasso.

Gertrude Stein and Alice B. Toklas at 27 rue de Fleurus, 1914.

was no one at home."[26] A principal bone of contention was Picasso's genius. "As for Picasso's late [i.e., cubist] work," Leo wrote Mabel Foote Weeks, "it is for me utter abomination. Somebody asked me whether I didn't think it mad. I said sadly, 'No, it isn't as interesting as that. It's only stupid.'"[27] Leo felt much the same way about Gertrude's work. Mutual admiration and love had turned not so much to hate as to intense irritation. They should have gone their separate ways long before.

Despite the exasperation that Alice and her "brother-in-law" (as Gertrude liked Alice to think of Leo) felt for each other, Leo found her presence "a godsend, as it enabled the thing to happen without any explosion."[28] And it is indeed astonishing, given the siblings' delusions of intellectual infallibility and delight in taking offense, that they managed to split up their magnificent collection without annihilating each other. Since the principals were no longer speaking, Alice brokered the *partage*. It was finally arranged that Leo would keep all the Renoirs and Matisses; Gertrude would keep all the Picassos; and they would split the few remaining Cézannes. The only problem was Cézanne's little painting of apples, which they both coveted and Leo insisted on keeping. "I'm afraid you'll have to look upon the loss of the apples as an act of God," he wrote to her.[29] Picasso consoled her with a Cézannesque watercolor of an apple.[30]

Because the Steins had never been permitted to modernize—above all electrify—the *pavillon* on the rue de Fleurus, Gertrude and Alice looked around for somewhere else to live. Shortly before Christmas, 1913, they announced that they had found an apartment in that most *recherché* building, the Palais Royal (where Cocteau and Colette would end their days); whereupon their landlady's agent relented and allowed them to install electricity and make extensive structural changes, as befitted a moderately well-off but exceedingly ambitious couple who expected to entertain a great deal. "We found we liked it best here after all," Gertrude wrote Mabel Dodge, "and so we are making ourselves a bit more comfortable."[31]

Gertrude celebrated her sibling's departure in a 150-page screed about herself and Leo entitled *Two: Gertrude Stein and Her Brother*. Towards the end of this wodge of words, which was not published until after her death, Gertrude is carried away on the wings of egomania, which she confused and occasionally conflated with genius: "She felt what she felt when she did what she did when she worked. She worked when she did what she did. She felt what she felt when she did what she did . . ." and so on until a final holy-rolling litany in praise of herself: "She is the anticipation of expression having immaculate conception. She is the anticipation of crossing. She is the anticipation of regeneration. . . . She is the rising having been arisen. She is the convocation of anticipation and acceptation. She is the lamb and the lion."[32]

In anticipation of their split, Gertrude and Leo had decided in October to sell three of their greatest Picassos: *Young Acrobat on a Ball* (1905), *Nu à la draperie* (1907) and *Three Women* (1908). Kahnweiler gave them 20,000 francs as well as *Man with Guitar* (p. 279), painted earlier in the year at Céret. To fill some of the holes on her walls, she subsequently bought three Juan Gris still lifes from him; she also acquired Picasso's 1902 *Blue House*, after it failed to reach its reserve at the Peau de l'Ours sale. Kahnweiler made a large, quick profit—around one hundred percent—on the Stein deal. Within a matter of weeks he had sold the *Young Acrobat on a Ball* to Morozov for a record 16,000 francs and the other two paintings to Shchukin in time for them to be included in his 1913 catalog. Kahnweiler had valued *Three Women* earlier in the year at 20,000 francs, so he is unlikely to have sold it for less than 15,000. As for *Nu à la draperie*, there is a mention of 12,000 francs in one of his stockbooks, but we do not know whether this is what he asked or received. It is safe to say that Kahnweiler would not have taken less than 25,000 francs for these two masterpieces.

At the beginning of April, 1914, Leo left Paris to settle in Settignano, outside Florence. To Mabel Weeks he did not hide his bitterness:

> I'm going to Florence a simple minded person of the "Old School" without a single Picasso, hardly any Matisses, only two Cézanne paintings & some aquarelles, & 16 Renoirs. Rather an amusing baggage for a leader in the great modern fight. But que voulez vous. The fight is already won and lost. . . . Cézanne and Matisse have permanently interesting qualities, Picasso might have had if he had developed his gifts instead of exploiting those he did not possess. The general situation of painting here is loathsome with its cubico-futuristic tommy-rotting. I don't believe it can last very long, however, as its effectiveness is soon seen through & when no longer curious it becomes a bore. It is, even on the part of the most distinguished representative, nothing better than an exploration of ingenuity.[33]

To his sister Leo tried hard to be jocular: "I hope that we will all live happily ever after and maintain our respective and due proportions while sucking gleefully our respective oranges."[34] Gertrude retaliated with the malevolently valedictory gift of a set of kitchen knives.

* * *

The network of dealers that Kahnweiler had set up to promote his artists in Germany was working out so well that he was ready to tackle another as yet unexploited market, the United States. Hitherto Picasso's American sales had been left in the hands of friendly patrons like Gertrude Stein; or Frank Haviland, whose well-intentioned efforts to help with commissions and sales had a way of leaving the people involved, particularly the artist, dissatisfied; or Stieglitz, whose 291 Gallery (backed in part by Haviland's brother, Paul) had had little success with his Picasso shows. What was Kahnweiler to do? The 291 Gallery was too amateurishly run to satisfy his very businesslike standards. Besides, instead of using Kahnweiler as a principal source of Picassos, Stieglitz had tended to use the Haviland brothers. At Gertrude Stein's instigation, Kahnweiler chose as his representatives two young men from a rival camp, who were also her protégés: the sculptor Michael Brenner and a painter called Robert Coady—partners in the recently opened Washington Square Gallery and both fervent champions of the modern movement.

Washington Square Gallery. Photograph from *The Morning Telegraph* (New York), December 6, 1914.

Brenner's knobbly head of Gertrude Stein confirms her description of him: "The sculptor who never finished anything. . . . He had an admirable technique and a great many obsessions which kept him from work."[35] His job was to stay in Paris and assemble stock, Coady's to run things in New York. Coady, whose rich mother provided the backing, was the more interesting and enterprising of the partners. A sullen-looking Irishman with huge ears, red hair and "a smile . . . more grim than ingratiating,"[36] he venerated Cézanne to the extent of translating and publishing Vollard's monograph on him. And yet he saw Cézanne and the other modern artists he admired in the distorting light of his other obsession, tribal art. There was more than a touch of lunacy to his theories.

> Cézanne was not French, it was the Negro blood of his mother that gave his canvases most of their qualities. Picasso, who has attempted to carry on Cézanne's principles and who has based his work on the Congo, is of Spanish blood—blood that has been in contact and mixture with that of Africa—Gris too is Spanish and Rivera is [of] . . . Spanish origin. . . . There was a Negro element in nearly every known epoch.[37]

For all his quirks, Coady deserves to be recognized as a pioneer promoter not just of Kahnweiler's cubists but of all forms of primitivism and popular culture. Through Max Weber he had met the Douanier Rousseau and acquired paintings by him. Besides dealing in African and Oceanic sculpture, he was one of the earliest sponsors of American Negro art—children's drawings especially, of which he owned, according to Mabel Dodge Luhan, several thousand. Besides primitivism, Coady's "aesthetic vision encompassed modern technology."[38] Like Léger, he saw great beauty in industrial machines—steam-hammers, railroad engines, jib-cranes—as well as in such manifestations of pop culture as storefronts and billboards. To promote his *idées fixes*, Coady launched a magazine, *The Soil* (1916–17), which published pieces by Gertrude Stein, Charlie Chaplin and Nick Carter, paintings by Cézanne, Rousseau and MacDonald Wright as well as Picasso, and photographs of those fashionable new icons, black boxers and heavy machinery. But he put across his views in such a clumsily provocative way that he made more enemies than friends. Fellow modernists were a favorite target. Coady claimed that Toto, the Hippodrome clown, had more appeal than Picabia and Brancusi. Gleizes, he complained, suffered from "Metzingitis."

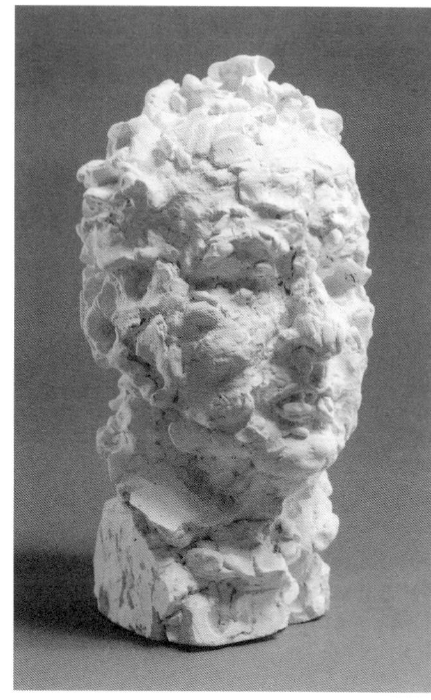

Michael Brenner. *Portrait Sketch of Gertrude Stein*, 1923–24. Plaster, ht: 39.1 cm. Hirshhorn Museum and Sculpture Garden, Smithsonian Institution: Gift of Mrs. Michael Brenner, 1977.

On February 1, 1914, Brenner signed a contract with Kahnweiler, whereby the Washington Square Gallery became the exclusive North American outlet for works by Picasso, Braque, Gris and Léger in exchange for a 2,500-franc guarantee. This was subsequently raised to 5,000 francs and, a month later, to 6,000 francs. The arrangement started with an informal show of drawings by Picasso along the lines of Stieglitz's 1911 exhibition. Since the shows that the Washington Square Gallery contracted to hold later in the year—ten works by Gris in October and ten works by Picasso in December—were canceled by the outbreak of war, Brenner and Coady have been written off as non-starters. However, once the contract was signed, Kahnweiler consigned several works to them; and after he fled to Switzerland, Picasso was induced to send them some more paintings, including the great 1914 painting of Eva in a feather boa on a green ground (p. 335), which they failed to sell. Brenner's fawning letters to Picasso, ingratiatingly spiced with boxing references, confirm that little came of these consignments, apart from the sale of three drawings in 1916.[39] During the war Coady's fellow Irishman and friend John Quinn became one of the gallery's best clients: he bought Gris's early masterpiece *L'Homme au café* and is likely to have been one of their few clients for Picasso. But Coady was too idealistic and at the same time too much of a curmudgeon to make a successful salesman. He preferred selling

Robert Coady. *Cosmopsychographical Organization*, 1916. Collage, reproduced in *The Soil*, December, 1916.

photographs of Kahnweiler's and Druet's stock to enthusiastic students—an activity that contributed to the dissemination of Picasso's (also Matisse's) work in America. The partnership was dissolved in 1918; Coady died three years later. None of his work survives except the illustration of a collage—a mishmash of cubism and fauvism in the form of Kahnweiler and Druet photographs—entitled *Cosmopsychological Organization.*[40] A suitable memorial to this confused man.

* * *

Report of the Peau de l'Ours sale in *La Revue Française*, March 15, 1914; from the cuttings collection of Kahnweiler's gallery.

Although the American market for Picasso's work did not get going until after the war, the French market took off in the last few months of peace. Since the 16,000-franc price that Morozov paid Kahnweiler for *Young Acrobat on a Ball* was not known to the general public, the 12,650 francs that a Picasso fetched at a Paris auction on March 2, 1914, was assumed to be a record and made much of in the press. The painting in question was the famous 1905 *Saltimbanques* that André Level had bought through Moline and Sagot for 1,000 francs in 1908. Level had been acting on behalf of the Peau de l'Ours, a collectors' consortium which he and twelve partners had formed in 1904. Each shareholder contributed 250 francs a year for ten years to provide Level with an annual budget of 2,750 francs with which to buy modern pictures.[41] The group's name derived from La Fontaine's fable "The Bear and the Two Companions," about two trappers who sell a furrier the skin of a huge bear before they have actually caught it. The bear evades capture and whispers to one of the trappers: "Don't sell the bear's skin [*la peau de l'ours*] until you've caught him." The investors had agreed to sell up the collection after ten years. Hence the auction at the Hôtel Drouot. Since Level was an enterprising man with excellent family, social and business connections in the *haute bourgeoisie* and had a flair for public relations, he found no difficulty drumming up extensive press coverage and turning the sale into a major social event. There was a lavish catalog and the Drouot's two best galleries had been spruced up, hung more attractively than usual and filled with flowers. The principal painters involved, Picasso and Matisse, refrained from attending the sale, but the art world was there in force: collectors such as Lefèvre, Kann and Dutilleul; critics including Apollinaire, Salmon, Raynal and the reactionary but popular Tabarant; French dealers like Vollard, Druet and Bernheim-Jeune; German dealers like Kahnweiler, Uhde, Flechtheim and Thannhauser; and not least a smart young curator, Paul Jamot, from the Louvre, whose presence made for much conjecture. There were also *amateurs* from *le tout Paris*, among them Prince Antoine Bibesco, the Antoine de la Rochefoucaulds and Paul Poiret.

For the art market the Peau de l'Ours sale was indeed a historic occasion. It was the first time a major group of modern works had come up on the block; what is more, they sold exceedingly well. However, Salmon goes much too far when he sees the sale in terms of the "*bataille d'Hernani*"—the riot that broke out at the first night of Victor Hugo's anti-monarchist play in 1830 and helped overthrow Charles X and establish the concept of an avant-garde.[42] The Peau de l'Ours sale went off peacefully. When Picasso's *Saltimbanques* (estimated at 8,000 francs) fetched the highest price, 12,650 francs—over twelve times what it had cost—far

Picasso. *Bowl of Fruit*, fall, 1908. Tempera on panel, 21×27cm. Öffentliche Kunstsammlung Basel, Kunstmuseum.

from there being any boos, the public applauded. Had *Les Demoiselles d'Avignon* been up for sale, things might have been very different, but the *Saltimbanques* was a symbolist painting, and by 1914 symbolism was far from shocking. Picasso's *Three Dutch Girls*, likewise painted in 1905, also did much better than expected: 5,720 francs. And the only cubist painting in the sale, a little panel entitled *Bowl of Fruit* (1908), was cubist in little else but its date; otherwise Poiret might not have paid 1,250 francs for it. The fourteen Matisses in the sale were marginally more "difficult," but on the whole Level had played safe, as befitted a canny businessman at the head of an investment group.

Kahnweiler rushed from the saleroom to give Picasso the news: his twelve works had made just under 20,000 francs. Since Level had taken the innovative step of paying the artists twenty percent of the proceeds—what was known as the *droit de suite* (it would become law six years later)—the artist was due just under 4,000 francs in royalties. Meanwhile Heinrich Thannhauser, who had bought the *Saltimbanques* for his Munich gallery, was telling the press that he would have paid twice as much. Mere sales talk! The dealer would never have bid as high as he did if his progressive nephew (and future partner), Siegfried Rosengart, had not shamed him into doing so. When the threat of war ruled out hopes of a quick profit, Thannhauser accused Rosengart of landing the gallery with a white elephant. "Look how I'm stuck with this painting," he moaned.[43] As soon as he could, he unloaded the *Saltimbanques* for no more than it had cost.

Picasso. *Bottle of Bass, Wineglass, Packet of Tobacco and Visiting Card*, 1914. Pasted papers and pencil on paper, 24×30.5cm. Musée National d'Art Moderne, Centre Georges Pompidou, Paris.

The publicity generated by the Peau de l'Ours prices—above all the fact that investors in the tontine had quadrupled their money in ten years—boosted the sales of modern paintings, especially those handled by Kahnweiler and his German confrères. It also enhanced Picasso's fame, and not only in France. The news was picked up by Spanish and American papers, and for the rest of his life the artist would suffer from being perceived as a celebrity. To thank Level, Picasso gave him a papier collé (including a bottle of Bass, a wineglass and a tobacco packet) personalized, as it were, with the recipient's visiting card, whose turned-down corner indicates that the caller has found nobody at home. In its humor, thoughtfulness and faintly mocking courtesy, this gift is typical of the artist. In 1918 Picasso would do an Ingresque portrait of Level; he would give him things to sell when he opened the Galerie Percier in 1925; and he would contribute a frontispiece—of what else but *saltimbanques*?—to his *Souvenirs d'un collectionneur* (1959).

Political reactions to the Peau de l'Ours sale were less reassuring. One ultraconservative newspaper, *Paris-Midi*, played on its readers' paranoia by claiming that Thannhauser's purchase of the *Saltimbanques* was part of a German campaign to demoralize France. "The great prices were attained by the grotesque and crude works of undesirable foreigners, and it was the Germans who paid or pushed up these prices," according to *Paris-Midi*'s columnist, Maurice Delcourt.[44] Modern art was the Germans' secret weapon, Delcourt asserted. Young French painters, who should know better, were being suborned into

> imitating the imitative Picasso, who turns everything into pastiche; finding nothing left to imitate, they sink into the mire of "*le bluff cubiste*." Thus the order and decorum of our national tradition will disappear little by little to

Picasso. *Portrait of André Level*, 1918. Pencil on paper. Private collection.

> the great joy of Mr. Thannhauser and his compatriots, who will soon stop buying Picassos; instead they will loot the Louvre, which will no longer be capable of defending itself against the effete snobs and intellectual anarchists who serve as their unwitting accomplices. The money that [the Germans] squandered yesterday [at the Peau de l'Ours sale] will have been well spent.[45]

These inflammatory words fell on ears still smarting from the outcome of the Dreyfus case: ears only too ready to believe that Jews and Germans were manning a Trojan horse all set to subvert French culture. The success of Kahnweiler's *Ostpolitik* undoubtedly encouraged chauvinist paranoia. Picasso, who had an acute sense of danger, tried to persuade his dealer to take out French nationality—unsuccessfully: the obligation to do military service, which naturalization involved, was incompatible with his pacifist beliefs. Picasso's prognostications were to prove well founded. The view of cubism as a German manifestation would come back to haunt him again and again during the war, culminating in the jeers of "filthy Huns" from philistines and xenophobes at the first night of *Parade*, in 1917. Picasso, Satie and Cocteau would be pilloried as "*les trois boches*."

* * *

Little or no information about the course of Eva's illness has survived, because she was determined to keep it a secret. We know the name of the specialist she consulted: Dr. Rousseau, 123, boulevard Montparnasse. We know that she had an operation sometime in the first half of 1914—presumably before leaving for Avignon in mid-June—and that it was not in the long run a success. We also know that the medical expenses were considerable. Picasso liked to shock people by saying that he should have left Eva with Marcoussis and landed *him* with her doctor's bills.[46] Once again, Picasso's misogyny comes across as a macho pretense, a typically Andalusian device to conceal his very unmacho compassion. Of course he cared.

We do not know the nature of Eva's cancer. The nailed-on breasts of *Woman in an Armchair* might suggest a mastectomy; even that the painting was in the nature of an ex-voto. (One can see why this latter-day Saint Agatha—the saint whose emblem is a pair of amputated breasts—was singled out for blasphemous veneration by the surrealists.) However, the emphasis on Eva's breasts is just as likely to have been a matter of fixation or cubist contrivance. Another possibility: given her bronchial attack in 1913 and the official story that she died of tuberculosis, Eva may have suffered from lung cancer. Whatever the cause, her ill-health is mirrored in her lover's work of the next two years. Flights of lightheartedness and rococo fantasy should not be taken at their face value. Picasso's use of sharp, bright colors is usually indicative of a heightened state of nervousness or of sexuality gone sour or sad or twisted. It seldom implies contentment.

20

Collectors, Dealers and the German Connection

D.-H. Kahnweiler on the terrace of the Hôtel Roma, 1913. Photograph by Braque. Archives Kahnweiler: Galerie Louise Leiris.

To enhance the exclusivity of his artists Kahnweiler never allowed Picasso, or any others in his stable (except, on one occasion, Braque), to have an exhibition in his gallery. Nor would he permit their reputations to be contaminated by showing alongside the Salon cubists. As a result, Picasso's work was less familiar to the Parisian art world than his memorably exotic name. Only the lucky few who had the entrée to his studio or the Steins' *pavillon*, or who visited Kahnweiler's to see what might be hanging on his walls or available in his photograph albums (much of the dealer's stock was usually out on consignment), were able to follow the progress of his increasingly hermetic style. Articles about his painting—not least by friends—were few, and seldom illuminating. Reproductions of his work were also rare; it would be another twenty years before an art journal would chronicle his current production. Picasso liked the reclusive image that Kahnweiler devised for him. It accorded with his increasingly hermetic life and work. Not for him the posturing and boasting of the lesser cubists, or, worse, the self-promoting antics and manifestos of the futurists.

Why, given his relative invisibility, would Picasso be perceived in modernist circles on both sides of the Atlantic as the hero of the modern movement, and why would he no less widely be perceived in reactionary circles as a charlatan, bolshevik or clown? The answer to both questions has to do with the success of Kahnweiler's *Ostpolitik*: his strategy of getting progressive young dealers like himself to put on exhibitions in Germany and thus establish a constituency and a market for his artists outside France. Built into the success of this strategy was a dangerous side effect. The more acclaim cubism generated in Germany, the more hostility it generated in France. Then as now, chauvinism and anti-Semitism went hand in hand with philistinism, and well before war broke out, the bigots who had hounded Dreyfus came to perceive cubism as a German-Jewish plot to undermine French culture. Were not the principal promoters of this subversive new cult mostly German Jews: Kahnweiler, Flechtheim and Thannhauser?

However, before going into the ramifications of Kahnweiler's *Ostpolitik*, let us take a look at the new breed of French Picasso collectors. They were few in number and all from the same prosperous Parisian milieu, the *haute bourgeosie*. The doyen of this group was not so much a collector as an animator and eventually a dealer, André Level. Notwithstanding a

Opposite: D.-H. Kahnweiler, fall, 1910. Photograph by Picasso. Archives Picasso.

mundane job as managing director of the Marseille Dock Company, Level had great taste and perspicacity—qualities that would recommend him to Picasso. An auction addict since the age of eighteen, he had started buying modern art as early as 1895, under the aegis of Vollard and the Bernheims. In due course his enthusiasm rubbed off on his three brothers—Emile, a banker, Jacques, an industrialist, and Maurice, a lawyer—and some cousins, Baron Curnieu and two banker brothers, Raoul and Max Pellequer. (Max would become Picasso's financial advisor and put together a major collection of his work, including the Blue period *Celestina* portrait). Level would start them off with Berthe Weill, Sagot or his favorite dénicheur, Lucien Moline, and then take them to see Vollard and Kahnweiler. After the famous Peau de l'Ours sale, he became one of Picasso's closest advisors.

Modigliani. *Roger Dutilleul,* 1918. Oil on canvas, 100×65cm. Private collection. This and the paintings on the opposite page were in Dutilleul's collection.

The most dedicated of Kahnweiler's Parisian Picasso collectors was a reserved young man called Roger Dutilleul: "The quintessential French haut bourgeois [Kahnweiler wrote], very enlightened, very fastidious, belonging to a vanished era but profoundly sympathetic."[1] Though well connected, Dutilleul was not particularly rich. He had started collecting while still a student. Later, he entered the cement business; and for the rest of his life most of his income went on modern painting. By sheer chance he had walked into Kahnweiler's gallery soon after it opened and had been delighted to find things he could afford. Low prices were the original attraction; however, he soon developed a discriminating eye for the most advanced art of the period. Dutilleul lived simply with a print-collector brother and never married, preferring to devote all his resources to collecting. "My pictures are my children," he used to say.[2] His other interests were stamp collecting and reports of billiard matches. Evidently an obsessive man: a kindly Cousin Pons.[3]

Dutilleul's small rooms were crammed with pictures: hung floor to ceiling, piled on furniture, stacked in closets. Frames were either simple wooden *baguettes* or old moldings that he refinished to match the paintings. Early on, he got rid of his larger canvases and concentrated on works that were smaller but the pick of the latest cubist crop. The first artists Dutilleul bought from Kahnweiler were Vlaminck and Derain, but he soon graduated to Picasso and Braque. Picasso would always be his hero, because he preferred art that was raw, instinctive and intense. He dismissed Matisse as decorative; and although he regarded himself as Kahnweiler's pupil, he never gave in to his cajoling and bought Juan Gris—too cerebral. By 1914, Dutilleul had amassed at least twenty-five Picassos and almost as many Braques, painted between 1907 and 1914: a cubist microcosm. And when he came home on leave during the war, he continued to buy from the dealers who had taken Kahnweiler's place. Thanks to the generosity of his industrialist nephew, Jean Masurel, much of this superb collection has been bequeathed to the Musée d'Art Moderne, Villeneuve-d'Ascq, at Lille.

No less important as a collector of cubism was André Lefèvre, who came from the same enlightened background as his friend Dutilleul, but was richer and less ascetic. Lefèvre loved literature as well as painting and assembled a major nineteenth- and twentieth-century library—including a batch of Proust's corrected galleys—which he kept in a bookcase of Balzac's. In 1907, André Level took Lefèvre to Brussels, then the principal

Braque. *La Roche-Guyon*, 1909. Oil on canvas, 73×60 cm. Musée d'Art Moderne, Villeneuve d'Ascq: Geneviève and Jean Masurel Gift.

Picasso. *Bottles and Fish*, 1909. Oil on canvas, 73×60 cm. Musée d'Art Moderne, Villeneuve d'Ascq: Geneviève and Jean Masurel Gift.

Picasso. *The Game of Chess*, fall, 1911. Oil on canvas, 33×41 cm. Private collection.

market for *art nègre*, to launch him as a collector of tribal art; and in 1910, he introduced him to Kahnweiler, who started him off buying works by Picasso, Braque and Derain.

Lefèvre did not have the money to splurge until after World War I. Success on the stock market enabled him to become one of the biggest buyers of cubist painting, particularly at the sales (1921–23) of Kahnweiler's sequestered stock, where he acquired numerous works by Braque, Gris and Léger, as well as his favorite, Picasso. A major influence on his taste was Max Jacob, whose drawings and manuscripts he collected and later donated to the museum at Quimper, in Brittany, the poet's birthplace. By 1927, when he was forty-five, Lefèvre had made enough money to retire and devote all his time to collecting. For the rest of his life, this reserved man continued to amass works by the modern masters he had been one of the first to appreciate; he also invested heavily in the younger generation. By the time he died, in 1965, Lefèvre owned more than three hundred works, including fifty-two Picassos. Thirty of these were left to the Musée d'Art Moderne and other French museums, on condition that they be reunited and exhibited every thirty years.[4] The remainder of the collection was auctioned in Paris at three successive sales (1966–67), which established new records for cubist paintings. The art world's dawning perception of cubism as the most gilt-edged of modern movements dates from these sales.

Picasso. *Repose*, 1908. Oil on canvas, 81×65cm (formerly in Lefèvre's collection). The Museum of Modern Art, New York.

Lefèvre's executor, Alfred Richet,[5] was another cultivated businessman—a collector, though in a more modest way than Lefèvre. As well as works by Picasso, he bought gouaches by Max Jacob. (Buyers of Jacob's amateurish drawings got a shot at acquiring Picasso's gifts to the poet.) Richet, whom Jacob acclaimed as "an admirable prose stylist,"[6] deserves recognition for two articles in *L'Intransigeant* (November and December, 1928), which help us understand what motivated him and many of his friends—all pillars of the Parisian bourgeoisie—to buy avant-garde art. They collected out of a desire for intellectual or spiritual fulfillment, Richet said—not acquisitiveness. Though they were exceedingly shrewd about money—and in some cases exceedingly tight with it—such men as Richet despised speculation and the notion of art as investment. That it might be a means of acquiring status never occurred to them. Buy for adventure, even fun, was Richet's message, never for profit. How right he proved. Discriminating collectors who buy out of sheer love do far better than those who buy for investment. Even allowing for devaluation, rising costs of insurance and threats of a capital levy, Kahnweiler's early clients would find that they had made an enormously profitable investment: Richet, Dutilleul and Lefèvre would live to see many of their Picassos worth more than a hundred times what they had paid.

Derain. *Portrait of Paul Poiret*, 1914. Oil on canvas, 101×73cm. Musée de Grenoble.

Two other Parisian collectors, from the very different world of *la haute couture*, deserve mention: Paul Poiret and Jacques Doucet. Both these men had started by building up magnificent collections of *dix-huitième* paintings and decorative arts. (Indeed Doucet was probably the greatest collector in the field since Lord Hertford assembled what came to be known as the Wallace Collection.) In 1912 they both decided to sell their eighteenth-century holdings and invest the proceeds in contemporary art. Poiret's taste ran to *arts décoratifs*: Raoul Dufy's textiles and miniature ceramic gardens, and Bakst's Ballets Russes extravaganzas. However, he bought some early Picassos out of the studio and at least one cubist painting (at the Peau de l'Ours sale). In 1916 Poiret would also arrange for the first public showing of *Les Demoiselles d'Avignon*. His sister Germaine Bongard turned part of her dress shop into a gallery dealing in cubist painting.[7] His other sister, Nicole Groult, also dabbled in dealing, when she was not promoting her lover, Marie Laurencin.

Doucet, on the other hand, put together one of the greatest collections of modern art in France (from Manet and Seurat to Picasso, Chirico and Duchamp), as well as the world's most comprehensive library of nineteenth- and twentieth-century literature, manuscripts and archival material. His advisors, André Breton and André Suarès, persuaded Doucet to concentrate on masterpieces. As well as acquiring *Les Demoiselles d'Avignon*, sight unseen, from the artist for 25,000 francs (paid in monthly installments of 2,000 francs), he owned several other Picassos: a major Rose period *Head of Harlequin* (1905), two superb cubist works, *Man with a Guitar* (1912) and *Ma Jolie* (1914), and many more.[8] Picasso would never forgive Doucet for "stealing" the *Demoiselles* from him; nor would he forgive himself for accepting 25,000 francs for it when, he claimed, he had turned down 200,000 francs in 1916. How could he have allowed this dressmaker to get the better of him? He refused to visit Doucet and see how well the painting looked on his staircase, and vehemently turned down the old man's offer to buy *La Danse* in 1925.[9]

Picasso. *Portrait of Jacques Doucet*, 1915. Black chalk on paper, 31.3×24.3cm. Musée Picasso.

* * *

By far the finest collection of Picasso's work in France belonged to foreigners: Leo and Gertrude Stein. Thanks to Gertrude's promotional flair —"hurrah for *gloire*" was her battle cry—the ensemble that her brother Leo had begun and she would complete proved to be the most effective vehicle for the dissemination of Picasso's reputation in Europe and, by word of mouth, in the United States. Nevertheless, the Steins' collection could not compare in magnitude with that of their principal rival, the Muscovite Maecenas Sergei Shchukin. True, the impact of his paintings was mostly confined to Moscow, but Moscow was becoming one of the most progressive art centers in the world. By opening his palace to the public every Sunday (spring, 1909, onwards) and exposing Russian artists like Tatlin and Malevich to the latest Picassos and Matisses, Shchukin helped them to make a major contribution to the modern movement.

Shchukin's Tolstoyan decision to share his aesthetic responses with others was prompted by grief. In 1907, his first wife had died very suddenly; then a brother had poisoned himself; and two sons, one a deaf-mute, had committed suicide.[10] In his loneliness this religious man (he was an "Old Believer") had adopted two orphans of the war with Japan, and he took to spending hours discussing his paintings with visitors and the students he allowed to make copies. Picasso's art belongs in cathedrals, Shchukin said,[11] hence the austerity and spirituality of some of his acquisitions.

Until war broke out, in 1914, Shchukin would buy an average of ten Picassos a year, many of cardinal importance. But his understanding of the artist's work did not always keep pace with the great forward leaps he was making, as Picasso complained to Gertrude Stein (September 18,

1912): "The day of my departure I ran into Monsieur Shchukin at Kahnweiler's; he has not yet bought the big painting like the large red one you have. He does not understand more recent work."[12] Within a few months, however, Shchukin's eye had sharpened and his taste toughened, and the last purchases he made before war broke out were nothing if not daring. In the end his collection covered most of Picasso's early phases, except for the brush with abstraction in 1910.

Shchukin was a dedicated proselytizer for modern art, always pressuring his more worldly friend Ivan Morozov to follow his adventurous lead. Morozov was the last survivor of three gifted brothers—Russian Rockefellers—who had inherited an enormous textile and banking fortune. Mikhail, the eldest, had been famously protean: an able historian who lectured at Moscow University; a man-about-town whose autobiographical play ran for many years; a gambler who once lost a million gold rubles at a sitting; and a progressive collector, who died (aged thirty-four, in 1904) owning some of the finest Tahitian Gauguins as well as other post-impressionist masterpieces. Arseny, the youngest brother, was no less of a phenomenon. At a party he gave for an entire regiment, he had the caviar served off a gigantic silver tray held by a stuffed bear.[13] And then one day in 1909, while he and his brother were waiting for Maurice Denis to supervise the hanging of some of his paintings, Arseny casually picked up a revolver that was lying around. "What if I were to kill myself?" he asked and blew his brains out.[14]

Picasso. Study for *Still Life with Skull*, 1908. Watercolor, gouache and pencil on paper, 32×24cm. Pushkin Museum of Fine Art, Moscow. This and the paintings opposite were in Shchukin's collection.

Ivan, the middle brother, was more conventional. He had first collected only Russian painting, starting with the nineteenth-century "Wanderers" and ending, just before the Revolution, with Larionov, Goncharova and Chagall. He ultimately owned more than 430 Russian works. As if to continue his dead brother's initiative, Morozov embarked on a second collection, devoted to Mikhail's favorite post-impressionists. And over the next ten years, he acquired (mostly from Vollard) thirteen Cézannes, several Gauguins and Van Goghs. All most commendable, but Shchukin felt that Morozov should advance more boldly into the modern field, so in 1908 he introduced him to Matisse and masterminded his acquisition of the three great Moroccan compositions of 1913. Shchukin also urged him to buy Picasso, but Morozov was not as open-minded as his mentor (nor as public-spirited: he preferred to show his collection to fellow tycoons, students complained). And he limited himself to three Picassos, two of them masterpieces: the cubist *Portrait of Vollard* (p. 173) and that key work of the Rose period, the *Young Acrobat on a Ball.*

* * *

Picasso's other great pre-1914 patron was a Czech: Dr. Vincenc Kramář. This cultivated son of a rich Prague businessman had studied art history in Vienna under the eminent Adolf von Hildebrandt and written a thesis on thirteenth-century Bohemian Gothic and also worked on Czech baroque. Far from inhibiting his understanding of modernism—the case with Bode and Berenson and most art historians of the day—knowledge of the art of the past made Kramář all the more discriminating about contemporary painting.[15] His enthusiasm for the modern movement had been nurtured by his studies of architectural history; also by the revelation of Gauguin. Surprisingly, Kramář did not visit Paris until 1910 (at the age of thirty-

Picasso. *Woman with Fan*, spring, 1909. Oil on canvas, 100×81 cm. Pushkin Museum of Fine Art, Moscow.

Picasso. *Table with Violin and Glasses*, 1913. Oil on canvas, 65×54 cm. State Hermitage Museum, St. Petersburg.

The Picasso Room in Sergei Shchukin's Moscow palace, 1913.

Vincenc Kramář, c. 1910. Národní Galerie, Prague. The paintings below and opposite formed part of his collection.

Picasso. *Head of Harlequin*, 1908. Gouache on paper, 62×47.5cm. Národní Galerie, Prague.

three), when he bought Derain's Cézannesque *View of Montreuil* (1909) from Kahnweiler. The following year, he focused on cubism. His first Picasso was the gouache of a harlequin (1908) that the artist had contributed to an auction (May 22, 1911) to raise money for a monument to Cézanne. Four days later, Kramář visited Vollard and bought a cast of the great 1909 head of Fernande. On May 31, he went to Kahnweiler's and snapped up three more cubist Picassos and a Braque.[16] These acquisitions would cement a lifelong friendship with Kahnweiler. Henceforth, whenever a new batch of Picasso's work arrived, the dealer would notify Kramář, who would take the next train from Prague and, the following morning, be waiting outside the gallery before it opened. In November, 1911, Kramář bought five Picassos that Kahnweiler had just received and then went on to Vollard's and bought three more—rather more cheaply.[17]

By 1914 Kramář had assembled a major cubist collection: some twenty paintings, a group of drawings and prints, and the bronze by Picasso, as well as works by Braque, Léger and Gris. He insisted that his collection—particularly the Picassos—did not reflect his personal preference. His goal was a didactic ensemble that would educate the public "to see in cubism the most important step in the formation of the avant-garde of our time. . . . I wanted to show that cubism is not a studio game . . . [but] a serious attempt to discover a new plastic concept rooted in reality."[18] As well as setting an example of enlightened, modern patronage, Kramář tirelessly promoted cubism in the local art journals he edited and exhibitions he organized.[19] He was no less active in his encouragement of Czech cubists: Filla, Kubišta, Procházka and Gutfreund. They should take their cue from the leaders of the pack, he insisted, not the *Ersatzkubisten* (the Salon cubists).[20]

Besides making regular visits to Kahnweiler's and Vollard's,[21] Kramář kept track of the latest developments in cubism by checking out the artists' studios, particularly Picasso's. The artist would communicate news of these visits to his small band of collectors so as to play them off against each other. As we have seen, in 1912, when he was manipulating Gertrude Stein into buying again, he told her that Kramář had been by and coveted the *Ma Jolie* that she was after. At the same time Kahnweiler's constant invocation of Kramář's name struck Picasso and Braque as excessive, and they teased the dealer with jokes at the Czech's expense.

The Kramář archive includes countless letters from Kahnweiler but only one from Picasso: a letter of May 27, 1911, introducing the collector to Ignacio Zuloaga, whose El Grecos he wanted to see.[22] Kramář was an associate of the art historian Max Dvořák, a pioneer in the rediscovery of El Greco, and had evidently spotted the umbilical link between him and Picasso. Did he, one wonders, realize how the *Demoiselles* related to the *Apocalyptic Vision*?

* * *

Picasso had little success with English collectors. The only one of Kahnweiler's artists to find favor there was Derain. His tasteful blend of modernity and traditionalism appealed to British art lovers. Picasso was too much for them, even the Blue and Rose periods. Only three or four of his cubist works found buyers, in each case someone associated with Bloomsbury. In October, 1911, Clive Bell—the engaging country gentleman

Picasso. *Still Life with Tenora*, 1911. Oil on canvas, 61×50cm. Národní Galerie, Prague.

Left: Picasso. *Woman in an Armchair*, spring, 1909. Oil on canvas, 100×79.5cm. Private collection, New York.

Above: Picasso. *Violin and Anchor (Souvenir du Havre)*, May, 1912. Oil on oval canvas, 81×54cm. Národní Galerie, Prague.

Left: Picasso. *Woman in an Armchair*, spring, 1910. Oil on canvas, 94×75cm. Národní Galerie, Prague.

Picasso. *Head of a Man*, 1913. Oil, charcoal, ink and crayon on sized paper, 62×46.5cm (formerly in Roger Fry's collection). Richard S. Zeisler, New York.

turned art critic—and his wife, Vanessa, bought *Jars with Lemon* of 1907 (much like the painting Picasso had exchanged with Matisse) from Kahnweiler for four pounds.[23] A year later, Vanessa Bell persuaded one of her admirers, Harry Norton, a Cambridge mathematician, to purchase a 1910–11 still life,[24] one of thirteen Picassos loaned by Kahnweiler to the Grafton Gallery's second post-impressionist exhibition, which Bell and Roger Fry had organized. The exhibition had generated a lot of *Punch* jokes and philistine protests but, apart from Norton's acquisition, very few sales. Bell also prevailed upon another "Bloomsberry," Goldsworthy Lowes Dickinson, to buy a fine drawing for Picasso's *Woman Combing Her Hair* (1906). Roger Fry was more adventurous. The *Head of a Man* of 1913,[25] which he had acquired from Kahnweiler and included in his second (1914) Grafton Group exhibition, was barely figurative. This cautious man had been softened up by Gertrude Stein, whom he would call on whenever he visited Paris. Fry's onetime mistress, the celebrated Bloomsbury hostess Lady Ottoline Morrell, also owned some fine Picasso drawings, but I have been unable to identify them. She is likely to have bought these in 1909 on a trip to Paris under the aegis of the rich Chicagoan Mrs. Emily Chadbourne, who took her to see her friends the Steins, also Picasso, Matisse and their dealers.

For British intellectuals who chose to see themselves as avant-garde, this was a shameful record—especially shameful in that, when war broke out in 1914, at least half the Picassos in England were hanging on the walls of the German embassy (see p. 323).[26] "The English audience . . . haven't got the sensibility to form," Roger Fry wrote to Gertrude Stein (March 5, 1913). "They'll take one's ideas as pure ideas but they can't fit them onto the picture at all."[27] The situation would be all too briefly redeemed, twenty years later, by Douglas Cooper, who assembled a collection that charted the development of cubism, year by year, subject by subject, medium by medium, through the work of its four principal artists: Picasso and Braque, Gris and Léger. England was not worthy of his collection, Cooper decided, and removed it to France.

* * *

Picasso. *Portrait of Dr. Claribel Cone*, 1922. Pencil on paper, 64×49.4cm. The Baltimore Museum of Art: Cone Collection.

As for American collectors of Picasso (in the United States as opposed to Paris), they, too, were few and far between. The situation would have been very different if Hamilton Easter Field's commission of eleven cubist panels had ever materialized. Field's failure of nerve was a tragedy for America as well as for cubism. Such interest in Picasso as there was can usually be traced back to the Steins. The artist had supplied Gertrude with a portfolio of drawings (mostly 1904–06) on sale or return, from which she kept friends like Harriet Levy and the Cone sisters supplied.[28] The Cones, whom she had started on their collection, would prove a disappointment. After 1907, they virtually ceased buying Picasso. Like Leo Stein, they were horrified at Picasso's "tommyrot" cubism.[29] Instead, they took up Matisse, and for the rest of their lives would remain faithful to him. Picasso, who developed into a more assiduous salesman for his work than he liked to admit, tried to woo them back in January, 1908, by sending them, via Gertrude, a present of a somewhat tubby drawing of himself, inscribed "*Bonjour Mlle. Cone.*" To judge by her nauseatingly folksy reply to Gertrude, Etta Cone took this as a joke: "Here comes your dear old letter, with the delightful sketch of Picasso and Fernando's [*sic*] nice wishes. Dey am sure nice folk . . . and tell Pablo that Fernando ought massage his tummy into shape again."[30] Apart from the 1905 portraits of Leo and of Michael's son, Allan, the 1922 portrait of Claribel and some minor early drawings and bronzes, the only Picasso of any consequence they would buy after 1907 was the pretty-pretty *Mother and Child* of 1922.

Even the rapacious Dr. Albert Barnes of Philadelphia, who made wholesale acquisitions in Paris in the years preceding World War I, owed much of his interest in Picasso and Matisse to the Steins. Barnes had been introduced to them by the American painter Alfred Maurer. The daunting doctor and the no less daunting Gertrude are both credited with bettering each other: he supposedly chased her round a dining-room table, "in pursuit not so much of her as of a canvas by Picasso and won it at a thumping good price";[31] she supposedly made him buy two Matisses when he had wanted only one. Barnes is also rumored to have offered Michael Stein $5,000 for a large Picasso and been rebuffed.[32] Realizing that he had met his match in Gertrude and Michael, the doctor befriended the unbusinesslike Leo and paid him to be his "advisor." After extorting most of Leo's remaining treasures for derisory prices, Barnes dispensed with his services.

Picasso. *Violin, Sheet Music and Bottle*, spring, 1914. Oil on oval canvas, 42×27cm. Barnes Foundation, Merion, Pa.

In 1913 Barnes bought some fine Blue and Rose period paintings from Vollard (including the vast *Blind Flower Seller*, for which he paid only $300). He subsequently boasted of having acquired sixteen drawings of 1905 circus scenes directly from Picasso for a dollar apiece.[33] The following year he also acquired five fine little cubist Picassos from Kahnweiler.[34] Under the influence of Leo Stein, Barnes would soon repudiate cubism, in two articles for *Arts and Decoration*.[35] In the first of these he hails Picasso "as a great artist and a great painter" (and Matisse as "a greater artist than painter"), and boasts of being "the first in America to hang Matisse and Picasso in a collection."[36] Although Barnes sees Picasso's style as "a welding of the essences of Greco and Cézanne," he dismisses cubism as "having fun with the public with cubes." In the second article, "Cubism: Requiescat in Pace," malice and vanity have blinded the doctor. Cubism was a "fiasco," the paintings "academic, repetitive, banal, dead"—unless of course they belonged to him, as he pointed out in yet another harangue. So erratic was Barnes's taste that he later resumed buying cubist Picassos.[37] However, his eye for Picasso never equaled his eye for Matisse.

Besides collectors like Barnes and the Cones, a number of young American painters discovered modern art on the walls of the rue de Fleurus *pavillon*. Admission to the Steins' Saturday evenings was no problem. "For form's sake and in Paris, you have to have a formula," Gertrude said, "everybody was supposed to be able to mention the name of somebody who had told them about it. It was a mere form, really anybody could come in."[38] The contacts that young Max Weber made through the Steins—with Picasso, Apollinaire and Douanier Rousseau—earned him the mantle of a prophet back in New York. His principal convert to the Picasso cult was the photographer and avant-garde impresario Alfred Stieglitz.[39] Weber had taught him everything, Stieglitz said.[40] It was largely at Weber's prompting that in March, 1911, he put on the first exhibition of Picasso's work in New York: eighty-three drawings and watercolors

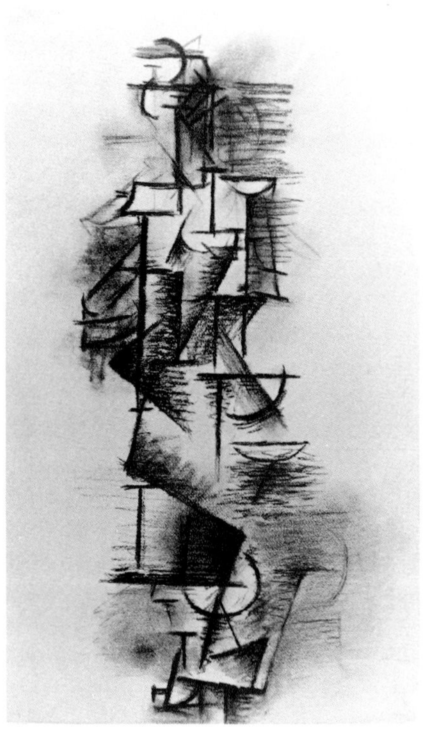

Picasso. *Standing Nude ("The Fire Escape")*, 1910. Charcoal on paper, 48.5×31cm. Metropolitan Museum of Art, New York. Photograph by Stieglitz from *Camera Work*, December, 1910.

Picasso. *Landscape (Two Trees)*, 1908. Gouache on paper, 48×63.5cm. Philadelphia Museum of Art: Louise and Walter Arensberg Collection.

(works that Haviland had arranged for Steichen and de Zayas to choose from the artist's portfolios), crammed onto the walls of the three small rooms that constituted his and Steichen's 291 Gallery.

This exhibition supposedly launched Picasso in America.[41] In fact only one drawing (a Blue period subject) sold: to Hamilton Easter Field, who paid countless visits to the show and finally shelled out eleven dollars for it. However, the presence in the Stieglitz bequest at the Metropolitan Museum of a major group of early Picasso drawings (including the cubist *Standing Nude* of 1910, known as *The Fire Escape*),[42] would suggest that Stieglitz kept a batch for himself. Gallery associates like Paul Haviland, Marius de Zayas (the Mexican caricaturist, who later published an interview with Picasso) and Agnes Ernst Meyer (known as the Sun Girl) are also likely to have made acquisitions. All three became collectors: Haviland of tribal art, de Zayas of cubist Braque and Picasso, and Mrs. Meyer of Cézanne, Brancusi and, to a lesser extent, Picasso.[43] Surprisingly, one of the gallery's more ardent supporters, Arthur Jerome Eddy—the perspicacious lawyer and critic from Chicago, also author of a well-argued book, *Cubists and Post-Impressionists* (1914)—never acquired anything later than the proto-fauve grinning hag of 1901 that ended up in the Arensberg collection.

Although he came of a prosperous (dry goods) family and his wife was the daughter of a rich brewer, Stieglitz was always pleading poverty. With some reason, he regarded his 291 Gallery as a public service rather than a business venture, so lack of sales did not bother him. However, this did bother Picasso, and he gave Haviland hell for letting him in for such a fiasco. Stieglitz subsequently acquired other works by the artist, but after a second show of Picasso, Braque and Matisse in 1914, which was largely assembled by Picabia and his dealer wife, his interest in cubism waned,[44] and a passion for Picabia's protean work took its place. After World War I, Stieglitz's avant-garde enthusiasms waned, and he devoted more and more of his mesmeric flair to photography and the paintings of his mistress, Georgia O'Keeffe, and his friend John Marin.

The painter Arthur B. Davies, who helped organize New York's Armory show (February–March, 1913), was another of Picasso's early American patrons. Unlike the genuinely modern-minded Weber, Davies was a schemer, whose switch to modernism had more to do with self-promotion than inner conviction. His attempt to enliven his coy nudes and mystical unicorns with a touch of cubist modernity engendered some very "awkward concoctions."[45] The Armory show was crucially important for the history of modernism in America, but it did little to enhance Picasso's reputation. Matisse and Brancusi proved far more popular. Davies was the only person to buy a Picasso (the relatively minor 1908 gouache *Two Trees*, for $243). Shortly afterwards, he acquired a major cubist painting from Kahnweiler, *Still Life with Musical Instruments* of 1913 (p. 362); and in the first Kahnweiler sale (1921), he would buy the 1912 *Nude Woman ("J'aime Eva")* (p. 223).[46] Davies was more a victim than a hero of the Armory show. His subsequent role as a patron of modernism "would be limited to introducing wealthy women such as Lillie Bliss and Abby Rockefeller to the pleasures of collecting contemporary art."[47]

* * *

Until the extensive files of Kahnweiler's correspondence with his German associates (recently discovered in storage at the Galerie Louise Leiris) are made available,[48] it will not be possible to evaluate the full range and complexity of the dealer's *Ostpolitik*. However, thanks to John Field, who questioned Kahnweiler at length about the German connection some thirty years ago, and to more recent researches by Pepe Karmel, it has been possible to piece together much of this unfamiliar story.[49] (For the sake of brevity, details have been relegated to the notes.) Since the more established German dealers—even the supposedly progressive Cassirers, who had done so well with impressionism that their motto was said to be "*Durch Manet und Monet zu money*"[50]—were averse to showing anything as radical as cubism, Kahnweiler was obliged to look elsewhere for representatives who would help carry out his ambitious plans. He had no problem finding them. Numerous young men of his generation and background preferred to apply the financial acumen they had inherited from their parents to trading in art rather than in wheat or coal or garments. This enabled them to reconcile the *tachles*—the profitable ventures—of stern Jewish fathers with the *shmonzes*—the spiritual concerns—of idealistic Jewish sons.[51]

Such men were Alfred Flechtheim of Düsseldorf, who came of an old established family of grain merchants; Hugo Perls of Berlin, who started by following his family into the law; and Justin Thannhauser of Munich, whose father, Heinrich, had switched from bespoke tailoring to picture dealing. Of these Alfred Flechtheim was the most progressive. To finance his passion for modern art, he toiled away in the grain exchanges of Paris, Moscow, Bucharest, Antwerp, London and Liverpool before returning to run the family business in Düsseldorf, also to transform the local art association, the Sonderbund Westdeutscher Kunstfreunde und Künstler, into one of the most enlightened bodies of its kind in the world.

On his trips to Paris Flechtheim had made friends with Uhde and the *dômiers*, and, not least, Picasso's suicidal friend, Wiegels, who was also from Düsseldorf. Flechtheim had already encountered Picasso at Sagot's, but it was Uhde who really brought them together. Friends remembered Flechtheim as a man of manic enthusiasm, gargoyle looks and irrepressible charm. Picasso liked him because he had an altruistic passion for his work and spoke Spanish. Flechtheim addressed him in the second-person singular—something Kahnweiler and Uhde never did. Picasso sold him things out of the studio, including the quintessential Rose period *Blue Boy* of 1905. By 1911, Flechtheim's private collection of Picasso was the largest in Germany.[52] Thanks to Uhde, he became a friend of Kahnweiler's, and later his principal German representative.

Otto Feldmann. *Alfred Flechtheim on the Telephone*, 1911. Pencil on paper, 35×23.5cm. Museum Ludwig, Cologne.

Despite a preference for policemen and athletes—when asked to identify the most important artistic event of the century, he unhesitatingly replied Max Schmeling's recent fight[53]—Flechtheim married a suitable Jewish woman, Betti Goldschmidt, but he soon scandalized her family by spending her entire dowry on paintings by Picasso, Braque, Girieud and Friesz, among others. Two years later, he was hailed as both hero and villain when he organized the great international exhibition (including sixteen Picassos) at the Sonderbund. Flechtheim's dream was to make a killing in the grain business and then set up in Paris as a private dealer who would manage, like Uhde or Goetz, to buy and sell paintings and yet

Picasso. *Man Reading a Newspaper*, summer, 1914. Pencil on invitation to opening exhibition at Flechtheim Gallery, Düsseldorf, December, 1913, 16×12.7 cm. Musée Picasso.

retain his amateur status. He never achieved this dream. After helping to mastermind the first-ever Picasso retrospective at Thannhauser's Munich gallery in 1913—the exhibition that would establish Germany as the most Picassophile country in Europe—Flechtheim had a breakdown for reasons that he described in a diary.[54] His father and uncle had made unwise investments, which had brought the family business, not to speak of young Alfred, to the brink of bankruptcy. His magnificent collection, which included Van Gogh's *Zouave*, five Cézannes, two Gauguins, works by Seurat, Rousseau and Munch and some ten Picassos (among them the *Blue Boy*, *Au Lapin Agile* and five cubist paintings) was worth at least 150,000 marks, but nobody, not even his "*lieber beau père*" Goldschmidt, was prepared to accept it as collateral. How else was Alfred going to settle his debts of 30,000 marks? Meanwhile he had fallen unhappily in love with the handsome Swedish artist Nils de Dardel; as a result Betti was threatening to leave him. The only solution to his woes, Flechtheim concluded, was suicide. He took out a large life insurance policy in favor of his wife and parents, and planned to have a fatal "accident" in March, 1914. Suddenly everything changed for the better. In September the Düsseldorf museum purchased his Van Gogh for 40,000 marks; and by Christmas his friends Paul Cassirer and Carl Sternheim had enabled him to abandon the troubled grain business and open a gallery in Düsseldorf. Within a few months it had prospered sufficiently for him to open a second gallery in Berlin, which would eventually become his headquarters. In his last diary entry (August 5, 1914), Flechtheim congratulates himself on staying alive, starting a new career, and winning back his self-respect, his fortune and his wife; at the same time he deplores the outbreak of war. "Everything's finished," he writes. He was wrong. After the war, in which he had a surprisingly successful career as a soldier, Flechtheim became one of the most adventurous modernist dealers of his day, until the Nazis chased him off to England in 1937.

Unlike Flechtheim, who regarded the promotion of modern art as a vocation, the Thannhausers were primarily interested in profits. After closing the stuffy Munich gallery he had run with F. J. Brakl, Heinrich Thannhauser opened a new venture, the Moderne Galerie. Since he had little understanding of modernism, he sent his son, Justin, to study art history in Berlin, Florence and ultimately Paris, where he dallied with the *dômiers* and bought his first Picasso. To justify the name of the new enterprise, Thannhauser put his premises at the disposal of Kandinsky's Neue Künstlervereinigung, which evolved into the Blaue Reiter. The second of these group shows (1910–11) included three works on paper by Picasso.[55] To generate even more publicity, father and son allowed the futurists to hold their principal German rally—a surefire source of headlines—in their gallery. The Thannhausers exploited the futurists' *succès de scandale* to the maximum, while handing out exculpatory cards which said "*Ohne Verantwortung der Galerie*" ("The gallery disclaims responsibility"). These cards may have reassured the burghers of Munich; they horrified young artists like Paul Klee.

No less cynically promotional was the Thannhausers' decision to mount the first full-scale retrospective of Picasso's work in February, 1913. The exhibition included 114 items: almost two-thirds of them paintings (including 29 from Kahnweiler and 13 from Flechtheim) and the rest watercolors,

Picasso. *Woman with Pears (Fernande)*, summer, 1909. Oil on canvas, 92×73 cm. The Estate of Florene M. Schoenborn. This and the paintings on the opposite page were all in Flechtheim's collection before 1914.

Picasso. *Woman Playing the Violin*, spring, 1911. Oil on canvas, 92×65 cm. Private collection, Krefeld.

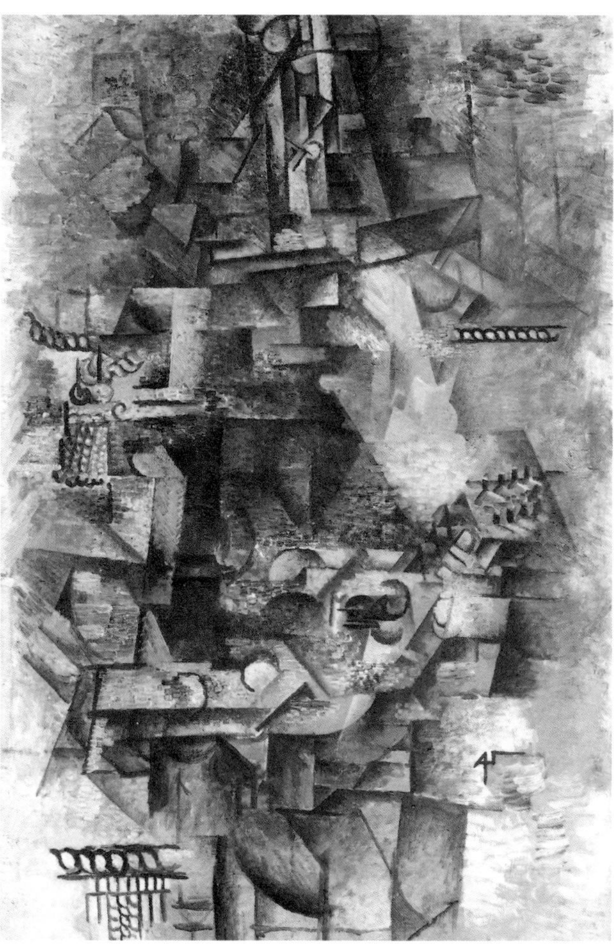

Picasso. *Woman with Mandolin*, 1911. Oil on canvas, 100×65 cm. Collection Beyeler, Basel.

Picasso. *Dead Birds*, 1912. Oil on canvas, 46×65 cm. Museo del Prado, Madrid.

drawings and etchings. In his catalog preface Heinrich Thannhauser did his specious best to isolate Picasso from expressionism and futurism—and even cubism; he also came out against manifestos. Hypocrisy let the Thannhausers in for a well-deserved attack by Max Raphael, the philosopher, economist and art historian, who was both a friend of Picasso's and a fan of cubism. In his previously quoted letter denouncing Pechstein for attacking cubism as intellectual and theoretical, Raphael took the opportunity to castigate "ambitious persons who have learned . . . to mobilize the press and exhibitions in order to promote publicity and business." "Americanization in art," he adds prophetically.[56] In fairness to the Thannhausers, it must be said that the publicity generated by their pioneer exhibition did much to establish Picasso's reputation in Mitteleuropa and boost his sales. When asked why he never visited this or any other exhibition of his work outside France—especially since Matisse realized the usefulness of personal appearances—Picasso said that he was too preoccupied with his work to leave his studio, least of all for a country whose language he could not understand.

Jules Pascin. *Justin K. Thannhauser and Rudolf Levy Playing Cards*, December 24, 1911. India ink and colored pencil on paper, 23×29cm. The Solomon R. Guggenheim Museum, New York: Gift of Justin K. Thannhauser, 1978.

The Perls family's involvement in Picasso's rise to fame started in 1910, when Hugo Perls, a Berlin magistrate, and his first cousin, Curt Glaser—a doctor of medicine and art critic who created the Berlin museum's modern print department—married two sisters, Käthe and Elsa Kolke, and spent their honeymoons together. On their way back to Berlin, they stopped in Paris and visited various private collections, including the dealer Josse Bernheim's, where they were impressed by a group of Blue period Picassos.[57] They also met Uhde, who sold them a portrait of Mateu de Soto, and Kahnweiler, who sold them a 1908 nude. Hugo's son, Klaus—subsequently a major New York dealer and collector—says that his father never really liked cubism: in 1912 Uhde sent him on approval the great 1909 *Seated Woman in Green* (p. 139)—a painting that had struck them all "like a thunderbolt" when they had seen it in Paris—advising him to hang it in his dressing room in order to get accustomed to it, but Perls returned it a few months later.[58] Early Picasso would always be Hugo Perls's passion, so much so that he gave up the law to become a *marchand amateur*, specializing in the Blue and Rose periods. For a source, he used Vollard, who had stockpiled Picasso's early work, rather than Kahnweiler, who dealt mostly in cubism. He claimed that "about four dozen Blues"—including *The Boy with a Pipe* and *Les Noces de Pierrette*—had passed through his hands.[59] Perls did so well as a private dealer that he and his wife, Käthe, eventually (1923) opened a gallery on Berlin's Bellevuestrasse and continued to specialize in early Picasso.

*　　　*　　　*

On a more modest level were a number of young art historians, painters, critics, musicians, who abandoned their vocations to open small contemporary galleries. Most of these men gravitated to Munich, traditionally the principal German art center. That they survived is a measure of the public's support for modernism. Since these dealers' clients were seldom as prosperous as Thannhauser's, there was a call for less costly items. Kahnweiler accordingly encouraged Picasso and his other artists to do multiples: prints and illustrated books, which would appeal to young art lovers

Picasso. *Head of a Man with Pipe*, 1912. Etching, 13×11 cm. Private collection.

of modest means. He was profiting from experience: as an apprentice at Tardieu's bank he had bought lithographs and engravings by Cézanne, Toulouse-Lautrec and Manet. Prints, Kahnweiler realized, could help in the dissemination of modern art; they could also generate extra income for the dealer as well as the artist. Picasso had acquired a small handpress in 1907, but he did not use it until 1909, when, at Kahnweiler's urging, he engraved two plates—pulled by the master engraver Eugène Delâtre—which were published in editions of a hundred. And until the war made copper plates scarce, he continued to do cubist engravings. (Braque, too, took up printmaking. Between 1907 and 1912 he executed as many as ten drypoints, although only two of them were published—likewise in editions of a hundred.) The cubist prints as well as Jacob's *Saint-Matorel* books, which Kahnweiler included with the consignments of paintings he dispatched to galleries in Germany and Eastern Europe, not only sold well; they helped promote his *Ostpolitik*. When war broke out, Kahnweiler's stock of prints would be sequestered with the rest of his property. But prints would eventually prove to be a gold mine for him: after World War II, he turned the market for Picasso's vast output of prints into such a lucrative business that it rivaled the market for his paintings.

Back, however, to Munich in 1912, when Hans Goltz, a dealer whom Paul Klee commended for his commitment to modern art, opened Die Neue Kunst Galerie. Goltz was the first dealer to show a cubist work in his window, presumably one of the Picassos he had borrowed from Kahnweiler.[60] In Cologne Kahnweiler's principal associate was Otto Feldmann, a writer and artist (his excellent drawing of Flechtheim is reproduced on p. 313), who opened a gallery, Der Rheinische Kunstsalon, in 1912. A year later, he took over most of Thannhauser's 1913 retrospective, before it went on to Stuttgart. Encouraged by this show's reception, Feldmann opened another branch, Die Neue Galerie, in Berlin. It was there in December, 1913, that he brought off his most imaginative coup: a major exhibition devoted to *Picasso und Negerplastiken* (Picasso and tribal sculpture). It consisted of 53 paintings and 13 drawings done between 1907 and 1913, 39 or 40 of them loaned by Kahnweiler.[61] Since no copy of the catalog has come to light, we have no details of the number, identity or source of the tribal sculpture; nor do we know whether it was assembled by Uhde, who is said to have written a catalog preface, or Kahnweiler's friend and mentor, Carl Einstein, who was already planning his pioneer book on *Negerkunst* (1915).

Besides being the second largest show of Picasso's work yet mounted, this exhibition is important for addressing an issue—primitivism as an influence on modern art—which concerned German and French painters at the beginning of the century as much as art historians today. Surprisingly, this peripatetic exhibition has been allowed to fade into oblivion.[62] The expressionists and their chroniclers preferred to forget that Matisse and the fauves, not to speak of Picasso and the cubists, had discovered African sculpture well before they had. In an effort to establish expressionist priority, Kirchner tried to falsify the record by altering the dates on his paintings. Primitivism was *their* preserve, the Brücke artists felt, and to prove it they went, insofar as they could, native. Kirchner's Dresden studio was so cluttered with exotic textiles and fetishes that it resembled the abode of a witch doctor; and Heckel's tented attic room was filled

Sam and Milli, performers from the Schumann Circus in Ernst Ludwig Kirchner's Dresden studio, 1910; photograph by Kirchner. Photo Archive Bolliger–Ketterer.

Selection of pictures included in the exhibition *Picasso und Negerplastiken*, 1913–14.

Left: Picasso. *Full-Length Nude*, spring, 1907. Oil on canvas, 93×43cm. Museo d'Arte Contemporaneo, Milan: Jucker Collection.

Below left: Picasso. Study for final version of *Three Women*, spring, 1908. Gouache on paper, 51×48cm. Musée National d'Art Moderne, Centre Georges Pompidou, Paris.

Below right: Picasso. *Woman with Mustard Pot*, winter, 1909–10. Oil on canvas, 73×60cm. Gemeentemuseum, The Hague.

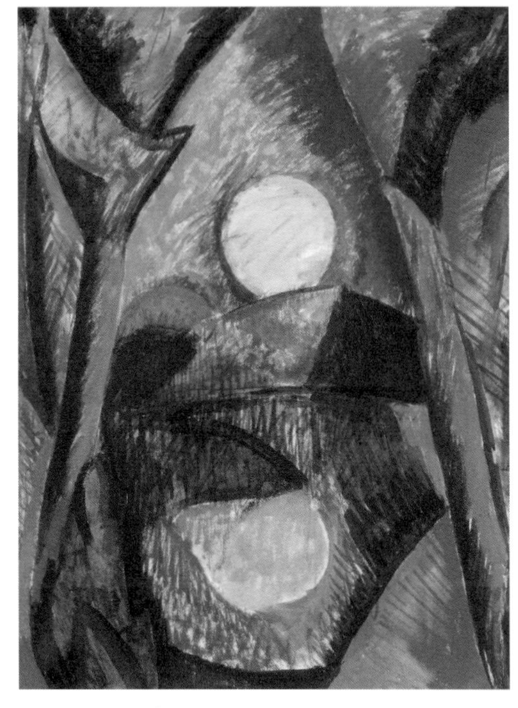

Picasso. *Landscape, Sunset*, August, 1908. Gouache on paper mounted on canvas, 62.5×47cm. Private collection.

Above: Picasso. *Bottle of Rum*, 1911. Oil on canvas, 61×50cm. Jacques and Natasha Gelman Collection.

Above center: Picasso. *Buffalo Bill*, spring, 1911. Oil on canvas, 46×33cm. Private collection.

Right: Picasso. *Shells on a Piano*, spring, 1912. Oil on oval canvas, 24×41cm. Whereabouts unknown. Kahnweiler photograph: Galerie Louise Leiris.

Above: Picasso. *Bouillon Kub*, 1912. Oil on panel, 27×21cm. Whereabouts unknown. Kahnweiler photograph: Galerie Louise Leiris.

Left: Picasso. *Head of Man with Mustache*, spring, 1912. Oil on canvas, 61×38cm. Musée d'Art Moderne de la Ville de Paris.

Right: Picasso. *Guitar*, summer, 1912. Oil on oval canvas, 72.5×60cm. Nasjonalgalleriet, Oslo.

with tribal masks, calabashes and primitive lutes supplied by a brother in the Cameroons. In search of the *Urmensch*, with whom they identified, some of them went on pilgrimages to primitive settlements: Nolde, who fancied himself a latter-day Gauguin, had joined an expedition to New Guinea; Pechstein had gone to the island group of Palau; Schmidt-Rottluff to the extreme north of Norway. All this was anathema to Flechtheim, who saw modern art as emanating from Paris and not Munich or Dresden and who dismissed the expressionists as "bill-posters." Picasso, he realized, had developed into a far more fearsome shaman without traveling farther than the Trocadéro.

Rudolf Grossmann. *Rudolf Levy and Wilhelm Uhde at the Dôme*, c.1910. Pen on paper. Whereabouts unknown.

One name is conspicuously absent from the roster of Kahnweiler's German outlets: that of Herwarth Walden, the charismatic owner of Berlin's Sturm gallery and magazine, also the anarchist hero of the Mitteleuropean avant-garde. "A total lack of plastic sensibility made [Walden] commit the most extraordinary blunders" is the excuse Kahnweiler gives for his rejection of him.[63] Walden was in the forefront of every progressive movement in Berlin, political and literary as well as artistic: an energetic promoter of expressionism and futurism, and an early champion of Kandinsky, Kokoschka and Chagall. Granted, he exhibited artists whom Kahnweiler condemned as *Ersatzkubisten*—Delaunay, Gleizes, Metzinger, Le Fauconnier and the like. But why ever not? Delaunay exerted a formative influence on Klee and Macke; and the others had a serious following in Germany. Kahnweiler apparently felt threatened by Walden—a free spirit who was far more open-minded, if less discriminating, than himself. He also felt threatened by Walden's adoption of Guillaume Apollinaire as his arbiter of taste. The Parisian artists whom the poet was urging Walden to promote were either anathema to Kahnweiler or, worse, artists who were under contract to him. (In partnership with Derain, Walden had actually bought and sold a Courbet.) Kahnweiler did not want his stable written about in the "blunder-filled" pages of Walden's *Sturm* magazine. Nor was he prepared to lend anything to the Sturm's 1912 show of Picasso's early drawings or to another one in 1913, where Picasso was ignominiously paired with Albert Bloch. Kahnweiler's refusal to cooperate with Walden is a measure of the narrowness that constituted his strength.

* * *

Picasso's success in Germany owed almost as much to Wilhelm Uhde as to Kahnweiler. The Prussian intellectual who had rejected puritanism and the Jewish intellectual who had rejected Mammon would be lifelong friends. Their dissimilarities were complementary. Kahnweiler focused on dealing, above all in cubism, to the exclusion of almost everything else except music. Though no less serious, Uhde was protean and gregarious; he delighted in the Parisian *vie de bohème* to the extent of writing a book about it. He prided himself on being a collector. Dealing was a matter of convenience: a métier he had drifted into when disapproving parents terminated his allowance. Thanks, however, to his Prussian punctiliousness, scholarly polish and gentlemanly charm, his amateur status would never be in any doubt. To his dying day, he described himself as a "man of letters." He was a man of more than that.

Marie Laurencin. *Portrait of Nils de Dardel*, 1913. Oil on canvas, 92.5×73cm. Musée Marie Laurencin, Nagano.

Besides being a leading *dômier*, Uhde presided over a salon of his own every Sunday. At these informal Franco-German gatherings artists

(Picasso, Braque, Marie Laurencin, Delaunay, Dufy, as well as assorted *dômiers*, such as Kisling) mingled with collectors, writers, academics and students from all over Europe. Uhde's stylish apartment on the Ile Saint-Louis epitomized the aesthetic taste of the period:

> faded brocades, heavy faience in rich, dark colors, a charming Egyptian mask, extremely modern, an austere madonna, a Saint Sebastian. And on the walls, the architectural art of Picasso, ecstatic, sad, troubling; the Gothic, balance, romanized . . . made earthly by Braque; the fantastic landscapes of Henri Rousseau; the canvases of Marie Laurencin.[64]

Picasso. *Head of a Woman*, early 1908. Gouache on panel, 27×21 cm. Whereabouts unknown (formerly in Uhde's collection). Kahnweiler photograph: Galerie Louise Leiris.

The only decorative features Uhde omits are the student banners from Heidelberg. In Paris he was looked after by his handsome valet, Constant; outside Paris, at Senlis, by a gifted housekeeper, Séraphine, whom he would later promote as a naïf painter. The household at Senlis also included two lovers. Together they constituted a family: Uhde was "Father"; the Swedish writer and painter Gustaf Hellstrom was "Mother"; and Flechtheim's friend Nils de Dardel was "Da-di-da-da," their "baby." After war broke out, Gertrude Stein chose to believe this "family" had been a nest of spies. She of all people should have known better.

Uhde worshiped youth—its energy and dazzle. Nostalgia for his student days at Heidelberg inspired two early novels,[65] which were more an emotional release than serious fiction. His admiration and affection for the charismatic young Picasso was likewise inspired as much by hero worship as by aesthetic discrimination. For his part, the artist derived comfort from Uhde's passionate support but would sometimes grumble that this admirer failed to keep up. After a period of Hegelian ratiocination, the thoughtful Prussian would usually come round to whatever had originally shocked or puzzled him—the use of Ripolin in 1913, for example—and continue to collect Picasso and urge his friends to follow suit. Unlike most other dealers, Uhde was altruistic in his promotion of cubism, also unusual in making a sharp distinction between his collection and his stock. He never put his favorite paintings—Picassos, Braques and Douanier Rousseaus—on the market. When his property was sequestered, in 1914, his fifteen Picassos included such masterpieces as *Fanny Tellier* (1910), *The Poet*, and *Man with Tenora* (both of 1911),[66] as well as his own famous portrait.

Uhde's coterie included a number of young homosexuals whom he urged to collect Picasso. They made little secret of their orientation, hence possibly their liberated attitude to modernism. Besides Uhde and Flechtheim there were several other Germans, Austrians and Scandinavians who gravitated to the avant-garde not so much out of fashion or flair or a perverse desire to be different as out of innovative compulsion: an urge to rally to Picasso as the rebel leader of modern art. Such a man was Rolf de Maré, a rich Swedish friend (and subsequently lover) of Nils de Dardel, Uhde's *homme fatal*. In due course de Maré would become a lesser but more adventurous Diaghilev. After the war he and his next lover, the brilliant dancer and choreographer Jean Börlin, whose "short life was an ardent, single, soaring burst of creativity,"[67] would stage ballets—among them Léger and Cendrars's *Création du Monde* and Picabia and Satie's *Relâche* (with an entr'acte by René Clair)—for their Ballets Suédois company. These ballets would do far more than *Parade* for modernism. De

Picasso. *Bottle, Guitar and Pipe*, fall, 1912. Oil on canvas, 60×73 cm (formerly in de Maré's collection). Museum Folkwang, Essen.

Maré, who was a gifted amateur musician, had started by collecting Spanish masters, including three El Grecos. He soon advanced to Courbet, Manet and Seurat, and by 1914 was buying Picassos from Flechtheim—notably the dazzling *Au Lapin Agile* (1905), a study for the *Demoiselles* and two or three cubist paintings: a *Woman with Mandolin* (p. 315) and the superb 1912 still life now in the Folkwang Museum, Essen.[68] After the war, de Maré made a number of purchases at the Kahnweiler sales as well as from his friend Flechtheim and ended up with the finest collection of Picasso in Scandinavia.

Picasso. *Pigeon in Its Nest, with Eggs*, spring–summer, 1912. Oil on canvas, 33×41 cm (formerly in Alphonse Kann's collection). Whereabouts unknown. Kahnweiler photograph: Galerie Louise Leiris.

Another rich young foreigner to appear on the Parisian art scene (circa 1910) was Alphonse Kann, an Austrian, naturalized British, who lived in great style at Saint-Germain-en-Laye—"almost too much of an *homme du monde*," according to Roché.[69] Kann had started collecting Van Goghs and Cézannes around 1908. But by 1912 he was acquiring some of the most advanced Picassos of the period.[70] Like Uhde, Kann made money out of his collection. Besides a fortune, he had inherited considerable business and artistic acumen; and for some thirty years he played the art market like the stock market, switching backwards and forwards between the nineteenth and twentieth centuries. In the face of the Nazi threat, Kann retreated to London, leaving behind a large part of his collection—major works by Degas, Picasso and Braque—to be confiscated and used by Göring in swaps for old masters. Some of the Picassos were recovered by his family after the war; other works had passed into the hands of his gigolos.

The collector closest to Uhde was Edwin Suermondt, scion of a patrician family of art patrons from Aachen, where a museum is named after a celebrated uncle. Suermondt had gone to Oxford, then Heidelberg, where he had met Uhde, who was ten years his senior. At Uhde's urging, the young man gave up the law to study art history under Wölfflin, for whom he did a doctoral thesis on Bosch. He subsequently joined Uhde in Paris and became a *dômier*. He was taken to Picasso's and Braque's studios and the Steins' Saturday evenings, where he seems to have been one of the good-looking young men whom Gertrude describes as clicking their heels and bowing and "making a very effective background to the rest of the crowd."[71] Suermondt was better off than the other *dômiers*; while still in his twenties, he was able, with Uhde's help, to put together a discriminating collection of Picassos.[72] During the war Suermondt contracted lung disease and was invalided out of the army. In 1919 he finally married, and fathered a daughter. Four years later, he was dead. The collection was inherited by his daughter, who would marry Flechtheim's Düsseldorf associate, Alex Vömel. The paintings are long since sold, but the Vömel gallery still exists.[73]

Picasso. *The Pont Neuf*, spring, 1911. Oil on canvas, 33×24 cm (formerly in Edwin Suermondt's collection). Private collection.

One of the few Picasso collectors in Germany to have left a record of their activities is Princess Mechthilde Lichnowsky: novelist, poet, playwright, Egyptologist, as well as ambassador's wife. Born Countess Arco-Zinneberg, she had married (1904) Prince Charles Max Lichnowsky, who was appointed German ambassador to London in 1912. Virginia Woolf described him as "a poor mind," whose Polish blood gave him the intuition of a village idiot, "so that he [saw] further than cleverer men."[74] Roger Fry wrote Woolf's friend Goldsworthy Lowes Dickinson that he found the wife "a very simple, brusque, unsophisticated creature who is really keen about art—of course in a German way—too intelligent."[75] Bloomsbury grew jealous of the princess's closeness to Fry: she even worked for his Omega Workshop. Princess Lichnowsky claims that the first time she saw a Picasso it was "love at first sight."[76] She proceeded to acquire at least three—possibly as many as six—examples of his work.[77] In 1914 (either shortly before or shortly after the declaration of war) she decided to buy three more important paintings from Thannhauser, including the *Saltimbanques*.[78] In her memoirs the princess claims to have cabled her husband for the necessary money. "Meanwhile on an idiotic impulse to extol my new passion . . . I mentioned my discoveries and my intention to buy them"[79] to Hertha Koenig—another rich woman (sugar-beet factories in the Ukraine), who wrote poetry and fiction and, like Princess Lichnowsky, supported Rilke—and rashly took her to see them at Thannhauser's. Twenty-four hours later, the Lichnowsky money arrived, but it was too late. The princess would have us believe that Hertha Koenig had bought the lot behind her back. However, a letter from Rilke to Koenig confirms that *he* was the person who persuaded her to buy the *Saltimbanques*: "This is one of the most decisive paintings of our time. Couldn't you save it and keep it? The right hands and the right wall need to be there before the art trade drives up the prices."[80] As for Princess Lichnowsky's Picassos, she loaned them to a Berlin museum. To Roger Fry's embarrassment, she remained in touch with him. While working for the Quakers on the western front, he was discovered to have a letter from her in his possession and was arrested as a spy. After her husband died, in 1928, the princess reclaimed her Picassos, sold them to Thannhauser and married an Englishman.

Hertha Koenig spent most of the war on her family estate, Gut Boeckel, in Westphalia. She had left the *Saltimbanques* in her Munich apartment, which she lent to friends—among them Rilke. While staying there at a particularly harrowing period of the war (June–October, 1915), Rilke's thoughts strayed nostalgically from the Picasso to the harlequins he had enjoyed watching in the Paris streets, and he was inspired to write the fifth of his *Duino Elegies* (dedicated to Koenig).[81] When the Nazis started cracking down on modern art, Frau Koenig sold the *Saltimbanques* as well as her other Picassos back to Thannhauser around 1934 and thenceforth limited her collecting to medieval sculpture.

An even more adventurous society woman was Lotte, wife of Paul von Mendelssohn-Bartholdy. Besides being an early collector of Van Gogh and the Douanier Rousseau, she purchased a Picasso as early as 1910: the *Moulin de la Galette* (1900). Thannhauser, who sold it to her, subsequently got it back and kept it in the private collection he later made over to the Guggenheim Museum. At first Frau Mendelssohn-Bartholdy confined herself to early works. However, Flechtheim encouraged her to experiment, and before 1914 she started to collect cubism: Picasso's so-called *Head of a Woman* of 1909 and his *Arlésienne* of 1912 (p. 240).[82] Frau Mendelssohn-Bartholdy also bought some great cubist Braques: a fine 1910–11 still life and that stormy set piece, the *Harbor Scene* of 1909 (p. 157). After World War I, she became a contributor to Flechtheim's *Querschnitt* and continued to collect modern painting, including several later Picassos, until the early 1930s, when the Nazis forced her and her husband to seek refuge, like the Flechtheims, in England. To keep going,

Picasso. *Head of a Woman*, spring, 1909. Gouache and black crayon on paper, 61.8×47.8cm (formerly in the Mendelssohn-Bartholdy Collection). Art Institute of Chicago.

they sold their Picassos back to Thannhauser and much of the rest of their collection to Emil Bührle, the Swiss armaments manufacturer.

* * *

Compared with the Germans, Austrian collectors were immune to Picasso's appeal, with one exception: Hugo von Hofmannsthal—poet, scholar, historian, librettist—who used his royalties from the libretto of *Der Rosenkavalier* (first performed in 1911) to buy the artist's bravura self-portrait *Yo Picasso* of 1901 from Thannhauser.[83] Not far off, in Budapest, however, there dwelt an incomparably colorful and comical collector, Marczell Nemes (or, as he preferred, de or von Nemes)—a character straight out of Hofmannsthal. By 1910, this Faninal (the parvenu in *Rosenkavalier*) had made enough money out of wood and coal and supported enough charitable causes to conceal his mysterious origins under the title Royal Advisor. Unlike most people who see art collecting as a quick and easy means of social advancement, Nemes had a surprisingly good eye and refreshingly advanced taste. The only trouble was that he came to regard himself as an artist and took to restoring his paintings himself. This Faninal did not start collecting—Munkácsy and minor Dutch masters—until he was forty (around 1906), but the discovery of El Greco, a year or two later, opened his eyes to "great art." And in no time he had virtually ruined himself buying everything from Rembrandt and Chardin to the impressionists and post-impressionists.

Picasso. *Woman with Mandolin*, early 1909. Oil on canvas, 92×73cm. State Hermitage Museum, St. Petersburg.

By 1910 Nemes had caught up with Picasso—cubist Picasso. Uhde compared him to "a horse-dealer" but admired his "astonishing sensibility,"[84] his capacity for falling instantly in love with a painting. This was the case with the great *Seated Woman in Green* of 1909 (p. 139) that Uhde had bought from Kahnweiler a few days before Nemes's visit to his gallery in 1910. Through one of his many agents Nemes offered Uhde four times what he had paid, and turned very churlish when this was not accepted. Nemes had better luck at Kahnweiler's, where he bought Picasso's no less important *Woman with Mandolin* (1909).[85] This and three other Picassos were included with works by Matisse, Rouault and Van Dongen in an exhibition at Budapest's Müvészház (Artists' House) that same year. Besides being a maniacally extravagant collector, Nemes was "a magnificent adventurer [who] bought castles in Bavaria, palaces in Venice and houses in Paris the way other people would buy a hat or an umbrella."[86] Soon he was deep in debt—dunned by Parisian dealers who had encouraged his folly. Through Kahnweiler, he sold Picasso's *Woman with Mandolin* to Shchukin, but he was too addicted to collecting to stop. After 1918 he continued to splurge, albeit on a smaller scale. His posthumous sale (1933) included no Picassos; he had presumably disposed of them privately.[87]

* * *

None of the collections that resulted from Kahnweiler's *Ostpolitik* has survived.[88] Those that were not dispersed after World War I fell victim to the Nazi condemnation of "*entartete Kunst*" ("decadent art"); or, since the more discriminating collectors and dealers tended to be Jews, to expropriation. Collectors who managed to get their paintings out of Germany were obliged to sell them to support themselves. Dealers were more fortunate, in that most of them were able to reopen their galleries in New York or Switzerland. Thannhauser, for one, did a thriving business buying back paintings from clients who had become refugees. Thanks largely to Nazi depredations, the pioneering role that German collectors played in thc dissemination of Picasso has gone unrecorded. Ironically, most of the major Picassos that Kahnweiler and his associates sold to Germany have ended up in America. As a result American collectors and museum directors are usually credited with establishing Picasso's fame. But we cannot leave the German connection out of account, especially if we bear in mind that the Steins, whose father had migrated from Bavaria in 1841, were of German extraction.

Below: Rudolf Herrmann. Poster for *Entartete Kunst* exhibition (with a profile of Flechtheim behind the tribal mask), 1938. Museum für Kunst und Gewerbe, Hamburg.

FETES
AVI
GNO
N

21

Avignon
1914

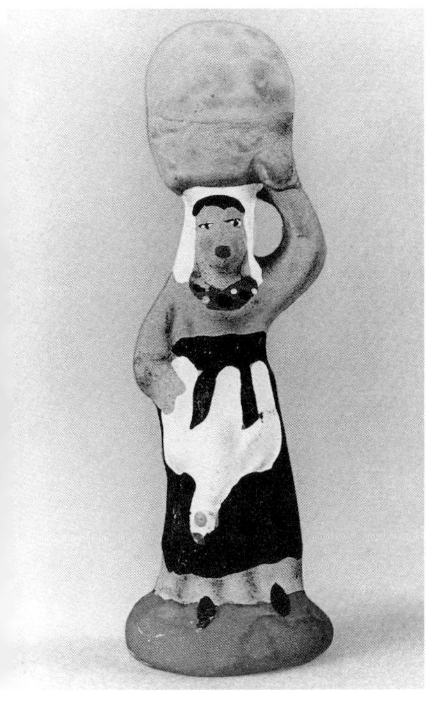

Woman with a Chicken. Provençal *santon* figure, painted terracotta. Private collection.

Opposite: Picasso. *Man at a Bar,* summer, 1914. Oil on canvas, 238×167.5cm. Private collection.

"ARTISTS TODAY ARE BEING DRAWN TO THE MIDI," Apollinaire told his readers (June 14, 1914).

> Instead of spending their vacations in Brittany or the area around Paris, as many artists of the preceding generation did, painters are now heading for Provence. They have even abandoned the Pyrenees; Céret is no longer the Mecca of cubism. . . . After visiting Nevers, Derain is now in Nîmes. Picasso is joining him there the day after tomorrow, and Braque is going to settle at Sorgues, near Avignon. The region will doubtless be receiving many other painters, among them Girieud, Lombard, perhaps even Friesz, Matisse and Edouard [Serge?] Férat."[1]

Apollinaire was right about the new trend, wrong about the details. Derain had not gone to Nîmes but to Avignon, where Picasso and Eva joined him on June 15.[2] After spending the day with the Derains, the Picassos (Eva now called herself Madame Picasso) left for nearby Tarascon, where they hoped to find a house for the summer. Picasso knew this town from previous trips in the region and thought it a good, quiet place to work. He also remembered it for its famous *santons* (Provençal crèche figures). Tarascon was close enough to Montfavet, where the Derains had found a house, and Sorgues, where Braque would arrive (by bicycle from Paris) on July 5. At the same time it was far enough away to preclude the day-to-day involvement with Braque that cubism had formerly necessitated—an involvement that Picasso no longer needed and that Eva, who was still regarded as a usurper by Braque's Marcelle and Derain's Alice, would probably have preferred to avoid.

Tarascon was, indeed still is, a sleepy Provençal town, halfway between Avignon and Arles and across the Rhône from Beaucaire. Like Beaucaire, it guards the entrance to the Rhône valley, which forms a wind tunnel down which the mistral roars. It was easy of access (the junction of the Nîmes–Saint-Rémy and Avignon–Arles railway lines), as well as unspoiled to the point of backwardness. Like other towns that had once depended from papal Avignon, Tarascon had a tradition of tolerance; it still boasted a Jewish quarter. Its arcaded main street was very much like Horta; and its shuttered, ocher houses, medieval castle and ramparts, not to speak of medieval drains, were reminiscent of Spanish towns. So was the almost total lack of distractions, apart from the occasional *cockade* (bull tease) and a festival in honor of the town's patron, Saint Martha, sister of Lazarus and Mary of Bethany. (On an evangelizing mission to Provence, Martha is reputed to have used holy water to slaughter the "Tarasque"—a satanic dragon that had been terrorizing the town.) Tarascon's Hôtel des Empereurs, where Picasso and Eva stayed, was reasonably comfortable, but it was no place to work. And, as usual in provincial southern towns, there were no houses for rent—no suitable ones, that is: Eva was an exigent *maîtresse de maison* and would have insisted on a modicum of domestic convenience. "The Tarasque has devoured everything," Picasso complained to Apollinaire, "but by the Feast of Saint Martha on the 28th, we will have tamed it."[3]

Edouard-Antoine Marsal. *Apotheosis of Mistral*; on postcard sent by Picasso to Apollinaire, June, 1914. Musée Picasso.

The Tarasque did not relent. Defeated in their search, Picasso and Eva returned to Avignon and put up at the Grand Nouvel Hôtel, just off the Place de la République, near the Palais des Papes. This time they were more successful in their quest. On June 23, Eva wrote Gertrude Stein, "This morning Pablo found a somewhat Spanish house in the city proper. He has to go and see the owner who is very rich (a freemason), quite charming and eighty-five years old. He believes that Pablo is a house-painter and wants to find him some work. It's about time we found a place where we can feel a little at home; this bohemian-style hotel life does us no good."[4] Two days later (June 25), Picasso sent Gertrude and Alice a sketch of an imaginary dog called Saucisson and the news that he and Eva were moving into 14, rue Saint-Bernard that very day.[5]

Besides keeping Apollinaire and Max Jacob informed of his whereabouts, Picasso sent them postcards of Edouard-Antoine Marsal's corny *Apotheosis of Mistral* (the celebrated Provençal poet had died earlier that year), with a promise that he would do an apotheosis of each of them. A week or so later (July 4), Apollinaire replied from Munich at greater length than usual, explaining the new form of versification he had devised: poems that were "ideograms" (he soon switched to calling them "calligrams"), in that they took their shape from their intrinsic subject instead of some accepted form of prosody. The letter included a sample for Picasso's delectation: "The Pipe and the Paintbrush." "You will see several more in the next number of *Les Soirées de Paris*," the poet promised.[6] Picasso was intrigued but not greatly impressed by Apollinaire's pictographic poems. When asked, years later, whether they might have been a response to papiers collés, the artist gave a dismissive shrug.

The rue Saint-Bernard house has been demolished, but Derain did a painting of it (bought by Roger Fry), so we have a record. It looks charming—Spanish, as Eva said, whitewashed and built around a little courtyard. There was one feature in which Picasso took pride: a mosaic floor which might have inspired the increasingly mosaic-like pointillism of his still lifes. For a studio Picasso made do with a poorly lit attic. "Very difficult to get used to working [there]," he told Kahnweiler.[7] The windows look small; also the house would have been overshadowed by the forbidding façade (almost two hundred yards long) of the Hôpital Sainte-Marthe. This grim eighteenth-century building had originated as an orphanage cum-workhouse, was later a barracks and, finally, more or less abandoned, except for one wing which housed the local art school. A small chapel-like building at Picasso's end of the Hôpital was a morgue. On the other side of the Hôpital loomed the ramparts, which had been remachicolated by Viollet-le-Duc. Adjoining the ramparts were the stables where cabbies kept their horses and *fiacres*. Reminiscing about Avignon

TARASCON - Vue d'Ensemble du Château du Roi René

54 AVIGNON.
La Cathédrale et le palais des Papes, vue prise du Beffroi.
ND. Phot.

2 TARASCON. — Gardians avec leur femme en croupe. — LL.

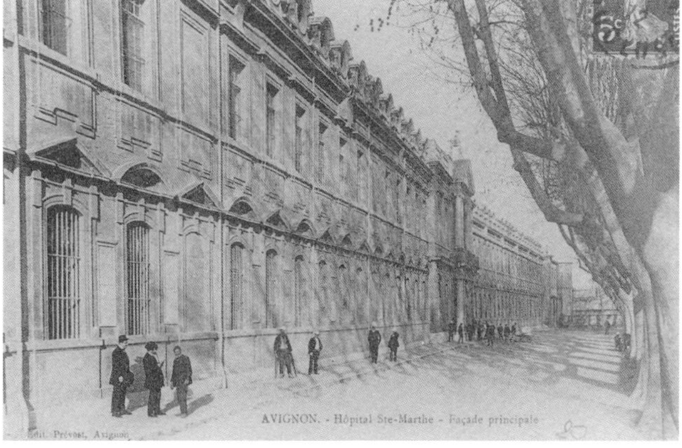

Top left: Château de Tarascon; on postcard sent by Eva and Picasso to Gertrude Stein and Alice Toklas, June 25, 1914. Beinecke Rare Book and Manuscript Library, Yale University.

Center left: Provençal cowboys in Tarascon; on postcard sent by Picasso to Gertrude Stein, June 14, 1914. Beinecke Rare Book and Manuscript Library, Yale University.

Top right: Palais des Papes, Avignon; on postcard sent by Picasso to Gertrude Stein, September 9, 1914. Beinecke Rare Book and Manuscript Library, Yale University.

Center right: Hôpital Sainte-Marthe, Avignon; postcard, c. 1910. Archives Municipales, Avignon.

Left: Derain. *Picasso's House in Rue Saint Bernard, Avignon,* 1914. Oil on canvas. Private collection.

Picasso said that one of the cabdrivers asked him to paint a sign advertising *Fumier à vendre* (manure for sale), and that he had come up with a colorful sign embellished with pointillistic flourishes. He urged me to track the sign down. "By now it must be worth a fortune." Since I lived nearby, I tried, but after forty years the trail had gone cold.

To do the housework, Eva engaged a maid; however, as she told Gertrude Stein, she developed such an affection for this woman—her only companion for much of the day—that she could not bring herself to order her around.[8] As she was obsessive about such matters, Eva ended by doing most of the cooking and housework herself. (Might the crotch-faced old crone in Provençal costume whom Picasso drew so memorably be the maid?) Eva also busied herself darning her stockings and Picasso's socks and, when war broke out, knitting balaclavas for the troops. Eva's letters to Gertrude and Alice evoke an atmosphere of snug bliss that is not entirely convincing. She is careful to keep quiet about her health, which was a recurrent source of worry; careful to convince these inquisitive well-wishers that she was *à la hauteur de la tâche*, up to the task of being a model companion, ultimately wife, to this most demanding and deserving of men. For all Eva's solicitude—in this respect she was a vast improvement on Fernande—and for all that Picasso evidently worshiped her, it is difficult to believe that someone who enjoyed whoring as much as he did never availed himself of Avignon's most notorious attraction, the brothel, which was (according to Max Jacob) as lavishly appointed as any in France.[9] It was also wrongly thought to have been the inspiration for *Les Demoiselles d'Avignon.*

Picasso. *Old Woman*, 1914. Pencil on paper, 29.8×20cm. Picasso Heirs.

The story that the house on the rue Saint-Bernard had belonged to Max Jacob's Avignonnaise grandmother likewise turns out to be apocryphal. In the margin of a letter to Kahnweiler Picasso notes that it was the birthplace of René Seyssaud—a very minor fauve, whose work he would have seen at Vollard's and Bernheim's.[10] Seyssaud and his friend Auguste Chabaud (who likewise exhibited at Bernheim's, also at the Armory show) figured among the artists Eva described to Alice Toklas: "Pablo has got to know some Avignon painters and sees them all the time."[11] Picasso's principal contact with local artists was the genial Marseillais, Pierre Girieud. Girieud was an intimate friend of Salmon and Paco Durrio and a pillar of the Lapin Agile, where his colorful canvas of a macaw hung close by Picasso's eponymous painting. Girieud had also executed a heavy-handed Gauguinesque portrait of Eva in 1911 and exhibited it the same year at the Salon d'Automne. (The *vernissage* of this Salon had inspired Picasso's amusing caricature of Girieud's friend the Avignon painter Alfred Lombard;[12] see p. 208.) Apollinaire mentions Girieud frequently but never very favorably in his art criticism. Picasso seems to have taken rather more interest in the "promising" but now forgotten Henri Doucet, the only local painter mentioned in his letters: apropos his mobilization in November, 1914, and his death in action a few months later.

Pierre Girieud. *Lesbos*, 1910. Oil on canvas. Whereabouts unknown.

Most of the above were part of a loosely associated group of painters, poets, collectors and musicians from southern and southwestern France who did not constitute a movement but, one way or another, had harnessed local patriotism to the cause of modern art. Some of them—patrons like Maurice Fabre, of Narbonne, Arthur Huc, of Toulouse, Gustave Fayet, of Béziers—had been among Picasso's earliest collectors; others he knew from Céret; yet others he now met in Avignon. These men were provincial and proud of it. They were also progressive: pioneer admirers of Cézanne, Van Gogh and Gauguin. Cubism may not have been entirely to their taste, but they were delighted to have its foremost practitioner in their midst. Avignon also boasted its own art movement, The Groupe de Treize, which had been founded to instill new life into local painting—a cause it signally failed to achieve. These painters and others from as far afield as Montpellier and Aix-en-Provence would get together at the Café Riche. Picasso followed their example; some of his mail is written on Café Riche writing paper. It was there that he would meet Braque and Derain when they came in from Sorgues and Montfavet; and after they were called up, it was there that he would forgather with Marcelle and Alice.

Folco de Baroncelli, c. 1900. Archives iconographiques du Palais du Roure, Avignon.

As for "the cream of Avignon society" that Picasso is said by Braque (in a letter to Kahnweiler, dated July 15) to have frequented,[13] only one person fits the bill: Folco de Baroncelli, Marquis de Javon, whose ancestors had come to Avignon with the pope in the fourteenth century. Most of the local noblesse were far too stuffy to be of interest to Picasso, but Baroncelli was a man after his own heart. Such was his passion for the bulls and horses of the Camargue that Baroncelli neglected his considerable properties, including the handsome, if dilapidated, Palais du Roure, in Avignon. By the time Picasso met him, he had lost most of his possessions; however, he had recently inherited the mantle of Mistral as head of the Félibrige—the society that the poet and his friends had founded in 1854 to protect the Provençal language, traditions and folklore—and was already a local legend.

Baroncelli was very small and fine-featured and so tanned and Indian-looking that when Sitting Bull came to the Camargue with Buffalo Bill, he supposedly made the marquis an honorary member of his tribe and gave him the name "Faithful Bird" and a "bonnet" of eagle feathers. Picasso's friend Jean Hugo (painter and great-grandson of Victor Hugo) has evoked Baroncelli:

> His beautiful minuscule hands were covered in rings. In mourning for some relation or other, he wore a shirt of violet velvet with very tight moleskin trousers and, like his retinue, a wide-brimmed hat. . . . He spoke in a singsong voice with the charming Avignon accent of which he was so proud. His manners were exquisite. He paid infinite compliments. . . .[14]

Camargue horsemen; on postcard sent by Eva to Gertrude Stein, June 28, 1914. Beinecke Rare Book and Manuscript Library, Yale University.

Baroncelli lived mostly in a reed-thatched cabin on an island in one of the Camargue's lagoons, surrounded by herds of wild bulls and horses, not to mention the cowboys on whom he doted. On his large white horse ("the smaller the rider, the larger the mount," he used to say), he devoted his days to rounding up the bulls and presiding over the *cockades* and other folkloric manifestations around which life in the Camargue revolved. The cult of the bull, which was such a feature of the Rhône delta before mass tourism sullied it, endeared this area forever to Picasso's Mithraic heart. Forty years later, when he resumed going to bullfights at Nîmes and Arles—often by way of Avignon—he liked to talk of the days when he was first exposed, thanks partly to Baroncelli, to the taurine traditions of Provence and Languedoc.

Like the herds of bulls, the swarms of gypsies who hung around Avignon on their way to or from their pilgrimage church at Les Saintes-

Picasso. *Man at a Bar*, 1914. Pencil on paper, 30×20cm. Picasso Heirs.

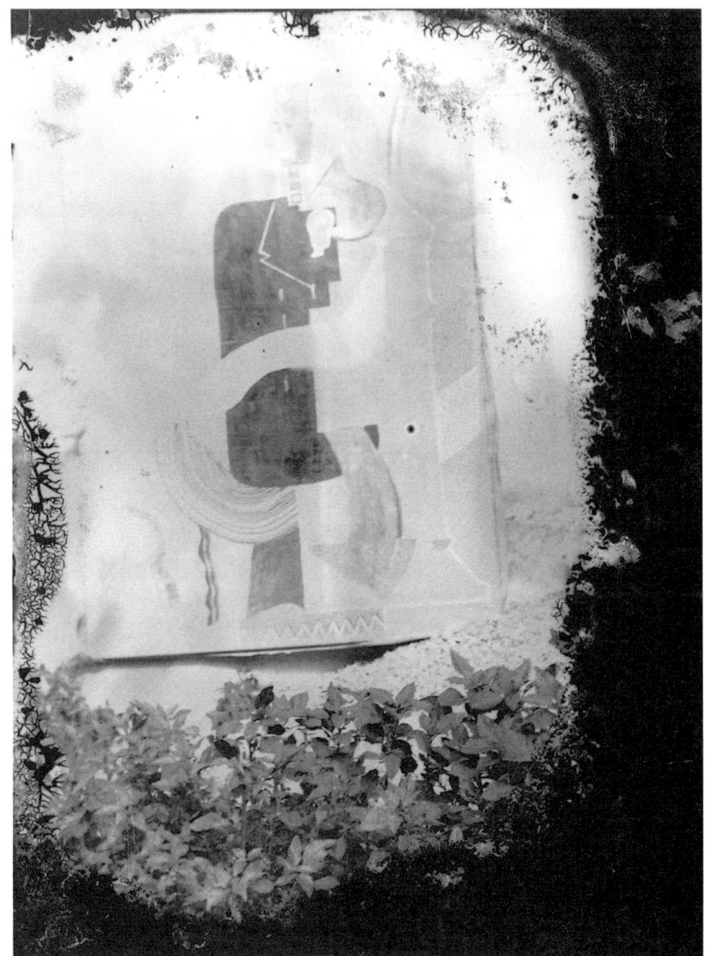

Man at a Bar in progress, 1914. Photograph by Picasso. Archives Picasso.

Left: Picasso. *Couple at a Table*, summer, 1914. Pencil on paper, 49.5×38cm. Picasso Heirs.

Maries-de-la-Mer reminded Picasso of Andalusia. At night the sounds of *cante jondo* could be heard from their encampments outside the ramparts. And on his visits to the flamingo-fringed lagoons of the Camargue he was transported back to the Marismas (the salt marshes) of the Guadalquivir, to the south of Seville, which are likewise the scene of a joyous and licentious pilgrimage, the Rocío. The light also recalled Spain. Spanish artists, including Picasso, had seldom shown much interest in simulating sunlight. But here in Provence Van Gogh and more recently the fauves had keyed their palette to it. And now Picasso followed suit. Maybe it was the very darkness of his studio, compared with the sunlight outside—perhaps, too, Eva's illness and the imminence of war—that inspired him to lighten and brighten his palette and give the final phase of cubism an unprecedented sparkle.

Processional boat at the pilgrimage church of Les Saintes-Maries-de-la-Mer.

* * *

"I've been doing only large canvases," Picasso wrote Kahnweiler on July 21, "or rather . . . thinking of doing them. I've begun one that's already fairly well along. . . . Things are moving and I hope the Good Lord does not want them to stop."[15] Only one really large painting has survived (238×167.5 cm): the *Man at a Bar* (often described as "Seated Man with Glass"). It is one of the most ambitious and experimental of the artist's later cubist compositions, also one of the least resolved. That it was not signed until much later (to establish the painting's authenticity rather than its completion) suggests that it had been set aside to be reworked, then left as it was. The image is so equivocal that Palau believes it to represent not one but two figures.[16] In fact there is only one: not seated but leaning against a pedestal or bar, as we can see from some of the preparatory drawings.[17] Picasso has taken outrageous liberties with arms and legs: a flipperlike left arm painted white reaches for a glass; a right one, resembling a length of blue colon, meanders across the painting, ending up in a ball of tiny fingers. The legs dangle: the left one, all too recognizable in the preliminary drawing, turns into what looks like a napkin over a waiter's arm. (We are evidently in the Café Riche.) The most legible area of this painting is the man's comical face: a rectangle of centrally parted hair,[18] scrotumlike eyes, a penis-shaped nose bisecting a mustache, a minute pearly-toothed mouth and a gigantic mandala-shaped ear. The fantastical deformations that Picasso makes of body parts would inspire Miró to do much the same in his surrealist paraphrases of eighteenth-century paintings, like the *Portrait of Mistress Mills in 1750* (after a mezzotint by George Engleheart). Miró extends and enlarges the bow on Mistress Mills's hat (top right-hand corner of the composition) much as Picasso extends and enlarges the similarly placed ear of the man in the Avignon painting.

Joan Miró. *Portrait of Mistress Mills in 1750*, 1929. Oil on canvas, 116.7×89.6cm. The Museum of Modern Art, New York: James Thrall Soby Bequest.

Unable, it would seem, to resolve this *Man at a Bar* to his satisfaction, Picasso tried out alternative ideas for the other large canvases he had in mind, among them several ribald combinations of a naked man and woman lolling together either side of a table. As so often when Picasso devotes a great many drawings to a specific project, he fails to come up with a painting. He simply lets his graphic imagination rip and, seeing himself once again as God the Creator, sets about redesigning humanity,

Picasso. *Eva in a Fox Fur with Sentinelle*, 1914. Pencil on paper, 31.5×23.5cm. Picasso Heirs.

Eva with Sentinelle, 1914. Archives Picasso.

though hardly in his own image. He plays outrageous tricks on the scale and nature of body parts, contriving heads out of bottle tops, hands out of things animate as well as inanimate (paws, hooves and flippers as well as pegs, doorknobs and tassels), feet out of what else but the feet of chairs and tables, and arms out of what else but the elaborately buttoned arms of an armchair. He also makes puns on limbs and lengths of intestine, breasts and binoculars, torsos and bottles and much else besides. Surrealism *avant la lettre*. Later in the year, when the weather turned cool, Eva must have taken to wearing one of those fox furs with beady little glass eyes and a clasp in the snout to snap onto the tail. In a drawing of a woman—evidently Eva—with one of these then fashionable accessories over her shoulder, Picasso amuses himself by contrasting the fox's sharp dead face with the sharp live face of the wearer and the even sharper *gueule* of the German shepherd crouched at her side. The artist relished his ingenious little joke sufficiently to substitute snoutlike clasps for women's noses in some of his other drawings.

The huge unfinished painting of the man with a glass can be seen as a rehearsal for the masterpiece of the Avignon period, the *Portrait of a Young Girl* (as the back of the canvas is inscribed). Like the great *Woman in an Armchair* of the previous summer, this is not so much of Eva as about her. It also has to be seen in relation to Matisse, specifically his great symphonic set piece, *Red Studio* of 1911—a painting in which furniture, sculpture, paintings and studio bric-à-brac are suspended in a wash of blood-red paint. *Red Studio* suggested to Picasso how he could use a field of intense color (bright green as opposed to bright red) as a spatial element. Color, which had formerly proved so difficult to integrate into cubism, has finally turned out to be the solution rather than the problem. Instead of painting space as if it were palpable, and dissolving forms in it, Picasso could now make do with an expanse of saturated color—an expanse that is flat yet appears to have depth and substance—in which, as *Red Studio* demonstrates, all manner of things could be suspended or to some extent dissolved in the paint's illusory depths.

Picasso devised a technique to enhance the ambivalent flatness of this painting still further. He made paper cutouts of the feather boa, glove, hat, et cetera, and then simulated them in paint on the canvas, shadowed in certain areas so that they appear to hover just above the paint surface. Like the famous trompe l'œil nail in Braque's 1909–10 still lifes, this technique enables Picasso to make an ironic comment on cubist notation and the function of papier collé. The strange thing about this "portrait" is that except for one pinkish hand (the other is gloved), Eva's frail body has vanished—vanished into the ground, as she herself would eighteen months later. As in H. G. Wells's *Invisible Man*, clothes are all we see of her: a hat trimmed with flowers, ribbons and a spotted veil (this was the era of heavily spotted veils); a feather boa, a lace jabot, two blue sleeves and, at the very center of the painting, something that could be one of Eva's Bon Marché corsage ornaments, to judge by the paper sketch.

Cutout sketches of a lightbulb (some with a filament, some with concentric red lines to suggest warmth) help us to identify the mysterious Montgolfieresque object, lower left. In the final painting Picasso has transformed it from a source of light into a source of heat by attaching it to a comically small log and placing it in front of the fireplace (the jagged

Left: Picasso. *Portrait of a Young Girl*, summer, 1914. Oil on canvas, 130×97 cm. Musée National d'Art Moderne, Centre Georges Pompidou, Paris.

Picasso. Cutouts relating to *Portrait of a Young Girl*, 1914. Musée Picasso.
Above: *Feather Boa*. Gouache on paper, 24×13 cm.
Below left: *Burning Log*. Oil on tracing paper, 15×8.5 cm.
Below center: *Light Bulb*. Pencil on both sides of paper, 10×5.8 cm.
Below right: *Light Bulb*. Oil on paper, 12×7.2 cm.

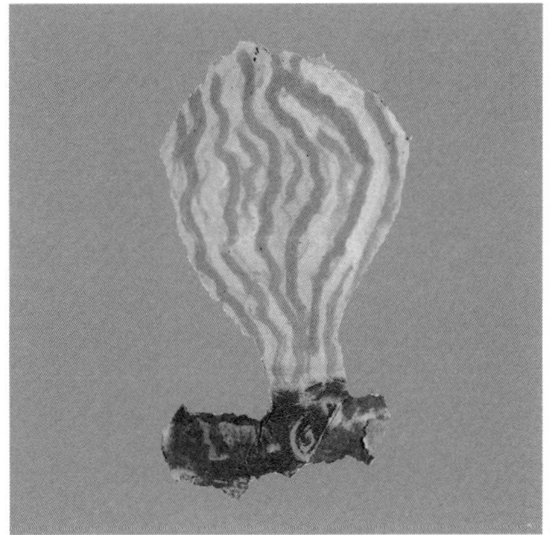

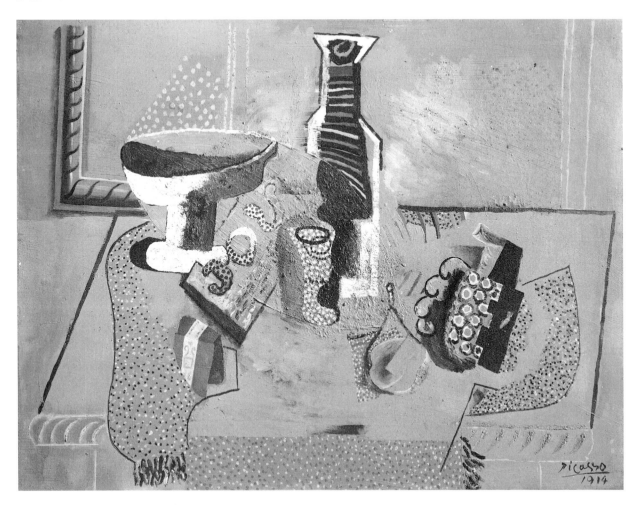

Above: Picasso. *Green Still Life*, summer, 1914. Oil on canvas, 60×79.5 cm. The Museum of Modern Art, New York: Lillie P. Bliss Collection.

Right: Picasso. *Still Life with Bottle of Maraschino*, summer, 1914. Oil and charcoal on canvas, 38×46 cm. From the collection of Mrs. John Hay Whitney.

Matisse. *Red Studio*, 1911. Oil on canvas, 181×219.1 cm. The Museum of Modern Art, New York: Mrs. Simon Guggenheim Fund.

black rent in the green ground on the left of the composition). But it still looks ambivalent, as does everything else in this painting, not least the one item that is monochromatic and three-dimensional: the gray cube sticking out of the black hole of a fireplace. Ostensibly part of the mantelpiece, this grim bit of grisaille suggests that all is not well beneath the green skin of paint and the pretty pointillist passages.

The influence of Matisse's *Red Studio* and *Blue Still Life* likewise explains why the objects and decorative motifs in another masterpiece of this period, the Museum of Modern Art's *Green Still Life*, look as if they are being absorbed into a pool of green paint. The newspaper is melting into the tablecloth, which is melting into the table, which is melting into the wall. To judge by telltale pentimenti left by the artist on the paint surface, certain items have already gone under. The rest of the Avignon still lifes are less monochromatic and rather more ornate; a style that has come to be known, misleadingly, as rococo cubism. "Decorated" would be more accurate: decorated not decorative. These paintings are the most lyrical examples of late cubism: colorful, witty, infinitely ingenious, and executed with a glitter that recalls Picasso's early training in *preciosismo* —the simulation of shimmering surfaces which permitted nineteenth-century Spanish painters like Marià Fortuny to demonstrate their virtuosity.[19] Maybe Picasso wanted to show his mistress how seductively he could paint. A sudden sweetness in his work usually reflects an uprush of tenderness. Why else come up with such mouthwatering displays of cookies, brioches, wafers, ladyfingers and fruit (apples, pomegranates, pears with leaves on, melons cut appetizingly open), as well as faceted flagons of Anis del Mono and straw-covered bottles of Negrita rum, diapered like a harlequin? Even such time-honored cubist objects as pipes, playing cards and newspapers are rendered with an unaccustomed degree of sensuousness.

The ingenious dovetailing of decorative elements suggests that Picasso had been looking closely at Juan Gris's recent work, while the *malerisch* delicacy reveals his continuing indebtedness to Braque's methods of enlivening paint surfaces: methods that Picasso would exploit ever more imaginatively—to Braque's eventual resentment. If only we could compare the two artists' work at this, their last, phase of very close contact, and chart their divergence in the light of Picasso's giant leaps in and out of cubism. Alas, we cannot: Braque spent the summer of 1914 reconditioning his new house at Sorgues—as a highly trained craftsman he insisted on doing everything himself—and did virtually no easel painting. It was only on July 25, a week before he was mobilized, that he was able to tell Kahnweiler, "I'm glad that I rented this house and am finally installed. The studio is very pretty. I've hung the walls with some paintings I had left here, and it's all ready for work."[20] Braque would not work in the studio until after his recovery from the war wound that would nearly blind him.

Braque standing outside the Villa Bel-Air, Sorgues, 1914. Archives Laurens.

The principal source for the innovations in the Avignon still lifes is to be found in Picasso's immediate past: above all in the painted bronze absinthe glasses and related constructions done earlier in the year in Paris. He had kept the constructions but sold all but one of the absinthe glasses to Kahnweiler, who was supposed to send him photographs of everything he had acquired so as to refresh the artist's memory. Picasso set great store by his memory—"a painter's most useful adjunct," he once said. Given his colossal output, he was very reliant on the black-and-white record that photographs provide—God forbid that he should repeat his hits any more than his misses—very reliant, too, on their help in enabling him to reconstruct the mystifying steps (mystifying above all to him) in his unrelenting progress. Hence the anxiety in what was probably his last letter to Kahnweiler before the war: "I've received a few more photos and am waiting for the others. They're not bad. Délétang has had a good touch of late. But the little glasses are really bad, it's hard to understand anything from them."[21]

These little glasses are the prototypes of images at the heart of many of the Avignon still lifes. Picasso would have needed to recall the different ways in which their different surfaces refract the light. Henceforth *verres à pied* (glasses with stems), more often than not fluted, take the place of musical instruments in Picasso's repertory. Indeed they recur so often that one has no choice but to see the fragile wineglass, with its wasp waist of a stem and lovingly delineated orifice, as a metaphor for Eva's fragility, sexuality and negativeness. (One is also reminded of Picasso's 1910 project to illustrate Cervantes's story about the young man who is convinced that his body is made of glass.) Never again would Picasso represent Eva as a guitar. And then what paradoxical games with transparency and opacity, not to speak of pointillism, these glasses enable Picasso to play. By using pointillism against itself, as if it were a form of camouflage, he atomizes the object. When Picasso returned to Paris and saw a convoy of camouflaged artillery lumber up the boulevard Raspail, he turned to Gertrude Stein and said, "We were the ones who did that."[22] For much of the war pointillism would be his camouflage.

Picasso. *Three Glasses*, 1914. Oil on packing paper, 30×15.5cm. Musée Picasso.

* * *

In the course of the summer—exactly when, we do not know—Picasso embarked on an experiment in pictorial relativity that would set off a radical change in his work. The experiment takes the form of a smallish, squarish naturalistic painting of an artist's studio, which came to light only after Picasso's death. The focal point is a nude girl holding a towel. To the girl's right, drawn but not painted, a seated man in working clothes leans on a table, gazing into space. Behind her is a notional green smudge of a landscape on an easel and a palette hanging from one of Braque's trompe l'œil nails—an indication that these seemingly naturalistic figures are situated in cubist space. Picasso portrays the girl as an artist's model, but she is evidently Eva: she has the same small-boned frame, the same girlishness, that we find in other representations of her. As for the lack of finish, I agree with Daix that it is intentional.[23] Picasso wants to play up the contrast between painting and drawing, as well as the contrast between cubist and perspectival space.

Picasso. *Glasses and Bottle*, 1914. Pencil on paper, 37.8×49.6cm. Musée Picasso.

Because this is a studio subject, the seated man has been identified as an artist: Picasso or an alter ego.[24] A mistake. The man is not an artist: he is an anonymous Cézannesque "*Cardplayer*" type, who personifies the Midi. He is brother to the mustachioed men in cafés—reading, smoking, drinking, playing guitars or cards or, as here, daydreaming—whom Picasso had repeatedly portrayed over the last three summers in the south. The

Cézanne. *Man with a Pipe*, 1890–92. Oil on canvas, 91×72cm. Pushkin Museum of Fine Art, Moscow.

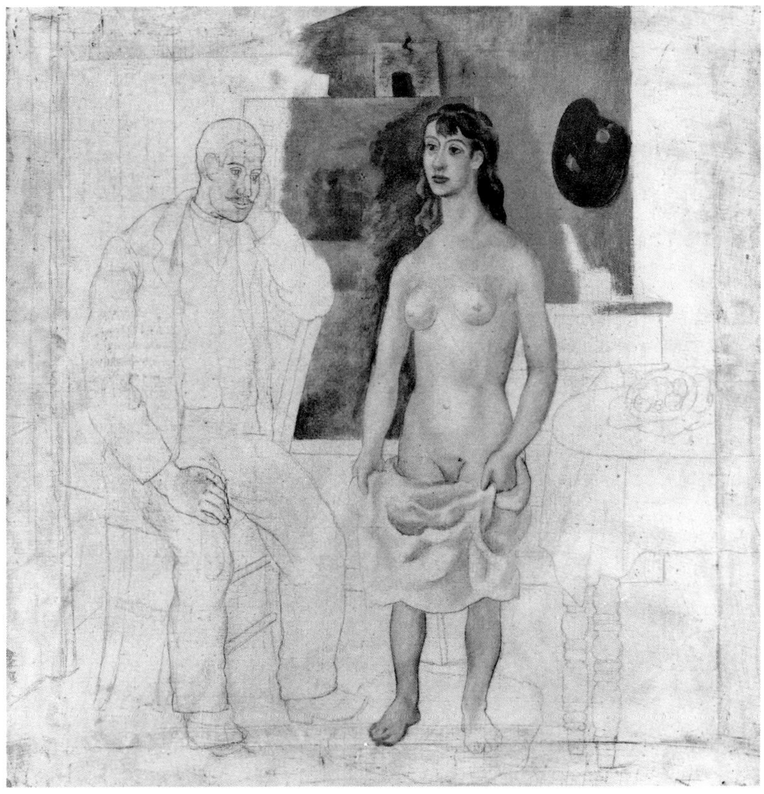

Picasso. *Seated Man and Artist's Model*, summer, 1914. Oil and pencil on canvas, 58×55.9cm. Musée Picasso.

Jean Auguste Dominique Ingres. Study for *Andromeda*, c. 1819. Oil on canvas, 45.8×37cm. Fogg Art Museum, Harvard University: Bequest of Grenville L. Winthrop.

Derain. *Portrait of Iturrino*, 1914. Oil on canvas, 92×65cm. Musée National d'Art Moderne, Centre Georges Pompidou, Paris.

Picasso and Derain. *Still Lifes*, summer, 1914. Oil on tiles, 54×54cm. (overall). Yale University Art Gallery: The Philip L. Goodwin, B.A. 1909, Collection (Gift of James L. Goodwin, 1905, Henry Sage Goodwin, 1927, and Richmond L. Brown, 1907).

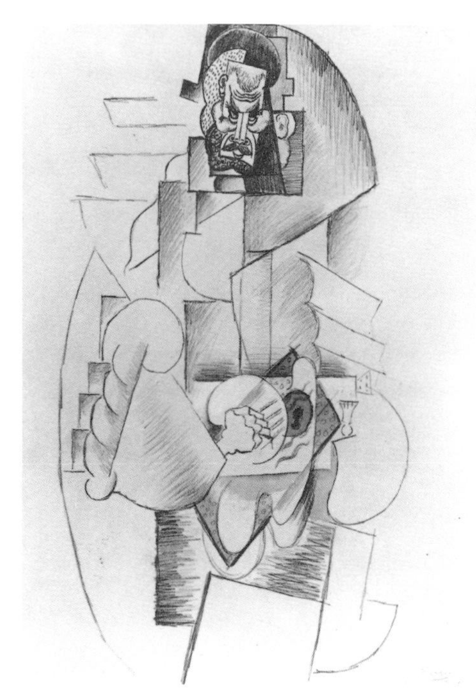

Right: Picasso. *Man in a Hat, Playing a Guitar (Iturrino)*, summer, 1914. Watercolor and pencil on paper, 49.7×38cm. Galerie Berggruen, Paris.

disparity between the two models—the Cézannesque peasant and the Ingresque nude—is allegorical: it reflects the disparity between the two great nineteenth-century masters who preside over this period of change. In the artist-and-model compositions he did at the end of his life Picasso puts himself into the picture and uses the creative act as a metaphor for the procreative act. Here, however, he keeps himself right out of the picture. If the figures look alienated—seemingly in a different space and time warp—it is because they relate not to one another but to Picasso, just as in one of the greatest of all studio paintings, *Les Poseuses*, the models relate only to Seurat.

This studio scene may also owe something to Derain. He and Picasso were once again in regular touch, as we know from Derain's painting of the Avignon house. Meanwhile Picasso had just acquired Derain's fine painting of a girl in a shawl (1914)—was it because the modeling of the face owes so much to his portrait of Gertrude Stein?[25] Also, in a sly act of one-upmanship, Picasso proposed to Derain that they should each paint still lifes on the tiles that had come loose in Derain's kitchen and incorporate them into a fourfold panel. They could then give it to Kahnweiler—for his birthday on June 25.[26] By comparison with Picasso's tough little still lifes, Derain's attempts at cubism recall the genteel decorations of Duncan Grant and Vanessa Bell.

Derain. *Girl with Shawl*, 1914. Oil on canvas, 61 × 50 cm. Musée Picasso.

Derain emerges with rather more glory from another confrontation with Picasso. When Iturrino, the Basque painter who had shared his first show at Vollard's, passed through Avignon, Picasso did a striking drawing of him—a lifelike mask of this dramatic-looking man grafted onto a synthetic cubist figure—while Derain devoted one of his greatest portraits to him. Derain could hardly have made a better case for traditional representationalism. His portrait may have been instrumental in persuading Picasso to give figuration another try. Besides the studio painting, he did a number of naturalistic drawings in the course of summer: still lifes of fruit, bottles of ink and the inevitable glasses, also studies of an aging muscle-builder—sometimes clothed, sometimes unclothed—who looks like a professional model. Picasso may even have shared a model with Derain. Though he was a poor draftsman—facile yet weak—Derain was always advocating drawing from life. He was also forever invoking the sacred name of Cézanne, whose shadow falls across Picasso's work one more time.

Braque was apparently too busy renovating his new house to see much of Picasso. However, as he wrote Kahnweiler on July 25, he hoped that Picasso would once again become his neighbor: "Picasso paid me a visit. He is still fond of Sorgues. He would like to find something here."[27] Interestingly enough, Picasso had expressed a similar wish, a month earlier, to Derain, who had likewise assured Kahnweiler (June 21) that "Picasso may soon become my neighbor."[28] Picasso's letters to Kahnweiler and Gertrude Stein fail to mention any such intentions on his part. He evidently chose to keep his distance, as did Eva. The pursuer, it appears, was now the pursued. Cubism had virtually run its course, and Picasso no longer needed a co-worker.

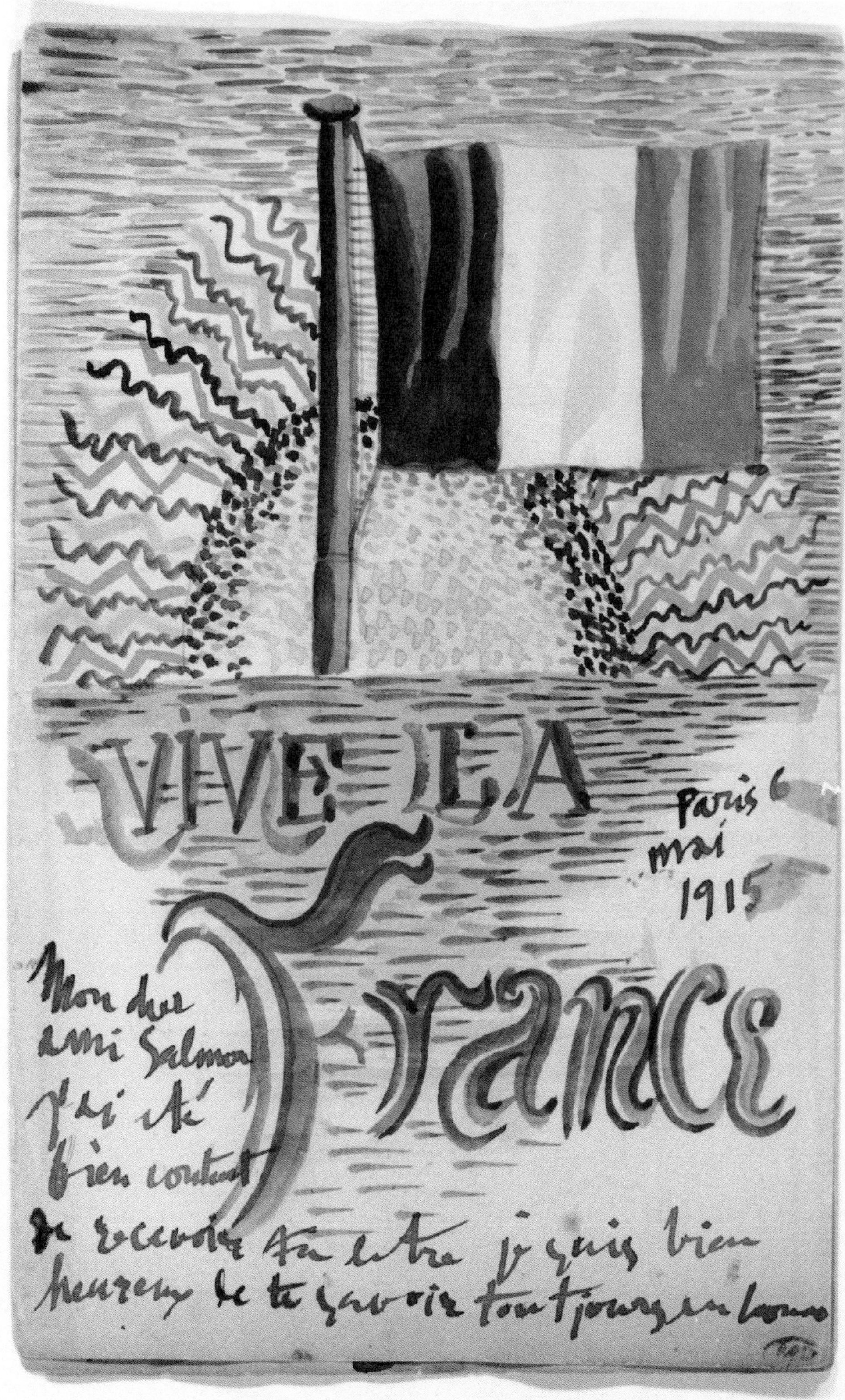
VIVE LA
France
Paris 6
mai
1915
Mon cher
ami Salmon
j'ai été
bien content
de recevoir ta lettre je suis bien
heureux de te savoir toujours en bonne

22

Outbreak of War

"If there had been a bit more cubism, that is to say modern ideas, the war would not have taken place."[1]
(Apollinaire, November, 1915)

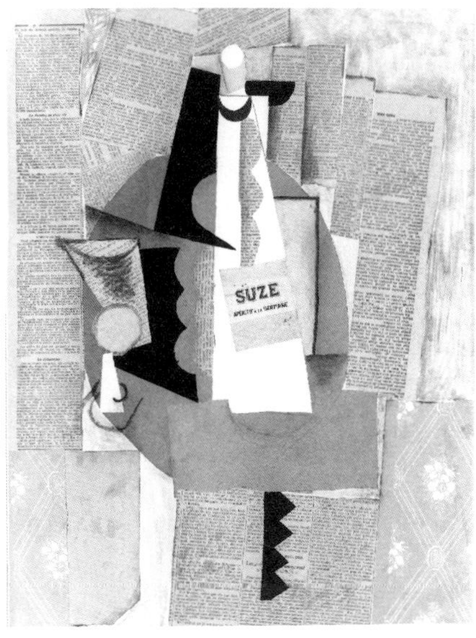

Picasso. *Glass and Bottle of Suze (La Suze)*, fall, 1912. Pasted papers, gouache and charcoal, 64.5×50cm. Washington University Gallery of Art, St. Louis: University purchase, Kende Sale Fund, 1946.

BEYOND HORROR AT THE PROSPECT OF WAR, there is no evidence whatsoever in letters or statements by Picasso or his friends as to where he stood ideologically. Kahnweiler, who was a fervent socialist, saw no trace of socialism in Picasso's views; he was apolitical, he said—only an anarchist in that he was a free spirit and a Spaniard. There is nothing to the contrary in Picasso's French police dossier, beyond the fact that he had once been the roommate of an alleged anarchist, Pere Mañach.[2] However, an apolitical stance does not preclude convictions of one kind or another. In general terms Picasso was a liberal humanist, adamant on one issue only: he always was and always would be a pacifist. This was not an easy line to take in World War I. Pacifists were usually denounced as traitors or shirkers, even by someone as progressive as Apollinaire.

Years later, Picasso confirmed his pacifism in a conversation with Daix:

> One day I brought [Picasso a photograph of] the *Glass and Bottle of Suze* [papier collé], because in it I had found an account of a huge demonstration against the Balkan War (between 40,000 and 100,000 people were estimated to have attended) held on November 17, 1912, at Pré-Saint-Gervais, a suburb of Paris, in a place called Butte du Chapeau Rouge. There were speeches by German, Russian and French socialists, anarchists and pacifists, and cries of approval: "*A bas la guerre!*" "*Vive la révolution sociale!*" In France this was a great event in the history of the Socialist Party's anti-war struggle. . . . I asked Picasso if he had included [the newspaper clipping of] the speech on purpose. He said, "Of course . . . because it was an important event involving a hundred thousand people. . . . Oh yes, I found that in the newspaper, and it was my way of showing I was against the war."[3]

When Daix asked Picasso why he had buried his pacifism in a papier collé which would not emerge until 1922, the artist laughed and said, "Well, I knew that people would find this later and understand."[4] According to Daix, "Picasso did not intend to create a manifesto proclaiming his political ideas. Rather, it was something that played a private role at one moment or another in his art."[5]

Picasso. Letter to André Salmon decorated with flag and "Vive la France," May 6, 1915. Gouache, watercolor and India ink on paper, 17.5×11.1cm. Musée Picasso: Gift of M. et Mme. Alain Mazo.

Picasso's pacifism was instinctive—probably atavistic. The conviction that war and warriors were stupid and evil stemmed from his Andalusian birthright as much as its counterpart, machismo, did. In Andalusia, according to David Gilmore, violence, above all of the saber-rattling variety, is regarded as uncouth.[6] Andalusians set a high value on *formalidad*—

Picasso with Sentinelle, 1914. Archives Picasso.

civility, with its emphasis on self-restraint and self-control. This is the more necessary because Andalusian men are aggressive. But their weapon is mockery rather than the knife or the gun. And they direct their physical aggression towards animals—that is to say, bulls—or, sexually, towards women. "The emphasis is entirely upon sexual aggressiveness with virtually no stress on pugilistic prowess. . . . In Andalusia, physical toughness, fighting and athletic bravado are strongly devalued."[7] Picasso's pacifism was reinforced by the conviction that his art took priority over all other considerations and that his well-being, not to say his life, must never be put at risk. In the circumstances there could be no question of his joining the Foreign Legion, as several foreign-born artists were doing; just as there had never been any question of his adopting French nationality, as he had, provocatively, urged Kahnweiler to do. Picasso was never tempted, for the same reason that Kahnweiler was never tempted: it would have involved the unthinkable obligation of military service.

As for going back to Spain, that, too, was out of the question. Life was too provincial. Besides, as someone who was perceived by the French as owing everything to France, Picasso could not afford to look as if he were deserting his adopted country in its hour of need. And then there was the problem of Eva's poor health: she could not be expected to leave her native land. All in all, it made far more sense to stay put, even if regulations pertaining to aliens were more than ever stringent and snarled in red tape.

Picasso's first response to the imminence of war was characteristically pragmatic. Anticipating the closure of Kahnweiler's gallery and the collapse of the market for his work, he dashed up to Paris with Eva a day or two before the declaration of war (July 30 or 31), and withdrew all the money from his bank account. "*C'était le coup de maître*," Serge Férat wrote Soffici.[8] According to Matisse, the sum amounted to 100,000 gold francs.[9] Picasso's peasantlike approach to money triggered rumors of gold ingots stashed under his bed.[10]

Crowds outside the Banque de France, Paris, in the last days of July, 1914.

Besides bourgeois panic—thousands of French people had joined this eve-of-the-war run on the banks—Picasso had another urgent reason for the trip to Paris. Foreigners—especially painters, writers and students from Spain—were more than ever suspected of political or cultural subversion and subject to strict surveillance. All the more need for papers to be in order, strings to be readied for pulling, as well as money to be at hand. As Gris wrote Kahnweiler from Collioure the day war was declared, "Foreigners, summoned to the Town Hall to reveal their closest secrets, have been involved in a mass of fines and proceedings for not having their papers in order, and some have even been threatened with expulsion."[11] Picasso, whose fear of the authorities had been exacerbated by *l'affaire des statuettes*, would have been anxious to conform to the letter of the law. No less worrying, he was still owed 20,000 francs by Kahnweiler for the batch of work (including the bronze absinthe glasses) that he had handed over earlier in the summer. Since the dealer was off on a vacation that would end in exile, Picasso had good reason to be pessimistic about the fate of his money, just as he would soon have good reason to fear for the fate of his recent work. Most of his friends were away from Paris. Gertrude and Alice were in London; however, Picasso and Eva had the concierge let them into the rue de Fleurus to check the installation of some picture brackets.

After twenty-four hours at the most, Picasso returned with Eva to Avignon, nest egg in hand. He was just in time to go to the station with Braque and Derain, who had been mobilized. As patriotic reservists, both of them were unashamedly pro-war, impatient to fight—in contrast to Picasso, who made no secret of his views. "I never saw [Braque and Derain] again," Picasso told Kahnweiler, who tried years later to explain away this *boutade* as a metaphor: "He did see them again, but . . . he meant that it was never the same."[12] Metaphor or not, these words have been taken much too seriously. Picasso's intimacy with Braque was indeed waning, but Henry Hope (author of a pioneer monograph on Braque) was misinformed in his assertion that they "had a personal quarrel just before the war."[13] Leighten has further embellished the legend: "The argument that [Picasso] and Braque reportedly had on the platform of the train station in Avignon . . . may well have concerned Picasso's pacifism, or in any case his refusal to join the war."[14] Both Picasso and Braque assured me that they took leave of each other on the friendliest terms. As his letters to Marcelle from the front reveal,[15] Braque continued to send Picasso affectionate messages and never included him in his vehement castigations of *fainéants* (shirkers), like Delaunay. "You remember how [Delaunay] went on about his patriotism," Serge Férat wrote Soffici. "Well the bastard ran off to Biarritz the day mobilization was ordered and profited from some previous heart problem to get invalided out."[16] Another despised *fainéant* was Gleizes, who joined up and then, after marrying Juliette Roche in 1915, arranged for her politically powerful father to have him demobilized so that they could go off to New York together.[17] (If Braque turned against Juan Gris, it was not because he was a shirker—like Picasso, he was a Spanish national—it was because Braque felt that "the former cartoonist" had muscled in on cubism and to some extent appropriated his place while he was off fighting.) And although in the years between the wars Picasso and Braque would grow apart—socially and politically as well as artistically—and say scathing things about each other, the bonds between them were never severed. According to Dora Maar, Picasso's most abiding male friendship, apart from those with his Quatre Gats cronies, would always be with Braque.[18]

Alice Derain photographed by D.-H. Kahnweiler at the Derains' rue Bonaparte apartment, 1914. Archives Kahnweiler: Galerie Louise Leiris.

As for the group's dependents, Braque had arranged for Marcelle to stay on in his new house at Sorgues until things were more settled. Derain gave Picasso his dog, Sentinelle, to look after but, in the event of disaster, entrusted his wife, once Picasso's mistress, to the protection of Matisse. Meanwhile she stayed on at Montfavet, where her sister joined her, and they "wandered around like souls in torment."[19] Alice, who liked to live well, found herself very short of money, as did everybody else who depended on Kahnweiler for their income—with the notable exception of Picasso.

* * *

For Kahnweiler, the war came just as he was enjoying his first taste of victory. Virtually all the best young Paris-based artists were under contract to him. Their work, above all Picasso's, was attracting worldwide attention and selling well, especially in Germany and Russia. Kahnweiler had proved to his far from confident family that he was as successful in his chosen field as they were in theirs. He and his wife had moved to a larger apartment (rue Georges-Sand), where he had installed an ever-growing private collection, including portraits of himself by Van Dongen and his wife by Derain, and African sculpture.

Although he prided himself on his foresight, Kahnweiler had refused to consider the possibility of war (*"Je n'ai pas voulu y croire jusqu'à la dernière minute"*).[20] At the end of July, he, his wife and little Zette had left on a mountain-climbing vacation in the Bavarian Alps. Only when the Germans started calling up reservists did he see the danger of being corralled into the kaiser's army. With all haste he and his family crossed into Switzerland and headed for Italy. The outbreak of war, Kahnweiler said, was "something absolutely dreadful, a laceration, beyond description, because it was obviously impossible for me to fight for Germany."[21] A "laceration," too, because it put paid to his dreams of fame and fortune for his artists, not to speak of himself, the godfather of cubism. Success would not come his way again for another thirty-five years. After World War II, Picasso would resume using Kahnweiler as his dealer, thus enabling him finally to profit from his acumen and make a vast fortune as well as achieve more prestige than any other modernist dealer. The artist had total faith in Kahnweiler's discretion, so he entrusted him with much of his confidential business, but he would never again let him have any real control.

Lucie and Daniel-Henry Kahnweiler in their rue Georges-Sand apartment, 1913. Archives Kahnweiler: Galerie Louise Leiris.

Back, however, to the first months of the war. Kahnweiler stayed on in Italy, unable to decide what to do. He was obliged to be very circumspect, for fear that the German authorities might penalize him for draft-dodging and confiscate the works he had consigned to dealers in Munich and Düsseldorf. Communications with business associates and family members had to be clandestine. Kahnweiler's problems with the French authorities were even worse. There was nothing against his returning to Paris and reclaiming his property—the apartment with his collection, the gallery with his stock—provided he joined the Foreign Legion: an option that his pacifism ruled out. Alternatively, he could have accepted Brenner and Coady's offer to ship him and his stock to New York, where he could have continued to deal out of their gallery. This would have been the best solution, had he taken it soon enough. Cautious as ever, Kahnweiler finally chose exile in neutral Switzerland, where he could live off the charity of his old friend Hermann Rupf, the Bernese haberdasher with whom he had shared lodgings when he first came to Paris. Exile meant that everything he owned was subject to sequestration. His stock was moved to a damp storage-place on the rue de Rennes until, at Kahnweiler's request, it was transferred back to the gallery that was no longer his. If most of his artists had not been fighting for their lives at the front, they might have resisted the government's confiscation of their recent work. Picasso was the more resentful for not being at the front; and he set about fighting the sequestration, which he blamed entirely on Kahnweiler.

Derain. *Portrait of Madame Lucie Kahnweiler*, 1913. Oil on canvas, 92×73cm. Musée National d'Art Moderne, Centre Georges Pompidou, Paris.

Once settled in Bern, Kahnweiler registered as a dealer so that he could negotiate the sale of whatever he had been able to rescue from former associates like Flechtheim and Thannhauser. Unfortunately, apart from Rupf and his friend Hadorn, few of the Swiss showed much interest in modern art. In his frustration, Kahnweiler enrolled in a philosophy class at the University of Bern. He reread Kant and Hegel and immersed himself in the ideas of Alois Riegl, Worringer and Wölfflin, as his wartime writings reveal.[22] Under the influence of Rupf, a diehard socialist, Kahnweiler brought his unfocused leftism almost but not quite to the point of serious commitment. He was apparently scared off by Rupf's doctrinaire friend Robert Grimm; this fervent radical tried hard and unavailingly to bring him together with Radek and Zinoviev. Although he was too cautious to consort with Bolsheviks, Kahnweiler established lifelong friendships with subversives of a different stripe: artists who shared his exile, such as Paul Klee, Hans Arp and the young Romanian poet Tristan Tzara, who would inaugurate the dada movement at Zurich's Café Voltaire in 1916. Kahnweiler approved of the movement's nihilism but disapproved of its iconoclasm, especially when directed against his sacrosanct artists. "Cathedrals made of shit" is how the dadaists would soon be describing cubist paintings.

In the course of 1916, Kahnweiler would express his newfound concepts in his seminal *Der Weg zum Kubismus*, a subjective and dogmatic account of *his* cubism. *Der Weg* abounds in illuminating ideas—some of them way ahead of their time—but these did not commend the text to Picasso or Braque. When it was finally published in France (1921), both of them complained that it was too theoretical, too Germanic—the kind of Teutonic cant that Picasso used to silence with a volley of shots from his revolver. Chauvinist attacks on cubism for supposedly being German-inspired would greatly intensify the artist's allergy to the whole panoply of German *Geisteswissenschaft*. Picasso was also, I suspect, annoyed with Kahnweiler for singling out the Cadaqués paintings for special praise—they had supposedly "shattered the enclosed form"—when he had originally turned all but one of them down. The essay inevitably suffers from being written in isolation, without access to archives and photographs, let alone the artists involved. However, considering he had little but the paintings he had sold to Rupf and his memory to go on, Kahnweiler's study is surprisingly reliable.

Cover of Kahnweiler's *Der Weg zum Kubismus*; design based on Louis Marcoussis's 1910 painting of the Sacré-Cœur.

The worst hit of Kahnweiler's stable was Juan Gris. He could not return to Spain, as he had skipped military service, or Paris, as he feared (groundlessly) that his return ticket was no longer valid. Meanwhile he was stranded without a penny at Collioure, where the authorities were threatening him with expulsion. Fortunately, a local family, whose son Gris had known in Madrid, came to the rescue; otherwise he and his wife would have starved. Fortunately, too, Picasso's innate charity won out over resentment, and he sent Gris money. Matisse, who had stayed on at Collioure, was also supportive, as was Gertrude Stein, who had started to collect Gris's work a few months earlier. She sent Gris 200 francs and, with Matisse's help, proposed a scheme whereby she and Brenner, the Paris-based American dealer, would provide him with 125 francs a month in return for paintings. Gris, who was punctilious to the point of folly, wrote and asked Kahnweiler, his dealer in exile, for permission to go ahead with this fair-minded arrangement. Kahnweiler invoked the terms of their contract and refused to countenance any such exchange. All the artist's work belonged contractually to him, he maintained. "If everything belongs to you," Gris replied in an uncharacteristic show of spirit, for which he later apologized, "either I should stop working or I should hand over my entire output to the Custodian of Enemy Property."[23] After some

Modigliani. *Juan Gris*, c. 1915. Oil on canvas, 55×38 cm. Metropolitan Museum of Art, New York: Bequest of Miss Adelaide Milton de Groot, 1967.

unseemly haggling, Kahnweiler agreed to send 125 francs a month to Gris's sister in Madrid, who would then transfer the funds to Paris. Although this scheme left Gris open to charges of trading with the enemy, it gave Kahnweiler the illusion of still being in business. And it enabled the craven artist to hoodwink Gertrude into believing that he was being sent money by his family and therefore in no further need of her help. When she discovered the truth, Gertrude was understandably furious and refused to have anything to do with the artist until after the war. Gris did not wriggle off the hook of Kahnweiler's contract until April, 1915, whereupon he signed up with Léonce Rosenberg.

Apollinaire in uniform, 1914. Photograph by G. Meunier. Collection P.M.A.

* * *

As for Apollinaire, the outbreak of war triggered a series of events that would culminate in his death. At the end of July, he had gone to Deauville to work on an illustrated gossip column for *Comœdia* magazine. He had traveled there in the writer André Rouveyre's chauffeur-driven car, together with a couple of pet toads called Di and Do, who first repelled and then enchanted him.[24] Late in the evening of July 31, they were in the casino when general mobilization was announced. They immediately drove back to Paris, stopping en route at Rouveyre's house in Fontainebleau, where Apollinaire dashed off a poignant article, "La Fête manquée," in which he meditates on "the end of the party." He invokes a portent he had seen the previous morning: "A marvellous Negro dressed in a robe of . . . silvery blue and dawn pink, bicycling through the streets of Deauville . . . towards the beach. At last he reached the sea and apparently dived in. Soon all that was left of him was a sea-green turban, gradually engulfed by . . . waves."[25] Apollinaire also wrote a charming poem, "La Petite Auto," about his drive from Deauville. It ends:

> We arrived in Paris
> At the moment mobilization notices were being posted
> We understood my friend and I
> That the little car had driven us into a new epoch
> And that although both of a ripe age
> We had just been born. [26]

Louise de Coligny-Chatillon; photograph, c. 1914.

Although there was no need for Apollinaire to enlist—friends had invited him to spend the war in Spain or Switzerland—he hastened to do so. But on August 24 his application was adjourned, presumably because of his record as a former jailbird. With no military or journalistic obligations, Apollinaire felt free to go off and enjoy himself, as only he knew how. After obtaining a *laisser passer*, he left for Nice on September 3 and immediately embarked on a roller-coaster affair with a well-born *allumeuse*, Louise de Coligny (known as Lou), who vacillated between extremes of frigidity, depravity and disdain. Maddened by her teasing advances and capricious rebuffs, Apollinaire went back to the recruiting office. This time he was accepted for the artillery; what is more, accepted by Lou, who, albeit briefly, became his devoted slave—happy to smoke opium and be whipped and sodomized by him, as confirmed in his exceedingly explicit love poems to her: for instance, the litany to Lou's nine orifices: "*O Portes de ton corps / Elles sont neuf et je les ai toutes ouvertes.*" ("O, Gates of your body / They are nine and I have opened them all.")[27] The

Picasso. *Guillaume de Kostrowitzky Artilleur*, 1914. Ink on paper, 23×12.5cm. Private collection.

affair was too combustible to last. In despair, Apollinaire volunteered for an intense course of cavalry training and found consolation of a kind in discipline and drill. Meanwhile he continued to write Lou ecstatic poems.

Wartime letters from Apollinaire to Picasso are few and far between. However, Picasso's have survived, and they are touchingly warm and affectionate. On February 7, 1915, the artist sent the poet some tips on camouflage: "I'm going to give you a very good tip for the artillery. Even when painted gray, artillery and cannons are visible to airplanes because they retain their shape. Instead they should be painted very bright colors, bits of red, yellow, green, blue, white like a harlequin."[28] "*Je te [sic] embrasse mon vieux frère*" is how he ends up. A few months later, Picasso signs off with a calligram of his own that is even more succinct than Apollinaire's "Pipe and Paintbrush": a tricolor drawing of his hand, inscribed, "To wish you good day my hand becomes a flag."[29]

Apollinaire's compatriots Louis Marcoussis and Adolphe Basler had also joined the French army. "[Marcoussis] came to see me yesterday to show off his sergeant-major's stripes," Gris wrote Raynal. "He was furious, because in my ignorance I called him 'corporal.'"[30] Basler had a more serious reason for fury, but not with Gris. Before the war, he had eked out his living as an art critic by working as an amateur dealer and, on a trip to New York, had foolishly left his group of important Picasso drawings with Stieglitz as collateral for a small loan. Now that Basler was a penniless *poilu*, the rapacious Stieglitz was out to appropriate his Picassos.[31] Another Pole, Kisling, who had once been under contract to Basler, had volunteered for the Foreign Legion, been wounded and invalided out. Serge Férat, still a Russian citizen, had signed up as an orderly and was working at the Italian military hospital in Paris. The American dealer Brenner had likewise joined the nursing corps—as a stretcher bearer. Even Modigliani had tried to enlist but proved too far gone to pass his medical. Pascin, who was Bulgarian, had made his way to New York, where he acquired American nationality. Picabia had put his driving skills and car at the service of the French army, until he, too, decided to head for New York. Chagall, who had been caught by the war in Vitebsk, stayed on in Russia and, after the October Revolution, became the local commissar for fine arts. Severini, recently married to Paul Fort's daughter, had contracted tuberculosis; his patriotic set pieces of flags, planes, guns and slogans were surely devised as a sop to French chauvinism. The newly wed Marie Laurencin was in particularly bad odor with Picasso and Braque, not to mention her former lover, Apollinaire, for having fled with her German baron to Spain. She stayed there for the rest of the war prettifying her style and dallying, like her husband, with Spanish ladies and gentlemen, and hanging out with the Picabias, Gleizes and other refugees from the war.

Although as profoundly anti-war as Picasso, Matisse had tried to enlist: "[He] has been revisioned three times and doesn't go on account of his eyes," Gertrude told Henry McBride.[32] Elsewhere she fantasizes that Picasso's Bateau Lavoir neighbor Herbin was "so tiny that the army dismissed him. He said ruefully the pack he had to carry weighed as much as he did. . . . He was returned home inapt for service and he came near starving."[33] There is no truth in this, nor in Stein's claim that Metzinger was also let go for being "undersize."

Derain as a military bicyclist, August, 1914. Archives G. Taillade.

Léger (left) in the trenches, 1916. Private collection.

As for Picasso's friends in uniform, Braque was soon made a second lieutenant; Derain was stationed at Lisieux, in Normandy, training to be a bicyclist, "but so far has been laid up with a leg";[34] Vlaminck was working in an army paint shop at Le Havre; Raynal and Salmon were both on active service—Salmon very broke and dependent on handouts from Picasso and other friends. Léger, whose work Picasso had come round recently and rather grudgingly to accept, turned out to be one of the more gallant of the Montparnasse artists. Until he was gassed in 1917 and invalided out of the army, Léger was a sapper in the engineering corps and constantly in the thick of action: Verdun, Aisne, Argonne. Whenever he could, he drew or painted (sometimes on shellcases). The sketches he made at Verdun just before the French counteroffensive in October, 1916, are all the more vivid for being done on the spot. And in the compositions he painted later in the studio—*La Partie de cartes* and *Les Foreurs*—he evokes mechanized warfare more powerfully than any other modernist. The war inspired Léger's concept of *éléments méchaniques*, which enabled him to visualize a woman's strapping thighs in terms of the highlit cylinder of a gun-barrel. Léger had transformed Cézanne's celebrated dictum into a machine aesthetic. For the rest of his life, Léger loved to recount how his intrepid and famously amorous wife, Jeanne, helped by her young maid, Kiki (later celebrated as "Kiki of Montparnasse," the lover of Kisling, Man Ray and many more), dressed up as a *poilu* and made her way to Verdun in order to sleep with her "*mec*" in the trenches. She was arrested and nearly shot as a spy, but she finally found Léger in a dugout—drawing. After making love, she returned to Montparnasse, a heroine.[35]

*   *   *

Picasso. *Head of a Soldier in a Képi*, 1911–15. Oil on canvas, 63×51 cm. Private collection.

The fact that "Avignon" appears more often in Picasso's cubist work than any other place-name confirms his special affection for the town. "We're thinking of staying here until the end of the war," Picasso wrote (September 11) to Gertrude Stein and Alice Toklas,[36] who were still in England. They evidently preferred being stranded in London to being strafed in Paris. Given his feelings against the war, it is surprising that Picasso decorated his letters (especially ones to Apollinaire) with tricolor flags and bellicose slogans. Eva was surely a jingoist; however, I suspect that these patriotic effusions were a tongue-in-cheek bow to what would now be called political correctness. In much the same spirit Picasso composed one of the finest of his Avignon still lifes around a corny little vase emblazoned with crossed tricolor flags and the words, "*Vive la . . .* ," which he cunningly leaves the beholder to complete. An ironical use of patriotic kitsch was Picasso's only possible response to warmongers.

"We're not badly off here," Picasso's letter to Gertrude continues, "I'm even working a little, but I feel very worried when I think of Paris, my house there and all our things."[37] Picasso was in fact working intently. On September 22, Max Jacob, who had been turned down by the army, wrote to Kahnweiler, who was still in Italy: "Galanis [a young Greek painter who had joined the French army] has brought me news from Avignon. Our Picasso, it seems, is doing some of the best work he has ever done."[38] No doubt about it, Avignon suited him. There was no risk of air raids,

Fernand Léger. Study for *La Partie de cartes*, 1915. Pen on paper, 19×13.5cm. Private collection.

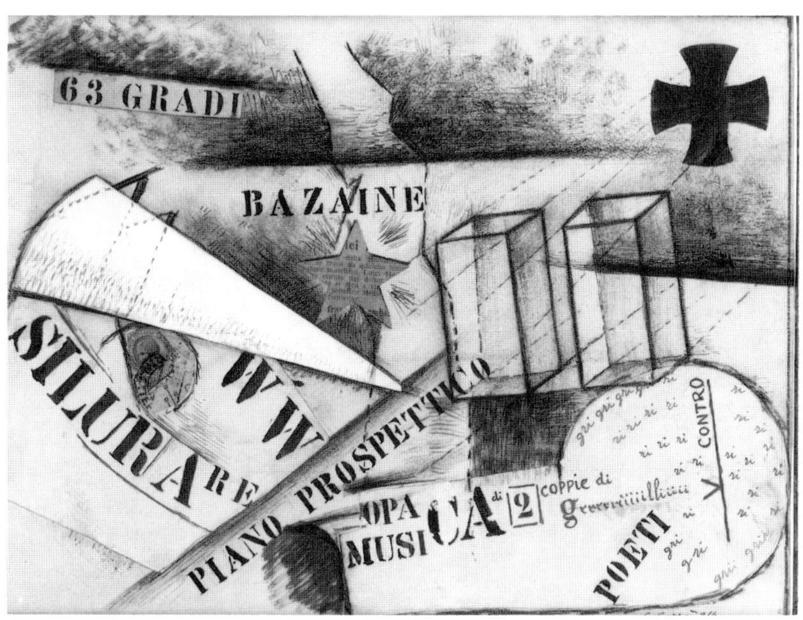

Carlo Carrà. *Joffre's Angle of Penetration on the Marne Against Two German Cubes*, 1914. Pasted papers, newsprint, postage stamp, pencil, conté crayon, ink and white on paper, 25.5×34.3cm. Private collection.

Picasso. *Playing Cards, Wineglasses and Bottle of Rum ("Vive la . . .")*, 1914–15. Oil and sand on canvas, 54×65cm. Private collection.

which had first hit Paris on August 30; and although the Germans had advanced as close as twenty miles from Paris, that was still several hundred miles from Provence. And now, as a result of the battle of the Marne (September 6–10), the enemy was being forced to withdraw.

Porte Saint-Lazare, Avignon, with poster for *Kub*; postcard, c. 1914. Archives Municipales, Avignon.

However far they were from the front, foreigners were not safe from the chauvinism that was sweeping France. Leaders of the fanatically right-wing Action Française, like Léon Daudet (son of Provence's most famous writer, Alphonse Daudet), kept xenophobia on the boil. Even French nationals were not safe. According to Max Jacob, poor Marcelle (still not married to Braque) found herself briefly "arrested as a spy in Avignon, and then released without having been raped."[39] Alice Derain was also detained. Shopkeepers with foreign-sounding names were obliged to emblazon their storefronts with explanatory signs and *Vive la France* banners, or risk being looted; innocent photographers were accused of espionage and in one case almost lynched. Picasso lay low and kept out of trouble, but by virtue of being a cubist and a former target of philistine attacks from the left as well as the right he had reason to be on his guard.

Within days of the outbreak of war, spy mania erupted in a particularly bizarre, and to Picasso, menacing form: "*l'affaire du bouillon KUB*." To advertise their famous soup concentrate, the French branch of the German Maggi corporation had erected hundreds of huge billboards in highly visible locations all over France. Besides the enormous letters *KUB*, which had a distinctly German connotation, given that the letter *K* is seldom used in French, the signs carried code numbers of purely administrative significance.[40] To paranoid elements in the military, the positioning of these eye-catchers was strategic, and the real purpose of these reference numbers was to provide information about neighboring targets, sources of supply and so forth to advancing German troops. Amazingly, even the minister of the interior went along with this madness. He instructed the *préfets* of every department to destroy or paint out all *KUB* billboards, especially ones along railroad tracks or adjacent to important viaducts and road junctions. Newspapers urged motorists and cyclists to go out and annihilate these "*machiavéliques*" signposts. A mob six hundred strong paraded around the town of Lille singing patriotic songs as they tore down the billboards. All over France children went on similar rampages, egged on by local bigots. Meanwhile the police neglected more serious duties to arrest some of Maggi's salesmen not only for being spies but for supposedly foisting cans of poisoned milk on French babies.

Looting of a Maggi dairy in Paris, August, 1914.

Picasso had cause for alarm as he had included one of the *KUB* billboards in a landscape two years earlier (p. 240) and used the word as a visual/verbal pun in a number of cubist compositions. (So had Braque, whose still life of a violin in front of a Mozart/Kubelick poster makes a similar pun.) What is more, Picasso had been publicly attacked by Vauxcelles as "*le chef des messieurs cubistes, quelquechose comme le père Ubu-KUB*."[41] If a simple billboard could be construed as a signal to the enemy, what about his recent paintings with their fragmented words, arcane pictorial code and diagrammatic appearance—works that had found great favor with German dealers?[42] Sure enough, these dealers would soon be denounced as German agents, who had used the cubists to infiltrate French culture and destroy it from within. One of the worst of the rabble-rousers was a reactionary anti-Semite called Tony Tollet, who gave lectures attacking "the Influence of the Judeo-German Cartel of Parisian Painting Dealers on French Art":

> I want to speak to you of the crushing and pestilential influence that the cartel of art dealers has had on French art [his jeremiad begins]. I want to show you the strategies they have used to corrupt French taste . . . how they have imposed works bearing the hallmark of German culture—Pointillist, Cubist and Futurist, etc.—on the taste of our snobs. Everything—music, literature, painting, sculpture, architecture, decorative arts, fashion, everything—has suffered the destructive effects of our enemies' asphyxiating gases.[43]

LES VACANCES DU MAITRE CUBE

Joseph Hémard. *Les Vacances du Maître Cube.* Cartoon in *La Vie Parisienne,* July 13, 1912. Bibliothéque Nationale, Paris.

Picasso's gradual switch to legibility and Ingresque notation has been seen as a response to these chauvinistic attacks.[44] There may have been some such link, but I doubt it, just as I doubt the wisdom of seeing Picasso's classicism as analogous to the *retardataire* "*rappel à l'ordre*" that the chaos of war would engender. In this context we should never forget that Picasso was very conscious of his role as "*le peintre de la vie moderne,*" very conscious of his mission to work against the grain rather than with it. Tailoring his art to contemporary fashions or canons of beauty or taste would have been unthinkable. He would always pride himself on being a jump ahead of the Zeitgeist.

* * *

For all that Avignon was far from the front, the town was deeply committed to the war effort. Refugees from Alsace and Lorraine were lodged in schools, seminaries, factories, as well as the Alhambra Cinema and Palace Theater. Other buildings had been requisitioned as military hospitals (including the Hôpital across from Picasso's house) and were already overflowing with wounded soldiers. Troops were quartered in the Hôtel de Ville, municipal theater, courthouse and Palais des Papes, not to speak of garages and stables. The society painter Jacques-Emile Blanche provides a vivid account of life there in the first weeks of the war (September 19, 1914):

> Avignon looked so papal yesterday that one was amazed to be confronted by the military at every turn. I never saw so many uniforms in my life. Avignon is a factory processing canon-fodder.
>
> There is a regiment of the Foreign Legion as well as troops (of all kinds): Russians, Poles, Italians, Greeks, Egyptians; two squads in red and blue uniforms going off on manoeuvres; several negroes and mulattos among them. If you press on as far as the station, there are Indian soldiers. From morning to night and night to morning, the Côte d'Azur line supplies the Front with armed tribes from the East and the Far East, Alexander's legions, displaying all shades of skin and all manner of weapons. Thomas Cook's representatives apologize to us, their clients of old, for being no earthly use. Albion's former tourists in khaki puttees and caps, revolvers in their holsters, have taken over the stations of the Paris–Lyon–Mediterranée line and are treating their comrades from the Himalayas to a tour of the Champagne district [a principal battle zone], a few days in Paris, followed perhaps by a grave on Christian soil. Madness![45]

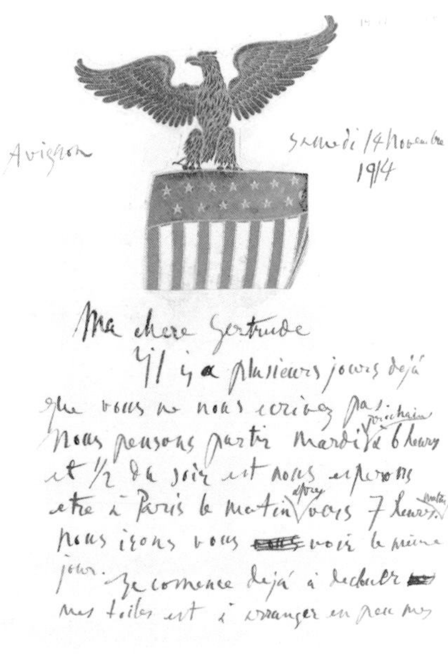

Avignon samedi 14 novembre 1914

Ma chere Gertrude
Il y a plusieurs jours déjà que vous ne nous écrivez pas. Nous pensons partir mardi prochain à 6 heures et 1/2 du soir et nous esperons être à Paris le matin vers 7 heures et nous irons vous voir le même jour. Je commence déjà à déclouer mes toiles et à arranger un peu mes pinceaux et couleurs.
C'est tout.
Bien des choses à Alice et bien à vous Picasso
A bientôt

Nous venons de recevoir une lettre de Alice Eva la remercie et dit qu'elle est bien gentille

Picasso. Letter to Gertrude Stein decorated with the American flag. November 14, 1914. Beinecke Rare Book and Manuscript Library, Yale University.

Blanche goes on to wonder whether or not it might be undignified for Avignon's Saracen battlements to have so many Peek Freans and Huntley and Palmer vans parked in their shade. One of his last vignettes of Provence in the second month of the war is of watching two amputees trying out their newly acquired wooden legs in the gusty white dust of the mistral.

Such was the background to Picasso and Eva's Avignon life. Although they had decided to sit out the war there, the town was beginning to resemble a base camp. To Gertrude and Alice in London, Picasso sent a postcard of a regiment leaving Avignon for the front: "We are full of enthusiasm for France," Picasso wrote, and Eva added, "*Vive la France*."[46] The two of them began to have second thoughts about staying on. By October Paris seemed to be out of immediate danger. People who had fled the city were returning. On October 6, Picasso wrote Gertrude that he might have to make a trip to the capital between the 15th and 20th;[47] he was waiting for news of a check, presumably from Kahnweiler for the 20,000 francs still owed him. Wishful thinking. The dealer was hiding out in Siena; unable to return to France, where the authorities had already sequestered his personal property and the stock of his gallery; unable to repatriate to Germany, where pacifists risked being jailed or even shot; unable, it would seem, to get a visa for his wife, her illegitimate child, and himself to settle in Switzerland. Meanwhile Kahnweiler continued to pay the rent of his Paris gallery, where his sequestered stock was back in storage. If the dealer could afford to pay his landlord, why not his artists? Picasso lived in hopes, but the longed-for check never materialized, and he became more and more worried.

Picasso would soon have an even more pressing reason for going to Paris. Around the middle of October, Eva suffered a recurrence of the cancer for which she had been operated on earlier in the year. In a letter from the two of them, dated October 19, Eva asks Gertrude, who had recently returned from London, to find out whether her specialist, Dr. Rousseau, was in Paris—if need be, send round her maid to inquire. "As quickly as possible," Picasso adds. "Her operation has still not healed. We have seen a doctor here but without knowing anything about him, we don't have much confidence. Perhaps we'll go back to Paris to get the doctor to treat her and completely cure her of all her troubles."[48] A week later, Eva writes to Alice: "I am not ill; all the same I have to see a doctor in Paris. We think of returning in three weeks. I hope the German planes are not frightening."[49] She sends friendly greetings to Mildred Aldrich, but has sharpish things to say about Alice Derain, who had returned to Paris the week before: "I don't know why she wants Brenner's address, perhaps to bring off a '*coup de trafalguar*' [an underhand move]. If you see her again, don't let her know we're returning. She'll find out soon enough." Eva was no kinder about Marie Laurencin: "Like you I think she's an idiot, yet she'll go to Heaven."[50]

On November 14, Picasso sent Gertrude a letter, including a collage of a cutout eagle and part of an American flag, with the news that they were taking the night train on Tuesday (November 17) and would come and see her the following day.[51] He said he had already started to pack up his considerable accumulation of canvases, portfolios and sketchbooks, easels, brushes and paints. And then there were the animals to see to:

Derain's dog, Sentinelle, as well as his own and Eva's three cats. Back in Paris, he would feel closer to the war—all the more so for being a vigorous thirty-three-year-old male who was not in uniform, a prime target for women proffering white feathers. As Gertrude said, "The old life was over."[52]

Postcard from Picasso to Gertrude Stein showing a regiment leaving Avignon for the front, September 11, 1914. Beinecke Rare Book and Manuscript Library, Yale University.

LE
OURI

23

Wartime Paris

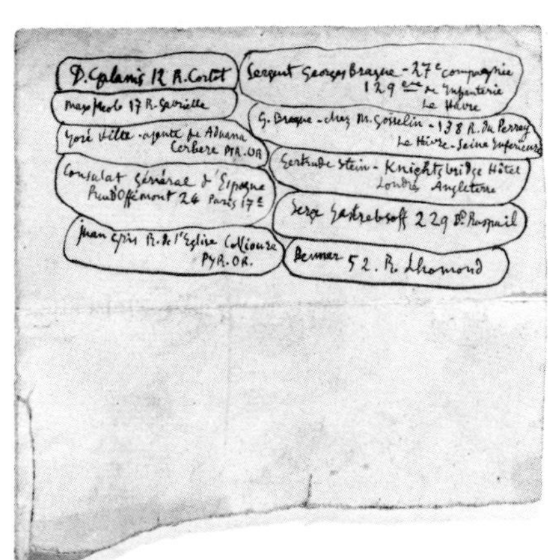

Notes by Picasso on the whereabouts of his friends at the start of the War. Archives Picasso.

Opposite: Picasso, *Man with Dog (rue Schœlcher)*, spring, 1915. Etching and engraving, 27.8×21.8 cm. Musée Picasso. The view from the window (upper left) looks over the Cimetière Montparnasse towards the Tour Eiffel.

BACK IN PARIS, PICASSO FOUGHT to rescue Kahnweiler's vast holdings of his cubist work from the grasp of the custodian of enemy property. As we have seen, everything was back in storage at the rue Vignon gallery—everything, that is, except for the photographic plates, which Délétang, the photographer, kept at his studio.[1] Since he had sold most of the items, Picasso had no legal claim on Kahnweiler's stock. However, the last lot of paintings, drawings and sculptures had not been paid for, and Picasso was adamant that this was his property and should be returned to him. He also felt that he had a stronger moral claim to the works that Kahnweiler had acquired from him than the custodian of enemy property. Couldn't these be made available to collectors?

Picasso needed an enterprising lawyer, and who better to recommend one than André Level, the organizer of the Peau de l'Ours sale earlier in the year? Besides being an astute and fair-minded businessman, Level was a pioneer believer in artists' rights; he also had powerful connections at most levels of the French establishment. Level suggested Maître Henri Danet, and on December 2 he took Picasso to see him at his office, 85, rue de Richelieu. Little could apparently be done until a sequestrator was appointed to deal with Kahnweiler's case. Meanwhile the legal situation was far from clear. On December 28, Danet wrote Picasso that a Monsieur Nicolle had been put in charge of the dealer's sequestration.[2] Six weeks later (January 21, 1915), Level told Picasso that Danet had succeeded in getting Nicolle to start on an inventory of Kahnweiler's stock and an accounting of monies owed to the gallery (among others, Shchukin owed "a very large sum," and Léonce Rosenberg 12,000 francs).[3] Given the arcane nature of cubism and the fact that much of Kahnweiler's business was transacted in German, these tasks proved more complicated than the sequestrator had envisaged. As soon as they were completed (sometime in May?), Danet moved to have Picasso's unpaid works exempted—without success. Nor did he succeed in getting the sequestrator to come up with the 20,000 francs that was owed on them.

These setbacks enraged Picasso, and his feelings for Kahnweiler curdled into hatred. He chose to forget the services the dealer had done him and remember only the negative things: his niggardliness at moments of crisis, and the times he had failed to buy much of his recent work and Vollard had had to come to his rescue. Old resentments came flooding back. Picasso talked menacingly of liquidating the gallery, suing and bankrupting Kahnweiler—anything to get revenge. To his surprise, the artist found himself alone in this attitude. None of his fellow cubists (Braque, Léger and Gris) or the former fauves (Derain and Vlaminck) had anything like Picasso's savings to draw on, and yet they accepted their losses with stoic grace. "Because most of us were away at the war," Braque said, "and had more urgent preoccupations."[4]

The letters that Kahnweiler sent Picasso in Avignon during the first weeks of the war have not survived. (They were probably handed over to Danet.) The dealer apparently promised to pay Picasso the 20,000 francs he owed him, plus interest, as soon as he could. In a long letter of self-justification written in 1920 Kahnweiler complains that Picasso refused to answer his communications. He allows that this could have been out of fear of the French authorities: after all, communicating with the enemy was a felony. "But then," the dealer goes on, "you instituted proceedings against me and ever since you seem to pursue me with a hatred that seems quite unjustified on your part."[5]

Kahnweiler's principal advisor, the Swiss moneychanger Eugène Reignier, who had stayed on in Paris, tried to patch things up—with no success. Picasso put the worst interpretation on everything. Informed that Kahnweiler's account at the Banque Française was empty, Picasso concluded that the dealer had made off with the gallery's funds; whereas the government had imposed a moratorium, and the bank, which had been in the habit of guaranteeing Kahnweiler's line of credit up to a certain sum, had been forced to suspend all such arrangements. To make matters worse, not just Shchukin and Léonce Rosenberg but many other creditors had declined to pay up; hence the lack of assets. Kahnweiler felt that Picasso had no right to blame him for a situation that was not his fault. For his part, Picasso thought Kahnweiler very much to blame: he had shown no foresight whatsoever. Why had he not arranged to have his stock shipped out of the country when there was still time—if not to New York, then to Switzerland? At the very least, he could have had the works which had not been paid for returned to the artists in question. Picasso had a point. If he continued to rail against Kahnweiler for almost a decade, it was surely because he had been cruelly exploited by unscrupulous dealers when he first lived in Paris and could see Kahnweiler's conduct only in the blackest light. True, by 1914 Picasso was much richer than anyone else in the dealer's stable, but he had once been much poorer. That is why the specter of poverty put him in such a panic, also why he felt justified in using Kahnweiler as a scapegoat for his animosity and fears. "*Le marchand—voilà l'ennemi,*" his indictment of Léonce Rosenberg, and by implication Kahnweiler, late in 1918 was a cry from the heart.[6]

Juan Gris. *Portrait of D.-H. Kahnweiler*, 1921. Pencil on paper, 32.5×26cm. Musée National d'Art Moderne, Centre Georges Pompidou, Paris.

Even more urgent than Picasso's need for redress against Kahnweiler was his need to find a substitute for him. For the next two years, he would play the field. Vollard, the dealer for whom Picasso continued to have the highest regard, was no longer available. He had closed his gallery for the duration of the war and was masquerading as a "scholar" who devoted his time to memorializing his friends Cézanne and Renoir in lavish *livres d'art* and giving lectures under the auspices of the French Information Services in Spain and Switzerland.[7] By now Vollard had made enough money to live simply but sybaritically without sacrificing much of his cherished stock. He was less than ever interested in having artists

Picasso. *Portrait of Ambroise Vollard*, August, 1915. Pencil on paper, 46.5×32cm. Metropolitan Museum of Art, New York: The Elisha Whittelsey Collection (The Elisha Whittelsey Fund, 1947).

Picasso. *Portrait of Léonce Rosenberg*, 1915. Pencil on paper, 45.7×33cm. Private collection.

under contract. However, two Parisian dealers who had started up shortly before the war were most eager to step into Vollard's or Kahnweiler's shoes: Léonce Rosenberg and Paul Guillaume.

Rosenberg had begun to buy Picassos in 1913, and by the time war broke out he owned twenty important Picassos as well as ten Braques, five Juan Grises and twenty Herbins.[8] In 1914, Rosenberg had joined the French flying corps as a liaison officer, but his duties were far from onerous, and he managed to keep his gallery functioning throughout the war. His ambition was to take over all four of Kahnweiler's cubist artists and reassemble them under the banner of his Galerie de l'Effort Moderne. In April, 1915, Rosenberg put Gris under contract. He would take delivery of paintings when he came on leave, slapping varnish onto surfaces (often as not the sides of plywood packing cases, since canvas was scarce and expensive) which had not had time to dry out: hence the *craquelure* and warping of many of Gris's panel pictures. Rosenberg made overtures to Picasso through Level and soon started buying from him on a regular basis. Later in the year, Picasso did a handsome Ingresque drawing of Rosenberg in uniform, standing, appropriately, in front of the great *Harlequin* painting he had just bought. The quality of the drawing implies a certain regard for the sitter, who had indeed saved the artists from the financial problems caused by Kahnweiler's flight. Rosenberg did everything to inveigle Picasso into a long-term arrangement. However, as the artist would soon discover, the dealer had more flair than substance. As a historian of cubism has written:

> His culture was vast but rather superficial. . . . He claimed to have nothing to learn about cubism, but painters soon realized that he had little notion of its nature or depth. The commitments into which he launched himself with such enthusiasm turned out to be extremely weak in theoretical discernment as well as financial stability.[9]

Rosenberg is "too futile for us," Apollinaire wrote Max Jacob (March 14, 1916) after visiting his premises: "It's deplorable, the most authentic things look like so much junk. . . . Not at all the right setting for Picasso's work. In this ambiance *chefs d'œuvre* sink to the level of *hors d'œuvres*."[10] Picasso came to the same conclusion; after 1917, he would sell less and less to Rosenberg. In due course, his younger, infinitely more professional, more sharply focused brother, Paul, would take Léonce's place and profit from his eye and flair as well as his failings. Paul would eventually make off with all his brother's best painters.

To avoid accusations of sibling rivalry, Paul Rosenberg let his partner, Joseph (Jos) Hessel, make overtures to Picasso. Although Marie Laurencin had written Roché from Madrid, as early as February, 1915, that Picasso was rumored to be signing up with "my dealer Hessel,"[11] nothing would transpire until July, 1917, when the artist agreed to be represented by a syndicate consisting of Hessel, Paul Rosenberg (Léonce refused to take part) and Georges Bernheim, to be backed by Nathan Wildenstein.[12] Meanwhile Picasso was becoming ever more adept at selling his own work. Towards the end of 1915, Laurencin wrote again to Roché from Málaga of all places: "Doubtless to infuriate me, someone has written me from Paris that Picasso is more and more rolling in gold."[13]

Rosenberg's principal rival was Paul Guillaume. The brilliant young son of a *garçon de recettes* (uniformed bank messenger), Guillaume had

Giorgio de Chirico. *Portrait of Paul Guillaume*, 1915. Oil on canvas, 79×57.2cm. Musée de Grenoble: Gift of Albert Barnes, 1935.

started out working for a garage which imported raw rubber from Africa for motor tires. One day, the rubber cargo included a bonus, a sculpture from Gabon. This transformed Guillaume's life. He became so fascinated that he used his earnings to finance the study of this unfamiliar art form. In due course he made contact with African dealers in tribal artifacts and set up as an importer and a "runner." By the time he was twenty-one (1912), Guillaume had put his humble origins behind him and totally reinvented himself. A supremely suave and confident young man with a great talent for public relations, he set about paying court to Max Jacob and Apollinaire. They were so awed by his eye for *art nègre* and his determination to dominate the market for African and Oceanic as well as modern art that they introduced him to their painter and collector friends.

Picasso was no less impressed and, according to "Baron" Mollet, helped steer Guillaume towards one of his first great coups. Intrigued by the Chiricos at the 1913 Salon des Indépendants, Picasso had asked Apollinaire to track down the painter. Together, they had visited Chirico's basement studio and were "so enchanted by what they saw that they decided to do everything possible to promote his work."[14] They chose the unknown Guillaume, who planned to open a gallery in February, 1914, to launch the unknown Chirico. After some prodding, Guillaume contracted to pay the artist a hundred francs a month for his entire production.

The war closed Guillaume's first gallery; it propelled him in and out of the army, in and out of yet another gallery. By the end of 1915, his affairs had begun to prosper. Max Jacob had found him, albeit briefly, a backer—an extremely perceptive dealer in antiquities called Joseph Altounian—and introduced him to Modigliani and Derain, whose reputations this brilliant impresario would do much to promote. Guillaume also kept in contact with his other touchstone, Apollinaire, who was at the front. Late in 1915, he asked the poet how best to corral Kahnweiler's cubists.

> I fear that Kahnweiler's painters are already taken [Apollinaire replied], above all Picasso, but have a try all the same. I think Picasso would have to be guaranteed 50,000 francs a year. The others less, but go and see the wounded Lieutenant Braque, who is convalescing at the Hôtel Meurice.[15]

Apollinaire double-checked with André Level, who replied on February 17, 1916, that

> [Léonce] Rosenberg as well as Paul Guillaume strike me as having a future, the one as much as the other. I like the decisiveness and faith of the former. I know the latter less well, but have already had occasion to appreciate his taste, which is discerning and not without assurance, as my purchases from him bear out. [16]

Paul Guillaume in uniform, 1914. Archives Paul Guillaume, Paris.

Rather than tie himself down to a contract with one or the other of these dealers, Picasso preferred to play them off against each other—at least for the time being. Besides, he still had hopes of New York—not so much of Coady and Brenner, who talked big, sold little and took forever to settle their debts, but of Marius de Zayas, whom Picasso regarded as a friend. With Stieglitz, his partner in the 291 Gallery, de Zayas was in the process of starting a new enterprise —a more commercial version of 291 —to be called the Modern Gallery. It was backed by Picabia, Paul Haviland and their forceful former colleague, Agnes Ernst, who had married the investment banker Eugene Meyer. A few weeks before the outbreak of war, de Zayas had gone to Paris with Mrs. Meyer to acquire works for a show of Picasso, Braque and primitive art. And between Kahnweiler and Picabia's wife, Gabrielle Buffet, who was a *marchand amateur*, he had assembled eighteen Picassos and several Braques. By the time de Zayas was ready to leave Paris, war was imminent. The prescient Paul Guillaume loaded him down with as much tribal sculpture as he could stow in his trunk; de Zayas also took back enough paintings for a Douanier Rousseau show. Although their original exhibit was not a financial success, the Modern Gallery's idealistic partners felt morally obliged to continue their support of modernism. And so de Zayas returned to Paris in late October, 1915, and had no difficulty persuading Picasso to let him have seven more cubist works on consignment, including that cubist masterpiece the 1914 *Portrait of a Young Girl* (p. 335) and the 1915 circular wood relief, then known as *Still Life in a Garden*.[17]

Marius de Zayas at the 291 Gallery, 1913. Photograph by Stieglitz. De Zayas Archive, Seville.

De Zayas found cubism hard to sell to American collectors. Hamilton Easter Field, who had once aspired to be a cubist patron, showed no interest in acquiring things. As his work was selling better in Paris, Picasso had the more important paintings shipped back from New York. Some months later (September 14, 1916), he sent de Zayas a friendly but businesslike letter concerning the remaining, unsold items: five paintings (valued at 2,500 francs) and six drawings (valued at 2,000 francs).

> Since I would like to settle this business as soon as possible . . . I will give you the lot for the sum of 3,700 francs which you would have to send me right away. If this is not agreeable to you, I would like you to ship them back to me. . . . I sold the portrait back here that I had sent to America, of a woman in a feather boa seated in an armchair in front of a fireplace [*Portrait of a Young Girl*] and for the price I was asking. A hearty handshake from your friend who loves you, Picasso.[18]

Picasso does not mention that he had either just sold, or was about to sell, another major recent work that de Zayas had returned to him, *Man in a Bowler Hat* of 1915 (p. 369), to the same buyer: the artist's perceptive new friend Eugenia Errazuriz.

Picasso. *Glass, Pipe, Dice and Ace of Clubs (Still Life in a Garden)*, summer, 1914. Painted wood and tin, diam: 34cm. Musée Picasso.

Thanks to de Zayas's enthusiasm, however, the Modern Gallery chalked up a few successes. The Walter Arensbergs bought the magnificent *Seated Nude* of 1910 from one of the gallery's two shows and various lesser items. The biggest collector of Picasso in the United States, the Irish-American lawyer John Quinn, made most of his purchases through his Paris agent, the ubiquitous Roché. All the same de Zayas managed to sell him the highly important 1908 gouache *Five Nudes in a Forest* (the origin of the monumental *Three Women*), and a fine cubist head of 1910.

Ironically, Quinn's most important Picasso acquisition came about not through evangelists of modernism like de Zayas or Stieglitz but through an enterprising woman, Harriet C. Bryant, who was more of a decorator and an *antiquaire* than an art dealer. Early in 1915, Miss Bryant had commissioned Walter Pach, a young American painter/critic, also one of Quinn's advisors, to go to Paris and find modern paintings for an exhibition she proposed to hold in March at the Carroll Galleries, which she ran. As an art student, Pach had frequented the Lapin Agile, where, Roché said, he had bored habitués to tears singing "savage melodies" at inordinate length.[19] Pach had supposedly met Picasso and must also have

Above: Picasso. *Seated Nude*, fall, 1910. Oil on canvas, 98.5×77 cm. Philadelphia Museum of Art: Louise and Walter Arensberg Collection.

Top left: Picasso. *Standing Female Nude*, spring, 1910. Oil on canvas, 97.7×76.2 cm (formerly in John Quinn's collection). Albright-Knox Art Gallery, Buffalo, N.Y.

Left: Picasso. *Still Life with Musical Instruments and Fruit Bowl*, 1913. Oil on canvas, 100×81 cm (formerly in Arthur B. Davies's collection; photograph before restoration). Private collection.

learned how to charm Vollard, for he managed to persuade this most intransigent of dealers—more intransigent than ever, now that he had closed down his gallery and sold paintings only for gold—to let the Carroll Galleries have five major Picassos on consignment.[20] Vollard must have suspected Quinn, who was known to operate in mysterious ways, of backing this transaction; otherwise he is unlikely to have been so forthcoming. Sure enough, before the Carroll Galleries exhibition opened, Quinn had written him, commending Miss Bryant's initiative and offering to buy all five Picassos. Vollard accepted. Later in the year, Quinn added a sixth painting, an early cubist still life—probably one of the ones the dealer had bought from Picasso on his return from Horta in 1909. In all, Quinn's purchases amounted to 21,500 francs. Two years later, he would acquire the great 1906 *Two Nudes* from Vollard for 12,000 francs and thus become the largest collector of Picasso in America—a far more discriminating one than his rival whom he referred to as "that brute Dr. Barnes." Quinn's purchases were in the nature of a portent: America was taking the place of Germany in the dissemination of Picasso's work.

*   *   *

Meanwhile Picasso had every reason for concern about Eva's health. In mid-January, 1915, she underwent yet another operation, which did no more to arrest the cancer than the first one. On February 7, Picasso told Apollinaire that Eva had been in a nursing home for almost a month. "I've been very worried and haven't had a moment to write to you, but now that she seems to be getting better, I'll write more often."[21] In the days following the operation, Picasso took his meals with Hélène d'Oettingen and Serge Férat. They had a telephone, so he could keep in touch with Eva's doctors. "That's why I can't come and lunch or dine with you," he explained to Gertrude Stein and Alice Toklas.[22] There was a further advantage to life chez "ces Russes." Although Serge worked until very late at the Italian hospital, Hélène still managed to entertain what was left of the Montparnasse intelligentsia. Guests brought attractive women.

Giorgio de Chirico. *Picasso Dining with Serge and Hélène and Léopold Survage*, 1915. Pen on paper, 32.5×23.5cm. Desshau Trust.

With Eva confined to a nursing home, Picasso cast around for a mistress. There was no shortage of candidates. He fancied Irène Lagut, but she belonged to Serge, so he did not pursue her—at least for the time being. And then there was a friend of hers, a painter and set designer called Hélène Perdriat, who was one of Roché's mistresses (he called her "*La Reine*"). She was famously available. But Picasso was not interested in a casual fling; he was in search of someone who was not only attractive but bright enough to hold his interest and understanding enough to realize that his work came first. And so he embarked in greatest secrecy on a romance which, if he had had his way, would have ended at the altar.

Gaby Depeyre, the girl in question, lived nearby on the top floor of a building on the boulevard Raspail. How they met we do not know. André Salmon claimed to have urged Picasso to go and see her sing or dance in a local cabaret. He refers to her as "Gaby la Catalane."[23] But Salmon is far from reliable. Gaby was a Parisienne: a liberated Montparnasse girl—a friend possibly of Eva or Irène Lagut. As to when the affair began, Serge wrote Soffici on December 13, 1915, that Eva was dying, but that Picasso had had "another woman in his life for seven months."[24] I suspect that they had met even earlier—in January or February, at the time of Eva's operation. Discretion would have been called for on both sides. Picasso would not have wanted Eva to hear about a serious involvement on his part. Gaby would likewise not have wanted her other lover, Herbert Lespinasse—the American-born engraver and poet whom she would eventually marry—to be embarrassed by her escapade, though he is likely to have known about it.

Gaby Depeyre, c. 1915–16. Archives Picasso.

Gaby was twenty-seven years old when she first met Picasso. She was a gentle beauty with a classic profile that inspired images as incisive as the decoration on a Greek mirror back. This time round, Picasso did naturalistic drawings of his mistress—portraits that aimed to please and flatter her rather than extend the frontiers of his art. Instead of expressing his feelings publicly, as he had done with Eva, by inscribing "*Ma Jolie*" and other loving messages on cubist still lifes, most of which he promptly sold, Picasso expressed his passion for Gaby privately. To the margins of portrait drawings and watercolors he added inscriptions of love-letter length, intended for her eyes alone. Since he could not risk keeping any references to Gaby around the studio for Eva to find, Picasso gave her virtually this entire mini-œuvre, and for forty years she kept it hidden away. It was not until the end of her life that Gaby decided to put her Picasso memorabilia on the market, and foolishly erased many of his adoring messages, but enough of them remain to show how vulnerable Picasso was to love. He would prove even more vulnerable to *chagrin d'amour.*

Three summery Provençal interiors that Picasso did for Gaby reveal that they must have made a secret trip to the south in the summer or fall of 1915. True, there is no record of the artist's leaving Paris at this time, but the rusticity of the rooms—the earthenware pots, rush-bottomed chairs, Provençal *bahuts* (chests), bundles of *serment de vigne* (kindling made of vine prunings), *tommettes de Marseille* (floor tiles) and the open fireplace with the cooking pot on the hob—proclaim the Midi. Picasso would not have taken Gaby to Céret or Sorgues or Avignon for fear of being recognized. Instead he is likely to have gone somewhere new, somewhere quiet and by the sea. Where else but the unspoiled fishing village of Saint-Tropez, which had yet to be discovered by more than a few painters, among them Gaby's future husband?[25] One of the earliest settlers, Herbert Lespinasse had bought a picturesque house on the baie des Canoubiers, where the luminaries of Montparnasse—Kisling and his Kiki, the Pascins, the newly married Nils de Dardels—liked to come and unwind.[26] After being awakened by shots from the host's revolver, guests would forage for water and firewood and spend the rest of the day sailing in Lespinasse's fishing boat or skinny-dipping off his beach. Whether Lespinasse was there or not, Gaby is likely to have had the run of this retreat. For his part, Picasso would have yearned to escape from Paris, from the shadow of Eva's illness, from the stigma of being a noncombatant during some of the worst carnage of the war—and what better sanctuary than the shores of the cleansing, revitalizing Mediterranean? Picasso's main problem would have been to find a convincing pretext for leaving Eva for a few days.

Picasso. *Reviens mon amour . . .*, 1916. Watercolor on paper, 17.5×13cm. Musée Picasso.

One of the more charming records of this honeymoon-like trip is a watercolor of a Provençal kitchen which carries a lovelorn inscription, likewise in watercolor. Picasso invokes "the little staircase that ascends to

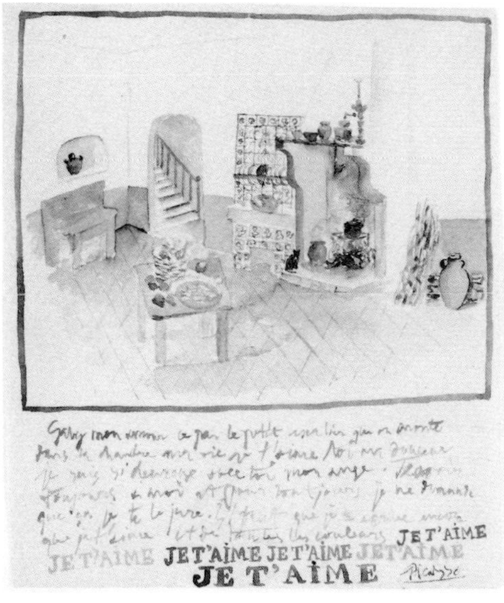

Top left: Picasso. *Provençal Kitchen*, 1916. Watercolor on paper, 17.5×15.3cm. Musée Picasso.

Top center: Picasso. *Provençal Dining Room*, 1916. Watercolor on paper, 17.5×11cm. Musée Picasso.

Top right: Picasso. *Provençal Bedroom*, 1916. Watercolor on paper, 17.5×13cm. Musée Picasso.

Left: Picasso. *Gaby Depeyre*, 1915–16. Pencil on paper, 28.5×22.5cm. Picasso Heirs.

Picasso. *Je t'aime Gaby.* February 22, 1916. Watercolors and photographs pasted on paper (each oval 4.2×3.5 cm; sheets with inscriptions 6.5×17.5 cm, 3×13.2 cm). Musée Picasso.

the bedroom" and ends up, "*Je t'aime de toutes les couleurs*" (I love you in every color), followed by the phrase "*JE T'AIME*," reiterated six times in six different colors. Typical of Picasso to have had the imagination, infatuation and childishness to think up this and another sentimental conceit: his name artfully entwined with hers. Calligraphic lovemaking.

Besides the interiors and portrait drawings, Picasso gave Gaby a number of love tokens: some small panels of decoration, which may have been projects for embroidery; a matching necklace of wooden beads, each painstakingly painted with a different geometrical motif; and a collection of cameo-size gouaches (an allegorical portrait of Gaby beneath a hovering putto, and three mildly cubistic still lifes—intricate little variations on the same theme). These were evidently contrived to please Gaby's unsophisticated eye; they also reveal that Picasso no longer had any problem reconciling representationalism and decoration with the demands of synthetic cubism. (Significantly, the only painting of importance that Picasso gave Gaby, *Peonies* of 1901,[27] is very traditional.) Gaby—or might it have been Picasso?—had this collection of miniatures, each of which bears a different declaration of love on the back, framed together with photographs of the two of them. An emblematic motif at the center proclaims once again, *JE T'AIME*. Picasso had never made such eloquent pictorial love to Eva, nor would he ever pay any other woman the compliment of such sentimental inscriptions, let alone of an exclusive style.

In a self-portrait drawing he gave Gaby, Picasso depicts himself mockingly as a conventional, if covert suitor, cap in one hand, box of chocolates in the other. He is glancing up at the studio window, where his beloved is on the lookout, waiting for Diego Rivera (in the background) to disappear so that she can signal to Picasso that the coast is clear. A note of bourgeois propriety is usually present in the drawings he did of Gaby. Her looks were well attuned to the artist's emerging neo-classicism: however, the idiom he devised for her alternates between the sugary classicism of late Renoir and the more astringent classicism of Ingres. A drawing done around this time for an old-masterish composition of three Gaby-like nudes in a landscape suggests that Picasso had taken a look at Renoir's *Judgment of Paris*—a subject that would have been relevant to his private life. His acquisition, shortly after the war, of two of Renoir's obese nudes confirms Picasso's perverse preference for the aged impressionist's gamiest phase. This quirk of taste recalls Wagner's confession late in life: "I adore Rossini, but don't tell the Wagnerians."[28]

Picasso. *Self-Portrait as Suitor*, [illegible] Pen and ink on paper, 15×11.5cm. Sala Gaspar, Barcelona.

Picasso. *Three Graces*, 1915–16. Pencil on paper, 23.5×23.5cm. Picasso Heirs.

* * *

Now that most of his cronies, except for Max Jacob, were off fighting, the *bande à Picasso* had virtually ceased to exist. And the artist, who depended so heavily on the company and support of friends, had to make do with casual acquaintances—for the most part expatriates—who hung out at the Dôme or the Rotonde or Hélène d'Oettingen's. Gone was the close, backbiting camaraderie of the old days. Wartime life in Montparnasse had a desperation, which was irritating but distracting. The expatriates included a number of Italians, not least Severini, who might have died of tuberculosis if Picasso, Max Jacob and Gertrude Stein had not raised the money to send him to Barcelona to be treated by Ramon Reventós.

Amedeo Modigliani at the Bateau Lavoir, 1915. Photograph probably by Paul Guillaume.

Modigliani was also a problem—more so than ever now that Dr. Alexandre, his Svengali, who believed that drugs like opium and hashish stimulated an artist's imagination, had been mobilized. According to Max Jacob, Modigliani was currently living with "a great English poet [Beatrice] Hastings: drunken, musical (a pianist), bohemian, elegant, dressed in the manner of the Transvaal and surrounded by a gang of bandits on the fringe of the arts."[29] Hastings (born Emily Alice Haigh and South African not English) was known as "the wild colonial girl." She worked as a journalist in Paris for A. R. Orage's *New Age*, and kept a tally of her numerous lovers by making notches in the headboard of her bed. She was also celebrated for having attended the Quat'z' Arts ball wearing a trompe l'œil dress that Modigliani had painted onto her naked body. Besides being Modigliani's longest-lasting mistress, Hastings had passionate affairs with Ezra Pound, Katherine Mansfield, Orage and Raymond Radiguet, as well as brief encounters with André Breton, Wyndham Lewis and Picasso. Picasso apparently procured her for Apollinaire when he came on leave. This

> gained me [Hastings wrote] the gift of a painting from M. Picasso "in eternal gratitude" on a straw handbag I had. The painting had red stars and a black glass and green grapes and something in delicate whites and greys which may be a table-cloth or temples in the clouds—it depends which way you look at it.[30]

Apollinaire used some of Hastings's traits—not least her promiscuity—for his portrayal of Maude, the beautiful English femme fatale in his roman à clef *La Femme assise.* Love for Maude drives the Picasso character, Pablo Canouris, almost to suicide. *La Femme assise* usually keeps more or less to the truth. In this case, however, Apollinaire also draws on Irène Lagut for Maude, which is confusing, as Irène is the book's protagonist under the name of Elvire. Apollinaire's reasons for doing this will become clear in Chapter 25. An early feminist who wrote some excellent books, including a novel about a cancer ward, *Madame Six*, Hastings deserves to be rescued from the oblivion which befell her well before she became an alcoholic. She gassed herself and her pet mouse in 1943.

Under pressure from Max Jacob and André Salmon, Picasso had come to like Modigliani and his work well enough to acquire a major painting—he painted over it when canvas became scarce—and sit to him for a portrait more than once.[31] However, he had no patience with Modigliani's addictions and frequently made jokes at his expense. "Why does he always get blind drunk in Montparnasse," he once asked, "never on the grands boulevards?"[32] One evening (July or August, 1916), Modigliani had arrived at Picasso's studio and consumed an entire bottle of Anis del Mono. Hans Arp, who was present, wrote Hilla Rebay that he lay "prostrate on the floor whimpering about all the savageries he had seen."[33]

And then there were the "metaphysical" Chiricos. When the Germans had closed in on Paris, Giorgio, his younger brother, Andrea (who wrote, composed and, later, painted under the name of Alberto Savinio), and their mother had taken refuge with Paul Guillaume in Normandy. Like most other refugees, they had returned to Paris after the Germans were stopped at the Marne. Until he and his brother left to join the Italian army in the summer of 1915, Chirico saw rather more of Picasso than he later admitted—often at Hélène d'Oettingen's, as recorded in Chirico's

Modigliani. *Beatrice Hastings*, 1916. Oil on canvas, 65×46cm. Private collection.

Giorgio de Chirico. *The Child's Brain*, 1914. Oil on canvas, 80×65cm. Moderna Museet, Stockholm.

caricature of the baroness, her lover Survage, Serge and Picasso lunching under the Douanier Rousseau's self-portrait. Although Picasso's admiration for Chirico's work dates from 1913, it was not until 1915 that he saw how the man he had come to call "*le peintre des gares*" (the painter of railroad stations) could assist him in his transition from cubism to a modernist concept of classicism. To detect Chirico's influence we need only compare the eerie portrait of his bare-chested slug of a father, *The Child's Brain*, with Picasso's *Man in a Bowler Hat*: a parodic "Monsieur Dupont" image, with his buttoned-up waistcoat and mustachioed smirk.[34] The feather-shaped eyebrow in the Picasso is a mocking reference to the feathery eyelashes and body hair of Chirico's clammy parent. The phallic top of the easel in the upper right-hand corner of the Picasso mimics the large red penis of a chimney in the upper right-hand corner of *The Child's Brain*. A snide acknowledgment, I suspect, of the parallel between the no less penile bookmark in Chirico's foreground volume and the masturbatory finger marking a place in Picasso's penitent Magdalen's book (see p. 118). In other paintings Picasso appropriates the empty frames and framed images from Chirico's paintings and uses them to imply the flatness that a picture within a picture generates; also, ironically, to italicize things and give them a heightened degree of reality—for which Apollinaire had yet to invent the term "surreal." Chirico does not seem to have appreciated the covert compliment that Picasso was paying him. It would not be long before Chirico turned against the modernists who had formerly befriended him. Eventually Picasso turned against Chirico, but not against his early work. In 1936 he acquired an album of his "metaphysical" drawings and some manuscripts from Paul Eluard.

As for Picasso's Spanish friends, he preferred the ones who had remained in Spain and made no demands on him to the Parisian expatriates. He still saw the Catalan sculptor Gargallo, who had settled in Paris in 1912, but he tended to avoid Juan Gris, the "sorcerer's apprentice," and Pichot, who had sided with Fernande. Picasso would always be drawn to South Americans, and in 1915–16, he saw a great deal of Manuel Ortiz de Zarate, the defiantly bohemian descendant of conquistadors who had once wielded great power in Chile. To escape his family, Ortiz had emigrated to Italy, where he lived by copying Guido Reni altarpieces and selling them to parish priests. Modigliani, whom he had met as early as 1904 in Rome, encouraged him to move to Paris. There he blossomed into a major Montparnasse personality and a minor cubist painter. Apollinaire called Ortiz "the only Patagonian in Paris."[35] Max Jacob warmed to him because he, too, claimed to have had visions.[36] A Swiss friend, Emile Le Jeune, described Ortiz seated on the terrace of the Rotonde envisioning "a golden-age . . . when a painter would only have to describe a picture to get paid."[37] Conceptual art *avant la lettre*. Picasso loved Ortiz for his wit and warmth and soaring spirit. The two of them brought out the mischievous side in each other, much as Picasso and Manolo had once done.

Picasso. *Man in a Bowler Hat*, 1915. Oil on canvas, 130×89.5cm. Art Institute of Chicago: Gift of Mrs. Leigh B. Block in memory of Albert D. Lasker.

In the spring of 1914, Ortiz had brought a young Mexican cubist, Diego Rivera, who was having his first show at Berthe Weill's, to Picasso's studio:

> I went to Picasso's studio [Rivera wrote] intensely keyed up to meet Our Lord, Jesus Christ. The interview was marvelous. Picasso's studio was full of his exciting canvases. . . . As for the man . . . a luminous atmosphere

> seemed to surround him. My friends and I were absorbed for hours, looking at his paintings. . . . He let us see his most intimate sketchbooks. . . . Picasso asked me to stay and have lunch with him, after which he went back with me to my studio. There he asked to see everything I had done from beginning to end. . . . We had dinner together and stayed up practically the whole night talking. Our thesis was Cubism—what it was trying to accomplish, what it had already done, and what future it had as a "new" art form.[38]

Modigliani. *Diego Rivera*, 1914. Ink and colored crayon on paper, 30×22cm. Private collection.

Henceforth Picasso would be Rivera's "*maestro*." A month or two after this meeting, Rivera left for Spain. Because of the war he did not return to Paris until the spring of 1915. When he reappeared, Picasso gave him a warm welcome—something he would soon regret. Rivera's mistress, the Russian painter Marevna (Vorobov), who may have resented Picasso's lack of response to her advances, claimed that in the course of long technical discussions about their work, Rivera became convinced that Picasso was out to steal his cubist ideas. Since Rivera's theories stemmed from Gleizes and Metzinger and involved much talk of the fourth dimension—everything that was anathema to Picasso—this is unlikely. "He sickens me, Pablo does," Rivera supposedly told Marevna. "If he pinches something from me, it'll always be Picasso, but as for me, they'll always say I copy him. One of these days I'll chuck him out, or I'll shove off to Mexico." According to Rivera, they nearly came to blows: "[Picasso] left when he saw me pick up my Mexican stick and . . . threaten to break his [head?]."[39] That there was a scintilla of justice to Rivera's accusations will emerge in Chapter 26.

And lastly the Russians, many of whom had stayed on in Paris, as if in anticipation of the Revolution. Years later, Picasso observed that long before he married Olga Khokhlova, so much of Mother Russia had rubbed off on him from the expatriates he frequented that a barber assumed him to be Russian. "Their smell was on me," he said.[40] Serge and Hélène had given Picasso his first taste of Russian extravagance. Hélène is even supposed to have had a brief affair with him around this time;[41] however, in view of his involvement with Gaby and hers with Survage, this is more likely to have taken place well before the war. Meanwhile, an even feistier, more eccentric Russian woman had come to play a dominant role on the Montparnasse scene: dynamic little Marie Wassilieff.

A grant from the tsarina had enabled Wassilieff to come to Paris (circa 1905) and study art. "I was as beautiful as the madonna," she told an interviewer.[42] Another boast: she had once been accosted by a little old man, who turned out to be the Douanier Rousseau. He took her back to his studio, played the violin for her and asked her to marry him. "I couldn't do it," Wassilieff said. "His breath was so awful; he smelled of death."[43] Through her great friend and fellow chiromancer, Max Jacob, Wassilieff had visited the Bateau Lavoir and met Picasso. She had also briefly enrolled at the Académie Matisse: an experience which inspired her to start, around 1912, her own Académie Russe, later known as the Académie Wassilieff. The professor was Fernand Léger, into whose hand students were expected to press five francs whenever he corrected their work. After the war closed down her school, this indefatigable woman spent her days nursing and her nights running her studio on the avenue du Maine as a canteen for impecunious artists and writers. (Picasso's former friend Paco Durrio started up a similar venture in Montmartre).

Thanks to Wassilieff's flair and energy, her canteen was an instant success. As a soup kitchen, it was allowed to stay open long after the curfew obliged cafés to close, though not to serve wine or liquor, which of course it did. The canteen soon developed into an "international cultural center," where people could eat and drink cheaply and find companionship. Wassilieff hung the walls with works by Picasso, Modigliani, Léger, Chagall and an assortment of her own artifacts—pseudo-African sculptures and caricatural dolls of the regulars (including Picasso). To dispel wartime gloom, she would shade the lights with colored paper and encourage people to put on skits. Jacob was always ready to perform a campy little song or dance. Picasso liked to play the torero, using a tablecloth as a cape and a girl with index fingers held up to her ears as a charging bull. To shouts of *Olé*, he would dispatch her with an imaginary sword. Far gone on drink and drugs, the narcissistic Modigliani would slowly strip naked, while ceremoniously reciting Dante or Lautréamont. ("Oh, the beautiful Renaissance youth!" English and American girls were said to sigh.)[44] There was no shortage of music—classical, popular or bizarre (Zadkine's "Camel's Tango" or Africans performing on nose flutes), no shortage, either, of political arguments and fights. Only when her canteen was about to be wrecked would the minuscule Wassilieff stop the horseplay.

Modigliani. *Marie Wassilieff*, c. 1915. Oil on canvas, 72×54 cm. Private collection.

One of Wassilieff's regulars and lovers was Trotsky, whose admiration of Picasso's work may have resulted from meetings in the canteen. Wassilieff's liaison with Trotsky would have disastrous consequences. In 1917, she was indicted as a revolutionary agent and put under *résidence surveillée*; even her illegitimate child was taken from her. (The baby was cared for by Fernand and Jeanne Léger.) Eventually she was cleared of all charges, and the canteen was saved from closure. For Picasso and the survivors of his Montmartre *bande*, Wassilieff's raffish evenings were a distraction from the horrors of war and brought back the old days at the Lapin Agile before tourists were allowed in. Where better to fête artists like Braque and Léger after they returned wounded from the war?

* * *

Despite the changing pattern of his life, the friends in whom Picasso put the most confidence at this unhappy time were still Gertrude Stein and Alice Toklas. Much as they relished gossip, they were good at keeping secrets and, therefore, to be trusted with the details of Eva's illness—details which Picasso divulged to virtually no one else. Since the rue de Fleurus was only a few minutes away from the rue Schœlcher, the two ménages saw much of each other that winter and spring—a time when the Germans renewed their raids on Paris. One evening in March, 1915, the four of them were dining chez Stein when an air-raid alarm sounded—the first zeppelin attack. Since Gertrude's *pavillon* was not bombproof, they took shelter in the concierge's more solidly built quarters. After waiting in vain for the all-clear, they returned to the studio. By the light of a candle under a table Gertrude and Picasso talked away until two in the morning, while Alice's "knees knocked together as described in poetry and prose."[45] Eva, who had only recently emerged from a clinic, tried to sleep beside her on the sofa, while the new Breton maid did the dishes.

Alice was so apprehensive of the bombing and Gertrude so apprehensive of shortages and soaring costs that they decided to go to Spain, where life was safe and cheap. The war had left her short of ready money, so Gertrude was obliged to sell a painting from her collection. Her brother Michael, who had gone in for Matisse rather than Picasso, made the choice easy for her. On the eve of the war he had loaned nineteen of his Matisses to an exhibition in Berlin; and although they were the property of a neutral American, they had been sequestered by the Germans. As consolation, Michael now asked Gertrude to sell him her last remaining Matisse, the fauve *Femme au chapeau*—the foundation stone of her and Leo's original collection—for $4,000. She accepted. Picasso would have been relieved that no more of his paintings were sacrificed.

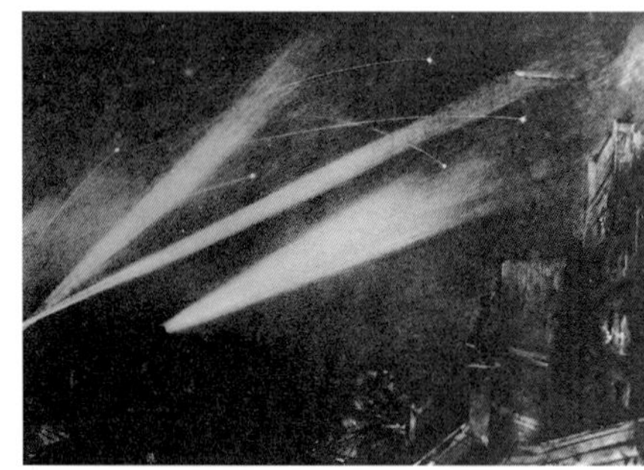

View from Montmartre of the zeppelin raid on Paris, March 21, 1915.

In mid-March Gertrude and Alice and their maid, Jeanne, left for Barcelona, then moved on to Palma de Mallorca, where they took a furnished house. They were so delighted with their abundant garden, with their disgustingly behaved deerhound (which they had named Polybe Bouton Geborue Reinach)—above all with each other—that they stayed away for over a year. In the course of their Mallorcan sojourn Gertrude produced the "most authentic and accessible . . . of her 'difficult' writing,"[46] also some overtly sexual pieces, in which she extols Alice as "her sweetheart, her little dove, her gay baby, her dear wife. There are kisses and caresses for 'Mrs' and promises from her devoted husband that he will be faithful, true, hard-working, flourishing, successful, rich and adoring."[47] When Gertrude and Alice returned to Paris, towards the end of June, 1916, they would continue to see Picasso insofar as their Red Cross work permitted. During the year in Palma, however, Gertrude had become such a totally committed husband to Alice that her ties with Picasso began to unravel—a process that the artist's marriage, two years later, would accelerate. Although she continued to collect (mostly Juan Gris), Gertrude would never buy another Picasso; and for all their mutual affection, she would never again be his confidante—his "buddy." On his side, Picasso found it increasingly difficult to accept Gertude's view of herself as a fellow genius. Alice would eventually replace her in his affections.

*   *   *

The principal member of the original *bande à Picasso* to be *réformé* (exempted from military service) was Max Jacob. As the German army drew ever closer to Paris, the poet felt he better do something about the cache of manuscripts he had left with his friends the Fillaciers at Enghien. This town, where Parisians still go to gamble, was not yet threatened; nevertheless Jacob made a great to-do about leaving on a rescue mission—by tram. The Fillaciers' house turned out to be an oasis of peace and plenty. He spent a month there, sorting through his work of the last ten years and helping out at a local hospital. When the Germans were halted at the Marne, Jacob returned to Paris with three hundred of his favorite poems. The best of these would be published in 1917 as *Le Cornet à dés*: a collection that would make his reputation, albeit in a restricted circle, as a major poet. Back in Paris, Jacob tried to enlist, as his three brothers had already done, but he was turned down. His finances had always been precarious—now more than ever. The war had dispersed most of his friends and put paid to the genteel scrounging to which needy poets traditionally resort. Jacob had to think up new strategies: by claiming to be an out-of-work tailor (his father's trade), he became eligible for welfare. Meanwhile he could always eat for next to nothing (65 centimes for a three-course meal) at Marie Wassilieff's or one of the canteens that Gertrude Vanderbilt Whitney had set up for starving artists and writers in Paris.

Jacob's antidote to wartime misery was wartime promiscuity. His biographer, Andreu, puts this delicately: Max carried his "desire to please" to excessive lengths.[48] To Maurice Raynal, who had been badly wounded, Jacob wrote that the artists' canteens enabled people to express their natural instincts without regard for decency, thus enabling them to forget national and other concerns. The deeper Jacob wallowed in what he chose to regard as sin, the more obsessive was his fear of the devil and the greater his need for atonement. For him the only way out of this vicious circle was a change of faith. Ever since his vision of Christ in 1909, Jacob had longed to be received into the Catholic Church. However, the Church was loath to accept someone perceived as a *mauvais sujet*: a self-dramatizing fraud, a drug addict, a dissolute homosexual and, as bad if not worse, a down-at-heel pauper and a Jew.

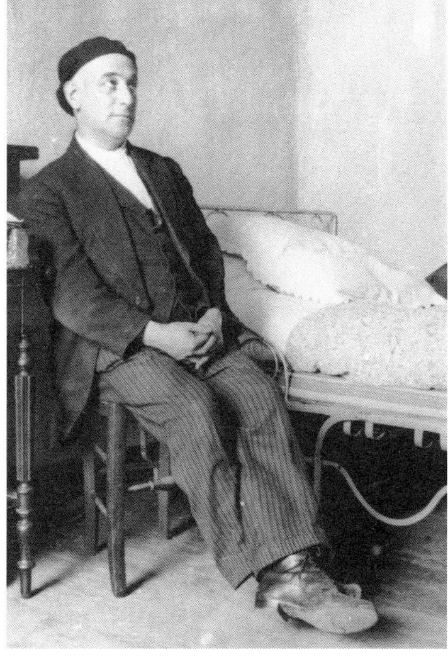

Max Jacob in his room at the monastery of Saint-Benoît, June, 1922.

One evening towards the end of 1914, Jacob was recounting his difficulties with the Church to some friends in a café, when a genial dwarf at a neighboring table declared that there was no real problem: he had only to go and see Cardinal Amette, archbishop of Paris, who would arrange everything. When Jacob objected that a cardinal was far too eminent for his humble needs, the dwarf, who was called Pica (coincidentally, Diaghilev's nickame for Picasso), directed him to the father superior of the Notre Dame de Sion convent, which specialized in the conversion of Jews. After initial confusion—the superior mistook him for someone called Vigourel (conceivably the proprietor of the boulevard Raspail bar)—Jacob related his visions, made an act of contrition and was accepted for instruction. "Sometimes I am so overwhelmed with tears," he wrote Raynal in November, 1914, "and I feel so Catholic that my style suffers."[49]

Father Ferrand, who took charge of the "interminable" instructions, told Jacob that his faith was more emotional than rational. Jacob disagreed. In his account of his conversion Jacob says, "I believe in God because I have seen a God."[50] By the same token he believed he had actually seen hell: "There is an herb that makes me see demons. I drank an infusion of that herb [henbane] and I saw demons. I must believe what I saw. . . . My description tallies with other descriptions."[51] Jacob's overwhelming fear of the devil played as important a role in his conversion as his love of God.[52] But we should never forget that the poet's religious feelings remained as deeply rooted in his ambivalent passion for Picasso as they had been in 1909; and he was still apt to identify the loved one with Satan as well as with Christ—sometimes both at the same time—depending on the loved one's not always kindly attitude towards him.

The process of conversion was anything but smooth. To believe Jacob—more difficult than ever on this occasion—he celebrated the feast of the Immaculate Conception in a daylong debauch with three women, "one of whom was undergoing a nervous breakdown."[53] There were other lapses from virtue, moments of moral torment and doubt and problems with dissolute friends, whom Jacob could not live without, despite—or

Picasso. *Max Jacob*, 1915. Pencil on paper. Private collection.

was it because of?—their "horrendous" vices. These pressures triggered another vision: this time in a Montmartre cinema, where Paul Feval's film *La Bande des habits noirs* was playing. All of a sudden the screen seemed to change into a sort of sheet, on which a figure very like the Christ in the 1909 vision appeared to Jacob, except that this time he had some children under his cloak. "I could only conclude that the affection I have always felt for children found favor with Him, who was giving me renewed proof of His protection."[54]

Visions did not find favor with the Church, unless they were experienced by eminent ecclesiastics or deranged girls. Jacob's baptism was repeatedly delayed. His instructor was called up and another had to be found; the chapel needed repairs; his choice of godmother, Sylvette Fillacier, proved unacceptable; his godfather, Picasso, was unable to track down proof of his own baptism. Were the priests testing his sincerity? Very possibly. Not many of Jacob's friends took his conversion, let alone his visions, seriously. Picasso was one of the few who did. Not that this made him the less mocking. "A good Catholic," he would later tell Max, "is a man who has a large apartment, a family, servants and a motor car."[55] And he urged Jacob, who was most offended, to take the baptismal name of Fiacre—the patron saint of gardeners, after whom cabs had been named. The saint was also renowned for curing "*le fic saint Fiacre*" —that is to say, hemorrhoids and fistulas.[56] Picasso's suggestion was thus a mocking allusion to Jacob's anal proclivities; also to one of his earliest published poems about a cab horse outside the Grand Hôtel. Since it was dedicated to Picasso, this poem had come to be known as "*le cheval de Picasso.*"[57] Four years later, the artist would refer to it when Jacob was run over and seriously hurt on his way to the first night of *Le Tricorne.* "So you were run over by a *fiacre*," Picasso said. "You see I'm a prophet." Deeply wounded, Jacob replied that it was not a cab but a private car.[58]

As well as undergoing instruction, Jacob sat to Picasso for one of the first and finest of his Ingresque portrait drawings. "It is very handsome," he wrote Apollinaire (January 7, 1915), "simultaneously like my grandfather and an old Catalan peasant and my mother."[59] Picasso, who showered Apollinaire with drawings and caricatures of himself, did not give this drawing to Jacob: he would have sold it, as he sold virtually everything else that the artist had made over to him. The following year, however, Picasso would relent and give him a later version, duly inscribed. Anticipating its eventual appearance on the market, the artist got it back in 1933 or 1934, when Jacob asked for a handout of 10,000 francs. "Yes," Picasso replied, "but return the drawing you have of mine."[60] Not since *Les Demoiselles d'Avignon* had one of Picasso's works caused such consternation among his followers as the highly finished 1915 portrait. When it was published, in 1916, in *Elan* (Ozenfant's magazine), the more dogmatic cubists inveighed against it as a counterrevolutionary step—as *retardataire* in its way as Jacob's conversion to Catholicism.

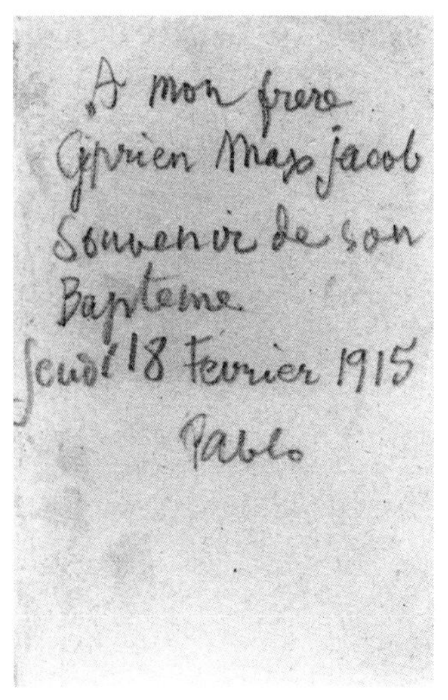

Picasso's inscription in the copy of Thomas à Kempis's *Imitation of Christ* he gave Max Jacob for his baptism, February 18, 1915. Bibliothèque Municipale, Orléans.

Finally, on February 18, 1915, Jacob was received into the Church in the Notre Dame de Sion chapel. Instead of Fiacre, he took Picasso's seventh name, Cyprien, because it was associated with magic. (Cyprien of Antioch and Cyprien of Corinth had both practiced magic; Cypris was also another name for Venus and thus of occult significance to this former mage.) Picasso presented his godson with Thomas à Kempis's *Imitation of Christ,*

Max Jacob in top hat, 1915. Archives Picasso.

inscribed, "To my brother Cyprien Max Jacob. In memory of his baptism." Eva could not attend the ceremony: she was in hospital. A few days later, Jacob would have an audience with the archbishop of Paris, thanks presumably to Pica's intervention. For the occasion he borrowed Picasso's top hat—inside which the artist had written his name in large letters—and was photographed outside the Bateau Lavoir. By April Picasso and Jacob had once again drifted apart. On April 24 the artist wrote Apollinaire: "I see Max from time to time. Our dog has bitten him on the hand. He has recovered. The bite inspired a poem."[61]

* * *

For the rest of 1915 Eva would be in and out of the hospital. By early November, she was back in a clinic for the last time. Despite his terror of illness and death, Picasso behaved with exemplary concern. Every day he took the Métro to Auteuil and sat by her bed, watching her die. On December 9, he wrote to Gertrude Stein in Mallorca:

> Don't be surprised if I've never written to you since you left. But my life is hell—Eva is still ill and gets worse every day and now she has been in a nursing home for a month. . . . My life is pretty miserable and I hardly do any work. I run backwards and forwards to the nursing home and I spend half my time in the Métro. I haven't had the heart to write you.
>
> However I've done a picture of a Harlequin that I think in my opinion and several people's opinion is the best I've ever done.[62]

This great *Harlequin* painting, in which Picasso mourns the dying Eva, will be discussed in the following chapter. Even still lifes done around this time reflect the imminence of her death. In the *Still Life with Bottle of Anis del Mono*, for instance, Picasso shamanistically paints the white ground of the ace of clubs the blackest of blacks. Traditionally the ace of clubs is a good-luck card, but for Picasso (and Apollinaire) it also symbolized the anus. In Picasso's favorite book, *Les Onze Mille Verges*, Apollinaire describes how a bomb explodes in a brothel and leaves the whores sprawled in salacious positions, "the ace of clubs presented to the gaze of lecherous soldiers . . . an admirable display of assholes."[63] This painting also includes a coded self-portrait: himself as a harlequin in the guise of an anthropomorphic bottle of Anis del Mono, whose facets have been transposed into diapering. Another, no less disturbing painting that relates to Eva's death depicts a seated woman reading a newspaper and wearing an elaborate hat with a mauve veil—a traditional emblem of mourning. It is decorated with a large white bird, which seems to have come alive and is about to ascend heavenwards.

Picasso evidently took a sketchbook to the clinic, to judge by a drawing of a nun in a coif (shades of the boy dressed up as a nursing nun, in his first major work, *Science and Charity*). He also drew the dying Eva in her nightdress, which has the same scalloped edge as the chemise she wears in *Woman in an Armchair*. As in the painting of her in the hat with the bird, Eva's face is a dead-looking, brick-shaped thing, embellished with a large phallic nose. She is foreshortened like Mantegna's *Dead Christ* in the Brera, the soles of her feet thrust out at us as if to imply that she was destined to leave the room "feet first."[64] The only sign that this is not a corpse is the way Eva's right arm is folded behind her head—same as in another done on this occasion, which likewise attests to his anguish,

Right: Picasso. *Nun*, 1915. Pencil on sketchbook page, 20×13.5cm. Marina Picasso Collection: Courtesy Galerie Jan Krugier, Geneva.

Below: Picasso. *Still Life with Bottle of Anis del Mono*, fall, 1915. Oil on canvas, 46×54.6cm. The Detroit Institute of Arts: Bequest of Robert H. Tannahill.

Above: Picasso. *Seated Woman (Eva) Wearing a Hat Trimmed with a White Bird*, 1915–16. Oil on canvas, 80×65cm. Private collection.

Right: Picasso. *Eva on Her Deathbed*, 1915. Pencil on paper, 16×24.5cm. Private collection.

psychic turmoil and anger at Eva's leaving him. Picasso could not forgive anyone close to him for dying.

Eva died sooner than expected—on December 14, 1915, "almost without any suffering," as Serge Férat wrote Soffici.[65] Picasso "may be a great artist," Marie Laurencin wrote Roché; "all the same he is a wretched man. After the ensuing loneliness, that's not funny either."[66] The funeral bordered on black farce. Members of Eva's family were shocked by the strange-looking bohemian mourners—what was left of the *bande à Picasso*—whom they were meeting for the first time. But what upset everybody, not least Juan Gris, who gave a report to Raynal, was the behavior of Max Jacob.[67] Although Max had recently been received into the Catholic Church, he behaved like anything but a good convert. Was he perhaps testing God's patience? It was a very cold day and the funeral cortège took a very long time to get from the clinic to the cemetery. En route Max repeatedly stopped for a drink. The drunker he became, the more macabre were the jokes he cracked. Meanwhile he had taken a liking to the coachman in charge of the hearse. After insisting that the man join the mourners in prayer at Eva's graveside, he went off with him. Picasso was furious. He retaliated by allowing Jean Cocteau, who had been paying court to him since June, to take over as his court jester.

24

Picasso and Cocteau

Romaine Brooks. *Portrait of Jean Cocteau,* 1914. Oil on canvas, 250×133cm. Musée National d'Art Moderne, Centre Georges Pompidou, Paris.

Opposite: Self-portrait photograph by Picasso in his rue Schœlcher studio, 1915–16. Archives Picasso.

A FEW MONTHS AFTER EVA'S DEATH, in spring, 1916, Axel Salto, a Danish critic, visited the rue Schœlcher studio and recorded his impression:

> [Picasso] had on a grass-green sweater and baggy trousers of brown velvet such as French artists still wear. He is small in stature and built like a bull-fighter. His skin is sallow and his wicked black eyes are set close together; the mouth is strong and finely drawn. He reminded me of a racehorse, an Arab with a well-shaped neck. People said that he had secret powers and could kill a man by looking at him; they said other strange things too. There was something massive and supernatural about him. He was amiability itself, showing me all his possessions, including a peepshow where you looked through a glass and saw a starry sky with angels flying about. I saw Henri Rousseau's picture of the European potentates standing together under a canopy. . . . Also pictures by Derain and Matisse and watercolours by Cézanne. His own first work, which hung over the bed, was painted at the age of twelve: a picture of a golden-haired girl in a vermilion skirt. The delicate features were finely observed . . . [and] it was shown with unmistakable pride. . . . The later picture, *Demoiselles d'Avignon,* was hanging in the studio. . . . Picasso, who is thirty-four, is said to have . . . embarked on new phases of development, opening the way towards forms of art that cannot be predicted. . . . One feels that the potentialities are as manifold as combinations on a chess-board.[1]

* * *

So vast was the cultural divide between Montparnasse and the *quartiers bourgeois* that Picasso and the young literary dandy Jean Cocteau might have been living in two different cities instead of a few kilometers apart. They might never have met if Cocteau, in a bid to reinvent himself as a modernist, had not made a determined effort to involve Picasso in his machinations. At first he had counted on Gleizes, whose fiancée, Juliette Roche, was a friend of his, to introduce him to the cubists—the only group synonymous with the avant-garde. Cocteau's strategy was to prevail upon Gleizes to paint a full-length portrait of him in uniform. It was not a great success. "Witty and distinguished," said Picabia, "but I wish I knew whether it portrayed an old lady or a pot of flowers."[2] By the beginning of 1915, Cocteau realized that he had better address himself directly to Picasso, who was rumored to be edging back to a classical style. As he had never met the artist, he looked around for a go-between. A suitable candidate was at hand: Edgard Varèse, one of the most theoretically advanced composers of his time, whose goal was to capture the fourth dimension in music. Varèse, whom Cocteau had met casually before the war, knew Picasso from Bateau Lavoir days, and had been in the studio (circa 1912–13) when the artist had had one of his blazing rows—cubism versus classicism—with Manolo. This had ended with Manolo "pointing to one of Picasso's cubic women [saying]: 'Anyway, in spite of all your cubism, Pablo, you can't keep me from being your contemporary.'"[3]

Edgard Varèse, c. 1917.

The first step in Cocteau's pursuit of Picasso was to write (March 13, 1915) his painter friend Valentine Gross for the address of Varèse, who was currently her lover. Cocteau had a valid reason for approaching him: he was planning a "revolutionary" production of *A Midsummer Night's Dream* and wanted Varèse to be the musical director and orchestrate the various "interpolations" he had chosen: Satie's *Cinq Grimaces* as well as four pieces by Ravel, Stravinsky, Florent Schmitt and Varèse himself. But, above all else, Cocteau wanted the composer to introduce him to Picasso.

Hitherto the meeting between Picasso and Cocteau has always been said to have occurred in December, 1915.[4] However, a dated letter in the Picasso archives reveals that they had already met by July 5: "Cher Monsieur Picasso, Could I perhaps come and see you on Wednesday morning? I need to ask you a detail about our Russian protégé."[5] Their first encounter must, therefore, have taken place a few days, possibly a week or two earlier, as Varèse—recently invalided out of the army with lung trouble—was in contact with Cocteau by early June and had left Paris to convalesce by the end of the month. Accounts of the Picasso/Cocteau meeting differ. Cocteau said that Varèse took him to the rue Schœlcher studio.[6] Varèse said that they had to go to Madame Cocteau's apartment, because her son was ill.[7] I believe Varèse.

For Cocteau, this was "the greatest encounter of his life." He was so awed "by the terrible eyes that pierced like gimlets and the intelligence that poured from him as if from the 'rose' of a watering can"[8]—that he for once kept quiet. Nor was Picasso very talkative. "There were long silences," Cocteau told Cabanne in 1960. "Varèse couldn't understand why we looked at each other without saying anything. When Picasso spoke, his syntax was visual. One immediately *saw* what he was saying."[9] Cocteau had been looking for a "masculine god" to worship. His previous hero, the dashing fighter pilot Roland Garros, who had taken him on reconnaissance flights over enemy lines, had been shot down and taken prisoner in April. Picasso fitted Cocteau's bill to perfection. He was "more than a prodigy, he was a miracle . . . and he appeared after a feminine period, whose charm had to be combated."[10] What did he get from his first meeting with Picasso? Cabanne asked. "An electrical charge," Cocteau replied.[11]

As for Picasso, he wanted nothing to do with Cocteau—to believe Max Jacob, who had followed his meretricious career in the pages of various *revues de luxe* with envious disapproval. Far from discouraging Cocteau, rebuffs brought out his resourcefulness. And he set about inveigling Picasso into friendship. He left little presents for him with the concierge at the rue Schœlcher, and unleashed a barrage of flattery beyond anything the artist had ever known. (By 1916 he would address letters to "Le Prince Pablo de Picasso.") This would have been counterproductive had Cocteau been less beguiling and Picasso less inured to the attentions of poets who doubled as Rigolettos. The artist soon found the company of

Valentine Gross, c. 1912. Private collection.

this infinitely diverting young man to be just the solace he needed at this vulnerable phase: torn between secret love for Gaby Depeyre and wrenching pity for Eva. In addition Picasso was ill—the problem seems to have been an ulcer—and he would not recover for a year or more.

Cocteau was undoubtedly charming, decorative, mercurial, witty: a passable poet and *feuilletonist* and a dazzling conversationalist. Even Edith Wharton said she had "known no other young man who so recalled Wordsworth's 'Bliss was it in that dawn to be alive.'"[12] But he was also, many people felt, on the make, frivolous, treacherous, snobbish—a poseur whose principal claim to fame was a book of very light verse, called *Le Prince frivole*, and the concept of *Le Dieu bleu*, a chichi orientalist ballet for Diaghilev, which had flopped.[13] By the age of twenty-six, Cocteau had managed to irritate much of the *beau monde* he was out to conquer, also most of the literary establishment, with the notable exception of Proust, who introduced him into his great novel as Octave, the dandy son of a rich manufacturer, with the nickname, "In the Soup."[14] Proust describes Octave as having "brought about a revolution in contemporary art at least equal to that accomplished by the Ballets Russes."[15]

At this painful moment of "shedding his skin," Cocteau was fortunate in the friendship of Valentine Gross: a gifted young beauty from Boulogne—"my swan," he called her (she had a long neck)—who had done a series of drawings of Nijinsky and other dancers in action: all the more valuable for matching specific movements to specific bars of music. Thanks to her musical as well as artistic sensibility, Valentine had already established herself as a luminary with a literary and musical salon. She was one of those women in whom everyone confides; also the first of a succession of upwardly mobile young beauties to be known as "*la petite sœur des riches*." Fond as she was of Cocteau, Valentine knew that the clever young men who attended her Wednesdays—Léon-Paul Fargue, Valéry Larbaud, Gaston Gallimard—would have melted away if she had ever imposed him on them. When François Mauriac, who had known him very early on, chided Cocteau for leaving his former friends without looking back, the poet had replied: "Had I looked back, I'd have turned into a pillar of SUGAR."[16] Another old friend, Marcel Jouhandeau, dubbed him "*l'ange du mensonge*" (the angel of lies). And André Gide, on whom he fawned, likewise took against him. Gide told Cocteau to change his affected handwriting; he also encouraged his lover, Henri Ghéon, to denounce Cocteau's verse in print: "To discern, among the gifts, which are his own and which are borrowed, would require very patient analysis."[17]

Nijinski in *L'Après-midi d'un faune*, 1912. Photograph by Adolphe de Meyer. Bibliothèque Nationale.

Even Diaghilev had reservations. Although he called Cocteau "Jeanchik" and challenged him to "astound" him—something Picasso would do far more effectively—the impresario did not (according to Stravinsky) really trust him either as a collaborator or as a friend. He particularly resented the way Cocteau chased after his beloved Nijinsky and popped up whenever the dancer was being rubbed down by his masseurs.[18] Nor did Bronislava Nijinska approve of the way her brother had fallen under the influence of this young man "with hollow rouged cheeks, thick, dark curly hair above a high forehead and very large black eyes. Always elegantly dressed, he heightened his complexion with lipstick." She made a point of asking who this man was and why he wore makeup. "It's very Parisian," Nijinsky told her. "He advises me to do the same . . . rouge my cheeks and lips.

Anna de Noailles and Etienne de Beaumont, 1914. Private collection.

It's the poet, Jean Cocteau."[19] The Cocteaus' neighbor, the Comtesse de Chevigné, on whom Proust partly based his Oriane de Guermantes, was likewise put out when Cocteau prostrated himself, the better to fondle Kiss, her Pomeranian. "Careful," she snorted. "I don't want him covered in face powder."[20]

In his quest for a persona, Cocteau had cultivated and ultimately identified with the aristocratic Romanian poetess Comtesse Anna de Noailles —a sacred monster of daunting affectation and preciosity. So closely did he base his handwriting on hers that on receiving a *pneumatique* from him, the comtesse declared this was the first time she had ever corresponded with herself. "*Anna-mâle*," as Cocteau was known in certain circles, soon rounded on his benefactress. To her face he continued to be ingratiating; behind her back, he mimicked her and denounced her as a mindless pilferer, whose only aim was to please. If he was to figure on the crest of the new wave, Cocteau realized, he would have to jettison this *démodé* role model and the image that went with it.

Cocteau's next *beau idéal*, Comte Etienne de Beaumont (Radiguet's Comte Orgel), was altogether more suitable and would leave an indelible mark on his disciple's character. Beaumont, whom Cocteau met in 1913, was also precious and mannered and almost as snobbishly censorious as Proust's Charlus, Robert de Montesquiou. However, he considered himself the most progressive member of the *gratin*. And with some justice: in the 1920s he would become a leading patron of modern painting and music, of Picasso and Satie in particular. Henceforth Cocteau would do what he could to ape the count's sharp, aristocratic look (beautifully caught in Picasso's portraits), the *racé* timbre of his voice, and, not least, his spiteful wit. The day after his wife, Edith, died, Beaumont would send three of her best friends telegrams, "*A très bientôt ma petite chérie*," signed Edith.[21]

* * *

Reims Cathedral on fire after the German bombardment, September 19, 1914.

When war broke out, Cocteau joined the Red Cross. From supervising milk distribution at railroad stations he managed to switch to a fashionable ambulance unit. This was run by Misia Godebski, a formidable lion huntress formerly married to Thadée Nathanson (director of *La Revue Blanche*). Misia, who was in the process of divorcing her second husband, the newspaper ogre Alfred Edwards, to marry the flashy Catalan muralist José María Sert, had persuaded Paris fashion houses to lend her a convoy of delivery vans. Misia led the way in an enormous Mercedes driven by the political cartoonist and fashion illustrator Paul Iribe, dressed like a deep-sea diver—with Paul Poiret at his side.[22] With Cocteau decked out in a vaguely naval uniform designed by Poiret, Misia's cavalcade advanced on the ravaged city of Reims. The ruins of the cathedral, Cocteau said, resembled "a mountain of old lace" or "a woman at whom vitriol had been thrown."[23] He was appalled to watch a priest prying open the jaws of dying soldiers with a knife in order to administer the Last Sacrament.

Back in Paris, Cocteau and Iribe launched a stylish propaganda journal called *Le Mot*.[24] The shrill jingoistic tone was calculated to appeal to the worst fears and prejudices of its chauvinistic readers, not to speak of the authorities in charge of mobilization. Cocteau even had a column called "Atrocités." As Steegmuller observes, he made the most of "the only kind of wartime atrocity laid to the German armies in Belgium that has not

Cocteau in uniform, c. 1916. Private collection.

Cocteau at the front, c. 1916. Private collection.

been proved—the amputation of the hands of children."[25] He also commended himself to that arch-chauvinist Léon Daudet (brother of his great friend Lucien) by castigating "the rich poverty of *Der Rosenkavalier*," and (in an unsigned article) the francophile art patron Count Kessler, as well as "*le boche Strauss and l'autrichien Hofmannsthal.*"[26] Cocteau had it in for Strauss and Hofmannsthal because their Diaghilev ballet, *La Légende de Joseph* (1914), had been a hit whereas his own *Dieu bleu* (1912) had been a failure. No less self-serving was his attack on Max Reinhardt, for putting on a lavish "Anglo-Saxon" production of *A Midsummer Night's Dream* in Berlin. "In Paris, in the midst of war, a group is planning to answer Reinhardt," he wrote. "They [who else but Cocteau?] promise us a sensationally new staging and French music . . . for our ally Shakespeare."[27] No less cynical was Cocteau's put-down of Wagner, especially in view of his strategy for keeping in with the Germans in World War II: making a film, *L'Eternel Retour*, based on *Tristan and Isolde*.

In December, 1914, Cocteau resumed ambulance work, this time with Etienne de Beaumont's lavishly accoutered unit.[28] What with uniforms "like Argentine policemen's," which Beaumont had dreamed up for his team, the convoy "resembled a circus on the move," according to Bernard Faÿ, who served with them.[29] The hotel where they spent the first night turned out to be the British commander-in-chief's headquarters. Beaumont and Cocteau caused a stir by coming down to dinner in silk pajamas, one in black, one in pink, and jangling gold ankle bracelets. On arriving at the front, the ambulances proved extremely popular, as they were equipped with showers. Cocteau supervised this facility, photographing and on occasion seducing the Zouaves and Senegalese sharpshooters, and even writing a poem about them, called "La Douche."[30] Eventually there was a scandal. Outraged by Cocteau's passion for one of his men, a jealous *goumier* (Moroccan) sergeant threatened to hack the flirtatious poet to pieces. The incident might have ended in court-martial or murder had it not been for Beaumont's cool cajolery and diplomacy.

On leave Cocteau worked hard to project a more serious image. He made every effort to distance himself from his past as a society pet in order to ingratiate himself with the modernists. This involved visualizing the Parisian cultural situation in quasi-political terms of "an artistic right and an artistic left, which were ignorant and disdainful of each other for no valid reason and which it was perfectly possible to bring together."[31] Cocteau had a simplistic solution: to convert Diaghilev to modern painting; to reconcile modern artists, especially Picasso, to the sumptuous aesthetic of the ballet; and to coax the cubists out of their isolation and persuade them to abandon "their hermetic Montmartre folklore of pipes, tobacco packages, guitars and old newspapers."[32] There was only one person capable of reconciling right and left, Cocteau felt: himself. He personally would constitute the bridge—as it were, the Pont Neuf—between the bourgeoisie and bohemia and pass himself off as a "professor of modernism."

To activate this process, Cocteau needed an eye-catching vehicle, and what better than the burlesque *Midsummer Night's Dream* he had envisaged as an Anglo-French riposte to Reinhardt? He planned to put this on at the Cirque Médrano, with three famous clowns, the Fratellini brothers, as the comics. Unlike Reinhardt, Cocteau proposed huge cuts and, to make the play topical and patriotic, retainers in allied uniforms, Hippolytus

Albert Gleizes. Costume design for Hippolyta in *A Midsummer Night's Dream*, 1914. Gouache on paper, 27×21cm. Musée des Beaux-Arts, Lyon.

in a Phrygian bonnet and Theseus as "a nightmare General French." For the décor Cocteau approached both Lhote and Gleizes. Lhote, who had recently opened a shop selling Louis-Philippe and Biedermeier furniture, was not up to it—"a bad painter ignored by the good ones," as Reverdy said of him.[33] Gleizes did some costume designs and proposed imaginative ways of projecting "sets" onto colored floor cloths but did not stay around to execute them. Two days after their marriage, he and Juliette Roche fled to New York. And so Cocteau pinned his hopes on Picasso. Now that he had access to the studio, he used all his charm and wit, eloquence and flattery, to involve the artist in his plan for a modern ballet or theatrical production that would involve the circus and/or burlesque. There was not as yet any talk of *Parade*; Cocteau wanted Picasso to work on his version of *A Midsummer Night's Dream*.[34]

*　　　*　　　*

That Picasso rapidly succumbed to Cocteau's charm should not have surprised his friends. In between bouts of manic work, Picasso needed to be amused, above all now that he was depressed by his own as well as Eva's illness, and lonely because most of his friends were away at the front. Cocteau provided just the distraction he needed. The poet's sense of paradox was very much to Picasso's taste: his ability to take an idea, turn it upside down, back to front, inside out, distort or transform it, make it vanish and reappear, as if he were a conjuror. Even his critics conceded the nimble dazzle of his wit, the high camp of his mimicry. The censorious Gide was sufficiently fascinated by Cocteau's description of life as an *ambulancier* to describe him mimicking bugle calls, the whistle of shrapnel and a Red Cross lady screaming, "I was promised fifty wounded. . . . I want my fifty wounded."[35] On the score of his conversational prowess, Cocteau is sometimes compared with Oscar Wilde. And although he lacked Wilde's intellectual integrity and generosity of heart, he had the same ability to electrify the most inert or philistine company. As someone who was often present at Cocteau's bravura performances in the 1950s, I can only say that I have never heard a raconteur to equal him.

Cocteau was obsessed with having his portrait painted. As a very young man he had sat for Jacques-Emile Blanche, Bakst, Romaine Brooks and many more. Now he was determined that Picasso should paint him in his new "Ingresque" manner. As he well knew, an insidious sitter could easily wheedle his way into an artist's confidence. With this in mind, he appeared at the rue Schœlcher studio (probably in early July, 1915, if Cocteau is correct in claiming that he did this on his second visit), wearing a harlequin costume under his raincoat. Picasso did not like being coerced. He put the importunate poet off with vague promises and kept the harlequin costume.[36] The summer went by without any sign of a portrait. On September 25, Cocteau tried a different tack. "My portrait must be painted," he wrote, "because I am going to die," and he enclosed some army tobacco vouchers—very welcome: tobacco was in extremely short supply—and said he was "writing lots of things about him [Picasso] for New York" (none of which can be traced).[37] At some point Cocteau learned that Picasso was at work on a harlequin painting. Might this be his portrait? he wrote the artist on February 6, 1916.[38] To believe Cocteau, it was indeed of him, or had started by being of him. However, that could

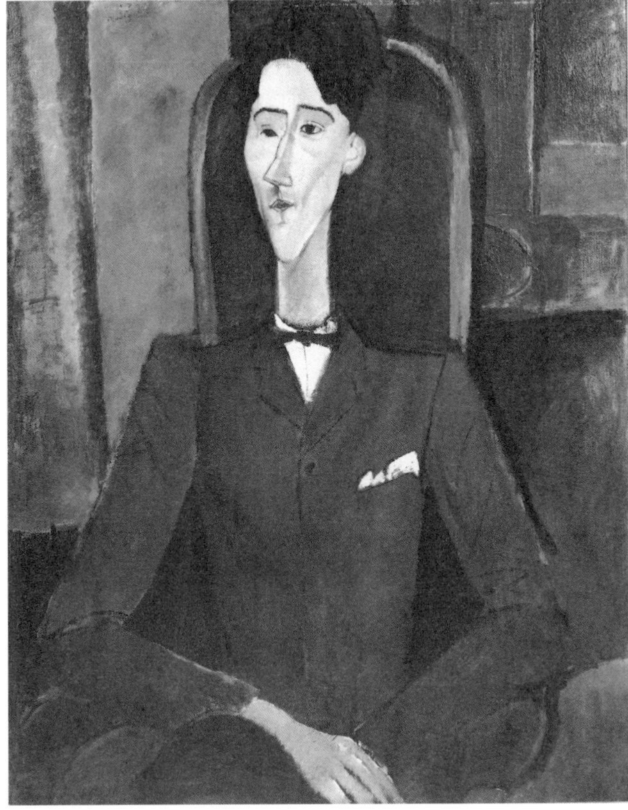

Above: Modigliani. *Jean Cocteau*, 1915. Oil on canvas, 97×80cm. The Henry and Rose Pearlman Foundation, Inc.

Above left: Jacques-Emile Blanche. *Jean Cocteau*, 1912. Oil on canvas, 91×72cm. Musée des Beaux-Arts, Rouen.

Left: Moïse Kisling. *Jean Cocteau in the Studio*, 1916. Oil on canvas, 73×60cm. Petit Palais, Geneva.

Above: Matisse. *Interior with Goldfish*, 1914. Oil on canvas, 146.5×112.4 cm. The Museum of Modern Art, New York: Gift of Florene M. Schoenborn and Samuel A. Marx.

Left: Picasso. *Harlequin*, fall, 1915. Oil on canvas, 183.5×105 cm. The Museum of Modern Art, New York: Acquired through the Lillie P. Bliss Bequest.

Far left: Picasso. *Dancers*, 1915–16. Pencil on lined paper, 27.3×21 cm. Musée Picasso.

Left: Picasso. *Dancers*, 1915–16. Pencil on paper, 29×22.5 cm. Musée Picasso.

have been wishful thinking on his part. Picasso supposedly made it more and more abstract, until it was no longer recognizable. The painting that best fits Cocteau's description is the great *Harlequin* on a black ground that Picasso had begun a few months before Eva died. This might, indeed, have started as a portrait of Cocteau, but it ended up as an allegorical portrait of Picasso. The diamond-patterned costume had apparently triggered the artist's recurrent identification with harlequin: not the playful commedia dell'arte figure that Cocteau had in mind but the "her-lequin" of medieval legend—a soul escaped from hell. Picasso's *Harlequin* also has another derivation in his own recent watercolors of two dancers. Successive studies depict these figures dancing ever more closely together— seemingly spotlit on the circular floor of a cabaret or stage, and sometimes observed by spectators in boxes to right and left. If Gaby performed in a Montparnasse cabaret, as Salmon says, the shimmying girl might conceivably be her.

When he tackled the large canvas, Picasso merged the dancing couple (himself with Gaby? or with Eva?) into a single harlequin. All that is left of the girl is two or three layers of shadow, each on a slightly skewed axis, onto which harlequin's motley rocket of a body has been superimposed. His bottle-top head is as dehumanized as Chirico's dummies; the tiny, toothy mouth is the more eerie for its rictus of a grin, and the eyes all the beadier for being minimal—birdlike. Harlequin's hands are hardly visible: minuscule paws, one white, one black, holding a white rectangle, which has been left mysteriously blank—seemingly a canvas or a mirror or a variation on Veronica's veil. Because it looks deceptively unfinished, no one has ever remarked (at least in print) that this rectangle contains a vital clue to the painting's meaning: the unpainted area to the right is unmistakably a self-portrait in profile. When Matisse saw this painting, he thought it was Picasso's greatest work to date—not least because, as he rightly said, it derives in one important respect from his *Interior with Goldfish* of 1914. The Matisse is also in the Museum of Modern Art, but the nature of the link between these two encoded self-portraits has gone unrecognized.[39] A very rough sketch reveals that Matisse originally envisaged a figure on the right-hand side of the canvas, but whittled this down to a minimal cubistic construction.[40] The only clue that this painting is self-referential is the white rectangle, which stands for a palette, with the artist's thumb stuck prominently through it—a feature borrowed from Cézanne. There is something very moving about these two great rivals communicating secretly with each other through cryptic passages in their work. By depicting himself cubistically, Matisse pays tribute to the movement he had once denounced, but which, as he now admitted, had "spurred him on to some of his finest moments."[41] The white rectangle, which Picasso would have immediately recognized as a quotation from Cézanne's self-portrait with a palette, is a way of returning the compliment and at the same time getting in a sly, conspiratorial dig. No less moving is the way that Picasso hides yet draws attention to himself, spotlit against the blackness of Eva's mortal illness and the blackness of war. And how typical of him to use motley to suggest mourning and leave us in the dark as to where we are—Golgotha, no-man's-land, or the Bal Bullier.

*　　　*　　　*

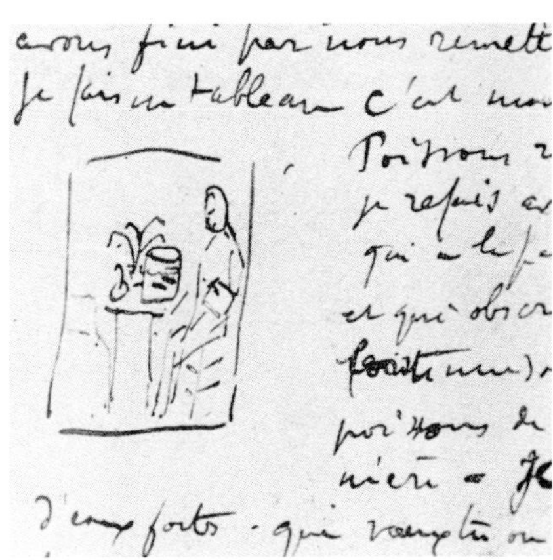

Matisse. Rough sketch of first idea for *Interior with Goldfish* on a postcard sent to Charles Camoin, fall, 1914. Archives Camoin.

Cézanne. *Self-Portrait with Palette*, 1885–87. Oil on canvas, 92×73cm. Bührle Foundation, Zurich.

Back doing ambulance work at the very end of 1915, Cocteau waited in vain for a word from Picasso. "We train huge rats to sit up and beg like little dogs," he wrote Valentine on February 2, 1916, but "not a word from Picasso. He has forgotten how to write since he has taken to collage" (a reference, presumably, to his romance with Gaby rather than the artistic process he had invented).[42] Cocteau's pranks still raised military hackles: it was not so much that he took the regimental mascot, a nanny goat, for walks, but that the long gauze bandages he used as a leash were in very short supply. When he came on Easter leave at the end of March, Cocteau found Picasso more than ever in need of consolation. At four in the afternoon on March 17, Apollinaire had been severely wounded. A shell fragment had pierced his helmet. "I didn't realize I'd been hit," he said, "and went on reading (the *Mercure de France*) until all of a sudden blood came pissing down."[43] At first the damage did not appear to be serious. Once the shell fragment was removed, the wound began to heal. It was only after Serge Férat had pulled the necessary strings to have Apollinaire moved to the Italian hospital in Paris that paralysis unexpectedly set in. On May 9, the poet had to be trepanned. Picasso, who was devastated, checked the medication with Apollinaire's doctor. When told they were using a Chilean "miracle" balm made of herbs from the pampas, "*la baume de fier à bras*," he was much relieved.[44]

Apollinaire wounded, 1915. Photograph by Paul Guillaume. Bibliothèque Nationale.

Apollinaire's absence from the scene worked to Cocteau's advantage in his cultivation of Picasso. So did the fact that Max Jacob was out of favor. Cocteau seldom lost an opportunity to denigrate the court jester whose place he was taking. "Claude Anus," he called him in a letter to Gleizes, "a meddlesome creature given to prancing around the sacristy. . . good-hearted but grubby."[45] And to Valentine he compared Jacob to a convent gardener "who smuggles dirty books to the good sisters."[46] He was always careful to lavish praise on Jacob's writing but apt to temper it with sneers about "the back of the shop smell."[47]

"God hates Cocteau," Jacob complained to Maritain,[48] but Max would soon relent and do his former enemy many kindnesses. And Cocteau, to his great credit, would be one of the only friends to intervene with the Germans when the Gestapo arrested Jacob at the end of World War II. In the course of this Easter leave, which lasted over a month, Cocteau became Picasso's Leporello.

> [He] keeps taking me to the Rotonde [Cocteau complained to Valentine, a few months later]. I never stay more than a moment, despite a flattering welcome from the circle (perhaps I should say the cube). Gloves, cane and collar astonish these artists in shirtsleeves—they have always regarded them as the emblems of feeble-mindedness. Too much sitting around cafés makes for sterility.[49]

Be that as it may, Cocteau stayed long enough to make useful contacts with what he called "the left," among them Modigliani and Kisling, who both set about painting portraits of him in a studio on the top floor of the Rotonde. One of the many drawings Modigliani did of Cocteau bears the inscription: "I, the undersigned, author of this drawing, swear never to get drunk again for the duration of the war. Modigliani."[50] As cafés closed early, Cocteau would sometimes take Picasso to meet his smart friends. The artist was not averse to this. He felt at ease in grand houses. He, too, was of noble lineage; what is more, his uncle Salvador had married into

Apollinaire. *Serge Férat at the Italian Hospital*, 1917. Watercolor on paper. Whereabouts unknown.

the Malagueño aristocracy. "I'll dine with the duke" is how he ends one of his notes.[51] Through Cocteau Picasso made one friendship of the utmost importance: with a rich Chilean *femme du monde*, Eugenia Errazuriz, who would fall platonically in love with him, acquire some of his greatest recent paintings and facilitate his *entrée* into Parisian society.

In the course of his long Easter leave, Cocteau did everything he could to further his ballet/theater project. Undaunted by his failure to interest Diaghilev, Stravinsky or anybody else in his earlier *David* ballet and by the cancellation, when it was already in rehearsal, of *A Midsummer Night's Dream*, he set about recycling these two aborted projects—the burlesque biblical spectacle and the burlesque Shakespearean production—into a burlesque circus ballet. Cocteau hoped this would prove entertaining enough to appeal to sophisticated elements on the right and provocatively modern enough to ensure the collaboration of Picasso and the no less exigent Erik Satie. Since persuading Valentine Gross to organize a dinner so that he could meet him, Cocteau had been courting the composer. Sometime in April, he went to hear Satie and Ricardo Viñes play his four-hand *Morceaux en forme de poire*. He immediately asked Satie to collaborate on a ballet, provisionally to be called *Parade*. Under the impression that Cocteau merely wanted to adapt his *Morceaux* for the ballet, the composer wrote Valentine that he hoped "the admirable Cocteau will not use my old pieces. Joking apart, don't you think we should do something new?"[52] Eventually Satie would do just that. Meanwhile Picasso held back from a commitment. Did he suspect, like Satie, that Cocteau's ideas would need whittling down and sharpening? They were too pretentious to inspire much confidence: "May *Parade* distill all the involuntary emotion given off by circuses, music halls, carrousels, public balls, factories, seaports, movies, etc. etc."[53]

On May 1, a day or two before his leave ended, Cocteau's wish finally came true. Picasso did his portrait: not painted but drawn, and not in harlequin costume but in uniform. And then the elegant *ambulancier* returned to the battlefront. His unit was ordered to the Somme in preparation for the big July offensive, so Cocteau was not in Paris during the third week in May, when Diaghilev made a quick trip to Paris. In his absence their mutual friend, Eugenia Errazuriz, took the impresario on a first visit to Picasso. Diaghilev was puzzled by the work, deeply depressed by the view over the cemetery, but much impressed by the man. What, if anything, was discussed we do not know. Picasso still had reservations about working in that suspect field the ballet—especially on a project whose seriousness and feasibility were in doubt.

* * *

For the first few weeks on the Somme, Cocteau withstood the carnage—"hunting for the dead—horrible discoveries of wretches battered to pulp. . . . The very sheds are groaning"—and then collapsed, apparently with battle trauma or shell shock.[54] On July 8, he was sent back on sick leave to Paris, and there, despite dizzy spells, tics, headaches and immense fatigue, he threw himself into a very different battle—the battle for *Parade*. On August 11, he wrote vaingloriously to Stravinsky, who was in Switzerland: "In a week I shall return to my post on the Somme, where big guns

Picasso. *Jean Cocteau*, May 1, 1916. Pencil on paper. Private collection.

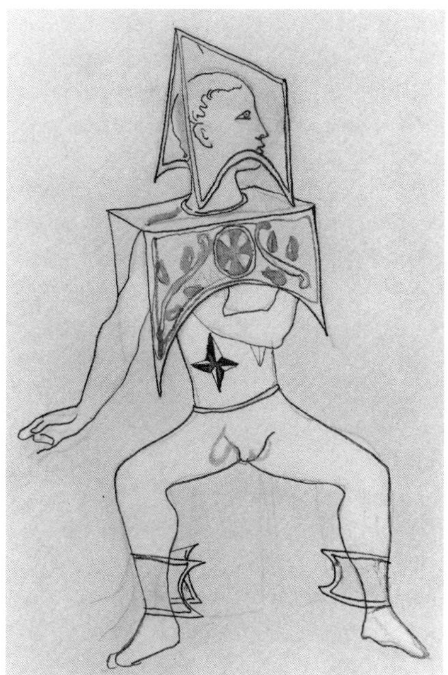

Jean Cocteau. Costume design for *David*, 1914. Pen and ink, crayon and pastel on paper, 25.7×20cm. Archer M. Huntington Art Gallery, The University of Texas at Austin.

camouflaged as if by Bakst or the Cubists are shaking all Picardy."[55] At the same time he and his well-connected mother were pulling every possible string to have his sick leave prolonged and prevent his going back to the front. To Valentine there was no talk of "returning to my post." Instead he moaned that "no one would recognize me. With my lackluster eyes and my poor hair all destroyed by the Somme."[56] Finally on November 24, thanks to his mother's friend Philippe Berthelot, director of political affairs at the Quai d'Orsay, Cocteau was given a cushy job in the war information office, Later, he would have the gall to claim that he had "left the war" because he was enjoying it too much. This enjoyment had disgusted him, he said. "As soon as I made that discovery, I arranged to leave, taking advantage of being sick."[57]

Pierre Auguste Renoir. *Misia Natanson*, 1904. Oil on canvas, 92.1×73cm. National Gallery, London.

Apart from loss of nerve, Cocteau had another pressing reason for not returning to the front. His *Parade* project had angered his old friend and sometime enemy Misia Sert. Foreseeing problems with this difficult woman's vanity and deviousness, Cocteau had taken the precaution of letting her think that *Parade* had really been her idea. However, after returning from a summer spent in Sitges with Diaghilev—she claimed to be the only woman he could stand—Misia realized that Cocteau had hoodwinked her. With the connivance of the younger, prettier and more gifted Valentine Gross, he had inveigled "her" Satie into writing new music for a project suspiciously like a rehash of the *David* ballet that Diaghilev and Stravinsky had turned down in 1914. How dare he? In her role as musical arbiter, she had decreed that only Satie's earlier pieces were to be used for a ballet. She and Diaghilev were going to take *Parade* away from him, she told Cocteau, and "begin all over again with Satie."[58] Enraged at the implication that he was past his prime, Satie fought back at the woman whom he and his coterie had nicknamed Tante Brutus and *la faiseuse d'anges* (slang for abortionist), because she enjoyed stabbing her friends in the back and aborting their schemes; also Tante Truffaldin, because she behaved like the treacherous valet in the commedia dell'arte.[59]

Jacques-Emile Blanche. *Portrait of Eugenia Errazuriz*, 1890. Pastel on paper, 163.8×97.8cm. Private collection.

Misia struck fear into Cocteau by making a conspicuous fuss of the convalescent Apollinaire. Hence Cocteau's refusal to accompany Picasso on a visit to the wounded poet in the hospital. As he wrote to Gleizes: "[Apollinaire], very tiresome with his Bolivar beard, his scar and his C[roix] de guerre. . . . Picasso I love. People are trying to set us against each other, but I refuse to listen to their mischief-making and to his friends, who accuse him of 'stealing their inventions.'"[60] Picasso, who had yet to meet Misia, kept aloof from the intrigue. Satie stood firm: on August 8, he wrote to Valentine, "It's happened! I've broken with Tante Truffaldin. What a bitch!"[61] Meanwhile Misia rallied her forces. She persuaded Stravinsky to let Cocteau have a piece of his, or rather her, mind. Cocteau, as he reported to Valentine (August 13), did not give way. "It's great to be in the thick of the dogfights of great art," he wrote. "In due course the quibbling fades away leaving . . . sweetness and light in its wake."[62] The quibbling was indeed about to fade away. Within ten days, Cocteau miraculously managed to get a definite commitment out of Picasso, overcome Diaghilev's doubts, neutralize Stravinsky and in so doing triumph over "Tante Truffaldin."

*   *   *

How Cocteau brought the *Parade* negotiations to a triumphant conclusion has never been fully explained. Satie, who was jealous of Stravinsky, certainly did his best to wreck Misia's plans. Her role as bad fairy in the birthing of *Parade* has always been recognized. But nobody has identified the good fairy, who saved the day for Cocteau: Eugenia Errazuriz. Cocteau had known Eugenia since before the war. In 1915 he had urged his mother to call on her in London. "Of her celebrated beauty there remains a kind of Abbé Constantin charm," he told his mother, "and some canvases by famous painters [among them Sargent, Orpen and Boldini]."[63] After Eugenia's return to Paris, Cocteau brought her together with Picasso. And an *amitié amoureuse* rapidly developed between them. Besides a passion for the artist—"she looks at him with eyes of love ["*les yeux doux*"], Roché wrote in his diary (July 21, 1916)[64]—Eugenia turned out to have a passion for his recent work. Picasso enjoyed her company, enjoyed talking Spanish with her, but given the age gap, her piety and his other involvements, there was no question of an affair. She supplanted Hélène d'Oettingen in his life and, to some extent, Gertrude Stein.

Picasso. Study for costume of French Manager in *Parade*, 1917. Pencil on paper, 27.8×22.6cm. Musée Picasso.

As a close friend and occasional backer of Diaghilev and Stravinsky, Eugenia was uniquely placed to save *Parade* from Misia's meddling; and save it she did—more for Picasso's sake than Cocteau's. Also maybe for her own: she disliked Misia; so would Picasso, although later, at his wife's insistence, he would sometimes accept her invitations. Picasso's revenge on Misia was conceptual. In one of his *Parade* designs he had decorated the French manager's sandwich board with chopped-up words as if to advertise a concert. It reads: "*Grand Con[cert] Miss Cert Merd.*" It was not, of course, used. What was Misia like? I once asked Picasso. We happened to have been to see Garbo in *Camille*, a film version of *La Dame aux camélias*. "Remember the conniving old duenna who played the role of Garbo's friend?" he said. "That was Misia to the life." So much for the story—put about by her—that they had once been lovers.

Picasso's regard for Eugenia was such that he supposedly gave her what is arguably his most important painting of the war years, the monumental *Seated Man* of 1916. (See Chapter 26.) He also sold her two other major works, the famous 1914 *Portrait of a Young Girl* and the 1915 *Man in a Bowler Hat.* More than anyone else, it would be Eugenia who briefly transformed Picasso, for better or worse, from a Montparnasse bohemian into the casually elegant lion of what Max Jacob would call his "duchess period." She took him to the Tower of Babel ball (*Soirée Babel*) that Etienne de Beaumont gave in his magnificent *hôtel particulier.* (The ball lived up to its name, Cocteau reported: "Madame Errazuriz chattered away in Spanish with Picasso, Serge [Diaghilev] in Russian with Massine, and Satie in Sauterne with me!")[65] She would groom him for his audience with her friend the king of Spain in 1917; she would preside over his marriage to Diaghilev's ballerina Olga Khokhlova; and where else would the Picassos spend their honeymoon but at her villa at Biarritz?

When she met Picasso, Eugenia had just turned fifty.[66] She had been born into an old Chilean silver-mining family, which was believed, at least by Picasso, to have a touch of Inca blood. A great beauty, she had married José Tomás Errazuriz, an amateurish painter of landscapes. Finding the Chilean *beau monde* stifling, the newlyweds moved to Europe, and after a summer in Venice, where her looks captivated Sargent, they settled in Paris. Eugenia distinguished herself by disdaining eighteen-ninetyish ostentation and froufrou and adopting a minimalist style in dress and decoration. In this respect, she was the antithesis of her overblown rival-to-be, Misia, whose velvet-hung rooms were chockablock with gilded furniture, rock-crystal galleons, and portraits of herself by Renoir, Lautrec, Bonnard and Vuillard.

William Orpen. *Portrait of Eugenia Errazuriz*, c. 1900. Oil on canvas, 76×63.5 cm. Private collection.

After 1900, the Errazurizes moved to London. When the Ballets Russes arrived on their first triumphant visit in 1911, Eugenia made herself indispensable to Diaghilev, who set great store by her taste. (She would later help him form a collection of modern pictures, including works by Picasso, for Massine.) He also counted on her support—much as he did on Misia's—with fund-raising and what would later be called public relations. Back in France after her husband's death, in 1913, Eugenia resumed her role as an arbiter of modernism. When Proust refers in his last volume to society ladies ("touched by art as if by heavenly grace") dwelling "in apartments filled with cubist paintings, while a cubist painter lived only for them, and they lived only for him,"[67] he was writing from experience. He had happened to call on Eugenia as she was moving into her new house—a *dépendance* of Etienne de Beaumont's mansion—and unpacking the great cubist paintings that Picasso had given or sold her.

Eugenia had a genius for spotting genius. Through Diaghilev she had met Stravinsky, whom she came to regard as her composer. During the war she sent him a thousand francs a month; if it was late, the composer would complain to Misia, who would—on at least one occasion—send him two thousand francs. She also kept him supplied with that increasingly rare commodity tobacco. In return he gave her a major notebook and dedicated scores to her. Later Eugenia would adopt Blaise Cendrars as her poet and Le Corbusier, who designed a villa for her at the Chilean resort of Viña del Mar,[68] as her architect. Picasso was of course her painter.

In the tussle over *Parade* Eugenia would have perceived that success depended not so much on Cocteau, the originator of the project, whom not even Diaghilev really trusted, as on the infinitely more creative Picasso. But Picasso would not commit himself. He had good reason to fear that any involvement with the "decadent" Russian ballet (a spectacle he had never even seen) and the no less "decadent" Cocteau might bring *"le peintre de la vie moderne"* into disrepute. If Eugenia could get Picasso to stop procrastinating and commit himself to *Parade*, she knew that Diaghilev would go ahead with it. In her cool way, Eugenia was as skilled at bringing people together as Misia was at driving them apart. She also had the advantage of a more modern sensibility towards painting, which is why Diaghilev, whose understanding of contemporary art was far from sure, looked to her for guidance. Exactly what steps Eugenia and Cocteau took we do not know. At all events they prevailed. Picasso would say only that Eugenia had been very helpful. When the Ballets Russes presented a gala *répétition générale* on May 11, 1917, the two rival ladies were very much in evidence. Paul Morand contrasts them: "Misia dressed to kill in a silver tiara . . . Madame Errazuriz got up as a Spanish nun."[69]

*　　　*　　　*

On August 24, 1916, Cocteau and Satie sent Valentine a triumphant postcard, confirming that Picasso had agreed to do the décor. *Parade* was finally a reality. "Picasso is moulting," he wrote Valentine at greater length a week later, "undergoing a transformation—Saturday night we begin real work."[70]

Mikhail Larionov. *Stravinsky, Diaghilev, Cocteau and Satie*, c. 1917. Pen on paper. Private collection.

25

Irène Lagut

Picasso. *Elvire Palladini (You-You)*, 1916. India ink on paper, 22.5×27.5cm. Picasso Heirs.

Picasso and Pâquerette. Detail of photograph taken by Cocteau, August 12, 1916.

Opposite: Irène Lagut, c. 1915. Service du Patrimoine, Menton.

GABY'S REFUSAL OF PICASSO'S OFFER of marriage dealt a mortifying blow to his pride and made his sense of isolation all the more painful. He would always find it difficult to function on his own. And so, once again, he was in quest of a wife. Two dazzling young women had recently entered his life: Elvire Palladini,[1] nicknamed You-You, and Emilienne Pâquerette Geslot, known simply as Pâquerette—one of Poiret's star mannequins. You-You was a wild-looking beauty whom Picasso depicts in the nude, offering herself up to him. No drawings of Pâquerette have been identified but she appears in the delightful sequence of snapshots that Cocteau took of Picasso and some of his friends (among them Max Jacob, Modigliani, Kisling, Salmon) on August 12, 1916.[2] Pâquerette was the quintessential Parisian model—tall, cool, dressed in the height of *outré* fashion and "very nice," according to Gertrude Stein,[3] who returned from Mallorca in June, 1916, and was back in contact with Picasso. The artist did not contemplate marrying either You-You or Pâquerette. But they consoled him when, as often happened, his next choice of a wife, Serge Férat's bisexual mistress, Irène Lagut, made herself unavailable.

The ramifications of Irène's affair with Picasso are easier to follow if we know about her convoluted past. A principal source for this is the novel *La Femme assise*, which Apollinaire—Picasso's accomplice in the girl's abduction—wrote about this bizarre interlude. Despite an incongruous subplot concerning some Mormons, the novel (which had many working titles: *Les Clowns d'Elvire, Les Caprices de Bellone, Irène de Montparnasse, Paris pendant la guerre*) is supposedly true to life in that Irène herself provided the story as well as the illustrations.[4] And insofar as one can check, the novel, which was not published until 1920, two years after Apollinaire's death, and then in a very poorly edited version, keeps to the facts of her affair with Picasso.[5] We should, however, allow for the misogyny and censoriousness that afflicted the last two years of the writer's life. Far from seeing Irène in a favorable light, as she had every reason to expect, her collaborator portrays her as a tease—an unprincipled good-time girl with a taste for other good-time girls. Especially insulting was his identification of Irène with *La Femme assise* (the seated woman) of the title. This was a reference not so much to one of Picasso's favorite subjects (though that too) as to the allegorical figure on the forged Swiss five-franc coins that had flooded Europe when Apollinaire was a child. The title implies that for all their charms, liberated women like Elvire/Irène are worthless fakes.

There are two possible reasons for Apollinaire's bias. After watching Irène repeatedly encourage and discourage Picasso, accept and refuse his proposals of marriage, Apollinaire, who had also been the victim of traumatic rejections, may have felt like avenging his old friend's wounded pride as well as his own. Apollinaire also had a score of his own to settle with Irène—a score which explains his emphasis on her lesbianism. "She liked women the way a man does," he says. And again, towards the end of *La Femme assise*, he enumerates her six current lovers. Besides Nicolas/Serge, he lists a Piedmontese clown and an armless *mutilé de guerre*. She did not love any of them, Apollinaire claims; her only true loves were two women. One of them, called Corail, is based on red-headed Ruby Kolb. Shortly after becoming Apollinaire's mistress, Ruby had gone off with Irène to Brittany, where the poet joined them. Might they have had a *ménage à trois*? Back in Paris, the two women went to the circus every Saturday evening, and were photographed with their arms round each other's waists. Ruby Kolb was "*La jolie rousse*," the mistress the poet would marry six months before he died. She is better known as his widow, Jacqueline Apollinaire.

Irène Lagut and Ruby Kolb, c. 1915. Collection P.M.A.

In *La Femme assise* Picasso is called Pablo Canouris (a Spanish/Albanian painter with the eyes of a bird and "hands of celestial blue");[6] Irène is Elvire (like Picasso's girlfriend You-You); Serge Férat is Nicolas Varinoff; Hélène d'Oettingen is Princess Teleschkine; and Apollinaire calls himself Anatole de Saintariste. However, Apollinaire's mean-spirited account is not our only source of information about Irène. For one thing, until recently, she was very much alive in an old people's home in Menton (she died at the age of one hundred and one in 1994). Like a lot of old ladies with a gallant past, Irène was not particularly forthcoming. Fortunately, she gave two major interviews—one to Marie-Jeanne Durry in *Les Lettres Françaises* (1969), another on French television four years later (that is to say, when she was eighty)—which provide a convincing, albeit sanitized, version of events.[7] If Irène was reticent about Picasso, we should remember that he was still alive at the time of these interviews. She would not have wanted to offend him. Fortunately some of the letters she wrote at the time of her affair with Picasso have survived and, where it has been possible to check, her story proves remarkably close to Apollinaire's.

She was born, Irène tells us, on January 3, 1893, in a small village near Maisons-Laffitte, about twelve miles from the center of Paris, to a peasant family originally from the Jura. (Hence Gertrude Stein's description of her as "a very lovely woman who came from the mountains and wanted to be free.")[8] Her father was a mailman. After leaving school at the age of fifteen, she was put to work in the post office—a far cry from being free. She was soon liberated from drudgery by a local doctor, who seduced her and set her up in Paris. Her parents had the police charge him with violating a minor, but Irène refused to testify against him, and he was acquitted. Already a grave beauty with a childish laugh, Irène was only too happy to let her seducer encourage her precocious taste for group sex and other women. The doctor supposedly introduced her to an elderly Russian (a Monte Carlo pickup, according to Apollinaire). She would have us believe that he was so struck by her resemblance to a daughter, who had recently committed suicide, that he took her to live with him in St. Petersburg.

Mikhail Larionov. *Apollinaire and Ruby*, 1915. Pencil on paper, 42×27 cm. Private collection.

Irène describes her protector as a leading lawyer, a great friend of Rodzianko, president of the Duma. He kept her in considerable style, before passing her on to a twenty-six-year-old grand duke, who, according to *La Femme assise*, was vastly rich and vicious, with an entourage of pretty boys, masochistic generals, and middle-aged businesswomen of daunting depravity. This sounds too much like Apollinaire's pornographic masterpiece, *Les Onze Mille Verges*, to be entirely credible. However, there is independent confirmation from the usually well-informed Alice Halicka (Marcoussis's Polish wife) that Irène had indeed been "sold to" a Russian nobleman,[9] that she had contracted typhoid, lost most of her hair and been packed off back to Paris with a third-class ticket. "Homesickness" is Irène's reason for her return. At the frontier she was taken off the train —because her papers were not in order, she says, and she was a minor. As she was over twenty, there must have been another, less creditable reason for detaining her. At all events she claims to have been rescued by "the aide-de-camp of a Grand Duke I knew," who told the authorities that he would be responsible for her, and on they went to Paris.

Irène Lagut. Illustration from the prospectus for *Les Clowns d'Elvire*, 1916. Collection P.M.A.

Back in France in the spring of 1913, Irène headed for Montparnasse and (according to Apollinaire) went to work in a music hall. There she fell in love with a chorus girl (Mavise Baudarelle, in *La Femme assise*): in fact one of two daughters—Vigoureux by name, hence known as the "Vigourelles"—of the owner of the boulevard Raspail bar where Picasso, Apollinaire and the *Soirées de Paris* group regularly forgathered. Down the street was the apartment that Serge Férat shared with his "sister." As soon as Irène moved in with the Vigoureux family, she caught Serge's eye. Not only was she a beauty, she was fresh from St. Petersburg. Despite her lesbian involvement, she embarked on an affair with him and settled into his comfortable and secluded studio.[10] In August she accompanied Serge and his "sister" on a trip to Sorgues to visit Braque, in the course of which Hélène took against Serge's beautiful working-class mistress.

For all his kindness to Irène, Serge often left her alone for days at a time while he edited *Les Soirées de Paris* and attended to his demanding "sister." Irène did not mind this—at least at first—because she could draw and paint. She took to copying the Douanier Rousseaus that hung in the studio, and soon turned into a not very good *faux naïf* painter. Apollinaire raved about her work. In a silly preface to Irène's 1917 exhibition, he would describe her as "one of those singular Satanesses of art who keep the magnificent uncertainty of our time gushing away."[11] You will not attract attention, he told her, if you are not perceived as evil.

Serge's friends—Picasso, Apollinaire and Max Jacob—took a great liking to Irène. She was sexy and high-spirited and a demon dancer who liked to end her evenings at the Bal Bullier. She personified the "new girl"—reckless, classless, amoral—who emerged in the course of the war. Nevertheless, she was surprisingly affectionate and loyal (rather than faithful) to her protective, undemanding lover. It was only after the outbreak of war, when Serge volunteered to be a medical orderly, that problems arose. Day after day she was left alone in the hot, airless studio; the only sign of life was a recurrent shriek from the concierge's parrot: "Brr, it's cold!" "I was so bored that I made up with my family and am spending some time with them,"[12] she wrote Ardengo Soffici from Maisons-Laffitte on June 24, having evidently placated them by claiming to be married. The possessive

Hélène d'Oettingen. Private collection.

Hélène continued to insist that Serge spend all his free time with her.

> I feel totally abandoned, [Irène wrote Soffici again on August 11, 1915] Serge hasn't dined with me once in the last three weeks. . . . People are trying to tear us apart. Words are being put into his mouth. I know he loves me, but selfishly. His sister has come up with a pretext that restaurant food is bad for him, so I am condemned to go out alone. . . . I am not prepared to play the role of victim, but that is what my life is like and it's not funny for a girl of twenty-two.[13]

Ardengo Soffici, c. 1914. Soffici Archive.

Hélène became ever more vindictive. She pretended to be ill so that Serge had to spend nights at her apartment rather than his studio. In February, 1916, Irène wrote Soffici that she would never be happy again, that she was left alone until late at night, when Serge would come back from the hospital, grouchy and exhausted.[14] He claimed (according to Apollinaire in his novel) to have sworn off sex for the duration of the war but had successive affairs with women who worked with him. So cavalier was Serge's attitude to Irène that he may, consciously or not, have made her available to Picasso (as, later in life, admiring friends like Eluard and Penrose would make their women available to the great man). The night before he left for a Russian ambulance unit on the western front, Serge announced that he had a lot of shopping to do and was obliged to dine with his sister. Would "Pablo" (we are back in *La Femme assise*) take Elvire/Irène to his private box at the local cinema, where he and his friends were in the habit of going night after night to see the *Fantômas* films or the sensational *Mystères de New York*?

Irène would have been easy enough for Picasso to seduce. However, her loyal nature, not to speak of her other affairs and aspirations to spiritual freedom, made it unlikely that she would leave an easygoing protector like Serge for someone who, for all his charisma, was known to be maniacally possessive. As for Picasso, he was not interested in yet another casual affair; he wanted a wife—Irène and only Irène—and he was prepared to go to any lengths to get her. The assumption of divine power had always come naturally to him, especially now that he was beginning to be perceived as a classicist. Why not assume the role of a classical deity? Why not abduct Irène just as Jupiter had turned himself into a bull and abducted Europa? No wonder Ovid's *Metamorphoses* would later inspire a suite of engravings and some remarkable drawings.

Picasso's villa at 22, rue Victor Hugo, Montrouge.

Apollinaire was only too ready to act as Picasso's accomplice. The operation to relieve the pressure on his brain had left him prone to violent swings of mood, but the prospect of behaving like a character in a novel by his hero, the Marquis de Sade, would have raised his morale. He could then write about the episode. Actually he had to some extent already done so: in 1907 Apollinaire had published a story called "L'Albanais," based on something that may or may not have happened to an Albanian friend of his, Faïk bég Konitza.[15] It is about a man who can liberate himself from an unrequited passion only by abducting another girl. Life, Apollinaire realized, could be made to mirror art, just as art could be made to mirror life. And so he inserted a recycled version of "L'Albanais"—the blueprint for Irène's abduction—into his roman à clef about this event, as if it were an incident in "Pablo's" past. Like Picasso, Apollinaire fed on himself.

For some time Picasso had been eager to leave the cavernous rue Schœlcher studio, with its memories of Eva and its outlook over a wilderness of tombs—a most unsuitable view for someone prone to melancholy and black superstition. He was also eager to move away from the frantic hub of Montparnasse—that cluster of cafés: Dôme, Rotonde, Coupole—where he was increasingly the object of envious attention. During the summer he found the hideaway he needed for his peace of mind as well as the *enlèvement* of Irène: a villa of remarkable ugliness, secluded behind a row of spiky railings. It belonged to a lawyer and was conveniently situated at Montrouge, a dim suburb a subway stop or two beyond Montparnasse.

Jacques Doucet, the couturier and collector, who would later buy *Les Demoiselles d'Avignon*, has given the best description of Picasso's "*château de Montrouge*": the dream house of an elderly petit bourgeois who had done moderately well in the haberdashery business, with

> pokey rooms giving on to a suburban street, a little kitchen garden to hang out the washing, two or three rows of vegetables tended by Picasso's enterprising maid, who had hoped to realize a cherished dream of raising rabbits, but after acquiring a pair to breed from, the police dog [got them]. . . . Picasso is happy there. He draws a lot but paints little. . . . I have a vague idea that he is retrogressing and is going to dump cubism to the great dismay of his followers, who, lacking his great gifts, won't know what to do.[16]

Picasso. *Self-Portrait at Montrouge*, 1917. Black chalk and watercolor on paper. Private collection.

Besides seclusion, no. 22, rue Victor Hugo, had the advantage of being on the road to Arcueil, where Picasso's old acquaintance and new associate Erik Satie lived. Now that they were working together on *Parade*, they would often accompany one another home in the blackout, sharpening and refining Cocteau's meretricious, modernistic scenario. When it was time to go their separate ways, they would doff their hats and take formal leave of each other—"*Bon soir, Monsieur Picasso,*" "*Bon soir, Monsieur Satie.*" Picasso did not officially move to Montrouge until his lease on the rue Schœlcher ran out in October, 1916.[17] Meanwhile he used the place for clandestine affairs. Eugenia Errazuriz found him a *bonne à tout faire* and gave him "a marvelous rose pink silk counterpane." "Where did that come from Pablo, asked Gertrude Stein. Ah ça, said Picasso with much satisfaction, that is a lady. It was a well known chilean society woman who had given it to him. It was a marvel."[18] So was the wallet she gave him on September 28. The artist kept it forever, and it is still among his effects in the Musée Picasso.

Did Gertrude—back in Paris after more than a year in Mallorca—realize that she had to some extent been supplanted? Eugenia made no claims to genius, but she was extremely cultivated, extremely well off and every bit as perceptive about modern painting as Gertrude. What is more, there was nothing she would not do for Picasso. Gertrude's armor-plated ego was probably proof against any suggestion that her fellow genius might have found another protectress. In any case, now that Verdun was over, she and Alice were off to do their bit for the war. Around the time Picasso left for Rome, they set out for the provinces in the Ford van they called Auntie to organize the distribution of American medical supplies to army hospitals. On their rounds in Provence, the two women called on the convalescent Braque, much to his embarrassment. He complained that they "wore boy-scout uniforms with green veils and colonial hats;"[19] and had attracted so much attention in Avignon that the police had asked to see his papers as well as theirs. Braque was outraged.

Gertrude Stein and Alice Toklas visiting a hospital in the course of their war work, c. 1918. Beinecke Rare Book and Manuscript Library, Yale University.

Irène Lagut. *Portrait of Picasso*, c. 1916. Ink on paper, 21×16 cm. Private collection.

On the appointed day—sometime early in August, 1916—Picasso and Apollinaire invited Irène out for the day. As she told one of her interviewers, they took her from bar to bar, restaurant to restaurant, plying her with champagne, "until, without knowing exactly how or why, I found myself in Montrouge."[20] And there Picasso locked her up, just as he had locked up Fernande Olivier eleven years earlier, when he had first taken her to live with him. As Apollinaire's Picasso character, Pablo Canouris, says in his heavy Spanish accent: *"Pour aboir braiement une femme, il faut l'aboir enlebée, l'enfermer à clef et l'occouper tout le temps."* ("To have a woman properly you have to make off with her, lock her up and devote all your time to her.") Picasso turned out to be an inept jailer. As he later told Dora Maar, Irène managed to undo a bolt on the shutters and escape back to Serge.[21] Not, however, for long. Nor were the shutters proof against thieves. Later there would be a burglary. To Picasso's great relief, all they took was his silver—no art.

In her interviews Irène is studiously vague about her *enlèvement*, especially the date. She implies that it brought a brief affair with Picasso to an end. In fact it happened some months into their relationship; and shortly afterwards she returned to live with him at Montrouge. Letters to Soffici reveal that this affair had started in the spring of 1916 and would continue its roller-coaster course until the beginning of 1917.[22] The fiasco of the abduction seems to have made Picasso more determined than ever to get Irène away from Serge. Blandishments would alternate with harassment and threats.

Picasso's blandishments were largely a matter of advancing Irène's career as an artist and to that extent were successful. He insisted that she quit the Académie Julian, where she had recently enrolled. The teaching would turn her into a hack, he said. "Above all develop your faults."[23] She did so: there was no improvement. Then he persuaded galleries to take an interest in her work. Henceforth, Irène would find her pictures hanging alongside Picasso's. She claims that this embarrassed her: she did not want to appear *intéressée* (on the make)—all the more so since she evidently was. Enough of her admirer's fame rubbed off on her to create a demand for her feeble pastiches of Marie Laurencin. Picasso even saw that her work was included when *Les Demoiselles d'Avignon* was exhibited for the first time, in July, 1916.

> Since the war [a woman journalist wrote of the *vernissage*], painters no longer terrify the bourgeoisie with their outlandish outfits. Excellent little paintresses now wear coats and skirts of a sober cut and hats of delicate pink. In their midst, their mentor Picasso, sporting an English cap, speaks about his art with intelligence and good humor. Here at least is someone who does not pose as an artist who is misunderstood. He warmly vaunts the genius . . . of a young beginner, whose first name is Irène and who is very pretty. "[Her work] is a revelation," he says.[24]

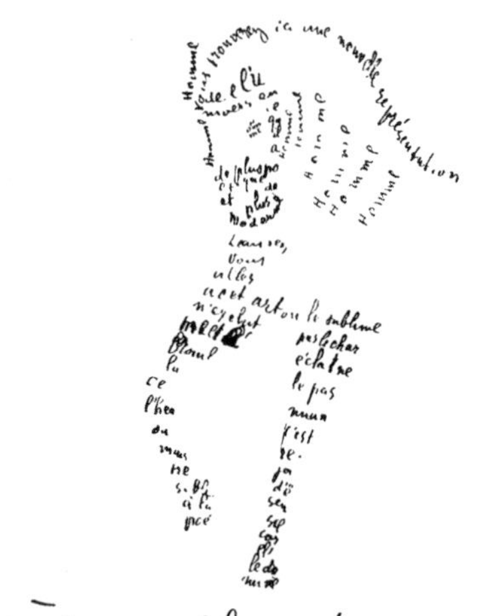
tout terriblement
Guillaume Apollinaire

Apollinaire. Calligram from catalog of the first "Soirées de Paris" exhibition—*Paintings by Léopold Survage, Drawings and Watercolors by Irène Lagut*—held at Madame Bongard's Gallery, January, 1917. Bibliothèque Historique de la Ville de Paris: Fonds Apollinaire.

Since sweet words and love tokens had failed to win over Gaby, Picasso resorted to *force majeure* in his siege of Irène. The account in *La Femme assise* of what transpired one night when Elvire/Irène had managed to lock her admirer out of her apartment has the ring of truth, especially "Pablo's" combination of macho violence and childish cajoling, all in the heavy Andalusian accent we have already heard: *"Elbirre, oubrre-moi, je te aime, je te adore et si tu ne m'obéis pas, je te touerrai avec mon*

Nude photograph of Irène, c. 1914, found among Picasso's effects. Archives Picasso.

Picasso. *Nude*, 1916. Pencil on sketchbook page, 32×24 cm. Picasso Heirs.

rebolber." ("Open up, Elvire, I love you, I adore you and if you don't obey me I'll kill you with my revolver"—presumably the famous revolver that had once belonged to Jarry, the one Picasso had used to scare off bores when he lived in Montmartre.) "Love, that's me. Love is peace, and I am love because I am neutral, and he [Varinoff/Serge] stands for war. War is not love, it's hatred. Therefore you detest him and you love me, my little Elvire. Open up, open up to your Pablo who adores you."

So much for Apollinaire's version. Let us now hear Irène's version of events, as communicated to Soffici on September 15, 1916, from Bénodet in Brittany, where Serge had taken her to recover from her ordeals. If the letter sounds as if she were justifying herself to Serge rather than Soffici, it is perhaps because Serge was looking over her shoulder:

> I have just had a terrifying at the same time profoundly idiotic experience. Picasso fell in love with me much too seriously and had recourse to the lowest tricks, when he saw that his attempt to get me away from Serge had failed.
>
> Picasso stole a nude photograph from me, which I had never shown Serge for fear that he would give me hell. [Picasso] was always brandishing it at me saying, "this will come in very useful one day." Finally, when Serge's sister returned home from Nice, he went to her and said, "Irène is a whore. For proof you only have to see what she wears when she gets photographed. She has cuckolded Serge. Even I have slept with her." And he did everything he could to have me thrown out into the street so that I would be forced to go and live with him. He's the vilest man one could possibly imagine. There are a whole lot more details but they are impossible to write down. Fortunately Serge does not believe a thing, because he is aware of Picasso's modus operandi, how at every exhibition he has his pictures hung next to mine. The success of my work is probably due in large part to this, hence my disgust with painting. The strategies for getting ahead are so sordid; it all depends on one's backing not on one's work.
>
> This saga has dragged on for months. Now, I'm here with Serge for three weeks to get a bit of rest.[25]

Irène's story of being blackmailed by Picasso over the photograph follows the version in *La Femme assise* so closely that it is hard not to believe Apollinaire's account of the rest of the drama, more especially since it was written, a year later, at Bénodet with Irène by his side. Canouris/Picasso did indeed put his threats into practice. He showed the compromising photograph and letters to Teleschkine/Oettingen, who delightedly showed them to her brother. The brother hastened back home to confront his mistress with the evidence. "He told her that it was useless to deny these allegations, that Pablo himself had confirmed them, and that he was going out so that she could pack her suitcases and leave." When Varinoff/Serge returned, he found a strong smell of gas and the studio door locked from the inside. With the concierge's help, he broke in: Elvire/Irène lay asphyxiated by the gas stove. A doctor was summoned and she was with some difficulty resuscitated. She managed to persuade Varinoff that there was no truth to Pablo's accusations, that they were part of a plot to get her away from him; and they were briefly reconciled.

Given his closeness to Picasso, Apollinaire is unlikely to have invented this story. Picasso could be very ruthless when his passions were aroused. That there had been a brush with tragedy is hinted at by Max Jacob, who was also staying in Brittany (with Liane de Pougy and her husband, Prince

Ghyka). "By his side at Bénodet," Max wrote his friends the Altounians, "Serge has the tragic Irène, the capricious Irène, the inescapable Irène—I cannot say more."[26] Besides being privy to the story, Max knew how wayward Irène was. So wayward, indeed, that after telling Soffici her tale of woe, she returned to Paris and resumed her affair with Picasso. At some point Serge, too, contemplated suicide, and Apollinaire had "to shut him up in a closet to prevent him harming himself."[27] The unfortunate cuckold had so much respect for Picasso's genius that he would always forgive him. Picasso liked that.

In the course of the next four months, there seem to have been further breakups, further reconciliations. Marie-Jeanne Durry (one of Irène's interviewers) cites a letter, now lost, which Picasso wrote Irène on November 30, 1916.[28] She had caused him sorrow, much sorrow, Picasso says, but he did not hold this against her. In order to forget her he had been at pains to keep out of her way, but now that she had sent him such a sweet note, he looked forward to seeing her the following day. Irène, it would seem, was not prepared to let either of her lovers—the gentle white Russian or the bold black Spaniard—off her hook. At the bottom of the page Picasso, who often used his work to manipulate the women in his life, did a watercolor of Irène in a red dress on a prancing white horse riding up towards the sun, while Picasso in the familiar red, white and green harlequin costume urges her on. There is no limit to the help your harlequin can provide, he seems to be saying. From the description, this watercolor relates to the sketches he was doing for the *Parade* curtain.

Picasso. *Nude*, 1916. Detail of pencil drawing on sketchbook page, 32×24cm. Picasso Heirs.

Sometime after receiving this letter, Irène moved in with Picasso for several weeks—between the beginning of December, 1916, and mid-January, 1917. We saw almost nobody, Irène says:

> There was the dog, the cat, the bird. . . . True, we had people over. . . . Max came to lunch with us, Cocteau came to lunch with us, because at this point we were going to . . . or rather Picasso had decided to marry me. I was not altogether sold on the idea. It was at the time he was doing the décor for *Parade* . . . . After getting married (the witnesses were to be Apollinaire and Cocteau), we were going to leave for Rome. Instead I escaped. I went back to Serge."[29]

Drawings of Irène nestling in a high-backed chair by the fire, clutching a cat or her white bulldog, Bob, evoke the snug intimacy of life in this suburban hideaway, with which "*l'Andalou de Montrouge*," as Valentine's future husband, Jean Hugo, called him, "in his espadrilles, cummerbund and cap,"[30] was so contented. "*L'Andalou de Montrouge*" evidently took pride in his lace-curtained love nest.

Yes, Picasso *had* painted her portrait in the course of their affair, Irène said, but she returned it when she left him. I have been unable to trace any such painting. However, there are a few representational drawings of her; and the numerous *Femmes assises* of 1916, sometimes wearing the smart hats Irène liked, evidently refer to her. The only other painting in which she admits to figuring (alongside a young man)—the famous *Lovers* (National Gallery, Washington)—dates from 1923, six years after she left Picasso.[31] It would appear that the affair started up again in 1922–23, when he was beginning to tire of married life.

After the first break with Picasso (in 1917), Irène had not remained with Serge Férat for long. She soon embarked on a romance with Raymond

Picasso. *Irène Lagut*, 1915–16. Pencil and wax crayon on paper, 49×31 cm. Picasso Heirs.

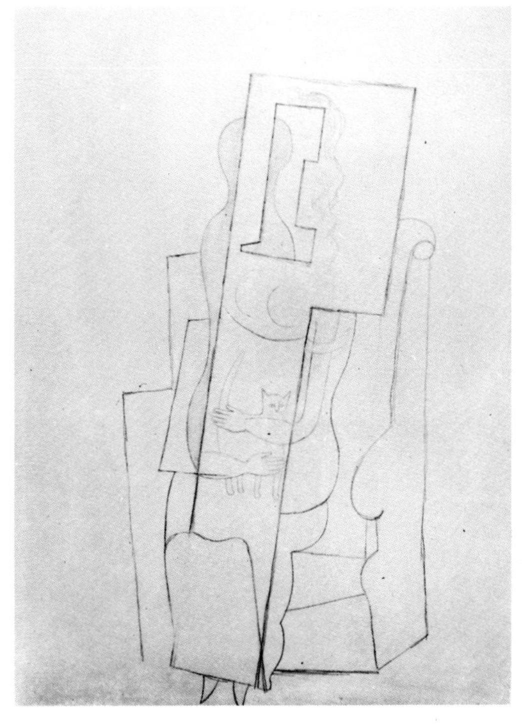

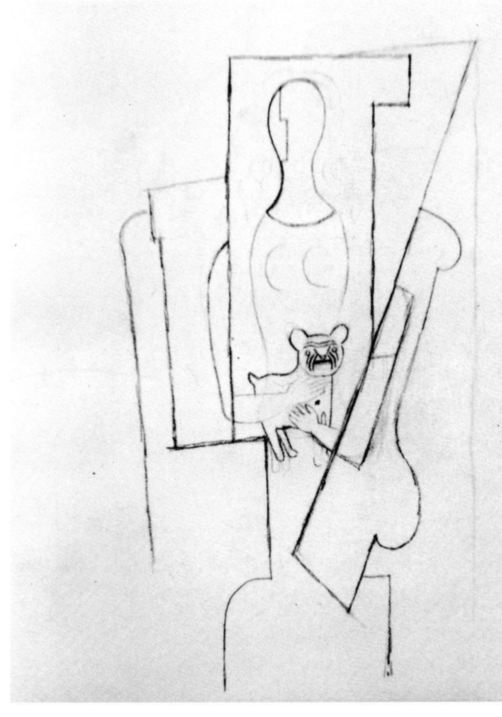

Picasso. *Irène Holding a Cat* (top) and *Irène Holding a Dog* (above) drawn in the artist's studio, 1916. Pencil on sketchbook pages, each 32×24 cm. Picasso Heirs.

Picasso. *Woman with Hat in an Armchair,* 1915–16. Watercolor and crayon on paper, 22.5×17.5 cm. Private collection.

Picasso. *Lovers,* 1923. Oil on canvas, 130.2×97.2 cm. National Gallery of Art, Washington, D.C.

X-radiograph of Picasso's *Portrait of Olga* (1923), showing a *Woman in an Armchair* of 1915–16. Laboratoire de recherche des Musées de France.

Picasso. *Portrait of Olga,* 1923. Oil on canvas, 116×80.5 cm. Musée Picasso.

Radiguet—the prodigious seventeen-year-old writer whose poems she was illustrating—apparently with the blessing of his lover, Cocteau. In 1921 she moved to a studio on the faubourg Saint-Jacques and became the mistress of the young composer Georges Auric. By this time her décors and costumes were having a mild success in the small world that revolved around Cocteau and the Bœuf sur le Toit nightclub. After once again taking up with Picasso, Irène predictably let him down. She had decided once and for all to forfeit her cherished freedom and marry a straitlaced surgeon who disliked her bohemian friends. According to Dora Maar, Picasso continued to keep up with Irène.[32] Sometime in the 1940s, her need for freedom reasserted itself and she left the surgeon for a woman.

A palimpsest of superimposed images, which might relate to Irène, has recently emerged in X-radiographs of a 1923 portrait of Olga. A label on the stretcher reveals that Braque had shipped this canvas to Picasso in Céret—probably in 1912, after he had eloped with Eva. There are faint traces of a cubist figure underneath much stronger ones of a seated woman in red, black and blue.[33] This image includes a fur tippet, as do certain terminal watercolors of Eva done in 1915. However, it also resembles some Irènes of 1916. After this enchanting but maddening *allumeuse* walked out in 1923, Picasso may well have felt like hiding the mess of his wartime amours under a thick coat of white paint embellished with a *comme il faut* image of his wife.

Irène Lagut. *Two Women and a Bird,* c. 1917. Watercolor on paper, 24×16cm. Private collection.

If Picasso portrayed Irène less often than his other great loves, it is hardly surprising. Irène was constitutionally incapable of giving herself up to him body and soul. And unless he had emotional as well as physical possession of a woman, Picasso could not internalize her image; and embark on the physiognomical analysis, pictorial lovemaking, let alone the fiendish manipulation—deification followed by a degrading process of psychosexual dissection—which endow the portraits of his wife, Olga, or Marie-Thérèse Walter or Dora Maar with such wrenching intensity. A further consideration: In his work of 1915–16, Picasso was concerned with exploring and expressing his own feelings rather than anyone else's. Nineteen-sixteen, the year of his on-again, off-again affair with Irène, may have been a year of darkness and confusion in his work, but it was also a year of darkness and confusion for the entire world. Picasso was a pacifist, and the grief, loneliness and alienation of his personal life was enormously amplified by the escalating carnage on the battlefront. His statement in 1945 that although he had never actually painted it, the war was in everything he did at the time applies to his work in World War I as much as in World War II.[34] Apart from some comical drawings of Apollinaire as a warrior, the only overt reference to the war in Picasso's work occurs in an earlier composition (circa 1911), which Picasso partly painted over in 1915 (see p. 350). He has left enough of the khaki-colored cubist paint surface free to form the silhouette of a pipe-smoking soldier in a peaked *képi.* The result is a skillful exercise in metamorphosis rather than a statement about the war. A covert allegorical approach would always work best for Picasso. What better confirmation of this than the power with which his *Harlequin* and *Seated Man* of 1915–16 conjure up the blacked-out night of the soul?

26

Picasso's *Chef d'œuvre inconnu*

Picasso. *Woman in an Armchair*, 1915–16. Gouache and watercolor on paper, 30×23cm. Private collection, France.

Opposite: Picasso. *Seated Man*, 1916. Oil on canvas, 200×132cm. Private collection.

PICASSO'S FIRST EFFORTS TO ESCAPE FROM CUBISM were tentative and sporadic: fraught, one would imagine, with doubts and fears. It took almost as long as World War I for cubist images to give way to eye-foolingly lifelike ones. The artist's protracted rebirth as a classicist does not, however, mean that cubism should be seen as a finite chapter in his development. Cubism went underground. Picasso would continue to draw on the discoveries that he and Braque had made for the rest of his life, and his most original paintings and sculptures almost always turn out to be rooted in them.

In the course of experimenting with figuration, Picasso kept to the same still-life objects—musical instruments and things associated with café life: bottles, glasses, newspapers and pipes—that had constituted his and Braque's cubist repertory. As for his figures, he restricted himself mostly to that other cubist icon, the seated man. Previously, Picasso had endowed most of his seated men with a vestigial identity. They were poets, *aficionados* or guitarists, and were labeled accordingly with the usual cubist indicators. (Earlier still, at the time of the Blue period, Picasso had used his seated men symbolically to allegorize the senses as it were in reverse: sight allegorized by a blind man, taste by a starving man, and so on.) However, the seated man who emerges in Picasso's work after 1911 has no symbolical or allegorical meaning; he is a kind of lay figure, on whom Picasso could project (much as Cézanne did with his apples) his own sensations.

The seated women in Picasso's wartime work are not nearly as numerous as their male counterparts, and they are far from anonymous. Almost all of them can be identified as one or another of the women in the artist's life—Eva, Gaby, Irène. Nor is there any question of portraying them in cafés or similar public places. Picasso liked to keep his women under lock and key and therefore depicts them at home, often as not naked and ensconced in the depths of a *fauteuil* (armchair). In his obsessively superstitious way, the artist invests armchairs with a deep symbolical significance. Fifty years later, he told Malraux, "When I paint a woman in an armchair, the armchair implies old age or death, right? So, too bad for her. Or else the armchair is there to protect her . . . like negro sculpture."[1] In the light of this admission, we can assume that the labial armchair in the 1913 painting of Eva implies death, whereas the huge all-enveloping armchair at Montrouge, in which Irène often sits, implies protection. When the heavily bandaged Apollinaire is portrayed in this same piece of furniture, it might well imply death as well as protection.

Compared with Eva's, or for that matter Irène's, *fauteuil*, the seated man's hard little chair is of no more consequence than himself. But just as a simple melody can inspire complex variations, the seated man engendered a number of drawings of such intricacy that the basic subject ceases to matter. What they are really about, one feels, is drawing as a sequential act: a creative process which, as the artist demonstrates, feeds on itself. By studying his drawings *en série*, Picasso always hoped to understand how his eye and hand coordinated with his imagination. He said he never did.

"They're better than before, aren't they?" Picasso said provocatively to Kahnweiler[2] when (spring, 1914) he showed him two figurative drawings of a seated man which were evidently a response to the recent Cézanne exhibition in Paris. Kahnweiler, who had come to see himself as the impresario of cubism, did not hide his dismay at this counterrevolutionary twist. He was downright horrified a year or two later when photographs reaching him in Switzerland revealed that by 1917 classicism had spread to Picasso's paintings.[3] For better or worse, Kahnweiler's enforced absence freed the artist from pressure to go on toeing the cubist line. Indeed, these first manifestations of classicism can to some extent be seen as a way of provoking the dealer he had come to loathe. For the next three years Picasso would tirelessly examine the various options open to him by repeatedly drawing his seated man. The fact that there are at least a hundred times as many drawings of this subject as there are paintings is a measure of Picasso's obsession; it also testifies to the wartime shortage of paint and canvas.

Picasso. *Apollinaire in an Armchair*, 1916. Pencil on paper, 31×23cm. Private collection.

Sometimes Picasso draws the seated man with arms folded, sometimes holding a musical instrument. But most of the time he portrays him with his left elbow on a table, thoughtfully or absentmindedly holding his chin in his hand. His other hand usually clasps a pipe, which is often depicted as if it were some kind of wartime prosthesis. Only a man could paint a pipe, Picasso said; women had no right to do so, because they did not smoke them. The pipe, held, as a rule, at crotch level, had come to have a certain macho significance; it functions as a label that identifies otherwise sexually indeterminate figures as male.

Picasso's feelings for Cézanne are supposed to have been wholly reverential. To my mind, this was true only before 1910. Later, Picasso became ever more intent on challenging, mocking and measuring himself against a mentor whose shadow he wanted to assimilate as well as escape. At various times he would acknowledge Cézanne as a mother, father and even grandfather, but he would also denounce him as someone who meant no more to him than Harpignies (the last and most boring survivor of the Barbizon school).[4] He was, of course, joking, but Cézanne had to be transcended—exorcised—metaphorically killed, just like his father. This is surely what Picasso had in mind when he submitted Cézanne's quintessential image to ever more ruthless cubistic transformations.

We can usually tell where the drawings were done: figures done in Avignon are evidently farm laborers—they have a relaxed, rustic air—whereas the ones done in Paris tend to look parodically urban. The

Above: Picasso. *Seated Man*, summer, 1914. Pen and sepia ink on paper, 20.9×21.8cm. Musée Picasso.

Right: Picasso. *Man at a Bar*, 1914. Pencil on paper, 48×38cm. Picasso Heirs.

Below left: Picasso. *Seated Man*, 1914. Pencil on paper, 31.3×23.8cm. Marina Picasso Collection: Courtesy Galerie Jan Krugier, Geneva.

Below right: Picasso. *Seated Man*, 1916. Pencil on sketchbook page, 31×24cm. Picasso Heirs.

Picasso. *Seated Man*, 1914. Pencil on paper, 30×20cm. Picasso Heirs.

Picasso. *Seated Man*, 1915. Pencil and India ink on paper, 20×13.5cm. Marina Picasso Collection: Courtesy Galerie Jan Krugier, Geneva.

difference in nuance is considerable, but all it actually required were a few minimal adjustments—flicks of pen or pencil—to the cubist shorthand that Picasso had devised for physiological and sartorial details. A collar or the lack of one could establish the basic seated man as a buttoned-up citizen or a Provençal peasant. To do this representationally would have been less succinct, less ingeniously metamorphic and far more laborious. Picasso's highly finished drawings of Vollard and Max Jacob in the virtuoso manner of Ingres took a great many sittings, in the course of which the artist seems once and for all to have internalized the image of the seated man. These meticulous portraits also enabled Picasso to extend his vocabulary of signs for starched collars and buttoned vests, which came in handy when he was in a mocking mood and wanted to turn his seated man into a bourgeois symbol.

"Down with style!" Picasso proclaimed in one of his more messianic moods. "Does God have a style? He made the guitar, the harlequin, the dachshund, the cat, the owl, the dove. Like me. The elephant and the whale, fine—but the elephant and the squirrel? A real hodgepodge! He made what doesn't exist. So did I."[5] We should heed Picasso's cry. Instead of seeing his *Seated Men* in terms of a stylistic contrast, we should see these alternative modes as the verso and recto of the same coin. When Ansermet expressed astonishment that Picasso should switch from a cubist drawing to a naturalistic one, the artist replied, "But don't you see the result is the same?"[6] Picasso was always out to harness drawing to his own ends; out to develop his graphic powers to such a pitch of suppleness and versatility that questions of style would no longer impinge. As a classicist, he was inclined to envision his art primarily in terms of drawing, and drawing primarily in terms of line: line so tense and incisive that it did not need the support of secondary contours (as Cézanne's often did) or the addition of shading or hatching. And it is this dazzling linear dexterity and versatility that enabled him to keep his coin (cubist one side, classical the other) spinning so fast that it no longer matters which side is which. Style was beside the point: nobody would pay attention if one always said the same thing in the same words and the same tone of voice is how Picasso put it.[7]

Facility was another of Picasso's bugbears. To keep facility at bay, he said that he had to make things as difficult as possible for himself. A case in point is the multiplicity of legs in several of the seated man drawings: as many as ten in some of them (the man's, the chair's, the table's). Most artists would have been at pains to avoid such a diabolical compositional problem; Picasso made a virtue of it in displays of graphic ingenuity that no other artist in history, except perhaps Leonardo, has ever commanded. The multiplicity of legs enables the artist to indulge in pictorial counterpoint of utmost complexity, to play negative and positive space off against each other until the eye reels; and at the same time make ingenious pictorial puns on the seated man's animate legs and feet and the chair and table's wooden ones. Another idiosyncratic device: Picasso often gives the seated man a concertina-like sleeve that looks as if it contains successive elbows. Sometimes he simply wants to make a pictorial pun between the bends in the arm of a *fauteuil*, such as he had in his studio, and the bends in the arm of the man seated in it. Sometimes he turns out to have borrowed this device from Jarry, some of whose earliest images of Ubu include an arm that has as many twists as an intestine.[8] Having one body part mimic or parody another body part is a contrivance to which Picasso will have frequent recourse.

These drawings enabled Picasso to keep eye, hand and imagination at a maximum pitch of coordination, but they also enabled him to circle a subject, approach closer and closer, with a view to doing a major painting. Picasso's first large version of the subject—the *Man at a Bar* with the Avignon poster in the background—is the ambitious failure that is discussed in Chapter 21: the painting whose contortions look ahead to the surrealist paraphrases of Miró. A year would pass before Picasso had another stab at doing a major painting of the subject that was so firmly wedged in his mind. Sometime in the early summer of 1915, just as he was finishing the *Man in a Bowler Hat*, he took an even larger canvas and embarked on a seated man, this time out-of-doors. This masterpiece would preoccupy him for more than a year, during which he would exorcise this obsessive subject by painting over and over it until the seated man was literally wiped out. In the process he would also exorcise cubism. Two or three months later, Picasso would begin his other great wartime painting, the Museum of Modern Art's *Harlequin*. As Eva's cancer entered into its final phase, he worked intensively on these two canvases. The *Harlequin* would be finished before Eva died; the *Seated Man* would undergo successive repaintings, in the course of which Picasso tries out his effects in a series of related drawings and watercolors, also some still-life paintings—guitars on mantelpieces—which have a curious anthropomorphic resemblance to the vanishing figure in the big canvas.

Alfred Jarry. *Ubu Roi*, 1896. Lithograph published in *La Critique*, 24×32cm.

By the end of October, Picasso felt that both these large paintings were finished. On November 3, 1915, he wrote a letter to Léonce Rosenberg, confirming the sale to him of the *Harlequin* and *Man Seated in Shrubbery* (as the *Seated Man* was originally called) as well as three watercolors of dancers for 8,500 francs (4,500 francs on account; the balance to be paid by the end of January).[9] Rosenberg took delivery of the *Harlequin*, but Picasso was unwilling to relinquish the other painting: he needed to rework it. Months went by; finally on April 14, 1916, Picasso again informed Rosenberg that the painting was ready; and again failed to hand it over.[10] Further reworking ensued. At some point a sizable addition was made at the top, and the area of canvas formerly nailed to the sides of the stretcher was used to form a white border and enhance the flatness. In the end Rosenberg never got the painting. On November 22, 1916, Picasso sent the dealer an official letter confirming "that by mutual accord we have annulled the sale of the picture, *Man Seated in Shrubbery* (4,000 francs), which I had undertaken to deliver to you."[11] He had decided to give this painting, which he said he "would not even have given his father,"[12] to his mother figure, Madame Errazuriz.

So great was his regard for Eugenia that Picasso may have been this prodigal, but I doubt it. For all his generosity with his work, Picasso is unlikely to have given away a painting that was conceived to be as much of a breakthrough as *Les Demoiselles d'Avignon*. The story of the gift could well be a fiction devised for Rosenberg's benefit, to cover up its sale to someone else, who was not only a very close and supportive friend but a leading arbiter of avant-garde taste. Why leave the fate of this painting, which meant so much to him, to the discretion of a dealer in whom he had less and less confidence? After this abortive transaction, the dealer continued to court Picasso but soon lost out to his shrewder, more effective brother, Paul Rosenberg, who would remain Picasso's (and Braque's) principal dealer until 1939. By presiding over the forced sales of Kahnweiler's sequestered stock in 1921–22, Léonce Rosenberg would forfeit Picasso's goodwill forever. Braque used his fists to make *his* feelings felt.

The big painting has not as yet been X-rayed. However, Picasso photographed himself in front of it on two separate occasions: seemingly when it was more or less finished the first time round—that is to say in September or October, 1915—and when it was finally signed, a year or so later. In the first photograph the painting is true to its original title, *Man Seated in Shrubbery*. We can see how, in the interests of monumentality, Picasso has taken his seated man out-of-doors and enclosed him in a vast, pyramidal scaffolding of rectilinear planes, set off against foliage and an expanse of sky. That the seated man was much easier to detect in the painting's earlier state is confirmed by Martín Luis Guzmán, a writer and hero in Pancho Villa's revolutionary campaigns. After a visit to Picasso's studio with Diego Rivera in August, 1915, Guzmán reported that the figure "with his hand on his cheek etched itself into one's memory."[13] That is no longer the case.

Rivera in his studio with *Zapatista Landscape* on the easel, 1915.

The cantankerous and egotistical Rivera was less favorably impressed. To understand why, we have to go back to the spring of 1914, when Rivera had paid a visit to Picasso and been overwhelmed by what he saw. Within a year Rivera's love turned to hate. After returning in the summer of 1915 from a prolonged sojourn in Spain and being shown the *Seated Man*, he accused Picasso of stealing from him: specifically from his 1915 *Zapatista Landscape* (*The Guerrilla*). This "Mexican trophy," as Rivera called it, was an outdoor still life. It included a sombrero, rifle, serape, cartridge belt and ammunition box piled up pyramidally against a backdrop of mountains: "the accoutrements of a civil war and revolution existing in the sky-blue realm of the artist's detached consciousness."[14] To integrate his rebel trophy into the landscape, Rivera had flanked it with passages of white and green paint scumbled over a black ground in imitation of foliage. Rivera guarded this formula jealously: it was virtually his only original contribution to cubism. Hence his rage when Picasso went ahead and borrowed it for two 1915 still lifes in which he takes objects out of the studio into the open air. In the *Seated Man* he uses this motif rather more flagrantly to situate the figure in a garden. (Later Picasso would reconcile indoors with outdoors by setting still lifes on a table in front of an open window with sky or sea or neighboring buildings beyond.)

Rivera also deluded himself that another device—the portrayal of objects by their absence, that is to say, by their silhouettes and shadows[15]—was his innovation. An obvious example of this in Picasso's work is the puzzling white silhouette like an ice cream cone in his *Still Life in a Landscape*, referred to above. As a related drawing confirms, it represents a bunch of grapes in a fruit dish. Rivera uses a remarkably similar device in his 1916 *Still Life with Flowers* in the Metropolitan Museum. This time the shoe is on the other foot: Picasso had used negative space as early as 1905 for the dog in his *Death of Harlequin* and again and again in cubist compositions.

Self-portrait photograph by Picasso with *Seated Man* in progress, fall, 1915. Archives Picasso.

Diego Rivera. *Zapatista Landscape (The Guerrilla)*, 1915. Oil on canvas, 144×123 cm. Museo Nacional de Arte, Mexico City.

Picasso. *Still Life in a Landscape*, 1915. Oil on canvas, 62×75 cm. Algur H. Meadows Collection, Meadows Museum, Southern Methodist University, Dallas, Tx.

Home Life Insurance Company Building (1893–94), Broadway, New York; from *Architectural Record*, May, 1910.

French gun at the front, summer, 1915, camouflaged with what were described by the press as "futuristic representations of trees."

By accusing Picasso of plagiarism, the little-known Rivera made a name for himself; worse, he gave cubist hacks a pretext for barricading studio doors against the artist to whom they owed so much. Whenever Picasso appeared, they pretended to be terrified that he was going to rob them of their little studio secrets. "I was present at interminable confabulations outside half-open doors," Cocteau said in describing what happened when Picasso took him round the Montparnasse studios. "We used to have to wait until [the artists] had locked up their latest pictures. They were just as mistrustful of each other. This state of siege nourished the silences of the Rotonde and the Dôme. I remember one week when everybody was whispering and wondering who had stolen Rivera's formula for painting trees by scumbling green on black."[16] Even Max Jacob could not resist teasing Picasso for making off with Rivera's little gimmick. In the second of two maddeningly facetious chronicles of "*La Vie artistique*" that he contributed to the New York–based magazine *291*, he has his fictitious art critic say to a fictitious woman painter, "I have seen a Mexican trophy of yours that I was tempted to take for a Picasso. If this misapprehension does me no credit, it may prove to be very much to yours."[17]

The fuss kicked up by Rivera may explain why, in the course of reworking his big painting, Picasso eliminated much of the foliage. The artist had no compunction about stealing, least of all from people who had taken far, far more from him. He used Rivera's trademark rather as he might have used a bit of wallpaper that had caught his eye. Furthermore he exploited its ambivalence: it could transform indoors into outdoors, or blur the difference between the two. Besides appropriating Rivera's greenery, Picasso gave an open-air look to his *Seated Man* by using rows of large dots (pointillistic they are not) to suggest the fenestration of that wondrous new phenomenon, the skyscraper—the tallest thing made by man. These skyscraper "windows" enormously enhance our perception of this amorphic figure's scale; they will do the same for the *Seated Man*'s even more gigantic offspring, the Managers in *Parade*. It was Gertrude Stein who had opened Picasso's eyes to skyscrapers, some years earlier, when she had shown him "the first photograph of a skyscraper." The scale had astonished him. "Good God, he said imagine the pangs of jealousy a lover would have while his beloved came up all those flights of stairs to his top story studio."[18] (Picasso's studio was on the top floor; so was Gaby's.) He also had another source of skyscraper material: in the issue of the *Architectural Record* where Burgess's "Wild Men of Paris" appeared, there was a profusely illustrated article on these buildings.

Picasso puts these dotted passages to many other uses: to set up pictorial rhythms, also to unify things, as he and Braque had unified the heterogeneous objects in cubist still lifes. Above all he uses dots—black on white, white on black, multicolored ones—as a form of camouflage, just as he had told Apollinaire the artillery should do (see p. 349). (Ironically, the camouflage units of the French army took a reciprocal interest in modern art, to the extent that they named their regimental mascots "Picasso" and "Matisse.")[19] Besides camouflaging the seated man, the dots cloak him in an element of painterly mystery, mystery that has its roots not only in art but in literature: specifically Balzac's *Le Chef d'œuvre inconnu*.

Balzac's story fascinated Picasso, just as it had Cézanne. He identified with the mad old genius who is the hero and would devote some of his

Self-portrait photographs by Picasso in his studio, 1915–16. Works in progress include *Man at a Bar* (top left and right), *Guitar on a Pedestal Table* (bottom left) and *Seated Man* (bottom right). Archives Picasso.

finest book illustrations to it. And towards the end of his life, when he returned to themes and subjects from the past, Picasso would once again find inspiration in *Le Chef d'œuvre inconnu.* The story concerns a fictional seventeenth-century artist of incomparable technique, Master Frenhofer, who tantalizes his friends, Poussin and Porbus, by telling them that he has been working for ten years in secret on perfecting his masterpiece, *La Belle Noiseuse* (The Mischievous Beauty), a flawlessly beautiful painting of a flawlessly beautiful woman, imbued with "that indescribable something, perhaps the soul itself, that envelops the body like a haze." The two younger artists ache to see it. When old Frenhofer finally allows them into his studio (on the rue des Grands Augustins, where Picasso would later make a point of having a studio), they are appalled to see nothing there

Picasso. *Seated Man*, 1915–16. Gouache on paper, 26.5×21 cm. From the collection of Mrs. John Hay Whitney.

> but confused masses of color and a multitude of fantastical lines that go to make a dead wall of paint. . . . In a corner of the canvas as they came nearer, they distinguished a bare foot emerging from the chaos of color, half-tints and vague shadows that made up a dim formless fog. Its living delicate beauty held them spellbound. . . . "There," Porbus continued, as he touched the canvas, "lies the utmost limit of our art on earth."[20]

The Picasso is as indecipherable as the Frenhofer. Besides two rudimentary eyes and a pipe that establishes the figure's otherwise indeterminate sex, the only decipherable element in this *chef d'œuvre inconnu* of Picasso's—for that is what this painting represents—is the merest tip of a foot. Who, then, is this seated man buried deep inside this semblance of a skyscraper? As in the other great work of the period, the *Harlequin*, the subject turns out to be self-referential. This is a painting about the act of painting—a magic act, Picasso always said. The artist has done a vanishing trick; he has melted into the cosmic darkness of paint, taking cubism with him. Significantly, he photographed himself more often in front of this *Seated Man* than in front of any other painting—out of narcissism, to judge by a photograph taken in front of the *Seated Man*'s predecessor, the 1914 *Man at a Bar.* In the first of these Picasso keeps his cap on but strips down to his underpants. In the second he is barechested, and the skintight underpants are, to say the least, revealing. There is, however, another angle to the narcissism. The urge to superimpose himself photographically onto this masterpiece is akin to the urge to superimpose a covert self-portrait onto the *Harlequin*—stamp his ego on it. Although this magnificent painting stands in somewhat the same relationship to the end of cubism as the *Demoiselles* stands in relation to the beginning, it is relatively little known—seldom exhibited and never given its due except, ironically, by Cocteau, who was the only one of the artist's friends in a position to watch "the young man seated in a garden" disappear over the years "and give place to a magnificent metaphor of lines, forms and colors, where Picasso reigns, alone in the world. None of his other attainments equals it."[21] He incorporated the composition into a caricature of Picasso and devoted the first section of his Mallarméan pastiche, *Ode* (written in 1916), to an evocation of it.[22] If little further attention was paid to the *Man Seated in Shrubbery*, it was largely because the painting had the good fortune to hang in a succession of extremely private collections. Madame Errazuriz ceded it to Etienne de Beaumont,

Jean Cocteau. *Picasso Cubiste*, c. 1917. Graphite pencil on paper, 26×19 cm. Private collection.

who left it to his nephew Henri, who relinquished it to the present owner. The first time most scholars got a glimpse of this masterpiece was when the *Seated Man* was loaned to the Museum of Modern Art retrospective in 1981.

Picasso. Illustration for Balzac's *Chef d'œuvre inconnu*, 1927. Etching, 19.4×27.8 cm.

Picasso. *Scene in Frenhofer's Studio* (*Suite 347*, no. 64), May 5, 1968. Engraving, 41.4×49.6 cm.

27

Parade

"Parade *is a kind of portrait of you. So let me offer it to you."*[1]
(Cocteau to Satie, December, 1916)

Satie and Valentine Gross, August, 1916. Photograph by Cocteau. Private collection.

In the first week of September, 1916, Diaghilev arrived in Paris and gave his *Parade* team the go-ahead. Short of money as usual, he neglected to sign the requisite contracts, but at least Picasso and Satie could start work. As Cocteau deluged him with ever more fanciful ideas, Picasso began to have doubts—doubts that he shared with Satie on their long walks home in the blackout. Within a matter of days Cocteau sensed there was a conspiracy against him.

> Make Satie understand [he wrote Valentine on September 4], if you can cut through the fog of aperitifs, that I really do count for something in *Parade*, and that he and Picasso are not the only ones involved. I consider *Parade* a kind of renovation of the theater, and not a simple "pretext" for music. It hurts me when [Satie] dances around Picasso screaming "It's you I'm following! *You* are my master!"[2]

Satie continued to do exactly this.

> *Parade* is changing for the better [he wrote Valentine on September 14], behind Cocteau's back! Picasso has ideas that please me better than those of our Jean. How unfortunate! And I am for Picasso! And Cocteau doesn't know it! What's to be done? Picasso tells me to go ahead and follow Jean's text, and he, Picasso, will work on another text, his own—which is astounding, prestigious. . . . Knowing Picasso's wonderful ideas, I am heartbroken to be obliged to compose according to those of the good Jean, less wonderful oh yes! Less wonderful! What's to be done! What's to be done!—Write and advise me. I'm going crazy."[3]

The devious Satie knew exactly what had to be done. He wrote a short note informing Cocteau that Picasso had "some curious and new ideas for *Parade*."[4] This prompted a meeting, and on the 20th Satie told Valentine that everything had been arranged—"Cocteau knows everything. He and Picasso have reached an agreement. What luck!"[5] The strategy worked. Not to worry about Satie, Cocteau boasted to Valentine (September 22), "I can reassure you on that score. The good Socrates [Satie] is stirring things up between Picasso and me—because of differences of vocabulary, he fears that one is talking white and the other black. Picasso and I have decided to lie to Satie so that he won't know what we are up to."[6] Cocteau was of course the one being lied to. Picasso and Satie continued to work behind his back to keep *Parade* pared down to essentials right up to the ballet's first night. In 1921, Cocteau would avenge himself after a

Opposite: American Manager in *Parade*, 1917. Bibliothèque Nationale.

fashion. When Rolf de Maré wanted Picasso to do the décor for the Ballet Suédois production of *Les Mariés de la Tour Eiffel,* Cocteau vetoed the idea. Picasso's creations "were too powerful," he said. "They engrossed too much of the audience's attention."[7] De Maré, who had become a friend as well as a major collector of Picasso, would bitterly regret using Irène Lagut instead.

For all that he had written *musique d'ameublement,* Satie was not prepared to have his music serve as a background to Cocteau's secondhand bruitism: mechanical noises that mimicked the din of modern life and, the poet felt, would serve the same purpose as bits of papier collé and trompe l'œil in a cubist composition. Nor did Satie like the idea of verbal and aural enhancements "issuing from an amplifying orifice"[8] (a cross between a modern barker's megaphone and an ancient oracle's mask). Picasso had similar reservations. The prospect of doing décor that would be just that, décor, would not have appealed to him, especially for a gimmicky *Gesamtkunstwerk* whose principal purpose was to propel Cocteau to the summit of avant-garde stardom. Picasso agreed with the young poet Pierre Reverdy, who described Cocteau as "the sandwich man of the period" and asked him why, coming from so far and setting out so late, should he push ahead of everyone else.[9]

As a seemingly conciliatory gesture, Satie agreed to incorporate some of "Jean's noises"—trains, sirens, airplanes, revolver shots and the like —into his score, but he did not conceal his distaste and, with Picasso and Diaghilev's connivance, had the noises suppressed at the first performance. When Cocteau realized he had been double-crossed, he had a terrible tantrum and moaned that his masterpiece had been irreparably harmed. To Satie's irritation, he succeeded in having some of the noises restored at the ballet's revival in 1921. "Cocteau is sticking to the boring 'tricks' of 1917," Satie complained to Valentine (December, 1920). "He's worn Picasso and myself to a pulp. It's a mania with him. *Parade* is by himself, alone. All right, I say. But then why didn't he do the décor and costumes, or write the music for this wretched ballet?"[10] Picasso was less indulgent. When Cocteau failed to do what he was told, the artist gave him "*une bonne paire de gifles*" (a good slap). André Gide, who went backstage after the first performance, noted in his diary that he had "found Cocteau walking up and down in the wings, older, tense, uneasy. He is perfectly aware that the sets and costumes are by Picasso and that the music is by Satie, but he wonders whether Picasso and Satie aren't really by him."[11]

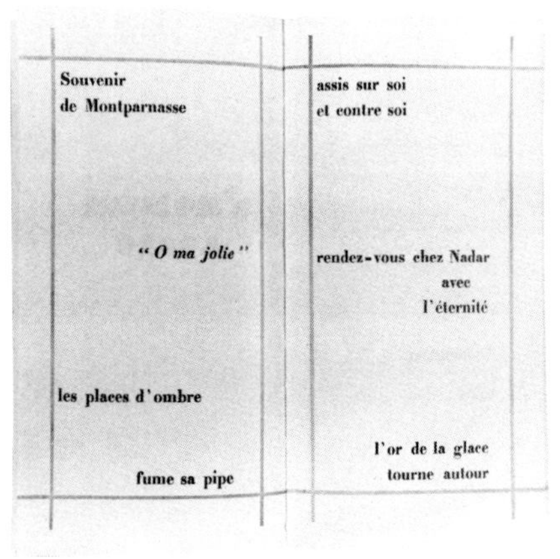
Souvenir
de Montparnasse
"O ma jolie"
les places d'ombre
fume sa pipe
assis sur soi
et contre soi
rendez-vous chez Nadar
avec
l'éternité
l'or de la glace
tourne autour

Cocteau. Opening pages of *L'Ode à Picasso,* 1919.

To ingratiate himself with Picasso, Cocteau set about writing him an *Ode.* By mid-October this modish piece was ready and the poet was reciting it to anyone who would listen. Picasso's reactions have not been recorded. Modernists were dismissive. An exception was Angel Zarraga, a popular decorative painter, whom Picasso liked. He sent Roché a report: "That astonishing gift for free association that Cocteau handles so adroitly . . . very stark, perhaps too much so."[12] (Zarraga's letter is more interesting for a scarcely believable anecdote about Picasso's childhood: how he would attach little "*cartouches*"—cartridge cases—filled with ink to the bodies of flies, which would then fly around the room, dripping ink on his schoolmates' exercise books and the teacher's bald head.) As a career move, the publication of *Ode* in 1919 was not a success. Cocteau's brazen attempt to duplicate Mallarmé's innovative *mise-en-page* for "Un Coup de dés jamais n'abolira le hasard," with its fastidious use of "abstract" space and musical resonance, is exactly the sort of rip-off that triggered the violent "Cocteauphobia" of the dadaists and surrealists. Benjamin Péret would liken Cocteau to an "angel's turd" and Radiguet as the "*pelle*" (literally a shovel; it can also mean a French kiss) to scoop it up. André Breton would castigate him for "[living] off the cadavers of those of the first rank."[13] With the help of Soupault and Eluard he would see that Cocteau became "the most hated man in Paris."

Serge Diaghilev, c. 1915. Photograph by Sasha.

Besides the "noises off" and special effects, Picasso was bothered by the superficiality of *Parade*'s modernism. It was not much more than symbolism in a flashy, futurist guise: anathema to Picasso, who had had a hard enough struggle to cleanse his own work of symbolist traits. Also it was too literary, too otherworldly. The hokiness in which Cocteau proposed to shroud his performers—the Chinese Conjuror, the Little American Girl, the Acrobats—harked back to *Petrouchka*, Diaghilev's allegorical ballet about street entertainers. Until Picasso put his foot down, Cocteau had intended to emphasize "the occult element" by evoking a whole other dimension of his characters' lives—the dimension "on the other side of the showman's booth."[14] Stage directions appended to Satie's original score oblige the Conjuror to mime the cutting of his own throat, to the shrieks of missionaries whose eyes and tongues are being torn out. And the Little American Girl (Mary Pickford with a dash of Pearl White) is expected to dance her "Steamboat Rag" (originally called "*Titanic* Rag"), which Satie had adapted from Irving Berlin, to the added accompaniment of typewriters, a Morse-code machine tapping out SOS's and a disembodied voice intoning: "Cube tic tic tic tic on the hundredth floor an angel has made its nest at the dentist's tic tic tic *Titanic* toc toc *Titanic* sinks brightly lit beneath the waves . . . ice-cream soda tic tic." Very thin stuff.

These little strategies "to expand character" struck Picasso as superfluous. He had never worked for the theater before but he had an inherent sense of it. Time and again, this sense had manifested itself in his painting, not just in figure compositions—*Les Demoiselles d'Avignon* being the most obvious example—but in still lifes. Picasso has a way of dramatizing the most mundane confrontations, transforming a fruit dish and a water jug into star performers on a canvas "stage": an impression that the gilded proscenium arch of a frame helps to enhance. He welcomed the prospect of bringing his images to life on a real stage, especially once he saw how he could exploit the theater, rather than have the theater exploit him. *Parade*—his *Parade*, as distinct from Cocteau's—would provide Picasso with an opportunity to come up with far more than décor, though that too. In the theater—above all the Châtelet, which was one of the largest in Paris—he would be able to deploy far vaster effects than in the studio; to work more freely than ever before in three dimensions; and to explore the breakthrough he had made in 1912–13 with his cardboard constructions. That the preparatory work on *Parade* would be done in Rome was a bonus: it would enable him to escape the war and his on-again, off-again engagement to Irène, catch a restorative glimpse of the Mediterranean and, who knows, find a wife.

In September, Diaghilev had given the *Parade* collaborators five months to do their preparatory work, five months before they were to leave for

Apollinaire. *Les Oiseaux chantent avec les doigts*, 1916. Watercolor over pencil on paper, 16×10.8cm. Musée Picasso.

Rome, where sets and costumes would be executed. As usual, Picasso left everything to the last. Nevertheless, when Diaghilev returned to Paris early in January, he was able to approve the maquettes that Picasso showed him. (He had caught cold, so "Pica" had to transport his work to the Hôtel Edouard VII). On January 11, the artist signed a contractual letter:

> Confirming our verbal agreement, I accept to undertake the production (sets, curtains, costumes and properties) of the ballet "PARADE" by Jean Cocteau and Erik Satie.
>
> I will make all the necessary designs and models and I will personally supervise all the work of carrying them out.
>
> All the designs will be ready by March 15, 1917.
>
> For this work you are to pay me the sum of five thousand francs, and if I have to go to Rome, a thousand francs extra. The drawings and models remain my property.
>
> Half the sum named must be paid me on delivery of the designs and models, and the other half on the day of the first performance.[15]

Cocteau was so fretful that things would not be ready in time that Picasso had to put his mind, somewhat firmly, at rest: "I am working on the project almost every day. I hope no one disturbs me."[16] By February 12, everything was ready. Satie sent word to Roché, who was in New York, that he had finished his work (not strictly true: he had yet to do the orchestration); and that the "*beau décor, costumes & rideau de Pic-Picas-Casso*" were also ready.[17] Among the projects was a maquette for the drop curtain. It was the only glimpse of *Parade* that Picasso permitted Jacques Doucet, the great collector and couturier, when he paid a visit to Montrouge: "Hardly cubist at all," Doucet reported to Roché (March 31, 1917), "with harlequins."[18] How much of the Montrouge material was ultimately used we do not know. Once Picasso arrived in Rome and started to work on a daily basis with Massine, the choreographer, and the team that painted the scenery and made the costumes, he would radically revise his maquettes and unleash a torrent of new ideas.

The way Picasso plays cubist elements off against figurative ones generates much of the energy in *Parade*. To judge by the sketch Doucet presumably saw and some magnificent drawings of harlequins, in one of the Montrouge sketchbooks (it also includes a number of seated Irènes), Picasso started work in a relatively representational idiom—an idiom harking back not so much to Ingres as to his own work of the Rose period and to the time-honored imagery of the commedia dell'arte, on which ballet had traditionally drawn. Cocteau does not mention harlequins in his original treatment, so they were presumably Picasso's suggestion—an allusion possibly to the costume that Cocteau had left in the studio. Since one of the harlequins resembles him, the artist may even have envisaged a character in *Parade* who would be a projection of himself: a playful counterpart, perhaps, to the Managers, which he had devised to give Cocteau's scenario some structure: "What a forceful man [Diaghilev] was," Picasso told Brassaï. "He always had a conductor's baton in his hand, and when someone didn't obey him—well he hit them with it."[19] This might explain the puzzling drawing of a stocky harlequin (mustachioed but otherwise not unlike Picasso), who menaces a top-hatted Manager type with *his* baton. In the end the Montrouge drawings played no role in

Picasso. Study for *Parade* curtain, 1916–17. Watercolor on paper, 27.3×39.5 cm. Musée Picasso.

Picasso. *Harlequin (Self-Portrait?)*, 1916. Pencil on paper, 30.5×22.9 cm. Picasso Heirs.

Picasso. *Manager and Harlequin*, 1916. Pencil on sketchbook page, 22.9×30.5 cm. Picasso Heirs.

the gestation of *Parade*. Rather, they paved the way for a number of seductive gouaches and paintings of seated harlequins—a synthesis of cubist flatness and trompe l'œil modeling, but this time free of tragic, self-referential overtones.

When Picasso embarked on *Parade*, the *Seated Man* painting, which had preoccupied him for the last year, would still have been in the rue Schœlcher studio. He had not yet given it to Eugenia Errazuriz—indeed may still have been working on it. Having allowed his other *chef d'œuvre inconnu*, the hitherto unexhibited *Les Demoiselles d'Avignon*, to be exhibited that summer,[20] Picasso may well have wanted to bring the revolution that the *Demoiselles* had initiated nine years earlier to a grand finale in another huge, ambivalent, unresolvable masterpiece. Meanwhile the "curious and new ideas," which had so impressed Satie, were taking the form of three gigantic Managers (later reduced to two), based on the *Seated Man*. Massine remembers the artist's doing the maquettes for these figures in Rome, but these would have been working drawings executed after seeing Depero's large cardboard constructions for another Diaghilev ballet, *Le Chant du Rossignol*. With Depero's help, Picasso was able to come up with animated structures for his Managers that were almost as big as Catalan *gegants* (the papier-mâché processional figures that he had depicted for a Barcelona newspaper in 1902).[21] At the Joffrey Ballet's revival of *Parade*, in 1973, it was apparent that although the Managers upstaged Massine's choreography, they held Cocteau's flimsy scenario together and punctuated the action. They also added a note of pathos by making the performers—here Picasso was having a dig at the tyrannical Diaghilev—look vulnerable and small. The overpowering effect that the Managers must have had was even more apparent to anyone lucky enough to see Picasso's original constructions—albeit a bit battered—on their last recorded appearance, at Richard Buckle's Diaghilev exhibition in London in 1955.[22] They were a revelation: one of Picasso's most imaginative attempts to merge painting and sculpture. Since then they have apparently been destroyed.

French Manager in *Parade*, 1917.

*   *   *

In an effort to salvage Apollinaire's sinking spirits, Picasso and some of the poet's friends (Max Jacob, Reverdy, Juan Gris, Blaise Cendrars and the Belgian poet Paul Dermée) decided to honor him with a banquet on the last day of 1916. The pretext was the publication of his fantastical, partly autobiographical roman à clef *Le Poète assassiné*, though this had actually occurred some months earlier. Apollinaire had cobbled this book out of as many as eight earlier projects, some of them dating back as far as 1903. The resultant ragbag, albeit of genius, is of some relevance to Picasso's work. The plot, such as it is, ends with the murder of Croniamantal, the Apollinaire-like poet, and the erection of a monument to him by his artist friend, "L'Oiseau de Benin" (Picasso). The day after the murder, L'Oiseau de Benin, accompanied by Tristouse Ballerinette (Marie Laurencin) and other grieving friends, make for a clearing in the Bois de Meudon, where they dig a hole shaped like the poet and surround it with a wall. This concept—premonitory earthworks—would haunt Picasso when he was commissioned to design a memorial to Apollinaire, and the committee turned down one imaginative project after another.

Above: Modigliani. *Apollinaire*, c. 1916. Pencil on paper, 17.5×11.2 cm. Private collection.

Top left: Irène Lagut. *Apollinaire on Horseback*, November 28, 1916. Pen and ink on paper. Collection P.M.A.

Left: Performers in Apollinaire's "surrealist drama in two acts and a prologue" *Les Mamelles de Tirésias*, 1917. Collection P.M.A. The costumes were designed by Serge Férat.

For the banquet, the friends rented an imposing room in the Palais d'Orléans on the avenue de Maine and summoned an eclectic group of admirers to a large and, considering wartime shortages, lavish lunch. Apollinaire found some of the mocking names that Max Jacob had invented for the dishes offensive and insisted on changing them: for instance, *Bisquits de mimetisme* to *Hors d'œuvres cubistes, orphistes, futuristes.* The guests included Salmon, Gide, Cocteau, Cendrars, Fénéon, Paul Fort, Jules Romains, Jacques Copeau, Braque, Matisse, Vlaminck and, rather surprisingly, Bakst. Picasso arrived with You-You. This does not mean that he had broken with Irène. She probably stayed away out of discretion; most of the guests were friends of Serge's.

The banquet ended in a free-for-all: "rows and people screaming at each other," Gris wrote Raynal.[23] The first speaker, Madame Alfred Mortier—a big-bosomed, chauvinist who wrote books of impregnable boredom under the name of Aurel—was indignantly shouted down, and so was the next one, P.-N. Roinard, for bringing out an ominously voluminous manuscript. Only the popular novelist Jacques Dyssord made himself heard. Meanwhile fights broke out between Cendrars, who had lost an arm in the war, and a journalist; it then spread to rival factions of cubists, orphists and futurists. Radishes and bits of bread flew across the room. Apollinaire finally calmed things down by reciting a poem and making a toast. His dinner, Apollinaire wrote Raynal, who was in the trenches at Verdun, was exactly what it should have been: "A magnesium flash, explosive, dangerous, brief, carried to the brink of paroxysm. The air was thick with menacing stumps."[24] Cocteau, who was desperate to neutralize Apollinaire's prejudice against him, sent him an ingratiating note on two separate postcards, suggesting a meeting, at the same time poking fun at Bakst: "that huge, gentle, yellow-booted slug has kept an unforgettable memory of the banquet. He missed the onrush of the negroes and *Shéhérazade's* suicide. . . . Long live the banquets of Verlaine and Apollinaire. Long live the rigolo-repast the day of Mallarmé's burial."[25]

Tributes rained down on Apollinaire's great bandaged head. In his honor a group of budding poets, headed by Reverdy, had founded a review, *Nord-Sud* (named after the Métro linking the "twin centers of art and letters," Montmartre and Montparnasse). Young admirers gathered every Tuesday evening in the Café Flore to pay him homage; editors besieged him for contributions; ever-increasing numbers of his books were sold. But none of this rekindled Apollinaire's energy or genius. Far from confirming him as a leader of the avant-garde, the one and only performance of his burlesque "*drame lyrique*" about the birthrate in Zanzibar, *Les Mamelles de Tirésias* (sets by Serge Férat; costumes by Irène Lagut; rehearsal space courtesy of Hélène d'Oettingen), triggered a pretentious protest from a group of cubist artists that included Gris, Hayden, Kisling, Lhote, Lipchitz, Metzinger, Rivera, Severini. They claimed that this admittedly flimsy piece reflected badly on their "*recherches plastiques*" and brought the modern movement into disrepute. That Apollinaire was deeply wounded emerges from his fine letter to Gris:

> I'm notifying you that our friendship is over. I do not admit that in the name of I don't know what principle people can condemn this or that aesthetic in the domain of art or of letters. . . . As between you and me I take things very seriously. I have never deserted my friends at critical junctures.

LES MAMELLES DE TIRÉSIAS DRAME

Serge Férat. Drawing for cover of Apollinaire's *Les Mamelles de Tirésias.* Edition Sic, 1918. Private collection.

> If they drop me the moment they sense I am under attack, they are no longer my friends. That's why I bid you goodbye. . . . Meanwhile don't forget that the play is surrealist and that the word cubist has been strictly banished."[26]

Apollinaire thought that Blaise Cendrars—supposedly a friend—was behind the attacks on him. He was probably right. The one-armed Cendrars had no compunction about mocking a fellow *mutilé de guerre.* In any case, by the end of the war the wounded were too numerous to be sacrosanct. "I'm appalled by Apollinaire's assumption of absurdity," Cendrars wrote. "He's like a cracked bidet. His scar has nothing glorious about it, it emits the fresh farts of his Victory. Don't attribute too much importance to Apollinaire's wind."[27]

* * *

Two weeks after the Apollinaire banquet (January 14, 1917), "*les admirateurs du peintre Braque*" organized a banquet at Marie Wassilieff's studio to celebrate the artist's discharge from the army after a long and painful convalescence. It was almost as *déchainé* as the Apollinaire affair, but much more upbeat. The committee consisted of Picasso, Apollinaire, Juan Gris, Max Jacob, Metzinger, Reverdy, Paul Dermée, Wassilieff, Matisse and his former pupil Walter Halvorsen. They limited themselves to thirty-five guests, who were charged six francs a head. Wassilieff supposedly let Beatrice Hastings have "the final say about the guest list"[28]—presumably out of respect for her former lover Modigliani. As Hastings insisted on bringing her new beau, the sculptor Alfredo Pina, there was bound to be trouble. Sure enough, at the end of dinner a very drunken Modigliani burst into the studio at the head of a mob of uninvited artists and models, only to be confronted by the jealous Pina brandishing a revolver. Before he could fire, Wassilieff, who was barely five feet tall, pushed Modigliani down the stairs. To prevent further irruptions, Picasso and his guest, Ortiz de Zarate, locked the door and pocketed the key until Matisse prevailed upon them to return it to Wassilieff.[29] From then on, everyone behaved themselves as well as alcohol permitted.

Marie Wassilieff. *Braque Banquet,* January, 1917. Collection Claude Bernès.

Wassilieff had taken trouble with the decorations: barbaric hangings, black tablecloths, red napkins, white plates, and laurel wreaths for Braque and Marcelle. The main course was turkey. Wassilieff entertained the guests with her Cossack "dance of the little fish," and Max Jacob "was at his most brilliant and witty in two impersonations—of a colonel and Braque's mother."[30] Everyone danced till dawn, not least the guest of honor and Derain, who were still prancing around at six in the morning, brandishing the bones of the turkeys they had eaten. Picasso behaved with unwonted innocence, according to Wassilieff's unpublished memoirs: "singing some song or other for the ears of his Pâquerette."[31] Once again Irène may have kept away out of discretion; or had she finally gone back to Serge?

Braque in Henri Laurens's studio, 1915. Photograph by Laurens. Archives Laurens.

Studio high jinx, redolent of the first act of *La Bohème,* provided an escape valve for the tensions—the guilt and the *Schadenfreude*—which afflicted the many noncombatant guests. But it was only a temporary one. Apollinaire and Braque had been wounded where they had most to lose, in the head. And no amount of lionization could assuage their bitterness and rage. Apollinaire, who had been awarded the Croix de Guerre, had

Above: Braque in his studio at Sorgues, 1917. Archives Laurens.

Left: Braque. *Still Life with Guitar and Glass*, 1917. Oil on canvas, 60×92 cm. Rijksmuseum Kröller-Müller, Otterlo.

nearly ended up paralyzed: Braque, who had twice been mentioned in dispatches and also awarded the Légion d'Honneur and Croix de Guerre for gallantry, had nearly ended up blind—a trauma that had radically changed his disposition. Despite his enjoyment of extrovert pursuits, Braque had always been something of an introvert and he now grew steadily more so, developing ultimately into a visionary, who would increasingly identify painting with *poésie.* This emerges in his aphorisms—the fruit of sickbed meditations—which are a key to understanding his cubist as well as his post-cubist work. Braque's head wound initiated a metaphysical process which would lead him to a state of *néant* (nonexistence). "I have made a great discovery," he said many years later. "I no longer believe in anything. Objects don't exist for me except insofar as a rapport exists between them, and between them and myself. When one attains this harmony, one reaches a sort of intellectual *néant*—what I can only describe as a state of peace—which makes everything possible and right."[32] Notions such as these would make Picasso extremely impatient. "Next thing, he'll invoke the fourth dimension!"

Braque's attitude towards Picasso inevitably changed. He and, above all, Marcelle were upset by Picasso's offhand quips about Braque being his "ex-wife," whom he had never seen again after their farewells at Avignon station. However, if they did not keep in contact as closely as they had in the past, it was not out of animosity but because Braque spent so much time at Sorgues, where he still had a house. When Braque was wounded, Picasso had been stricken. Sickness upset him almost as much as death. Nevertheless he visited his "pard" in the hospital and at the Hôtel Meurice, where he convalesced, and was very supportive when he resumed painting. Picasso would always regard Braque as his closest male friend, but that does not mean that the converse was necessarily true. In later years, when they lived far apart, it was always Picasso who asked anxiously for news of Braque, seldom the other way around. Given Braque's increasing conservatism and detachment from the world, his coolness was to be expected. Veteran's umbrage must also have played a part in it. After all he had been through, how could Braque not resent the fellow mountaineer for streaking ahead to fame and fortune while he was stuck in the trenches? Whatever his feelings may have been, Braque seldom if ever took them out on Picasso. Instead he took them out, a year or so later, on another noncombatant Spaniard, Juan Gris. He felt that Gris had slipped into his place at the helm of cubism; and so he had. Usually such an honorable man, Braque behaved meanly. After using many of Gris's methods to jump-start his work in 1917, he refused to have his paintings hung in the same gallery. For Gris, who had hitherto been Braque's fervent admirer, this rejection was very hard to bear.

When he left the hospital and resumed painting, Braque had the greatest difficulty adjusting to the aftermath of cubism. In a courageous but not entirely successful bid to reestablish parity with Picasso, he set about painting a very large synthetic cubist *Musician.* Though a bit narrower, it is eight inches taller than Picasso's *Seated Man*; and it is strikingly similar in composition, concept and surface embellishment. There are even the same contrasts of confetti-like pointillism with larger "skyscraper" dots; and the eyes are set in a head shaped like a set square. The most noticeable difference is the *Musician*'s ramrod rigidity, and the whiff of "Salon"

Braque. *Musician*, 1918. Oil on canvas, 221.3×113 cm. Öffentliche Kunstsammlung Basel, Kunstmuseum.

cubism. True, Braque had been seeing Metzinger, but the rigidity could also be a legacy of the disciplines of war. Inevitably, parallels with Picasso are very striking—so much so that I cannot help wondering whether, consciously or not, Braque may not have roped himself to his fellow Alpinist one last time. For better or worse, the experiment did not work. Braque's future triumphs would necessitate his being very much on his own. So would Picasso's.

* * *

A week before the Braque banquet, Louise Faure-Favier, Apollinaire's columnist friend, had visited Wassilieff's studio and reported that the artists she met there discussed nothing but their work. She attributed this to Picasso, "the leader of the pack, who no longer has the air of a joyful master always ready to play skittles (*billes*) with his disciples. Even that young artist Mlle. Irène, queen of beauty, now has only one aim, to make great progress in painting."[33] Evidently, the two of them were still together, what is more, still planning to marry, to judge by a letter Picasso wrote Cocteau on January 15: "It says in my passport that I must leave France within three days (I got it yesterday). . . . I suppose we leave tomorrow. I shall drop a note on Diaghilev, telling him the same as you."[34] The "we" presumably refers to Irène. Since the exit visa would no longer have been valid for next month's trip to Rome, Picasso must have had another urgent reason for leaving France. What else but the need to present his fiancée to his mother and sister and old friends in Barcelona?

Picasso. *Irène Lagut*, 1917. Pencil on paper, 27.5×23cm. Picasso Heirs.

As head of his family, Picasso was still under pressure to live up to his position—marry and produce a son and heir. He had been punctilious about taking his first two fiancées, Fernande and Eva, to meet his parents, and, later in the year, he would present the woman he would ultimately marry, Olga, to doña María. Picasso would certainly have wanted to do the same with Irène. Whether or not they actually left for Spain we do not know. My own belief is that they never did; that the prospect of parental acceptance and the commitment it implied would have scared Irène, the free spirit, into breaking with Picasso once and for all; and that instead of going to Barcelona and then on to Rome on what Picasso envisaged as a wedding trip, she walked out on him—on or around January 16.

Cocteau later tried to turn the voyage to Rome to his own narcissistic advantage. In a television interview in the 1960s, he claimed that Picasso had said to him, "Since we're to make a wedding trip, we'll go and tell Gertrude Stein about it." So they called on Gertrude, and Picasso supposedly announced, "*Voilà*—we're leaving on our wedding trip,"[35] implying that Cocteau was taking Irène's place as the bride-to-be. Gertrude's memory is slightly but significantly different. "One day Picasso came in and with him and leaning on his shoulder was a slim, elegant youth. It is Jean, announced Pablo, Jean Cocteau and we are leaving for Italy. . . . He was very lively at the prospect of going to Rome."[36]

Jean Cocteau. *Picasso*, Easter, 1917. Pen and ink on paper. Musées de la Ville de Paris.

Satie was supposed to accompany Picasso and Cocteau to the city he liked to call "Rhum." He had already spent most of his advance from Diaghilev on luggage—articles that this man who never traveled never needed. At the last moment he decided not to go on this great adventure. He preferred the safety of his hideaway at Arcueil, to which nobody was ever granted admittance. As Cocteau said, Satie was "a bottle that should never be shaken."[37] There was another possible reason for his staying behind. Satie, who was sensitive about his indigence, had been outraged by the terms that Cocteau had arranged with Diaghilev:

> Given the importance of the libretto of *Parade*, the collaborators agree between them that only Monsieur Cocteau will receive the royalties due after each performance until these amount to 3,000 francs—the whole of which sum he agrees to cede to Erik Satie. Over and above this sum, the royalties will be shared between the composer and the librettist in the usual way.[38]

The indignity of this arrangement—the cheek of prosperous young Cocteau getting himself paid more than impoverished old Satie, and then fobbing him off with charity—prompted a bitter letter to Valentine:

> Cocteau is definitely a bounder and a shit. I don't want to see him any more—ever. He has every right to be a creep but not to this extent. . . . I regret, dear friend, I cannot compliment you on this loathsome bird—and such a tough one. This is not a reproach. It's an observation—sad. . . . What a chilblain to get on one's legs!"[39]

Valentine also received a report from Cocteau (February 15): "We leave tomorrow without Satie. Impossible to take along this *étrange paquet avec papates* [weird sack of potatoes]. . . . To the Minister, who asked [Satie], 'Do you know Rome?' . . . he replied, 'By name, only by name.'"[40] For his part, Satie was happy to stay behind. He still had the orchestration of *Parade* to do; also a score for the *Life of Socrates*, which Princesse Edmond de Polignac had commissioned. This time he claimed to have found the perfect collaborator—"never importunate—a dream": Plato.

Alfred Frueh. *Erik Satie*; on postcard sent by Picasso to Apollinaire, September 22, 1918. Archives Picasso.

"Picasso laughed," Cocteau said of their departure on the Rome express, "when he saw our painter friends (the doctrinaire cubists) . . . dwindling bodily as the train drew further away."[41] Cocteau was better placed than anybody else to assess the significance of Picasso's departure from Montparnasse. For the last eighteen months, he had been the most assiduous visitor to the studio, and he had watched Picasso slowly lowering the curtain on cubism as he transformed his *Seated Man* into its apotheosis. Cubism—what Cocteau punningly called "*la chute des angles*"—was indeed dwindling. Even Gris, who had carried synthetic cubism to new heights, was trying to liberate his work from its burden of theory. Meanwhile hangers-on persisted in systematizing things. Rivera, for instance, had come up with a mysterious picture-making contraption—he called it *la chose*—which could apparently give any image an authentic cubist look. A kind of camera obscura, it was constructed out of "sight vanes" (mobile planes of glass and gelatine). Its inventor claimed it had enabled him to discover the secret of the fourth dimension.

And then there was the fracas that became known as "*l'affaire Rivera.*" After a dinner Léonce Rosenberg gave for his artists at Lapérouse, the guests had adjourned to André Lhote's sumptuous studio, where Reverdy, who held forceful views on the purity and integrity of cubist painting, launched into a polemical harangue. Convinced that he was being attacked, Rivera gave him a mighty slap, at which Reverdy screamed and pulled Rivera's hair. To stop the fighting, Metzinger suggested a duel. Whereupon Rivera held out a conciliatory hand, which Reverdy refused, and ungallantly left. "This is the most serious event of the season," Max Jacob reported to Doucet. "*It will be necessary to take definite sides.*

Reverdy's side, Braque, Gris and surely Picasso, Ribera's [Jacob's name for Rivera] side will perhaps be Metzinger, Lhote, Maria Goutièrres, Marevna."[42] This foolish studio brawl was symptomatic of the dissolution of cubism.

Nor was all the squabbling factional. Reactionary elements were still attacking the cubists as pro-German. Perhaps because she had been shouted down at the Apollinaire banquet, the appalling Madame Aurel stepped up her chauvinistic campaign against modern French art in a sanctimonious pamphlet entitled *The Commandment of Love in Post-War Art.* ("When I saw [our art] imitated *en Bochie,* I realized why. . . . In promoting [it], Germany helped us kill off our resources of uprightness.")[43] Very soon the barbarian dadaists would be at the gate, although another three years would go by before Picabia came out with his anti-cubist manifesto. This man, whose wife had done very well out of dealing in their paintings, dared to accuse the cubists of being venal: of having "cubed negro sculptures, cubed violins, cubed illustrated newspapers, cubed shit and the profiles of young girls, and were now cubing money."[44]

Olga Khokhlova as one of the twelve princesses in *The Firebird,* 1916. Archives Picasso.

So much for the "dwindling cubists" that the Rome express was leaving behind in Paris. What was ahead for Picasso? By carrying him off to Rome, *Parade* would totally change his life. Diaghilev's ballet company would provide him with a brilliant new *tertulia* and above all a bride, Olga Khokhlova, whom Picasso would love passionately and possessively for a time and then, in his misogynistic way, love to hate. Her cool, melancholy beauty and lithe dancer's body would prove a perfect vehicle for his emergent classicism. She would change Picasso in another respect. At Olga's behest, he adopted, insofar as he could, the trappings of convention. Old friends need not have worried. It would not take Picasso long to lose patience with this masquerade and hang a sign on his studio door proclaiming "*Je ne suis pas un gentleman.*"

No less important, the trip to Rome would put Picasso back in touch with the Mediterranean. The inland sea that had cradled him would always regenerate his spirits, not to speak of his passion for the ancient world. Now that he had finally traveled to Rome and, more to the point, Naples, this passion would gradually take over his work. And just as he had appropriated the sacred fire, first of Christian, then of tribal, art, Picasso would now set about appropriating not merely the trappings of classicism (Pompeian frescoes, engraved mirror backs, Flavian busts, phallic amulets and other miracle-working artifacts) but their numinous power. The "*intercesseurs*" in which he had formerly put his faith—tribal ones as well as the saints who had protected him in early life—would give way to Hermes, Mithras and so many more. Under their auspices Picasso would evoke that animal mix of lethargy and ferocity, priapism and tenderness that still characterizes life on the shores of the Mediterranean. No longer would Picasso mythologize himself as Christ but as Dionysos presiding over Eleusinian mysteries; as Jupiter transforming himself into a bull; as Pygmalion in search of new metamorphic tricks to turn. Nor would he always suit the subject to the mode: classical subjects or themes are not necessarily treated classically, and vice versa. As he said time and again, it was all the same thing.

Cocteau's conversion to classicism was a simple matter of turning his coat. Within months of sending Valentine two postcards of the Elgin marbles to say that "this atrocious frieze runs up the whole expanse of Picasso's staircase. It personifies the drama of official marble" (September 12, 1916),[45] he would kowtow to classicism as if he had never been anything but a fervent admirer. And in due course he would redecorate his mind with yet another set of aesthetic clichés. Like a hairdresser putting a plaster cast of Apollo in his shop window, someone said. A call to order was too much of a *diktat* for Picasso. He still saw himself as a rebel leader of art: "A new David"—as he would tell Adolphe Basler—who would rise up and sweep away all the "mannerism" into which art had fallen. When it comes to Vlaminck, he said, "I myself would like to be in charge of the guillotine." Picasso continued, "As soon as I get home, I'm going to have a go at painting the *Horatii*! . . . Yes, the time has come."[46] This was more of a *rappel à la révolution* than a *rappel à l'ordre*.

Often as not, Picasso's apparent respect for the canons of classical beauty turns out to be ironical or tongue-in-cheek. Often as not, he sets the canons up the better to knock them down or mock them—for instance, the outrageous liberties he takes with proportions that are traditionally sacrosanct. Granted, a classical idiom would enable Picasso on occasion to be nostalgic or loving or proudly proprietary (as in the earlier portraits of Olga), but there is often something in his figures' gaze or comportment to suggest that there is more *accidie* than *luxe, calme et volupté* to these idylls. The nymphs are paying each other too much attention. The men have woken up; restless, they are throwing stones. There will soon be a pursuit, playful at first, then not so playful, ending in dark Dionysiac doings in dark Dionysiac groves. Picasso will depict these scenes with godlike indulgence: on Olympus rape is no crime. It is as if he wanted to prove Plutarch wrong, that "the great god Pan" was no longer dead, now that Picasso had returned to the classical scene.

Picasso. *Bathers*, summer, 1918. Pencil on paper, 23×31.9cm. Fogg Art Museum, Harvard University: Gift of Paul J. Sachs, Class of 1900. A testimonial to my friend W. G. Russell Allen.

Short Titles and Notes

Abbreviations of archives and libraries where original documents are located:

Archives Picasso	Picasso Archives at the Musée National Picasso, Paris
Archives Vollard	Archives Vollard, Manuscrits du Louvre et des Musées Nationaux, Paris
Beinecke Library	Stein papers and correspondence in the Collection of American Literature, Beinecke Rare Book and Manuscript Library, Yale University
Fonds Joseph Altounian	Documents and drawings of Max Jacob. Collection Cruz-Altounian
Kahnweiler Archive	Papers and photographs of D.-H. Kahnweiler, Galerie Louise Leiris, Paris
Ransom Center	Diaries and correspondence of Henri-Pierre Roché at the Harry Ransom Humanities Research Center, The University of Texas at Austin
Rosenberg Archive	Picasso/Rosenberg correspondence, Centre Georges Pompidou, Paris
Soffici Archive	Papers of Ardengo Soffici, Florence

Short titles of catalogs used to identify works by Picasso:

B.	Georges Bloch. *Pablo Picasso. Catalogue de l'œuvre gravé et lithographié.* 4 vols. Bern: Kornfeld & Klipstein, 1968–79.
Baer	Brigitte Baer. *Picasso Peintre-Graveur.* 7 vols. Bern: Kornfeld, 1986–96.
C.	Sébastien Goeppert, Herma Goeppert-Franck and Patrick Cramer. *Pablo Picasso, Catalogue raisonné des livres illustrés.* Geneva: Patrick Cramer, 1983.
D.B.	Pierre Daix and Georges Boudaille. *Picasso: The Blue and Rose Periods.* Trans. Phoebe Pool. Greenwich, Conn.: New York Graphic Society, 1967.
D.R.	Pierre Daix and Joan Rosselet. *Picasso: The Cubist Years 1907–1916.* Trans. Dorothy S. Blair. Boston, Mass.: New York Graphic Society, 1979.
JSLC	Arnold Glimcher and Marc Glimcher, eds. *Je suis le cahier: The Sketchbooks of Picasso.* New York: The Pace Gallery, 1986.
MP	*Musée Picasso: Catalogue sommaire des collections.* 2 vols. Paris: Réunion des Musées Nationaux, 1985, 1987.
MP Carnets	*Musée Picasso: Carnets: Catalogue des dessins.* 2 vols. Paris: Réunion des Musées Nationaux, 1996.
MPB	*Museu Picasso: Catàleg de pintura i dibuix.* Barcelona: Ajuntament de Barcelona, 1984.
PF.I	Josep Palau i Fabre. *Picasso: Life and Work of the Early Years 1881–1907.* Oxford: Phaidon, 1981.
PF.II	Josep Palau i Fabre. *Picasso: Cubism 1907–1917.* New York: Rizzoli, 1990.
S.	Werner Spies. *Picasso: Das plastische Werk.* Stuttgart: Gerd Hatje, 1983.
Z.	Christian Zervos. *Pablo Picasso.* 33 vols. Paris: Cahiers d'Art, 1932–78.

Short titles of principal sources cited in the notes:

Adéma	Pierre-Marcel Adéma. *Guillaume Apollinaire.* Paris: La Table ronde, 1968.
Andreu	Pierre Andreu. *Vie et mort de Max Jacob.* Paris: La Table ronde, 1982.
Ansen	Alan Ansen. *The Table Talk of W. H. Auden.* Princeton, N.J.,: Ontario Review Press, 1990.
Apollinaire 1913	Guillaume Apollinaire. *The Cubist Painters—Aesthetic Meditations.* Trans. Lionel Abel. New York: Wittenborn, rev. ed. 1949. Originally published as *Les Peintres cubistes—Méditations esthéthiques.* Paris: Figuière, 1913.
Apollinaire 1977	Guillaume Apollinaire. *Œuvres en prose I.* Paris: Gallimard, "Bibliothèque de la Pléiade," 1977.
Ashton	Dore Ashton. *Picasso on Art: A Selection of Views.* New York: Viking, 1972.
Assouline	Pierre Assouline. *L'Homme de l'art: D.-H. Kahnweiler 1884–1979.* Paris: Balland, 1988.
Baldassari	Anne Baldassari. *Picasso Photographe, 1901–1916.* Paris: Musée National Picasso, 1994.
Basler	Adolphe Basler. *La Peinture . . . Réligion Nouvelle.* Paris: Librairie de France, 1926.
Baudelaire	Charles Baudelaire. *Selected Writings on Art and Artists.* Trans. P. E. Charret. Harmondsworth: Penguin, 1972.
Bell	Vanessa Bell. *Selected Letters of Vanessa Bell.* Ed. Regina Marler. London: Bloomsbury, 1993.
Billy	André Billy. *Avec Apollinaire: Souvenirs inédites.* Paris: La Palatine, 1966.
Bolger	Doreen Bolger. "Hamilton Easter Field and His Contribution to American Modernism." *The American Art Journal* 20:2 (1988), 78–107.
Braque 1957	Georges Braque interviewed by John Richardson. "The Power of Mystery." *Observer* (London), Dec. 1, 1957.
Brassaï	Brassaï. *Picasso and Company.* Trans. Francis Price. Garden City, N.Y.: Doubleday, 1966. Originally published as *Conversations avec Picasso.* Paris: Gallimard, 1964.
Breunig	LeRoy C. Breunig, ed. *Apollinaire on Art: Essays and Reviews 1902–1918.* Trans. Susan Suleiman. New York: Viking, 1972. Originally published as Guillaume Apollinaire. *Chroniques d'Art.* Paris: Gallimard, 1960.
Burgess	Gelett Burgess. "The Wild Men of Paris." *Architectural Record* 27:5 (May 1910), 400–14.
Cabanne	Pierre Cabanne. *Pablo Picasso: His Life and Times.* Trans. Harold J. Salemson. New York: Morrow, 1977. Adapted from *Le Siècle de Picasso, 1: 1881–1937.* Paris: Denoël, 1975.
Caizergues and Seckel	Pierre Caizergues and Hélène Seckel. *Picasso/Apollinaire: Correspondance.* Paris: Gallimard, 1992.
Chapon	François Chapon. *Mystère et splendeurs de Jacques Doucet 1853–1929.* Paris: Jean-Claude Lattès, 1984.
Cooper	Douglas Cooper. *Picasso Theatre.* London: Weidenfeld and Nicolson, 1968.
Cousins	Judith Cousins, with the collaboration of Pierre Daix. "Documentary Chronology." In *Picasso and Braque: Pioneering Cubism.* New York: The Museum of Modern Art, 1989 (Rubin 1989).
Daix 1977	Pierre Daix. *La Vie de peintre de Pablo Picasso.* Paris: Seuil, 1977.
Daix 1988A	Pierre Daix. "L'Historique des *Demoiselles d'Avignon* revisé à l'aide des carnets de Picasso." In *Les Demoiselles d'Avignon.* Paris: Réunion des Musées Nationaux, 1988.
Daix 1988B	Pierre Daix. "Les Trois Périodes de travail de Picasso sur *Les trois femmes* (automne 1907–automne 1908), les rapports avec Braque et les débuts du cubisme." *Gazette des Beaux-Arts* (Paris), series 6, 3:1428–29 (Jan.–Feb., 1988), 141–54.

Daix 1992 — Pierre Daix. "The Chronology of Proto-Cubism: New Data on the Opening of the Picasso-Braque Dialogue." *Picasso and Braque: A Symposium.* New York: The Museum of Modern Art, 1992, 306–21.

Daix 1993 — Pierre Daix. *Picasso: Life and Art.* Trans. Olivia Emmet. New York: HarperCollins, Icon Editions, 1993. Originally published as *Picasso Créateur: La Vie intime et l'œuvre.* Paris: Seuil, 1987.

Daix 1995 — Pierre Daix. *Dictionnaire Picasso.* Paris: Robert Laffont, 1995.

Daix and Rosselet — Pierre Daix and Joan Rosselet. *Picasso: The Cubist Years 1907–1916.* Trans. Dorothy S. Blair. Boston: New York Graphic Society, 1979. Originally published as *Le Cubisme de Picasso. Catalogue raisonné de l'œuvre 1907–1916.* Neuchâtel: Ides et Calendes, 1979.

Derain — André Derain. *Lettres à Vlaminck.* Paris: Flammarion, 1955.

Durry — Marie-Jeanne Durry. "Irène Lagut." *Les Lettres françaises,* Feb. 12–18, 1969.

Faure-Favier — Louise Faure-Favier. *Souvenirs sur Guillaume Apollinaire.* Paris: Grasset, 1945.

Favela — Ramón Favela and James K. Ballinger. *Diego Rivera: The Cubist Years.* Phoenix: Art Museum, 1984.

Faÿ — Bernard Faÿ. *Les Précieux.* Paris: Librairie Académique Perrin, 1966.

FitzGerald — Michael C. FitzGerald. *Making Modernism: Picasso and the Creation of the Market for Twentieth-Century Art.* New York: Farrar, Straus and Giroux, 1995.

Flam — Jack D. Flam. *Matisse: The Man and His Art 1869–1918.* Ithaca: Cornell University Press, 1986.

Flechtheim — *Alfred Flechtheim: Sammler. Kunsthändler. Verleger.* Ed. Stephan von Wiese and Monika Flacke-Knoch. Düsseldorf: Kunstmuseum, 1987.

Fleuret — Fernand Fleuret, "Le Secretaire et Dame coupable ou les dernières Aventures du Baron d'Ormesan," *La Boîte à perruque.* Paris: Les Ecrivains Associés, 1935, 175–212.

Freeman — Judith Freeman. *The Fauve Landscape.* New York: Abbeville Press, 1990.

Fry — Edward F. Fry. *Cubism.* New York/Toronto: McGraw-Hill, 1966.

Geelhaar — Christian Geelhaar. *Picasso: Wegbereiter und Förderer seines Aufstiegs 1899–1939.* Zurich: Palladion/ABC Verlag, 1993.

Gibson — Ian Gibson. *Federico García Lorca.* London: Faber and Faber, 1989/1990.

Gilot — Françoise Gilot with Carlton Lake. *Life with Picasso.* New York: McGraw-Hill, 1964.

Golding — John Golding. *Cubism: A History and an Analysis 1907–1914.* London: Faber and Faber, 1959 (rev. ed. Cambridge, Mass.: Harvard University Press, 1988).

Häger — Bengt Häger. *Ballets Suédois.* Trans. Ruth Sharman. London: Thames and Hudson, 1990.

Halicka — Alice Halicka. *Hier: Souvenirs.* Paris: Editions du Pavois, 1946.

Henderson 1983 — Linda Dalrymple Henderson. *The Fourth Dimension and Non-Euclidean Geometry in Modern Art.* Princeton, N.J.: Princeton University Press, 1983.

Henderson 1988 — Linda Dalrymple Henderson. "X Rays and the Quest for Invisible Reality in the Art of Kupka, Duchamp, and the Cubists." *Art Journal* (Winter, 1988), 323–40.

Hoffmeister — Adolf Hoffmeister. *Visages écrits et dessinés.* Trans. François Kerel. Paris: Editeurs français réunis, 1964.

Hugo — Jean Hugo. *Le Regard de la mémoire.* Arles: Actes Sud, 1983.

Jacob — Max Jacob. *Chroniques des temps héroïques.* Paris: Louis Broder, 1956.

Johnson — Ron Johnson. "Picasso and the Poets." Unpublished manuscript, [1988].

Kahnweiler 1920 — Daniel-Henry Kahnweiler. *The Rise of Cubism.* Trans. Henry Aronson. New York: Wittenborn, Schultz, 1949. Originally published as *Der Weg zum Kubismus.* Munich: Delphin, 1920.

Kahnweiler 1946 — Daniel-Henry Kahnweiler. *Juan Gris: His Life and Work.* Trans. Douglas Cooper. New York: Abrams, 1946. Originally published as *Juan Gris: sa vie, son œuvre, ses écrits.* Paris: Gallimard, 1946.

Kahnweiler 1949	Daniel-Henry Kahnweiler. *The Sculptures of Picasso.* Trans. A. D. B. Sylvester. London: Rodney Phillips, 1949.
Kahnweiler 1956	Daniel-Henry Kahnweiler. *Letters of Juan Gris.* Trans. Douglas Cooper. London: Privately printed, 1956.
Kahnweiler 1961	Daniel-Henry Kahnweiler. *Mes Galeries et mes peintres: Entretiens avec Francis Crémieux.* Paris: Gallimard, 1961.
Karmel	Joseph Low Karmel (Pepe Karmel). "Picasso's Laboratory: The Role of His Drawings in the Development of Cubism, 1910–14." Doctoral thesis, Institute of Fine Arts, New York University, 1993.
Klüver	Billy Klüver. *Un jour avec Picasso.* Trans. Edith Ochs. Paris: Hazan, 1994.
Klüver and Martin	Billy Klüver and Julie Martin. *KiKi's Paris: Artists and Lovers 1900-1930.* New York: Harry N. Abrams, Inc., 1989.
Kostenevich and Semyonova	Albert Kostenevich and Natalya Semyonova. *Collecting Matisse.* Paris: Flammarion, 1993.
Lagut	Unpublished interview with Irène Lagut by Jean-José Marchand and Philippe Colin. "Archives du XXème Siècle." Radiodiffusion Télévision Française, 1973.
Lanchner and Rubin	Carolyn Lanchner and William Rubin. *Henri Rousseau.* New York: The Museum of Modern Art, 1985.
Laporte	Geneviève Laporte. *Un Amour secret de Picasso.* Monaco: Editions du Rocher, 1989.
Leighten	Patricia Dee Leighten. *Re-Ordering the Universe: Picasso and Anarchism, 1897–1914.* Princeton, N.J.: Princeton University Press, 1989.
Leonard	Sandra E. Leonard. *Henri Rousseau and Max Weber.* New York: Richard L. Feigen & Co., 1970.
Level	Brigitte Level. *Correspondance de Guillaume Apollinaire: André Level.* Paris: Aux Lettres Modernes, 1976.
Lichnowsky	Fürstin Mechtilde Lichnowsky. *Heute und Vorgestern.* Vienna: Biegland Verlag, 1958.
Luhan	Mabel Dodge Luhan. *Movers and Shakers.* Albuquerque: University of New Mexico Press: 1936/1987.
Madsen	Axel Madsen. *Sonia Delaunay: Artist of the Lost Generation.* New York: McGraw Hill, 1989.
Malraux	André Malraux. *Picasso's Mask.* Trans. June Guicharnaud with Jacques Guicharnaud. New York: Da Capo Press, 1994. Originally published as *La Tête d'obsidienne.* Paris: Gallimard, 1974.
Marevna	Marevna Voborev. *Life in Two Worlds.* London: Abelard, Schuman, 1962.
McBride	Henry McBride. "Hamilton Easter Field's Career." *The Arts* 3:1 (Jan. 1923).
McCully	Marilyn McCully, ed. *A Picasso Anthology.* London: Arts Council of Great Britain, 1981.
Mellow	James R. Mellow. *Charmed Circle: Gertrude Stein and Company.* New York: Praeger, 1974.
MoMA Symposium	*Picasso and Braque: A Symposium.* Organized by William Rubin, moderated by Kirk Varnedoe, proceedings ed. Lynn Zelevansky. New York: The Museum of Modern Art, 1992.
Monod-Fontaine 1984A	Isabelle Monod-Fontaine et al. *Donation Louise et Michel Leiris: Collection Kahnweiler-Leiris.* Paris: Museé National d'Art Moderne, Centre Georges Pompidou, 1984.
Monod-Fontaine 1984B	Isabelle Monod-Fontaine et al. *Daniel-Henry Kahnweiler, marchand, editeur, écrivain.* Paris: Musée National d'Art Moderne, Centre Georges Pompidou, 1984.
O'Brian	Patrick O'Brian. *Pablo Ruiz Picasso.* New York: Putnam, 1976.

Olivier 1933 — Fernande Olivier. *Picasso and His Friends.* Trans. Jane Miller. New York: Appleton-Century, 1965. Originally published as *Picasso et ses amis.* Paris: Stock, 1933. Page references in the notes are to the published English version; however, citations are frequently made from the new, unpublished trans. by Michael Raeburn and Christine Baker.

Olivier 1988 — Fernande Olivier. *Souvenirs intimes.* Ed. Gilbert Krill. Paris: Calmann-Lévy, 1988. Trans. Michael Raeburn and Christine Baker (unpublished); n.p. refers to unpublished text from the original manuscript.

Otero 1984 — Roberto Otero. *Recuerdo de Picasso.* Madrid: Ministerio de Cultura, 1984.

Painter — George D. Painter. *Marcel Proust: A Biography.* London: Pimlico, 1996.

Palau i Fabre 1990 — Josep Palau i Fabre. *Picasso: Cubism, 1907–1917.* Trans. Susan Branyas, Richard-Lewis Rees and Patrick Zabalbeascoa. New York: Rizzoli, 1990. Originally published as *Picasso: Cubisme, 1907–1917.* Barcelona: Polígrafa, 1990.

Palau i Fabre 1991 — Josep Palau i Fabre. "Picasso i Horta." *Butlletí del centre d'estudis de la terra alta* 15–16 (Sept., 1991), 2–22.

Parmelin — Hélène Parmelin. *Picasso Says.* Trans. Christine Trollope. London: Allen and Unwin, 1969. Originally published as *Picasso dit . . .* Paris: Gonthier, 1966.

Penrose — Roland Penrose. *Picasso: His Life and Work.* London: Granada, 1981. Originally published London: Gollancz, 1958.

Pierre — José Pierre. *Marie Laurencin.* Paris: Somogy, 1988.

Podoksik — Anatoli Podoksik. *Picasso: La Quête perpétuelle.* Paris: Cercle d'Art, 1989. Originally published as *Picasso: Vechnyi Poisk.* Leningrad: Aurora, 1989.

Rewald — John Rewald, ed. *Paul Cézanne Letters.* New York: Hacker Art Books, 1976.

Richardson 1959 — John Richardson. *Georges Braque.* Harmondsworth: Penguin Books, 1959.

Robbins 1964 — Daniel Robbins. *Albert Gleizes: 1881–1953.* New York: The Solomon R. Guggenheim Museum, 1964.

Robbins 1985 — Daniel Robbins. "Jean Metzinger at the Center of Cubism." In *Jean Metzinger in Retrospect.* Iowa City: University of Iowa Museum of Art, 1985, 9–23.

Rubin 1972 — William Rubin. *Picasso in the Collection of The Museum of Modern Art.* New York: The Museum of Modern Art, 1972.

Rubin 1983 — William Rubin. "From Narrative to 'Iconic' in Picasso: The Buried Allegory in *Bread and Fruitdish on a Table* and the Role of *Les Demoiselles d'Avignon.*" *Art Bulletin* (New York) 65:4 (Dec., 1983).

Rubin 1984 — William Rubin. "Picasso." In *"Primitivism" in Twentieth-Century Art,* 1. New York: The Museum of Modern Art, 1984, 241–343.

Rubin 1989 — William Rubin. *Picasso and Braque: Pioneering Cubism.* New York: The Museum of Modern Art, 1989.

Rubin, Seckel, Cousins — William Rubin, Hélène Seckel and Judith Cousins. *Les Demoiselles d'Avignon.* New York: The Museum of Modern Art, 1994.

Sabartès — Jaime Sabartès. *Picasso: Documents iconographiques.* Trans. Félia Leal and Alfred Rosset. Geneva: Pierre Cailler, 1954.

Salmon 1912 — André Salmon. "Histoire anecdotique du Cubisme." In *La Jeune Peinture française.* Paris: Société des Trente, Albert Messein, 1912.

Salmon 1956 — André Salmon. *Souvenirs sans fin: Deuxième époque (1908–1920).* Paris: Gallimard, 1956.

Salmon 1957 — André Salmon. *Modigliani: Le roman de Montparnasse.* Paris: Seghers, 1957.

Salmon 1961 — André Salmon. *Souvenirs sans fin: Troisième époque (1920–1940).* Paris: Gallimard, 1961.

Sarrazin — Arlette Sarrazin-Verdaguer. *Picasso et La Rue des Bois.* Les Amis du Vieux Verneuil: *Bulletin* 43 (Sept., 1992).

Schapiro — Meyer Schapiro. *Cézanne Watercolors.* New York: Knoedler's, 1963.

Seckel — Hélène Seckel. *Max Jacob et Picasso.* Quimper: Musée des Beaux-Arts, 1994.

Severini	Gino Severini. *Tutta la vita di un pittore.* Milan: Garzanti, 1946.
Schneider	Pierre Schneider. *Matisse.* Trans. Michael Taylor and Bridget Stevens Romer. London: Thames and Hudson, 1984. Originally published as *Matisse.* Paris: Flammarion, 1984.
Shattuck	Roger Shattuck. *The Banquet Years: The Origins of the Avant-Garde in France —1885 to World War I.* New York: Vintage Books, 1968. Originally published 1955.
Silver	Kenneth Silver. *Esprit de Corps: The Art of the Parisian Avant-Garde and the First World War, 1914–1925.* London: Thames and Hudson, 1989.
Simon	Linda Simon. *The Biography of Alice B. Toklas.* Garden City, N.Y.: Doubleday, 1977.
Stallano	Jacqueline Stallano. "Une relation encombrante: Géry Pieret." In *Amis européens d'Apollinaire* (Actes du seizième colloque de Stavelot, Sept. 1–3, 1993). Paris: Presse de la Sorbonne Nouvelle, 1995, 10–29.
Steegmuller 1963	Francis Steegmuller. *Apollinaire Among the Painters.* New York: Penguin Books, 1986. Originally published New York: Farrar, Straus and Giroux, 1963.
Steegmuller 1986	Francis Steegmuller. *Cocteau: A Biography.* Boston: Nonpareil Books, 1986. (The author of the present work has retranslated several of Cocteau's letters and reminiscences.)
Stein 1933	Gertrude Stein. *The Autobiography of Alice B. Toklas.* New York: Vintage Books, 1961. Originally published New York: Harcourt, Brace, 1933.
Leo Stein	Leo Stein. *Appreciation: Painting, Poetry and Prose.* New York: Crown, 1947.
Steinberg	Leo Steinberg, "The Philosophical Brothel," *October* (New York and Cambridge, Mass.) 44 (spring, 1988), 7–74. Revised version of "The Philosophical Brothel," *Art News* (New York) 71:5 (Sept., 1972), 20–9, 71:6 (Oct., 1972), 38–47.
Toklas 1954	Alice B. Toklas. *The Alice B. Toklas Cookbook.* New York: Anchor, 1960. Originally published New York: Harper Brothers, 1954.
Toklas 1963	Alice B. Toklas. *What Is Remembered.* New York: Holt, Rinehart and Winston, 1963.
Uhde 1928	Wilhelm Uhde. *Picasso and the French Tradition.* Trans. F. M. Loving. New York: Weyhe, 1929. Originally published as *Picasso et la tradition française.* Paris: Editions des Quatre Chemins, 1928.
Uhde 1938	Wilhelm Uhde. *Von Bismark bis Picasso: Erinnerungen und Bekenntnisse.* Zurich: Oprecht, 1938.
Vallentin	Antonina Vallentin. *Pablo Picasso.* Paris: Albin Michel, 1957. Trans. as *Picasso.* Garden City, N.Y.: Doubleday, 1963.
Vallier	Dora Vallier. "Braque: La peinture et nous." *Cahiers d'Art* (Paris), (Oct., 1954).
Varèse	Louise Varèse. *Varèse: A Looking-Glass Diary, I, 1883-1928.* London: Davis-Poynter, 1973.
Watson	Steven Watson. *Strange Bedfellows: The First American Avant-Garde.* New York: Abbeville Press, 1991.
Weiss	Jeffrey Weiss. *The Popular Culture of Modern Art: Picasso, Duchamp and Avant-Gardism.* New Haven and London: Yale University Press, 1994.
de Zayas	Marius de Zayas. "How, When and Why Modern Art Came to New York." Intro. and notes by Francis M. Naumann. *Arts Magazine* (New York) (Apr., 1980), 96–126.
Zilczer 1975	Judith K. Zilczer. "Robert J. Coady, Forgotten Spokesman for Avant-Garde Culture in America." *American Art Review* 2 (Nov.–Dec., 1975), 77–89.
Zilczer 1986	Judith K. Zilczer. "Robert J. Coady, Man of *The Soil.*" In Rudolf E. Kuenzli, ed. *New York Dada.* New York: Willis Locker & Owens, 1986, 31–43.
Vol. I	John Richardson. *A Life of Picasso 1881–1906.* New York: Random House, 1991.

INTRODUCTION pp.3–9

1 Parmelin, 106.

2 See Vol. I, 327.

3 Stein 1933, 59.

4 Adéma, 117.

5 Seckel, 59.

6 Liane de Pougy, *Mes cahiers bleus* (Paris: Plon, 1977), 193–4.

7 Guillaume Apollinaire, *Journal intime* (Paris: Editions du Limon, 1991), 145.

8 Apollinaire would eventually use Raoul Dufy to illustrate *Le Bestiaire ou Cortège d'Orphée* (1911).

9 Salmon 1961, 100.

10 Seckel, 51.

11 See Vol. I, 180.

12 Daix 1995, 380.

13 Luhan, 30.

14 Baudelaire is quoted by Christian Geelhaar, "The Painters who had the right eyes: on the reception of Cézannes Bathers," in Mary Louise Krumrine, *Paul Cézanne: The Bathers* (London: Thames and Hudson, 1990), 285.

1 "LE PEINTRE DE LA VIE MODERNE" pp.11–27

1 The exhibition *Les Demoiselles d'Avignon*, curated by Hélène Seckel, was shown at the Musée Picasso, Paris (Jan. 26–Apr. 18, 1988), and at the Museu Picasso, Barcelona (May 10–July 14, 1988).

2 A revised and amplified version of the catalog in English was subsequently published by the Museum of Modern Art, New York, in 1994; see Rubin, Seckel, Cousins. Leo Steinberg's essay "The Philosophical Brothel" was first published in *Art News* (New York) 71:5 (Sept.) and 71:6 (Oct.), 1972; see Steinberg.

3 Herbert T. Schwarz, *Picasso and Marie-Thérèse Walter, 1925–1927* (Montmagny, Quebec: Editions Isabeau, 1988), 116.

4 That Steinberg turns out to be guiltier than Cooper of "patent inaccuracy" is borne out by his references to the verso of the Cooper drawing: in "The Algerian Women and Picasso at Large," *Other Criteria* (New York: Oxford University Press, 1972), 168; and in his justly celebrated essay "The Philosophical Brothel" (see Steinberg). In his *Other Criteria* essay he rightly claims the drawing is "vastly significant for the history of twentieth-century art," but for the wrong reasons. He sees it as the first example of Picasso's desire "to make recto and verso cohabit in the same contoured image." Thrown off by the buttoned vent in the back of her jacket, Steinberg has mistaken not only the smartly dressed Fernande for a nude, but her "rump" (his word) for her pelvis. When he republishes this drawing in 1988 (Steinberg, 56), he silently emends the title from *Standing Nude* to *Standing Woman (Woman in a Riding Habit)*. This, too, is erroneous—not Steinberg's fault: he took it from Gary Tinterow's entry in his catalog *Master Drawings by Picasso* (Cambridge, Mass., 1981) of the Fogg Art Museum's Picasso drawing show. Picasso specifically inscribed a related sketch "*costume-tailleur*." This means a tailored suit, not a riding habit, something that Fernande is most unlikely to have owned.

5 Baudelaire, 432.

6 Ibid., 430–2.

7 Daix 1995, 97–8.

8 Baudelaire, 434.

9 Vol. I, 470.

10 Ibid., 471.

11 Salmon 1912; trans. in Rubin, Seckel, Cousins, 244.

12 Rubin, Seckel, Cousins, 45, 130 n.153.

13 See Vol. I, 429, for an account of the purchase of this painting.

14 When I first published this material in "Picasso's Apocalyptic Whorehouse," *New York Review* (New York) (Apr. 23, 1987), 40–7, the question was raised as to whether Zuloaga had the painting shipped to his property in Spain instead of Paris. Given the parallels between the El Greco and the Picasso, not least of scale and format, the answer seemed self-evident. My hunch has now been confirmed. Seckel and Cousins have published a letter, dated June 14, 1907, from Zuloaga to Paul Lafond, author of an article on his collection, confirming that "my collection is divided in two. The best things are here in Paris and the rest are in Eibar." (See: Rubin, Seckel, Cousins, 151.) Since the *Apocalyptic Vision* was the finest El Greco in Zuloaga's collection and is illustrated in the article, there can be no further cause for doubt.

15 In the course of relining by the Prado restorer in 1880, the entire top and a strip along the left-hand side of this painting, which had deteriorated, were removed. See Richard Mann, *El Greco and His Patrons* (Cambridge: Cambridge University Press, 1986), 142–3.

16 A receipt from Picasso in the Archives Vollard—11 pictures for 1,100 francs—is dated Sept. 14, 1907. My special thanks to Gerrard White for bringing this document to my attention.

17 According to Annette Rosenshine, the Steins were responsible for the acquisition of Picasso's second studio. Max Jacob also recalled that Picasso had rented an ill-lit room on the floor below his studio. See Rubin, Seckel, Cousins, 148 n.1.

18 Burgess, 408.

19 Leo Stein, 174.

20 Another possibility is that Picasso worked from photographs, as Matisse did at the time, specifically from studies of the nude in *L'Etude Académique*, a magazine for art students published between 1904 and 1908; see: Elizabeth Hutton Turner, "Who is in the brothel of Avignon? A case for context," *Artibus et Historiae* 9 (1984), 139–57.

21 Wilhelm Boeck and Jaime Sabartès. *Picasso* (London: Thames and Hudson, 1955), 38.

22 Rubin, Seckel, Cousins, 57–8, 130 n.169. Mary Mathews Gedo in "Art as Exorcism: Picasso's *Demoiselles d'Avignon*," *Arts Magazine* (New York) 55:2 (Oct. 15, 1980), 83 n.55, assumes that the disease took the form of syphilis.

23 In Vol. I, 238, I suggested that Picasso had given Dr. Fontbona *Woman by the Sea* in exchange for services performed for a girlfriend. Francesc Fontbona has kindly corrected this error and supplied me with the diagnosis which his great-uncle had informally disclosed to members of his family.

24 See Vol. I, 218–19. Among Picasso's personal effects in the Archives Picasso is an address book dating from the first years of his residence in Paris. Among the names listed is Dr. Julien [*sic*], chaussée d'Antin 12.

25 Picasso to Kahnweiler, Dec. 2, 1933; in Daniel-Henry Kahnweiler, "Huit Entretiens avec Picasso," *Le Point* (Souillac and Mulhouse) 7:42 (Oct., 1952), 24.

26 Otero 1984, 31.

27 Rafael Santos Torroella, "Sobre un artículo de Lluís Permanyer: 'Les demoiselles d'Avignon,'" *Hoja de Lunes* (Barcelona) (Jan. 25, 1982), 16.

28 These spoof identities were a part of a studio farce still being played out, fifty years later, at La Californie, where a hideous tapestry version of the *Demoiselles* dominated the studio—*"beaucoup plus fort que l'originale,"* the artist used to tease American museum directors by saying ("much better than the original"). Woe betide the earnest pedant who dared to question him about the women's identities. If Picasso's mood was good, there might be a whole new cast—Madame de Gaulle, his potter's wife, Gina Lollobrigida. If it was bad, the offender would be frozen out.

29 Otero 1984, 31.

30 Gilot, 84.

31 Toklas 1963, 35.

32 Daix 1993, 71.

33 Salmon 1956, 221.

34 Ibid. Pellerin was so struck by this song that he used it to distract his fellow soldiers during World War I bombardments.

35 Kahnweiler 1946, 9.

36 Guillaume Apollinaire, *Guillaume Apollinaire: Journal Intime, 1898–1918*, ed. Michel Décaudin (Paris: Limon, 1991), 42. The entry is dated Feb. 27, 1907.

37 Stallano, 15. My thanks to Peter Read for making this publication available to me.

38 Biographical information about Pieret appears in Willard Bohn, "Géry Pieret au bord du Pacifique," *Que Vlo-ve* 22 (Apr.–June 1987), 8–11, and Stallano.

39 Alice Halicka, *Apollinaire familier* (Paris: La Table ronde, Sept., 1952), 93.

40 Fleuret, 181.

41 Ibid., 176.

42 Olivier 1933, 183.

43 Stallano, 27.

44 "The art critic and his roommate . . . Géry Pieret called each other '*tu*,' and lived in the closest possible intimacy. A nice world" (*La Voix française*). "If M. Apollinaire provided his secretary with a bed, those who are familiar with Polish morals will know that there was nothing surprising or criminal about it" (*Le Siècle*). See Stallano, 22.

45 Steegmuller 1963, 166.

46 Géry Pieret's account was originally published in *Paris-Journal* (Aug. 29, 1911).

47 Apollinaire's 1915 account is trans. in Steegmuller 1963, 167.

48 Stallano, 17.

49 Malraux, 11.

50 Alfred H. Barr, Jr., *Picasso: Forty Years of His Art* (New York: The Museum of Modern Art, 1939), 59–60.

51 The outbreak of war delayed publication of Picasso's disclaimer. It did not appear until 1942, in the foreword to Vol. II of Zervos's *catalogue raisonné*.

52 Zervos's text is trans. in Rubin, Seckel, Cousins, 216.

53 Pierre Daix, "Il n'y a pas d'art nègre dans *Les Demoiselles d'Avignon*," *Gazette des Beaux Arts* (Paris), ser. 6, 76:1221 (Oct., 1970), 247–70.

54 Pierre Daix in conversation with the author and Marilyn McCully.

55 Françoise Gilot in conversation with the author.

56 Romuald Dor de la Souchère, *Picasso à Antibes* (Paris: Fernand Hazan, 1960); trans. in Rubin, Seckel, Cousins 1994, 216.

57 All but one of the subjects in Carnet 10 relate to the *Demoiselles*, especially the second one from the left, and to another sizable painting, the markedly tribal *Nu à la draperie*.

58 I have been able to identify no more than fourteen. There may well be others. Stein kept six of these canvas-backed sheets for himself and his sister, and eventually sold off the remainder to collector friends. These included the Cone sisters of Baltimore and Horace Titus, who assembled a group of fine works on paper by Picasso and Juan Gris for his wife, Helena Rubinstein.

59 Picasso told me this apropos the finest of these sketchbook pages, which I illustrated in *Pablo Picasso: Watercolors and Gouaches* (London: Barrie and Rockliff, 1964), 30.

60 Leo Stein, 175.

61 For further discussion, see Rubin 1984, passim.

62 Florent Fels, "Opinions sur l'art nègre," *Action* (Paris) 3 (Apr., 1920), 23–7; Cocteau's reply to the same questionnaire was no less dismissive: "*L'art nègre* has become as boring as *le japonisme Mallarméen*."

63 Florent Fels, "Chronique artistique: Propos d'artistes—Picasso," *Les Nouvelles littéraires* (Paris), 2:42 (Aug. 4, 1923); trans. in Rubin, Seckel, Cousins, 216.

64 Gilot, 266.

65 Picasso to Leo Stein, Apr. 27, 1907 (Beinecke Library).

2 RAYMONDE pp. 29–45

1 See: Seckel, 60; also Salmon 1956, 328.

2 André Salmon, *La Négresse du Sacré-Cœur* (Paris: Gallimard, 1968; originally published in 1920), 167.

3 Seckel, 60.

4 Salmon 1956, 328–9.

5 Palau i Fabre 1990, 46–7.

6 Two related drawings (Z.VI.1010, PF.II.304), done a year or so later, reveal that Picasso contemplated doing an ambitious composition inspired by the *castellers*: an ascending mass of densely packed figures culminating in a couple of naked women instead of a boy. Nothing came of this unique stab at futurist dynamism. Nor did anything come of a 1917 project for a folkloric ballet on the theme of the *castellers*, with décor by Picasso, which Eugeni d'Ors proposed to Diaghilev.

7 This painting is uncannily like a double Chan mask from the middle Sepik, although no example of such an object is known to have reached Europe at this period. See, e.g., Alfred Bühler, Terry Barrow, Charles P. Mountford, *Oceania and Australia: The Art of the South Seas* (London: Methuen, 1962), 68, which shows a mask, now in Basel, collected in 1956.

8 Picasso in conversation with the author; see also Vol. I, 417–8.

9 Salmon 1956, 329.

10 Z.XXVI.262

11 Seckel, 60. Note that the original account—Henri Herz, "Contribution à la figure de Max Jacob," *Europe* 489 (Jan., 1970), 137–41—is slightly different.

12 Salmon 1956, 329.

13 Seckel, 64 n.39.

14 Fernande to G. Stein, Aug. 8, 1907 (Beinecke Library).

15 Daix 1988A, 514. Palau i Fabre 1990, 68, mysteriously attributes these names to Picasso's pets.

16 The five heads have been X-rayed, but not the whole composition.

17 See, e.g., William Rubin in Rubin, Seckel, Cousins, 130–3; David Lomas, "A Canon of Deformity: *Les Demoiselles d'Avignon* and physical anthropology," *Art History* (Norwich), 16:3 (Sept., 1993), 424–6; and Michael Leja, "'Le Vieux Marcheur' and 'Les Deux Risques': Picasso, Prostitution, Venereal Disease, and Maternity, 1899–1907," *Art History* (Norwich) 8:1 (Mar., 1985), 66–81.

18 Chapon, 332.

19 Rubin, Seckel, Cousins, 224.

20 Vallentin, 149.

21 Uhde 1938, 142.

22 Kahnweiler to G. Stein, [1933] (Beinecke Library).

23 Kahnweiler's visit is recounted in Kahnweiler 1946, 9, and Kahnweiler 1961, 44.

24 D.-H. Kahnweiler, "Picasso et le Cubisme" (Lyon: Musée de Lyon, 1953); trans. in Rubin, Seckel, Cousins, 238.

25 Brassaï, *The Artists of My Life*. Trans. Richard Miller (London: Thames and Hudson, 1982), 206, 208.

26 Françoise Gilot told the author that according to Picasso, Kahnweiler and Lucie Godon met in London, where she was working, and not in Paris; also that Picasso was fascinated by the name Godon because it derived from "Goddam" and denoted French people who collaborated with the English in the Hundred Years' War.

27 Jean Lorrain, *Poussières de Paris* (Paris, 1899), 143–4.

28 Picasso would also have known the version of Loïe Fuller's "*danza serpentina*" which was performed, seemingly on water (the dancer was in a boat and was illuminated from the shore with projections of light), at the Festa Modernista in Sitges in 1895.

29 Baer 17.

30 Daix 1993, 78.

31 Daix 1988A, 518.

32 See Vol. I., 385. Rubin 1984, 268, sees this tracing as an early image of his own hand functioning with the thaumaturgic power of the shaman.

33 Picasso may also have had Fernande's hand in mind, particularly since she is known to have had "the Napoleonic forefinger, quite as long, if not a shade longer than the middle finger." Stein 1933, 19.

34 Daix and Rosselet, 185 n.28.

35 Salmon (in 1912) claimed that "a holiday interrupted the painful experiments. Upon his return, Picasso resumed work on the large test-canvas." Rubin, Seckel, Cousins, 245.

36 Christopher Green thinks that *The Harvesters* was inspired by memories of Gósol. See "Figure into Landscape into *Tableau-Objet*: Placing Picasso's Cubist Landscapes," *Picasso Landscapes 1890–1912* (Barcelona: Museu Picasso, 1994), 29.

37 This painting of two harlequins, one very tall, one very short, is now in the Barnes Collection. Rouart wrote to Picasso several times in the spring of 1907 concerning the purchase of the painting and also extending invitations.

38 Eugène Rouart to Picasso, July 10, 1907; in Rubin, Seckel, Cousins, 152.

39 Rubin, Seckel, Cousins, 150.

40 Denys Sutton was told by Alice Derain that Picasso visited Avignon with Derain in the course of the summer. There is no evidence that either of them went there, except the memory of Derain's widow, who at the time was still married to Maurice Princet. Derain spent most of the summer at Cassis on the Côte d'Azur.

41 Stein 1933, 64.

42 See Vol. I, 417.

43 Schneider, 207 (quoting Gaston Diehl).

44 Kahnweiler 1920, 7.

45 Salmon 1912; trans. in Fry, 85.

46 Vallentin, 150.

47 Fernande to G. Stein, Sept. 19, 1907 (Beinecke Library).

3 CÉZANNE AND PICASSO pp. 47–57

1 Daix 1995, 181.

2 Fernande to G. Stein, Aug. 8, 1907 (Beinecke Library).

3 Fernande to G. Stein, Aug. 24, 1907 (Beinecke Library).

4 Fernande to G. Stein, Sept. 2, 1907 (Beinecke Library).

5 Fernande used the surname Belvallé (once spelled Belvalet) in signing three letters to Gertrude Stein around this time (Sept. 2, 16, 19, 1907), perhaps in honor of the reconciliation with her "aunt." However, her friends believed that this was her real name. Two years earlier, Apollinaire's painter friend E.-M. Poullain wrote the poet: "Tu sais que Fernande s'appelle Bellevallée. Max qui est fâché avec eux appelle Picasso le lys dans la belle vallée." See Peter Read, *Picasso et Apollinaire: Les métamorphoses de la mémoire 1905/1973* (Paris: Jean-Michel Place, 1995), 30. We know that Fernande's mother's name was Lang, and it seems likely that Belvallé was the name of her adoptive parents. However, it has proved impossible to confirm this—the name does not appear in the commercial directory among the accessory-makers on rue Réaumur, where the family had its business. It is conceivable that it was the name of Fernande's real father, whose identity is unknown.

6 See ch. 1, note 16, above.

7 Stein 1933, 19.

8 Ibid.

9 Level purchased the *Saltimbanques* in late 1907; in a note dated Jan. 24, 1908, Level says that a framer is coming to measure the painting; FitzGerald, 275 n.37.

10 An excellent account of the Peau de l'Ours sale in 1914 is given in FitzGerald, 15–46.

11 Fernande to G. Stein, Sept. 16, 1907 (Beinecke Library).

12 Vol. I, 464.

13 Simon, 48–9.

14 Ibid., 58.

15 Ibid., 63.

16 After World War I, Annette returned to Europe. Alice saw that Gertrude shunned her, but it no longer mattered: she was on her way to Zurich to have Dr. Jung undo the damage done by "Dr." Stein. Later Annette did a stint with Gurdjieff, and in the 1960s ended up in Berkeley, where she found not only a following among the students but an analyst who gave her LSD therapy.

17 Fernande to G. Stein, Sept. 16, 1907 (Beinecke Library).

18 Stein 1933, 25.

19 Ibid., 95.

20 Ibid., 12.

21 Harold Acton, *More Memoirs of an Aesthete* (London: Methuen, 1970), 175.

22 Schapiro, 11.

23 Parmelin, 72.

24 Schapiro, 15.

25 "Treat nature by means of the cylinder, the sphere, the cone, everything brought into proper perspective so that each side of an object or a plane is directed towards a central point." Cézanne to Bernard, Apr. 15, 1904; in Rewald, 301.

26 Gilot, 124–5.

27 The catalog lists 56 items, but some last-minute additions are not included.

28 Rainer Maria Rilke, *Letters on Cézanne*; ed. Clara Rilke, trans. Joel Agee (London: Jonathan Cape, 1988), 78.

29 Ibid., 43.

30 Ibid., 28–9.

31 Ibid., 46.

32 Ibid., 47.

33 Ibid., 57–8.

34 Ibid.

35 See Vol. I, 336–7.

36 Brassaï, 79.

37 Parmelin, 114.

38 Christian Zervos, "Conversation avec Picasso," *Cahiers d'art* X:7–10 (1935), 178.

39 *Grandes Baigneuses*, 1900–06 (National Gallery, London), was listed as no. 17 and *Grandes Baigneuses*, 1899–1906 (Philadelphia Museum of Art), as no. 19 in the catalog of the 1907 Salon d'Automne.

40 Cézanne to Roger Marx, Jan. 23, 1905; in Rewald, 313.

41 Braque in conversation with the author.

42 See Vol. I, 408–9.

43 W. H. Auden, "Woods," *Collected Shorter Poems* (New York: Random House, 1967), 257.

44 Picasso in conversation with the author.

45 Stein 1933, 22.

46 Ibid.

47 Daix 1988B, 143.

48 It is unlikely that the first version of the *Three Women* and the sketches for *Friendship* were completed within ten days or so of the opening of the Cézanne exhibition, especially in view of Picasso's statement to Cooper that *Nudes in the Forest*—the first manifestation of the *Three Women* theme—dates from the fall of 1907.

49 Kahnweiler 1920, 7.

4 RENDEZ-VOUS DES PEINTRES pp. 59–77

1 Vallier, 14.

2 Marcelle Braque in conversation with the author.

3 Uhde 1928, 39.

4 Vallier, 13.

5 For information concerning Braque's family background, see Richardson 1959.

6 Vallier, 13.

7 Richardson 1959, 3.

8 This *Cercle* would organize a major fauve show in 1908.

9 Vallier, 13.

10 Claude Lepape and Thierry Defert, *Georges Lepape ou l'élégance illustrée* (Paris: Herscher, 1983), 22.

11 Stein 1933, 61.

12 Ibid.

13 Olivier 1933, 103.

14 Laurencin to Roché, Apr. 12, 1906 (Ransom Center).

15 Laurencin to Roché, Apr. 28, 1906 (Ransom Center).

16 Laurencin to Roché, June 13, 1906 (Ransom Center).

17 Laurencin to Roché, Aug. [23], 1906 (Ransom Center).

18 In his personal address book, Picasso lists the name Paul Filippi [*sic*] (presumably Paulette), at 35 avenue des Gobelins (Archives Picasso).

19 Paul Fort, *Mes Mémoires: toute la vie d'un poète (1872–1943)* (Paris: Flammarion, 1944), 44.

20 Salmon 1957, 71.

21 Ibid.

22 Jean Mollet, *Les Mémoires du baron Mollet* (Paris: Gallimard, 1963), 93–4.

23 Olivier 1933, 76.

24 Roché Carnet 26:15, May 18, 1906 (Ransom Center).

25 Roché Carnet 47:5, Apr. 22, 1909 (Ransom Center).

26 Olivier 1933, 43.

27 Roché Carnet 32:21, Dec. 23, 1906 (Ransom Center).

28 Laurencin to Roché, July 11, 1907, Carnet 37:4 (Ransom Center).

29 Faure-Favier, 51.

30 Apollinaire 1977, 256.

31 Marie Laurencin, *Le Carnet des Nuits* (Geneva: Pierre Cailler, 1956), 40.

32 Olivier 1933, 85–7.

33 Pierre, 16.

34 Ibid., 72.

35 For a perceptive analysis of Laurencin's involvement with Apollinaire and the group at the Bateau Lavoir, see Julia Fagan-King, "United on the threshold of the twentieth-century mystical ideal: Marie Laurencin's integral involvement with Guillaume Apollinaire and the inmates of the Bateau Lavoir." *Art History* (Norwich) 11:1 (Mar., 1988), 88–114.

36 Fagan-King says nine; ibid., 97.

37 Salmon 1956, 177.

38 Another possible link was Fernande's "adoptive sister" Antoinette, the mistress of the fauve Othon Friesz, with whom Braque spent the summer of 1906 in Antwerp, but Fernande is silent on this relationship. In Olivier 1933, 16, Fernande refers to this girl as "one of my close relatives who was married to a painter."

39 Salmon 1961, 182.

40 Richardson 1959, 5.

41 Braque in conversation with the author.

42 Richardson 1959, 6.

43 Braque in conversation with the author.

44 See Vol. I, 306.

45 Clive Bell, *Since Cézanne* (London: Chatto and Windus, 1922), 211.

46 Derain, 98.

47 Salmon 1961, 179.

48 Vlaminck and F. Sernanda, *D'un lit à l'autre* (1902); and Vlaminck, *Tout pour ça* (1903).

49 Shattuck, 61.

50 See Derain.

51 Derain signed a receipt for 3,300 francs from Vollard in exchange for 89 paintings and 80 drawings (Archives Vollard).

52 Freeman, 179.

53 This comment inspired Gertrude Stein's "Sacred Emily," in which the words "Rose is a rose is a rose is a rose" appear for the first time; see Simon, 279, n.79.

54 Derain, 154.

55 Derain to Matisse, Mar. 8, 1906; in Freeman, 201.

56 Cited by Georges Duthuit, "Le Fauvisme," *Cahiers d'Art* IV (1929), 29.

57 RoseAnna Warren, "A Metaphysic of Painting: The Notes of André Derain," *The Georgia Review* (Athens) 32:1 (spring, 1978), 141.

58 Derain, 146–7.

59 Maurice Vlaminck, *Tournant Dangereux* (Paris: Stock, 1929), 98.

60 Purrmann to Barr, Mar. 3, 1951; in Alfred J. Barr, *Matisse, His Art and His Public* (New York: The Museum of Modern Art, 1951), 94 n.3, 533.

61 Golding, 140 n.2, sees the masklike face of the central figure in Derain's *Bathers I* as the first example of a synthesis of Cézanne and tribal art; he suggests that it was inspired by a Congolese mask in the collection of Paul Haviland, brother of Picasso's friend Frank Burty Haviland. However, Flam finds this suggestion "clearly unacceptable, for there is no African influence . . . in the painting." See Jack Flam, "Matisse and the Fauves," in *"Primitivism" in 20th Century Art* I (New York: The Museum of Modern Art, 1984), 219.

62 Kahnweiler 1961, 45–6.

63 Golding believes they may have worked together in Derain's sculpture studio.

64 Apollinaire 1913, 16.

65 See Vol. I, 306.

66 Information about Princet's life was kindly supplied to me by Linda Dalrymple Henderson.

67 Derain, 221.

68 Jennifer Mundy, "Conservative Art can also be Good Art," *The Art Newspaper* (London) (Jan., 1991), 14.

5 THREE WOMEN pp.79–91

1 Toklas 1963, 35.

2 Olivier 1988, n.p.

3 Stein 1933, 27–8.

4 Toklas 1963, 35.

5 Olivier 1933, 133.

6 Ibid., 133–4; see Vol. I, 325.

7 Stein 1933, 20.

8 For many years part of this panel was lost; it has now been put back together again.

9 Vol. I, 316.

10 Toklas 1963, 36.

11 Stein 1933, 26.

12 Toklas 1963, 133.

13 Ibid., 36.

14 Daix 1992, 311, has finally set the record straight.

15 Braque in conversation with the author.

16 Z.II*.5 and other related studies also exerted an influence on Braque.

17 Olivier 1933, 97–8.

18 Seckel, 65.

19 A letter from Fernande to Gertrude Stein, undated but evidently written during her separation from Picasso (fall, 1907), confirms that she will be bringing Madame Vorvane, i.e., Marcelle, to tea the following Friday (Beinecke Library). Marcelle would therefore have been known to the *bande à Picasso* well before the end of 1907.

20 Françoise Gilot in conversation with the author.

21 Kahnweiler to G. Stein, [1933] (Beinecke Library). Denise Laurens has also confirmed that Marcelle and her mother-in-law, the wife of Henri Laurens, had been old friends but that "Marcelle was not free when she met Braque."

22 Judith Cousins in conversation with Marilyn McCully reports that Carl Einstein was a witness at the wedding of Georges and Marcelle Braque in the early 1920s.

23 Daix 1995, 143.

24 Burgess, 401.

25 Stein 1933, 64.

26 Ibid., 65.

27 Ibid., 18.

28 Pierre Daix, "Derain et Braque," *André Derain: Le peintre du "trouble moderne"* (Paris: Musée d'Art Moderne de la Ville de Paris, 1994), 78.

29 Braque's appointment in Feb., 1908, is confirmed on a postcard from "L.M."; Cousins, 349. Freeman, 109, has suggested that Picasso also painted "L.M."

30 Burgess, 405.

31 Cousins, 351.

32 Fernande to G. Stein, June 17, 1910 (Beinecke Library).

33 Inez Haynes Irwin, Apr. 14, 1908; in Rubin, Seckel, Cousins, 156.

34 Burgess, 408; 401; 406.

35 Burgess to Inez Haynes Irwin, May 22, 1908; in Rubin, Seckel, Cousins, 156.

36 Burgess to Inez Haynes Irwin, May 29, 1908; ibid.

37 In Vol. I, 324, I suggested that the curious appearance of Wiegels (who apparently signed his paintings G. Wiegels) may have contributed to the androgynous looks of Picasso's young *saltimbanques*. Gautherie-Kampka disputes this on the grounds that Wiegels's official request for change of domicile from Düsseldorf to Paris dates from Aug. 3, 1906, that is to say, post-*saltimbanques*. However, this does not preclude Wiegels's having resided in Paris prior to 1906. See Annette Gautherie-Kampka, "Le Cercle des artistes du café du Dôme: 1903–14," doctoral thesis (Lyon: Université Lumière, 1993).

38 Olivier 1988, 228. See also Vol. I, 324.

39 Olivier 1988, n.p.

40 In March, 1908, Picasso was distressed to learn that his Uncle Salvador, the distinguished doctor whom he had rebelled against when he was a student, was seriously ill. He wrote his cousins Concha and María: "I've just received a letter from Lola telling me that your father is very ill, and you can imagine the state I am in having just heard the news. Write me every day if there is any new development since I am worried the whole time." (Reproduced in facsimile in Ricardo Huelin y Ruiz-Blasco, *Pablo Ruiz Picasso* [Madrid: Biblioteca de la Revista de Occidente, 1975], 404.) Picasso's uncle died on Mar. 31, 1908.

41 Daix 1995, 203.

42 On stylistic grounds, the late Anatoli Podoksik claimed that these memento moris date from late 1907, that is to say, six to nine months before Wiegels's suicide; Podoksik, 154. For once I cannot agree with him. The inclusion of a mirror reflecting a framed sketch for the Boston *Standing Nude* (spring, 1908) in the more finished memento mori points to a later date. As for the unusually expressionistic style and dissonant color, it is no more typical of late 1907 than it is of summer, 1908.

43 Vol. I, 324.

44 Olivier 1933, 73.

45 Olivier 1988, n.p.

46 This drawing also appears to be a preparatory sketch for a small bronze sculpture.

47 J. B. de C. M. Saunders and Charles D. O'Malley, *The Illustrations from the Works of Andreas Vesalius of Brussels* (Cleveland: World Publishing, 1950), 29.

48 See Daix 1988B.

49 Marilyn McCully has pointed out that although Matisse's painting is known in English as *Bathers with a Turtle*, the type of chelonia represented is, in fact, a common Mediterranean tortoise (*Testudo graeca* or *Testudo hermanni*), often kept as a household or studio pet. Cécile (Lucie) Vidil, a model at Matisse's Academy, was photographed nude circa 1911 in the studio of her lover, Per Krogh, standing next to a small tortoise (Klüver and Martin, 42); Fernande also recounts that among the animals Picasso kept at the boulevard de Clichy studio from 1909 were two dogs, three cats and a tortoise (Olivier 1988, n.p.).

50 Picasso to the Steins, May 26, 1908 (Beinecke Library).

51 Picasso to Leo Stein, June 14, 1908 (Beinecke Library).

52 Ibid.

53 Baldassari, 177.

6 LA RUE-DES-BOIS pp.93–99

1 Picasso to the Steins, Aug. 14, 1908 (Beinecke Library).

2 Malraux, 137.

3 Sarrazin, 13.

4 The villagers were equally dismissive of Picasso. They called him the "*barbouilleur*" (dauber); Sarrazin, 14.

5 Olivier 1988, n.p.

6 Lanchner and Rubin, 61.

7 Ibid., 11.

8 Malraux, 135.

9 Lanchner and Rubin, 48.

10 Madsen, 65–6.

11 Cousins, 353.

12 Vallier, 14.

13 Quoted by John Russell, *Georges Braque* (London: Phaidon, 1959), 8.

14 Braque 1957.

15 Ibid.

16 The role of *passage* has been discussed and disputed at considerable length by William Rubin and Leo Steinberg in an exchange of articles: Leo Steinberg, "Resisting Cézanne: Picasso's *Three Women*," *Art in America* (New York) 66:6 (Nov.–Dec., 1978), 115–33; William Rubin, "Pablo and Georges and Leo and Bill," *Art in America* (New York) 67:2 (Mar.–Apr., 1979), 128–47; Leo Steinberg, "The Polemical Part," ibid., 114–27.

17 Alfred J. Barr was the first to define *passage* in English in *Cubism and Abstract Art* (New York: The Museum of Modern Art, 1936); for further discussion see Daix 1995, 672–3.

18 Vallier, 16.

19 Olivier 1988, n.p.

20 Ibid.

21 Fernande to Apollinaire, Aug. 21, 1908; in Caizergues and Seckel, 69.

22 Ibid., 70.

23 Olivier 1988, n.p.

24 Vallentin, 157.

25 Picasso to the Steins, Sept. 13, 1908 (Beinecke Library).

7 THE COMING OF CUBISM pp.101–121

1 Although Kahnweiler apparently changed his exhibition schedule, Monod-Fontaine 1984B, 98, has traced an exhibition catalog, *Peintures de Pierre Girieud. Grès de Francisco Durio* (Oct. 25–Nov. 14, 1908); for further discussion, see Cousins, 436 n.65.

2 The first printed mention of "cubes" occurs in Vauxcelles's review (*Gil Blas*, Nov. 14, 1908) of Kahnweiler's exhibition of Braque's work. And the first actual mention of "cubism"—that convenient but misleading term—occurs in a muddle-headed article (*Mercure de France*, Apr. 16, 1909) by Charles Morice, in which Braque is castigated as being "on the whole a victim—setting Cubism aside—of an admiration for Cézanne that is too exclusive or ill-considered." For further discussion, see Cousins, 435–6 n.62.

3 Vallier, 18.

4 Guillaume Apollinaire, *Mercure de France*, Jan. 16, 1909.

5 Vallier, 18.

6 Golding, 15. For further and extensive discussion of the history of cubism, see Golding's well-documented and thoughtful study.

7 Picasso to de Zayas, 1923; in Fry, 168.

8 Gilot, 272.

9 Picasso in conversation with the author.

10 Roger Allard, "Die Kennzeichen der Erneuerung in der Malerei," *Der Blaue Reiter* (Munich, 1912), 35–40; in Fry, 70.

11 Picasso to Zervos, 1935; in Ashton, 10.

12 Richardson 1959, 9.

13 *Paris-Journal*, Jan. 1, 1912; in Cousins, 388.

14 Vallier, 14–16.

15 Ibid., 16.

16 Ibid.

17 Golding, 7.

18 Apollinaire 1913, 23.

19 Cousins, 355.

20 See Vol. I, 392.

21 Albert Kostenevich, "Russian Collectors of French Art: The Shchukin and Morozov Families," *Morozov and Shchukin —The Russian Collectors* (Essen: Museum Folkwang, 1993), 72–3, cites the 1908 article by Pavel Muratov, which lists the major works in Shchukin's collection: no Picassos are included.

22 See letters from Shchukin to Matisse, May–July, 1908; in Kostenevich and Semyonova, 161–2.

23 Olivier 1933, 119.

24 Ibid.

25 Ibid.

26 Jacqueline Picasso in conversation with the author.

27 Olivier 1933, 118.

28 Cousins, 359.

29 For further discussion of the identity of the portrait, see Lanchner and Rubin, 126.

30 Picasso to Florent Fels (*Propos d'artistes*); trans. in Shattuck, 67.

31 Judith Cousins and Hélène Seckel, "Eléments pour une chronologie de l'histoire des *Demoiselles d'Avignon*," in *Les Demoiselles d'Avignon* 2 (Paris: Musée Picasso, 1988), 562.

32 Ibid., 33–4.

33 Madsen, 84.

34 Leo Stein, 191.

35 Ibid., 182.

36 Stein 1933, 103.

37 Mellow, 139.

38 Shattuck, 66.

39 Laporte, 31.

40 Olivier 1933, 68.

41 Ibid.

42 Salmon 1956, 57.

43 Besides those names mentioned in this account, the guests included Braque, Ramon and Germaine Pichot and her sister and brother-in-law (the Fornerods), the Ageros, René Dalize, Jacques Vaillant and almost certainly Wilhelm Uhde and his bride, Sonia, who would soon transfer her affections to Delaunay. Juan Gris, who lived in the Bateau Lavoir, and Manolo are also likely to have been present.

44 Olivier 1933, 69.

45 Ibid.

46 Seckel 68, 69 n.35.

47 Olivier 1933, 92.

48 Ibid., 66.

49 Shattuck, 61.

50 Ibid.

51 Seckel, 69 n.31.

52 Léger in conversation with the author.

53 This work is thought to be *Paysage exotique*, 1908 (no. 217 in Dora Vallier's *catalogue raisonné* of Rousseau's works).

54 Daix and Rosselet, 241.

55 The late Edward Fry once showed me a photograph of a drawing for this painting, which turned out to be a fake after a lost drawing.

56 John Klein, "New Lessons from the School of Chatou: Derain and Vlaminck in the Paris Suburbs," in Freeman, 141.

57 First pointed out by Jane Lee in "L'Enchanteur pourrissant," *Revue de l'art* (Paris) 82 (1988), 60 n.9.

58 Ibid., 52.

59 See Vol. I, 225.

60 Baldassari, fig. 77.

61 Ansen, 34.

62 The late Christian Geelhaar, who was the first scholar to study this painting in the light of *Carnaval au bistro*, felt that the study for the still life in the margin of the *Carnaval* drawings was the point of departure for *Bread and Fruit Dish on a Table*. Rubin is convinced that "the margin sketch was made during the execution of *Bread and Fruit Dish on a Table*." At Rubin's urging, Geelhaar subsequently changed his mind. I think he was right the first time, and that the juxtaposition of these studies explains the eucharistic theme. See Rubin 1983, 624.

63 Daix and Rosselet, 252.

64 Braque in conversation with the author.

65 Baldassari, 112.

66 Daix 1995, 519, credits Dominique Bozo with pointing out this painting's link to Braque and Apollinaire.

67 Willard Bohn, "In Pursuit of the Fourth Dimension: Guillaume Apollinaire and Max Weber," *Arts Magazine* (New York) 54 (June 1980), 166–9.

68 Albert Gleizes, Oct. 4, 1912; in Henderson 1983, 61.

69 Ibid., 53.

70 Braque 1957.

8 THE SECOND VISIT TO HORTA pp. 123–137

1 Fernande to Toklas, May 15, 1909 (Beinecke Library).

2 Ibid.

3 Fernande and Picasso to G. Stein, May 16, 1909 (Beinecke Library).

4 Ibid.

5 The so-called Guayaba group had been meeting in the studio on riera Sant Joan that Picasso had shared with Carles Casagemas, in 1901, and Angel de Soto, in 1903. To make way for the construction of the Via Laietana in 1908, the building, and with it the trompe l'œil murals Picasso and Casagemas had executed in 1901, was demolished.

6 O'Brian, 171.

7 Vol. I, 498 n.29.

8 These drawings look so far ahead that Palau has mistaken a study (PF.II 384) for *Le Pont Neuf* (spring, 1911) as one of this series; PF.II, 135.

9 Daix 1993, 94.

10 See p. 165.

11 Fernande and Picasso to G. Stein, [late July], 1909 (Beinecke Library).

12 Membrado is a very common name in Horta and not all of its bearers were related. Tobies Membrado was the brother of Joaquim Membrado, but the brothers were apparently unrelated to Josefa Sebastià Membrado (although I suggested that possibility in Vol. I, 105), who was the daughter of Joaquim Sebastià Andreu and whom Picasso had drawn during his first stay in Horta in 1898.

13 Fernande to Toklas, June 15, 1909 (Beinecke Library).

14 Fernande to Toklas, [July], 1909 (Beinecke Library).

15 Fernande to Toklas, June 28, 1909 (Beinecke Library).

16 Fernande to Toklas, June 26, 1909 (Beinecke Library).

17 Ibid.

18 Ibid. According to Palau i Fabre 1991, 19, when the *tonto* would enter the local bar he would immediately go to Fernande and salute her with a thumb and fist gesture, which she would return.

19 Fernande to Toklas, June 26, 1909 (Beinecke Library).

20 Ibid.

21 Fernande to G. Stein, [mid-July], 1909 (Beinecke Library).

22 Malraux, 138.

23 Picasso to G. Stein, June 24, 1909 (Beinecke Library).

24 Palau i Fabre 1991, 20, recounts that Picasso told him that he had painted the palm trees in the Horta scene because they made a good effect.

25 There was no brick factory in Horta; rather the buildings depicted are said to have been at that time a series of olive oil presses, known locally as "the factory." Maria-Lluisa Borràs, on the other hand, has proposed that a brick factory did in fact exist, but it was located on the River Ebro in Tortosa, where Picasso and Fernande had stayed on their journey to Horta; see Albert Kostenevich in *Impressionisti e post-impressionisti dai musei sovietici*, 2 (Lugano: Thyssen-Bornemisza Foundation, 1987), 126. However, the chimney, which Borràs (and Palau) have associated with brick factories, could equally represent the chimneys where the olive leaves and branches are burned. These are still a feature of the local countryside.

26 Fernande to Toklas, June 15, 1909 (Beinecke Library).

27 The images of the man with his arms folded are usually thought to date from earlier in the year, but since they portray the same man as Z.II*.166, which Picasso told Daix was painted in Horta (Daix and Rosselet, 246), they were presumably done at the same time. The Centre Picasso d'Horta believes the model to be the younger brother of Manuel Pallarès, Salvadoret. However, contemporary photographs show Salvadoret to be a young man with huge ears and narrow sloping shoulders, quite unlike the build of the so-called *Athlete*.

28 The photograph of the *guardia civil* is located in the Archives Picasso. It was unavailable for reproduction here because of a forthcoming publication by the Musée Picasso concerning Picasso's stay in Horta.

29 Paul Hayes Tucker, "Picasso, Photography and the Development of Cubism," *Art Bulletin* (New York), 64:2 (June, 1982), 293, was the first to point out the similarity of Picasso's use of *passage* to its "counterpart" in photography "known as halation . . . a variety of blurring effects a camera can produce." Similar effects are evident in Picasso's paintings as well as his photographs, where roofs fade off into other areas and these other areas fade off into the sky.

30 Stein 1933, 91.

31 McCully, 64.

32 Stein 1933, 90.

33 Rubin 1983, 645.

34 Palau i Fabre 1990, 144, suggests that the painter merged "the primitive idea of the cone, inspired by the mountain of Santa Barbara" and linked it to the face of Fernande. He also compared the twist of the mountain to the twist of her neck.

35 Leighten, 111.

36 Baldassari, 192.

37 Daix 1995, 186.

38 Drawings for the Anis del Mono bottle and other still-life objects, including a ceramic *botijo* (drinking vessel) in the shape of a cock (water or wine is poured through the tail and drunk through the beak), appear in one of Picasso's Horta sketchbooks (Picasso Heirs).

39 Vol. I, 102–3.

40 Pallarès died aged ninety-eight, in 1974.

41 Roberto Otero in conversation with the author.

42 Picasso to the Steins, [July], 1909 (Beinecke Library).

43 James Joll, *The Anarchists* (London: Eyre & Spottiswoode, 1964), 236.

44 Temma Kaplan, *Red City—Blue Period: Social Movements in Picasso's Barcelona* (Berkeley: University of California Press, 1992), 99–101.

45 Vol. I, 72–3.

46 Picasso to the Steins, [July], 1909 (Beinecke Library).

47 Picasso to the Steins, [August], 1909 (Beinecke Library).

48 Picasso and Fernande to the Steins, [July–August], 1909, (Beinecke Library).

49 Fernande to G. Stein, [mid-July], 1909 (Beinecke Library).

50 Fernande to G. Stein, [late August] (Beinecke Library).

51 Fernande to G. Stein, Sept. 7, 1909 (Beinecke Library).

9 FAREWELL TO BOHEMIA pp. 139–151

1 Vol. I, 456.

2 In the 1930s Picasso told Julio González that with the early cubist paintings "it is only necessary to cut them out—the colors are the only indications of different perspectives, of planes inclined from one side or the other—then assemble them according to the indications given by the color, in order to find oneself in the presence of a 'Sculpture'"; quoted in Marilyn McCully, "Julio González and Pablo Picasso: A Documentary Chronology of a Working Relationship," *Picasso: Sculptor/Painter* (London: Tate Gallery, 1994), 219.

3 Picasso owned two casts of this Venus; when he acquired them we do not know.

4 The dealer had bought the plaster in 1910 and lost no time casting it in bronze.

5 In the late 1950s the Paris dealer Heinz Berggruen acquired one of the two original plasters from the Jacques Ullman collection. Ullman had acquired it from Edouard Jonas, who had purchased a share of the Vollard inheritance from the dealer's sisters. In exchange for allowing a second edition of bronzes to be made (in 1959)—numbered from one to nine—Picasso received the original and a third of the casts.

6 Daix 1977, 105, and Werner Spies, *Picasso: Das plastische Werk* (Stuttgart: Gerd Hatje, 1983), 53, think these plasters antedate the large head. Like Rubin 1972, 203 n.2, I think they postdate it. Karmel, 272 n.18, thinks that they were done in 1911.

7 Palau i Fabre 1990, 165, mistakes this for a self-portrait.

8 Rubin 1984, 340 n.182.

9 Kahnweiler 1949, 3.

10 Olivier 1933, 139–40.

11 The Steins' purchases were *Houses on the Hill, Horta de Ebro* (Z.II*.161), *The Reservoir* (Z.II*.157) and *Head and Shoulders of a Woman* (Z.II.*167). Haviland bought *Factory at Horta* (Z.II*.158) in 1909, but according to Podoksik, 176, it was in Kahnweiler's possession when it was bought by Shchukin in 1910–11.

12 Picasso to Apollinaire, Jan. 10, 1910; in Caizergues and Seckel, 75.

13 Stein 1933, 96.

14 Olivier 1933, 135.

15 Ibid., 136.

16 Françoise Gilot, "From Refuse to Riddle," *Art and Antiques* (New York), (summer, 1992), 57.

17 Olivier 1933, 137.

18 Ibid., 135.

19 Olivier 1988, n.p.

20 Olivier 1933, 135, 153.

21 Ibid., 153.

22 Fernande to G. Stein, June 17, 1910 (Beinecke Library).

23 Olivier 1933, 143.

24 Stein 1933, 110.

25 Fernande, Picasso, Cremnitz, Ramon and Germaine Pichot to Gertrude, Dec. 29, 1909 (Beinecke Library).

26 Olivier 1933, 139.

27 Ibid., 154.

28 Ibid., 144.

29 Ibid.

30 Andreu, 56.

31 Olivier 1988, 242.

32 Andreu, 57.

33 Ibid., 57–8.

34 Max Jacob, *La Défense de Tartuffe* (Paris: Gallimard, 1964), 108.

35 Seckel, 70.

36 Leroy C. Breunig, "Max Jacob et Picasso," *Mercure de France* 1132 (Dec. 1, 1957), 594.

37 For further discussion of the various accounts, see Seckel, 71.

38 Ibid., 72.

39 Seckel, 73 n.17.

40 Ibid.

41 Picasso to Xavier Gonzales (1938); in Daix 1995, 782.

42 Braque in conversation with the author.

43 Vol. I, 186.

44 There seem to have been two mandolins in Picasso's studio: one long-necked, one shortish. Karmel, 120.

45 Vallier, 16.

46 Z.XXVI.390; Daix and Rosselet, 250.

47 Penrose, 165.

48 Ibid.

49 *La Maison Tellier*—about a country outing organized by a madam for her girls—was one of Guy de Maupassant's best-known stories. Vollard published a deluxe edition in 1935 illustrated with Degas's brothel monotypes (some of which Picasso acquired in 1958).

50 Penrose, 165.

51 Pepe Karmel in conversation with the author.

10 CADAQUÉS—1910 pp. 153–165

1 Gibson, 145.

2 Fernande to G. Stein, June 17, 1910 (Beinecke Library). Klüver and Martin, 37, have dated a photograph of Matisse and his family taken in Collioure, summer, 1910.

3 Picasso to Apollinaire, [June 29], 1910; in Caizergues and Seckel, 76–7.

4 Ibid., 12–13.

5 Gibson, 144.

6 The house was located directly on the water, near the plaça ses Herbes. Palau (Palau i Fabre 1990, 488) has mistakenly suggested that the house was situated on the central plaça de Federic Raholà.

7 Fernande to G. Stein, July 14, 1910 (Beinecke Library).

8 Dawn Ades, *Dalí* (London: Thames and Hudson, 1982), 39.

9 Gibson, 144.

10 Ibid.

11 Palau i Fabre 1990, 487.

12 Although there is no record in the Archives Picasso to suggest that Dalí actually sent these cards every year, Pichot's nephew has claimed that family legend has it that the year Picasso did not receive one of these cards, he became nervous (Antoni Pixtot [who uses the Catalan spelling of his name] in conversation with Marilyn McCully).

13 Palau (Palau i Fabre 1990, 488), was told this by Alice Derain.

14 Fernande to G. Stein, July 14, 1910 (Beinecke Library).

15 Braque in conversation with the author.

16 Karmel, 91.

17 Ibid.

18 The relevance of X-ray photographs to cubism was first proposed by Stephen Kern in *The Culture of Time and Space: 1880–1918* (London: Weidenfeld and Nicolson, 1983), 147. It is further studied in Henderson 1988.

19 Henderson 1988, 324.

20 MP Carnets 1.20, 2r.

21 Daix and Rosselet, 258, catalog the work as *Man Rowing*.

22 Anne Carnegie Edgerton, "Picasso's 'Nude Woman' of 1910," *Burlington Magazine* (London), 122:928 (July 1980), 499–503.

23 For instance, the drawing (PF.II.534) which Palau entitles *Arabesque of Sails and Waves* represents one of those old-fashioned, semi-cylindrical blotters: a desk-set accessory.

24 Seckel, 76, 84 n.3.

25 Cousins, 367.

26 Kahnweiler wrote Picasso: "*Vous avez dont ce qu'il y a à faire en changeant la 'justification.' Si le rectangle noir sur la page blanche, vous paraît trop petit, on peut l'enlargir y et l'allonger. Faites-moi donc un dessin du rectangle comme vous le voyez sur une feuille de papier du format.*

Je viens de voir Braque à qui j'ai montré le prospectus. Il trouve le caractère très joli et comme moi il est d'avis qu'il n'est pas trop petit" (Archives Picasso).

27 Andreu, 70.

28 Palau interprets the rosette as "the outline of Mademoiselle Léonie's face converted into a sort of subliminated and fantasized rose. . . . An anchored boat is cleaved within the head" (Palau i Fabre 1990, 183).

29 Picasso sent Derain a postcard soon after his arrival in early July: "*Nous sommes dejà a Cadaques. Je espere que tes promesses des visites vont se realiser. Pour arriver[?] ici se tres facille si tu veux je te donnerai des detailles.*" My thanks to Jane Lee for making a copy of this document available to me (Derain Archives, Chambourcy).

30 Salvador Dalí, "Sant Sebastià," *L'Amic de les Arts* (Sitges) 16 (July 31, 1920); in Gibson, 183.

31 Salmon relates Derain's view to El Greco's *View of Toledo*, which had been included in the 1908 Salon d'Automne retrospective. He even congratulates the artist on restoring El Greco to his rightful glory. See Jane Lee, *Derain* (Oxford: Phaidon, 1990), 33.

32 Lucian Freud remembers Picasso humming "Tipperary" for him and declaring that it was a favorite of his.

33 Olivier 1988, 240.

34 Brassaï, 238.

35 Ibid.

36 Fernande to G. Stein, Aug. 10, 1910 (Beinecke Library).

37 Cousins, 368.

38 Fernande to Toklas, Aug. 12, 1910 (Beinecke Library): "*En ce moment est ici avec nous un ami d'enfance de Pablo de Barcelone lequel est revenu avec nous.*"

39 Rubin 1989, 64. Rubin believes Picasso began work on two of the narrower panels before he left Cadaqués.

40 Fernande to G. Stein, July 14, 1910 (Beinecke Library).

41 Kahnweiler 1920, 10. Had Kahnweiler not been writing from memory (the outbreak of war had stranded him in Switzerland without access to his photographic records), he might have been more cautious about dating this vital "shattering of the enclosed form" specifically to Cadaqués.

11 CUBIST COMMISSIONS AND PORTRAITS pp. 167–181

1 I am indebted to William Rubin, who was the first scholar to resurrect the Field commission (in Rubin 1989, 63–9) and to identify the various paintings (sometimes reworked) that constituted the series. Hamilton Easter Field's cousin John Field has also kindly provided me with information concerning the family and the project.

2 Bolger, 87.

3 Ibid., 82.

4 According to John Field.

5 Bolger, 87.

6 Critical response to Matisse at the 1910 Salon is given in Flam, 282.

7 Picasso generally used standard French canvas formats, which are as follows (in centimeters):

No.	Figure (F)	Paysage (P)	Marine (M)
0	18×14	18×12	18×10
1	22×16	22×14	22×12
2	24×19	24×16	24×14
3	27×22	27×19	27×16
4	33×24	33×22	33×19
5	35×27	35×24	35×22
6	41×33	41×27	41×24
8	46×38	46×33	46×27
10	55×46	55×38	55×33
12	61×50	61×46	61×38
15	65×54	65×50	65×46
20	73×60	73×54	73×50
25	81×65	81×60	81×54
30	92×73	92×65	92×60
40	100×81	100×73	100×65
50	116×89	116×81	116×73
60	130×97	130×89	130×81
80	146×114	146×97	146×89
100	162×130	162×114	162×97
120	195×130	195×114	195×97

8 Daix 1977, 115 n.19.

9 McBride, 3.

10 Stieglitz to Hamilton Easter Field, Oct. 21, 1911 (Beinecke Library).

11 There appears to be no other reference to the Field commission in any of Kahnweiler's writings or gallery records that it has been possible to consult.

12 McBride, 3.

13 None of the panels was sold to a Russian collector, as Field or Laurent later believed (Bolger, 87).

14 Only the Uhde portrait was probably finished in the spring (in time for the May show of Picasso's work at Uhde's gallery on rue Notre-Dame-des-Champs).

15 A letter from Fernande to Gertrude Stein, June 17, 1910 (Beinecke Library), confirms that Picasso was at work on the Vollard portrait.

16 Uhde 1938, 155.

17 Gilot, 49.

18 Vol. I, 199.

19 Ibid., 195.

20 Olivier 1933, 144.

21 Breunig, 122–3.

22 Ibid., 123

23 Confirmed by Dora Maar to the author.

24 Gilot, 73.

25 Ibid.

26 Ashton, 64.

27 Dora Maar in conversation with the author.

28 Rubin 1984, 310.

29 Baldassari, 118.

30 Gris to Picasso, May 31, 1917; Gris to Picasso, Aug. 7, 1917 (Archives Picasso).

31 Kahnweiler 1961, 61.

32 Salmon 1961, 278.

33 Severini, 149.

34 Discussed in Chapter 14.

35 The exhibition held at the Galerie Boëtie in October, 1912, was called the Section d'Or and included the Puteaux group (notably Gleizes, Marcel Duchamp and Jacques Villon). Works were shown by more than thirty painters, many of whom had participated in the cubist manifestation of the Salon des Indépendants the previous year. Although Delaunay and Le Fauconnier abstained, Gris was added to this group.

36 Salmon 1961, 277.

37 Cocteau, *Le Passé defini* II (Paris: Gallimard, 1953), 159.

38 Picasso in conversation with the author.

39 Francis Berthier, "La merveilleuse et grande aventure de Roger Dutilleul," in *La Collection Dutilleul* (Paris: Galerie des Arts, [1983]), 60.

40 Gris to Kahnweiler, Feb. 17, 1920; in Kahnweiler 1956, 78.

41 Stein 1933, 111.

42 Olivier 1988, 240.

43 Ibid., 243.

44 Ibid., 242.

45 Ibid., 241.

46 Ibid.

47 Stein 1933, 136.

48 Fernande to G. Stein, July 5, 1911 (Beinecke Library).

12 SUMMER AT CÉRET—1911 pp. 183–197

1 Picasso and Fernande to Apollinaire, Aug. 24, 1911; in Caizergues and Seckel, 88.

2 Picasso to Fernande, Aug. 8, 1911; in facsimile in original French edition of Olivier 1933.

3 Picasso to Braque, July 25, 1911; in Cousins, 376.

4 Ibid., 375–6.

5 The description of the composition appears in Picasso's letter of July 25, 1911, to Braque, quoted in part in Rubin 1989, 54 n.3

6 Picasso to Braque, July 25, 1911; in Cousins, 375.

7 I am indebted to Michael Raeburn for this suggestion.

8 Braque to Kahnweiler, Sept., 1911; in Cousins, 380.

9 Picasso to Braque, July 25, 1911; in Cousins, 376.

10 It is not without relevance that Japanese strippers refer to a certain erotic movement as "doing the accordion."

11 Olivier 1988, 232. Fernande mentions Déodat de Séverac in connection with Henri Bloch, that is to say, circa 1905. The earliest extant letter from Déodat to Picasso is dated 1908 (Archives Picasso): Déodat encourages Picasso (and, he hopes, the Derains) to vacation with him in Carcassonne.

12 For the most accurate study of the *cobla* instruments in Picasso's Céret paintings, see: Lewis Kachur, "Picasso, popular music and collage Cubism (1911–12)," *The Burlington Magazine* (London) 35:1081 (Apr., 1993), 252–60.

13 Olivier 1988, 226.

14 Karmel, 156–8, notes the connection between the drawings and photograph.

15 For example, Z.VI.1161, Z.XXVIII.154, Z.VI.1147, Z.XXVIII.28, Z.XXVIII.168

16 The legend of the Pont du Diable is as follows: after an engineer had made two unsuccessful attempts to build a bridge across the river Tech, the Devil proposed to him that he (the Devil) would construct it during the night, so long as he was given the soul of the first person to cross the bridge. As he worked away he conjured up sweet Catalan music so that the townspeople would not awaken. At dawn the engineer foiled the Devil by getting a black cat to cross the bridge; the cat awoke a cock, which startled the Devil, who failed to place the last stone. For tricking him, the Devil told the engineer that he would try to demolish the bridge. The Céretans then built two more bridges so that the Devil's prediction would fail to come true.

17 Gilot, 76.

18 Vallier, 16.

19 Rubin 1989, 56 n.35.

20 Karmel in conversation with the author.

21 Richardson 1959, 26.

22 Rubin 1989, 24, describes him as an accordion player, but the artist confirmed to Hope, Cooper, Leymarie and myself that he is a guitarist. Braque told some of us that the bar in question was at Marseille, others that it was at Le Havre. Le Havre is more likely, given that he had repeatedly visited his parents there in 1911, but had not been to Marseille since Nov., 1910.

23 Picasso to Fernande, Aug. 8, 1911; see note 2 above.

24 Cousins, 382.

25 Picasso misdated this letter Aug. 17. Braque had written on the 15th that he planned to be in Limoges on the 17th.

26 Golding, 91.

27 MoMA Symposium, 110.

28 Braque was so pleased with this engraving that he did a painting after it known as *La Table de Bar* (Romilly 117).

29 Rubin 1989, 45. A short version of the first four chapters of Kahnweiler's book was published as "Der Kubismus," in *Die Weißen Blätter* (Zurich–Leipzig), (Sept., 1916), 209–22. The book itself appeared in 1920. See Fry 160. For further discussion see Mark Roskill, "Braque's *Papiers Collés* and the Feminine Side to Cubism," MoMA Symposium, 223.

30 According to Dora Maar in conversation with the author

31 Quoted in Rubin 1989, 44. This article would subsequently be the basis for Soffici's pioneer book *Cubismo e altre*, which would appear in 1913. Soffici's text would then be adapted to a Russian version by Aksenov, which was published in 1917 (with a cover by Soffici's Russian girlfriend, the artist Alexandra Exter).

32 Rubin 1989, 43.

13 L'AFFAIRE DES STATUETTES pp. 199–205

1 Pieret to Apollinaire, [1911]; in Stallano, 20.

2 Fleuret, 177.

3 Ibid.

4 Pieret to Apollinaire [1911]; in Stallano, 20.

5 Pieret to Apollinaire, May 8, 1911; ibid.

6 Steegmuller 1963, 170.

7 Fleuret, 184.

8 Apollinaire to Gide, June, 1911; in Adéma, 187.

9 Apollinaire to Picasso, July 24, 1911; in Caizergues and Seckel, 85.

10 Apollinaire claimed in an interview in *Le Matin* (Sept. 13, 1911) that Pieret left his apartment on the rue Gros for good on Aug. 21.

11 Steegmuller 1963, 168.

12 Olivier 1933, 147–8.

13 Steegmuller 1963, 174.

14 Ibid., 175.

15 Salmon 1956, 117. Pieret's letters have subsequently disappeared. According to various accounts, they were last in the possession of the Paris police.

16 Steegmuller 1963, 176.

17 Olivier 1933, 149.

18 Ibid.

19 Penrose, 178.

20 Gilbert Prouteau (*Paris Presse*, June 20, 1959); in Steegmuller 1963, 188.

21 Daix 1993, 141–2.

22 Roché Carnet 51:1 (Ransom Center).

23 Adéma, 153.

24 Cecily Mackworthy, *Guillaume Apollinaire and the Cubist Life* (New York: Horizon Press, 1963), 140.

25 Serge Férat to Soffici, July 24, 1912 (Soffici Archive).

26 Robert Couffignal, *L'Inspiration biblique dans l'œuvre de Guillaume Apollinaire* (Paris: Minard/Lettres Modernes, 1966), 139.

27 Steegmuller 1963, 198.

28 Ibid.

29 "Le Satyre masqué," "Le Vol de la Joconde," *Le Passant* (Paris), 4 (Nov. 18, 1911).

30 Stallano, 13, says he signed his articles "Jouven" or "Jean Loupoigne."

31 Les Treize, "Les Lettres. Les poètes et les présages," *L'Intransigeant* (July 27, 1924), 2.

32 Halicka, 47.

14 THE OTHER CUBISTS: JACKDAWS IN PEACOCKS' FEATHERS pp. 207–219

1 Steegmuller 1963, 187.

2 Breunig, 114.

3 Ibid., 183.

4 See Vol. I, 333.

5 Breunig, 151.

6 Umberto Boccioni, Carlo D. Carrà, Luigi Russolo, Giacomo Balla, Gino Severini, "The Exhibitors to the Public," Feb. 5, 1912; trans. in Joshua C. Taylor, *Futurism* (New York: The Museum of Modern Art, 1961), 127.

7 Kahnweiler 1961, 46.

8 Robbins 1985, 13.

9 Ibid., 18.

10 Cousins, 380.

11 McCully, 92.

12 Cabanne, 143.

13 Ibid.

14 Cousins, 381.

15 Golding, 149.

16 Fry, 59–60.

17 Kahnweiler to Robbins; in Robbins 1964, 17 n.13.

18 Assouline, 176.

19 Pierre, 52.

20 Assouline, 177.

21 Robbins 1985, 19.

22 Ibid.

23 Robbins 1964, 30.

24 According to Douglas Cooper.

25 Vallier, 19.

26 Daix 1995, 813.

27 Albert Gleizes and Jean Metzinger, "Cubism" (1912); in Robert L. Herbert, *Modern Artists on Art* (Englewood Cliffs, N.J.: Prentice-Hall, 1964), 4.

28 Braque in conversation with the author.

29 Caizergues and Seckel, 94.

30 Apollinaire to Soffici, Jan. 9, 1912 (Soffici Archive).

31 Late in life Sonia Delaunay confirmed to John Field that she and her husband had always thought Picasso "a shit."

32 Stein 1933, 98.

33 Mellow, 98.

34 Breunig, 67.

35 Ibid., 212.

36 Madsen, 75–6.

37 Stein 1933, 98.

38 Madsen, 91.

39 As Delaunay certainly knew, Seurat had used divisionism to "deconstruct" the Eiffel Tower twenty years earlier.

40 See Vol. I., 448.

41 Golding, 149.

42 An early-nineteenth-century director of the Gobelins tapestry factory, M.-E. Chevreul had written the treatise *Principles of Harmony and Contrast of Colors* in 1839.

43 Madsen, 100.

44 See Vol. I, 274.

45 Because of the war the book did not appear until 1918, and then under the title *Calligrammes.*

46 Apollinaire's use of "*l'esprit nouveau*" appears in his celebrated defense of *Parade* in 1917.

47 Picasso to Apollinaire, [Feb. 27, 1913]; in Caizergues and Seckel, 100–1.

15 MA JOLIE—1911–12 pp. 221–233

1 Olivier 1988, 250.

2 Severini, 115–35.

3 Olivier 1933, 169.

4 Severini, 151.

5 Ibid., 150.

6 Elizabeth Cowling and Jennifer Mundy, *On Classic Ground: Picasso, Léger, de Chirico and the New Classicism 1910–1930* (London: Tate Gallery, 1990), 195.

7 Ibid.

8 Sabartès, 314.

9 Ibid.

10 Picasso to Kahnweiler, June 12, 1912; in Cousins, 395.

11 Sabartès, 314, was the first to cite the lyrics "O Manon, ma Jolie, mon cœur te dit bonjour" as the source for *Ma Jolie*. Maurice Jardot, in *Picasso: Peintures 1900–1955* (Paris: Musée des Arts Décoratifs, 1955), no. 28, identified this refrain as coming from "Dernière chanson," a well-known song of the period, written by Harry Fragson (1911) after a motif from a dance by Herman Finck, "Dans les ombres."

12 Stein 1933, 111.

13 Picasso to G. Stein, Apr. 30, 1912 (Beinecke Library).

14 Picasso to G. Stein, May 1, 1912 (Beinecke Library).

15 Picasso to G. Stein, May 8, 1912 (Beinecke Library).

16 Stein 1933, 141.

17 Picasso to Kahnweiler, June 12, 1912; in Monod-Fontaine 1984B, 110.

18 Gilot, 74. For further discussion of the *Still Life with Chair Caning*, see MoMA Symposium, 150–1, 186–7.

19 Daix 1993 (French ed.), 120.

20 Cabanne, 151.

21 Braque to Marcelle, Apr. 27, 1912; in Cousins, 389.

22 Apollinaire 1913, 23.

23 Severini, 141; trans. Jennifer Franchini in Gino Severini, *The Life of a Painter* (Princeton, N.J.: Princeton University Press, 1995), 96.

24 Daix 1995, 130.

25 Ibid.

26 Linda Nochlin, "Picasso's Color: Schemes and Gambits," *Art in America* (New York), 68:10 (Dec., 1980), 112.

27 Nochlin (ibid.) reminds us that scallop shells are the traditional badge of the pilgrim, i.e., of someone who travels on foot; hence Picasso's *retardataire* portrayal of them.

28 Toklas 1954, 30.

29 Severini, 151–2.

30 Picasso to Braque, May 18, 1912; in Cousins, 390.

31 Michael Stein to G. Stein, June 19, 1912 (Beinecke Library).

32 Leo Stein to G. Stein, May 29, 1912 (Beinecke Library).

33 Ibid.

34 Laporte, 44.

35 Daix and Rosselet, 312.

36 Severini, 139.

37 Serge Férat to Soffici, Oct. 21, 1912 (Soffici Archive).

38 Fernande to Apollinaire, July 11, [1912–18]; in Caizergues and Seckel, 212.

39 Roland Dorgelès, *Le Figaro littéraire* (Paris), (Dec. 29, 1962); in Olivier 1988, 251.

40 See Vol. I, 311.

16 SORGUES—1912 pp.235–257

1 Picasso to Kahnweiler, May 20, 1912; in Cousins, 391.

2 Picasso to Kahnweiler, May 24, 1912; in Monod-Fontaine 1984A, 166.

3 Ibid.

4 Picasso to Kahnweiler, May 25, 1912; in Monod-Fontaine 1984B, 110.

5 Picasso to Braque, May 25, 1912; in Cousins, 392.

6 Picasso to Braque, May 30, 1912; ibid., 393.

7 Picasso to Kahnweiler, June 1, 1912; ibid.

8 Picasso's list of paintings is reproduced in Monod-Fontaine 1984A, 166–7.

9 Picasso to Kahnweiler, June 5, 1912; in MoMA Symposium, 342.

10 Picasso to Kahnweiler, June 7, 1912; in Cousins, 394.

11 The painter Joaquim Sunyer had been Fernande's lover around the same time that she met Picasso in 1904; see Vol. I, 312.

12 Picasso to Kahnweiler, June 12, 1912; in Cousins, 394–5.

13 Ibid.

14 Picasso to Kahnweiler, June 17, 1912; ibid., 395.

15 Picasso to Kahnweiler, June 19, 1912; ibid., 396.

16 Picasso to Kahnweiler, June 20, 1912; ibid.

17 Braque in "Testimony against Gertrude Stein"; in McCully, 64.

18 For a discussion of the palimpsest-like nature of Picasso's Céret and Sorgues paintings, see Karmel.

19 Picasso in conversation with Kahnweiler, Dec. 2, 1933; trans. in Rubin, Seckel, Cousins, 223.

20 Picasso to Kahnweiler, June 25, 1912; in Cousins, 397.

21 Picasso to Kahnweiler, June 26, 1912; ibid.

22 Picasso to Braque, June 27, 1912; ibid.

23 Vol. I, 221.

24 Daix 1993, 405 n.19.

25 Z.XVIII.267, 299–305.

26 Palau i Fabre 1990, 261.

27 Palau i Fabre 1990, 316, says that Kahnweiler went to Sorgues to get the "fresco" back to Paris. There is no evidence for this.

28 Picasso to Kahnweiler, July 9, 1912; in Cousins, 399.

29 Picasso to Braque, July 10, 1912; ibid.

30 Ibid., 400.

31 Rubin 1984, 305 and n.168.

32 Malraux, 13.

33 Vallier, 14.

34 Braque to Kahnweiler, Aug. 16, 1912; in Cousins, 402.

35 According to Denise and Claude Laurens in conversation with the author and Marilyn McCully.

36 Braque to Kahnweiler, Aug. 24, 1912; in Cousins, 402.

37 Vallier, 14.

38 Rubin 1989, 23.

39 Gilot, 76–7.

40 Braque to Kahnweiler, Sept. 27, 1912; in Cousins, 404.

41 Picasso to Kahnweiler, Aug. 21, 1912; in Cousins, 402.

42 Daix 1993, 406.

43 Braque to Kahnweiler, [Sept. 16], 1912; in Cousins, 403.

44 Picasso to G. Stein, Sept. 18, 1912 (Beinecke Library).

45 Picasso to Kahnweiler, Sept. 17, 1912; in Cousins, 403.

46 Braque to André Verdier; in Rubin 1989, 40.

47 Fry, 147.

48 Duncan Grant to Clive Bell, Feb. 26, 1914; in Richard Shone, *Bloomsbury Portraits* (London: Phaidon, 1993), 130. My thanks to Richard Shone for bringing this lettter to my attention.

49 Picasso to Braque, Oct. 9, 1912; in Cousins, 407.

50 Daix and Rosselet, 287.

51 See Leighten, 121–42. A more openminded, contextual reading of this work is to be found in Weiss, 11–12, who draws attention to "ephemerality and the play of the pun" as "salient contents and qualities of collage."

52 Cousins, 412.

53 Earlier in the year (April–May) at Dalmau's gallery in Barcelona, essentially the same group of Section d'Or artists exhibited together. Among the works shown was Duchamp's *Nude Descending a Staircase.*

54 Picasso to Braque, Oct. 31, 1912; in Cousins, 410.

55 Cousins, 411.

56 Ibid.

57 MoMA Symposium, 153.

58 Braque to Kahnweiler, Aug. 24, 1912; in Cousins, 403.

59 Braque in conversation with the author.

60 Ibid.

61 Elizabeth Cowling, "The fine art of cutting: Picasso's *papiers collés* and constructions in 1912–14," *Apollo* (London), (Nov., 1995), 16 n.7.

62 Ibid., 15.

63 Vol. I, 110.

64 André Salmon, *La Jeune sculpture française* (Paris: Albert Messein, 1919); in Elizabeth Cowling and John Golding, *Picasso: Sculptor/Painter* (London: Tate Gallery, 1994), 57.

65 André Salmon, *L'Air de la Butte* (Paris: La Nouvelle France, 1945), 82.

66 Vanessa Bell to Duncan Grant, Mar. 25, 1914; Bell, 160.

67 Ibid.

68 Baldassari, 107, has suggested that the photograph was taken in Picasso's Bateau Lavoir studio, but there is nothing to suggest that this was the case.

17 LIFE IN MONTPARNASSE pp. 259–269

1 Jacob, 95.

2 Breunig, 409.

3 Klüver and Martin, 11.

4 Palau i Fabre 1990, 306–7, thinks that the vertical scaffolding in the artist's 1912–13 work derives from the half timbering that is such a feature of this building.

5 Another explanation of their relationship was that they had shared a wet nurse.

6 Jacob, 26–7.

7 Olivier 1933, 174.

8 Ibid.

9 Serge Férat to Soffici, July 24, 1912 (Soffici Archive).

10 Billy, 84–5.

11 Jacob, 26.

12 Ibid.

13 Faure-Favier, 15.

14 Stein 1933, 158.

15 Rubin 1972, 91.

16 Only one painting on glass has survived, *Violin and Newspaper* (Z.II**.764).

17 Jeanine Warnod, *La Ruche & Montparnasse* (Geneva/Paris: Weber, 1978), 34.

18 Ibid., 60.

19 Marevna, 179.

20 Olivier 1933, 127–8.

21 Fernande to G. Stein, Apr., 1911 (Beinecke Library).

22 Picasso to Roché, Apr. 7, 1911 (Ransom Center).

23 Z.XXVIII.17, 18, 32. In 1966 Picasso identified one of these drawings for Zervos, who was preparing this supplement to his *catalogue raisonné*; see Roberto Otero, *Forever Picasso*, trans. Elaine Kerrigan (New York: Abrams, 1974), 121.

24 Picasso to Kahnweiler, July 25, 1912; in Cousins, 401.

25 Georges Carpentier, *Ma vie de boxeur* (Amiens: Leveillard, 1921), 26.

26 Karmel, 180.

27 Cousins, 382.

28 Roché Carnet 47:6, Apr. 25, 1909 (Ransom Center).

29 See Vol. I, 327.

30 André Salmon, *Paris-Journal* (Oct. 13, 1911); in Karmel, 180.

31 Claude Meunier, *Ring Noir* (Paris: Plon, 1992), 49.

32 Ibid., 48.

33 Ibid., 48 n.1.

34 Fabian Lloyd [Cravan], *L'Echo des sports*, June 10, 1909.

35 Details of French canvas sizes are given in Chapter 11 n.7, p. 457.

36 Assouline, 189.

37 Compare the contract that Matisse signed with Bernheim-Jeune in September, 1909: canvases brought between 450 and 1,875 francs according to size; in addition, Matisse received 25 percent on all sales; see FitzGerald, 32–3.

18 CÉRET AND BARCELONA—1913 pp. 271–283

1 G. Stein to Mabel Dodge Luhan, Dec., 1912; in Luhan, 29.

2 Picasso to G. Stein, Dec. 23, 1912 (Beinecke Library).

3 MP Carnets I.17, 3r.

4 Edward F. Fry, "Picasso, Cubism and Reflexivity," *Art Journal* (New York), 47:4 (winter, 1988), 306 n.30.

5 As well as a 75-page sketchbook, there are at least 200 of these drawings according to Karmel. See Karmel, 259ff.

6 Alexander Babin in conversation with Marilyn McCully.

7 Kahnweiler to Picasso, Mar. 4, 1913 (Archives Picasso).

8 Vol. I, 284. Baldassari, 17–18, has established that Picasso originally worked from a photograph for this painting.

9 Kahnweiler to Picasso, Mar. 4, 1913 (Archives Picasso).

10 Kahnweiler to the author.

11 Picasso to Kahnweiler, 1913; in Monod-Fontaine 1984A, 170.

12 Picasso to Kahnweiler, Mar. 29, 1913; in Cousins, 416.

13 Picasso to Kahnweiler, Apr. 11, 1913; ibid.

14 Seckel, 96.

15 Ibid., 107 n.4.

16 Ibid., 98.

17 Ibid.

18 Ibid., 107 n.9.

19 Ibid., 98.

20 Ibid.

21 Ibid., 85 n.24.

22 Andreu, 89–90.

23 *Gil Blas* (Sept. 2, 1913); in Cousins, 422.

24 Picasso to Braque, Apr. 23, 1913; in Cousins, 416.

25 Derain to Kahnweiler, July 11, 1913; in Cousins, 420.

26 According to Picasso's nephew Xavier Vilató in conversation with the author.

27 Vol. I, 82.

28 According to Jacqueline Picasso in conversation with the author.

29 Eva to G. Stein, May 14, 1913 (Beinecke Library).

30 Ibid.

31 Palau i Fabre 1990, 249.

32 Seckel, 102.

33 Eva to Toklas, June 11, 1913 (Beinecke Library).

34 Eva to G. Stein, [June], 1913 (Beinecke Library).

35 Seckel, 179.

36 Ibid., 101.

37 Vol. I, 422.

38 Seckel, 103, 108 n.24.

39 Daix 1993, 132.

40 Eva to G. Stein, July 10, 1913 (Beinecke Library).

41 Eva to G. Stein, July 14, 1913 (Beinecke Library).

42 Eva to G. Stein, July 18, 1913 (Beinecke Library).

43 Eva to G. Stein, July 22, 1913 (Beinecke Library).

44 Schneider, 269.

45 Picasso acquired this painting from his friend Mopse Sternheim (daughter of the writer and collector Carl Sternheim) shortly before she was taken off to a Nazi concentration camp, where she was lucky to survive.

46 Eva to G. Stein, July 22, 1913 (Beinecke Library).

47 Ibid.

48 *L'Indépendant* (Perpignan), Aug. 9, 1913; in Cousins, 421.

49 Kahnweiler 1946, 16.

50 See Vol. I, 180–1.

51 Daix 1993, 408 n.23.

52 *Gil Blas*, Sept. 2, 1913; in Cousins, 422.

53 In a letter dated Aug. 16 to Kahnweiler, Gris states that Picasso had already left Céret; in Kahnweiler 1956, 1.

54 Picasso to Kahnweiler, August 19, 1913; in Cousins, 421.

19 WOMAN IN AN ARMCHAIR pp. 285–299

1 Steegmuller 1986, 137.

2 Arvid Fougstedt, *Svenska Dagbladet*, Jan. 9, 1916; trans. in Klüver, 46.

3 Penrose, 190.

4 Adéma, 232.

5 Schneider, 733.

6 See Vol. I, 417.

7 Matisse to Simon Bussy, May 20, 1911; in Schneider, 732.

8 Picasso to G. Stein, Aug. 29, 1913; in Cousins, 422.

9 Daix 1993, 133.

10 Ibid.

11 Jack Flam, *Matisse: A Retrospective* (New York: Levin, 1988), 294.

12 Schneider, 734.

13 Vol. I, 280 (top center).

14 Ibid., 49–50.

15 Françoise Gilot in conversation with the author.

16 MoMA Symposium, 107.

17 See Vol. I, 359–67.

18 Karmel in conversation with the author.

19 MoMA Symposium, 79–90.

20 For further discussion of the sexual connotations of this work see Weiss, 29.

21 *Glass and Packet of Tobacco* in the Musée Picasso (MP 44).

22 According to Ron Johnson, in his unpublished manuscript "Picasso and the Poets."

23 Werner Spies, *Picasso: Das plastische Werk* (Stuttgart: Gerd Hatje, 1983), 74.

24 Gilot, 321.

25 John Golding, "Introduction," in *Picasso: Sculptor/Painter* (London: Tate Gallery, 1994), 22.

26 Mellow, 200.

27 Ibid., 201.

28 Ibid., 202.

29 Leo Stein to G. Stein, undated (Beinecke Library).

30 See Vol. I, 397.

31 Mellow, 206.

32 Gertrude Stein, *Two: Gertrude Stein and Her Brother and Other Early Portraits* (New Haven: Yale University Press, 1951), 88, 108–9.

33 Leo Stein to Mabel Weeks, April, 1914 (Beinecke Library).

34 Leo Stein to G. Stein, undated (Beinecke Library).

35 Stein 1933, 115.

36 Zilczer 1986, 33.

37 Zilczer 1975, 84.

38 Zilczer 1986, 32.

39 Zilczer 1975, 80.

40 Ibid., 85.

41 FitzGerald, 270 n.2, notes that there were thirteen partners. Two of the eleven voting shares had been split. Since Level was an admirer of Picasso, the fund ended up owning twelve of his works, chief of which was the huge 1905 *Saltimbanques*, which he had bought through Moline and Sagot.

42 Salmon 1956, 259–60.

43 According to Angela Rosengart in conversation with the author.

44 Maurice Delcourt, "Avant l'Invasion," *Paris-Midi*, Mar. 3, 1914.

45 Ibid.

46 According to Dora Maar in conversation with the author.

20 COLLECTORS, DEALERS AND THE GERMAN CONNECTION pp.301–325

1 Assouline, 91.

2 Dutilleul described his early acquisitions and the influence of Kahnweiler in Roger Dutilleul, "L'art et l'argent. La parole est aux collectionneurs," *Art présent* (special no., 1948). My thanks to Savine Faupin for bringing this to my attention. For further discussion of Dutilleul and other collectors, see Malcolm Gee, *Dealers, Critics and Collectors of Modern Painting: Aspects of the Parisian Art Market Between 1910 and 1930* (New York and London: Garland Publishing, 1981).

3 Eponymous hero of Balzac's novel (1847), one of the "scenes of Parisian life" in *La Comédie humaine*.

4 Besides the Picassos, Lefèvre's bequest included 30 Légers, 23 Grises, 21 Laurenses, 15 Modiglianis, 15 Mirós, 15 Massons, 6 Braques (among them his cubist masterpiece, the *Man with Guitar* of 1914), 5 Klees and many items by the lesser artists whom Kahnweiler took up in the twenties and thirties after Picasso, Braque and Léger had deserted him for Paul Rosenberg.

5 Richet's daughter Michèle was on the staff of the Musée Picasso long before it opened. As conservateur en chef honoraire, she was responsible for the first catalog of the museum's collections.

6 Max Jacob, *Les propos et les jours: Lettres 1904–1944*, ed. Didier Gompel-Netter and Annie Marcoux (La Pierre-qui-vire: Zodiaque, 1989), 270.

7 During the war Germaine Bongard opened the Galerie Thomas in her house on rue de Penthièvre. The first exhibition (Dec., 1915) included works by Picasso, Derain, Matisse, Léger, Kisling and Modigliani.

8 Z.VI.686; Z.II*.354; Z.II**.527.

9 Chapon, 312.

10 Kostenevich and Semyonova, 11.

11 See Vol. I, 393.

12 Picasso to G. Stein, Sept. 18, 1912 (Beinecke Library).

13 Beverly Whitney Kean, *All the Empty Palaces: The Merchant Patrons of Modern Art in Pre-Revolutionary Russia* (New York: Universe, 1983), 108.

14 Ambroise Vollard, *Recollections of a Picture Dealer*, trans. Violet M. Macdonald (Boston: Little, Brown, 1936), 132.

15 Kramář was the first scholar/collector in the cubist field, and in 1921 he brought out *Kubismus*, a history of cubism, which closely follows Kahnweiler's recently published account.

16 For details of these acquisitions, see Jiří Kotalík, "Pablo Picasso a Praga," and the catalog in *Cubisme a Praga: Obres de la Galeria Nacional*, Barcelona: Museu Picasso, 1990.

17 See Geelhaar, 30–1, who gives details of the prices Kramář paid, Kahnweiler's being substantially higher than Vollard's for works of equivalent size.

18 Hoffmeister, 239–40.

19 Kramář helped the Artists' Group (Skupina výtvarných umělců) mount exhibitions in 1912, 1913 and 1914, drawing on Kahnweiler's stock as well as his own ever-expanding collection. The 1913 show included as many as thirteen Picassos.

20 In 1919, when Czechoslovakia gained its independence, Kramář was appointed director of what soon became the Národní (National) Galerie. Because his own collection was destined for the museum, he limited himself to acquiring only three, albeit major, Picassos (including the 1909 *Landscape with a Bridge*). However, at his death in 1960, some of the smaller Picassos secretly passed to his family.

21 Kramář also acquired works from Sagot (whose eulogy he wrote in one of his art journals); see Hoffmeister, 329.

22 Picasso to Kramář, May 27, 1911 (Národní Galerie, Prague).

23 Z.II*.32; Vanessa Bell to Virginia Stephen, [Oct. 19, 1911]; in Bell, 109.

24 Z.II*.241.

25 Z.II**.431.

26 The Oxford collector Sir Michael Sadler, who had acquired major works by Gauguin and Kandinsky in 1911, bought several Picassos but no date of purchase is known.

27 Roger Fry to G. Stein, Mar. 5, 1913 (Beinecke Library).

28 See Vol. I, 404. The Cones had a brother, Moses. He never bought Picasso, but in 1906 his wife acquired a drawing for the *Woman with Loaves* (1906).

29 The only faintly "difficult" Picasso in the Cone collection, a study for *Nu à la draperie* of 1907, was bought by Etta Cone from Gertrude Stein in the early 1930s to help her out financially.

30 Brenda Richardson, *Dr. Claribel & Miss Etta: The Cone Collection* (Baltimore: Museum of Art, 1985), 101. See also Vol. I, 410.

31 Ira Glackens, *William Glackens and the Ashcan Group* (New York: Crown, 1957), 216.

32 Harriet Levy has confused a Picasso with a Matisse. Cited in Howard Greenfield, *The Devil and Dr. Barnes: Portrait of an American Collector* (New York: Marion Boyars, 1989), 44–5.

33 Ibid., 46.

34 Two heads of 1907 (Z.II*.11 and 12) and three still lifes of 1908, 1911–12 and 1914 (Z.II*.95, Z.II*.322 and Z.II**.495).

35 Alfred Barnes, "How to Judge a Painting," *Arts and Decoration* 5:6 (Apr., 1915), 217–20, 246–50; "Cubism: Requiescat in Pace," *Arts and Decoration* 6:3 (Jan., 1916), 121–4.

36 Works by both Matisse and Picasso were already represented in various American collections, including those of Harriet Levy, Alfred Stieglitz and the Cone sisters.

37 At the third of Kahnweiler's forced sales in 1923, Durand-Ruel acquired four major works on paper for Barnes.

38 Stein 1933, 13.

39 Stieglitz's conversion to Picasso had also been instigated by that other great American photographer Edward Steichen, a frequent visitor to Paris from 1900 onwards and an habitué of the Steins' salon.

40 Leonard, 47.

41 Critical reactions were not as foolish or philistine as one might expect. True, Arthur Hoeber of *The New York Globe* (Mar. 29, 1911) described the drawings as "the gibberings of a lunatic," but the *New York World* (Apr. 16, 1911) hailed them as "a new thrill in town in the world of art," and the *Evening World* critic (Apr. 1, 1911) found that Picasso could "draw and paint with the consummately beautiful mastery of a Millet or a Degas" and that even in "the weird geometrical jumbles . . . there must surely be something doing of large impact for the future"; these reviews also appeared in *Camera Work* 36 (Oct., 1911).

42 Z.II*.208.

43 Watson, 80. According to John Field, Mrs. Meyer bought "a recent still life" from Kahnweiler in 1914.

44 Stieglitz's later acquisitions included the 1902 painting *A Woman Ironing* inscribed to Sabartès, the faceted bronze *Head of Fernande* of 1909 and a related drawing, a 1912 papier collé, *Bottle and Glass*, and a number of fine early drawings.

45 Watson, 173.

46 Z.II*.54 (*Two Trees*); Z.II**.364 (*Nude Woman "J'aime Eva"*); Z.II**.759 (*Still Life with Musical Instruments and Fruit Bowl*).

47 Watson, 173. After his death Davies's effects were sold at auction in April, 1929, the depth of the Depression. Cézanne watercolors went for $100, Picasso drawings (including a major study for the Museum of Modern Art's *Two Nudes* of 1906) for $60 and $70, a Matisse bronze for $90.

48 Paper deterioration is the reason for their unavailability.

49 Some of this material has appeared in John Richardson, "Picasso und Deutschland vor 1914," *20 Jahre Wittrock Kunsthandel*, Düsseldorf: Wolfgang Wittrock Kunsthandel, n.d. [1994], 10–31.

50 *Lustige Blätter* 1899; illus. in Flechtheim, 98.

51 Peter Demetz, in Walter Benjamin, *Reflections: Essays, Aphorisms, Autobiographical Writings* (New York: Harcourt Brace Jovanovich, 1978), ix.

52 In addition to *Blue Boy* (Z.I.271) it included, among others, *Boy Holding a Vase* (Z.I.272), also of 1905, *The Watering Place* (Z.I.265) and *Two Brothers* (Z.I.304), both of 1906, and *Woman with Mandolin* (Z.II*.270) of 1911.

53 Flechtheim, 21.

54 Flechtheim's 1913–14 diary is published in *Neue deutsche Hefte* (Gütersloh) 135:3, 1972, 44–60.

55 Pierre Daix and Georges Boudaille, *Picasso: The Blue and Rose Periods*, trans. Phoebe Pool (Greenwich, Conn.: New York Graphic Society, 1967), list two works (Z.I.200, 224) as having been shown at Thannhauser's gallery in 1909, possibly in the first N.K.V. exhibition. From Kahnweiler's notebooks John Field has identified two of the three works shown in 1910 as Z.II*.41 and Z.II*.140 (illustrated in the catalog). The third was a still-life drawing.

56 McCully, 91–2.

57 Although Perls maintained they saw Blue period Picassos, there is no record of any early works by the artist at Bernheim's. My thanks to Hector Feliciano for pointing this out to me.

58 The story of the "*Blitzbild*" (now in the Von Abbe Museum, Eindhoven) is told by Hugo Perls in his memoirs (*Warum ist Kamilla schön? Von Kunst, Künstlern und Kunsthandel*, Munich: Paul List, 1962, 14–15), though he remembers being sent the painting by Kahnweiler rather than Uhde. He also implies that he kept it and sold it himself to the Dutch museum. However, it was back with Uhde before 1914, as it was included in the sale of works sequestered from him.

59 Hugo Perls in conversation with John Field.

60 Other dealers in Munich whom Kahnweiler kept supplied included the stylish dilettante Georg Caspari—composer, violinist, theater critic—who in 1913 opened a gallery of nineteenth- and twentieth-century painting in the old Eichthal palace. Shortly after the gallery opened, Kahnweiler sent him the 1903 *Portrait of Madame Soler* (Z.I.200), which he sold for 3,500 francs (more than Vollard was obtaining for Blue period paintings). An exhibition Caspari held in March, 1914, included several Blue period works: the late 1901 *Portrait of Mateu de Soto with Sculpture* (Z.I.94, which belonged to Hugo Perls), the 1902 *Seated Woman in a Hood* (Z.I.119, which had belonged to Gertrude Stein); see "Munich letter," *American Art News* (New York) 12:26 (Apr. 4, 1914), 5. Another Munich gallery that specialized in Blue period Picassos was the Neue Kunstsalon, owned by Max Dietzel and Paul Ferdinand Schmidt.

61 According to John Field, Kahnweiler, in his Notebook 2, lists forty works (as well as forty-six photographs), which were sent on Nov. 14, 1913, to the Neue Galerie, Berlin, "Picasso Exhibition." Michael Raeburn's comparison with the information given in Daix/Rosselet enables the majority of the works to be firmly identified: Z.II*.12, 11, 22(?), 40, 41, 42, 103, 57, 78, 77, 148, 141, 147, 104, 211, 247, 291, 249, 271, 267, 251, 245, 292, 250, 255, 309, 310, 282, 275, 295, 303, 320, 286, 244, 254, 314, 359, 357; Z.II**.426, 384.

62 After Berlin, Feldmann's *Picasso und Negerplastiken* show traveled to Emil Richter's gallery in Dresden, one of Die Brücke's principal dealers. There it was augmented with fourteen Rose period drawings from Kahnweiler as well as other loans (possibly from Flechtheim). Later (Feb.–Mar.) a modified version of the exhibition was shown at the Galerie Miethke in Vienna. In April, 1914, it launched a new gallery in Zurich, belonging to Gottfried Tanner, a cousin of the Bernheim-Jeunes; in May the show made its last stop at the Kunsthalle in Basel. I owe the discovery of this hitherto undocumented exhibition to John Field's researches.

63 Kahnweiler 1946, 205 n.22.

64 Uhde 1928, 35.

65 *Vor den Pforten des Lebens* (1902); *Gerd Burger* (1903). Uhde also wrote a little book about *Paris* (1904), illustrated with works by the impressionists.

66 Z.II*.235, 285, 288; illustrated on pp. 151, 188, 104.

67 Michel Fokine quoted in Häger, 280.

68 Z.II*.270; Z.II**377.

69 Roché Carnet 73, June 10, 1916 (Ransom Center).

70 Kann acquired the beautiful little *Still Life* (Z.II*.283) of 1911, also *Violin (Jolie Eva)* (Z.II*.342), *Pigeon in Its Nest, with Eggs* (Z.II*.346), both of 1912, and the great 1915 *Harlequin* (Z.II**.555).

71 Stein 1933, 96.

72 Suermondt's Picasso's included *Seated Harlequin* of 1901 (Z.I.79), *L'Escritoire* (Z.II*.232) of 1911, the small 1911 *Pont Neuf* (Z.II*.248), three or four other paintings and a number of drawings. He also owned Douanier Rousseau's balletic *Football Players* and a magnificent pair of Braque still lifes (1909), all now in the Guggenheim Museum.

73 According to John Field, Uhde's collector friends included a wealthy young landowner from Silesia, Paul (Oscar?) Huldschinsky, who had a fine collection of old masters. His first acquisition in the modern field was a remarkably ugly 1901 *Flowerpiece* (D.B.V.28) from Uhde, but he ended up with at least ten works on paper by Picasso, none of which figures in the sales catalogs of the Huldschinsky collection (1928, 1931). Another such collector was Franz Kluxen of Münster (also listed in catalogs as Kluxen of Boldixen, an island in the North Sea), about whom little is known. However, if Field's re-creation of his collection is correct, he was one of the earliest (he started in 1910) and most serious buyers of Picasso in pre-1914 Germany. Each of Kluxen's paintings charted an important stage in the artist's early development: one of his first still lifes; a *Mädchenporträt* of 1904, which could be the famous Blue period *Girl with the Helmet of Hair* (Z.I.233); the ferociously striated *Vase of Flowers* (Z.II*.30) of 1907; the *Woman with the Black Hat* (Z.II*.178) of 1909 that ended up with Bienert; and *The Woman Playing the Violin* (Z.II*.256) of 1911 that was sold to another early collector, Hermann Lange of Krefeld. There may also have been drawings. By 1920, all the Kluxen Picassos that can be traced had changed hands. Kluxen may have been a victim of the war or of hard times.

74 Virginia Woolf, *The Diary of Virginia Woolf* 1 (London: Hogarth Press, 1977), 146.

75 Roger Fry to Goldworthy Lowes Dickinson, May 31, 1913; Denys Sutton, *Letters of Roger Fry* 2 (London: Chatto & Windus, 1972), 370.

76 Lichnowsky, 190.

77 Princess Lichnowsky's Picassos probably included the 1904 *Portrait of Suzanne Bloch* (Z.I.217), *Blue Boy* (Z.I.271) of 1905 that Flechtheim had bought directly from Picasso, and a "*Madonna*" of 1905.

78 The other two Picassos were probably the *Blind Man's Meal* (Z.I.168) and a *Sleeping Pierrot*: probably *The Death of Harlequin* (Z.I.302) which Uhde had once loaned Rilke.

79 Lichnowsky, 190.

80 Rilke to Hertha Koenig, Nov. 4, 1914; in Geelhaar, 73.

81 See Vol. I, 336–7.

82 The Mendelssohn-Bartholdys' collection included *Head of a Woman* (Z.I.206) and *Portrait of Angel de Soto* (Z.I.201) of 1903; *Boy with a Pipe* (Z.I.274), 1905, and *Boy Leading a Horse* (Z.I.264), 1906, also a 1909 *Head of a Woman* (Z.II*.140) and *Arlésienne* (Z.II*.356), 1912.

83 Vol. I, 192.

84 Uhde 1938, 153.

85 *Seated Woman in Green* (Z.II*.197); *Woman with a Mandolin* (Z.II*.133).

86 Uhde 1938, 154.

87 The only other Hungarian to collect Picasso before World War I was Baron Ferenc Hatvany: a Blue period *Mother and Child* (D.B.XI.21), which he gave the Szépmüvészeti Múzeum, and possibly a 1909 gouache of a standing nude (D.R.247).

88 Collectors in Hamburg, where Picasso was held in high regard, included Max Leon Flemming—a friend of Uhde and Flechtheim—who owned five or six Picassos; a lawyer named Rauert, who bought the Blue period *Portrait of Mateu de Soto* (Z.I.94) from Georg Caspari in Munich; a collector named Henry Simms, who loaned two Picassos to Thannhauser's 1913 exhibition (a 1903 painting and a "*Spanish Clown*" of 1908); and Dr. Oscar Troplowitz, who left a group of impressionists and the *Absinthe Drinker* (Z.I.120) of 1902 to the Kunsthalle, where it remained until Hitler had it confiscated and included in the 1939 sale of "*entartete Kunst*" at the Fischer Gallery, Lucerne. In Frankfurt Ludwig and Rosy Fischer bought one of two Tuileries garden scenes (1901) that Thannhauser had acquired in Paris as well as *The Mourners* (Z.I.52; also 1901). In Cologne Pierre Leffmann owned the monumental *Actor* (Z.I.291) of 1904–05, but relinquished it to another collector in 1912. This was the year that Kahnweiler sold the Wallraf-Richartz Museum the large, dull conversation piece *The Soler Family* (Z.I.203) of 1903, one of the very few Picassos the Nazis might actually have liked; yet they condemned it to be sold. And from Cologne's fourth International Sonderbund (1912)—the exhibition that inspired New York's Armory show—a Wilhelmine architect from Düsseldorf, Wilhelm Kreis, acquired the large 1903 Blue period panel known as *Tragedy* (Z.I.208). Kreis sold this

to Herr Schubert of Bochum; it ultimately went through Chester Dale to the National Gallery, Washington.

In Wuppertal-Elberfeld there were several collectors. By 1913, the New York–born painter Adolf Erbslöh owned one if not two still lifes of 1907–08; the prominent banker Baron August von der Heydt—a progressive collector despite close links to the kaiser—owned a 1901 *Man in a Cloak* (Z.I.16) and a Rose period watercolor of a circus family (Z.I.281), which he later gave to the museum in Wuppertal that bears his name; and that otherwise discriminating collector Julius Schmits owned the clumsy *Mother and Child* (Z.XXI.290) of 1901. In Breslau there was at least one unidentified Picasso, according to a report in *Cicerone* of an exhibition of *Werke moderner Kunst aus Breslauem Privatbesitz* in the Schlesisches Museum. And in Dresden the principal collector of modern art was Flechtheim's friend Ida Bienert. Her first acquisitions date from before 1914. During World War I, she bought the early cubist *Woman in a Black Hat* (Z.II*.178), which had previously belonged to Franz Kluxen.

21 AVIGNON—1914 pp.327–341

1 Breunig, 406.

2 Picasso to Apollinaire, June 13, 1914: "Nous partons demain . . ."; in Caizergues and Seckel, 111.

3 Ibid., 112.

4 Eva to G. Stein, June 23, 1914 (Beinecke Library).

5 Eva to G. Stein, June 25, 1914 (Beinecke Library).

6 Caizergues and Seckel, 119.

7 Picasso to Kahnweiler, July 21, 1914; in Cousins, 430.

8 Eva to G. Stein, Nov. 10, 1914 (Beinecke Library).

9 Seckel, 63 n.18.

10 Picasso to Kahnweiler, July 21, 1913; in Monod-Fontaine 1984B, 122.

11 Eva to G. Stein, Oct.26, 1914 (Beinecke Library).

12 In 1912 and 1913, Girieud and Lombard (with the help of Cézanne's friend the poet Joachim Gasquet) tried without much success to organize a Salon de Mai at Marseille.

13 Braque to Kahnweiler, July 15, 1914; in Cousins, 429.

14 Hugo, 148–9.

15 Picasso to Kahnweiler, July 21, 1914; in Monod-Fontaine 1984B, 123.

16 Palau i Fabre 1990, 408.

17 A drawing for this composition of a man at a bar (not in Zervos), confirms this analysis; see Marilyn McCully, *Picasso: A Private Collection* (London: Cacklegoose Press, 1993), 94–5.

18 Palau (Palau i Fabre 1990, 408) mistakes the hair for a crown ("an open allegory of Picasso's ideological leanings, shielded in religion"), thereby compounding the artist's pun.

19 See Vol. I, 18.

20 Braque to Kahnweiler, July [25], 1914; in Monod-Fontaine 1984B, 123.

21 Picasso to Kahnweiler, July 21, 1914; in Cousins, 430.

22 Stein 1933, 23.

23 Daix 1995, 681.

24 I am greatly indebted to Kenneth Silver's perceptive study *Esprit de corps* (see Silver), but cannot accept his identification of the seated man as an artist, nor the nude drawing he publishes, 67, as a study for the girl. This depicts Gaby Depeyre and therefore dates from at least a year later. The Musée Picasso has entitled this painting *The Painter and His Model*—to my mind, incorrectly.

25 Derain's *Portrait of Lucie Kahnweiler*, 1914 (Musée National d'Art Moderne, Paris), is also indebted to the Gertrude Stein portrait.

26 Zervos and others have mistakenly cataloged this painting as being on wood.

27 Braque to Kahnweiler, July [25], 1914; in Cousins, 430.

28 Derain to Kahnweiler, June 21, 1914; in Cousins, 428.

22 OUTBREAK OF WAR pp.343–355

1 Apollinaire to Madeleine Pagès, Nov. 19, 1915; in Guillaume Apollinaire, *Tendre comme le souvenir* (Paris: Gallimard, 1952), 263.

2 My informant, who has had access to Picasso's pre-1914 police dossier, prefers to remain anonymous.

3 Daix 1992, 74–6.

4 Ibid., 76.

5 Ibid.

6 David D. Gilmore, *Aggression and Community: Paradoxes of Andalusian Culture* (New Haven: Yale University Press, 1987), 131.

7 Ibid.

8 Serge Férat to Soffici, Aug. 5, 1914 (Soffici Archive).

9 Gris to Kahnweiler, Oct. 30, 1914; in Cousins, 432. FitzGerald, 278 n.65, has published the accounts Picasso kept in a small sketchbook that now belongs to Marina Picasso. The entries cover the last four months of 1913 and the whole of 1914; all of them, except one for 100 francs, are identified with a *k* for Kahnweiler. The entries are as follows: 15,850.15 francs on Oct. 15, 1913; 4,950 francs on Nov. 15, 1913; 3,250 francs on Dec. 22, 1913; 5,688 francs on Apr. 4, 1914; 1,650 francs on May 11, 1914; and 12,400 francs on June 8, 1914. Since Kahnweiler had agreed (on Mar. 4, 1913) to pay Picasso 27,250 francs for a selection of recent works and a few earlier paintings, his income for 1913 was at least 51,400 francs—a very considerable sum. The June 8 payment was the last Picasso would receive from Kahnweiler until after the war, when he would receive the 20,000 francs (with interest) that the dealer had owed him since 1914.

10 Reported by Douglas Cooper to the author.

11 Gris to Kahnweiler, Aug. 1, 1914; in Kahnweiler 1956, 6.

12 Kahnweiler 1961, 59.

13 Henry R. Hope, *Georges Braque* (New York: The Museum of Modern Art, 1949), 74.

14 Leighten, 144.

15 These letters have not as yet been made available to scholars; however Braque's heirs, Claude and Denise Laurens, have confirmed their gist.

16 Serge Férat to Soffici, Aug. 5, 1914 (Soffici Archive).

17 Juliette Gleizes told John Field she had also persuaded her father to arrange for the exemption from military service of four other painters, including Metzinger and Picabia. See also Silver, 413 n.27.

18 Dora Maar in conversation with the author.

19 Marcelle to Braque, Aug. 3, 1914; in Cousins, 431.

20 Kahnweiler to Derain, Sept. 6, 1919; in Monod-Fontaine 1984B, 123.

21 Kahnweiler 1961, 66.

22 Yve-Alain Bois, "Kahnweiler's Lesson," *Representations* (Berkeley), (spring, 1987), 33–68.

23 Gris to Kahnweiler, Nov. 6, 1914; in Kahnweiler 1956, 16.

24 Margaret Davies, *Apollinaire* (New York: St Martin's Press, 1964), 246.

25 Ibid., 247.

26 "La Petite Auto" was originally published in *Calligrames: Poèmes de la Paix et de la Guerre*, 1918.

27 Apollinaire enclosed "En allant chercher des Obus" in a letter to Louise de Coligny, May 13, 1915.

28 Picasso to Apollinaire, Feb. 7, 1915; in Caizergues and Seckel, 129.

29 Picasso to Apollinaire, Apr. 24, 1915; ibid., 133.

30 Gris to Raynal, Feb. 15, 1915; in Kahnweiler 1956, 25.

31 Evidence of Stieglitz's harsh treatment of Basler during the war can be traced in their 1915 correspondence (Beinecke Library), where the money owed on the Picasso drawings is a recurrent subject.

32 G. Stein to McBride, Jan. 20, 1915 (Beinecke Library).

33 Stein 1933, 159.

34 G. Stein to McBride, Jan. 20, 1915 (Beinecke Library).

35 The drawings that Jeanne Léger brought back from the front were published forty years later by Douglas Cooper. *Fernand Léger: dessins de guerre 1915–1916* (Paris: Berggruen, 1956).

36 Picasso to G. Stein, Sept. 11, 1914 (Beinecke Library).

37 Ibid.

38 Jacob to Kahnweiler, Sept. 22, 1914; in Max Jacob, *Correspondance* I, ed. François Garnier (Paris: Editions de Paris, 1953), 99.

39 Seckel, 115 n.26.

40 Jean Jacques Becker, *1914: Comment les Français sont entrés dans la guerre* (Paris: Presses de la Fondation National des Sciences Politiques, 1977), 505–8. I am grateful to Michael Raeburn for bringing this article to my attention. For an excellent account of the outbreak of war and its impact on artists in France, see Silver.

41 At the time of the Salon des Indépendants (1912), Louis Vauxcelles (in *Gil Blas*) christened Gris's *Portrait of Picasso* "Père Ubu-Kub"; Cousins, 389.

42 On Oct. 27, Apollinaire wrote André Level that he had met "a Polish painter, who said that he had been brought to Nîmes, shackled like a spy, for being a cubist. His drawings had been mistaken for plans, diagrams, etc."; see Level, 8.

43 Silver, 8.

44 See, for example, Silver, 71.

45 Jacques-Emile Blanche, Sept. 19, 1914, *Cahiers d'un Artiste: Juin–Novembre 1914* (Paris: N.R.F., 1915), 205–6.

46 Picasso and Eva to G. Stein, Sept. 11, 1914 (Beinecke Library).

47 Picasso and Eva to G. Stein, Oct. 6, 1914 (Beinecke Library).

48 Picasso and Eva to G. Stein, Oct. 19, 1914 (Beinecke Library).

49 Eva to Toklas, Oct. 26, 1914 (Beinecke Library).

50 Ibid.

51 Picasso to G. Stein, Nov. 14, 1914 (Beinecke Library).

52 Stein 1933, 142.

23 WARTIME PARIS pp.357–377

1 Because these photographs were stored on Délétang's premises, they escaped sequestration. Thus Kahnweiler's invaluable archive has survived intact at the Galerie Louise Leiris.

2 Henri Danet to Picasso, Dec. 28, 1914 (Archives Picasso).

3 André Level to Picasso, Jan. 21, 1915 (Archives Picasso).

4 Braque in conversation with the author.

5 Kahnweiler to Picasso, Feb. 10, 1920 (Archives Picasso).

6 FitzGerald, 3.

7 On Mar. 27, 1915, Gertrude Stein wrote Henry McBride: "The war doesn't matter to [Vollard]. He says it gives him so much time to perfect his [Cézanne] manuscript at which he has been working for five years" (Beinecke Library).

8 Christian Derouet, *Juan Gris: Correspondance, Dessins 1915–1921* (Valencia: IVAM Centre Julio González, 1990), 79 n.19.

9 Ibid., 13.

10 Apollinaire to Jacob, Mar. 14, 1916; in Seckel, 128.

11 Laurencin to Roché, Feb. 19, 1915 (Ransom Center).

12 For further discussion, see FitzGerald, 87–90.

13 Laurencin to Roché, [1915], Carnet 65 (Ransom Center).

14 Jean Mollet, "Les Origines du Cubisme: Apollinaire, Picasso et Cie.," *Les Lettres Françaises* (Paris, Jan. 3, 1947). In his unreliable and anti-modernist *Memorie della mia vita* (first published in 1945), Chirico gives a very different account of things. Far from acknowledging Picasso's early encouragement, he denounces him. Mollet's circumstantial version of events is more convincing.

15 Apollinaire to Paul Guillaume, July 1, 1915; in Jean Bouret, "Une amitié esthétique au début du siècle: Apollinaire et Paul Guillaume 1911–1918 d'après une correspondance inédite," *Gazette des Beaux-Arts* (Paris) ser.6, 76:1224 (Dec., 1970), 373–99.

16 Level to Apollinaire, Feb. 17, 1916; in Level, 78.

17 Traditionally dated 1914, Z.II**.830 is more likely to date from 1915, when Picasso started using Rivera's foliate scumbling.

18 Picasso to de Zayas, Sept. 14, 1916 (Rodrigo de Zayas Archives, Seville). I am grateful to Francis M. Naumann for bringing this letter and his well-documented article concerning de Zayas to my attention (see de Zayas).

19 Roché to Quinn, July 11, 1922; in B. L. Reid, *The Man from New York: John Quinn and His Friends* (New York: Oxford University Press, 1968), 207.

20 Z.I.96, 115, 202, 336; Z.II*.194.

21 Picasso to Apollinaire, Feb. 7, 1915; in Caizergues and Seckel, 128.

22 Picasso to G. Stein and Toklas, [Jan., 1915] (Beinecke Library).

23 Palau i Fabre 1990, 466.

24 Serge Férat to Soffici, Dec. 13, 1915 (Soffici Archive).

25 Picasso told me that he had known Saint-Tropez long before its "discovery."

26 See Klüver and Martin, 144–5.

27 Pierre Daix identifies this work as no. 28 in the 1901 Vollard show in Daix 1993 (French ed.), 442.

28 Ansen, 17.

29 Seckel, 115 n.4. For information about Hastings's life see Stephen Gray, "A Wild Colonial Girl: Reconstructing Beatrice Hastings," *Current Writing* (Durban) 6:2 (1994), 115–26, kindly brought to my attention by the author.

30 *New Age* (London) 9 (July 1, 1915).

31 Picasso later acquired Modigliani's *Jeune fille brune, assise* (1918), now in the Musée Picasso, Paris.

32 Halicka, 65.

33 Hans Arp to Hilla Rebay, [July or Aug.], 1916; in Joan M. Lukach, *Hilla Rebay* (New York: Braziller, 1938), 17.

34 Daix 1993, 145.

35 Klüver, 48.

36 Seckel, 137 n.13.

37 Klüver, 48.

38 Favela, 76, 80.

39 Marevna, 181–2.

40 Picasso to the author.

41 Cabanne, 171.

42 Youki Desnos, *Les Confidences de Youki* (Paris: Fayard, 1957), 43.

43 Ibid., 44.

44 Marevna, 62.

45 Stein 1933, 157. Two zeppelin raids occurred on Mar. 22, 1915.

46 Mellow, 222.

47 Simon, 99.

48 Andreu, 96.

49 Jacob to Raynal, Nov. 30, 1914; in Andreu, 97.

50 Andreu, 98.

51 Gerald Kamber, *Max Jacob and the Poetics of Cubism* (Baltimore: The Johns Hopkins Press, 1971), xxii.

52 Ibid.

53 Andreu, 99.

54 Andreu, 100.

55 Seckel, 124 n.15, points out that Picasso cannot have said this until after 1921.

56 Ibid., 113–14.

57 See Vol. I., 464.

58 Hélène Henry, "Max Jacob et Picasso: Jalons chronologiques pour une amitié: 1901–1944," *Europe* (Paris), 492–3 (Apr.–May, 1970), 206.

59 Jacob to Apollinaire, Jan. 7, 1915; in Seckel, 116.

60 Seckel, 139 n.48.

61 Picasso to Apollinaire, Apr. 24, 1915; in Caizergues and Seckel, 132.

62 Picasso to G. Stein, Dec. 9, 1915 (Beinecke Library).

63 Ron Johnson points this out in his unpublished study. See Johnson.

64 Palau i Fabre 1990, 460.

65 Serge Férat to Soffici, Dec. 13–14, 1915 (Soffici Archive).

66 Laurencin to Roché, [1916] (Ransom Center).

67 Gris to Raynal, Dec. 18, 1915; in Seckel, 121.

24 PICASSO AND COCTEAU pp.379–393

1 McCully, 125–6.

2 Pharamousse [Picabia], "Odeurs de partout," *391*, I, 4.

3 Picasso was quoted by Varèse in a lecture he gave some years later; see Varèse, 54.

4 Billy Klüver's publication of earlier Cocteau correspondence to Picasso has allowed us to revise the date of their first meeting; see Klüver, 89 n.94.

5 Cocteau to Picasso, July 5, 1915 (Archives Picasso); who this Russian protégé might have been is unclear.

6 Cocteau said in "Lettre à Paris," *Du* (Zurich) (1961), that he was taken to Picasso's studio by Varèse; Cooper, 16 n.6.

7 Cooper, 16 n.6.

8 Jean Cocteau and André Fraigneau, *Entretiens* (Paris: Editions du Rocher, 1988), 21.

9 Cabanne, 176.

10 Ibid.

11 Ibid.

12 Steegmuller 1986, 71.

13 *Le Prince frivole*, Cocteau's second book of poetry, was written in 1910. *Le Dieu bleu* was first performed by Diaghilev's Ballets Russes in 1912.

14 Painter II, 162.

15 Ibid., 163.

16 Steegmuller 1986, 149.

17 Ibid., 60.

18 Monique Lange, *Cocteau: Prince sans royaume* (Paris: Jean-Claude Lattès, 1989), 128.

19 Ibid., 126.

20 Steegmuller 1986, 53.

21 According to the author.

22 Jacques-Emile Blanche, Jean Cocteau, *Correspondance* (Paris: La Table ronde, 1993), 39 n.*c*.

23 Jean Cocteau, *Thomas l'imposteur* (Paris: Editions de la Nouvelle Revue Française, 1923), 61; Abbé Mugnier, *Journal: 1879–1939* (Paris: Mercure de France, 1985), 277.

24 *Le Mot* was published irregularly from Nov. 18, 1914, until July 1, 1915.

25 Steegmuller 1986, 130.

26 Ibid., 129.

27 Ibid., 132.

28 According to Faÿ, 32, Cocteau was with the unit in December, 1914 (Steegmuller does not agree with Fay; see Steegmuller 1986, app. III).

29 Faÿ, 30.

30 Steegmuller 1986, 142.

31 Ibid., 138.

32 Ibid., 139.

33 Christopher Green, *Cubism and Its Enemies* (New Haven and London: Yale University Press, 1987), 11.

34 According to Louise Varèse: "As I remember, Varèse once mentioned that Picasso was to have joined the [*Midsummer Night's Dream*] group" (Varèse, 116).

35 Steegmuller 1986, 123.

36 See Cooper, 19 n.19. Picasso confirmed to Cooper that Cocteau was dressed in the Harlequin costume and that it became one of his studio properties.

37 Cocteau to Picasso, Sept. 25, 1915 (Archives Picasso).

38 Cocteau to Picasso, Feb. 6, 1916 (Archives Picasso).

39 When I first noticed the hidden profile in the 1915 *Harlequin*, I checked to see whether anyone else had spotted it. There was no mention in Rubin 1972 nor in any other of the Museum of Modern Art's publications. I was, therefore, surprised to find in one of the notes to Kirk Varnedoe's self-portrait section of *Picasso and Portraiture* (New York: The Museum of Modern Art, 1996), 177 n.43, that "the possible [*sic*] existence of this profile . . . has long been a matter of curiosity among those who have worked with the painting at The Museum of Modern Art."

40 Matisse to Camoin, [late Oct.], 1914: "I'm doing a picture, it's a picture of the *goldfish* that I'm redoing with a person who is looking on with a palette in his hand." Flam, 397.

41 Flam, 362.

42 Cocteau to Valentine Gross, Feb. 2, 1916; Steegmuller 1986, 145, suggests that "collage" may be a reference to new pictures by Picasso or to a new friend "with whom he was collé."

43 Adéma, 285.

44 Billy, 113.

45 Cocteau to Gleizes, Aug. 13, 1916 (Gleizes archives, Musée National d'Art Moderne, Paris).

46 Cocteau to Valentine Gross, Aug. 13, 1916; in Steegmuller 1986, 164.

47 Ibid.

48 O'Brian, 219.

49 Cocteau to Valentine Gross, Aug. 13, 1916; in Steegmuller 1986, 163–4.

50 Steegmuller, 150 n*.

51 Cooper, 326.

52 Satie to Valentine Gross, Apr. 25, 1916; in Steegmuller 1986, 147.

53 Cocteau to Stravinsky, Aug. 11, 1916; ibid., 162.

54 Cocteau to Valentine Gross, July 8, 1916; ibid., 157.

55 Cocteau to Stravinsky, Aug. 11, 1916; ibid., 159.

56 Cocteau to Valentine Gross, Sept. 12, 1916; ibid.

57 Ibid., 122.

58 Ibid., 162.

59 Ibid., 163 n*.

60 Cocteau to Gleizes, [Aug.], 1916; ibid., 164.

61 Cocteau to Valentine Gross, Aug. 8, 1916; ibid., 163.

62 Cocteau to Valentine Gross, Aug. 13, 1916; ibid., 164.

63 Jean Cocteau. *Lettres à sa mère I: 1898–1918* (Paris: Gallimard, 1989), 164, 165 n.4. Pierre Caizergues notes that L'Abbé Constantin is a character in a novel by Ludovic Halévy (1882) about the lives of simple, virtuous folk.

64 Roché Carnet 74, July 21, 1916 (Ransom Center).

65 Cocteau to Misia Sert [1916]; in Steegmuller 1986, 169.

66 See John Richardson, "Eugenia Errazuriz," *House and Garden* (New York) (April, 1987), 76–84.

67 Painter II, 340.

68 The villa was never built. A pupil eventually erected a version of it in Japan, improbably roofed in thatch.

69 Paul Morand, *Le Journal d'un attaché d'ambassade: 1916–1917* (Paris: Gallimard, 1996), 236.

70 Cocteau to Valentine Gross, Aug. 24, 1916, and Aug. 31, 1916; in Steegmuller 1986, 165.

25 IRÈNE LAGUT pp.395–405

1 Palau i Fabre 1990, 467, claims that Palladini came from a family of Italian actors, although he gives no evidence for this assertion.

2 Cocteau's twenty-one snapshots are reproduced in Klüver.

3 Stein 1933, 169.

4 Only one illustration was ever published: in the Societé Littéraire de la France catalog for 1917.

5 *La Femme assise* was assembled from material Apollinaire had developed over several years. The part concerned with Mormons (which is only tenuously related to the story of Elvire/Irène) was composed long before the rest of the book. According to Michel Décaudin's "Notes" to *La Femme assise* (Apollinaire 1977, 1329–35), the first mention of a novel about Mormons was made on Nov. 7, 1912, in *Paris-Midi* by André Billy, who announced that "Apollinaire has chosen the title for his next novel: La Mormonne et le Danite." Papers in the Bibliothèque Littéraire Jacques Doucet confirm that numerous notes concerning Mormons, the Far West and the life of American Indians, all of which later appear in *La Femme assise*, were collected between 1911 and 1914. In addition, the passage on Montparnasse before the outbreak of war had appeared in the *Mercure de France* (Mar.–Apr., 1914).

Apollinaire did not embark on Irène Lagut's story until later. André Salmon announced in *L'Eveil* on Apr. 7, 1917: "Guillaume Apollinaire has completed *Irène de Montparnasse ou Paris pendant la guerre.*" Later (Aug. 26, 1917) Apollinaire wrote Jacques Doucet that he had finished the novel known as *La Femme assise.* A poorly edited version of this book was published posthumously in 1920; a revised edition appeared in 1948.

6 Apollinaire adapted the character of Pablo Canouris (Picasso) from a story entitled "L'Albanais," which was originally published in *Messidor* (Sept. 7, 1907). He had intended to recycle it in *Le Poète assassiné* (1916), but changed his mind. The story is based on another friend of Apollinaire's, the Albanian Faïk bég Konitza, and relates how, in order to overcome his hopeless love for an unfaithful English girlfriend, which has nearly driven him to suicide, he carries out an old Balkan custom and abducts a young girl from the streets of Cologne (Brussels in *La Femme assise*). He says of his countrymen that "the only woman that really belongs to us is one we have taken, the one we have tamed."

7 Durry, 6–7, and Lagut. Irène Lagut was also filmed by the BBC in 1993, at the time of her 101st birthday.

8 Stein 1933, 169.

9 Alice Halicka in conversation with John Field.

10 In a letter from Serge Férat to Soffici, Aug. 17, 1913 (Soffici Archive), he says that "Irène will write"; that is to say that by that date Irène Lagut was not only living with Férat but she was already a friend of Soffici's.

11 Guillaume Apollinaire, preface to *Peintures de Léopold Survage; Dessins et Aquarelles d'Irène Lagut* (Première exposition des "Soirées de Paris"), Chez Madame Bongard, Jan. 21–31, 1917.

12 Irène Lagut to Soffici, June 24, 1915 (Soffici Archive).

13 Irène Lagut to Soffici, Aug. 11, 1915 (Soffici Archive).

14 Irène Lagut to Soffici, Feb. 10, 1916 (Soffici Archive).

15 See note 6 above.

16 Jacques Doucet to Roché, [1916] (Ransom Center).

17 The secretive Picasso evidently wanted to conceal the fact that he had been using the Montrouge house as a *rendez-vous d'amour* since the summer. This explains why he did not notify his friends about the new address until October. Henri-Pierre Roché wrote in his diary on Sept. 4, 1916: "[Picasso] is going to move to Montrouge. So much the better. A house that belongs to a notary . . . it's all the same to him" (Ransom Center).

The actual move took place the following month: Picasso wrote Max Jacob, "I am deep in house-moving and you will arrive just in time to give me a hand" (O'Brian, 217). On Oct. 14 André Level wrote Picasso, "Good luck moving out" (Archives Picasso); in an undated letter written sometime after Oct. 7 Cocteau wrote Misia Sert: "Picasso is moving—I'm helping him and so is Apollinaire" (Steegmuller 1986, 168).

Among Picasso's papers is an Official Change of Domicile (from rue Schœlcher to rue Victor Hugo) dated Oct. 19, 1916 (Archives Picasso).

18 Stein 1933, 169. The date of Stein's return to Paris from Mallorca would have been after the British offensive in the Battle of Verdun (i.e., early August); the visit to Picasso would surely have occurred soon after Gertrude and Alice were once again settled in Paris.

19 McCully, 64.

20 Lagut, 23.

21 Dora Maar in conversation with the author.

22 Irène first mentions her involvement with Picasso in a letter to Soffici dated Sept. 15, 1916 (at which time she and Serge had been together in Brittany for some three weeks). She apologizes for not having answered his letter written some two months earlier, but says that the Picasso affair had preoccupied her (Soffici Archive).

23 Lagut, 11.

24 Louise Faure-Favier, "Echos-Vernissage," *Paris-Midi* (July 15, 1916), 2. Three works by Irène Lagut are listed in the catalog of the Salon d'Antin (July 16–31, 1916, Galerie Barbazanges): 68, *La cage*; 69, *Vase de fleurs*; and 70, *Portrait.*

25 Irène Lagut to Soffici, Sept. 15, 1916 (Soffici Archive).

26 Max Jacob to the Altounians, Sept. 3, 1916 (Fonds Joseph Altounian).

27 Adéma, 158.

28 Durry, 7–9.

29 Lagut, 23–4.

30 Hugo, 134.

31 Lagut, 25.

32 Dora Maar in conversation with the author.

33 See L. Faillant-Dumas's report on X-radiographs taken by the Laboratoire de recherche des musées de France in *Une Nouvelle Dation* (Paris: Réunion des Musées Nationaux, 1990), 28.

34 Peter D. Whitney, "Picasso Is Safe," *San Francisco Chronicle*, Sept. 3, 1944; cited in Alfred H. Barr, Jr., *Picasso: Fifty Years of His Art* (New York: The Museum of Modern Art, 1946), 223.

26 PICASSO'S CHEF D'ŒUVRE INCONNU pp.407–417

1 Malraux, 138.

2 Kahnweiler 1961, 74.

3 Cabanne, 196.

4 Basler, 12.

5 Malraux, 18.

6 Daix 1995, 196.

7 Malraux, 18–9.

8 My thanks to John Field for pointing this out to me.

9 Picasso to Léonce Rosenberg, Nov. 3, 1915 (Rosenberg Archive).

10 Picasso to Léonce Rosenberg, Apr. 14, 1916 (Rosenberg Archive).

11 Picasso to Léonce Rosenberg, Nov. 22, 1916 (Rosenberg Archive).

12 "J'aime tant que je ne l'aurais pas donnée même à mon père." Picasso is quoted in Hugo, 279.

13 Favela, 109.

14 Favela, 107–8.

15 Ibid., 130.

16 Ibid., 110.

17 Max Jacob, "La Vie artistique," *291*, 12 (Feb., 1916); in Seckel, 126.

18 Stein 1933, 50.

19 Schneider, 733.

20 Honoré de Balzac, *Le Chef d'œuvre inconnu* (1845 version) (Paris: Garnier–Flammarion, 1991), 69–70.

21 Jean Cocteau, *Picasso* (Paris: Stock, 1923), 11.

22 Jean Cocteau, "L'Homme assis," in *L'Ode à Picasso: poëme 1917* (Paris: A la Belle Edition, 1919).

27 PARADE pp.419–433

1 Cocteau to Satie, Dec., 1916 (Patrimoine de la Ville de Menton).

2 Cocteau to Valentine Gross, Sept. 4, 1916; in Steegmuller 1986, 167.

3 Satie to Valentine Gross, Sept. 14, 1916; ibid.

4 Satie to Cocteau, Sept. 15, 1916; in Cooper, 333.

5 Satie to Valentine Gross, Sept. 20, 1916; in Steegmuller 1986, 167.

6 Cocteau to Valentine Gross; Sept. 22, 1916; in Steegmuller 1986, 168.

7 Häger, 29.

8 Steegmuller 1986, 165.

9 Seckel, 139 n.53.

10 Satie to Valentine Gross, Dec. 13, 1920; in Cooper, 20.

11 Steegmuller 1986, 232.

12 Angel Zarraga to Roché, Oct. 23, 1916 (Ransom Center).

13 See Alexandra Parigoris, "Pastiche and the use of tradition," *On Classic Ground* (London: Tate Gallery, 1990), 306.

14 Cooper, 20.

15 Richard Buckle, *Diaghilev* (London: Hamish Hamilton, 1979), 321.

16 Picasso to Cocteau, Feb. 1, 1917; in Cooper, 327.

17 Satie to Roché, Feb. 12, 1917 (Ransom Center).

18 Jacques Doucet to Roché, Mar. 31, 1917 (Ransom Center).

19 Brassaï, 184.

20 *Les Demoiselles d'Avignon* was exhibited in July, 1916, at the Salon d'Antin; see Rubin, Seckel, Cousins, 164ff.

21 Vol. I, 247.

22 These costumes had been loaned by the widow of Colonel de Basil, Diaghilev's successor.

23 Gris to Maurice Raynal, Jan. 10, 1917; in Kahnweiler 1956, 44.

24 Apollinaire to Maurice Raynal, Jan. 27, 1917; in Adéma, 298.

25 Cocteau to Apollinaire; in Pierre Caizergues and Michel Décaudin, *Correspondance Guillaume Apollinaire, Jean Cocteau* (Paris: Jean-Michel Place, 1991), 15.

26 Apollinaire to Gris, June, 1917; in Adéma, 315.

27 Blaise Cendrars to Hélène d'Oettingen; in Adéma, 302.

28 Pierre Sichel, *Modigliani: A Biography of Amedeo Modigliani* (London: W. H. Allen, 1967), 404.

29 Klüver and Martin, 71.

30 Seckel, 142.

31 Ibid.

32 Braque 1957.

33 Louise Faure-Favier, *Paris-Midi*, Jan. 9, 1917, 2.

34 Picasso to Cocteau, Jan. 15, 1917; in Cooper, 326.

35 Steegmuller 1986, 174.

36 Stein 1933, 172.

37 Ornella Volta, *Satie/Cocteau: Les Malentendus d'une entente* (Bordeaux: Le Castor Astral, 1993), 29.

38 Ibid., 28.

39 Satie to Valentine Gross, Feb. 15, 1917; ibid., 29.

40 Ibid.

41 Cooper, 21.

42 Seckel, 150 n.43.

43 Silver, 404 n.13.

44 Picabia, "Manifeste Dada," *391* 12 (March, 1920), trans. in William A. Camfield, *Francis Picabia: His Art, Life and Times* (Princeton, N.J.: Princeton University Press, 1979), 140.

45 Steegmuller 1986, 137.

46 Basler, 13.

Index

Works by Picasso are listed by title (or subject) following the general index. References to illustrations are in *italics*.

INDEX OF WORKS

Text Permissions and Picture Credits

Grateful acknowledgment is made to the following for permission to quote copyright material:

ARCHIVIO SOFFICI: Excerpts from letters from Serge Férat and Irène Lagut to Ardengo Soffici; printed by permission of Valeria Soffici.

THE ESTATE OF FERNANDE OLIVIER: Excerpts from unpublished manuscript memoirs by Fernande Olivier; printed by permission of the Estate of Fernande Olivier. Excerpts from letters written by Fernande Olivier to Gertrude Stein and Alice Toklas; printed by permission of the Estate of Fernande Olivier and the Beinecke Rare Book and Manuscript Library, Yale University. Excerpts from *Picasso et ses amis*, reprinted by permission of the Estate of Fernande Olivier. Excerpts from *Souvenirs intimes*, edited by Gilbert Krill, © 1988 by Calmann-Lévy, reprinted by permission of the publishers and the Estate of Fernande Olivier.

THE ESTATE OF GERTRUDE STEIN: Excerpts from *The Autobiography of Alice B. Toklas* by Gertrude Stein, © 1933 and renewed 1961 by Alice B. Toklas. Rights throughout the world excluding the United States and Canada are controlled by the Estate of Gertrude Stein; reprinted by permission of Random House, Inc., and the Estate of Gertrude Stein.

HARRY RANSOM HUMANITIES RESEARCH CENTER: Brief excerpts from letters from Henri-Pierre Roché housed in the Carlton Lake Collection at the Harry Ransom Humanities Research Center at the University of Texas at Austin; reproduced by permission.

ILLUSTRATIONS

In most cases full credits are included in the captions, but the following additional credits are due.

Photographs of works in the following museums were supplied by the Réunion des Musées Nationaux: Musée Picasso, Archives Picasso, Musée d'Orsay, Musée du Louvre, Musée de l'Orangerie, Musée des Antiquités Nationales, Saint-Germain-en-Laye, Musée Réattu, Arles.

Photographs of works in the Museum of Modern Art, New York, and other photographs provided by the Museum (5a, 140, 314b) are © 1996 The Museum of Modern Art, New York. The painting on p.304a was acquired by exchange through the Katherine S. Dreier Bequest and the Hillman Periodicals, Philip Johnson, Miss Janice Loeb, Abby Albrich Rockefeller and Mr. and Mrs. Norbert Schimmel Funds.

Works illustrated from the Baltimore Museum of Art are from the Cone Collection, formed by Dr. Claribel Cone and Miss Etta Cone of Baltimore, Maryland.

Photographs of works in the Art Institute of Chicago are © 1996 The Art Institute of Chicago, All Rights Reserved. The drawing on p.323 is from the Charles L. Hutchinson Memorial Collection.

Photographs of works in the Cleveland Museum of Art are © 1996 The Cleveland Museum of Art.

Photographs of works in the Barnes Foundation are © 1996 by the Barnes Foundation, All Rights Reserved.

Photograph 385b is © 1996 Trustees of Princeton University.

The drawing on p.389b from the Archer M. Huntington Art Gallery is from the Severin Wunderman Collection, 1995.

Photographs of works in the National Gallery of Art, Washington are © 1996 Board of Trustees, National Gallery of Art, Washington. Photograph 404b is from the Chester Dale Collection.

Photographs of works in the Jacques and Natasha Gelman Collection were kindly supplied by the Metropolitan Museum of Art, New York.

The work in photograph 53a from the Museum of Fine Arts, Boston, is from the Bequest of Robert Treat Paine II.

The work in photograph 252 from the Jane Voorhees Zimmerli Museum was acquired with the Herbert D. and Ruth Schimmel Museum Library Fund.

Photograph 433 is reproduced by courtesy of the President and Fellows, Harvard University

Photograph 317b is © 1996 Dr. Wolfgang & Ingeborg Henze-Ketterer, Wichtrach/Bern.

Photograph 413a is reproduced with permission of the Instituto Nacional de Bellas Artes y Literatura, Mexico City.

Grateful acknowledgment for supplying photographs is made to all those named in the captions, to collectors who prefer to remain anonymous and to the following:

Jack Abraham: 252
Acquavella Galleries, Inc.: 73a, 162b, 194a
Muriel Anssens: 238, 303b
Archivio Fotografico Soprintendenza B.A.S. di Milano, su concessione del Ministero Beni Culturali e Ambientali: 259
Archivo CENIDIAP-INBA: 412a, 413a
Studio Basset: 215, 384
Yves Berrier: 5b, 58c, 180a, 198, 204, 219, 260b, 261b, 348a, 396a, 397a, 425a, 425c
Galerie Beyeler, Basel: 52a
BFI Stills, Posters and Designs: 154a
Bibliothèque Nationale: 424
Martin Bühler: 247b
Raymond Chabert: 239a
Christie's, London: 408
Douglas Cooper Archives: 315c
M. Coppens: 139
Peter Cox: 218b
Detroit Institute of Arts Founders Society: 124a, 376b
Ursula Edelmann: 132b
Finarte: 221
Fundación Picasso, Málaga: 270, 277
Giraudon: 75
Grosvenor Gallery: 363
Tom Haartsen: 210a, 291a, 428b
David Heald: 188b, 191b, 316
Michael Herling: 128a
Paul Hester, Houston: 240a
George Holmes: 389b
H. Humm: 177b
Bernd Kirtz: 121
Billy Klüver and Julie Martin: 228a, 350a, 397b, 419, 427a
Bob Kolbrener 40a
Galerie Jan Krugier, Geneva (photos by Patrick Goetelen): 125d, 278b, 350b, 376a, 377b, 409c, 410b
Kunsthaus Zurich: 169b
Kunstmuseum Basel: 163b, 227b
Lefevre Gallery: 182, 365d
Galerie Louise Leiris: 188a, 315a
Gérard Leyris: 203b, 206, 400b
Guy Loudmer: 211a
Arxiu Mas: 193a
Mathews: 122
Nasjonalgalleriet, Oslo (photos by J. Lathion): 83, 319f
Francis Naumann: 361a
Photothèque des Musées de la Ville de Paris: 172, 319e, 430b
Eric Pollitzer (courtesy of Pierre Matisse Foundation): 106
Rheinisches Bildarchiv: 313
Roger-Viollet: 197a, 266cd, 344b
Galerie Rosengart, Lucerne: 326, 368b
Roumagnac: 281a
Saporetti: 96b, 318a
Steven Sloman; 284
Sotheby's, London: 208
Sotheby's, New York: 351b
Lee Stalsworth: 296a
Stoppenbach and Delestre: 77, 85a
Jim Strong, Inc.: 336b
Soichi Sunami 416a
E. V. Thaw & Co: 251c
M. Thrun: 325
Total (Division Peintures): 225a
Didier Tragin/Catherine Lancien: 385a
Sylvaine Vaucher, Geneva: 322b
Graydon Wood: 209b